RHETORICAL AND CRITICAL APPROACHES TO PUBLIC RELATIONS II

This volume illustrates the application of rhetorical theory and critical perspectives to explain public relations practices. It provides a systematic and coherent statement of the crucial guidelines and philosophical underpinnings of public relations. *Rhetorical and Critical Approaches to Public Relations II* addresses the rhetorical/critical tradition's contribution to the definition of public relations and PR practice; explores the role of PR in creating shared meaning in support of publicity and promotional organizational efforts; considers the tradition's contributions to risk, crisis, and issues dimensions of public relations; and highlights ethics, character, and responsible advocacy. It uses a rhetorical lens to provide practitioners with a sense of how their PR campaigns make a contribution to the organizational bottom line.

Robert L. Heath, Ph.D., is Professor Emeritus of Communication at the University of Houston. He has published 17 books, and has contributed chapters and articles on issues management, public relations, crisis communication, risk communication, environmental communication, emergency management, rhetorical criticism, and communication theory.

Elizabeth L. Toth, Ph.D., is Professor and Chair of the Department of Communication at the University of Maryland, College Park. She has published books, journal articles, and book chapters on gender and public relations.

Damion Waymer, Ph.D., is Assistant Professor of Communication at Virginia Tech. His teaching and research interests include public relations and organizational rhetoric, and he has published his work in scholarly communication journals.

COMMUNICATION SERIES
Jennings Bryant/Dolf Zillmann, General Editors

Routledge
Taylor & Francis Group

NEW YORK AND LONDON

RHETORICAL AND CRITICAL APPROACHES TO PUBLIC RELATIONS II

Edited by

Robert L. Heath
Elizabeth L. Toth
Damion Waymer

Routledge
Taylor & Francis Group

NEW YORK AND LONDON

First published 2009
by Routledge
711 Third Avenue, New York, NY 10017, USA

Simultaneously published in the UK
by Routledge
2 Park Square, Milton Park, Abingdon, Oxon OX14 4RN

Routledge is an imprint of the Taylor & Francis Group, an informa business

© 2009 Taylor & Francis

Typeset in Galliard by Swales & Willis Ltd, Exeter, Devon

Library of Congress Cataloging in Publication Data
Rhetorical and critical approaches to public relations II/edited
by Robert L. Heath, Elizabeth L. Toth, and Damion Waymer.—2nd ed.
p. cm. — (Communication series)
Public relations—Moral and ethical aspects.   2. Communication in marketing.
3. Corporations—Public relations—Moral and ethical aspects.
I. Heath, Robert L. (Robert Lawrence), 1941–
II. Toth, Elizabeth L.   III. Waymer, Damion.
HM1221.R44 2008
659.2—dc22
2008031872

ISBN 10: 0–8058–6423–7 (hbk)
ISBN 10: 0–8058–6424–5 (pbk)
ISBN 10: 0–203–87492–7 (ebk)

ISBN 13: 978–0–8058–6423–6 (hbk)
ISBN 13: 978–0–8058–6424–3 (pbk)
ISBN 13: 978–0–203–87492–9 (ebk)

CONTENTS

ILLUSTRATIONS

Figures

Tables

CONTRIBUTORS

Linda Aldoory, Ph.D., is Associate Professor of Communication and Affiliate Faculty of Women's Studies at the University of Maryland, College Park. She is also editor of the *Journal of Public Relations Research*. Aldoory's research focuses on gender, power, and diversity in public relations and in health communication. In addition to her research and teaching, Aldoory consults for various health and social service agencies, including the U.S. Centers for Disease Control and Prevention and the Department of Homeland Security.

Jane Stuart Baker is a graduate student in the Department of Communication at Texas A&M University.

Josh Boyd (Ph.D., Indiana University) is an Associate Professor of Communication at Purdue University. He studies organizational rhetoric in contexts such as corporate and sports discourse, and he is thankful to have published research with his father and with his former graduate students.

Suzanne Boys, Ph.D., is Assistant Professor, University of Cincinnati. She received a Bachelor of Science in speech-language pathology from the University of Cincinnati in 1996; a Masters of Arts in communication from the University of Cincinnati in 2002, writing a thesis on the discursive construction of the teacher role by international graduate students; and a Ph.D. in communication from Texas A&M University in 2007. Her dissertation research on the Roman Catholic clergy sex abuse crisis developed a dialogical model for understanding crisis communication. Boys's research interests include public relations, crisis communication, non-profit organizing, dialogue, and the functions of silence in organizational communication. The courses she teaches include Communication in Organizations; Organizational Image, Identity, and Issues Management; Public Relations Case Studies; Crisis Communication; Organizational Cultures, and Organizational Diversity.

Lars Thøger Christensen (Ph.D., Odense University, 1993) is Professor of Communication at the Department of Marketing and Management, the University of Southern Denmark. Also, he is Adjunct Professor at the Copenhagen Business School where he established the CBS Center for Corporate Communication. His research and teaching interests include critical and postmodern approaches to the broad fields of organizational and corporate communications. In addition to six books, his research appears in *Organization Studies, European Journal of Marketing, The New Handbook of Organizational Communication, The Handbook of Public Relations, Communication Yearbook,* and elsewhere.

Charles Conrad is Professor of Communication at Texas A&M University and former editor of *Management Communication Quarterly.* He teaches classes in Organizational Communication, Organizational Rhetoric, and Communication, Power, and Politics. His research currently focuses on the symbolic processes through which organizations influence popular attitudes and public policies. He currently is working on a book manuscript that develops a "close comparison" of the communication-organization-health policy nexus in Canada and in the U.S.A.

W. Timothy Coombs is a Professor in the Department of Communication Studies at Eastern Illinois University and the 2002 recipient of the Jackson Jackson and Wagner Behavioral Science Prize for his crisis research. He has published in the *Journal of Public Relations Research, Public Relations Review, Journal of Public Affairs, Management Communication Quarterly, Journal of Business Communication, Journal of Communication Management,* and *Corporate Reputation Review.* He has written or co-authored four books including *Ongoing Crisis Communication* and *It's Not Just Public Relations.*

Chris Cudahy is at Atlantic Baptist University, Moncton, New Brunswick, Canada.

Sarah Bonewits Feldner (Ph.D., Purdue University, 2002) is an Assistant Professor in the Diederich College of Communication at Marquette University. Her primary area of teaching and research is organizational communication with an emphasis on organizational rhetoric. Her work largely focuses on issues of organizational mission, legitimacy, and identity. Some of her recent work has appeared in *Communication Studies* and the *International Journal of Strategic Communication.*

Kathy R. Fitzpatrick is Professor of Public Relations at Quinnipiac University in Hamden, Connecticut. A licensed attorney and accredited public relations professional, she has been teaching, writing, and counseling on matters related to public relations, law, and ethics for more than 20 years. Fitzpatrick is the co-author of *Public Relations Ethics and Journalism Ethics* (with Philip Seib) and the lead editor of *Ethics in Public Relations: Responsible Advocacy.* Her current research focuses on U.S. public diplomacy.

Robert L. Heath, Professor Emeritus of Communication at the University of Houston, has published 17 books including *Terrorism: Communication and Rhetorical Perspectives* (2008), *Today's Public Relations* (2006), *Encyclopedia of Public Relations* (2005), *Responding to Crisis: A Rhetorical Approach to Crisis Communication* (2004), and *Handbook of Public Relations* (2001). Heath also recently co-edited *Communication and the Media* (2005), volume 3 of the series Community Preparedness and Response to Terrorism, and *Rhetorical and Critical Approaches to Public Relations* (1992). He has contributed chapters and articles on issues management, public relations, crisis communication, risk communication, environmental communication, emergency management, rhetorical criticism, and communication theory. He is co-editor of the forthcoming *Handbook of Crisis and Risk Communication*.

Rachel L. Holloway is an Associate Professor and head of the Department of Communication at Virginia Tech. Her scholarly work on political rhetoric includes multiple articles, book chapters, and two books: *In the Matter of J. Robert Oppenheimer: Politics, Rhetoric and Self-Defense* (1993) and *The Clinton Presidency: Images, Issues, and Communication Strategies* (1996) (with Robert E. Denton, Jr.). Holloway is a past chair of the Public Relations Division of the National Communication Association.

Øyvind Ihlen is a Post Doctoral Research Fellow at the Department of Media and Communication, University of Oslo; and Associate Professor at Hedmark College, both in Norway. He has published in journals such as *Public Relations Review, Journal of Public Relations Research, Journal of Communication Management, International Journal of Strategic Communication, Corporate Communications: An International Journal, Journal of Public Affairs*, and *Business Strategy and the Environment.*

Roy Langer (Ph.D., Copenhagen Business School, 2000) is Professor of Corporate Communication in the Aarhus School of Business, University of Aarhus, Denmark. Langer has produced extensive research on stealth and undercover marketing at the crossroads between PR and marketing and in related areas; and he has published his research in journals such as *Corporate Communications, Psychology & Marketing, Corporate Reputation Review, Publizistik, Qualitative Market Research*, and more. He is serving as an editorial board member for a number of international journals and an active member of research communities within media, communication, and marketing studies.

David McKie is a Professor at Waikato Management School. He has published three books, over 20 book chapters, and over 40 journal articles. He is currently working on three books: on *Influencing Israel*, on *Leadership*, and on *Action Inquiry and Workplace Creativity*. As CEO of RAM (Results by Action Management) International Consulting, David also works as a change, leadership, and strategic communication consultant in private and public sectors in Asia, Europe, the Middle East, and the U.S.A.

Rebecca J. Meisenbach (Ph.D., Purdue University, 2004) is an Assistant Professor in the Department of Communication at the University of Missouri-Columbia. Her research focuses on intersections among identity, ethics, and rhetoric, with particular attention to non-profit and gendered organizing. She currently is studying the negotiation of stigma and occupational identities among fund raisers. Her recent work has appeared in *Communication Monographs, Communication Yearbook, Management Communication Quarterly*, and the *International Journal of Strategic Communication*.

Debashish Munshi is Chairperson and Associate Professor of Management Communication at the University of Waikato in New Zealand. He is a journalist-turned-academic whose research brings theoretical perspectives from such other disciplines as cultural studies, media studies, postcolonial studies, and subaltern studies into the study of management in organizations. He is (with David McKie) co-author of *Reconfiguring Public Relations: Ecology, Equity, and Enterprise* (2007).

Lan Ni (Ph.D., University of Maryland at College Park) is an Assistant Professor in the Jack J. Valenti School of Communication at the University of Houston. Her research focuses on strategic management of public relations, relationship management, identification of publics, and intercultural communication. Her work has been accepted for publication in *Public Relations Review, Journal of Communication Management*, and *Journal of Public Relations Research.*

Michael J. Palenchar is an Assistant Professor at the University of Tennessee's School of Advertising and Public Relations. He has more than 20 years of academic and professional experience, and his research has been published in among others the *Journal of Public Relations Research* and *Public Relations Review*. His first book, *Strategic Issues Management* (2nd ed.), is co-authored with Robert L. Heath, and he is the co-recipient of the 2000 and 2007 National Communication Association's Pride Award for top published article in public relations.

Ron Pearson was a Professor at Mount Saint Vincent University, Halifax, Nova Scotia, Canada, until his death in 1990. His rhetorical and critical scholarship in public relations inspired us all. We miss his brilliant challenges to the public relations profession and its body of knowledge.

Karen Miller Russell is Associate Professor at the Grady College of Journalism and Mass Communication at the University of Georgia. She conducts research on the history of public relations, and was awarded the Nafziger-White Award from the Association for Education in Journalism and Mass Communication for best dissertation, in 1995, and the Pathfinder Award, made annually by the Institute for Public Relations in recognition of the best public relations research program, in 2001.

Ashli Quesinberry Stokes is an Assistant Professor at the University of North Carolina at Charlotte. She pursues a wide variety of research in public relations and rhetoric, specializing in rhetorical approaches to analyzing public relations controversies. Most recently, Dr. Stokes co-authored a textbook about international public relations. She has also published in *Public Relations Review*, the *Southern Communication Journal, Studies in Communication Sciences*, the *Encyclopedia of Public Relations*, and has authored several book chapters.

Maureen Taylor is the Gaylord Family Chair of Strategic Communication in the Gaylord College of Journalism and Mass Communication at the University of Oklahoma. She earned a Ph.D. in Public Affairs and Issues Management from Purdue University in 1996. Taylor's research interest is in international public relations, nation building, and civil society campaigns. Taylor has conducted civil society research in Malaysia, Bosnia, Croatia, Kosovo, Serbia, Jordan, and Sudan.

Elizabeth L. Toth, Ph.D., is Professor and Chair of the Department of Communication at the University of Maryland, College Park. She has published *Women in Public Relations: How Gender Influences Practice*; *Public Relations: The Profession and the Practice*; *The Future of Excellence in Public Relations and Communication Management: Challenges for the Next Generation*; *The Gender Challenge in Media: Voices from the Field*; and *Rhetorical and Critical Approaches to Public Relations*. She has also published numerous articles and book chapters on gender and public relations.

Sarah Hagedorn VanSlette is an Assistant Professor in the Department of Communication and Theatre Arts at John Carroll University in Cleveland, Ohio. Her research interests include organizational rhetoric, rhetorical approaches to public relations, and international public relations. VanSlette received her M.A. and Ph.D. from Purdue University, where Josh Boyd was her advisor. She would like to thank him for his continued guidance and support, especially on their co-authored line of research on outlaw discourse.

Damion Waymer, Assistant Professor of Communication at Virginia Tech, earned his B.A. at the College of Charleston and earned both his M.A. and Ph.D. at Purdue University. His teaching and research interests include, generally, public relations and organizational rhetoric. More specifically, his research uses public relations and communication theories to explore the ways that marginalized or underrepresented publics can and do gain access to voice, as well as what strategies are available to them to challenge various issues they might encounter. Some of his work along this line of inquiry is published in scholarly journals such as the *Journal of Applied Communication Research*, the *Journal of Family Communication*, and *Qualitative Inquiry*.

Jennifer Willyard received her Ph.D. in Communication from Texas A&M University. She specializes on the intersection of organizational and political rhetoric and currently works in Austin, Texas, as an independent consultant.

INTRODUCTION

Robert L. Heath
University of Houston

When the first volume of *Rhetorical and Critical Approaches to Public Relations* was published, compliments emphasized one point: We in public relations and organizational rhetoric were slowly initiating the dawn of an era when meaning and the ethical judgment that accompanied it had arrived with enthusiasm and commitment. Most discussions of public relations prior to that time had focused on social scientific constructs and theory building that emphasized the processes of communication and relationships building. Many were saying, "but public relations is also about meaning." Many said, "perhaps public relations is primarily about meaning." That point is emphasized in spades in classic works such as *Unseen Power* by Scott Cutlip (1994).

Even today, especially in U.S. based journals that attend to academic discussions of public relations, most of the research features process in terms of variable analytic discussions rather than judgments of meaning and the ways it is formed. That trend is much less the case in such journals based outside of the United States. Also, some of the U.S. based publications that have recently emerged are emphasizing more of a meaning approach using variously the assumptions and principles of the rhetorical heritage, social constructionism, discourse analysis, and critical theory. Other journals that do not include "public relations" in their titles provide insightful discussions relevant to the practice and teaching of public relations as being vital to the collective making of meaning that defines commercial transactions and relationships between organizations, between them and individuals, society, and their physical and social environments. Some of these address the role that meaning plays in society and the way that organizational spokespersons work constructively as well as unreflectively or self-interestedly to discuss the ways that meaning is shaped which in turn influences marketplace activities and public policy decisions. Some critiques suggest that organizations assume individuals targeted in their campaigns are delusional and naively willing to accept corporate interpretations of very important matters.

Scope of our Study

For the wholeness, its total role in society, of public relations to be understood, appreciated, and evaluatively guided and corrected, academics and practitioners need constant and insightful discussions of the way meaning is socially constructed and enacted. What interests are served? Is the relationship between competing and cooperating interests balanced and proactive? Is it narrowly self-interested and reactive? Does it lead to enlightened choices, or clouded and even misled judgments? As the challenge to solving this dialectic, one can imagine that instead of merely helping one organization at a time to be effective, discourse needs to be engaged and shaped in ways that take the scope and purpose of making society more fully functioning.

Typically, scholarship and best principles address how to make individual practitioners effective, and in doing so, to make organizations effective—and even less ineffective. In this last approach, a substantial underpinning theme stresses the reality that since organizations need resources held by others, they are wise to mitigate conflict and to work to at least accommodate to others if not collaborate with them to make meaningful changes. Having set that outline, however, the question is what role does discourse play in conflict, promotion, image, reputation, relationship, and other factors of organizational success and the functioning of society. And, even more powerfully, the thrust of rhetoric can help define the organization, give it rationale, and set it in the context of society which is fundamentally all about meaning which provides insights and allows for enlightened choice. Rhetoric can help participants in social dialogue, even combatants, define conflict—the means for mitigation, accommodation, collaboration, and qualitatively superior relationships.

One of the central themes in public relations research, regardless of methodology and heuristics, is how do individuals as part of society make choices? What do they prefer? What do they oppose? Who do they like, and dislike? With which organizations do they identify, and against which do they unite? What products and services do they adopt as part of their lifestyle? What shapes their lifestyle? What ethical standards guide individual, organizational, and societal decisions? Who or what shapes these standards and sanctions their violation as well as rewards their compliance? What identities do people adopt? Are these identities ones that lead to individual and collective enrichment or alienation resulting from marginalization? What is the rationale of power and control in a society? What hegemonies shape individual and collective decisions and who benefits—or suffers—from these interpretative frames of reference, points of view, themes, or narratives as each writer or thinker might prefer to call them?

These and many other questions are explored in this book, as they are by other thinkers in other publications. The goal here, however, is keenly focused on understanding, righting, and supporting various approaches to the teaching and practice of public relations. We, as many others do, believe that since public relations is "an unseen power," its practitioners must be reflective and judicious in how they plan and execute their professional skills. They must have character sufficient to the wise management of their role in society. They must be substantial participants in strategic decisions, not merely the pawns used to implement such decisions.

What's in a title? As we created the first volume, we were worried that the word rhetoric in the title would fuel the hostility of critics of the field. Way too many people, and we find them teaching public relations as well, think of rhetoric as either vacuous discourse or manipulative, button-pushing strategies to cloud judgment, manage meaning, and control actions through "propaganda." These persons see rhetoric and propaganda as synonymous. Perhaps those opinions actually serve as the best rationale for the title, at least one of the key words. Since time began, humans have engaged in discourse to settle individual and collective matters. They have also bashed each other over the head and unleashed increasingly devastating techniques of warfare. That, for us, is the rationale and process of rhetoric—as discussed and elaborated for more that 2500 years in Western thought. It is about decision making where words supporting thoughts and based on reasoned discourse obtain appropriate outcomes to enlighten choices and guide preferences. It features influence. It acknowledges, however, that influence is a two-way street. Rhetoric has eternally wrestled with matters of enlightened choice and the dynamics of discourse best thought of in terms of statement and counter-statement. The very rationale for rhetoric is the reality that decisions need to be collective and socially responsible, but even then, who decides what is socially responsible? Is that an individual or collective endeavor?

Threads to be Unraveled

Although rhetorical theory has its own body of ideas and principles, it connects intellectually and ethically with others. One of these is social constructionism and another is discourse analysis. We can include critical studies in the list. We concur with Hallahan (1999) who saw this logic as being relevant to public relations inbound and outbound. It supports organizational planning by getting and understanding socially constructed frames which constitute the opinion community in which the organization operates. Knowing this is the basis of understanding rhetorical problems (Bitzer, 1968, 1987; Heath, 2001), essentially the conditions set by society for the acquisition and use of resources. "Similarly, outbound public relations communications involve attempts to define reality, as least as it relates to client organizations, for the many publics on whom the organization depends" (Hallahan, 1999, p. 206). And Hallahan stressed the point that "because defining reality is the very essence of communication, constructionists would argue that the process is neither inherently good nor bad" (Hallahan, 1999, pp. 206–207).

As media scholars began to focus on perspectives, or frames, those with a rhetorical background realized that one of the recurring principles of rhetoric had found additional voice. Perspectives, or frames, are not incidental, but vital to science, social science, and humanities. They are basic to public relations because its discourse is about something which becomes vital to decision making as it is given perspective, or frames. Rather than conceptualizing the process as "sharing information," we realize that it requires that, but also demands that the information be interpreted and judged before recommendations are advanced and conclusions formed. "Framing is a critical activity in the construction of social reality because it helps shape the perspectives through which people see the world" (Hallahan, 1999, p. 207). Such interpretations can be either overly positive or negative. Is it not the tendency of public relations practitioners to present the object of their case in as rosy a picture as possible? Also do spokespersons at times become overly negative in the condemnation of something they oppose? Too much attention to positive or negative attributes can ignore or marginalize other attributes. If we feature the positives, for instance, of urban renewal, we can miss the socially constructed reality, that it assumes the marginalization of poor people, the undesirables who need to be removed for renovation and beautification.

Gordon and Pellegrin (2008) drew on the usual sources of influence regarding the rationale of social construction theory to extract three central tenets they found to be especially relevant to public relations theory and practice.

> One tenet is that conceptions of reality (including of ourselves) are created through social interaction. A second tenet is that human institutions are created through social interactions and cannot exist independently of human agreement. Finally, a third tenet is that the constructed world of everyday life is itself an important element in the maintenance and reconstruction of social reality, human institutions, and ourselves. (p. 105)

One might reason that however foundational the first two principles are, the last is most centrally informative of public relations theory and practice.

As they continued in their discussion of social construction and public relations, Gordon and Pellegrin (2008) claimed that "An orientation that focuses on the making of meaning through human interaction offers routes to redefine, refine, reformulate, and restructure ourselves and our methods relating to both the practice and study of public relations" (p. 104). As discussed, "Discourse, from the constructionist orientation, is both a product of human interaction and a mechanism through which social realities are constructed" (p. 104). Although we might at times believe without reservation that meaning is promulgated, we should remember: "From the constructionist orientation, knowledge is itself a human product as well as an ongoing human production. Social constructionism, in short, contends that reality is a social construction that is created, maintained, altered, and destroyed through the process of human interaction" (p. 105). Such discussions do not deny fact, or avoid the word-thing dichotomy. They ponder this relationship and conclude: "Social constructionism does acknowledge a physical world independent of human interpretation" (p. 105). The key is not the denial of the physical world but the adoption, preferably through dialogue, of a functional view of it.

Taking a constitutive approach to public relations, Stokes (2005) approached its study from the normative perspective that features communication rules. Norms are socially constructed and implemented collectively through various rewards and sanctions. Regulative rules guide what is, can be, and should be done to create, maintain, or terminate a relationship. Constitutive rules guide interpretations. These rules are created and shared (see Heath, 1994) as narrative means for making collective interpretations. This analysis provides a "lens that reveals how public relations discourse shapes, reflects, and is constrained by the larger public sphere. The reciprocal influence of public relations and the media crafts and reinforces important shifts and trends in the trajectory of public debate" (Stokes, 2005, p. 556). "A constitutive analysis illustrates how public relations forums are created

and maintained, and substitute gestures of corporate transparency for corporate honesty and goodwill" (p. 556).

Markets, audiences, and publics are created and shaped through discourse. They can define themselves, through the normative expectations they create for themselves and for those who hold resources they want and need. But, such definitions often also reflect the resources they hold which organizations want and need. As a market takes on the constitutive rules of being that market, it may yield to messages provided by businesses, for instance. Herein lies the rationale for identification. "PR texts help populate our culture with messages that encourage certain meanings over others" (Stokes, 2005, p. 558).

Legitimacy is a vital topic in public relations, and can draw nicely on the rationale of social construction. "Despite the central role of legitimacy in social and organizational life, we know little of the subtle meaning-making processes through which organizational phenomena, such as industrial restructuring, are legitimated in contemporary society" (Vaara, Tienari, & Laurila, 2006, p. 789). Vaara et al. (2006) distinguished five "legitimation strategies: (1) normalization, (2) authorization, (3) rationalization, (4) moralization, and (5) narrativization" (p. 789). Insights can be achieved that help us decide which and when discursive strategies are effectively and ethically used when legitimating industrial restructuring in the media. "Legitimacy is a prerequisite for institutionalization and institutionalization is key to understanding the resources of legitimacy" (p. 791). The key to understanding this problem rests with language and shared meaning. "From this perspective, *legitimacy means a discursively created sense of acceptance in specific discourses or orders of discourse*" (p. 793, italics in original). Legitimacy by normalization "seeks to render something legitimate by exemplarity" (p. 798). "Authorization is legitimation by reference to authority" (p. 799). This discourse authorizes claims and establishes recurring authorizations and authorities. "Rationalization is legitimation by reference to the utility or function of specific actions or practices" (p. 800). "Moralization is legitimation that refers to specific values" (p. 801). Narrativization is legitimation that occurs when "telling a story provides evidence of acceptable, appropriate, or preferential behavior" (p. 802). The potency of narrativization results from dramatic structures that make some matter concrete and dramatic. And, thus the power bases of legitimacy become the result of and the playing out of narratives that define the norms of influence and shape interpretations (Heath, 1994) used as the rationale for enlightened choice.

Rhetoric presumes that no one necessarily has the best thoughts, makes the best decisions, and offers infallible advice. In fact, it presumes that every statement should suffer counter-statement. It believes, perhaps naively, that humans are capable of engaging in discourse that brings out the best in them and their efforts to live and work together. However naive that may seem, it presumes that all voices deserve to be heard, and regarded. Decisions ultimately are collective.

Problematics of Publics

How can we best understand this collective decision making? One of the key tools in that effort is the understanding of a public. Over the past two decades, a substantial and enlightened discussion has transpired among those interested in defining the concept and in integrating that logic into theory and criticism. Here we make no effort to capture, reflect on, or augment that robust discussion. But, we feel that it is necessary to point out problematics regarding the use of that term in discussions such as ours. Thinking about these problematics is vital to any reasonable and coherent analysis of the role of public relations in society.

First, it can be assumed that publics are only relevant to businesses. In fact, that is not true. Non-profits and governmental organizations also have publics, those individuals in varying degree of awareness, involvement, and organization whose awareness, choices, preferences, and actions can affect the well-being of one or more organizations.

Second, publics often are seen as stakeholders, collectives that have something that the focal organization wants or needs. But, they are also stakeseekers; they want something in exchange from the focal organization. This stake exchange is part of the logic of power resource management that defines the quality of relationships between an organization and its various publics; it is the logic of resource dependency theory which features interdependency.

Third, we often think of publics as critics of the target organization. They often are, but they also may want to and do support the organization. Such analysis suggests that one of the ways to conceptualize publics is how well their interests are respected and aligned with those of the focal organization. A brief example: During the *Exxon Valdez* crisis in Prince William Sound, Alaska, publics of various kinds targeted hostility toward the company and they faulted its management strategies and operational plans. Nevertheless, other publics also supported Exxon and wished it speedy and safe recovery. That conflicting opinion was palatable in a city such as Houston, Texas. So the issue position shared by or in conflict between an organization and its publics is important. And, that set of dynamics needs to realize well that there often are many publics. Environmental groups can be publics of one another—perhaps in support, but also disagreement. Similarly, we can have agreement and disagreement between industry groups (intra-industry and inter-industry).

Finally, when discussing public relations, many critics complain that the rationale for public relations theory is wrongly biased to help organizations (especially businesses) accommodate to publics in ways that often mask and otherwise do not solve problems and resolve issues—and the attendant conflict. We must balance such concerns, not only by how we view publics and organizations, but also by realizing that any public may itself have one or more publics. Even as we conceptualize environmental activists, can we not imagine that they have supporting and opposing publics, including the organization that they target? This logic, it seems, becomes clearer when we think of stakeholding and stakeseeking. During the *Exxon Valdez* crisis, did not various activist groups, industry groups such as commercial fishing, and the Alaskan government not have Exxon as its public—and seek stakes which it held? In various ways, fascinating ways, each group sought various stakes from Exxon. They needed Exxon's goodwill and financial resources, as Exxon needed and wanted theirs of various kinds. The government wanted cleanup and restoration. The affected industries wanted compensation. Activist groups not only wanted cleanup, but they also wanted punitive legislation—which they got.

As we have learned to think that not only the ostensibly or actually offending organization is suffering crisis, so too are various publics in support and conflict with one another. Thus, during crisis discussions about Hurricane Katrina we might focus on the federal administration, especially the Federal Emergency Management Agency (FEMA), or state and local government to address failings that led to crisis. But, close examination reveals that other groups, even families and individuals, were experiencing crisis. Cities and relief organizations suffered crises in various ways. As in the case of discussing organizations and publics, we need to keep the perspective that our target is the specific lay of the land, the publics, organizations, and even crises that are being discussed. Our theoretical telescope needs to give us focus, but our theory must be broad and accurate enough to not leave us myopic in how we define and use terms to fully understand what public relations can and should do to make a society more fully functioning. This requires understanding the specific and appropriate cast of characters, their relationships, and the meaning that drives these relationships and emerges from them.

As a Part of the Classroom

What then does this book mean for the classroom, and how can it best be used? That question focuses on the reality that each book is very likely to serve scholars by offering statements that agree with theirs and support them, as well as serving for the starting point in fruitfully corrective discussions that can continually refine and enhance the profession.

But, what about the classroom? For those who suppose that rhetoric is the teaching of the craft of manipulation, we hope they are disabused of that opinion and offered a better perspective—a more useful and accurate frame by the presentation of cases and sharing of analysis that follows in this book. Since the time of the ancient Greeks, the first Western thinkers to formally and systematically study rhetoric as the art of public discourse, thinkers have realized it was an art, not a science. There are no levers to be pulled or buttons to be pushed to control the minds, opinions, and actions of others. Humans are too complex and discourse is too tricky and uncertain. No one who has seriously studied rhetoric, and who recognizes the role of criticism, is misled into such a narrow and dysfunctional sense of the art to think that it is a stealth bomber that can get through appropriate defenses. And, so, that theme underpins our rhetorical and critical approach. It is an art. It is not a stealth bomber.

Thus, an attempt to use this book to teach in a prescriptive way can be frustrating. It does not lead itself to the classroom dedicated to a "rules based logic" of communication strategy: If X outcome, with audience Y, then apply strategy Z. We don't believe that rhetoric, criticism, or public relations works that way. It first of all requires reflection, and an awareness of what is the prevailing rhetorical question in some matter and what are the ethical and strategic options available and even required to address that problem.

One approach to the use of this book is to have it serve as the basis of dialogue—discourse that invites and even provokes students to engage several key questions. What is public relations? What role or roles does it play in society? How can it and should it be used to engage others in discourse? How can it and should it be used in the attempt to influence others' judgments and actions? Now, that line of questions presumes that students might have been rewarded in some other class with X points for selecting from multiple choice, true false, or short identification in answer to "what is public relations?" Can it be so reduced? Can that view be enlarged by discussion, using thoughts relevant to rhetoric and critical judgment? The teacher using this book, then, might find it useful to ask students to write several short papers.

The first paper could challenge the students to ferret out and use principles of rhetoric and criticism to define public relations. Such effort will bring students to think of themselves and their profession, and what good or harm they can do for society and even specific individuals and key organizations.

The book is divided into four sections. The first serves most generally as the foundation for the rest of the book. It is not designed or presumed to address all of the principles of rhetoric and criticism that are discussed and applied later, but the study needs a foundation. The first section, which is most relevant to the discussion of public relations as public relations, lays out the assumptions that people, including students and practitioners, make and should make when thinking about how discourse works and what role it serves in society. Those chapters can help students extract principles, which can even be stated as bullet points, that can guide their professional practice. They may realize that rhetorical strategies and critical assumptions are inseparable from views on the nature of society, collective decisions, and the roles of government and business.

Those principles, which can be expanded and refined as the students read more, can also ask and help them address a few more questions. What role does public relations play in society? What does that mean for my identity, who I think I am and who I want to be, as a member of the society? How can these thoughts sustain me in the practice of public relations over the years? As one of the editors has asked students over the years: If you sat next to a person on a plane who claimed to be a pediatric neurosurgeon, can you say with reasonable pride, "I am in public relations"? Or do we hide that fact, use a different job title, or change the conversation? Does public relations, and how each of us would and should practice it, serve society? Do we blanche when we tell our parents that is our major? A hint: One student in answering the question framed by the hypothetical neurosurgeon once wrote: "I would say, I am in public relations. I could help you and children by working to raise money for those who could not afford the best surgery? I could publicize your practice and that of your profession so that parents and guardians could better understand what services are available and how to get them? I could lobby for government support of those who need the services, but who are too poor to pay? I could help create and publicize foundations?" Should that student have received high marks for the essay?

A question for a second short essay paper could ask students to read additional chapters, draw on the principles selected and justified in the first paper, and discuss how rhetorical and critical approaches to public relations can serve marketing—image or reputation creation, publicity, promotion, and other activities relevant to the market place—the ways organizations of all types generate revenue and earn resources they need to operate effectively.

A third question (and a third short paper) could focus more on issues, crises, risks—the highly contentious aspects of the mutually beneficial relationships, or highly contentious relationships between people and organizations. Some who think of public relations only consider it to be a part of marketing, the selling of goods and services—the development of reputation and brand equity. Others think of it narrowly as issues management with issue communication, as crisis communication, and even risk communication. But the reality is that both of these broad challenges are part of what public relations practitioners do, and should do—rhetorically and critically. Public relations is not just buzz, or hype. It deals with real and fundamental questions of how well and responsibly (even respectfully) people associate with one another, and how and what roles organizations play in that relationship.

What responsibilities do organizations have for standing before the community where they operate to report on a crisis, to discuss an issue, or to address risks that concern one or more publics? Can one carefully crafted statement, issued by a company spokesperson, make a crisis go away? Can one carefully crafted statement make concerned citizens accept a risk that they believe is too great for them to bear?

After reading, discussing, and thinking about this book, what conclusions should students draw? A final short essay paper could address that line of inquiry. If we seriously believe that the character of practitioners is a key aspect of their ethical practice, is that not the closing theme? Aristotle, as featured in various chapters, reasoned that facts—the ability to prove propositions foundational to discourse—and character were the two universal standards of the excellent rhetorician. Obliquely, Plato set that standard, but then denigrated rhetoric and assigned it to be a craft similar to cookery. Isocrates and Quintilian both thought character and service to society were the primary signs of a good rhetor and responsible rhetoric.

We are prone, perhaps, in our time, to say that the best practitioner is he or she who works on behalf of some sponsor but with the goal of making the organization, its relationships, and the society in which it operates more fully functioning. Is that line of reasoning a solid rationale for the final paper? Who am I as a person, not just a corporate puppet, who aspires to be a public relations practitioner? Can I serve my employer well if I lack character and put the interest of my employer before or above other interests? Is the balance needed one that brings power, control, and interest together for collective and mutually beneficial outcomes?

More implicitly than explicitly, the analysis that is developed in the following chapters offers insights at three levels of analysis in keeping with the timeless challenge of George Herbert Mead (1934). He reasoned that analysis of the human condition requires examination of mind, self, and society. He was interested in how people think, the cognitive aspects of their mind, as well as their development of a sense of self, who they perceive themselves to be. Finally, he asked that both of those points of analysis be centered on the larger question of society. More recently, Motion and Leitch (2007) have used discourse analysis and European sociological analysis to augment the three focal points advanced by Mead. They reason that analysis of public relations and the work of practitioners needs to address matters of ideation (mind), identity (self), and relationship (society).

Finally, is the rationale for rhetoric, and therefore for public relations, to give effective voice to interests, concerns, hopes, information, evaluations, doubts, uncertainty, power, control, and such? Is that voice one among many? If so, what should that voice do in inviting and responding to other voices? How can we cooperate—and compete? How can we bring sound character to play? How can we reasonably and seriously look for agreement without abandoning principle? As strange as it might seem, especially for a tradition and a profession, each of which is often maligned, to think that they actually are inherently socially responsible. And, as Burke (1946) asked, "How can a world with rhetoric stay decent, how can a world without it exist at all?" The fact he raised this question demonstrates the paradox of rhetoric, with its companion lines of analysis: social constructionism, constitutive approaches to shared meaning, intersubjectivity, discourse analysis, and critical studies. The answer is in the doing and the doing of it well in ways that make society more fully functioning.

Final Thoughts

If the editors or authors leave the reader with the belief that a rhetorical and critical approach is inherently manipulative or otherwise prone to distort the quality of societal dialogue, then we have failed. Nothing is further from the minds and purposes of those who worked to create the first and now second volume. Also, we hope not to imply that we encourage students to think that if they are clever enough they can control opinions, manage meaning, and engineer consent. We seek to open minds to the challenges rather than provide or even suggest that public relations is formulaic—or always beneficial and good no matter how it is practiced. We are mindful that the flaws in discourse, which are the flaws in human nature, are going to translate into the flaws of individual, organizational, and societal relationships. The question is whether one individual or one organization can put matters right or even better by engaging in some more "constructive process" or whether the matter is to co-create meaning that can foster harmony where there has been unhealthy conflict, marginalization, manipulation, or alienation. In short, as we have discussed above and will stress in the chapters that follow, meaning counts; it counts for individual, organizational, and societal success.

References

Cutlip, S. M. (1994). *The unseen power: Public relations. A history*. Hillsdale, NJ: Lawrence Erlbaum.

Bitzer, L. (1968). The rhetorical situation. *Philosophy and Rhetoric, 1*, 1–15.

Bitzer, L. (1987). Rhetorical public communication. *Critical Studies in Mass Communication, 4*, 425–428.

Burke, K. (1946, October 22). Letter to Malcolm Cowley, Burke File, Pennsylvania State University.

Gordon, J., & Pellegrin, P. (2008). Social constructionism and public relations. In T. L. Hansen-Horn, & B. D. Neff (Eds.), *Public relations: From theory to practice* (pp. 104–121). Boston: Pearson.

Hallahan, K. (1999). Seven models of framing: Implications for public relations. *Journal of Public Relations Research, 11*(3), 205–242.

Heath, R. L. (1994). *Management of corporate communication: From interpersonal contacts to external affairs.* Hillsdale, NJ: Lawrence Erlbaum.

Heath, R. L. (2001). A rhetorical enactment rationale for public relations: The good organization communicating well. In R. L. Heath (Ed.), *Handbook of public relations* (pp. 31–50). Thousand Oaks, CA: Sage.

Mead, G. H. (1934). *Mind, self, and society.* Chicago, IL: University of Chicago Press.

Motion, J., & Leitch, S. (2007). A toolbox for public relations: The *oeuvre* of Michel Foucault. *Public Relations Review, 33,* 263–268.

Stokes, A. Q. (2005). Metabolife's meaning: A call for the constitutive study of public relations. *Public Relations Review, 31*(4), 556–565.

Vaara, E., Tienari, J., & Laurila, J. (2006). Pulp and paper fiction: On the discursive legitimation of global industrial restructuring. *Organizational Studies, 27*(6), 789–810.

SECTION ONE

RHETORICAL HERITAGE AND CRITICAL TRADITION

Theoretical traditions develop because humans have an innate desire to classify, explain, order, predict, understand and/or clarify their worlds, phenomena, and the unknown. We as humans are by nature conceptual beings. Similarly, ancient and today's scholars of communication and public relations develop theories, and offer them for debate and testing. However, our individual and scholarly theories, that find support, then begin to shape and influence how we see phenomena, what we see (and don't see), as well as why we interpret what we see in the ways that we do.

The opening assertion about the conceptual nature of human beings leads us to ask the following questions: (1) How are we taught and do we choose our systems of classification and labeling? (2) Can each individual's perception of a pattern differ from another person's perception of the same pattern? (3) If so, which perception of the pattern is the TRUE pattern (if there is such a pattern)? (4) If any one person's perception of the pattern is the only opinion or is among the minority opinion pertaining to that pattern, is it given adequate exposure in the scholarly literature and in society more broadly? (5) Is that minority opinion or theory valued? (6) Is it silenced? This is not an exhaustive list of questions raised; however, the possible answers to these questions are addressed in this first section.

The authors of Section One provide rhetorical and critical theory frameworks that have developed around the organizational practice of public relations. Our choice of rhetorical and critical theory frameworks is not exhaustive; but, these frameworks represent some of the most influential and powerful conceptualizations in the scholarly literature. As well, they suggest directions that this line of inquiry is taking since the 1992 *Rhetorical and Critical Approaches* was published. A lot has happened since then. More will build on these foundations.

Chapter 1 discusses the rhetorical tradition and its import to the study of public relations. This discussion reasons that rhetoric is dialogic, and it is a contest among multiple voices. As such, spirited debate is the essence of the rhetorical heritage, and this heritage is rooted in the belief that people as individuals (and publics as more collective voices) have the right and the ability to obtain and judge messages and make enlightened decisions accordingly. Moreover, as voices relevant to the dialogue in society, various publics engage in this conversation to make enlightened choices about products, services, organizations, issues, crises, and risks. If there is no difference of opinion, there is no need for rhetoric. And because there are differences of opinion, rhetoric instantiates the democratic process.

Although the rhetorical and critical approaches at times have different end results in mind, they are both useful when scholars explore the meaning derived by publics and organizations as they both (re)negotiate relationships that are mutually beneficial to them. With this said, chapter 2 wrestles with the opening six questions raised that frame this introduction, in a call for pluralistic studies in public relations. This chapter highlights the sociopolitical nature of theory building and theory usage in public relations, but more importantly highlights the strength of studying and researching in a rich, multi-theoretical discipline. In a similar vein, it is widely accepted that questioning a theory's usefulness is wiser than questioning its truthfulness because any truth can be represented in a variety of ways, depending on the theorist's orientation. Said differently, Anderson (1996), quoting Dewey, argued that "there is no single reality; instead there are as many realities as there are acceptable epistemological lines of action" (p. 40). Furthermore, Anderson stated:

> Our observational evidence was shown to be corrupted by our theories. Theory itself was shown to be better explained by sociological rather than evidentiary practices. And the evidence we did generate was shown to be promiscuous rather than fruitful. The conclusions are stunning: observations are arguments, theories are sociopolitical practices, and truth is plural. (p. 4)

If truth is plural, and if all communication theories are mutually relevant when addressed to a practical world in which we live (Craig, 1999), then our discipline can only benefit from the pluralism of theoretical approaches called for in chapter 2.

Although from a rhetorical theory standpoint, publics have the ability to express opinions about and interpret information from organizations, as well as judge organizational messages and make enlightened decisions based on those messages, some critical scholars argue that issues of power and hegemony thwart that process of enlightened choice and as such that hidden power and privilege must be exposed by the critical scholar for the betterment of the profession and society as a whole. It is not enough that (from the rhetorical standpoint) the "good organization, communicating well" sets forth the most persuasive, valid, sound, winning argument; rather, from a critical standpoint, questions of access and fairness almost indelibly emerge. Was the more powerful rhetor (the organization with more money and more resources) able to restrict or otherwise unfairly and inappropriately slant the public discussion to being only among other powerful rhetors? Whose interests are being served and agendas being forwarded by the said "enlightened decision"? Does the policy and power that results from dialogue make society better or merely privilege the most economically powerful voice? Does apparent "power" differences (such as deep pockets) really distort the dialogue, or in fact does that power discredit the voice of the powerful in the minds of various critics?

Chapter 3 pushes our theoretical envelope and intellectual domain, putting the integrative themes of chapter 2 into practice. In this chapter, public relations students and scholars alike are challenged to broaden their reading (as it provides a list of theorists and a brief synopsis of their works) and theoretical toolbox so that students, scholars, and practitioners can develop theories that can better inform our understanding of the practice and field of public relations.

Taking the rhetorical tradition and applying it to a specific theoretical approach, chapter 4, in part, argues for a theory of civil society and discusses how building a civil society is indeed a rhetorical process. Arguments are presented; various kinds of sense must be made of what is in the best interest of society and its members; building civil society is a rhetorical give and take. The author believes that such a worldview as citizenry coming together to build community is not ideal but underway in many nations of the world.

And as this introduction highlights theoretical traditions and public relations, this discussion would be incomplete if it did not take into account the various perspectives on public relations history. Chapter 5 appears unchanged from the first version of this volume. Its author Ron Pearson died as his promising career was being launched. His friends believe that this chapter is one of his most lasting legacies. Pearson illustrated that even accounts of history come with embedded values and rhetorical choices. Moreover, this chapter remains relevant to explaining why public relations practice has evolved as it has. It continues to make the compelling case that the value of information and the shaping of arguments is never purely neutral, but necessarily occurs within several competing worldviews.

Critical scholars attempt to unveil the hidden powers that alienate and marginalize portions of society. One such hegemonic force that operates in both our profession and society is issues of gender. From a feminist theory approach, chapter 6 highlights how gender can impact public relations texts and contexts, adversely affect both men and women in the profession, as well as marginalize persons globally. Aldoory argues that gendered norms of society provide the basis on which society and organizations make rhetorical choices, especially those that constrain the practice and practitioners of public relations.

Theoretical traditions can get replaced by competing views for multiple reasons. One reason is that scholars in the field may disagree with the scope, generalizability, and application of a theory. Scholars have found problems with many communication theories (see Reddy's 1979 conduit metaphor) and public relations theories (see J. E. Grunig, 2001, past, present, and future of Excellence theory). However, these theories are still used to explain many portions of communication activities. Although competing views have surfaced, these theories still manage to live on. Thus, as students of public relations it is important to know that having many scholars that disagree with a theory does not necessarily lead to the theory getting dismissed completely.

Typically theories get replaced when they become obsolete. New research conducted may explain an existing phenomenon better than the current theory; current theory may no longer adequately and sufficiently explain a phenomenon; or time, people, and/or the phenomenon being studied can change. Thus, a theory can get replaced by competing views if the existing theory is no longer seen as significant or is deemed trivial.

As students and practitioners being exposed to the field and theories of public relations, continually ask yourselves how certain theoretical frameworks shape the way you approach and study communicative and public relations phenomena. Ask yourselves how another theoretical approach might better explain the topic in question. Ask yourselves how other perspectives might better inform how you could or should approach various scenarios in your work environments.

This text, *Rhetorical and Critical Approaches to Public Relations II,* in its totality is a representation of what the editors believe to be a rich representation of the rhetorical and critical theoretical approaches to public relations today. The histories of these approaches are long and long-lived, and one can hope that this volume and the chapters within highlight the vibrancy of these approaches and further contribute to the literature, theory building, and practice of this field that is public relations.

References

Anderson, J. A. (1996). *Communication theory: Epistemological foundations.* The Guilford Press: New York.

Craig, R. T. (1999). Communication theory as a field. *Communication Theory, 9,* 119–161.

Grunig, J. E. (2001). Two-way symmetrical public relations: Past, present, and future. In R. L. Heath (Ed.), *Handbook of public relations* (pp. 11–30). Thousand Oaks, CA: Sage.

Reddy, M. J. (1979). The conduit metaphor: A case of frame conflict in our language about language. In A. Ortony (Ed.), *Metaphor and thought* (pp. 285–310). New York: Cambridge University Press.

1

THE RHETORICAL TRADITION
Wrangle in the Marketplace

Robert L. Heath
University of Houston

What is public relations? What role does it play in society? What role should it play or how should it serve society? When does it not serve society or when does it discredit itself by doing disservice to society? How are young people inspired to study for entry into the profession? What motivates them to go to work with enthusiasm during their career? Does it rely on supplying information? Does it use persuasion? Does it both inform and persuade? Does it motivate? Does it collaborate, negotiate, and resolve conflict? Does it use misinformation, disinformation, and engage in propaganda? Can it help make society more fully functional? If so, how can it help accomplish that end? Can it make society less functional? If so, how does it accomplish that end? Do activist groups and governmental agencies engage in public relations, or is it only a discipline that is unique to companies, the private sector? How is the social impact of public relations (and the organizations that engage in it) affected by what practitioners do (processes) and by what they say and write (meaning)?

One can imagine that each answer to those questions reflects the way any person defines public relations, sees its role in society as constructive or destructive, and assumes it to be rewarding of their time, ingenuity, talents, ethics, and sense of personal self-worth. If we announce to our parents, friends, or even complete strangers that we are "in public relations," do we shudder and then shy away from further conversation on the matter?

Plenty of definitions of public relations can be found; the same is true of rhetoric. The discussion of rhetoric is ancient; it was a robust part of educating citizens in ancient Greece and the Roman Empire. Today scholars are attentive to its nature and role in society, as is evident by the extensive coverage of this topic in the *International Encyclopedia of Communication* (Donsbach, 2008), which devotes a section to the topic including an entry on "Rhetorical Theory of Public Relations" (Ihlen, 2008; see also Ihlen, 2002). Rhetoric and public relations take their rationale from efforts humans make to influence one another, and to be influenced—necessary to society. As Gaines and Gronbeck (2008) observed, "The rhetorical impulse may be conceived as the desire to express one's thoughts in a way that affects the thoughts of others" (p. 4382). Is that also the rationale for public relations? And is the challenge to achieve influence but without managing meaning to the advantage of one entity at the disadvantage of one or more others?

In such matters, the most important challenge to each practitioner is to rely on definitions that satisfy him or her in ways that also reflect a responsible answer to these questions. By responsible, one can mean a definition that could be proudly discussed in public that reflects a balance between many interests, some that may be dramatically at odds with one another. As much as it might startle some, the rhetorical heritage helps us define public relations and set our sails on that matter. Effective, ethical, and responsive public relations depends on knowledge of and support for ethical, reflective, and savvy management as the centerpiece in academic research and public relations practice.

In moving toward a definition that melds public relations and rhetoric, one principle from the rhetorical heritage endures. Ancient Roman teaching of rhetoric brings us to champion this sage advice to a speaker: Be a good person who can therefore speak well (Quintilian, 1951). This definition emphasizes the judgment that the character of the speaker (organization in our times) is a vital part of the likely impact of any message and the role (whether constructive or destructive) the communicator plays in society. As organizations have replaced individuals as key figures in society (Cutlip, 1994; Heath, 2008a), we must analyze what it means to be a good organization communicating well. Here is a definition for consideration:

> Public relations is the management function that entails planning, research, publicity, promotion, and collaborative decision making to help any organization's ability to listen to, appreciate, and respond appropriately to those persons and groups whose mutually beneficial relationships the organization needs to foster as it strives to achieve its mission and vision.
>
> (Heath & Coombs, 2006, p. 7)

The legendary John W. Hill (1958) (co-founder of Hill & Knowlton) advised us to understand management as the initial step toward appreciating the roles and challenges facing public relations professionals. He cautioned,

> It is not the work of public relations—let it always be emphasized—to outsmart the American public in helping management build profits. It is the job of public relations to help management find ways of identifying its own interests with the public interest—ways so clear that the profit earned by the company may be viewed as contributing to the progress of everybody in the American economy. (p. 21)

He added, "Big companies, if they are properly managed, have a keen sense of public responsibility. They guide their policies in keeping with the public interest and make sure that each of their plants is a good neighbor in its respective community" (p. 39). Hill's position squares with the advice offered by Quintilian and captures the richness of the rhetorical tradition as the rationale for the responsible practice of public relations.

Seeing the need for management to learn from the variety of positions being advocated by various voices, Hill (1958) observed, "Good corporate public relations depend, first, upon sound policies truly in the public interest and second, upon clear and effective communication, explanation, and interpretation of policies and facts to the public" (p. 163). The interests of each private and public sector organization can never be indifferent to the public interest, but must achieve symmetry or harmony with that interest. This logic values a synergism between both interests based on process, ethics, and co-creation of shared meaning. It assumes that relationship development must be mutual for each organization to obtain resources held by its stakeholders. Those resources are required for the organization to succeed. Both interests can be adjusted to one another by organizations moving closer to the public interest by understanding and appreciating it as well as communicating about the ways in which the organization operates in the public interest. From this position, Hill (1963) reasoned:

> Business managements are concerned with the problems of conducting their corporate or industry affairs in ways that they may feel are contributive to public progress. They must arrive at effective policies that go far beyond their economic and operating functions into the complex realms of social, governmental, and political relationships. The large majority pushes forward into these policy areas as a matter of choice. But in terms of the long-range survival of corporate enterprise, there is little choice involved; it is a matter of essentiality. (p. 230)

Rhetoric is often seen as telling lies, distorting, spinning the truth, and manipulating, but the rhetorical heritage believes no communicator or manager can be effective without first being a good listener who wants to know, appreciate, and respect what others believe and think—and why they hold those positions. And such persons want to know why others act as they do based on the information they know and interpret and opinions they believe or reject. In this way, public relations and the rhetorical heritage focus attention not narrowly on the self-interest and opinions of the organization but on the persons whose goodwill is needed for the organization to succeed. In this way, public relations and rhetoric are inherently other oriented.

Set against Hill's perspective on public relations is the view of Edward Bernays (1955) that public relations can help engineer consent. Both grew up professionally in an era when practitioners' skills were honed by engaging in what was called propaganda. This concept guided public communication during World War I and continuing into World War II. Hill and other modern pioneers of the public relations profession realized that propaganda was a term suffering from substantial disrepute as it became associated with manipulation, especially lying and deception. A recent version of the engineering approach was presented by Madden (1997) who reasoned that public relations is like a stealth bomber, capable of influencing opinion because it penetrates minds like a stealth bomber penetrates radar systems undetected and without meeting resistance. Those communication options might win for a while but ultimately fail as does any profession that builds its rationale on them. Propaganda is the essence of asymmetry. Rhetoric is inherently symmetrical, focusing ultimately on the quality of ideas that result from the process of public statement and counterstatement (Heath, 2001). Any truly ethical public relations practitioner (especially those informed on the principles of rhetoric) realize that each statement must be carefully made and soundly supported because it can and likely will encounter counterstatement. To serve society, and help people make enlightened choices, it must be able to stand in the face of resistance, doubt, and challenge.

With these propositions in mind, we conclude that the nexus between the rhetorical heritage and public relations is squarely this: Both deal with "unsettled matters." Where there is choice, where choice is required by various circumstances, and people are free to make such choice, that is the realm of rhetoric. For that reason, it offers an excellent rationale for understanding the ethical practice of public relations which has the responsibility to serve communities of interest, and not merely one interest, of the organization paying for the professional service. On this basis, we explore the topic of rhetorical foundations for public relations in more detail during this chapter, as throughout this book.

Pillars of Public Relations Theory

Communication, especially in the rhetorical tradition, does not consist of one entity putting ideas and meaning into the minds of others. Meaning is the constitutive and attributive interpretations one person makes of the statements and actions of another. Practitioners are in the *message and meaning business*. For this reason, public relations theory and professional best practices require a solid understanding of messages and the meaning they can create—as well as how they can fail to adequately address rhetorical problems confronted by their employers, clients, and others in society. The rhetorical heritage provides an evolving body of strategic and critical insights to help practitioners be effective and ethical as they participate in the process by which society creates meaning—or meaning is created in society. Rhetorical theory has combined with organizational communication theory to feature the reality that all actions—the enactment of meaning—by organizations is rhetorical. As well as engaging in ethical processes of public relations, practitioners recognize that meaning matters (Heath & Frandsen, 2008).

To flesh out these conclusions, the rest of this section explores the theoretical foundations of various theories to understand and critique their usefulness for creating the theory and supporting the practice of public relations.

Systems theory, as well as its derivative *structural functionalism*, is useful for understanding and improving the processes of public relations, but it fails to help practitioners and scholars understand what messages are strategically and ethically relevant to each of the many adjustments required for information to flow and relationships to be in balance. Heavily focused on process, systems theory does not explain the role of ethics, language, and meaning in the efforts to foster or correct imbalance or achieve balance.

If practitioners and academics are to use discourse to make society more fully functional (Heath, 2006), they must know and share facts, but realize they do not come to us with inherently granted conclusions; although they may have a scientific origin and meaning, they also are burdened by political implications. Campbell (1996), comparing scientists for whom "the most important concern is the discovery and testing of certain kinds of truths" to "rhetoricians (who study rhetoric and take a rhetorical perspective) would say, 'Truths cannot walk on their own legs. They must be carried by people to other people. They must be explained, defended, and spread through language, argument, and appeal'" (p. 3). From this foundation, Campbell reasoned, rhetoricians take the position "that unacknowledged and unaccepted truths are of no use at all" (p. 3). The rhetorical tradition is founded on facts; since the age of Aristotle, rhetors have been required to assert and demonstrate their propositions by producing fact. Gaudino, Fritsch, and Haynes (1989) and others have indicted the assumption that "if you knew what I know we would agree," as though sharing information is the sole solution to public relations problems and the theory of how those problems can best be solved.

Rhetorical theory features the role information, fact, plays in shaping knowledge and opinions as well as being convincing and motivating actions. It addresses the ways evaluations are debated and confirmed or challenged. It contests the wisdom of various policies, identities, and reputations. As people compete through public and private debate to assert the strength of their ideas framed in propositional discourse, their statements exhibit an invitational quality (Foss & Griffin, 1995). As such, Burke (1969b) defined it as the "use of suasive devices for the transcending of social estrangement" (p. 208).

Rhetoric is inherently dialogic, a contest among multiple voices. Each voice knows that others may disagree—or agree. Assuming that alternative views have merit, they are set before interested parties for consideration. Spirited debate is the essence of the rhetorical heritage that believes in the right and ability of people to obtain and judge messages and make enlightened decisions accordingly.

Rhetoric instantiates the democratic process because it presumes that any position voiced in public must be sufficiently compelling to withstand vigorous critiques by other rhetors who believe their competing ideas have merit. For decades, large companies and governmental agencies—as well as various non-profits—have been viewed variously as tyrants and as valued sources of fact, evaluation, recommendation, and relationship through identification. Any view offers the opening of debate, public scrutiny.

A rhetorical perspective realizes that people interpret information by advocating contestable propositions regarding its accuracy, sufficiency, and relevance. As advocates for various interpretations of the data, participants in symmetrical communication seek to advance their views as being accurate and supportable and in mutual interest. They defend and attack conclusions and recommendations based on the data and premises available. Their discourse is often a clash of perspectives. Data are meaningless until interpreted; interpretation requires advocacy. Advocacy invokes propositional language and counter persuasion, in contrast to what we might call propaganda. This rhetorical perspective offers an epistemic, advisory, and invitational rationale for public relations.

Critical studies, such as those that have been primarily inspired by European thinkers, complete the troika of the pillars for public relations. Some lines of critical investigation grow from the rhetorical heritage. Other approaches to criticism draw heavily on social, sociopolitical theory to investigate and critique the roles large organizations play in the quality of the discourse of society, and in the quality of society itself. Critical studies both constitute an application of rhetoric to advocate qualitatively superior options and to judge the quality of the processes and procedures of discourse. While not indifferent to process, critical theory explores the deficits of systems theory and rhetoric by invoking ethical standards, ideological underpinnings, through discourse analysis steeped in the ethics of social democracy (see Cheney & Christensen, 2001).

Rhetoric to the Rescue

Because of profound misunderstanding of the rhetorical heritage, founding public relations theory and practice on rhetorical theory can be as risky in our times as it was to use propaganda as the rationale for public relations nearly 100 years ago (Fearn-Banks, 2005; Heath, 2005; Lubbers 2005a, 2005b). What we need is a way to address the current mistaken and politicized view of rhetoric as "mere," "hollow words," or something that can and should be "turned down," a stance often taken to discredit or even mute opponents. Out of the 1960s era of social protest, the cynical "rhetorical position" called others' expression on any matter "mere rhetoric." We hear, especially in political debate or in reaction to critics, the request to "turn down the rhetoric." That view of rhetoric suggests that if we make heartfelt and sincere statements with sharp words and pointed facts then we somehow distort the way that debate, advocacy, and dialogue should occur. In fact, that assumption flies in the face of the rhetorical heritage which since the golden age of Greece has focused on one central theme: How can statements be given more impact to make points that are worthy of consideration in and reconciliation by society.

Let's frame rhetoric a bit more before discussing various perspectives on rhetoric, key strategies and contexts, and ethics. Central to the heritage of rhetoric is a keen interest in how discourse can make society more fully functioning (Heath, 2006). The role of rhetoric enters where there is difference of opinion, doubt, uncertainty, and even firmly held opinions which may be wrong. Words and other kinds of symbolic discourse that work against an end of supporting sound choice are not "mere rhetoric," but are inappropriate rhetoric. Support for this line of reasoning came from Cutilip (1994) who observed, "only through the expertise of public relations can causes, industries, individuals, and institutions make their voice heard in the public forum where thousands of shrill, competing voices daily re-create the Tower of Babel" (p. ix). Through dialogue, individuals and groups co-create and negotiate identity, interest, and socially relevant meaning (Mead, 1934). Rhetoric enters the human experience because people have different views, different opinions, and prefer different actions. To the extent that collective and coordinated behavior is useful and even necessary, difference needs to be reconciled. We assume that better ideas can defeat inferior ones.

Rhetoric is the rationale for effective discourse. It consists of a well-established body of critical principles and strategic guidelines regarding how messages need to be proved, structured, framed, and worded. It is interested in how each message needs to be designed to be informative and persuasive. Because rhetorical theory arises out of disputes and differences of opinion, it offers guidelines on how people can negotiate differences and work together in collaborative decision making. It informs, creates divisions, and bridges divisions. It advocates, convinces, and motivates. It motivates people to make one choice in preference to another. If people everywhere shared the same information, opinion, and motives, there would be no need for rhetoric.

At its best, it is founded on the substance of good reasons (Wallace, 1963) to make society better for all. At its worst, it can engage in deception, manipulation, slander, character assassination, distortion, misinformation, and disinformation. Such motives tend to lead to some interests being privileged at the expense of others.

Champions of the rhetorical heritage believe that free and open discourse is the best answer to the misuse of the art. Some see rhetoric as competing voices (see Burke, 1969a; Brummett, 1995; L'Etang, 1996), each of which can enrich the search for truth and sound judgment. The best corrective for deception is public debate. In that format, one side of a controversy can be demonstrated to be false, manipulative, or deceptive. Public discourse, the forum of rhetoric, allows for combatants to challenge, correct, and elevate the discourse of society. Defending that view, Lentz (1996) reasoned: "Truth should prevail in a market-like struggle where superior ideas vanquish their inferiors and achieve audience acceptance" (p. 1). Rhetoric is ethical because it empowers participants to engage in dialogue, private or public. It confronts choice between having ideas, opinions, and actions "engineered" through propaganda or having them forged through the collective contest of ideas.

A rhetorical rationale of public relations views it as constructive dialogue, a wrangle in the marketplace of ideas, preferences, choices, and influence. Rhetoric is relevant to any context in which humans are compelled to make enlightened choice (Nichols, 1963). It is the rationale of suasive discourse which can and should lead to enlightened choices. That theme sets a firm, ethical, and socially responsible view of rhetoric and public relations. As Wallace (1963) advised, our discourse should prepare us to think back on important decisions; "statements that are evoked by the need to make choices in order that we may act or get ready to act or to appraise our acts after their doing" (p. 241). With that in mind we ask practitioners, in what way, each day, do you help others and yourself (and clients) to make enlightened choices? These themes will be systematically examined in the remainder of this chapter.

Rhetorical Tradition: Wrangle in the Marketplace

Rhetoric is employed when matters of various kinds are to be decided, when they are unsettled, when differences of opinion prevail, and when people are uncertain as to which of several decisions is best. It assists managements as they decide what strategies are available to promote and publicize a product or service, and even to shape an organization's image. It guides how they engage in issue debate, manage risks, and respond during crises. The rationale for rhetorical theory is that it helps us understand the process of decision making, collective efforts, and the give and take of conversation, debate, advocacy, accommodation, negotiation, and collaborative decision making.

Rhetoric's role in unsettled matters, Burke (1969b) noted, rests on the fact that society is a marketplace of ideas, facts, values, and policies: "the Scramble, the Wrangle of the Marketplace, the flurries and flare-ups of the Human Barnyard, Give and Take, the wavering line of pressure and counter pressure, the Logomachy, the onus of ownership, the War of Nerves, the War" (p. 23). For this reason, Burke (1973a) concluded that democracy institutionalizes "the dialectic process, by setting up a political structure that gives full opportunity for the use of competition to a cooperative end" (p. 444).

In each battle waged to achieve some collective outcome, each statement is not independent of others but gains its meaning and importance by how it agrees, disagrees, or otherwise responds to other statements. "Rhetoric is thus made from fragments of dialectic" (Burke, 1969b, p. 207). Dialectic, the cooperative use of competition, progresses from division through merger to identification. "A rhetorician, I take it, is like one voice in a dialogue. Put several such voices together, with each voicing its own special assertion, let them act upon one another in cooperative competition, and you get a dialectic that, properly developed can lead to views transcending the limitations of each" (Burke, 1951, p. 203). Each moment's work in public relations, by this rationale, competes for time and space with many others. Discourse analysis predicts how and why some statements will succeed and others will fail, as well as which are responsible, ethical, and in the public interest. The theory and ethics that drive rhetoric center on the rationale for suasive discourse, the art of influence and being influenced.

Given its 2500-year Western heritage since the golden age of Greece, some consider rhetoric to be the queen (lady or grand dame, see Brummett, 1995; L'Etang, 1996) of communication studies. Campbell (1996) championed rhetoric as "the study of what is persuasive. Issues it examines are social truths, addressed to others, justified by reasons that reflect cultural values. It is a humanistic study that examines all the symbolic means by which influence occurs" (p. 8). Connecting the heritage of rhetoric to the spirit of democracy in Ancient Greece, Kennedy (1963) framed the discipline this way: "In its origin and intention rhetoric was natural and good: it produced clarity, vigor, and beauty, and it rose logically from the conditions and qualities of the classical mind" (p. 3).

Burke (1965) cautioned, "Let the system of cooperation become impaired, and the communicative equipment is correspondingly impaired, while this impairment of the communicative medium in turn threatens the structure of rationality itself" (p. 163). The dialectic goes like this. Environmentalists argue that green is good, including green products, to create that identification. Extending that logic, manufacturers of consumer products appeal for identification based on claims that their products are green and environmentally sound.

This dialectic progression demands "a third term that will serve as the ground or medium of communication between opposing terms. And whatever logical problems such a third term may give rise to, we are being logical in feeling the need for it" (Burke 1969a, p. 405). Rhetoric, linguistic transformation, grows through act and counteract. More specifically, the process moves from act, through counteract, to the lesson learned. In public relations, an organization or spokesperson suffers opposition based on what it does or says: "the dialectical (agonistic) approach to knowledge is through the act of assertion, whereby one 'suffers' the kind of knowledge that is the reciprocal of this act" (Burke, 1969a, pp. 39-40).

Which choice is best, most correct, wisest, and preferable? Aristotle believed that the communicator is obliged to prove such advice as he or she asserts. Proofs of several kinds are the substance of rhetoric. These proofs are made useful through the presentation of fact and reasoning. They feature values and reveal the character of the speaker. In this way, an audience could assess the credibility of all rhetors (spokespersons in this context) by considering the values on which they base their life and build their messages. The end to which all discourse should be aimed is the public interest, identifications that are mutually beneficial. Values and good reasons are classic ingredients of rhetorical discourse, along with a scrupulous interest in the soundness of arguments based on fact and flawless reasoning as the soundness of each perspective asserted for others to adopt.

Rhetoric as Function and Strategy

Concerns about sham presentation, lying, and manipulation have forced considered critical commentary on the topic of rhetoric. These comments help us discuss how public relations can and should foster dialogue, contribute to that dialogue, and serve many interests, not merely that of the spokesperson. Debate over the factors that make ethical and effective discourse reach back at least 2500 years to the time of Plato.

Plato: A Critic of Rhetoric

As do critics today, Plato conceived of rhetoric as cookery, what we might today call "public relations spin," where truth is not as important as its appearance. He scorned the use of deceit rather than means for discovering truth, improving knowledge, or forming enlightened policy. He feared that it was employed for evil ends and consisted of trickery aimed at achieving an outcome one party desired indifferent and even purposefully harmful to the interest of others. He doubted that rhetoric could avoid making false accusations and using contrived evidence for unethical ends. In its place, Plato preferred dialectic to disclose truth through focused interrogation of one person by another. He assumed one party in each exchange is more knowledgeable and therefore able to lead the other party to a predetermined truth.

Despite Kennedy's (1963) sense of ancient Greeks' love for public discourse logically crafted and eloquently presented, Plato (1952) caustically cautioned that "rhetoric is not an art at all, but the habit of a bold and ready wit, which knows how to manage mankind: this habit I sum up under the word 'flattery'" (p. 262). By such criticism, Plato forced generations of communicators to be mindful of ethics, but his narrowing distortion of the sociopolitical role of the rhetorical tradition denied people access to means by which to engage democratically in public discourse to share information, propose opinions, and seek mutually beneficial solutions to collective problems. Plato's cynical assessment of rhetoric, which is voiced even today, extends to public relations if it is vacuous, manipulative spin doctoring. To support socially responsible ends, public relations must put into play the best information evaluated by the most ethical observations in support of mutually beneficial choices that can help society to function better. Most, also, would prefer public debate to having decisions made by management elites along the lines of Plato's philosopher king.

Aristotle: Blending Rhetoric, Politics and Ethics

Aristotle, a pupil of Plato, enriched the rhetorical tradition by focusing on the ethics of the process and substance of public discourse as contributing to the good of society and supported by an articulated ethics. As did others, he featured the role of rhetoric in the training of citizens and the virtue of discourse in society.

He determined that rhetoric was strategically functional; it was designed to solve problems and achieve outcomes with audiences whose opinions might differ and which might respond to different appeals. He found three prevailing contexts: Deliberative (political communication, including legislative debate), judicial (what we would call litigation), and epideictic (occasional or special situation communication). Each context was defined by its unique purpose and desired outcome. Deliberative rhetoric demonstrates the expedience of some policy, what it is best to do under the circumstances. Forensic rhetoric deals with guilt and innocence. Epideictic rhetoric is concerned with matters of praise and blame. This last context has recently been wisely used to examine crisis communication (see Huxman, 2004, for instance; for an application of principles of deliberative rhetoric to crisis, see Johnson & Sellnow, 1995).

Aristotle observed three major kinds of proof: Logos (typically featured as the logic of fact and reasoning about facts), pathos (conceptualized as the emotionally relevant value judgments related to a case), and ethos (roughly thought of as credibility but more wisely conceived as character). As such, the rhetor mounting a case is expected to focus on some problem and to recognize how different audiences may perceive and address that problem as well as respond differently to various proofs.

The rhetorical canon featured five elements of each presentation: Invention, structure, substance, delivery, and mastery. How the case was built depended on the rhetor's skills at invention, knowing what could and must be said to draw the appropriate conclusion. Ideas are not presented randomly, but need to follow one of several well-defined structures. The invention of a specific perspective requires knowledge of the relevant substance. All of this material needs to be effectively delivered (verbally and nonverbally), and with confidence that comes from mastery of the case. Some might call this mastery gravitas: Communicating with authority drawn from character.

These functional outcomes, forms of proof, and strategic elements needed a sound theoretical glue to hold them together and give them a laudable role in society. To produce such glue, Aristotle set two high ethical standards for those who engage in rhetoric. One is the need to demonstrate through evidence the factual basis for any claims advocated. As Aristotle (1952c) viewed the relationship between the discovery and exposition of ideas, he concluded that rhetoric is "the faculty of observing in any given case the available means of persuasion" (p. 595). The essence of persuasion is demonstration "since we are most fully persuaded when we consider a thing to have been demonstrated" (p. 594). Truth as it can best be known emerges through proof and reasoning presented for others to consider. The second standard is to demonstrate through the values espoused that the communicator is a good person speaking for a good cause—the demonstration of character. The highest good is the effort to make society better, more fully functional. His inquiry led to the conclusion that persons who engage in rhetoric must have a profound understanding of the role of discourse in a society, preferably one more disposed to democratic dispute rather than royal proclamation.

Aristotle believed that the character or *ethos* of public speakers—the predominant form of communication in the golden age of Greece—was vital to their success or failure as well as the wholesomeness of their social participation. Persons with more credibility are more believable and trustworthy because they associate their lives, arguments, and purposes with higher order values: Truth, morality and virtue. What distinguishes a speaker's character? Aristotle (1952c) answered: "good sense, good moral character, and goodwill" (p. 623). Standards of each "good" are basic to rhetoric which "exists to affect the giving of decisions" by listeners (readers or viewers) who then decide among the positions presented to them (p. 622).

He thought openness of public discourse motivated communicators to seek the best—strongest and most ethical points of view—because ideas are contested in public where they receive penetrating analysis. Aristotle believed the process entailed the seeking of truth through the process of public advocacy rather than leaving truth to be known (in the Platonic sense) by the singular analytic efforts of a "philosopher king." Thus, Aristotle took a stand 2500 years ago that was comfortable with the contemporary preference for two-way symmetrical communication. As Aristotle would argue, neither side in some controversy is inherently correct or morally right, but the process of exchange can reveal the interests of both sides so they can achieve a win-win, integrative outcome based on collaborative decision making.

With rhetoric, people collectively make decisions and form policy for the public good. In the opinion of Aristotle (1952b), "if all communities aim at some good," the best are those which aspire to "the highest good" (p. 445). Thus, rhetoric is judged by the quality of the process and its outcomes: "A man [or woman] can confer the greatest of benefits by a right use of these [techniques], and inflict the greatest of injuries by using them wrongly" (p. 594). "Every state is a community of some kind, and every community is established with a view of some good; for mankind always acts in order to obtain that which they think 'good'" (p. 445). Good can either be prescribed by one philosopher king (elitism) or decided by the populace (democracy).

What according to Aristotle (1952c) is the source of persuasiveness? "A statement is persuasive and credible either because it is directly self-evident or because it appears to be proved from other statements that are so" (p. 596). Aristotle believed that "Persuasion is achieved by the speaker's personal character when the speech is so spoken as to make us think him credible. We believe good men [and women] more fully and more readily than others" (p. 595). In this way, he believed that rhetoric should foster enlightened choice. For Aristotle (1952c), rhetoric serves to give counsel "on matters about which people deliberate; matters, namely, that ultimately depend on ourselves, and which we have it in our power to set going" (p. 599). Aristotle thought bad judgment and unsound character undo persuasion:

> Men [or women] either form a false opinion through want of good sense; or they form a true opinion, but because of their moral badness do not say what they really think; or finally, they are both sensible and upright, but not well disposed to their hearers, and may fail in consequence to recommend what they know to be the best course. (p. 623)

When a rhetor recommends a conclusion or action, he or she does so "on the ground that it will do good; if he [or she] urges its rejection, he [or she] does so on the ground that it will do harm" (Aristotle, 1952c, p. 598). People and societies are evaluated by the ends to which they aspire (Aristotle, 1952c, p. 608). Rhetoric is used to explore ways of achieving happiness by making choices that will do good and prevent or at least minimize harm. He observed, "When we know a thing, and have decided about it, there is no further use in speaking about it" (p. 639). This logic, crafted centuries ago, supports the rationale for public relations in our day. It can guide promotion and publicity as well as the dispute over issues, the resolution of crisis, and the ethical management of risk.

Centering attention on the connection between communication and ethics, Aristotle (1952a) began his *Nichomachean Ethics* by noting that, "Every art and every inquiry, and similarly every action and pursuit, is thought to aim at some good; and for this reason the good has rightly been declared to be that at which all things aim" (p. 339). "Therefore, virtue is a kind of mean, since, as we have seen, it aims at what is intermediate" (p. 352). For him, the higher ethical position was one that struck an appropriate balance between ethical extremes; some see this position as a fatal flaw in his ethics. Yet he reasoned that ethics must recognize "that moral virtue is a mean, then, and in what sense it is so, and that it is a mean between two vices, the one involving excess and the other deficiency, and that is such because its character is to aim at what is intermediate in passions and in actions" (p. 354). He firmly believed that some actions and morals were bad in and of themselves: "But not every action nor every passion admits of a mean; for some have names that already imply badness, e.g. spite, shamelessness, envy, and in the case of actions adultery, theft, murder" (p. 352).

For Aristotle (1952a), "it is no easy task to be good. For in everything it is no easy task to find the middle" (p. 376). For him ethics is a balance between excess and deficit, something that is learned through thoughts and actions that pit extremes against one another. The search is for the middle between the extremes, a win-win midpoint. He was interested in the search for justice: "We see that all men [and women] mean by justice that kind of state of character which makes people disposed to do what is just and makes them act justly and wish for what is just; and similarly by injustice that state which makes them act unjustly and wish for what is unjust" (p. 376). Thus, the tug of ethics is the process of knowing a state and its contrary state. Thus, the state of lying and not telling the truth is known as a contrast to the state of telling the truth.

Aristotle's (1952b) *Politics* frames his thoughts on rhetoric as he began his treatise: "Every state is a community of some kind, and every community is established with a view to some good; for mankind always act in order to obtain that which they think good. But, if all communities aim at some good, the state or political community, which is the highest of all, and which embraces all the rest, aims at good in the greater degree than any others, and at the highest good" (p. 445). "Virtue, then is a state of character concerned with choice" (Aristotle, 1952a, p. 352).

In his *Rhetoric* (1952c), he argued that "Rhetoric is useful (1) because things that are true and things that are just have a natural tendency to prevail over their opposites, so that if the decisions of judges are not what they ought to be, the defeat must be due to the speakers themselves, and they must be blamed accordingly" (p. 594). In this statement, Aristotle blended advocacy and symmetry. However narrow or incorrect one instance of advocacy might be, it is statement that is likely to suffer counterstatement in search for the truth. Aristotle's view, similar to symmetrical public relations, assumes that each voice deserves to be heard and judged for the merits of what is said. The voice of a big business, an activist group, a non-profit or government agency is not inherently superior to others. One voice should not drown out others.

> No other of the arts draws opposite conclusions: dialectic and rhetoric alone do this. Both these arts draw opposite conclusions impartially. Nevertheless, the underlying facts do not lend themselves equally well to the contrary views. No: things that are true and things that are better are, by their nature, practically always easier to prove and easier to believe in. (p. 594)

Thus, for Aristotle, the strength of the case was not its deceit but its demonstration. Through demonstration, the targets of messages determine which is best. "Persuasion is clearly a sort of demonstration, since we are most fully persuaded when we consider a thing to have been demonstrated" (p. 594). Great good can be done by using rhetoric ethically. The opposite can lead to harm. The same is true of public relations. Thus, "rhetoric is an offshoot of dialectic and also of ethical studies" (Aristotle, 1952c, p. 595).

In these ways, Aristotle offered two important lines of analysis that help us understand and appreciate the connection between rhetoric and public relations. Each communicator puts his or her character on the line by the content of what is said, the manner in which it is presented, the interests that are advanced or harmed by a case, and the way it serves or harms society. Persons must prove their claims and aspire to the highest values in all that they do and say. To those who claim that rhetoric is hollow statements, Aristotle would say, such can be the case, but that is not the best rhetoric, nor the reason that it is vital to society. As we are wise to be, Aristotle would shun sham, spin, and the presentation of falsehood. Likewise, we are asked in matters of public relations to demonstrate our case, to be of sound character, seek the public interest, and examine the statement of others as we expect them to examine the quality of our presentations.

This standard is amplified by others in the rhetorical tradition such as Isocrates and Quintilian. And, we explore their ideas to see reasoning that can support our theory and practice of public relations. In contrast to the golden age of Greece, our modern world sees organizations speaking, even though they speak through individuals. Here is the ethical and practical peril of public relations. Can ancient theory keep us on the right path?

Isocrates: Rhetorical Training Depends on Social Responsibility

As did Aristotle's, Isocrates' opinions on rhetoric underscored how citizens need to prepare themselves to serve society. For this reason, his ideas must be considered by modern students and practitioners of public relations. He recognized the need for civic education, since each generation hands on to each following generation the reins of governance. How men and women are educated will shape how they govern. If they are educated to understand the power of persuasion and appreciate its responsible role for collective decision making in the public interest, they will act accordingly when it is their turn to lead society.

Isocrates (1929) observed that the first requirement of the effective communicator is "a mind which is capable of finding out and learning the truth and of working hard and remembering what it learns" (p. 293). Communication is not an art where a facile mind and a quick wit should be the rule; rather, a thinker devoted to truth can best serve society.

As did Aristotle, Isocrates (1929) observed that rhetoric is a responsibility of each citizen and an essential element of an effective and ethical society. To this end, he reasoned:

> because there has been implanted in us the power to persuade each other and to make clear to each other whatever we desire, not only have we escaped the life of wild beasts, but we have come together and founded cities and made laws and invented arts; and, generally speaking there is no institution devised by man which the power of speech has not helped us to establish. For this it is which has laid down laws concerning things just and unjust, and things honourable and base; and if it were not for these ordinances we should not be able to live with one another. It is by this also that we confute the bad and extol the good. Through this we educate the ignorant and appraise the wise; for the power to speak well is taken as the surest index of a sound understanding, and discourse which is true and lawful and just is taken as the surest index of a sound understanding, and discourse which is true and lawful and just is the outward image of a good and faithful soul. (p. 327)

The key to discourse is not its nature alone, but its role in the service to society. Sham and deceit may occur in the substance and strategies used by rhetors, but time will reveal those devices and their deficiencies (Isocrates, 1929). These are principles sound enough to guide the practice of public relations as a responsible profession serving many interests and making society more fully functional.

In Isocrates' view, society is the benefactor of the person trained to be an effective and ethical communicator. Each citizen—today, even corporate citizens—must learn and apply the principles of strategic and ethical communication. That end must not narrowly serve some participant's self-interest, but the collective interest of all. Through robust dialogue, as Isocrates argued, a better, more ethical society can be crafted. "With this faculty we both contend against others on matters which are open to dispute and seek light for ourselves on things which are unknown; for the same arguments which we use in persuading others when we speak in public, we employ also when we deliberate in our own thoughts" (Isocrates, 1929, p. 327).

Isocrates reasoned that no one can know with certainty what is the best path to achieve the most desirable outcomes. Reasoning, knowledge, and the ability to communicate were, in his opinion, essential tools to that end: "I hold that man [or woman] to be wise who is able by his [or her] powers of conjecture to arrive generally at the best course" (p. 335). Education in communication theory and skills is essential to be a worthy citizen: "when anyone elects to speak or write discourses which are worthy of praise and honour, it is not conceivable that he will support causes which are unjust or petty or devoted to private quarrels, and not rather those which are great and honourable, devoted to the welfare of man and our common good; for if he fails to find causes of this character, he (or she) will accomplish nothing to the purpose" (pp. 337–339). Not only the ends, but also the means of communication rest on sound ethical purpose. In the matter of means, character counts:

> the man [or woman] who wishes to persuade people will not be negligent as to the matter of character; no, on the contrary, he will apply himself above all to establish a most honourable name among his fellow-citizens; for who does not know that words carry greater conviction when spoken by men [or women] of good repute than when spoken by men [or women] who live under a cloud, and that the argument which is made by a man's [or woman's] life is of more weight than that which is furnished by words. (p. 339)

The ethical challenge, one can assume Isocrates would argue, has not changed over the past two thousand years: "Therefore, the stronger a man's [or woman's] desire to persuade his hearers, the more zealously will he [or she] strive to be honourable and to have the esteem of his fellow-citizens" (p. 339).

Citizens, Isocrates advised those of his age, need to serve the interests of others by being effective communicators. Concern for others should motivate and precede the development of expertise instead of the development of expertise and looking for interests to serve. One can argue the same is true today, including the ethical role of corporate citizens. Ours is an age of organizational rhetors, instead of individuals themselves speaking or writing for public evaluation. It is a citizenship responsibility to participate in responsible and responsive dialogue.

Quintilian: Teacher of Ethical Rhetoric and Ethical Speakers

Greek philosophers realized two basic facts. People must demonstrate good character and be effective communicators to be excellent citizens, enjoying the privilege of engaging in discourse and knowing how to meet the burden of responsible and reflective communication. Greeks offered this legacy to the Romans who followed.

Picking up this tradition, Marcus Fabius Quintilian took a perspective that supports the paradigm for public relations as the good organization communicating well. Each organization should strive to be moral and communicate well to satisfy the interests of its markets, audiences, and publics. Only propositions that are justifiable and ethical can sustain themselves against the scrutiny of counter rhetoric. Today's trend for large organizations to not only achieve higher standards of corporate responsibility but to report their success fits the trend to be good, do good, and communicate well.

On this point, Quintilian (1951) was firm: "My ideal orator, then, is the true philosopher, sound in morals and with full knowledge of speaking, always striving for the highest" (p. 20). Quintilian's mission was clear and relevant to public relations' ethical standards: "My aim is to educate the true orator, who must be a good man [or woman] and must include philosophy in his studies in order to shape his character as a citizen and to equip himself to speak on ethical subjects, his special role" (p. 20). This theme is central to the mission of *Rhetorical and Critical Approaches to Public Relations II.* It is dedicated to drawing upon thoughtful and well-reasoned advice to set high standards for professional development and best practices based on the rhetorical heritage.

Toward a definition of rhetoric, Quintilian reviewed the ideas of his predecessors. Among them was Plato, who disparaged rhetoric when it is used for base outcomes and developed through false reasoning. Plato, Quintilian believed, "regarded rhetoric in itself as a honorable thing to be used by a just man in securing what is just" (p. 98).

Quintilian (1951) considered social values to be an explicit or at least implicit part of each statement: "If a case is based on injustice, neither a good man [or woman] nor rhetoric has any place in it" (p. 106). The quality of discourse is inseparable from the character of the person who chooses the side of an issue as well as the language, form, and substance with which to address it. For the ancients, rhetoric took vitality not from what could be said to cleverly win some point of view, but how public dialogue could advance society by assisting people to make sound choices. As Grunig (1992) and others (see for instance, Berger & Reber, 2006) have argued, the excellent organization not only becomes so through communication but also communicates in ways that foster and demonstrate its excellence because of its character, its adherence to higher rather than narrow and self-interested standards and values.

These choices could be the purchase of products of services or on the choice of which candidate to vote for or which public policy to champion. Enlightened choices come down to which non-profit to support for the cause that it serves, as well as support each government agency and policy for the good it does to society.

Which company has the best reputation, demonstrates the best character? And, can an organization communicate well over time if it does not have sound character? Can an organization recover from a crisis if it cannot explain why the crisis occurred and what will be done to reduce the likelihood of that risk from manifesting itself again? These questions continue to arise in the practice of public relations. Each student of that science and art is welcome and wise to ask: To what extent can my professional development be made more solid by understanding the rhetorical tradition? The following sections address specific components of that challenge.

Rhetoric and Enlightened Choice: Addressing Rhetorical Problems

Senior practitioners often say that they are expected to solve problems. To meet that challenge, one can imagine that they are called on to address **rhetorical problems**. One of the most important advances in rhetorical theory in the twentieth century was the conclusion that each statement addresses or should address a rhetorical problem. And the quality of the rhetorical statement is connected to how well it addresses this problem (Bitzer, 1968).

Perhaps the problem could be marketing-driven. As such the rhetor should address this question from a customer's point of view: Why should I buy a specific product or service? Once a decision is formed to make such a purchase, the customer is confronted with making an enlightened choice by addressing this additional question: Why buy X instead of Y?

Character, that essential challenge of the rhetorical tradition, is reflected at the start of each moment of discourse—from the recognition that a problem exists and that it must be addressed in a particular way. Any individual or organization expresses its character through the principles and values revealed by the causes it champions and opposes, by what it does and says—the total enactment of the organization. All of what an individual or organization does can have meaning, and therefore be part of its rhetorical strategy. By how it addresses the rhetorical problem it can demonstrate its worth to participate in some matter's discussion and offer advice that can lead to a truly enlightened choice.

Character comes through in marketing recommendations, issues debates, risk communication, as well as crisis prevention and response. Character is reflected by whether the persons who craft and make a statement do so for their (or their organization's) self-interest or for mutual interest, focusing on the quality of their respect for the buyer's interest, for instance.

Bitzer (1968) reasoned that each rhetorical problem demands that a position should be taken—and idea asserted, and a choice recommended. Such problems can come to us by circumstances of nature. A rhetorical problem is an exigency, a constraint on why something must be said, how it must be said, by whom it must be said, to whom it must be said, and to what end it must be said. Such exigencies occur for many reasons: Natural disaster, concerns voiced by others about a public policy or the character of some organization, recognition of a problem that needs to be addressed, a choice such as that of a product or service, a matter of character, a matter of sound policy, or sufficient willingness and ability to be responsive to a crisis. These are a few of the very broad kinds of rhetorical problems likely to confront a public relations practitioner. One way to conceive of a rhetorical problem is to think of various questions that demand attention or are raised in ways that draw attention to them on the part of individuals who want to form a useful opinion on these matters or want some other entity, such as the organization itself, to form a mutually beneficial attitude embracing multiple interests.

Natural disaster: After Katrina, many people asked whether the city, state, and nation were properly prepared to prevent a catastrophe of that kind. Were the emergency response actions the best that could be expected? Since Katrina, we might ask whether the recovery is moving at a rate and in service to the original residents of New Orleans in a way that is truly and effectively responsive to their interests. Were the levees well designed and properly maintained? Are the new ones properly designed? Will they be well maintained? Are all of the needed efforts being made to put neighborhoods back in order for residents whose lives were turned upside down by the storm?

Concerns voiced by others: Is the climate changing? If so, and it appears that at least some changes are occurring, are they natural or created by or exacerbated by humans? What can be done to abate climate change and its consequences, if it is occurring? Will such actions be effective? What will happen if we do not respond quickly and ably? We can imagine that both a spokesperson for a major energy company and for an environmental group would recognize this rhetorical problem; they might analyze it differently and respond differently—at least at the outset of their discourse. It is likely, at least at the outset, that each would and probably should respond to the rhetorical problem differently. Over time, can the dialogue bring society to a better understanding of the problem and the formulation of reasonable solutions—and mutually beneficial relationships?

Recognition of a problem that needs to be addressed: Products and services are often touted as solutions to problems. Thus, marketing communication is often formulated with a problem-solution rationale. Non-profits, such as Habitat for Humanity, recognize problems and address them as rhetorical problems, thereby posing rhetorical problems for others. They ask donors and volunteers: Are you willing and able to help build houses for deserving citizens either by contributing money or labor—or both? Are you willing to contribute to cancer research, to support local theater, or to advance the quality of the environment, even to recycle or help save a species by protecting habitat? The rhetorical problem is to provide information and evaluation that helps volunteers, for instance, to make an enlightened choice on these matters.

Choices, such as products or services (or contributions to non-profits or support for taxes to be spent): If I have an ache or pain, should I take a remedy? Should I diet? Which diet is most healthy and effective? Should I buy brand X instead of another brand? Should I see the latest movie—or rent the DVD? Should I buy a group's CD or go to its concert? Should I contribute (or volunteer) to the symphony, public radio, the Audubon Society, or American Diabetes Association? The rhetorical problems of this kind are myriad. They drive the promotion and publicity industry. They raise funds to solve problems.

A matter of sound character: If prices, such as a gallon of gasoline, are increasing, is that due to market forces or price gouging? If a war is not going well, should we withdraw, thereby forcing the responsibility of responding on others, or should we maintain our military stance indefinitely? Once military personnel have suffered a physical or mental injury, what is the sufficient level of care for these young men and women? If a terrorist attack occurs, how should a society respond? If we are at a high level of corporate responsibility, what is an appropriate amount of compensation (wages, salary, and bonus) for our service? To what extent does compensation depend on the financial and social performance of the organization? If a company is engaged in bad business practices, how obligated is each employee to remain silent or speak out—blow the whistle? If we agree that organizations exhibit character, it is a short leap of intellectual faith to conclude that their character defines their persona. Who or what the persona of an organization is becomes part of the messages and is also a product of that message and the actions by the organization.

A matter of sound policy: Should government regulate the content of prime time television programming to make it "more family friendly"? Should women have access to safe birth control, including abortion? What limits, if any, should be placed on these choices by government? How severely should drunk drivers by punished? Should people be allowed to smoke in public? Can privatization provide better services than is typically provided by governmental agencies? What regulation should be placed on gun ownership and the use of handguns? Can food ingredient labeling be designed to be useful to persons who truly want to understand the health consequences of certain foods?

Crisis response: How should the target organization respond to demonstrate its willingness and ability to exert appropriate control and be responsive to others' interests: If a chemical manufacturing facility discharges a toxic chemical, what must its executives and spokespersons say and do? If a young school child is not properly attended to during a school day, what must be said and done and by whom? If a company hides debt so it is worth far less than it appears to be and says it is, what must be said and done, and by whom? If a student buys guns and kills fellow students on campus, what should be said and done, and by whom and for what interests?

Each rhetorical statement is a strategic response to a rhetorical problem. A rhetorical problem is an exigency that must be addressed because it raises or exhibits doubt on some matter relevant to the actions and choices made by an organization and those who are affected by the problem and who can affect the interests of the organization. This problem sets the conditions for an appropriate response. A crisis, for instance, might constitute a rhetorical problem. This problem is different depending on the cause of the crisis. If an organization needs good will, and they all do, how can it communicate in ways that advance and earn this good will?

Encouraging enlightened choice (Nichols, 1963): *Appeal to agree with one point of view, make one choice in preference to another—the rationale for rhetoric.*

The communicator is obligated to offer facts, reasoning, and evaluation that can help individuals to make an enlightened choice, one that reflects the best facts, reasoning, and evaluations. To solve this rhetorical problem, one should ask, what must and can be said to help various publics make enlightened choices?

As practitioners offer details and opinions that publics can use to make enlightened choices, the practitioners should guard against the paradox of the positive (Waymer & Heath, 2007) or its opposite the paradox of the negative. Public relations practitioners like other professional communicators (advertising professionals, for instance) tend to operate out of a "sell through positive statement" or "damn through insult, ad hominen attack, and innuendo" mentality. In featuring the positive aspects of a product, service, or policy (even organizational image) their presentation can be biased to ignore and even deny important negative details that truly should be considered for an enlightened choice. The same can be for the paradox of the negative, which is especially a problem with political attack communication. Such caution does not and should not lead us away from featuring positive or negative aspects of some matter that truly needs to be considered, but we should be wary of distorting the presentation so that it actually leads to an unenlightened choice.

Such analysis is also highly relevant to efforts to create, mend, and reaffirm an organization's image. As Aristotle reasoned, demonstration of the factuality of claims is essential to rhetoric. Baudrillard (1988) reasoned that image can be established at four levels based on the degree to which the alleged image corresponds to reality based fact: A reflection of reality, a mask or perversion of a basic reality, a mask for the absence of a basic reality, or the condition by which image bears no sense of reality. As the organization reestablishes or (re)presents (Cheney, 1992) its image, it can drift away from facts that define that image (the best for advising enlightened choice) to a complete absence, avoidance, or manufacturing of image devoid of fact and a sense of reality. Such rhetorical positioning can either foster enlightened choice or completely frustrate it.

Adjusting organizations to people and people to organizations: *Appeal to individuals outside of an organization to adjust their thinking to it or advocate inside the organization that management should adapt to or accommodate to the needs, expectations, and preferences of key publics* (Heath, 2007).

The rationale of rhetoric, according to Bryant (1953) required solving the rhetorical problem of how to get people to adjust to ideas and how to adjust ideas to them. Herein lies one of the major challenges of rhetoric and a rationale for collaborative decision making and relationship building.

Organizations may adapt to and serve people's interests. Individuals may be asked to adapt to organizations; as for instance, they are required to pay school taxes or invited to vote for a school bond. What must the school district say to demonstrate the need for the taxes or the bonds? Rhetoric entails appeals to people to make adjustments to one another and to ideas that can foster consensus, concurrence, and coordination (Bryant, 1953). Skilled communicators adapt ideas to people. They know that if ideas are too foreign to the interests and vocabulary of some public, they will be rejected. Ideas change slowly. A non-profit organization might, for this reason, ask that donors adapt to the ideals and mission of the organization by giving modest amounts of money to support its charity. The nature of its charity has to be adapted to the people, by demonstrating that it fits with their values and preferences. Rhetoric also invites people to adjust to ideas. They might not at first accept the rationale for giving, but over time they can be convinced that this charity makes the community a better place to live. But this approach focuses as well on the reality that an organization cannot maintain or build effective relationships if it is unwilling or unable to adapt to the publics to which it appeals and which may exert pressures on it.

Building a case based on good reasons: *Appeal to virtue, fact, and sound reasoning that offers positive solutions to personal and collective problems.*

Rhetorical scholars have argued that the substance of rhetoric is good reasons (Wallace, 1963) which promote the search for a higher vision of ourselves (Weaver, 1953, 1970). Wallace concluded, "when we justify, we praise or blame; we use terms like right and wrong, good and bad; in general we *appraise*" (p. 243). As was emphasized in the discussion of the rhetorical heritage, rhetoric serves the people of society by recommending choices that are enlightened by shedding light on which are the best because they do the most good, serve interests best without bringing unduly negative consequences. If we champion the notion that public relations must work to help make society more fully functioning, we will expect practitioners to give us good reasons for adopting some product or service, supporting a non-profit, encouraging a policy, or liking an organization because it does good. To be good requires practitioners to demonstrate reasons that endure over time and bring praise for what they add to the quality of life.

Two lines of analysis support this conclusion. One reasons that rhetorical discourse must search for ideas that truly reflect the interests of people in society, that which is good for them. Second, this search for good is never independent of ethics. The character of each speaker, that person's credibility, depends largely on the quality of the values that drive the person's life choices as well as underpin the reasons for or against any proposed action. This kind of statement responds to the rhetorical problem: What is the best advice we can bring to bear on each choice people are asked or want to make? Do the choices made and the actions taken achieve mutually beneficial outcomes?

Inviting people by using rhetoric as courtship: Invitation and identification: *Appeal based on the assumption that individuals **identify** with key terms, important points of view, products/services, organizations, causes, and policies.*

Burke (1969b) argued that rhetoric is a form of courtship—or courtship is a form of rhetoric. Either way, it is easy to see publicity and promotion especially as being organizational forms of courtship based on appeals to identification. Rhetoric "involves the use of verbal symbols for purposes of appeal" (Burke, 1969b, p. 271). Through naming and the identifications that result from it, "persuasion ranges from the bluntest quest of advantage, as a sales promotion or propaganda, through courtship, social etiquette, education, and the sermon" (p. xiv). It is in this sense "the use of language as a symbolic means of inducing cooperation in beings that by nature respond to symbols" (p. 43). Cooperation results from merger and identification. Rhetoric deals with "the ways in which the symbols of appeal are stolen back and forth by rival camps" (Burke, 1937, p. 365).

Desire for identification, transcendence, and perfection, according to Burke, are universal motives for the sort of choices rhetoric addresses and the problems it solves. Through rhetoric, ideas clash. "The role of opposition is by no means negligible in the shaping of society. The victory of one 'principle' in history is usually not the vanquishing, but the partial incorporation, of another" (Burke, 1968, p. 71). Harmony is possible because words allow us to reconcile opposites, which when viewed from "another point of view . . . cease to be opposites" (Burke, 1961, p. 336). Burke (1966) reasoned: "A character cannot 'be himself' [or herself] unless many others among the dramatic personae contribute to this end, so that the very essence of a character's nature is in a large measure defined, or determined, by the other characters who variously assist or oppose him [or her]" (p. 84).

Pursuing this theme, Burke (1969b) stressed the power words, especially idioms, have to create identification which he believed was one of the major outcomes of rhetorical discourse. For him, "Identification is affirmed with earnestness precisely because there is division. Identification is compensatory to division" (p. 208). Identification is possible because people use terms to define and name themselves. Identification, shared views of reality and identity, result from the human tendency to engage in merger and division. Identification focuses on the notion that although we are unique, each a separate organism, we nevertheless are in varying kinds of collective arrangements. Social order and coordination become the essence of how society is organized, rewards are dispersed, and relationships are maintained.

In its best sense, rhetoric is invitational, asking people to consider alternative points of view (Foss & Griffin, 1995). Foss and Griffin contrasted two approaches to persuasion. One assumes that the source's ideas are superior to those of the target audience. This view can be extended to assume that the source's ideas are imposed on the audience through skilled argument and even propaganda. In contrast, an invitational rhetoric offers reason for an alternative point of view and invites its consideration. This is a more symmetrical and democratic approach.

Where there is agreement and no problems require solution, rhetoric is not needed, a point demonstrated by the absence of any discussion of rhetoric by Sir Thomas More (1965) in his *Utopia*. The rationale for rhetoric, and public relations, comes from uncertainty, doubt, difference of motive, and difference of opinion. In ancient Greece and Rome, individuals spoke in public to advocate one point of view in contest with competing views. Today, in an increasingly global society, organizations tend to speak or otherwise communicate instead of people. Even when individual voices stand out, they do so because they speak for an institution, an organization, and even a nation. The newsworthiness of their case is not only where they agree with others, but also where they disagree. This is as true for the promotion of products as it is for the advocacy of going to war or seeking peace. The voice might be a publicist for a small company advocating the virtues of its product or the president of a mighty nation seeking support for some policy or course of action.

Rhetoric can emphasize difference, even carrying it to an absurd extreme. Public relations practitioners may communicate to differentiate one product or service from another. Activists offer publics a choice between one vision of the future versus another. Politicians focus on their opponents' unfitness and doubtful character. Zealots advocate one perspective that even calls for the destruction of advocates of different views.

In this sense, rhetoric is eternally coupled with the need for community, and the rationale on which each community operates (Leeper, 2001; Kruckeberg & Starck, 1988; Starck & Kruckeberg, 2001; Brummett 1990; Buber 1965). Society cannot function without rhetoric. McKerrow (1989) cautioned that discourse often is about power "as it serves in the first case to maintain the privilege of the elite" and "to maintain social relations across a broad spectrum of human activities" (p. 91). When it is working at its best, it serves society to foster enlightened choice. Its vitality originates from the reality that facts require interpretation, some values are better than others when making specific decisions, and policies always require contingency and expedience. People seek to identify with one another as part of their incentive to achieve a collectivity, which serves for the effective management of risk. They do so through shared idioms, perspectives, defining terms, and a sense of perfection.

Building identifications by shared perspectives, social construction of meaning, and connecting zones of meaning: *Appeal to share one point of view or perspective as opposed to another.*

A theme that runs throughout rhetoric, and by extension public relations, is that it rests on the ability to influence what people think and why they act as they do. Relevant to this theme are academic discussions that focus on concepts such as intersubjectivity and shared sense-making (Dervin & Frenette, 2001), and social construction of meaning. The assumption is that those who act in harmony with one another do so because of a shared sense of the world and the appropriateness and inappropriateness of various choices and related action. Disharmony is, by extension, predicated at least in part on the assumption that it results because people see the world differently and therefore have different expectations for the enactment of the life narrative (Heath, 1994) as an undirected play (Pearce & Cronen, 1980).

Rhetoric depends on shared meaning, which in turn centers on definitions of meaning. Perhaps no singular statement is more profound than that by Burke (1968) whose views applied the principles of linguistic relativity. By this logic, he concluded that words serve as terministic screens. That means, as they experience and react to some matter people draw on their interpretations of that experience. Burke developed his concept of terministic screens by viewing pictures at an art show that were of the same subject but "looked" different because they were photographed through different colored lens. Each lens was like a different "tribal vocabulary." It inspired a different view of the same scientific facts, the reality itself. He concluded:

> We *must* use terministic screens, since we can't say anything without the use of terms; whatever terms we use, they necessarily constitute a corresponding kind of screen; and any such screen necessarily directs the attention to one field rather than another.
>
> (Burke, 1973, p. 50)

Each terministic screen is a perspective. Each perspective, subject to various rhetorical influences, constitutes its unique way of thinking and acting. Thus, rhetoric, and public relations by that connection, works to create, change, abandon, and enact various perspectives, the shared terministic screens that allow for cooperation and competition as well as the forming and enacting of choices.

People identify with one another as they share perspectives. Thus, perspectives become the basis of rhetorical appeals. Advocates reason that one perspective is superior to its competitors. They court others to agree, to see the world in a particular way, and to prefer some actions instead of others. Public relations uses identification through publicity. It informs, evaluates, and recommends. For instance, practitioners might publicize a baseball team, an amusement park, or a brand of exercise equipment. What must and can be said to help various publics make enlightened choices?

For these reasons, people are inspired to champion sports teams, buy products, purchase services, support and oppose political candidates, and live their lives in all of the ways that can be and are influenced by words. Words stand between people and their physical realm. They influence people's judgment. One can imagine, for instance, that we respond to "our team," "our candidate," "our car," "our clothes," and "our causes." Knowing these terms, and responding to them as propositions, we know the actions that are appropriate, prescribed by the shared meaning of the terms. We live these narratives, these undirected plays.

Through co-authored, socially constructed narratives, each public achieves collective opinions, judgments, and actions that govern its preferences and behaviors. Organizations can adopt or seek to influence the narratives of society, by what they say and do. Co-created meaning leads to a sense of community through shared narratives which supply people with knowable and collective ways to act toward organizations and one another. Narratives voice expectations regarding how organizations should act toward one another and the people of society.

A rhetorical enactment view of public relations acknowledges that all of what each organization does and says becomes meaningful because of the shared interpretations and expectations people place on those actions and statements (Heath, 2001, 2008b). Markets can be influenced, as well as publics by what each organization does and says—and by what it does not do or does not say.

Publics offer competing perspectives through their rhetorical efforts that challenge the views and actions of organizations. For instance, activists in a community might be concerned about soot emitted from a manufacturing facility. They may call for higher standards of environmental aesthetics as well as public health and safety. These calls might include letters to opinion leaders, speeches and rallies, and lobbying efforts with appropriate regulators. Disgruntled customers vote with their feet, and credit cards. They support one business by making a purchase from it. At the same time, this choice makes a statement of a lack of support for competitors.

This analysis builds on Mead's (1934) view of the dialectic of mind, self, and society:

> Our society is built up out of our social interests. Our social relations go to constitute the self. But when the immediate interests come in conflict with others we had not recognized, we tend to ignore the others and take into account only those which are immediate. The difficulty is to make ourselves recognize the other and wider interests, and then to bring them into some sort of rational relationship with the more immediate ones. (pp. 388–389)

A society—people and organizations—learns from mistakes. As a profession, public relations can serve society by solving these mistakes, understanding problems, and offering solutions that invite thoughtfulness and willingness to overcome restraints to corrective actions. Public relations can serve organizations by making them good as a prerequisite for their being articulate. Thus, public relations can assist organizations' narrative enactments (Heath, 1994; Weick, 1987).

Fisher (1987) reasoned that humans live life as narrative—an ongoing story. What Fisher (1985, 1987, 1989) called the narrative paradigm assumes that "there is no genre, including technical communication, that is not an episode in the story of life (a part of the 'conversation') and is not itself constituted by logos and mythos" (Fisher, 1985, p. 347). Seeing people as storytellers—co-authors, Fisher (1987) reasoned, "A narrative perspective focuses on existing institutions as providing 'plots' that are always in the process of re-creation rather than existing as settled scripts" (p. 18). For this reason, "all forms of human communication need to be seen fundamentally as stories—symbolic interpretations of aspects of the world occurring in time and shaped by history, culture, and character" (p. xi). Fisher (1987) concluded that knowledge "is ultimately configured narratively, as a component in a larger story implying the being of a certain kind of person, a person with a particular worldview, with a specific self-concept, and with characteristic ways of relating to others" (p. 17). Narrative is not devoid of rational or ethical content. The substance of narrative is good reasons, "values or value-laden warrants for believing or acting in certain ways" (Fisher, 1987, p. xi).

Rhetorical statements create narratives that give meaning, direction, and coordination to persons' lives. We can imagine that narrative is one of the most characteristic forms of rhetorical statement. From childhood, we are taught that stories begin with "once upon a time" and may end "happily ever after." They might also have tragic endings. Narrative gives form and substance to rhetorical statements. Reporters use the form and substance in news reports. If the report is a crisis, then responding organizations engage in the narrative so that society eventually learns the "story" to account for what happened, why it happened, and what will be done to prevent its recurrence. Events, a standard public relations tool, are designed to have narrative form and content. Practitioners want audiences to pay attention to see who is doing what, why, how, when, and where. One of the major publicity events each year in the United States is the Academy Awards ceremony. Prior to the big night—and following it—stories are told about actors and other artists to attract audiences to see who won, why they won, what they wore, how they reacted to victory or defeat, and where the movie will be playing next.

Large organizations and activists often engage in advocacy and counter advocacy regarding narratives of the future. The focal question is whether certain products or services as well as operations and even lifestyles will lead to a tragic end or a "happily ever after" outcome. This competition asks listeners, readers, and viewers to adopt one narrative, vision of the future, and make choices based on that preference. Activists often compare a picture of a dire future to one that is better; they advocate changes to avoid the dire future and achieve the better one.

Rhetorical theory champions the spirit and principles of the First Amendment to the United States Constitution. The right to speak is testimony to the positive role that public discourse plays in society. Rhetoric is a body of principles and strategies that strengthens the voice and enlivens the ideas of competing points of view. As it informs the way individuals communicate for themselves, it also is relevant for the practice of public relations. It offers strategies and challenges, but ultimately rests on the principle that to be effective each individual or organization needs first to be ethical, good, and to be responsibly knowledgeable. The next section examines the heritage of the connection between rhetoric and advocacy.

Managing through advocacy: Facts and judgments: *Appeal created by bringing facts and evaluations to bear.*

A current view is that rhetoric is hollow words, words that do not have factual content; similarly, we hear complaints that public relations is sham and spin, nothing of substance to be trusted. That view is quite at odds with the rhetorical tradition. Nevertheless, that tradition wrestles with the reality that facts themselves are produced by empirical observations, made more accurate through careful scientific investigation. But once they are reported, the facts receive interpretation. Therein lies the possibility of bias and distortion. That fact does not discredit rhetoric. In fact it gives it more credence and relevance because the devil is not only in the detail, but also in the interpretation of the detail. Thus, we have the rhetorical problem of knowing the fact, interpreting the fact, and using it to make enlightened choices.

Advancing a line of discussion that includes consideration of the rhetoric of science, Scott (1976) reasoned that rhetoric is epistemic because it gives us a view of reality and can lead to a shared view based on empirical validity. That view is based on the rhetorical responsibility for fair, candid, and honest representation of each fact: A scientific foundation for rhetoric. Advocacy, internal as well as external to an organization, requires scrupulous attention to fact, getting the facts right and interpreting them fairly. One can imagine that such is more likely to be the case through advocacy where statements are set against one another for careful scrutiny rather than if one side presents its case as definition and imposes it through its will and rule. That debate is rhetoric, an observation that supports the claim that the scientific method is rhetorical.

Writers such as Cherwitz and Hikins (1986) have argued that rhetoric is valuable to the search for knowledge because it is by this means that people assert and challenge the claims about the nature of events, things, experiences, and all matters (including products and services). They believed that rhetoric is "*the art of describing reality through language*" (p. 62). Although the outcome of discourse is important, Cherwitz and Hikins advised that "*the process of striving for knowledge systematically is more important than the attainment of knowledge itself*" (p. 166). In keeping with this logic, Scott reasoned (1976) that rhetoric can be thought of as "*a* way of knowing not *the* way" (p. 259). And, since "reality is socially constructed" (Scott, 1976, p. 261), there can be a tendency and even incentive to conclude that no view is better than another. However satisfying that relativism is intellectually it can be a frustration to those seeking to make an enlightened choice.

In answer to some rhetorical problems, the communicator, the good person seeking to communicate well, asks what needs to be known and considered to make an enlightened choice. That approach presumes that each person targeted with the information is invited to consider the information and opinion as steps toward making a choice that is better than its alternatives. That strategic approach contrasts with the asymmetrical approach whereby the source pronounces a conclusion based on a fact or opinion that otherwise goes unexamined and refined. The excellence of rhetoric is not in the making of a statement but in sustaining statements as they suffer counterstatements. As Wallace (1963) reasoned, "the basic materials of discourse are (1) ethical and moral values and (2) information relevant to these" (p. 240).

Critical Judgment of Rhetorical and Public Relations

Throughout the chapter, we have suggested and implied that rhetoric, and public relations, can, must, and will be held accountable. It must meet certain standards, conform to carefully considered principles. Criticism is an art that requires knowing standards, realizing the sorts of strategic choices that can and must be made, and determining the strategic and ethical quality of the responses made in the face of those choices.

This chapter has tried to explain the rationale for rhetoric and set forth key standards in that rationale that allow critics and public relations practitioners to make ethical choices in what they do, how they do it, and for which ends. Rhetoric stands in judgment for how well it serves multiple interests, not just one interest. Making such choices is not easy. It carries a lot of responsibility. But, for that reason, it offers a solid rationale for the profession of public relations.

References

Aristotle. (1952a). *Nichomachean ethics.* (B. Jowett, Trans.). In R. M. Hutchins (Ed. in Chief), *Great Books* (Vol. 2). Chicago, IL: Encyclopedia Britannica.

Aristotle. (1952b). *Politics.* (B. Jowett, Trans.). In R. M. Hutchins (Ed. in Chief), *Great Books* (Vol. 2, pp. 445–548). Chicago, IL: Encyclopedia Britannica.

Aristotle. (1952c). *Rhetoric.* (W. R. Roberts, Trans.). In R. M. Hutchins (Ed. in Chief), *Great Books* (Vol. 2, pp. 593–675). Chicago, IL: Encyclopedia Britannica.

Baudrillard, J. (1988). *Simulacra and simulations.* In M. Poster (Ed.), *Jean Baudrillard: Selected writings* (pp. 166–184). Stanford, CA: Stanford University Press.

Berger, B. K., & Reber, B. H. (2006). *Gaining influence in public relations: The role of resistance in practice.* Mahwah, NJ: Lawrence Erlbaum.

Bernays, E. L. (1955). *The engineering of consent.* Norman: University of Oklahoma Press.

Bitzer, L. (1968). The rhetorical situation. *Philosophy and Rhetoric, 1,* 1–15.

Brummett, B. (1990). Relativism and rhetoric. In R. A. Cherwitz (Ed.), *Rhetoric and philosophy* (pp. 79–103). Hillsdale, NJ: Lawrence Erlbaum.

Brummett, B. (1995). Scandalous rhetorics. In W. N. Elwood (Ed.), *Public relations inquiry as rhetorical criticism: Case studies of corporate discourse and social influence* (pp. 13–23). Westport, CT: Praeger.

Bryant, D. C. (1953). Rhetoric: Its function and its scope. *Quarterly Journal of Speech, 39,* 401–424.

Buber, M. (1965). *Between man and man.* (R. G. Smith, Trans.). New York: Macmillan.

Burke, K. (1937, January 20). Synthetic freedom, *New Republic, 89,* 365.

Burke, K. (1951). Rhetoric—old and new. *Journal of General Education, 5,* 202–209.

Burke, K. (1961). *Attitudes toward history.* Boston: Beacon.

Burke, K. (1965). *Permanence and change* (2nd ed.). Indianapolis, IN: Bobbs-Merrill.

Burke, K. (1966). *Language as symbolic action.* Berkeley: University of California Press.

Burke, K. (1968). *Counter-statement.* Berkeley: University of California Press. (Originally published 1931.)

Burke, K. (1969a). *A grammar of motives.* Berkeley: University of California Press.

Burke, K. (1969b). *A rhetoric of motives.* Berkeley: University of California Press.

Burke, K. (1973). *The philosophy of literary form* (3rd ed.). Berkeley: University of California Press.

Campbell, K. K. (1996). *The rhetorical act* (2nd ed.). Belmont, CA: Wadsworth.

Cheney, G. (1992). The corporate person (re)presents itself. In E. L. Toth & R. L. Heath (Eds.), *Rhetorical and critical approaches to public relations* (pp. 165–183). Hillsdale, NJ: Lawrence Erlbaum.

Cheney, G., & Christensen, L. T. (2001). Public relations as contested terrain: A critical response. In R. L. Heath (Ed.). *Handbook of public relations* (pp. 167–182). Thousand Oaks, CA: Sage.

Cherwitz, R. A., & Hikins, J. W. (1986). *Communication and knowledge: An investigation in rhetorical epistemology.* Columbia: University of South Carolina Press.

Cutlip, S. M. (1994). *The unseen power: Public relations. A history.* Hillsdale, NJ: Lawrence Erlbaum.

Dervin, B., & Frenette, M. (2001). Sense-making methodology: Communicating communicatively with campaign audiences. In R. E. Rice & C. K. Atkin (Eds.), *Public communication campaign* (3rd ed.; pp. 69–87). Thousand Oaks, CA: Sage.

Donsbach, W. (2008). *International encyclopedia of communication.* Malden, MA: Blackwell.

Fearn-Banks, K. (2005). Davis, Elmer, and the Office of War Information. In R. L. Heath (Ed.), *Encyclopedia of public relations* (pp. 237–239). Thousand Oaks, CA: Sage.

Fisher, W. R. (1985). The narrative paradigm: An elaboration. *Communication Monographs, 52,* 347–367.

Fisher, W. R. (1987). *Human communication as narration: Toward a philosophy of reason, value, and action.* Columbia: University of South Carolina Press.

Fisher, W. R. (1989). Clarifying the narrative paradigm. *Communication Monographs, 56,* 55–58.

Foss, S. J., & Griffin, C. L. (1995). Beyond persuasion: A proposal for an invitational rhetoric, *Communication Monographs, 62,* 2–18.

Gaines, R. N., & Gronbeck, B. E. (2008). Rhetorical studies. In W. Donsbach (Ed.), *International encyclopedia of communication* (pp. 4382–4395). Malden, MA: Blackwell.

Gaudino, J. L., Fritsch, J., & Haynes, B. (1989). "If you knew what I knew, you'd make the same decision": A common misperception underlying public relations campaigns? In C. H. Botan & V. Hazleton Jr. (Eds.), *Public relations theory* (pp. 299–308). Hillsdale, NJ: Lawrence Erlbaum.

Grunig, J. E. (Ed.). (1992). *Excellence in public relations and communication management.* Hillsdale, NJ: Lawrence Erlbaum.

Heath, R. L. (1994). *Management of corporate communication: From interpersonal contacts to external affairs.* Hillsdale, NJ: Lawrence Erlbaum.

Heath, R. L. (2001). A rhetorical enactment rationale for public relations: The good organization communicating well. In R. L. Heath (Ed.), *Handbook of public relations* (pp. 31–50). Thousand Oaks, CA: Sage.

Heath, R. L. (2005). Antecedents of modern public relations. In R. L. Heath (Ed.), *Encyclopedia of public relations* (pp. 32–37). Thousand Oaks, CA: Sage.

Heath, R. L. (2006). Onward into more fog: Thoughts on public relations research directions. *Journal of Public Relations Research, 18,* 93–114.

Heath, R. L. (2007). Management through advocacy. In E. L. Toth (Ed.), *The future of excellence in public relations and communication management: Challenges for the next generation* (pp. 41–65). Mahwah, NJ: Lawrence Erlbaum.

Heath, R. L. (2008a). Power resource management: Pushing buttons and building cases. In T. Hansen-Horn & B. D. Neff (Eds.), *Public relations: From theory to practice* (pp. 2–19). New York: Allyn & Bacon.

Heath, R. L. (2008b). Rhetorical theory, public relations, and meaning: Giving voice to ideas. In T. Hansen-Horn & B. D. Neff (Eds.), *Public relations: From theory to practice* (pp. 208–226). New York: Allyn & Bacon.

Heath, R. L., & Coombs, W. T. (2006). *Today's public relations: An introduction.* Thousand Oaks, CA: Sage.

Heath, R. L., & Frandsen, F. (2008). Rhetorical perspective and public relations: Meaning matters. In A. Zerfass, B. van Ruler & K. Sriramesh (Eds.), *Public relations research: European and international perspectives and innovations* (pp. 349–364). Wiesbaden, Germany: VS Verlag.

Hill, J. W. (1958). *Corporate public relations: Arm of modern management.* New York: Harper & Brothers.

Hill, J. W. (1963). *The making of a public relations man.* New York: David McKay.

Huxman, S. S. (2004). Exigencies, explanations, and executions: Toward a dynamic theory of the crisis communication genre. In D. P. Millar & R. L. Heath (Eds.), *Responding to crisis: A rhetorical approach to crisis communication* (pp. 281–298). Mahwah, NJ: Lawrence Erlbaum.

Ihlen, Ø. (2002). Rhetoric and resources: Notes for a new approach to public relations and issues management. *Journal of Public Affairs, 2*(4), 259–269.

Ihlen, Ø. (2008). Rhetorical theory of public relations. In W. Donsbach (Ed.), *International encyclopedia of communication* (pp. 4395–4397). Malden, MA: Blackwell.

Isocrates (1929). *Antidosis.* (G. Norlin, Trans.). *Isocrates* (Vol. 2, pp. 182–365). Cambridge, MA: Harvard University Press.

Johnson, D., & Sellnow, T. (1995). Deliberative rhetoric as a step in organizational crisis management: Exxon as a case study. *Communication Reports, 8*(1), 54–60.

Kennedy, G. (1963). *The art of persuasion in Greece.* Princeton, NJ: Princeton University Press.

Kruckeberg, D., & Starck, K. (1988). *Public relations and community: A reconstructed theory.* New York: Praeger.

L'Etang, J. (1996). Public relations and rhetoric. In J. L. L'Etang & M. Pieczka (Eds.), *Critical perspectives in public relations* (pp. 106–123). London: International Thomson Business Press.

Leeper, R. V. (2001). In search of a metatheory for public relations: An argument for communitarianism. In R. L. Heath (Ed.), *Handbook of public relations* (pp. 93–104). Thousand Oaks, CA: Sage.

Lentz, C. S. (1996). The fairness in broadcasting doctrine and the Constitution: Forced one-stop shopping in the "marketplace of ideas." *University of Illinois Law Review, 271,* 1–39.

Lubbers, C. A. (2005a). Committee on Public Information. In R. L. Heath (Ed.), *Encyclopedia of public relations* (pp. 154–157). Thousand Oaks, CA: Sage.

Lubbers, C. A. (2005b). Four-minute men. In R. L. Heath (Ed.), *Encyclopedia of public relations* (pp. 337–338). Thousand Oaks, CA: Sage.

McKerrow, R. E. (1989). Critical rhetoric: Theory and praxis. *Communication Monographs, 56,* 91–111.

Madden, T. J. (1997). *Spin man: The topsy-turvey world of public relations . . . as tell-all tale.* Boca Raton, FL: TransMedia.

Mead, G. H. (1934). *Mind, self, and society.* Chicago, IL: University of Chicago Press.

More, T. (1965). *Utopia.* (G. C. Richards, Trans.). In E. Surtz, S. J. Hexter, & J. H. Hexter (Eds.), *The complete works of Sir Thomas More* (pp. 1–197). New Haven, CT: Yale University Press.

Nichols, M. H. (1963). *Rhetoric and criticism.* Baton Rouge, LA: Louisiana State University Press.

Pearce, W. B., & Cronen, V. E. (1980). *Communication, action, and meaning.* New York: Praeger.

Plato. (1952). *Gorgias.* (B. Jowett, Trans.). In R. M. Hutchins (Ed. in Chief), *Great Books* (pp. 252–294). Chicago, IL: Encyclopedia Britannica.

Quintilian, M. F. (1951). *The institutio oratoria of Marcus Fabius Quintilianus.* (C. E. Little, Trans.). Nashville, TN: George Peabody College for Teachers.

Scott, R. L. (1976). On viewing rhetoric as epistemic: Ten years later. *Central States Speech Journal, 27,* 258–266.

Starck, K., & Kruckeberg, D. (2001). Public relations and community: A reconstructed theory revisited. In R. L. Heath (Ed.), *Handbook of public relations* (pp. 51–59). Thousand Oaks, CA: Sage.

Wallace, K. R. (1963). The substance of rhetoric: Good reasons. *Quarterly Journal of Speech, 49,* 239–249.

Waymer, D., & Heath, R. L. (2007, May). The paradox of the positive: A flaw in the practice of communication and public relations. Presented at the International Communication Conference, San Francisco.

Weaver, R. M. (1953). *The ethics of rhetoric.* Chicago: Henry Regnery Company.

Weaver, R. M. (1970). *Language is sermonic* (Ed. by R. L. Johannesen, R. Strickland, & R. T. Eubanks). Baton Rouge, LA: Louisiana State University Press.

Weick, K. E. (1987). Theorizing about organizational communication. In F. M. Jablin, L. L. Putnam, K. H. Roberts, & L. W. Porter (Eds.), *Handbook of organizational communication: An interdisciplinary perspective* (pp. 97–122). Newbury Park, CA: Sage.

2

THE CASE FOR PLURALISTIC STUDIES OF PUBLIC RELATIONS

Rhetorical, Critical, and Excellence Perspectives

Elizabeth L. Toth
University of Maryland

Introduction

Looking to strengthen the body of knowledge in public relations, rhetorical and critical scholars are creating theory that conceives of public relations as a potent force in society. Theirs is a worldview focused not only on explaining how public relations functions in organizations, but also on the meaning-making between organizations and publics, as they develop, cocreate, negotiate, and maintain their relationships with one another. Rhetorical and critical scholars take a humanistic approach to their studies of public relations. They consider the organization as *speaker* or *rhetor*, who seeks to influence stakeholders, employees, media, government, activist groups, and society. Rhetorical and critical scholars believe that the symbolic properties of communication *construct* organizational and public expectations, beliefs and behavior, their agreements and disagreements, misunderstandings, and ongoing interactions.

This edited book attempts to illustrate the utility to public relations practice of rhetorical and critical theories. It makes the case that these two perspectives contribute to solving public relations problems, along with the Symmetry/Excellence theory, which is considered "to have done more to develop public relations theory and scholarship than any other single school of thought" (Botan & Hazelton, 2006, p. 6). This chapter proposes to update my previous assessment (Toth, 1992) in which I considered the contributions of three perspectives: rhetorical, critical, and systems theory. It hopes to provide some conceptual guidance for the reader of the contributed chapters in this book and continues to argue "the case for pluralistic studies" that make up the theoretical advances for understanding of and application to public relations. This chapter describes rhetorical, critical, and Excellence perspectives of public relations—definitions, units of analysis, and research contributions. It discusses their complementary nature and their differences, concluding that we should consider all theories as we seek answers to how and why public relations should work for a more fully functioning society.

"Theory" is a term that has several meanings, including "merely theory."

However, theory is not "mere," but something that we all use in our daily decision making, to help us predict what will happen if we choose to do "A" or "B." Theories are dynamic and evolving, just as human behavior is. Theories, such as rhetorical, critical, and Excellence, change over time. For example, rhetorical scholar Coombs (chapter 12) reflects on earlier crisis communication research as "the form approach," that explains how an organization should respond (Coombs, 1999). In chapter 12, Coombs argues that this early theorizing focused on defense strategies, but that more recent studies, using the rhetorical lens, are focused on more positive and accommodative actions. Coombs's most recent evolution in thinking about crisis communication fuses rhetorical and social science methods to create a situational crisis communication theory (chapter 12).

J. E. Grunig and Hunt first proposed press agentry, public information, asymmetrical and symmetrical models to describe the historical progression of public relations (1984). Then, based on research findings of CEO "most valued" public relations behavior, Grunig and co-authors proposed a new model of symmetry as two-way practice that combined symmetrical and asymmetrical models (2001). In 2001, he proposed that we just move all together beyond the models and consider instead four underlying dimensions of public relations: one-way vs. two-way; asymmetrical vs. symmetrical; mediated vs. interpersonal; and ethical vs. unethical (2001, p. 29). These two glimpses are but a few of the continuing efforts of many scholars to advance the practical and ethical practice of public relations and to shape its role in societies around the world. Like all other disciplines, theory grows or the disciplines stagnate.

Theory gives us explanations for why or how things happened as they did. When we are in the middle of solving a public relations problem, we need theory to guide us well or we risk making decisions based only on our own experiences or the experiences of those around us. This "best practices option" isn't always a poor approach, but it depends on how experienced we are and how sound our cases and role models are!

Theories may start out as ideas that develop through our own observations about things (the inductive approach) or we may reason why something is so, such as why students can't access their password protected e-files to learn their grades, and then test the usefulness (the deductive approach) of our reasoning. Grunig (2008) argued that theory building was a process of "thinking logically and systematically about concepts, definitions, measures and the relationships among them" (p. 91). These measures may be developed through social science research methods and be quantitative or qualitative, or they may be measures developed through reasoned judgments based on agreed-upon standards.

We use standards to assess theories, such as the rhetorical and critical theories presented in this book. Shoemaker (1997) included in her standards for evaluating theories such criteria as explanatory power, predictive power, how many problems can be handled by the theory, and how much can a theory organize existing knowledge. She suggested that we consider the parsimony or simplicity of the theory, whether the theory could be given a fair test in which it either succeeds or fails (falsifiability), the internal consistency of the theory, and the heuristic provocativeness, that is how much the theory generates new ideas and expands our knowledge.

In my previous introductory chapter (Toth, 1992), I sought to identify and define concepts for three theory perspectives: rhetorical, critical, and systems. Much has developed to strengthen the rhetorical and critical stances for understanding public relations. Rhetorical scholars have developed models to consider more practically the strategic choices that public relations practitioners must make. Critical theorists have added new insights with their assessments of organizational public relations, including the insights of feminist and postmodernism perspectives. Systems theory has lost much of its attraction to scholars because of its limited scope and organizing power that is at once rational and social science research based. Although still useful—and eternally foundational, as discussed by Heath in chapter 1 and acknowledged as contributing such concepts as the organizational environment, boundary-spanning, and symmetry (Toth, 1992), I've replaced this perspective with Symmetry/Excellence or Excellence theory, considered its own paradigm or worldview of public relations (Botan and Hazelton, 2006, p. 9).

Additional paradigms are beginning to add to our understanding of public relations, such as Botan and Taylor's (2004) cocreational perspective of organizations and publics making meaning together and McKie and Munshi's call for reconfiguring public relations all together (2007). Some of the authors in this book have sought to contrast their theories by exposing the weaknesses of others. I continue to discuss the advantages of each of three perspectives, and the advantage of plural theories to guide our discussion and learning about the public relations enterprise.

Rhetorical Perspectives of Public Relations

The study of rhetoric concerns itself principally with how individuals, groups, and organizations make meaning, through argument and counter-argument, to create issues, resolve uncertainty, compete to achieve a preferable position, or to build coalitions—to solve problems. Rhetorical scholars believe that symbolic behavior creates and influences relationships between organizations and publics, through what Burke coined and then later Heath (see chapter 1) calls the wrangle in the marketplace—people who use words, visuals, and actions symbolically to share and evaluate information, shape beliefs, and establish ways of working together. Communication is the central force by which organizations and publics reach interpretations or meanings of their relationships to one another. Heath has referred to these agreements as "zones of meaning" established through argument and counter-argument, always to be resolved but never fixed for very long. Such zones take on shapes and make connections—and then change—in ways similar to what chaos theorists refer to as fractals. Rhetorical scholars assume that the social collectivity is one of continual engagement of messages and meaning-making between speakers.

The unit of analysis most often used by rhetorical scholars is the "public record," the messages available to the majority of society because they are retrievable via published documents such as newspapers and magazines, but also such media as films, videos, websites, iPods, and mobiles. In our era of citizen journalists, one's messages may be heard and tape-recorded and documented for the entire world to hear. Take for example former President Clinton's reply to a citizen journalist at a Hillary campaign stop that a certain magazine author was a "scumbag" for publishing an unflattering portrait of President Clinton. Rhetorical scholars have studied the messages of organizations, which have been sent to their constituent groups, whether the messages appear in annual reports, online pressrooms, intranets, Internet social networks, and orientations for new employees. In all such studies they take a constitutive approach that audiences of various kinds shape and respond idiosyncratically to messages rather than "allowing" messages merely to enter their brains as magic bullets.

Sometimes, the unit of analysis is filtered by way of gatekeepers, such as media reporters, editors, or producers of news, and most currently individuals with their own blogs. Their involvement has become known as "third-party" endorsement because these third parties to the sending and receiving of messages lend an "objective" dimension to the messages that are distributed. When the resulting "opinion" of these mediated messages is interpreted as "negative" or "adverse," the public relations professional argues with the editors and producers of the information for "corrections," because messages so widely distributed set the agenda for the public discussion and if repeated often enough become indelible in their meanings. Consider the success of political "attack" ads, even when their messages are not relevant or are without factual basis. Former presidential candidate John Kerry was never able to recover from the Swift Boat ad attackers (former soldiers in Vietnam) who questioned his military contribution in Vietnam, even though Kerry had the medals to prove his valor, because Kerry did not immediately contest their accusations. Analysts pointed to Kerry's slow response as pivotal to Bush's eventual victory.

Rhetorical scholars are turning their attention to the publics' discourses or messages, recognizing publics as active participants in constructing the meanings of their relationships with organizations. Rhetorical scholars have recognized that publics have very active roles in determining what the issues will be, their resistance to organizational messages, their own identities and goal-oriented constructions. Through the use of the Internet, we have "Eco-Moms" and "Raw Food Advocates" who share information and build community through their communication around common problems.

Rhetorical scholar Hatfield (2006) studied online groups whose participants identified themselves as walkers, crewmembers, and past walk participants in the Avon Breast Cancer Walks. When Avon suddenly pulled out of sponsorship of the 3-day walk event it had consistently sponsored because it had bowed to pressure that too little of the proceeds went to research, Hatfield studied how online groups made meaning of Avon's departure. Avon had constructed community around the 3-day event because participants spent months training and fundraising for it. Avon's disruption of this community created a rush of discussion filled with frustration, blame, and confusion at the silence on the part of the corporate speakers. Some participants were willing to walk "regardless." The publics used counter-argument and dialogue with Avon as partners who "helped shape rhetorical discourse" (p. 857) eventually leading to a re-constituted walk, but with a loss of trust toward Avon.

Boys (chapter 15) examined the rhetorical strategies of two activist groups, the Voices of the Faithful (VOTF) and the Survivors Network of those Abused by Priests (SNAP), and their alignment against the United States Council of Catholic

Bishops. She found that their different beliefs and identities worked against them combining their efforts to pressure the Council to change its position. Stokes and Holloway (chapter 18) analyzed how a movie's rhetorical strategies created an activist public identity.

The rhetorical enterprise is to evaluate and criticize the symbolic effectiveness of messages. Messages are evaluated on their ethical value to the public interest, or as Heath argues "for a more fully functioning society" (chapter 1). Rhetoricians work primarily from a humanistic stance, meaning that rhetorical scholars argue that their personal judgments are their important contribution to the analysis of human interaction. Rhetorical scholars are not social scientists in search of the precisely defined variable analytic methods of gathering information that are comprehensive or mathematical enough to represent a sample or whole population. Rhetoricians are themselves their own measuring instruments, "making judgments based on their self-perceptions of events or texts rather than asking others for their interpretations of what the events or texts mean" (Toth, 2000, p.125). The rhetorical scholar's evaluations—often highly subjective—are in turn judged by his/her abilities to interpret the meanings of symbols and to use the best arguments and evidence at his/her disposal—and to make a compelling case to convince others. While some may see rhetorical theory as limited in scope to "mere symbolic interpretation," others have taken the stance that symbolic interpretation has the most explanatory power in understanding the way organizations and publics interact with one another.

Critical Perspectives of Public Relations

Critical perspectives of public relations have grown in influence and theoretical richness since my previous overview chapter on rhetorical and critical approaches to public relations, adding two sub-areas, those of feminist scholars and postmodern scholars to their theorizing about the value or lack of value of public relations in society.

Perhaps, the most startling introduction of critical theory to public relations occurred in an article by Dozier and Lauzen (2000) in which they moved away from their preference for social scientific measures found in the Excellence study to call for liberating the intellectual domain from the practice view of public relations. They sought to expand the range of research questions by "incorporating additional perspectives from critical theory" (p.3).

> Critical theory and research takes the public relations scholar outside the relationships between powerful organizations and publics with deep pockets, begging a different set of questions, raising different concerns, and employing different methodological approaches. Behind all these differences is an ideological orientation to the interests of activists rather than corporations and other organizations with deep pockets.
>
> (Dozier & Lauzen, 2000, p. 16)

Dozier and Lauzen introduced heuristically provocative ideas for public relations, including public relations as the invisible hand in organizational behavior, powerless publics, and irreconcilable differences between organizations and publics. They proposed that we look at public relations in social movements.

Critical scholars argue for a world of organizations bent on dominating those of lesser power. The use of public relations is instrumental (functional) in organizations in order to accomplish their private goals. Critical scholars, along with rhetorical scholars, focus on the symbolic processes of organizations. However, critical scholars approach organizations' and publics' messages, not to improve on their efforts to succeed in building relationships with one another nor to examine their efforts to contribute to a more "fully functioning society," but to disrupt our beliefs about organizations and publics. McKie and Munshi (chapter 3) jolt us to open ourselves up to entirely different disciplines and fields of study rather than continue an insular focus on public relations as a management function of organizations. They propose that we look at the larger sociopolitical world and other social surroundings and social impacts.

Feminist criticism belongs within the domain of critical studies. It focuses on gender, as a way of organizing society, a scheme for categorizing people based on biological differences (Powell, 1988; Grunig, Toth & Hon, 2000; and Aldoory, chapter 6). Because these social constructions are often unconscious and/or used stereotypically, men and women are constrained to believe and accept very narrow self-identities. In the public relations field, for example, although the majority of public relations professionals are women, the majority of the managerial positions are held by men. Some feminist scholars have criticized this imbalance, citing organizational preference for men in positions of power because of the stereotypical attributes of masculinity, such as competiveness, rationality, and individuality (Rakow, 1989). Women may prefer working for male managers over women because they too have been socialized to believe that women managers are "too soft" or "too unwilling to help a sister," which are still stereotypes feminists call our attention to as the means by which society and its organizations oppress individuals because of gender. Rakow (1989) argued that organizations most commonly value public relations that is "masculine," yet there are tendencies for public relations to swing back and forth between ideologies of "masculinity" and "femininity" such as relationship building and collaboration.

Postmodernism as a perspective also belongs within the critical theory paradigm. The postmodern lens introduced by Holtzhausen (2002) challenges public relations researchers and practitioners to stop "privileging" the theory of public relations as a "function of organizations to manage communication" (p. 251). She calls on us to stop searching for best practices, or ideal standards of practice, as if there were fixed steps or laws that would always lead to best solutions. She also challenged practitioners to recognize ever-present values and biases in public relations work that favor the powerful.

Postmodernists seek first to "deconstruct" rather than accept at face value the language of organizations and second to take a stance against such organizational biases as "racism, sexism, eurocentrism, bureaucracies, and colonialism" (Boje & Dennehey, 1993, p. 10). Five characteristics of postmodern thinking include: "an emphasis on individual realities rather than one; an ethically responsible society; accommodation of many diverse ideas and perspectives, including modernism;

resistance to positivism; and a philosophy of the immediate rather than seeking the ideal state of society" (Holtzhausen, 2000, p. 96).

The purpose of the critical perspective is to be confrontational and provocative. Boyd and VanSlette's (chapter 17) chapter on outlaw discourse in public relations uses the postmodern lens to look at and accept public relations discourse that jar us as inappropriate, unconventional, and outside of the law, such as Osama bin Laden's grainy desert home videos, for what such discourse says about the field of public relations. That is, rather than looking at the ways communication assists the organization's management function, the critical scholar is intent on answering such questions as posed by Deetz and Kersten (1983): "Whose interests are served by organizational goals?" What role do they play in creating and maintaining structures of power and domination? (p. 155). Ultimately, regardless of the research and theory approach, this may be the most compelling question facing academics and practitioners.

Critical theorists would argue against the idea of "the unit of analysis," and call it an artifact of social science research thinking. However, critical studies have considered retrievable texts from annual reports, speeches, and weblogs. Critical theorists have reviewed the processes of public relations, such as Woodward's (2003) practical critical theory. He argued that public relations work can be done with "participatory" planning that brings into the process the voices of previously ignored or suppressed publics and respects the place and locale (context and culture) in which public relations is to be carried out.

Critical theorists are humanistic in their conceptualizing and measurements; that is, they present their judgments because of their wide reading of human behavior. They marshal their evidence, expose faulty arguments, and/or provoke us with uncomfortably new ideas. Dutta-Bergman (2005) took critical exception to the positive meanings of civil society (see Taylor's chapter 4). He built a case for civil society as a means of serving the "transnational elite" (p. 267). He uses as his examples his critical observations of U.S. political intervention in the Philippines, Chile, and Nicaragua. Critical theorists have also used social science research methods such as case studies or content analyses, but always with an eye for exposing injustices. Chay-Nemeth (2001) used Foucault's method of archaeology and Strauss and Corbin's grounded theory approach to analyzing data from news articles, reports, and in-depth interviews to build a critical archaeology of publics in the Thai HIV/AIDs issue, revealing a government bias against accepting the humanitarian AIDs patient nursing by Buddhist monks.

Excellence Theory

Systems theory (structural functionalism) has been a central theoretical lens in public relations research because of its focus on how the organization interacted with its internal and external environments. Systems theory provided an important role for the public relations practitioner, that of boundary spanner, one who crosses between the organization and its environment in order to collect, listen, and bring in new information with which the organizational leadership could make choices, to accommodate or resist depending on the issues, problems, or opportunities that this new information represented. This foundational theory set the platform for decades of work to understand and improve the flow of information and make relationships more balanced as the rationale for public relations.

Although systems theory represented one line of theory included in the Excellence study's assessment of how public relations contributed to organizational effectiveness, three other theoretical lenses were also of equal importance: goal attainment, management-by-objectives, or the theory that organizations are effective when they achieve goals; strategic constituencies, which sought to prioritize groups or publics and their possible consequences for organizations; and competing values, which recognized the bridge between strategic constituencies and goals, "so that organizations attain the goals of most value to their strategic constituencies" (Grunig, Grunig, & Dozier, 2006, p. 33). The Excellence study drew on theories of sociology, psychology, coorientation, gender, organizational communication, and ethics as well. Murphy quoted Grunig and Grunig (2000) in finding that systems theory was not sufficient for measuring organizational effectiveness (2007, p. 123).

The Excellence theory (Grunig, Grunig, & Dozier, 2006, p. 32) included four units of analysis:

1. The program level; that is the traditional level that most practitioners evaluate, such as media relations, community relations, customer relations;
2. The functional level; that is the public relations function as a whole which can be audited by comparing the structure and processes of the department with other organizational units;
3. The organizational level; that is the contribution of public relations to organizational effectiveness; and
4. The societal level; that is the contribution of the organization to society.

J. E. Grunig (1997) defined communication as:

> behavior—of people, groups, or organizations, that consists of moving symbols to and from other people, groups, or organizations. Thus, we can say that public relations is an organization's managed communication behavior. Public relations professionals plan and execute communication for the entire organization or help parts of the organization to communicate. (pp. 242–243)

The role of communication is part of the Excellence theory of public relations, through its symmetrical/asymmetrical, one-way vs. two-way, and mediated vs. interpersonal communication, and ethical dimensions (Grunig, 2001, pp. 28-30). The symmetrical/asymmetrical dimension represented "the extent to which collaboration and advocacy describe public relation strategy or behavior" (Grunig, 2001, p. 29).

The symmetrical dimension, which has become the most theoretically contentious (provocative) concept of the Excellence study "proposed that individuals, organizations, and publics should use communication to adjust their ideas and behavior to those of others rather than to try to control how others think and behave" (Grunig, 2006, p. 156). Among other critics of symmetry, McKie and Munshi (2007) attacked it as "flawed, largely normative at best (and at worst, misleading in its promise of quality of exchange amid realities of uneven power), very restricted in practice, and to date, structured in support of exclusionary practices" (p. 36). However, despite critical scholars' derision of symmetry as too idealistic, too tilted toward the powerful, and too hegemonic generally, symmetrical theory is central in the discourses of public relations. Botan and Hazelton describe how critics have spoken up, but "either the field has failed to see enough merit in what they have said to develop their own paradigms, or they have limited their remarks to critiques and failed to conduct affirmative research, share their data and sufficiently open their own theories to critical discourse" (2006, p. 9). Critical theorists remain fixated on symmetry, perhaps because of its promise of power sharing.

Symmetry has been called by J. Grunig (2001) "a process oriented experience of collaboration, of mixed motives, collaborative advocacy, and cooperative antagonism" (p. 28). The theory of symmetry has changed over time, as theories do, to include its situational nature and also the mixed motives of organizations and publics as they seek to make meaning of their relationships. Dozier, Grunig, and Grunig (1995) reflected on the unexpected finding of both symmetrical and asymmetrical communication in their sample of organizations practicing excellent public relations. They changed their conceptualization of symmetry by proposing a new model of symmetry as two-way practice that recognizes the potential strategic influence of both organizations and publics in seeking to resolve problems toward a possible win-win zone.

The Excellence theory focuses on public relations as a strategic management function. It contains a set of theoretical standards for how to practice public relations most effectively (to achieve excellence) and what is contained in each of the standards. The Excellence theory presents a paradigm or worldview of public relations concerned with solving the problems of the professional domain, that is findings that seek to explain and improve how public relations functions in organizations; to argue that public relations strategy and practice is situational rather than routine; and to add to a call for generic principles of public relations that should operate in different cultures, with such qualifications as the media systems, culture (including language), level of activism, level of the economy, the level of economic development, and type of political system found in each society. It provides a set of theoretical benchmarks by which public relations practitioners can achieve greater functioning in their organizations.

Discussion

A review of rhetorical, critical, and Excellence theories suggests some complementary understandings. Rhetorical, critical, and Excellence theorists agree on the importance of communication as a force in public relations practice. For rhetorical scholars, communication and the meaning-making through communication are the central ideas of public relations practice. Critical scholars assert also that relationships between organizations and publics are socially constructed, made meaning of, but often through the lens of power and privilege—a dysfunction of societies and the organizations that disproportionately shape them. Feminist scholars would add gender as a powerful lens in the meaning-making process. Postmodernists would support this stance but would not want to go beyond the moment and situation in any way to make generalizations to other situations or points in time. Excellence study theorists prefer more control in defining communication; therefore, they test proposed meanings by asking public relations practitioners to report on whether they agree with hypothesized communication behavior as representative of their work. The assumption in this primarily quantitative approach is that there are standard and agreed-upon meanings of actions and activities, not to the depth of meaning that we gain by examining rhetorical analyses. Finally, rhetorical and critical scholars would argue that the meanings and resulting actions must be continually reinterpreted.

All three perspectives have begun recognizing the dialogic nature of public relations. Rhetorical scholars such as Heath (see chapter 1) argue that rhetoric concerns dialogue: "a dynamic exchange by which interested parties seek to induce agreement and action." Botan and Taylor (2004), in their "state of the field" article, posit a cocreational perspective, with publics becoming partners in the "meaning-making process." "The major relationship of interest is between groups and organizations and communication functions to negotiate changes in these relationships" (p. 652). They cite an emphasis in cocreational research on organizational–public relationships, community theory, coorientation theory, accommodation theory and dialogue theory, "but the most cocreational theory is symmetrical/excellence theory" (p. 652). Spicer summarized the state of rhetorical theory building as: "We seem to have arrived at a theoretical and pragmatic understanding that both persuasion and dialogue may be necessary independently or compatibly given the situation, the goals of the organization, the goals of the stakeholders, and existing external constraints" (2007, p. 28). The Excellence authors used the new model of symmetry as their means of illustrating the dialogical nature of organizations and publics advocating and collaborating together around situational problems.

These three perspectives share much crossover research and acknowledgment of comparative approaches. Aldoory, Reber, Berger, and Toth (2008) combined their interests in power and gender, using a quantitative and critical analysis of how men and women public relations practitioners use similar and different power strategies that seem to reflect organizational constraints on their behavioral and communication choices. Their analysis included how difference in gender led to different perceptions of barriers to obtaining power. Women sought power to obtain a "seat at the table," while men rarely mention it as a goal because it wasn't an issue for them.

Waymer and Ni (chapter 11) use a qualitative case study to provide a rhetorical analysis of how the relationship between managers and their employees are interpreted and power is accrued. They conclude by providing practical advice to public relations workers who want to understand the organization–employee contract more clearly.

Rhetorical, critical, and Excellence theories argue similarly that they seek to solve problems of the practice, by identifying poor arguments, revealing power differences, or by providing examples of best practices. Finally, complementary in the rhetorical, critical, and Excellence approaches to public relations is the "critical" stance. The respective critical intention may differ. The rhetorical theorists consider the use of ethical and unethical practices in the argument and counter-argument of organizations and publics. They raised our expectation of public relations as achieving a more "fully functioning society," that is our expectations that organizations must contribute responsibly to their societies in an increasingly global world. Critical scholars, including feminist scholars and postmodernists, look for biases and unconscious assumptions about organizational and public relations behavior and challenge our unconscious and stereotypical beliefs about seemingly neutral decision-making processes. The Excellence study recognized the importance of values and competing constituencies in examining how organizations defined, valued, and used public relations. Excellence theory author J. E. Grunig (2008) argued that public relations practitioners should evaluate the ethics and social responsibility of the organization and serve as ethics counselors to management. It is through the quality of relationships that organizations can claim to be contributors to society; and it is through the extent of ethics that public relations should be considered.

The rhetorical, critical, and Excellence perspectives may be becoming more intertwined in the sharing of commonalities in meanings of concepts, units of analysis, and efforts to build theory and connect to practice. I had initially wanted to call my chapter "betting on all the horses" because there is such an invigorating advance in public relations knowledge and theory building that all those engaged in it should be encouraged and acknowledged. Theorists working in the same domain are never without competition and contention. It is through our own arguments and counter-arguments that our theories achieve the criteria of explanatory power and organizing of knowledge for increased understanding of the field. Rhetorical and critical scholars have begun to provide more detailed explanations of the basis of their judgments, such as found in chapter 1 of this book. While previously I criticized rhetorical and critical scholars for not revealing their own assumptions, I challenge scholars of Excellence theories that they must also start with their assumptions about theory, units of analysis, and method.

Rhetorical and critical scholars contribute a much richer delineation of what is meant by communication. It is rhetorical and critical scholars who elaborate on how organizing and communicating are "inextricably interwoven dimensions of social life" (Cheney & Dionisopoulos, 1989, p. 136). Their powerful view of public relations drills down to the construction of meanings built, argued, and counter-argued, whether we are discussing messages, processes, planning, policy-making, or organizational structures. One advantage of the Excellence theory perspective is the asking of public relations practitioners to describe their roles and practices, so as to include their important voices in the meanings of what public relations is. On the other hand, the work of rhetorical and critical scholars is to confront those meanings and to test them within the social, economic, and political landscapes in which meanings are developed.

This chapter was intended to argue for accepting the differing assumptions and directions of rhetorical, critical, and Symmetrical/Excellence perspectives as important contributors to the knowledge of public relations. Happily, the research to understand public relations includes such a diversity of approaches.

References

Aldoory, L., Reber, B. H., Berger, B. K., & Toth, E. L. (2008, March). Provocations in public relations: A study of gendered ideologies of power-influence in practice. Paper presented to the Eleventh Annual International Public Relations Conference, Miami.

Boje, D. M., & Dennehy, R. F. (1993). *Managing in the postmodern world. America's revolution against exploitation.* Debuque, IA: Kendall/Hunt Publishing.

Botan, C. H., & Hazelton, V. (Eds.) (2006). Public relations in a new age. In C. H Botan, & V. Hazelton (Eds.), *Public relations theory II* (pp. 1-18). Mahwah, NJ: Lawrence Erlbaum.

Botan, C. H., & Taylor, M. (2004). Public relations: State of the field. *Journal of Communication, 54*(4), 645–661.

Chay-Nemeth, C. (2001). Revising publics: A critical archaeology of publics in the Thai HIV/AIDS issue. *Journal of Public Relations Research, 13*(2), 127–161.

Cheney, G., & Dionisopoulos, G. N. (1989). Public relations? No relationship with publics: a rhetorical-organizational approach to contemporary corporate communications. In C. H. Botan, & V. Hazelton (Eds.), *Public relations theory* (pp. 135–158). Hillsdale, NJ: Lawrence Erlbaum.

Coombs, W. T. (1999). Information and compassion in crisis responses: A test of their effects. *Journal of Public Relations Research, 11*, 125–142.

Deetz, S., & Kersten, A. (1983). Critical models of interpretative research. In L. L. Putnam, & M. Pacanowsky (Eds.), *Communication and organization: An interpretative approach* (pp. 141–171). Beverly Hills, CA: Sage.

Dutta-Bergman, M. J. (2005). Civil society and public relations: Not so civil after all. *Journal of Public Relations Research, 17*(3), 267–289.

Dozier, D. M., Grunig, L. A., & Grunig, J. E. (1995). *The manager's guide to excellence in public relations and communication management.* Mahwah, NJ: Lawrence Erlbaum.

Dozier, D. M., & Lauzen, M. M. (2000). Liberating the intellectual domain from the practice: Public relations, activism, and the role of the scholar. *Journal of Public Relations Research, 12*(1), 3–22.

Grunig, J. E. (1997). Public relations management in government and business. In J. L. Garnett, & A. Kouzmin (Eds.), *Handbook of administrative communication* (pp. 241–283). New York: Marcel Dekker.

Grunig, J. E. (2001). Two-way symmetrical public relations: Past, present, and future. In R. L. Heath (Ed.), *Handbook of public relations* (pp. 11–30). Thousand Oaks, CA: Sage.

Grunig, J. E. (2006). Furnishing the edifice: Ongoing research on public relations as a strategic management function. *Journal of Public Relations Research, 18*(2), 151–176.

Grunig, J. E. (2008). Conceptualizing quantitative research in public relations. In B. Van Ruler, A. T. Vercic, & D. Vercic (Eds.), *Public relations metrics research and evaluation* (pp. 88–119). New York: Routledge.

Grunig, J. E., & Grunig, L. A. (2000). Public relations in strategic management and strategic management in public relations: Theory and evidence from the IABC excellence project. *Journalism Studies, 1*(2), 303–321.

Grunig, J. E., Grunig, L. A., & Dozier, D. M. (2006). The excellence theory. In C. H. Botan, & V. Hazelton (Eds.), *Public relations theory II* (pp. 21–62). Mahwah, NJ: Lawrence Erlbaum.

Grunig, J. E., & Hunt, T. (1984). *Managing public relations*. New York: Holt, Rinehart and Winston.

Grunig, L. A., Toth, E. L., & Hon, L. (2000). Feminist values in public relations. *Journal of Public Relations Research, 12*(1), 49–68.

Hatfield, H. H. (2006). A rhetorical typology of studying the audience role in public relations communication: The Avon 3-day disruption as exemplar. *Journal of Communication, 56*(40), 836–860.

Holtzhausen, D. R. (2000). Modern values in public relations. *Journal of Public Relations Research, 12,* 96.

Holtzhausen, D. R. (2002). Towards a postmodern research agenda for public relations. *Public Relations Review, 28,* 251–254.

McKie, D., & Munshi, D. (2007). *Reconfiguring public relations: Ecology, equity, and enterprise.* London: Routledge.

Murphy, P. (2007). Coping with an uncertain world: The relationship between excellence and complexity theories. In E. L. Toth (Ed.), *The future of excellence in public relations and communication management: Challenges for the next generation* (pp. 119–172). Mahwah, NJ: Lawrence Erlbaum.

Powell, G. N. (1988). *Women and men in management.* Newbury Park, CA: Sage.

Rakow, L. (1989). From the feminization of public relations to the promise of feminism. In E. L. Toth, & C. G. Cline (Eds.), *Beyond the velvet ghetto* (pp. 287–288). San Francisco, CA: IABC Foundation.

Shoemaker, P. J. (1997). Criteria for evaluating theories. Available from P. J. Shoemaker, S. I. Newhouse School of Public Communications, Syracuse University, Syracuse, NY 13244.

Spicer, C. H. (2007). Collaborative advocacy and the creation of trust: Toward an understanding of stakeholder claims and risks. In E. L. Toth (Ed.), *The future of excellence in public relations and communication management: Challenges for the next generation* (pp 27–40). Mahwah, NJ: Lawrence Erlbaum.

Toth, E. L. (1992). The case for pluralistic studies of public relations: Rhetorical, critical and systems perspectives. In E. L. Toth, & R. L. Heath (Eds.), *Rhetorical and critical approaches to public relations* (pp. 3–15). Hillsdale, NJ: Lawrence Erlbaum.

Toth, E. L. (2000). Public relations and rhetoric: History, concepts, future. In D. Moss, D. Vercic, & G. Warnaby (Eds.) *Perspectives on public relations research* (pp. 121–144). London: Routledge.

Woodward, W. D. (2003). Public relations planning and action as "practice-critical" communication. *Communication Theory, 13,* 411–431.

3

THEORETICAL BLACK HOLES

A Partial A to Z of Missing Critical Thought in Public Relations

David McKie and Debashish Munshi
University of Waikato

Public relations faces challenges as an academic field and as a practice. The education of students influences how they see both society and the role of the profession in society; the practice of public relations influences society and how society sees *itself* and the profession. No discipline is an island. Public relations education cannot be independent of, or be indifferent toward, the society in which it operates. Without a sense of the different ways that society might be theorized, public relations students and practitioners are limited in their participation in broader dialogues about how public relations contributes to public communication. It is not enough to be technically proficient without being able to make informed contributions to debates about contemporary society and its future development.

Leading scholars are increasingly calling for public relations to change. Coombs and Holladay (2007) ask public relations to go beyond acting as a delivery system for the client to become "a protector of the public" (p. 39); Heath (2006) asks that public relations contribute to a "fully functioning society" (p. 94); Moloney (2006) argues for the provision of public relations aid for socially disadvantaged groups; and Ihlen and van Ruler (2007) propose broadening "the theoretical scope of public relations studies by applying the works of a string of prominent social theorists" (p. 243). Coming from a parallel perspective, this chapter reviews an array of leading thinkers, not necessarily just social theorists, and asks readers to open themselves to other disciplines to overcome public relations' lack of awareness of other fields and a lack of engagement with major academic currents over the past 40 years. It addresses this intellectual insularity by surveying theorists and theories that have already impacted outside their original disciplinary origins. These include anthropologists, cultural theorists, ecofeminists, philosophers, poets, novelists, scientists, and sociologists. The aim is to kick-start interest in a range of areas by taking stock of intellectuals and traditions, which have been influential elsewhere but virtually omitted from the field to date.

Since the gaps are massive, it was difficult to prioritize. Accordingly, in the innovative tradition of this volume's predecessor (Toth & Heath, 1992), we opted for formal experimentation by adopting the favourite postmodern form of the list, and by alphabetizing it to avoid hierarchy. Of course, despite the randomness of the fixed alphabetic order, the list is not unbiased. It reflects our sense of omissions that matter weighted toward the following: European political theory (as a continuing major influence on thinking about power and society); postcolonial and subaltern thinkers (as a corrective to ethnocentrism and as recognition of the economic power shift from West to East); and environmental and gender theory (as major and ongoing issues of our age). In further grouping these into five thematic clusters, we do not seek to argue their specific relevance for public relations students, but rather, in this age of Wikipedia, to stimulate readers on their own initiative to explore at least some of them as there are massive archives available online to guide further explorations.

Having criticized the extreme functionalism of public relations, and having used activist objections and critical theory to suggest how effectiveness in isolation for concerns for equity and justice can be socially counterproductive (McKie & Munshi, 2007), we do not seek to underpin our recommendations in that directly utilitarian way. Instead, we hope our A to Z selections will encourage readers to go away and think about things in a whole new way. There is far, far more in this world than is dreamt of in public relations "how to" books and textbooks, of which there are already enough.

Nevertheless, in responding to legitimate editorial demands for thematic clustering, we propose five groups: (1) disciplines that can usefully augment absences in the public relations body of knowledge and methods, such as Arjun Appadurai's anthropology and Asian studies, which, along with Jared Diamond's biogeography and transhuman history, offer a corrective to the lack of reflection on ethnocentricity in the field and in its massive geopolitical slant to the West rather than the East (see also the entry for X, "Missing X-factors"); (2) environmental and feminist concerns, captured in the three Es of ecocentrism, ecofeminism, and Eurofeminism, in an attempt to widen the field's current restricted focus on contemporary women and organizations, and to redress the neglect of ecological issues; (3) political theory with psychological dimensions, as we aspire to stretch the narrow bounds of politics and psychology in public relations thinking, particularly through "wild" thinkers from very different cultural formations: Frantz Fanon's fusion of psyche and colonialization and Slavoj Žižek's Lacanian-informed Marxism; (4) "othering" in a postcolonial context that does not disregard the value of pre-modern perspectives such as Maori and Native American worldviews, Queer theory's reframing of the normal, and Amartya Sen's revisionist perspectives on economics and identity; (5) artistic and scientific approaches, which are significantly absent in public relations, but which inform all relations from the neglected novelists and poets of South America to the post-quantum physics of Dinah Zohar. We further recommend that, if our selections do not catch your imagination, that you explore other contenders—and we warmly invite you to write and let us know your discoveries—for similar broad categories to our selected five.

Arjun Appadurai, Anthropology, and Complex Alignments

Arjun Appadurai makes for an alphabetical and alliterative starting point for this discussion. In his own words he acknowledges his base in two "As" (the fields of anthropology and South Asian languages and civilizations) that are neglected in public relations. At all sorts of levels, approaches and debates from anthropology have shaped qualitative research across all disciplines (Denzin & Lincoln, 2005). One brief way to indicate gains from anthropology would be to imagine public relations field research acknowledging the fundamental questions, and the sensitivity to context, raised by Holmes and Marcus (2005) in examining "The Challenge of an Anthropology of the Contemporary" (p. 1099):

> As the anthropologist arrives at the gleaming headquarters of a multinational pharmaceutical corporation in New Jersey, the imposing governmental offices of the Bank of Japan, the sprawling alternative arts space in an urban ward of Cape Town, the courtrooms of the War Crimes Tribunal in the Hague, or the research laboratories of the World Health Organization in Hong Kong, he or she is faced with unsettling questions. What do I do now? How do I start the fieldwork that is at the heart of my profession? How do I engage the human subjects who can enliven my research and can make my theoretical ideas anthropological? These are not just the questions that haunt the graduate student. . . . They are the deep preoccupations that arise on a more or less daily basis, and it is with a veritable ethnographic treatment of the politics and ecologies of such knowledge forms that every project of the ethnography of the contemporary begins. (p. 1102)

Appadurai's (1996) particular focus, on an "archive of lived actualities, found in all sorts of ethnographies about peoples who have lived very different sorts of lives from my own, today and in the past" (p. 11), makes his work relevant to many disciplines. Moreover, he deploys these detailed local foci to generate informed hypotheses for wider planetary patterns such as his five-dimensional framework for exploring what he calls "global disjunctures" (Appadurai, 1990, p. 296) or the critical breaks between economy, culture, and politics "(a) ethnoscapes; (b) mediascapes; (c) technoscapes; (d) finanscapes; and (e) ideoscapes" (p. 296). In this framework, ethnoscapes denote the "landscape of persons who constitute the shifting world in which we live: tourists, immigrants, refugees, exiles, guest workers and other moving groups" (p. 297); mediascapes, which present the massive dissemination of mediated images that blur the lines between fact and fantasy; technoscapes provide the background for the "global configuration of technology" crisscrossing "previously impervious boundaries" (p. 297) at ever increasing speeds; finanscapes chart the near-instantaneous movement of megamonies that destabilize countries and corrupt rulers; and ideoscapes that show how different nations and regions cohere around different meanings of keywords.

Appadurai's framework is especially relevant because public relations as a discipline straddles economics, politics, and culture. He provides a grid with the flexibility to accommodate continuities, and change, with an essential multidimensionality, which recognizes differences that make a difference, and how these connect with each other. Moreover, Appadurai makes a convincing argument for the primacy of the imagination in sculpting global movements as a flow, something for public relations to take note of in an almost-globalized world that requires the ability to engage with ongoing processes rather than static structures. Appadurai's expertise is not restricted to the academy as evidenced by his consultancy roles in the private and public sector organizations such as the Ford Foundation, UNESCO, and the World Bank.

Appadurai's (2006) most recent book, *Fear of Small Numbers: An Essay on the Geography of Anger*, examines the dark side of globalization. In it he interrogates why the spread of capitalist democracy occurs alongside violence, such as suicide bombings and ethnic cleansings, that injure innocent civilians indiscriminately right across the world. He finds answers in the increasing neglect of minority cultures by nation-states alongside the globalism from below in the form of the contemporaneous growth of minority cultures. Partly as a result of the global mediascape, national minorities feel that they make up a powerful majority culture internationally. The enlargement of communication technologies, accompanied by globalization-powered economic inequities, has exacerbated majority–minority clashes in already fluid situations. The extreme outcomes feature violent expressions of the desire to eradicate the other. His fresh perspectives on these questions, and his expertise in cultural relations, have much to offer contemporary and future public relations.

Diamond's Histories of the Past and the Future

Jared Diamond (1998) shows how "narrowly focused accounts of world history" (p. 10) limit human understanding. A biogeographer, an evolutionary biologist, and a physiologist, Diamond is famous for a number of popular writings that cross disiciplines. His most famous work is the Pulitzer Prize-winning, scholarly, yet readable, tome, *Guns, Germs, and Steel: The Fate of Human Societies* (Diamond, 1998). It delves deep into the core of history, geography, and science to explore how socio-environmental factors led to some societies becoming "disproportionately powerful and innovative" (p. 10). Without feeding myths of ethnocentric superiority, Diamond tracks human development from early modern times to account for the growth of advanced colonial civilizations. His ultimate explanation decenters human agency in favor of resource availability in terms of climate, food, geography, and shelter.

Diamond (2005) builds on this theme in his later *Collapse: How Societies Choose to Fail or Succeed*, by constructing "a five-point framework of possible contributing factors . . . to understand any putative environmental collapse" (p. 11). Four of these factors, according to him, are "environmental damage, climate change, hostile neighbors, and friendly trade partners" but it is the fifth factor—"the society's responses to its environmental problems" (p. 11)—that is particularly important. The significance of Diamond's work to public relations is evident in his call for businesses to work sincerely together with environmentalists. Emphasizing that the "public has the ultimate responsibility for the behaviour of even the biggest business" (Diamond, 2005, p. 485), he observes that "changes in public attitudes will be essential for changes in businesses' environmental practices" (p. 485). According to ecological planning professor William Rees

(2005), Diamond's book offers a necessary antidote to climate sceptics and those remaining "in the sway of a dangerously illusory cultural myth. . . . [since] most governments and international agencies seem to believe that the human enterprise is somehow 'decoupling' from the environment, and so is poised for unlimited expansion" (p. 15).

Eckersley, Ecocentrism, and Ecofeminism

The biggest challenge to the myth that human activity and the environment can be decoupled comes from ecological theorists and environmental activists. As the challenges of climate change increase, perhaps exponentially, their views are likely to grow in relevance. As the spate of apocalyptic titles proliferate, we suggest that evidence is mounting in favour of an ecocentric view whereby "all organisms are not simply interrelated with their environment but also constituted by those very environmental relationships" (Eckersley, 1992, p. 49).

Ecofeminists similarly reject human aspirations to master nature by placing humans and non-humans as an integrated part of the larger realm of nature. In particular they critique "what they see as the patriarchal tendencies of Western science and of the Western development model" (Kurian, 2000, pp. 58–59). For ecofeminists, these patriarchal tendencies are responsible not only for the oppression of women but the degradation of the environment as well. According to ecofeminists such as Shiva (1988), it is the prevailing development model that has had devastating effects on the world's poor, especially women. This devastation is often ignored or marginalized. The considerable literature connecting ecology and feminism offers a rich body of work for re-theorizing planetary possibilities. It includes not just theoretical deep green movements but practical on-the-ground activist experience and the dialogues between them. The relationship between women and the environment sheds significant light on a range of different human–nonhuman relationships. If we are to address what Connelly and Smith (2003) call the "failure within ecological modernisation to appreciate the diversity of values we associate with the non-human world" (p. 361), the literature on ecofeminism offers excellent guidance because it moves the spotlight from the material value of resources to a more philosophical value of such resources. It pushes public relations to think of natural resources beyond the needs of the current generation of human stakeholders to the larger aspirations of seeing Nature as something that we are committed to passing on to generations that are to follow.

The Fury of Frantz Fanon

Any discussion of the human influence on the degradation of the planet can only be explored in depth with a closer look at the toxic legacy of colonialism. It was not just the territorial subjugation of foreign lands by powerful nations that characterized colonialism but also the domination of certain sets of values over others as well. From a critical perspective, it is evident that colonial regimes resorted to "spin" in a big way as they sought to gloss over the cultural and environmental havoc wrought on the colonized world in the name of "development." One major thinker of the twentieth century who exposed the sugar-coated European discourses of colonization through his fiery prose was the Martinique-born French-Algerian philosopher-psychiatrist, Frantz Fanon.

Fanon (1952) first caught the public eye with his much-cited work *Black Skin, White Masks*, which talks about the black psyche in an overwhelmingly white world. His later work powerfully presents the devastation wrought by European colonization on the Third World, and, overall, it is a body of work that has influenced not only anti-colonial liberation movements in Africa but present-day champions of diversity of thought. Fanon's (1965) tempestuous *Wretched of the Earth* talks about how Europe actively trumpeted all that it did for the world but never acknowledged the trail of misery it left behind for the vast majority of the Earth:

> That same Europe where they were never done talking of Man, and where they never stopped proclaiming that they were only anxious for the welfare of Man: today we know with what sufferings humanity has paid for every one of their triumphs of the mind. (p. 252)

Fanon's work is particularly important because of his ability to focus clinically on the human psyche, and the psychopathology of colonialization and decolonialization, embedded in historical, political, and economic realities.

Kristeva and Eurofeminism

In the limited coverage of feminist interests, and, despite their prominence in the field, the almost complete absence of European women writers on the subject in public relations remains of concern. The European feminist tradition frequently differs from empirical research on the limiting effects of glass ceilings, through its greater concern with power at a macrolevel, and its willingness to engage with such fundamental questions as how gender could and should be constituted, and how accepting traditional discourses of gender predicated on the differences between male and female, can themselves continue inequities. However, this is not to prioritize either one: both are badly needed.

Bulgarian-born Julia Kristeva is unusual in public relations, but typical of Eurofeminism in expressing major concerns with taken-for-granted and universalized points of reference. Considerations of women in public relations concern glass ceilings, rather than the whole building's foundations. Kristeva's (1992) *Strangers to Ourselves*, for instance, suggests how to reshape thinking on integration through sensitivity to shifting configurations around otherness. This can be seen in the following quote where she scrupulously, if unfashionably, tracks the negative impact of the loss of moral and religious certainty:

> While in the most savage human groups the foreigner was an enemy to be destroyed, he has become, within the scope of religious and ethical constructs, a different human being who, provided he espouses them, may be assimilated into the fraternities of the "wise," the "just," or the

"native." In Stoicism, Judaism, Christianity, and even in the humanism of the Enlightenment, the patterns of such acceptance varied, but in spite of its limitations and shortcomings, it remained a genuine rampart against xenophobia. The violence of the problem set by the foreigner today is probably due to the crises undergone by religious and ethical constructs.

(Kristeva, 1992, p. 2)

But, having acknowledged that, Kristeva (1992) goes on to self-reflexively anticipate a future transcendence where an encounter with a foreign other, "beginning with the moment when the citizen-individual ceases to consider himself as unitary and glorious but discovers his incoherencies and abysses, in short his 'strangeness'" (p. 2), can help us to educate ourselves so that it is no longer a question "of welcoming the foreigner within a system that obliterates him but of promoting the togetherness of those foreigners that we all recognize ourselves to be" (pp. 2–3).

Maori and Native American Worldviews

In considering colonial contexts, we are especially conscious of the Maori heritage of the land we currently live and work in. Although the identity of modern-day New Zealand is enshrined in the Treaty of Waitangi signed between Maori Chiefs and the British Crown in 1840, organizational processes in the country have rarely drawn on Maori worldviews. Organizations routinely profess their bi-cultural goals but, as Tremaine (1997) says, these goals have remained "unrealised for years and little progress towards them have been achieved" (p. 286). Much of the public relations theory and practice in New Zealand is based on largely Western paradigms that do not explicitly acknowledge the fundamentally bi-cultural character of the country.

This tendency of undermining the epistemological traditions of first peoples (or other marginalized groups) is global as can be seen in the near absence of references to Native American traditions in the copious amounts of mainstream public literature published in the U.S. Yet, as Griffin-Pierce (1995) points out:

North America has two histories. One starts with Christopher Columbus's "discovery" of the "New World." The other starts millennia earlier, when a people began to spread across the vast continent, developing cultures and traditions as varied as the landscapes of North America. To understand one history, we must first know the other. (cover flap)

Although indigenous epistemologies continue to be perceived as marginal in mainstream terms, such epistemologies are alive and active in indigenous circles. As the prominent Maori scholar Linda Tuhiwai Smith (1998) shows, "increasing numbers of indigenous academics and researchers have begun to address social issues within the wider framework of self-determination, decolonization and social justice" (p. 4). The essence of the Maori worldview, according to Raginui Walker (1996), is in the notion of *Whakapapa* or genealogy. This genealogy is not just charted in genetic terms but also in terms of culture, society, epistemology, and identity. It is unique, yet diverse. It is fixed, yet fluid.

For many indigenous peoples, the central crisis underlying the crisis in neoliberal democracy and globalization is spiritual and "rooted in the increasingly virulent relationship between human beings and the rest of nature" (Grande, 2000, p. 354). Indigenous research agendas, as Smith (1998) says, revolve around the goal of self-determination and the four directions that the research agendas represent are "decolonization, healing, transformation and mobilization," all of which "are processes which connect, inform and clarify the tensions between the local, the regional, and the global" and "can be incorporated into practices and methodologies" (p. 116). Drawing on indigenous thought can help public relations scholars to break down what has been identified as the field's "asymmetric hierarchy of publics" (Munshi & Kurian, 2005, p. 514), which ignores the multiplicity of colonized publics "below the corporate radar" (p. 514).

Neruda and the Common Destiny

What ought to unite these multiple publics is their shared heritage and their shared future. Strong, persuasive, and sustainable communication need not be something that is directed by a dominant source cloaked in power. As the Nobel Prize-winning Latin American poet Pablo Neruda (1997) shows, the most evocative and meaningful communication depends on the sincerity of the source:

> I have often said that the best poet is the man who delivers our daily bread: the local baker, who does not think he is a god. He fulfills his majestic yet humble task of kneading, placing in the oven, browning, and delivering our daily bread, with a true sense of community. (p. 203)

Neruda's faith in the common person was derived from his own political leanings. Politics is what gave his poetry the sharpest edge and his works clearly showed that transformation of any kind needed the turbulence of politics. As the literary critic Rene de Costa (1979) says, the purpose of Neruda's epic *Canto general* was "to convert the reader to the cause, to show him that solidarity of the oppressed is necessary to overcome the oppressor" (p. 108).

Neruda's empathy with marginalized sections of the population resonates with calls for an acknowledgement of subaltern publics in the process of addressing issues of equity in public relations. In public relations practice it resonates with the technological shift that empowers individuals as authors in the new media rather than mere audiences for the old media. Formerly marginalized individuals and groups can now reach larger constituencies through web publishing. The power of the shift has been widely observed, especially in relation to the media, where citizen journalists are transforming news from lecture format to dialogue (Gillmor, 2004), and to business, where blogs on corporations are opening up conversations instead of traditional organization-centered media relations (Scoble & Israel, 2006).

Queer Theory's Impact on Knowledge

Few theories have had as turbulent and as dramatic an impact on a number of disciplines as Queer theory, which has productively rocked areas as diverse as cinema and genetics. Originating in the realm of gay and lesbian studies, Queer theory's resistance to clearly defined terms, for not just sex and sexuality but also as a non-normative, non-heterosexual, and non-essentialist concept, has projected it as a quintessential product that undermines founding assumptions of modernity. Just as gender studies has moved beyond binary oppositions of man and woman, Queer theory demonstrates "the impossibility of any 'natural' sexuality" (Jagose, 1996, p. 3).

For public relations and George W. Bush's attempt to divide the world into a Western "US" and an Islamic "THEM," Queer theory has a message: The world is not constructed in binary opposites. As Judith Butler (1990), a scholar straddling feminist theory and Queer theory, articulately puts it: "identity categories tend to be instruments of regulatory regimes, whether as the normalizing categories of oppressive structures or as the rallying points for a liberatory contestation of that very oppression" (pp. 13–14).

Notions of cultures, therefore, need to oppose an orchestrated "management" of diversity in which dominant cores mark out groups of "others" as a "carefully crafted strategy of constructing and controlling" (Munshi, 2005, p. 47).

Sen: The Art of Maintaining Equality and Allowing Identity

Nobel Prize-winning welfare and development economist Amartya Sen is as renowned for his acknowledgement of local contexts as he is for his work on giving economics a human face. One of the most important arguments of Sen is that the notion of equality is not always a simple matter of equally dividing resources. For instance, Sen (1992) argues that all the talk about equality in income distribution hides the "substantive inequalities in, say, well-being and freedom arising out of such a distribution given the disparate personal and social circumstances of each individual" (p. 30). Policies and practices that view equality in simplistic terms, therefore, only end up privileging the elite over those who are socially and economically disadvantaged. What this means for public relations is that a commitment to issues of equity might mean giving more time and resources to publics that are systematically marginalized. A rare example is Moloney's (2006) support for the practice of lobbying provided disadvantaged groups get communication aid along the lines of legal aid.

While scholars in organizational communication (Cheney, 2000) are beginning to draw on the work of Sen, public relations has remained largely aloof from his paradigm-shifting work. Public relations scholars and practitioners could bring a lot more balance to the field by re-examining the concept of equality in more complex terms and weighing the relative socio-economic standings of various stakeholders in formulating sustainable communication strategies. Sen (2001) is also suggestive in loosening restrictive ideas of identity and allowing individuals contextual freedom so that:

the same person can be of Indian origin, a Muslim, a French citizen, a US resident, a woman, a poet, a vegetarian, an anthropologist, a university professor, a Christian, an angler, and an avid believer in extra-terrestrial life. . . . Each of these collectives, to all of which this person belongs, gives him or her a particular identity, which are variously important in different contexts. (p. 49)

Uslar Pietri, Vargas Llosa, and the "Other" World of South America

Novels are neglected as a source of learning in public relations and, if space had permitted, we would have covered T with how Amy Tan's (1989, 1996) fiction opens eyes to the complexities of intercultural, crosscultural, and intergenerational communication. Works from South America lead us into the world of what the Venezuelan writer, Arturo Uslar Pietri (1997), calls "The Other America." That the states of the southern part of the American continent continue to live in the geographical and ideological shadow of their dominant northern neighbor, the U.S., is evident in the lack of adequate engagement in Western management and business with the Spanish- and Portuguese-speaking intellectual powerhouses of the region: "It has gone on for four centuries; it has been long, arduous, unending, this search for the identity of the sons of the other America, which is still called by such objectionable, almost provisional names as Spanish America, Latin America, Iberoamerica, and even Indoamerica" (Uslar Pietri, 1997, p. 208).

While the Venezuelan writer's call to those in the southern continent to carve out its own distinct identity has had a major impact on thinkers in cultural studies, the Peruvian novelist, Vargas Llosa's ideological adventures with the left, the right, and the center exemplify the complexity of the region. That Vargas Llosa grew up in the Bolivian town of Cochabamba is also interesting, given the town's highly publicized ideological struggles reflected in the recent saga of protests and the local government's flip-flop policies over the privatization of water. The rich art, history, society, and politics of the South American nations forms an integral part of Vargas Llosa's (1984) *Aunt Julia and the Scriptwriter* and his *Conversation in the Cathedral* (1993). As public relations scholars, the intellectual tradition of South America not only offers rich diversifications for our theory and practice but also makes us aware of the political complexities of a range of publics in different parts of the world.

Missing X-factors

Despite our familiarity with Tan and several other writers of Chinese origin based in the West, we must own up to our lack of grasp of theoretical perspectives from China. This gap is epitomized in our difficulty in finding an appropriate entry under X for this chapter. As any one in business and enterprise would know, China, a land where names with the letter X are fairly common, is one of the leading players in a shifting geopolitical world.

Žižek, Zohar, and New Zealand

The question of integrity is, of course, a key issue for public relations. As it grapples with issues of truth, falsehood, and spin, public relations could look to the works of Slovenian philosopher Slavoj Žižek who explores the ways in which certain ideological assumptions frame "truth" in specific ways. Žižek's work illustrates "how there is a basic fault-line that shows through in oppositional structures of truth and falsity, which ideology itself serves to conceal" (Wright & Wright, 1999, p. 53).

According to Žižek, despite the range of natural and human-made catastrophes in the world, liberal capitalism is projected as some kind of ideological reality that can be taken for granted. In legitimizing such a conception, the undercurrents of domination or even exploitation remain concealed, making it possible for institutions "*to lie in the guise of truth*" [italics in original] (Žižek, 1994, p. 8):

> When, for example, some Western power intervenes in a Third World country on account of violations of human rights, it may well be "true" that in this country the most elementary human rights were not respected, and that the Western intervention will effectively improve the human rights record; yet such a legitimization none the less remains "ideological" in so far as it fails to mention the true motives of the intervention (economic interests, etc). (p. 8)

Žižek is also editor of an MIT Press series, "Short Circuits." His series foreword notes that a "short circuit occurs when there is a faulty connection in the network—faulty, of course, from the standpoint of the network's smooth functioning" (Žižek, 2006, p. ix) but it is selected as the title for the series because "Is not the shock of short-circuiting, therefore, one of the best metaphors for a critical reading . . . to cross wires that do not usually touch" (p. ix). Reading Žižek (2006) is often akin to a kind of perceptual short circuit and his underlying premise "that Lacanian psychoanalysis is a privileged instrument of such an approach" (p. ix) is alien to any current critical activity in the public relations field. Nevertheless he has amassed a unique body of work capable of making connections across promotional culture (from Hitchcock to Mel Gibson's *Passion of the Christ*), with links to neuroscience research, philosophy, politics, and theology.

As our other selected Z, science commentator Danah Zohar (1997) reminds us in her book *Rewiring the Corporate Brain: Using the New Science to Rethink How We Structure and Lead Organizations*: "All the sciences of the twentieth century, both physical and biological, are holistic. They show that the world does not consist of separate isolated parts but rather of intricately interconnected systems. A change in any one apparent part affects the whole" (p. 11). She has since co-published, *Spiritual Capital: Wealth We Can Live By* (Zohar & Marshall, 2004), in which she defines spiritual intelligence as "the intelligence with which we access our deepest meanings, values, purposes, and highest motivations" (p. 3). In a message that encompasses contemporary crises from Enron to Iraq, Zohar and Marshall (2004) draw the conclusion that "It is only when our notion of capitalism includes spiritual capital's wealth of meaning, values, purpose, and higher motivation that we can have sustainable capitalism and a sustainable society" (p. 4). In interweaving issues of spirit with issues of sustainable business, Zohar and Marshall (2004) parallel the new openness in the social sciences that Denzin and Lincoln (2000) identify as "The potential for a new flowering of the human spirit" (p. 1060). Public relations, with a professed attachment to values, and proven capabilities in promulgation, would be the obvious field to cultivate such potential.

The intricacies and complexities of knowledge that Žižek and Zohar discuss, albeit in very different ways, emphasize that creative thought is characterized not only by ferment and questioning but also by an ongoing engagement with scholarship in other fields. In this kind of engagement, Žižek leads the way for "there is seemingly no field (literature, linguistics, psychoanalysis, film studies, philosophy, opera, theology, political theory, new media technologies, history, popular culture . . .) left untouched by Žižek" (Simmons, Molloy, & Worth, 2005, p. 30). In *From Z to A: Žižek at the Antipodes*, Simmons, Molloy, and Worth (2005) use a reversed alphabetical list that begins with "Z is for Žižek" and ends with "A is for Anything goes" (p. 30) because, for "Žižek, 'anything goes' with a citational rapidity and an encyclopaedic extension that leaves his readers breathless" (p. 30).

Conclusion

Our "A to Z" is less expansive than the Žižekian canvas but, hopefully, still stretches the citational range and ideas beyond the currently constricted frame of public relations. Innovative thinkers are as vital to practice as education and should inform present as well as future practitioners. This is in line with Hamel and Breen's (2007) *Future of Management* observations that people "often defend the *how* of a hoary old management process simply because they haven't thought deeply about other ways of accomplishing the goals that process serves" (p. 18) and their identification of "innovation's deadliest foe: the often unarticulated and mostly unexamined beliefs that tether you and your colleagues to the management status quo" (p. 126). In expanding the line of vision of public relations, our list provides links to social, cultural, literary, and scientific icons whose works and philosophies can guide the field out of its insular existence and anchor it more firmly in its cultural contexts, and as a participant voice in debates on desirable end goals for society rather than simply a means to achieving current targets.

Each of the five signposts we identify in this expanded line of vision help direct both students and practitioners to ways of transformative thinking that will change the perception of public relations as a narrowly defined tool to achieve corporate goals to one of building relationships at multiple levels and in a range of contexts. The first signpost is that of interdisciplinarity, which opens the field to insights from outside business into diverse realms such as anthropology, biology, and cultural studies, relevant to the complexities of contemporary globalization. In challenging the misleading notion of public relations as only a management function, this signpost adds essential directions for navigating the larger socio-political world. The second signpost foregrounds environmental and feminist critiques of business as usual. It points to the paramount importance of public relations in sustaining ecological equilibrium as well as incorporating gender issues beyond organizational glass ceilings. The third signpost directs us to the need for a more inclusive political and psychological consciousness in a field that currently sees activist groups as outside its domain rather than inside it. The fourth signpost indicates how "other" worldviews manifest in the philosophical as well as political traditions of indigenous and minority groups worldwide while the fifth signpost takes us directly to the hearts and minds of poets, novelists, and scientists who in different ways show how the art and science of public relations can be better crafted and more equitably practised. Ideally, while we hope individual letter entries will spark innovative thinking in public relations, we dream that students of the field will embrace the list holistically and keep extending it as a natural part of a learning profession alert to its social surroundings and social impacts.

References

Appadurai, A. (1990). Disjuncture and difference in the global cultural economy. *Theory, Culture, and Society, 7*(2–3), 295–310.

Appadurai, A. (1996). *Modernity at large: Cultural dimensions of globalization.* Minneapolis, MN: University of Minnesota Press.

Appadurai, A. (2006). *Fear of small numbers: An essay on the geography of anger.* Durham, NC: Duke University Press.

Butler, J. (1990). *Gender trouble: Feminism and the subversion of identity.* New York: Routledge.

Cheney, G. (2000). Thinking differently about organizational communication: Why, how, and where? *Management Communication Quarterly, 14*(1), 132–141.

Connelly, J., & Smith, G. (2003). *Politics and the environment: From theory to practice* (2nd ed.). London: Routledge.

Coombs, T., & Holladay, S. (2007). *It's not just PR.* Oxford: Blackwell Books.

de Costa, R. (1979). *The poetry of Pablo Neruda.* Cambridge, MA: Harvard University Press.

Denzin, N., & Lincoln, Y. (2000). The seventh moment: Out of the past. In N. Denzin & Y. Lincoln (Eds.), *The handbook of qualitative research* (2nd ed.) (pp. 1047–1063). Thousand Oaks, CA: Sage.

Denzin, N., & Lincoln, Y. (Eds.). (2005). *The handbook of qualitative research* (3rd ed.). Thousand Oaks, CA: Sage.

Diamond, J. (1998). *Guns, germs, and steel: The fate of human societies.* New York: W. W. Norton.

Diamond, J. (2005). *Collapse: How societies choose to fail or succeed.* New York: Viking Penguin.

Eckersley, R. (1992). *Environmentalism and political theory: Towards an ecocentric approach.* New York: State University of New York.

Fanon, F. (1957). *Black skin, white masks* (C. Farrington, Trans.). New York: Grove Press. (Original work published 1952.)

Fanon, F. (1965). *The wretched of the earth* (C. Farrington, Trans.). London: Macgibbon & Kee. (Original work published 1961.)

Gillmor, D. (2006). *We the media: Grassroots journalism by the people, for the people.* Sebastopol, CA: O'Reilly Media.

Grande, S. (2000). American Indian identity and intellectualism: The quest for a new red pedagogy. *International Journal of Qualitative Studies in Education, 13,* 343–360.

Griffin-Pierce, T. (1995). *The encyclopedia of Native America.* New York: Viking.

Hamel, G., & Breen, B. (2007). *The future of management.* Boston: Harvard Business School Press.

Heath, R. (2006). Onward into more fog: Thoughts on public relations' research directions. *Journal of Public Relations Research, 18*(2), 93–114.

Holmes, D. R., & Marcus, G. E. (2005). Refunctioning ethnography: The challenge of an anthropology of the contemporary. In N. Denzin & Y. Lincoln (Eds.), *The handbook of qualitative research* (3rd ed.) (pp. 1099–1113). Thousand Oaks, CA: Sage.

Ihlen, Ø., & van Ruler, B. (2007). How public relations works: Theoretical roots and public relations perspectives. *Public Relations Review, 33,* 243–248.

Jagose, A. (1996). *Queer theory.* Dunedin, New Zealand: University of Otago Press.

Kristeva, J. (1992). *Strangers to ourselves* (L. Roudiez, Trans.). New York: Columbia University Press.

Kurian, P. (2000). *Engendering the environment?: Gender in the World Bank's environmental policies.* Aldershot, England: Ashgate Publishing.

McKie, D., & Munshi, D. (2007). *Reconfiguring public relations: Ecology, equity, and enterprise.* London: Routledge.

Moloney, K. (2006). *Rethinking public relations: PR propaganda and democracy.* London: Routledge.

Munshi, D. (2005). Through the subject's eye: Situating the other in discourses of diversity. In G. Cheney & G. Barnett (Eds.), *International and multicultural organizational communication* (pp. 45–70). Creskill, NJ: Hampton Press.

Munshi, D., & Kurian, P. (2005). Imperializing spin cycles: A postcolonial look at public relations, greenwashing, and the separation of publics. *Public Relations Review 31*(4), 513–520.

Neruda, P. (1997). The Nobel address. In I. Stavans (Ed.), *The Oxford book of Latin American essays* (pp. 199–206). New York: Oxford University Press.

Rees, W. (2005, January 6). Contemplating the abyss. *Nature, 433,* 15–16.

Scoble, R., & Israel, S. (2006). *Naked conversations: How blogs are changing the way businesses talk with customers.* Hoboken, NJ: John Wiley.

Sen, A. (1992). *Inequality reexamined.* New York: Russell Sage.

Sen, A. (2001). The predicament of identity. *Biblio,* March–April, 48–50.

Shiva, V. (1988). *Staying alive: Women, ecology, and survival.* New Delhi: Kali for Women.

Simmons, L., Molloy, M., & Worth, H. (Eds.). (2005). *From Z to A: Žižek at the Antipodes.* Wellington, New Zealand: Dunmore Press.

Smith, L. T. (1998). *Decolonizing methodologies.* London: Zed Books.

Tan, A. (1989). *The Joy Luck club.* London: William Heinemann.

Tan, A. (1996). *A hundred secret senses.* London: Flamingo.

Toth, E., & Heath, R. (Eds.). (1992). *Rhetorical and critical approaches to public relations.* Hillsdale, NJ: Lawrence Erlbaum.

Tremaine, M. (1997). Towards the inclusive organisation. In F. Sligo, S. Olsson, & C. Wallace (Eds.), *Perspectives in business communication: Theory and practice* (pp. 283–290). Palmerston North, New Zealand: Software Technology.

Uslar Pietri, A. (1997). The other America. In I. Stavans (Ed.), *The Oxford book of Latin American essays* (pp. 207–215). New York: Oxford University Press.

Vargas Llosa, M. (1984). *Aunt Julia and the scriptwriter.* London: Pan Books.

Vargas Llosa, M. (1993). *Conversation in the cathedral.* London: Faber and Faber.

Walker, R. (1996). *Nga Pepa a Ranginui: The Walker papers.* Auckland: Penguin.

Wright, E., & Wright, E. (Eds.). (1999). *The Žižek reader.* Oxford: Blackwell.

Žižek, S. (1994). The spectre of ideology. In S. Žižek (Ed.), *Mapping ideology* (pp. 1–33). London: Verso.

Žižek, S. (2006). *The parallax view.* Cambridge, MA: The MIT Press.

Zohar, D. (1997). *Rewiring the corporate brain: Using the new science to rethink how we structure and lead organizations.* San Francisco: Berrett-Koehler.

Zohar, D., & Marshall, I. (2004). *Spiritual capital: Wealth we can live by.* San Francisco: Berrett-Koehler.

4

CIVIL SOCIETY AS A RHETORICAL PUBLIC RELATIONS PROCESS

Maureen Taylor
University of Oklahoma

The field of public relations has been growing in both breadth and depth during the past decade. While the contributions of Excellence theory (J. Grunig, 1992) cannot be ignored, the field of public relations is now benefiting from broader theories that help us to understand its role in communities across the world. Excellence theory, the first comprehensive normative theoretical framework in public relations, has now been joined by other theories including accommodation theory (Cancel, Mitrook, & Cameron, 1999), relation management theory (Ledingham & Bruning, 1998, 2000), and dialogue theory (Kent &Taylor, 2002). These theories provide alternative frameworks to think about organization–public relationships. Another theoretical framework that may hold value for understanding the broader societal contributions of public relations is civil society theory.

What is civil society? Civil society means many things to many different people. To some, it is a normative model of how people should participate in their communities. Civil society can be understood through a common community debate about scarce resources. For instance, one group of community members organizing to build a teen center. This group includes teens, parents, teachers and law enforcement officers. They argue that teens cause less trouble after school if there is somewhere for them to go that involves activities and supervision. They create flyers, post their arguments on their Facebook pages, and write letters to the newspaper. The group wants to communicate the key message that teens need a space to be safe and be teens.

Another side of the debate is comprised of groups fighting for a senior center. Older citizens are the fastest growing group in the United States and senior centers play an important role in their lives. The seniors have paid taxes for decades, vote, and know the town's decision makers. The group wants to communicate the key message that seniors deserve a space in town to pursue their interests. A third group also has an interest in the debate. The anti tax group, comprised of vocal citizens wary of tax increases, wants to stop public funding of any center. This group wants to communicate the key message that special spaces for any group should be funded by the private sector such as local businesses. The local business community, a fourth group with an interest in the topic, has been silent on the issue but the Chamber of Commerce is planning to discuss the situation at its upcoming meeting. Once they decide their position, they will distribute a news release to the local media organizations to explain their position.

The competing groups need to form alliances, reach out to the media, and meet with government and businesses leaders to garner support. Each side needs to frame its message, inoculate the public against counter-arguments, and persuade decision makers that their desired end will be the most beneficial to the community. The existence of debate and decision is the hallmark of civil society.

This example shows civil society as the process of groups advocating for a desired end. Civil society creates the conditions that allows individuals and groups to advocate. This idealized perception of civil society describes a process where people interact and negotiate decisions. Civil society is the "evolution of cooperation and trust among citizens" (Hadenius & Uggla, 1996, p. 1622). Civil society can be understood through activities such as civic education, media development, and conflict resolution. Civil society may also be understood when it is absent from a community. For instance, who amongst us has not read about the violence in Darfur or Iraq and wondered what processes and structures need to be in place to stop the violence?

Civil society is not without its critics. Some scholars claim that civil society is merely a catchphrase that perpetuates top-down relationships among groups and nations (Dutta-Bergman, 2005a, 2005b). In this perspective, civil society activities are intended to maintain relationships between the dominant and the dominated. Dutta-Bergman's depiction of the marginalized in the subaltern challenges a public relations approach to civil society. It is the intent of this chapter to show that civil society as a rhetorical public relations process may be able to overcome such criticisms.

This chapter proceeds from the assumption that civil society is a desirable and empowering process. It facilitates relationship building among members of a society and can also build international relationships. Civil society is a requisite for what Heath (2006) termed fully functioning society theory (FFST). Civil society is the process of interactions that lead to relationships, build trust, and create social capital. The purpose of this chapter is to explore how public relations can inform civil society theory. Civil society is not an outcome; it is a process grounded in rhetoric. More specifically, this essay argues that civil society could be understood as a socially constructed process that can be created, maintained, and changed by rhetorical public relations activities. The first part of this chapter explores how civil society has been discussed in different academic fields including political science, sociology, mass media, and organizational communication. The second part puts forth a public relations approach to civil society based on the different partners in civil society. Civil society as a public relations theory has not fully been explicated and it is hoped that this essay will provide the historical and theoretical contexts necessary for situating it within a rhetorical framework.

Disciplinary Approaches to Conceptualizing Civil Society

Various academic fields have considered the topic of civil society. Each approach reflects the values and paradigms of that specific field of study. Some fields have studied civil society from the individual acting in a society perspective (Hauser, 1998). Rhetoricians, for example, have sought to understand how citizen rhetors frame public policy and debate. Political scientists and sociologists have explored the concept from more macro, societal perspectives looking at the intersection of public participation in organizations that creates trust and social capital (Barber, 1998; Gellner, 1994; Putnam, 2000; Seligman, 1997). Media theorists have argued that the media are a foundation of national (Gross, 2002) and international (Jacobson & Jang, 2002) civil society. Each perspective that addresses a different dimension of civil society will be discussed in more detail below.

Civil Society's Greco-Roman Roots

Many scholars point to the Greeks and Romans as the first groups to conceptualize and practice some form of civil society. Gerald Hauser has written extensively about the concept of civil society and the public sphere. Hauser traced the concept of the public sphere back to the Greeks and Romans seeing it as a "discursive space in which individuals and groups associate to discuss matters of mutual interest and, where possible, to reach a common judgment about them. It is the locus of emergence for rhetorically salient meanings" (1998, p. 21). Hauser is not nostalgic for the days when only free men could participate in the public discourse that would determine how individuals would live their lives. Hauser is quick to admit that the concept of the public sphere in ancient times was hardly perfect. Rather, he simply sought to show that the concept of the "public" influencing the "private" has historic precedence. The Greco-Roman period is the beginning of how individual rhetors used language to advocate or refute policy decisions.

In Hauser's historical perspective, rhetorical democracy is premised on civil society. Hauser and Grim (2004) prefaced their volume dedicated to rhetorical democracy and civic engagement with these words: "One lesson from our ancient forbearers endures, however: the idea that democracy and rhetoric are inextricably linked. Tending to the business of democracy means tending to its rhetorical practices" (p. xi).

Hauser (1997) initially defined civil society as "the network of associations independent of the state whose members, through social interactions that balance conflict and consensus, seek to regulate themselves in ways consistent with a valuation of difference" (p. 277). Hauser (2004) later noted that "civil society's character is inherently rhetorical" (p. 9). Political agents operate in a rhetorical space and that space is what allows civil society to function. In ancient Greece, the public and the political were often synonymous.

Civil Society as a Political Activity

The field of political science has also considered the concept of civil society. Political science theorists including Gellner (1994) have linked civil society to economic development. Gellner saw political civil society linked to economic activity and argued that the strength of a nation could be found in the intersection of the two. Barber (1998) has also examined civil society as public participation in community life and policy decisions. As evidence of the growing interest in civil society research, Benjamin Barber now serves as an endowed chair of Civil Society at the University of Maryland. Civil society might have become one of those concepts that was discussed mostly by academics lamenting the ills of society; yet, one of the best-known contemporary political scientists, Robert Putnam of Harvard University, has bridged the academic-popular culture gap. Putnam published *Bowling Alone: The Collapse and Revival of American Community* in 2000. Putnam's research was based on both primary and secondary data about membership in community organizations. Putnam's research showed how Americans have become disconnected at two levels. First, they are disconnected from democratic institutions and processes that form the basis of decision making in America. The number of citizens voting in local and national elections is at an all time low. Participation in the political parties is also down from earlier years. Putnam's research noted a loss of faith in the political system and in government's ability to serve public needs.

While this is troubling for democracies, Putnam's other finding hits closer to home. Putnam's second research finding suggests that the loss of social capital is linked to a concurrent lack of trust in family, friends, and neighbors. At almost every level of society, there is a loss of trust and thus a loss of social capital. Putnam's work raised alarms because he warned that social capital created by "connectedness" is diminishing. Social capital is the invisible wealth of a community. While it can help to create tangible outcomes associated with economic wealth, in the civil society sector, social capital is best understood as an intangible asset. Social capital is a community benefit that is created by a system of trusting and supportive interconnected organizations (Burt, 1997; Doerfel & Taylor, 2005; Putnam, 2000; Taylor & Doerfel, 2005; Toth, 2006). Toth (2006), building from Hazelton's work on social capital and public relations, considered social capital as how "individuals in organizations build relationships to lead to overall decision making" (p. 514). Social capital is created when organizational members communicate and enter into relationships with others. The wealth of a community is in its relationships that provide new opportunities, information, and access to a variety of resources (Monge & Contractor, 2000).

Putnam provides an example of the enormous value of social capital (or the tragic consequences when there is a lack of social capital in a community). In an interview with Jason Marsh of the magazine *Greater Good*, Putnam reflected on the real outcome of diminished social capital in the United States. Using Hurricane Katrina as the backdrop, Putnam said that if the storm had hit an area of the country with a history of greater social capital (such as Minneapolis), then:

> the folks in St. Paul wouldn't have been standing with guns on the bridges across the Mississippi up there trying to keep people who were trying to flee devastated Minneapolis from getting into St. Paul. And that's exactly what happened in New Orleans.
>
> (Marsh, 2005–2006, p. 5)

Putnam added: "In some sense God aimed that hurricane exactly at the part of America that was most vulnerable: the place that has low social capital and ineffective government" (Marsh, 2005–2006, p. 5). Putnam's work has joined other scholars who fear major societal implications from the loss of social capital and trust.

Sociological Approaches to Civil Society

The activities of the "Chicago School" are an early example of how some researchers in the field of Sociology have studied civil society. During the early years of America's urban transition, graduate students at the University of Chicago went out into their community to help solve real social problems. Students sought to identify the root causes and cures for social ills in cities. This type of proactive sociological research is a foundation for later sociological work in civil society.

Sociologist Seligman linked the concept of trust with the development and sustaining of civil society (1997). Seligman argued that trust is a requirement for civil society. Like Putnam (2000), Seligman's research shows that individual trust is disappearing in America. In place of trust, Seligman noted that societies have enacted rules, constraints, and systems of control that now determine how interpersonal and organizational interactions should occur. The loss of individual, organizational, and political trust is a significant problem for the development of civil society. Trust in government, media, and other institutions is at an all time low (Seligman, 1997). Some have blamed the media for this diminished trust while others actually see the media as playing a role in enacting civil society.

Mass Media's Role in Civil Society

Alexander (1998, 2006) is one scholar who advocates for the important role of the media in building civil society. "The news is the only source of firsthand experience they [citizens] will ever have about their fellow citizens, about their motives for acting the way they do, the kinds of relationships they form, and the nature of the institutions they might potentially create" (2006, p. 80). Civil society assumes a free and independent media system that serves the public interest. The existence of such a free and independent media, however, may not be sufficient for civil society development.

Moy and Pfau (2000) presented their results of a multi method "inter connected" study in a book about civil society and trust in American institutions. Moy and Pfau studied how Americans viewed local government and political parties through the lens of media coverage and media consumption patterns. They found that the media's coverage of governmental and political issues may be actually undermining public trust in these institutions. Moy and Pfau's work specifically focused on a small Midwest city (Madison, Wisconsin), but it also has implications for global discussions of civil society. At the international level, two factors in particular underlie the mass media's role in civil society—globalization and the economic transitions of post communist nations.

Globalization has prompted many scholars to think about how traditional media outlets and traditional journalistic practices can remain relevant in a globalized world. Bardoel (1996) argued that the advance of the information society could actually be the end of journalism as we know it. Bardoel (1996) noted that in traditional models of media, journalists provided objective information and content that became the basis of community-based civil society discussions. Today, media organizations may find their niche in directing the flow of information to community members and facilitating public debates. Newspapers and electronic broadcasters now regularly invite citizens to voice their opinion through their outlets. The media have become the *space* for the discussion rather than the *providers* of the content that shape the discussion. The emergence of blogs, citizen journalism, and interactive websites now brings people from all across the world to facilitate new ways of processing information.

The traditional media, now joined by the new media formats, have the potential to bring media into the center of civil society. Jacobson and Jang (2002) have explored how the media can contribute to a globalized civil society through promoting peace and covering democratic struggles. Corry (2006) has problematized civil society and asked if civil society actions were merely limited to actions within a specific nation state. Corry argued that a transcendent civil society movement has emerged that extends beyond national borders. Thus, because of media coverage and media organizations, civil society is no longer just limited to activities within one nation.

A second factor influencing research about media's role in civil society has come from studying media transitions in post communist media societies. The former Soviet Union and its East Bloc allies all controlled their media sector and placed it under the direction of the government. Gross (2002) reported on the various ways that media, popular culture, and democracy are now being played out in Eastern Europe.

> Media studies can reveal the potential of mass communication to affect change, the constraints or opportunities of the sociopolitical reality, and nature of social culture. In the Eastern European case, media studies reflect a process of political, social, economic, cultural and individual transition, transformation, and adjustment.
>
> (Gross, 2002, p. 26)

It is the media's role in what Gross called "transition, transformation, and adjustment," that has prompted multiple studies about media and public opinion in post communist nations. There is considerable evidence from the newly formed nation of Bosnia on the role of the media in this transition and transformation. For instance, Taylor and Napoli (2003) and Botan and Taylor (2005) examined how much the public (as a complex of publics) trusts politically motivated and independent media in Bosnia. Their findings suggest that the independent media, those media not formally associated with a political party or government, are most trusted when Bosnians need information to make decisions. The media, however, require content for their news stories. What may seem like a reasonable relationship, however, could be flawed. Bentele (2004) reminds us that media and public relations "render each other possible" and thus need each other to foster a fully functioning society (2004, p. 491). However, rather than cooperating, media and public relations professions may actually be competing with each other to the detriment of both parties. This is unfortunate because content, or information subsidies (Gandy, 1982), come from different types of organizations operating in the civil sphere. Organizational communication scholars are now beginning to study these civil society organizations.

Civil Society as the Social Capital Created by Organizations

Social capital is created when organizations cooperate and work toward shared goals. Social capital, as Kennan and Hazelton (2006) noted, can be understood at the individual, organizational, or societal levels. Inherent in social capital are many structural, relational, and communicative dimensions. Alexander (1998) has conceptualized civil society as "private and public associations and organizations, all forms of cooperative social relationships that create bonds of trust, public opinion, legal rights and institutions and political parties" (p. 3).

Recently, organizational communication scholars have become interested in civil society. Lewis (2005) showed how the term "civil society" has gained increased interest in the organizational communication literature. According to Lewis, the civil society sector is the fastest growing sector across the globe. There are 1.8 million registered non-profits in the United States alone and millions more around the world. This growth provides unique opportunities for public relations research about civil society. Lewis suggested that organizational communication scholars should study topics including social capital, mission effectiveness, and accountability, governance and decision making, and volunteer relationships. The organizational communication literature has many examples of how civil society is enacted when organizations work together. For instance, Shumate, Fulk, and Monge (2005) examined networks of nongovernmental organizations (NGOs) as they worked on HIV prevention. They concluded that how effective an NGO is in gaining access to power networks predicts their ability to influence policy and engage in relevant dialogues. M. Stohl and C. Stohl (2005) found that NGOs are playing important roles in shaping debate and policy in both national and international contexts. NGOs are also providing services, information, and relationships that complement, rather than compete with, governmental activities. Doerfel and Taylor (2005) and Taylor and Doerfel (2003) specifically measured how these relationships create social capital in Croatia. They found that when organizations cooperate, social capital, in the form of relationships and information sharing, is enhanced.

Synthesis of Previous Civil Society Research

The scholarly considerations of civil society mentioned above are by no means representative of all of the different ways that civil society, social capital, and the civil sphere have been conceptualized. A complete analysis of all articles and books in these disciplines falls beyond the scope of this chapter. However, the assumptions of communication, relationships, and political participation already mentioned do provide clues on how civil society has been studied. What becomes apparent is that civil society has been viewed as an *outcome* of different types of activities. For instance, one could sum up the previous sections by focusing on how the existence or failure of civil society creates certain outcomes. Some might argue that trust in government (or diminished trust) is an outcome of media coverage. Others seem to be arguing that social capital (a desirable outcome) has been lost because people do not join bowling leagues or play bridge anymore. What is missing from these perspectives is the idea that *meaning making and relationships* enact civil society. Civil society is not an outcome; it is a process grounded in rhetoric.

Civil society, although most often conceived of as a sociological, economic, or political activity, is based on discourse. Discourse, and more specifically the use of language to persuade and create shared understanding, is at the heart of all aspects of civil society. It is through discourse that individuals and organizations can participate in the "wrangle of the marketplace" of ideas.

Civil Society as a Rhetorical Public Relations Process

Botan and Taylor (2004) argued that the best way to understand the emerging trends in public relations theory development is to look at the theories through the lens of a cocreational perspective. This perspective sees meaning and communication as that which makes it possible for people and groups to agree to shared meanings, interpretations, goals: "The major relationship of interest is between groups and organizations, and communication functions to negotiate changes in these relationships" (p. 652).

The strategic use of language and symbols forms the basis of the cocreational perspective. Using Kenneth Burke's view of rhetoric as identification in the *Rhetoric of Motives* (1969), Heath (1992) foreshadowed the important role that public relations plays in civil society in his "The Wrangle in the Marketplace" chapter for the 1992 volume of *Rhetorical and Critical Approaches to Public Relations*. The opening paragraph tells us:

> Rhetoric is vital to society. Society could not exist if people did not use words and visual symbols to share and evaluate information, shape beliefs and establish norms for coordinated social action. Through rhetoric, people—individually and on behalf of organizations—influence opinions, understanding, judgment, and actions. (p. 17)

Public relations uses language and other symbolic forms to inform, persuade, and to build identification and coalitions. Organizational use of language (and identification) creates a competition for media and public attention. These rhetorical activities are at the heart of the civil sphere. Heath described this nexus as a "rich mix of voices" (p. 25).

Perhaps the best way to explain civil society as a rhetorical activity is to focus on how organizations contributing to the "mix of voices" use rhetoric in the public sphere. Organizational systems, created by humans to achieve some goal, are a foundation of civil society. Communication, information exchange, and the coordination of activities are core functions of organizations. There are many partners in civil society. Taylor and Doerfel (2005) identified seven key partners in civil society initiatives in Croatia. This chapter expands on that list and elaborates on the rhetorical public relations processes of these Croatian and international organizations as they participate in civil society. It also ties the partners together in an example of civil society in Croatia.

Civil Society Partners

The foundation of civil society is *the public*. Civil society is premised upon an informed and empowered public. In a civil society, the public has the right and, more importantly, the desire to participate in local, regional, and national decisions. Moreover, the public feels safe when participating in all levels of community decision making. Believing that all voices in a civil society are heard can be considered a bit naive. Indeed, one of the major critiques of the concept of civil society is that while it can be empowering to individuals, it can also be used to silence voices. Individuals are empowered when they join societal institutions.

Societal institutions, such as religious organizations, professional groups (associations of doctors, lawyers, educators), universities, unions, and political parties, create the organizational fabric of civil society. In many societies, there is no mediating group or institution between the individual and the government. In other words, there are very few opportunities for individuals to influence those who govern them. Organizations and institutions independent of government control provide a means for citizens to articulate their needs.

Institutions can use rhetorical public relations to define issues and because these institutions are respected, their positions on issues are weighed carefully by those still deciding on their position. More importantly, through issues management, institutional definitions of the issue and its solution can influence policy makers. In a civil society, institutions must operate at both micro and macro levels of the society. Community groups, professional groups, activists, and others all use language to inform, persuade. Their public relations tactics such as news releases, media events, and positions on issues allow them to participate in civil society.

Sometimes the success of these organizations is influenced by how they build relationships with other likeminded groups. For instance, Taylor and Doerfel studied how a civil society network was able to push the public agenda and work toward democratization in Croatia. Taylor and Doerfel found that certain institutions gain influence when they cooperate with the media to set the public agenda.

The *media* are also key partners in ensuring that there is a civil sphere. Siebert, Peterson, and Schramm (1963) first codified the different types of media systems. Some media outlets are state-run and reflect the priorities and policies of the government. Other media organizations are owned by political parties. They reflect the positions of that group. Some media organizations are owned by wealthy oligarchs or corporations and reflect certain priorities. Some nations enjoy a variety of media organizations showcasing different perspectives, opinions, and agendas.

Media outlets have the potential to perform an important function in strengthening the civil sphere. They are expected to disseminate accurate information that citizens use to make decisions. Where do the media get this information? According to Gandy (1982), the media gain much of their content from public relations practitioners. Taylor (2000) noted the important role that NGOs play in providing information subsidies to independent media. This news content comes in the form of research, statistics, access to the people who are featured in human interest stories, and insight into policy issues.

The value of an independent, multifaceted media to the creation and maintenance of civil society is clear. The independent media also serve as watchdogs to ensure that government officials and businesses are held accountable for their actions. Government-run media cannot embody such a role. The independent media are "the most critical of all civil society institutions" because they allow for communication between institutions, NGOs, the government, and the public (Shaw, 1996, p. 31). Shiras (1996) summed up the role of the media when he noted: "given the media's critical role in mobilizing public support and influencing public policy, they are both observers and participants" in the civil society process (p. 109).

Today, newer forms of media have emerged and are participating, for better or worse, in the rhetorical sphere of civil society. The traditional concept of media was that of television, radio, or print outlets that covered news for a community. The dominant mass communication media had wide dissemination and allowed for shared interpretations of local, regional, national, and international events. Newer forms of media, with more niche audiences, are now competing outlets for news users. For instance, alternative newspapers that may only exist online are now attracting large numbers of readers. Web logs, now known as blogs, have emerged as watchdogs and commentators on current events. Many times the news coverage of these personalized news outlets is ahead of the corporate news media.

Nongovernmental organizations (NGOs) and social cause groups also use rhetoric and public relations to advocate for their positions. In the U.S. this organizational type is most widely known as nonprofits. Given the capitalist framework for organizing in the U.S., these organizations are categorized by their pursuit of service ends rather than economic ends. In the former communist countries that did not have a history of profit-seeking organizations, the term nongovernmental organization has emerged as the dominant way to describe organizations without a profit motive or government control.

There is incredible diversity of NGOs. Across the world, groups have organized to protect the environment, children, animals, consumer safety, women's rights, and minority issues. In other nations of the world, especially in societies that have been dominated by repressive governments, there is no tradition of social cause groups acting on behalf of social issues. Today, there is an emergence of NGOs throughout the world. When any type of media select a frame provided by a societal institution, the media extend that group's influence in the public sphere. These grassroots organizations work on behalf of issues, not profit. Rhetoric is their currency.

The *business community* plays a role in the development of civil society. Business organizations have opinions on issues such as regulation, licensing, and access to natural resources, price controls, immigration laws, and legal reform. It is to their advantage that their voices also be included in the civil sphere. And, an ancillary benefit gained by the civil society is that with business participation, communicative links with other civil society entities (government and media) are formed. The emergence of professional business associations performing watchdog activities (e.g., the Better Business Bureau), pro social activities (e.g., the Rotary Club), and advocacy activities (e.g., the Chamber of Commerce) are an important step in ensuring civil society. However, too much influence from the business community may impede civil society development.

Another partner in civil society is *governance*—the local, regional, and national leaders that participate in policy formation. This group also includes the class of civil servants in a nation that execute the day-to-day activities of governance (such as those who graduate from France's elite Ecole Nationale d'Administration (ENA) or the *nomenclatura* of Russia). Government leaders, as well as members of the bureaucracy that support government, need to be accountable to the aforementioned partners. Government leaders need to carefully monitor public opinion and be willing to adapt to the publics' changing needs. In a normative model of civil society, government leaders at all levels understand issues and resolve them in a manner that benefits those they lead. Government leaders take their cues from the civil society discourse.

Finally, *international organizations* have an important role in fostering civil society (INGOs). There are two types of international organizations: donor organizations and regulatory agencies. In developing and post crisis countries, the United Nations (UN), the United States Agency for International Development (USAID), and the George Soros Open Society Institute (OSI) provide financial and human resources to help facilitate development. These international donor organizations fund local groups that work to achieve societal goals. For example, in the wake of the tsunami disaster in Asia in 2004, INGOs such as UNICEF, World Vision, Oxfam, and Save the Children immediately opened offices in affected areas. These groups asked people and governments around the world for donations and assistance to serve those affected by the tsunami. They provided what the government of Indonesia could not deliver: rapid, nonpolitical aid to those who had lost everything. INGOs are especially important during the initial stages of a civil society transition because they work directly with indigenous organizations and provide important training to local civil society leaders. Other international organizations such as the World Bank, World Trade Organization and other regulatory groups also can shape discourse in the civil sphere.

M. Stohl and C. Stohl (2005) highlighted the relationships among NGOs and INGOs that shape policy at the national and international level. In areas such as international law and human rights, INGOs are defining issues, creating debates, working with the media, and using public relations tactics and campaigns to get citizens to pressure their governments to enact change. M. Stohl and C. Stohl reviewed some of the problems associated with policy making in the international arena. Their article showed how a network of "NGOs provided watchdogs, the expertise, databases, and the basic bureaucratic work for the UN, which was often immobilized by its inherent organizational contradictions" (p. 452). This network was able to accomplish an objective that the UN could not accomplish on its own—

passing the historic Universal Declaration of Human Rights. NGOs pressured governments, rallied citizens, and organized their efforts to shape the language of one of the most important documents in history.

These seven partners—the public, societal institutions, media, nongovernmental organizations, the business community, governance, and international organizations—create the foundation of civil society. While each partner has its own issues, its own needs, and will represent different citizen interests, it is the goal of civil society to have interrelated objectives among these different groups. When the rhetorical discourse of two or more partners converge, then there is a much greater opportunity for those groups to achieve their goals. An effective civil society rests in the intersection of all of these partners' interests. It is in this intersection of interests that the role for rhetorical public relations activities become most clear.

An important implication of these seven partners is that the structure of civil society is not hierarchical. Individuals often share multiple identifications and memberships among different civil society groups. For instance, a teacher may be in a teachers' union and belong to a religious organization. The small businessperson may serve as a locally elected official while at the same time belonging to the Chamber of Commerce. By looking at civil society from the rhetorical public relations perspective, it is evident that civil society structure is the antithesis of the centralized hierarchy in which power is reserved for the elite few. More importantly, looking at civil society from a rhetorical perspective allows us to understand the individuals and organizations that negotiate meaning and work toward shared objectives.

Civil Society Exemplar from Croatia

Perhaps the best way to illustrate civil society as a rhetorical public relations process is to provide a real world example. In 1999, Croatia was still recovering from the break up of the former Yugoslavia and a war with its neighbors. President Franjo Tudjman, although quite ill, still exerted control over the Croatian people and political system. The HDZ controlled most media outlets in the country and opposition candidates and reformists could not get media coverage.

When President Tudjman died in early December 1999, democracy activists in Croatia sought to disseminate balanced information about the January 2000 elections. Several international organizations (INGOs) worked with local media and NGOs to increase public access to balanced and objective information. A partnership of local community leaders, NGOs, professional associations (trade unions), media outlets, political candidates, local business owners, and INGOs emerged to create a balanced media environment and an active civil society community. Together, these seven partners cooperated to identify key issues, create public awareness, and motivate Croatians to hold their government accountable. This coalition held news conferences, worked with the media, held debates, sent out information about election registration, and outlined the platforms *of all political parties.*

American and Western European governments paid for information campaigns to educate voters about election issues. More specifically, donors funded new, independent media that challenged the news coverage of the politically controlled state media monopoly. Donors created the media channels that featured civil society messages and helped pay for the development of civil society campaigns. Donors provided support for organizations to *communicate their agendas* and *fostered the development of a media* that carried this content. For the first time, there was a rich mix of voices in Croatia advocating for different positions.

The elections in 2000 were a watershed moment for Croatia. The Croatian people elected a new parliament and the nationalist HDZ party lost power. Voter turnout was well over 90% of all eligible voters. With the election of a new parliament and President Stjepan (Stipe) Mesic, Croatia became a democracy. Croatia soon entered into discussions with the European Union and applied for membership in the EU. Croatia is expected to become a member of the EU in 2009. There were many different civil society partners that had to cooperate for Croatia to make this type of progress in such a short amount of time. The Croatian transition is an example of the enormous power of the social capital created by relationship building between civil society partners and the media.

Conclusions

The purpose of this chapter was to explicate a discourse-based framework of public in civil society. At the heart of civil society is discourse. This discourse is the nexus of civil society when it allows all interested parties to participate in the public sphere. There are critiques, however, of how public relations has been used to foster civil society. These critiques are valuable in that they remind us that theories almost always come with some baggage that begs the question of their ultimate value to theorists and practitioners.

Dutta-Bergman (2005a, 2005b) has pointed out that many foreign donor activities that fall under the guise of civil society assistance are actually imperialistic activities. This particular civil society assistance serves the interests of the nations donating the money rather than benefiting the people in the country. Dutta-Bergman's examples from the Philippines, Iraq, Chile, and Nicaragua are indeed troubling to those who see the great potential of public relations in civil society. Yet, his examples provide evidence as to why we should view civil society as a rhetorical process.

This chapter argues that the potential co-opting of civil society can be minimized if we focus on the *cocreation of meaning through rhetorical discourse*. When we view civil society as a process where all parties can use language and symbols to persuade, then public relations scholars, practitioners, and critical theorists have a rationale and a method for critiquing instances of anti civil society activities.

The role for public relations in civil society is quite clear. When we focus on meaning making, language, rhetorical argument, and persuasion, then we have enormous potential to see how public relations theory can serve civil society interests. The focus on meaning making also ensures that if one group, through money, access, or media ownership, tries to dominate the civil sphere, then other actors or organizations may be able to moderate the self-serving interests. The dominant theories of public relations can be complemented by civil society's interest in how individuals and organizations can participate in what Burke (1969) and Heath (1992) called the "wrangle of the marketplace."

References

Alexander, J. C. (1998). *Real civil societies: Dilemmas of institutionalization.* Thousand Oaks, CA: Sage.

Alexander, J. C. (2006). *The civil sphere.* Oxford: Oxford University Press.

Barber, B. (1998). *A place for us: How to make society civil and democracy strong.* New York: Hill and Wang.

Bardoel, J. (1996). Beyond journalism. *European Journal of Communication, 11,* 283–302.

Bentele, G. (2004). New perspectives of public relations in Europe. In B. van Ruler & D. Verčič (Eds.), *Public relations and communication management in Europe: A nation-by-nation introduction to public relations theory and practice* (pp. 485–496). Berlin: Walter de Gruyter.

Botan, C. H., & Taylor, M. (2004). Public relations: State of the field. *Journal of Communication, 54*(4), 645–661.

Botan, C., & Taylor, M. (2005). The role of trust in channels of strategic communication in building civil society. *Journal of Communication, 55,* 685–702.

Burke, K. (1969). *Rhetoric of motives.* Berkeley: University of California Press.

Burt, R. S. (1997). The contingent value of social capital. *Administrative Science Quarterly, 42,* 339–365.

Cancel, A. E., Mitrook, M. A., & Cameron, G. T. (1999). Testing the contingency theory of accommodation in public relations. *Public Relations Review, 25,* 171–197.

Corry, T. O. (2006). Global civil society and its discontents. *Voluntas, 17*(4), 302–323.

Doerfel, M. L., & Taylor, M. (2005). Network dynamics of inter organizational cooperation: The Croatian civil society movement. *Communication Monographs, 71,* 373–394.

Dutta-Bergman, M. (2005a). Operation Iraqi Freedom: Mediated public sphere as a public relations tool. *Atlantic Journal of Communication, 13,* 220–241.

Dutta-Bergman, M. (2005b). Civil society and communication: Not so civil after all. *Journal of Public Relations Research, 17,* 267–289.

Gandy, O. (1982). *Beyond agenda setting: Information subsidies and public policy.* Norwood, NJ: Ablex.

Gellner, E. (1994). *Conditions of liberty: Civil society and its rivals.* New York: Allen Lane/Penguin Press.

Gross, P. (2002). *Entangled evolutions: Media, democratization in Eastern Europe.* Baltimore: Johns Hopkins University Press.

Grunig, J. E. (1992). *Excellence in public relations and communication management.* Hillsdale, NJ: Lawrence Erlbaum.

Hadenius, A., & Uggla, F. (1996). Making civil society work, promoting democratic development: What can states and donors do? *World Development, 24*(10), 1621–1639.

Hauser, G. A. (1997). On public and public spheres: A response to Phillips. *Communication Monographs, 64,* 275–279.

Hauser, G. A. (1998). Civil society and the public sphere. *Philosophy and Rhetoric, 31*, 19–40.

Hauser, G. A. (2004). Rhetorical democracy and civil engagement. In G. A. Hauser & A. Grim (Eds.), *Rhetorical democracy: Discursive practices of civil engagement* (pp. 1–16). Mahwah, NJ: Lawrence Erlbaum.

Hauser, G. A., & Grim, A. (2004). *Rhetorical democracy: Discursive practices of civil engagement*. Mahwah, NJ: Lawrence Erlbaum.

Heath, R. L. (1992). The wrangle in the marketplace: A rhetorical perspective of public relations. In E. L. Toth & R. L. Heath (Eds.), *Rhetorical and critical approaches to public relations* (pp. 17–36). Hillsdale, NJ: Lawrence Erlbaum.

Heath, R. L. (2006). Onward into more fog: Thoughts on public relations' research directions. *Journal of Public Relations Research, 18*, 93–114.

Jacobson, T. L., & Jang, Y. (2002). Media, war, peace and global civil society. In W. B. Gudykunst & B. Moody (Eds.), *The handbook of intercultural and international communication* (pp. 343–358). Thousand Oaks, CA: Sage.

Kennan, W. R., & Hazelton, V. (2006). Internal public relations, social capital, and the role of effective organizational communication. In C. H. Botan & V. Hazelton (Eds.), *Public relations theory II* (pp. 311–338). Mahwah, NJ: Lawrence Erlbaum.

Kent, M. L., & Taylor, M. (2002). Toward a dialogic theory of public relations. *Public Relations Review, 28*, 21–37.

Ledingham, J. A., & Bruning, S. D. (1998). Relationship management in public relations: Dimensions of an organization–public relationship. *Public Relations Review, 24*, 55–65.

Ledingham. J. A., & Bruning, S. D. (Eds.). (2000). *Public relations as relationship management: A relational approach to the study and practice of public relations*. Hillsdale, NJ: Lawrence Erlbaum.

Lewis, L. (2005). The civil society sector: A review of critical issues and research agenda for organizational communication scholars. *Management Communication Quarterly, 19*, 238–267.

Marsh, J. (2005–2006). Rebuilding community after Katrina: An interview with *Bowling Alone* author Robert Putnam. *Greater Good*, 4–5.

Monge, P. R., & Contractor, N. S. (2000). Emergence of communication networks. In F. M. Jablin & L. L. Putnam (Eds.), *The new handbook of organizational communication* (pp. 440–502). Thousand Oaks, CA: Sage.

Moy, P., & Pfau, M. (2000). *With malice toward all: The media and public confidence in democratic institutions*. Westport, CT: Praeger.

Putnam, R. (2000). *Bowling alone: The collapse and revival of American community*. New York: Simon and Shuster.

Seligman, A. B. (1997). *The problem of trust*. Princeton, NJ: Princeton University Press.

Shaw, M. (1996). *Civil society and media in global crises: Representing distant violence*. London: Pinter.

Shiras, P. (1996). Big problems, small print: A guide to the complexity of humanitarian emergencies and the media. In R. I. Rotberg & T. G. Weiss (Eds.), *From massacres to genocide: The media, public policy and humanitarian crises* (pp. 93–114). Cambridge, MA: World Peace Foundation.

Shumate, M., Fulk, J., & Monge, P. R. (2005). Predictors of the international HIV/AIDS NGO network over time. *Human Communication Research, 31*, 482–510.

Siebert, F., Peterson, T., & Schramm, W. (1963). *Four theories of the press*. Urbana Champaign: University of Illinois Press.

Stohl, M., & Stohl, C. (2005). Human rights, nation states, and NGOs: Structural holes and the emergence of global regimes. *Communication Monographs, 72,* 442–467.

Taylor, M. (2000). Media relations in Bosnia: A role for public relations in building civil society. *Public Relations Review, 26,* 1–14.

Taylor, M., & Doerfel, M. L. (2003). Building inter-organizational relationships that build nations. *Human Communication Research, 29,* 153–181.

Taylor, M., & Doerfel, M. L. (2005). Another dimension to explicating relationships: Measuring inter-organizational linkages. *Public Relations Review, 31,* 121–129.

Taylor, M., & Napoli, P. (2003). Media development in Bosnia: A longitudinal analysis of citizen perceptions of media realism, importance and credibility. *Gazette, 65,* 473–492.

Toth, E. L. (2006). Building public affairs theory. In C. H. Botan & V. Hazelton (Eds.), *Public relations theory II* (pp. 499–522). Mahwah, NJ: Lawrence Erlbaum.

5

PERSPECTIVES ON PUBLIC RELATIONS HISTORY*

Ron Pearson (Deceased)
Mount Saint Vincent University

If all writing about the past is partly an effort to understand the present, a confusing and contradictory present would seem to call more insistently for historical analysis and explanation. This is particularly true for the profession and academic discipline of public relations. In spite of a consensus about the role of public relations in contemporary organizations—a consensus evident in the many definitions of public relations that stress its role as a management function—a long list of difficult questions about the profession remains. To what bodies of theory can public relations legitimately lay claim? Is there, or can there be, something called public relations theory? Is public relations a profession? Should the practice of public relations be regulated, licensed? What kind of education is required for the practice of public relations? Does the public relations curriculum belong in journalism departments, schools of business, schools of public affairs, or in a department all its own? To what set of values should public relations adhere? What makes the practice of public relations legitimate? In whose interest should public relations be practiced? What constitutes ethical public relations practice?

None of these questions is superficial. The fact that they have provoked discussion for most of public relations' history in the 20th century is part of the context within which any practitioner or scholar of public relations interrogates that history. The need to find answers is an important part of the historian's motivation. Burke (1957) suggested that all writers, including those who write history, write to work through personal problems. And Wise (1980) argued that a text of historical scholarship needs to be understood as a personal response on the part of its author to contemporary situational exigencies, just as the primary recorded texts of historical actors need to be understood as situationally conditioned. Similarly, Berkhofer (1969) emphasized that the situationally conditioned viewpoints of historical actors and historical scholars must be rigorously distinguished. Both the writer of history and the reader of historical texts must be careful to make this distinction.

When historical explanations differ, it is not merely because historians have access to different facts. There are no brute historical facts, only historians' interpretations of them. Indeed the so-called brute facts of history are often the interpretations

---

* A version of this chapter appeared in Pearson (1990).

of others, including historical actors themselves. No single, obviously correct public relations history exists; rather, there are a plurality of public relations histories. Indeed, this doctrine can be seen as a main conclusion following from the themes of postmodern rhetorical theory.

The principal themes of rhetorical theory are intimately related to the themes of philosophy. Taking a postmodern view, Baynes, Bohman, and McCarthy (1987) summarized these themes as (a) a concern with the concept of reason, (b) a scepticism about the concept of the human subject, (c) a scepticism about epistemology, and (d) a fascination with language. All of these are intertwined, and if they can be related to one, single, overriding concern, it is a wariness of the idea of foundationalism, the view that there is one, single reality "out there" that human minds, with varying degrees of accuracy, are able to picture, and that is the final arbiter of truth. One of the most vigorous attacks on this view is by Rorty (1979), who challenges the notion that the mind mirrors nature because it supposes that there are invariant, ahistorical rules—the methods of historical scholarship, for instance—for making in the mind an accurate and complete representation of reality. Rorty denies that these invariant rules exist.

Postmodern philosophy is sceptical about conceptualizing reason in a strong sense as that powerful searchlight, which is the same for all peoples in all times, used by the mind to illuminate reality, historical or otherwise, and see it for what it really is or was. Instead, reason is seen as much more contingent and conventional and bound up always with particular, historical views of what counts as rational. At the same time, these philosophers are not satisfied with the Cartesian (modern) concept of man as atomistic and autonomous, standing against the world and peering into it. Instead, relying on insights from phenomenology, many contemporary philosophers are more apt to eschew a subject/object dualism in favor of a view that stresses the mutual dependence of both, such that each plays a role in constituting the other. On this view, human consciousness is seen as having an intrinsically social character and, because the mind cannot be distinguished radically from the body, rationality must take into account feelings and desires.

The historian can no more escape that bit of him or herself that is always in things than he or she can experience a pure interiority empty of the things of which he or she is conscious. It is seen as more realistic to view knowledge as interpretation rather than representation. Once interpretation replaces representation as the dominant metaphor for how we know, then the data of experience are less well described as an experience of things as they are than as an experience of meaning. For one cannot properly be said to interpret a thing; rather one interprets what the thing means. As a result, language, symbols, and rhetoric should move to the forefront of our epistemologies.

Thus, studying public relations historians and their histories can reveal much more about their attitudes and philosophical perspectives than it does about precisely what happened in the past. These historians come to historical texts with different philosophies of history, different social, political, and moral philosophies, and even different assumptions about epistemology and ontology. Wise (1980) used the term *explanation form* to denote the framework of ideas and philosophical assumptions a historian brings to his or her work and he suggested that often one dominates as the master form. Outlining these perspectives and identifying these explanation forms is one valuable way of mapping the terrain within which arguments about public relations occur and of uncovering the sometimes unarticulated philosophies of public relations that are extant in management and public relations literature.

By identifying a range of perspectives that historians take toward public relations' history, this chapter argues the claim that there is no single, privileged interpretation of public relations' past. The historical texts discussed are selected purposefully to represent this range of perspectives. Studying these historians reveals much about contemporary discourse on public relations and suggests that this discourse is complex and many-sided.

The chapter begins with Hiebert's (1966) biography of Ivy Lee, a practitioner who is often called the father of public relations. Hiebert's approach to public relations history reveals one important perspective. To set it in relation to others, this section reviews explanations of public relations' evolution by the British historian Pimlott (1951), the American business historian Tedlow (1979), the Marxist communication theorist Smythe (1981) and Olasky (1987), the conservative American historian of public relations. After treating each historian singly, a final section draws conclusions about historical scholarship in public relations and suggests a model for interpreting it.

PR and the Flowering of Democracy: Hiebert

Following a suggestion of Wise, it is possible to identify in Hiebert's book on Lee a number of paired concepts that together give a sense of the central explanatory framework of the book. These pairs can also be understood as examples of what Barthes (1957/1972) calls symbolic codes, sets of paired signs which produce and organize meaning in a text. These pairs as they are found in Hiebert's book are listed as follows:

fiction, lies	vs.	truth
secrecy	vs.	openness
partisan	vs.	neutral
persuasion	vs.	understanding
image	vs.	reality
propaganda	vs.	education
publicity	vs.	public relations
muckraker	vs.	gentleman of the press

Hiebert acknowledged that categories like these are sometimes difficult to separate in real life but he suggested that Ivy Lee had at least made the distinctions in thought and in public statements, even if he sometimes failed to meet his own rigorous standards. Hiebert found in Lee the articulation of a set of ideal public relations values that are captured by oppositions like lies–truth. These values also represent for both Lee and Hiebert what is basic in the idea of democracy.

In 1921, according to Hiebert, Lee told a gathering at the Columbia University School of Journalism: "We live in a great democracy, and the safety of a democracy will in the long run depend upon whether the judgements of the people are sound. If the judgements are to be sound, they will be so because they have the largest amount of information on which to base those judgements" (p. 317). It was the task of public relations to assist in supplying that information. Hiebert's own introductory commentary unequivocally asserts: "Without public relations, democracy could not succeed in a mass society" (p. 7), and later, in a concluding paragraph: "Ivy Lee and public relations played a significant role in preserving the pluralism of American society by opening channels of communication and allowing opposing groups to understand each other" (p. 318).

Lee hoped at one time to become a lawyer and studied for a semester at Harvard Law School. But he was forced to give up these studies when his money run out. As the story is told—Hiebert cited Goldman (1948) but Goldman gave no source for this story—Lee arrived in New York City with only $5.25 after leaving Harvard and, after securing food and lodging, spent his last nickel on a subway ride to the offices of the *New York Journal*. As luck would have it, editor Charles Edward Russell gave him a job.

As a reporter, Lee apparently lacked the cynicism of many of his fellow journalists. He identified with the powerful businessmen he wrote about and generally thought they were good people, although misunderstood. Lee would probably have agreed with the 1908 statement of AT&T president Theodore Vail that if questions about investments, returns, and distribution are clearly and satisfactorily answered, "there can be no basis for conflict between the company and the public" (p. 87), a view that remains as the basis for much current public relations thinking and practice. Gaudino, Frisch, and Haynes (1989), for instance, suggested there remains a strong belief among practitioners—even among those who claim to practice two-way forms of communication—in the myth that "If you knew what I knew, you'd make the same decision" (p. 299).

Hiebert suggested that Lee's move to journalism from law is partly explained by the fact that the two professions have something in common. "Lee saw . . . an opportunity to combine his literary and legal interests; he could use his pen to account for and defend ideas and actions [of business] before the court of public opinion, that great new audience of American readers" (p. 39). But it is impossible to tell from the text whether Lee actually saw this relationship between journalism and law, or whether it is an explanatory construct of his biographer. Hiebert's interpretation suggests that if Lee could not serve justice and democracy as a lawyer, he would have to find another way. Indeed, he would have to invent one.

Hiebert, as much as Lee, is keenly interested in truth, justice, and democracy as ideals that inform the idea of public relations. Hiebert reported that, during his (Lee's) work for the Pennsylvania Railroad, Lee circulated to the press a "Declaration of Principles" to which he planned to adhere as a publicist for the railroad. Hiebert began a passage by quoting part of Lee's declaration:

> This is not a secret press bureau. All our work is done in the open. This is not an advertising agency; . . . Our matter is accurate. Further details

on any subject treated will be supplied promptly, and any editor will
be assisted most cheerfully in verifying directly any statement of fact.
Upon inquiry, full information will be given to any editor concerning
those on whose behalf an article is sent out. In brief, our plan is, frankly
and openly, on behalf of the business concerns and public institutions,
to supply to the press and the public of the United States prompt and
accurate information concerning subjects which it is of value and interest
to the public to know about. (p. 48)

There is little doubt that more current public relations could be practiced with
the rectitude evidenced in Lee's declaration and that the declaration is laudable.
But Hiebert wants this declaration to do a great deal; for, in the paragraph immediately following, he interpreted its significance in this way:

The statement brought about a revolution in relations between business
and the public. Where formerly business pursued a policy of "the public
be damned," from now on business increasingly followed a policy of
"the public be informed."

A few other companies saw the efficacy of Lee's advice. . . . (p. 48)

Within this second passage a contradiction appears. On the one hand Hiebert
took Lee's declaration as revolutionary; on the other he allowed that only "a few"
other companies followed Lee's advice. In fact, it is still a legitimate empirical
question whether the revolution as Hiebert understands it has ever taken place.
Certainly the modern corporation wants to be attuned to the values, attitudes, and
behaviors of its various publics and often tries to influence those behaviors and to
adjust its own policies to what it believes are public expectations. But it is an open
question whether this activity is quintessentially democratic. Yet for Hiebert, the
essence of the public relations revolution is a flowering of democratic values. In the
foregoing excerpts, Hiebert's allegiance to this view of public relations seems to
make it difficult for the biographer to separate his own view of what the fledgling
profession should be from what it is reasonable to believe about the way public
relations actually evolved. In other places in his book, it is plain that Hiebert *did*
appreciate that, "too much public relations is Machiavellian, concerned with maintaining power regardless of ethical considerations" (p. 317). But if Hiebert understood this, why did he write about a public relations revolution?

A similar tension exists in another of Hiebert's interpretations of Lee. This one
is particularly illuminating because it shows how the same set of facts might be
given radically different interpretations. Hiebert described Lee's early journalistic
exploits:

Lee's first big scoop of his career came from Grover Cleveland. The
president had recently retired from the White House to his home in
Princeton. In typical nineteenth century fashion he refused to make any
public statements. . . . One evening young Lee organized a group of his
fellow students to go to the Cleveland home and serenade the ex-president

with college songs and cheers. Cleveland was moved by the gesture and at length came out onto the front porch where he made a little speech to the students. Lee was in the front row, pencil and pad in hand, and took down every word. (p. 28)

As Hiebert reported the president "was moved," should a reader take this as an instance of Lee's sincerity, of his sincere desire to move others? For on the next page Hiebert said, "[Lee] . . . may not have been humble, but he was sincere . . . He was the original 'really sincere guy'" (p. 30). Or is it an example of Lee's cunning orchestration of an event—the pseudo-event about which Boorstin (1961) has written—which both Cleveland, and Lee's biographer, took at face value? It is important for Hiebert to support claims about Lee's sincerity and the transparency of his intentions, because Hiebert wants readers to accept that Lee believed that "the truth was the most effective way to flatter the people in a democratic society. . . . a policy of honesty was the most direct means to public approval" (p. 31). Yet it is not obvious that Lee was honest about his intentions with President Cleveland, for he may well have made use of a staged event to encourage the president to give a public statement.

Hiebert seems more interested in the idea he believes Lee articulated and stood for than he is in the man himself. It is Lee's idea, taken at face value as Lee articulated it on many occasions, with which Hiebert is concerned, for the idea, unlike the man, can be rendered purely, simply and powerfully. But the important question for an understanding of public relations historiography is not how wide a gap exists between Lee the man and the idea Hiebert finds in Lee's writing. Rather, it is more important to draw a conclusion about the nature of the explanatory categories Hiebert used to explain the evolution of public relations and to understand why he used them.

As noted at the beginning of this chapter, a host of questions surrounds the public relations profession. Most of them have to do with its legitimacy. Hiebert would certainly have been aware of them; he not only taught public relations but practiced it as well. Were he at all concerned about the profession's legitimacy at the outset of his research on Lee, his discovery of the core idea of public relations in the language of democracy would assure him that no profession was more worthy. Moreover, he can show that the view of public relations as democracy in action is not his own construct, but an idea that is part and parcel of public relations' history. Indeed, public relations can be seen as the obvious and predictable response to a set of historical conditions that threatened democratic ideals. On this view, its evolution is natural and explainable as the inevitable evolution of ever-adaptable democratic principles.

Wise (1980) suggested it is important to ask what an historian's explanatory ideas do for him or her, how they act as tools, as a strategic response to a problematic environment. The foregoing analysis suggests, that in the case of Hiebert, his depiction of the history of public relations provided a powerful tool in the debate that was then current, and continues to be current, as to the status of the profession. Moreover, this observation about Hiebert's purpose is not a new one. One reviewer of Hiebert's book (Garraty, 1966) noted:

Hiebert has been so impressed by the novelty of Lee's techniques and his enormous success, and has himself been so captivated by the public-relations mistique, that he fails to come to grips with the moral questions involved in the business or with the fact that his hero, after all, was essentially a lackey. He advances the startling . . . thesis that the public relations business is a bulwark of democracy. . . . That Lee believed this is understandable; that his biographer believes it is an indication of the extent to which he has absorbed his subject's values. . . . In short, he has produced a public relations man's biography of Ivy Lee. (p. 42)

Pimlott's Specialization Theory

One explanation of the evolution of public relations, as has been noted in the foregoing section, sees the profession as an element of maturing democratic ideals. Other explanations, some incorporating the democracy idea and some repudiating it, have been suggested. This and following sections examine some of these explanations to generate a broader perspective on the writing of public relations history against which Hiebert's work can be seen.

Pimlott (1951) introduced a discussion of public relations' evolution by denying that public relations can be explained as a "natural response" to the growth of the mass media; usually such explanations beg the question of why the response is "natural," he said. In making this point, Pimlott made an interesting critical point that any claim about the apparent "naturalness" of a state of affairs is at heart the statement of an ideological position and not the neutral description of "the way things are" that it appears to be. Indeed, Pimlott's position in a way presages the postmodern views described earlier. The attack on foundationalism is also an attack on any effort to privilege one point of view over another based on the claim that the privileged perspective reflects the ways things really are.

Pimlott argued that the quasi-professionalization of the public relations function in the early 1990s—a function that is recognizable in all stages in history in various nonprofessional forms—is an aspect of increasing differentiation of social functions generally. "This in turn was due to increasing wealth, expanding markets, population growth, technological progress—indeed, to all the circumstances which produced the Industrial Revolution . . ." (p. 233). Finally, he made this disarmingly modest statement that suggests he sees nothing revolutionary about the growth of public relations: "There is nothing dramatic about this reason for the evolution of the public relations specialist. Because it is not dramatic it tends to be overshadowed by more colorful theories" (p. 234).

Part of Pimlott's point is that people, leaders of any kind especially, have always been concerned with image. He noted New England businessmen of the mid-1800s attended to their own public relations just as they attended to their own accounting and other aspects of management. For Pimlott, a fundamental reason for the differentiation of public relations as a unique management function is increased complexity in society and increased specialization to deal with it. Here it is worth remarking that an important aspect of Hiebert's explanation is that business had come to be indifferent to its image and thus needed public relations. It is noted later that Tedlow, even more forcefully than Pimlott, questioned this basic assumption about business' lack of concern for its public image.

Having linked public relations' evolution to a general increase in specialization, Pimlott developed a number of related explanatory propositions:

1. Because of increased complexity and "bigness," it became more difficult for an organization to communicate with the public. Moreover, the "public" came to be understood as differentiated into a number of sub-publics—employees, customers, shareholders, etc. "As the organizations increased in size and the 'publics' along with them, they also became remote, more impersonal, more incomprehensible" (p. 235).

2. It became increasingly necessary to bridge this widening communication gap. As Pimlott put it: "It proved to be more efficient to be open than to be secretive. Employers worked better; dealers were more loyal; stockholders were more contended" (p. 236). He also noted new ideas about business' responsibilities resulted in a need by business to justify itself to society. But Pimlott did not cast this observation in the language of democratic rights and obligations; rather he suggested public relations' evolution can be partly understood as a sound business strategy to increase efficiency and productivity.

3. Pimlott acknowledged the mass media as a major contributing factor in the evolution of public relations, but he avoided the suggestion of technological determinism. Because of the structural changes described here, more demands were made of mass media channels. As media themselves became more complex, it became necessary for organizations to employ experts familiar with them.

4. Finally, it must be noted that for Pimlott, public relations is related to democracy, as the title of his book suggests, but the idea of democracy does not play the kind of fundamental explanatory role that it does for Hiebert. Instead he pointed as well to a wide variety of causes of change—economic, technological, social—and suggested that public relations is a rational, and highly functional, management response to the demands of a changing environment. With public relations, organizations and hence society generally will function more smoothly. Pimlott concluded that public relations' significance for society is twofold—it is highly functional for the smooth functioning of society and supportive of American democratic ideals.

They [public relations specialists] are experts in popularizing information. They play an essential part in "group dynamics" . . . The better the job of popularization, the more smoothly will society function, but also the greater the understanding which the plain citizen will have of his own place in relation to the big and seemingly inhuman groups whose interplay is important for the "dynamics of group behavior." The more that is understood about group dynamics and the working of the mass media the clearer will be the role of the public relations group. . . . And the easier will be the problem—though it will never be easy—of

adapting the mass media to the needs of American democracy and of
curbing the excesses of propaganda. (p. 257)

Before leaving Pimlott, it is worth characterizing in general terms the kind of
historical explanation he advanced. Pimlott developed the outline of a seemingly
neutral, functional explanation for public relations that, on the face of it, does not
express an ideological position. Organizations must survive by adapting or adjusting to their environments, and specialized public relations roles allow them to
do this. As noted later, Tedlow offered a similar functional explanation as well as
debunking one of public relations' most cherished myths.

The Myth of the Boerish Businessman: Tedlow

Tedlow (1979), a business historian at the Harvard School of Business
Administration, attacked one of the most revered beliefs of public relations—the
belief that business, prior to the coming of public relations, was secretive and insensitive, indeed contemptuous, of public opinion. Relying on a number of examples
for his evidence, Tedlow supports two claims: (a) American businessmen since
colonial times have been notoriously solicitous of public approval, and (b) only
politicians have rivalled them in the use of publicity to further their enterprises.

Tedlow also reviewed and reinterpreted some of the classic evidence for the
opposite view, namely, the 1882 statement by William Vanderbilt which appeared
on the front page of *The New York Times* in which he was reported to have said "the
public be damned," a phrase that is reported in most public relations textbooks and
interpreted there much as Hiebert interpreted it.

Tedlow returned to the primary document to see what the phrase looked like
in context. Vanderbilt apparently made his statement in response to a reporter's
question. Wondering why Vanderbilt ran one of his railroads at a loss, the reporter
suggested that perhaps it was for the public benefit. In part, Vanderbilt is supposed
to have replied: "The public be damned. What does the public care about the
railroads except to get as much out of them for as small a consideration as possible
. . . Of course we like to do everything possible for the benefit of humanity in
general, but when we do we first see that we are benefitting ourselves" (p. 5).
When taken in context, according to Tedlow, the statement expresses a sentiment
still much accepted today—that the primary responsibility of an executive is to a
company's shareholders. He argued the statement bears none of the venomous
overtones so many public relations historians have read into it. Additionally, he
claimed, Vanderbilt denied using the language attributed to him, further evidence
of even Vanderbilt's concern for maintaining a decorous public image. Referring
to the so-called robber barons generally, Tedlow concluded:

> It would be wonderfully tidy to show how these economically proficient
> but socially insensitive moguls were gradually forced to defend themselves
> in the public forum by making use of the developing profession of public
> relations counseling. This is the "scenario" constructed by numerous
> public relations men who have explored their field's past. Such a sequence

is not without some validity, but history is rarely so one-dimensional and it certainly is not in this case. (p. 3)

Two generally accepted explanations for the evolution of public relations, according to Tedlow, are (a) the appearance of PR follows a changed attitude on the part of business to its social responsibilities; and (b) it arose as a defense against anti-business sentiment. Tedlow accepted that these claims exhibit some degree of truth, but in the case of both he suggested the story of public relations is much more complex and ambiguous. He agreed that corporate liberalism and public relations sometimes appeared together, but noted also that many exponents of public relations were quite conservative and would not likely have accepted social responsibility arguments. He also allowed that there is a temporal coincidence between the beginnings of PR and the hey-day of the muckrakers. But he asked: "Why has not public relations diminished in importance with the decline of anti-business sentiment? . . . why did nonbusiness institutions which were not particularly scrutinized by the muckrakers, such as universities, churches, charities, and the armed services, follow the lead of business and experiment with press bureaus at the time?" (p. 16).

Essentially, Tedlow repudiated what he called the views associated with the Progressive period that saw a conflict between "the people" and "the interests." He said this picture ignores developments within the business world itself. Key among these developments are unprecedented rates of growth among corporations, increased rationalization and centralization of management, and the need for larger markets. These changes brought with them new management problems to which some of the responses included Taylor's scientific management, the birth of industrial psychology, welfare capitalism, advertising and, of course, public relations.

In his view, causal explanation in this context is more complex than many explanations of public relations' past suggest. Tedlow viewed public relations as one element of management's response to rapid change along a number of dimensions—economic, technological, and social. He interpreted public relations' history in terms of organizations learning how to function more efficiently and effectively in new environments with little recourse to the more ideologically-loaded language of democracy.

PR, the Consciousness Industry, and Capitalism: Smythe

Of the writers considered in this chapter, Smythe (1981) is the only one who has not written a book with "public relations" in the title, yet much of his writing deals implicitly with related issues. He is also one of the few writers who consider public relations from a Marxist perspective, a perspective that is rarely acknowledged in histories and texts that mention "public relations" in their titles. Smythe located the evolution of public relations in the same time frame and within the same set of economic and social changes as do the other authors. Yet his account of the ways in which the evolution of public relations is explained by these factors is radically different.

Smythe developed an explanation of public relations' evolution within what he called a materialist–realist theory of mass communication. Among the key propositions of this theory is the claim that in the core capitalist countries (Western Europe, United States, and Canada) the mass media are not preeminently in the business of producing newspapers, magazines, or television shows. Rather, they (a) produce audiences as commodities that are marketed to business organizations that want to advertise consumer goods, and (b) establish a daily agenda of news, entertainment, and information that defines *reality* for the people. Another way of describing these two mutually reinforcing purposes is to claim that the commercial media (a) mass market the consumer goods and services produced by monopoly capitalism, and (b) mass market the legitimacy of the capitalist system itself. Smythe distinguished mass media content as advertising, on the one hand, and the "free lunch" on the other. The free lunch is the news, entertainment, and information. Advertising is related to meeting the first objective listed here, the free lunch to meeting the second. The profession of public relations is an element of business' effort to influence the content of the free lunch.

Smythe situated the growth of public relations in the latter quarter of the 19th century and the early part of the 20th century in the United States— the same time period within which media began to address the twin objectives described earlier. What is of interest in this context is his explanation for these responses on the part of business. According to Smythe, business faced two major problems at the turn of the century. One was a population becoming increasingly hostile toward the practices of big business. Hiebert also described this period of crisis for capitalism, but where he (following Lee) ascribed it to a lack of mutual understanding among business and the public, Smythe said the public understood perfectly—that was the problem. Second was a need that was part and parcel of the "bigness" problem. The larger, "rationalized" business organizations with centralized managements needed larger, rationalized markets. Smythe wrote:

> The principal contradiction faced by capitalism in the last quarter of the nineteenth century was that between the enormous potential for expanding production of consumer goods and the overt political hostility of the workers and a fair proportion of the middle class . . . In the resolution of the principal contradiction, two problems were identified and solved: 1) The need for an unquestionable conquest by the business system of control of the state and its ideological apparatus. . . . 2) The task of winning the automatic acquiescence of the population to a "rationalized" system of monopoly capitalism . . . (p. 57)

It is the second problem in which public relations can be seen as playing a role, for Smythe also asserted:

> The second level was the long-range problem confronting the emerging monopoly-capitalist system. . . . that of establishing institutional relations which would win the acquiescence of the population. . . . this problem

was one of establishing the hegemony of the business system over people as "consumers." . . . It was a problem of establishing domination of consciousness through culture and communication. (p. 57)

Smythe's explanation of the evolution of public relations goes well beyond the core claims of classical Marxism because of the emphasis he placed on the role of consciousness in the maintenance of the capitalist system. At least in the core capitalist countries, capitalism ultimately came to be relatively successful in providing for the material wants of the proletariat, thus reducing the likelihood of the kind of revolution Marx predicted. The "crisis" that would precipitate a new order is not, therefore, an economic or material one, but a crisis of legitimation, or of consciousness. To the extent this is true, public relations can be explained as an element of capital's response. In earlier ages, the response to potential economic crises was the reallocation of material resources—a greater sharing of economic benefits. In current times, the appropriate response takes place in the realm of ideas. Galbra (1983) has also argued that although capital's power was once related to the control and allocation of material wealth, it is now related to the control and distribution of ideas or in capital's ability to persuade.

PR and the Specter of Socialism: Olasky

Olasky's (1987) recent analysis of public relations' history is provocative and is especially interesting when it is contrasted with Smythe's. Both Olasky and Smythe agree that public relations is a strategy that big business uses to control markets and to increase profitability. But whereas Smythe made his analysis from a leftist perspective, Olasky approached public relation history as a free-market conservative.

Echoing Tedlow, Olasky argued that a wrong-headed progressive interpretation dominates the writing of public relations history. For Olasky, the view includes the ideas that public relations has improved steadily since press agentry beginnings (the idea of progress) and that public relations practitioners are motivated by a sense of serving the public interest. He suggested that an honest reading of public relations' history, however, reveals no evidence that public relations practitioners are becoming more ethical and professional or that corporations have been operating to achieve anything but self-interest.

The thrust of his historical analysis is that corporate public relations activities have been designed to circumvent free market forces in favor of what he called collaborationism—alliances of large corporations with each other and with government. He described the creation of the Interstate Commerce Commission in 1887 and the ultimate public acceptance in the early 20th century of the idea of "regulated monopolies" for telephone and electrical utilities as public relations triumphs that benefited the regulated industries more than they served the public interest. Olasky sees in the public relations campaigns that railroads and utilities waged in favor of regulation a pitched battle between defenders of free enterprise and market forces and those who favored planning and the use of non-market drive policies to control and regulate. He wrote:

For over a century, many major corporate public relations leaders have worked diligently to kill free enterprise by promoting big government-big business collaboration. Over and over again, many corporate public relations executives have supported economic regulation with the goal of eliminating smaller competitors and insuring their own profits. (p. 2)

Olasky interpreted public relations history in the context of his reading of the United States Constitution. He pointed out that the framers of that Constitution wrote a document to safeguard the private rights of individuals. In the Constitution, Olasky found a philosophy of freedom and individualism that he believes is threatened by the specter of what he calls collaborationism. Moreover, he reinterpreted the contribution of Lee and Bernays, the premier figures in public relations history, to show how their philosophies were supportive of this collaborationism and showed little sympathy with philosophies of individualism.

Olasky's Lee is quite different from Hiebert's Lee. Whereas Lee in Hiebert's biography is portrayed as a champion of democratic ideals, in Olasky he is just the opposite, a master controller and propagandist who was firmly in the collaborationist camp and whose actions served only to reduce individual freedom and choice.

Olasky suggested that Lee's belief in collaborationism explains what had hitherto been difficult to understand, especially when Lee is seen as the champion of democracy in America, namely, Lee's sympathies for Stalin and the communist experiment in the Soviet Union. Olasky suggested that Lee saw "the United States moving closer to the Soviet Union in social perspective. 'The United States started with complete individualism, every man for himself,' and the Soviets have the opposite position, Lee wrote, but 'we have found it necessary to restrict the power of the individual'" (p. 51). Olasky also suggested that Lee saw movement toward a new cooperative social order as natural, inevitable, and progressive.

Lee also had unflattering views of the multitude, said Olasky, views that would have supported his belief that the public needed to be managed and administered for its own good. For Lee believed that rational discourse was lost on the masses and that the cause of collaborationism was better served by communication that played on the imagination and emotions of the public. In this application of Freudian psychology, with its emphasis on the role of the irrational and the hidden as motivators of human action, Lee would presage the views and practice of Bernays, the nephew of Sigmund Freud, and the man credited with first using the phrase "public relations."

In reinterpreting Bernays, and as a result of his own interview with him in 1984, Olasky discovered a philosophy of public relations that holds that, (a) because among the masses emotion is more powerful than reason, and (b) because there is no God watching over the world, (c) therefore, manipulation of these masses through public relations techniques is essential to prevent chaos and ensure public order. Olasky argued that this "rationale for public relations manipulation based on his lack of confidence in either God or man . . . was his [Bernays'] most significant contribution to 20th century public relations" (p. 83). As in Lee, the focus in Bernays is in protecting the whole from the parts, or the state from the people. Moreover, Olasky pointed out the obvious contradiction in this philosophy:

> Because a democratic society is considered to be one in which "the people" in general do rule, and an authoritarian society is often considered one in which a small group of people rule, Bernays was trying to square the circle by arguing, in effect, that we must kill democracy to save it. (p. 84)

Olasky also identified another similarity between Bernays and Lee—the affinity of their ideals with socialism. Whereas Lee's collaborationism led him to sympathize with Soviet ideals, Bernays too was a champion of increased economic centralization along with more economic planning and social control.

Historical Perspectives on PR: A Synthesis

The preceding discussion has compared and contrasted different approaches to the history of public relations and different explanations for the evolution of the new profession. What is initially most interesting about these approaches, however, is not their differences, but what they have in common. For all the historians discussed agree on a number of basic facts. Professionalized public relations is a practice that begins in the last decades of the 19th century and first two decades of the 20th century and arises in the context of significant economic, technological, and social changes associated with that time period. These include:

- a crisis of competition in business that led to monopoly capitalism,
- increased social organization and specialization in society generally,
- increased communication problems among groups,
- the advance of scientific approaches to marketing, management, and administration,
- advances in technology generally, especially in the techniques of mass communication,
- an increase in the general level of education, and
- changes in values, the rise of egalitarianism.

Where the historians differ, of course, is in the way they interpret these and related facts and the way they explain the causal relations among them.

- Hiebert, himself a public relations practitioner, emphasized the democratizing influence of public relations. The ideals driving his analysis are the democratic ideals of an informed and active citizenry. In Lee he saw a larger-than-life champion of these ideals. For Hiebert, public relations is part of the natural evolution of these ideals; the growth of the profession is explained partly by the evolution of democracy and partly by the historical role played by Lee, who saw the need for public relations as a bulwark against nondemocratic forces.
- Pimlott too acknowledged a relationship between public relations and democratic institutions, but he emphasized increased specialization of roles in

society as a key rationale for the growth of public relations. For Pimlott, there is little that is dramatic or revolutionary in the evolution of public relations. Rather, public relations is a useful social role and helps society function more smoothly.

- Tedlow, whose study of public relations was initially part of a doctoral dissertation in American history at Columbia University (his adviser was the same John A. Garraty whose comments on Hiebert were quoted earlier), focused on business efforts to manage change as a key explanatory factor. He discarded some of the basic explanatory myths of public relations' history and develops a functional explanation for the growth of the profession. Public relations evolves as a specialized organizational role because without it institutions would not easily adjust or adapt to environments that became increasingly dynamic and complex.

- Smythe explained public relations as business' response to a situation in which it needed to control the minds as well as the bodies of its publics in order to promote and secure organizational goals—growth and profit. In Smythe, there is no talk of social responsibility or of democracy. The self-interest of profit-seeking organizations in capitalist economies beset by a crisis of legitimacy is the key reason for public relations.

- Olasky focused on the way in which public relations activity threatens what he believes are basic American values—competition and the rights of individuals—values that are often associated with capitalism. With Smythe he saw public relations as a technique of organizations for promoting economic self-interest through the control of markets. But while the Marxist explanation of this phenomenon is that it is a logical and irreversible *outcome* of an ideology of individualism, for Olasky a return to these classic individualist values is the only cure. Smythe saw in public relations the scourge of capitalism, Olasky the spectre of socialism.

By way of effecting some kind of final synthesis or framework within which to view these varied approaches to public relations history, it is worth returning to some of Wise's (1980) considerations on the writing of history. Wise described what can be loosely called the three major paradigms or explanation forms within which American historical research has been carried out, although to his list a fourth category is added to accommodate Olasky. Making use of these paradigms provides one strategy for mapping the different philosophies of history that public relations historians bring to their work.

Progressive historians, who controlled the historical stage from about 1910 to 1950, according to Wise, saw life in America as relatively straightforward and unproblematic. For the progressive historians, said Wise, "Life in America could be made free and open and just if only people willed it so and labored hard to implement their wills. Progressives obligated themselves to lead the way toward a juster, more enlightened society" (p. 83). . . . "Progress was their Master Form, the single key which explains most everything they thought and did" (p. 87).

When Hiebert published his book on Ivy Lee in the mid-1960s, he was about 35 years old. He had grown up and been educated during a time when little seemed to stand in the way of progress in America; his book came out before the crises and disillusionment that marked the late 1960s. Thus, in spite of the fact Hiebert wrote *Courtier to the Crowd* after the period Wise identified with progressive history, his book seems to fit into the mold Wise claimed motivated most progressive historians. Public relations, for Hiebert, is an instrument of progress that, if only people would come to appreciate it, could play a role in making America "free and open and just."

Counter-progressives, on the other hand, tended to be suspicious of the idea of progress and viewed historical reality as much more complex and ambiguous than did the progressives. Wise situated counter-progressive historians after 1950. Pimlott, possibly, and Tedlow would seem to fit into this category. Tedlow especially attacked some of the truisms and assumptions of the "progress" view of public relations and paints a much more complicated and conservative picture of the evolution of public relations than does Hiebert. Olasky, it might be argued, fits this category because of his questioning of the progress view of public relations. Yet his writing is marked by a fervor that makes it appear more ideologically motivated than the work of Pimlott or Tedlow so that it seems helpful to provide a separate category for Olasky.

New Left historians, according to Wise, began writing in America after 1960. "In their picture, America has not been so much an idea as a structure of power. And that power is anything but innocent. The nation has not been misguided in its acts of oppression; it's been cold, and ruthlessly calculating, and has done what it's done to protect and extend itself. To the New Left, America has not been a blunderer, it's been a predator" (p. 94). Clearly, Smythe fits into this category. It could also be argued that the recent analyses of Gandy (1982) are motivated by a similar view of history.

New Right historians is a category Wise does not mention, but one like it seems necessary to classify Olasky's history of public relations. Olasky's neo-conservatism is not captured by any of the other categories. It might be argued that the analysis of Tedlow is a conservative one in that it does not probe the legitimacy of those organizational goals for which the new public relations role was seen to be functional. But Olasky's conservatism is different, for it is marked by a much stronger and more clearly articulated ideology.

These four historical categories are helpful for bringing some order to the various public relations histories discussed above. But it is also useful to employ categories that (a) emphasize logical distinctions instead of historical ones, and (b) suggest the basis for a model that may help ordering some of the assumptions working behind contemporary discourse about public relations. Thus one can identify what might be called a broad *management paradigm* that favors structural-functional explanation and which occupies a middle or central position. The core idea here is that public relations develops as a specialized role (i.e. as a structural innovation in organizations) because it is functional for organizational survival. This paradigm is an important and perhaps dominant one (Trujillo & Toth, 1987) within current public relations theory and one that stresses public relations' contribution to organizational management. The historical analyses of Pimlott and Tedlow especially seem to be made from within this perspective and are supportive of it.

It can also be argued that Hiebert's explanation fits within this dominant management paradigm in that it provides a rhetoric of legitimation for what otherwise is clearly an explanation positing organizational needs, that is, organizational self-interests, as the driving force in the genesis of public relations. Although the historical explanations of Hiebert, on the one hand, and Tedlow and Pimlott on the other, have differences, they serve each other well. But this is not because explanations that emphasize the functional value of public relations are without ideologies; indeed they are not without ideologies, for the needs of these organizations, in the achievement of which public relations plays an important, functional role, are, by and large, the needs of profit-making organizations in a post-industrial capitalist economy. Rather, it is because this latter ideology is made more palatable when reworked in the language of democracy and social responsibility.

Finally, if it is accepted that Tedlow, Pimlott and Hiebert together represent different aspects of a dominant perspective on public relations, it follows that the historical analyses of Smythe and Olasky articulate assumptions that are critiques of this dominant perspective. Smythe, of course, presents a critique from the left, and Olasky one from the right. For the leftist critique, the rhetoric of democracy and social responsibility falsely legitimate those organizational interests served by public relations because they do not take into account the real needs of individuals (for community, for instance) but rather emphasize false needs of individuals for unfettered freedom as consumers. From the right, the legitimating rhetoric is seen as hollow because it fails to recognize the rights of individuals and subsumes them under the rights and needs of institutions. From the left, public relations is seen as serving the private interests of individuals, from the right public relations is seen as threatening these interests.

References

Barthes, R. (1972). *Mythologies.* (A. Lavers, Trans.). New York: Hill & Wang. (Original work published 1957).

Baynes, K., Bohman, J., & McCarthy, T. (Eds.). (1987). *After philosophy: End of transformation?* Cambridge, MA: MIT Press.

Berkhofer, R. F. (1969). *A behavioral approach to historical analysis.* New York: Collier-MacMillan Limited.

Boorstin, D. J. (1961). *The image: A guide to pseudo-events in America.* New York: Harper Colophon Paperbacks.

Burke, K. (1957). *The philosophy of literary form.* New York: Vintage Books.

Galbraith, J.K. (1983). *The anatomy of power.* Boston: Houghton Mifflin.

Gandy, O. (1982). *Beyond agenda setting: Information subsidies and public policy.* Norwood, NJ: Ablex.

Garraty, J. A. (1966). Up from puffery. [Review of *Courtier to the crowd: The story of Ivy Lee and the development of public relations*] *Columbia Journalism Review, 5,* 41–42.

Gaudino, J. L., Frisch, J., & Haynes, B. (1989). "If you knew what I knew, you'd make the same decision": A common misconception underlying public relations campaigns. In C. H. Botan & V. Hazelton, Jr. (Eds.), *Public relations theory* (pp. 299–308). Hillsdale, NJ: Lawrence Erlbaum Associates.

Goldman, E. F. (1948). *Two-way street: The emergence of public relations counsel.* Boston: Bellman.

Hiebert, R. E. (1966). *Courtier to the crowd: The story of Ivy Lee and the development of public relations.* Ames, IA: Iowa State University Press.

Olasky, M. N. (1987). *Corporate public relations and American private enterprise: A new historical perspective.* Hillsdale, NJ: Lawrence Erlbaum Associates.

Pearson, R. (1990). Perspectives on public relations history. *Public Relations Review, 16*(3), 27–38.

Pimlott, J. A. (1951). *Public relations and American democracy.* Princeton, NJ: Princeton University Press.

Rorty, R. (1979). *Philosophy and the mirror of nature.* Princeton, NJ: Princeton University Press.

Smythe, D. (1981). *Communications, capitalism, consciousness and Canada.* Norwood: Ablex.

Tedlow, R. S. (1979). *Keeping the corporate image: Public relations and business. 1900–1950.* Greenwich, CT: JAI.

Trujillo, N., & Toth, E. L. (1987, August). Organizational perspectives for public relations research and practice. *Management Communication Quarterly, 1*(2), 199–231.

Wise, G. (1980). *American historical explanations: A strategy for grounded inquiry.* Minneapolis: University of Minnesota.

6

FEMINIST CRITICISM IN PUBLIC RELATIONS

How Gender Can Impact Public Relations Texts and Contexts

Linda Aldoory
University of Maryland

Gloria Steinem (2008, January 8) has written, "Gender is probably the most restricting force in American life, whether the question is who must be in the kitchen or who could be in the White House." She was specifically talking about the 2008 U.S. presidential primary race, but her words resonate for every woman, and for every person who engages in feminist research. Her words are important because of the critics of feminism who argue that there is no longer any gender oppression in the U.S. These critics point to increasing numbers of women in the professional world and increasing numbers of women in political and economic leadership positions—for example, having Hillary Rodham Clinton as a frontrunner in the presidential primary for the Democratic Party allegedly attests to the lack of problems women face today. If this is the case, then feminist researchers (such as myself) have no more reason to study gender as a constraint on communication, on organizational life, or on public relations professionals.

Steinem's comment, however, points to some realities faced by both men and women who work and live in a society where communication—for example, public relations, media, speeches—create gendered norms. Gendered norms are assumptions and expectations about how to believe and how to act that are based on whether someone is a woman or a man. These gendered norms influence the way organizations are structured, the way professions are practiced, and the way people think about themselves. Thus, there is a continual need to study and critique how communication—and in this particular case, public relations—encourages gendered norms and constrains the public relations profession and professional. This study and critique of gender and its constraints has been labeled feminist research.

When public relations researchers engage in feminist research, they face challenges, because anything with the label "feminism" has been inaccurately stereotyped as man-hating, and radical. As Stephen (2000) noted, "feminist scholarship that takes an activist stance, that avows and celebrates a political dimension to scholarship, or that employs narrative methodology may run afoul of traditional preferences for dispassionate scholarship conducted using methodologies suitable for larger samples" (p. 194). Stephen (2000) argued that this is why feminist writings in communication, and in public relations in particular, are almost invisible in the journals and in the discourse about the professions. Stephen coded 31,500 research articles published in 70 communication journals between 1962 and 1997. For the majority of these journals, 0 to 5% of their articles were about gender and/or feminism. In public relations, the percentages in Stephen's study were no better. Out of 103 articles published in *Journal of Public Relations Research*, 8 were found to address gender/feminism/women. For *Public Relations Review*, only 16 of 574 (3%) articles addressed gender/feminism/women (pp. 208–209). As Stephen concluded, the history of feminist research in our field has been a struggle in an environment of "inhospitable institutional reception" (p. 194).

Perhaps public relations can learn some lessons from rhetorical approaches to communication, since Stephen (2000) found that a high proportion of feminist studies were published in rhetorical journals. In particular, a type of feminist research called feminist criticism can help to uncover the gendered constraints of the public relations profession and individual professionals. It is my goal in this chapter to show how a feminist critical approach can be useful to public relations. In order to achieve this goal, I begin by defining the concepts of feminism and feminist research, and feminist communication. I summarize the feminist research that has been done in public relations. I then explain what feminist criticism is and what it looks like in public relations. I offer examples of published studies that model feminist criticism in public relations. Finally, I develop lessons learned, and conclude with the hope that readers will understand that Steinem's comment about gender—as the most restrictive force in society—holds true, but that in public relations we can find ways of addressing this problem, in research and in practice. In particular, I hope to offer a sense of both the challenges and opportunities male and female students need to address as they progress towards being part of the public relations profession.

Feminism and Feminist Research

Feminism has been defined in a thousand ways, all of which have been contested. Dow (1996) defined feminism as "a set of political ideas and practices—developed through feminist movements, dedicated to the progress of women and the transformation of patriarchy" (p. xxiii). Liao (2006) argued that empowerment of women is a central concept in feminism (p. 106). Empowerment means that individuals have a sense of ability and confidence within that might be used to change something in their lives. Liao (2006) said, "Feminism grows out of social and political movements aiming to bring justice into society so the marginalized can choose their positions instead of being pushed into positions where they are" (p. 106).

Contemporary feminism has been criticized for its focus on the sole experiences of white, middle-class, heterosexual women (Dow, 1996; Few, 2007). Black feminist theory arose from black feminists "feeling far removed" from the feminism that was often only white (Few, 2007). Subsequently, many feminists today broaden their definition of feminism to be: the fight against oppression of *racial-ized* women, and historically and politically marginalized groups of people. Further, postmodern feminists have argued that all oppression—whether due to ethnicity, sexuality, ability, or history—should be exposed, critiqued, and eliminated (Liao, 2006). Wackwitz and Rakow (2004) defined feminist goals in this broad way:

> to expose practices of injustice and discrimination, to subject ideological and institutional systems of oppression to interrogation from the margins, to seek out and confront our own internalized attitudes of prejudice and depreciation of self and other, and to develop theories accounting for these oppressive practices, systems, and attitudes. (p. 7)

Rush and Grubb-Swetnam (1996) defined a feminist as a person "who believes in equal rights for everyone, including women, and when women are denied their rights, especially women" (p. 499).

These broader definitions of feminism highlight the fact that men have also been oppressed and are also constrained by a gendered society. While men have traditionally been demonized for their role in women's oppression, postmodern feminism views their complicity as part of the ideology that favors masculinity over femininity. This perspective—where feminism is greater than just women—is helpful in public relations. In today's public relations, over 85% of the profession are women, but less than 20% of management in public relations are women. This type of situation places demands on men as well as women to make changes that are equitable for everyone. Further, over 90% of the public relations profession remains white; what may be racialized discrimination in the profession should, therefore, be just as much a concern for feminist researchers (Grunig, Toth, & Hon, 2001).

Feminist Research

Reinharz (1992) offered a rather interesting understanding of what is "feminist research." She defined feminist research as (1) research conducted by people who identify themselves as feminist; (2) research that is in journals that publish only feminist research or in books that identify themselves as such; and (3) research that has received awards from organizations that give awards to people who do feminist research (p. 6). Reinharz explained, "The simple criterion of self-identification . . . allows me to go directly to the work of people who take the label for themselves and to avoid deducing what feminist research is from the standpoint of my personal definition. This approach rejects the notion of a transcendent authority that decides what constitutes 'feminist'" (p. 7). Reinharz's definition eliminates the necessity of measuring a piece of research against some feminist "norm." If the author(s) claim to be feminist, then the work is feminist.

Even with its variety and debates, feminist research has illustrated certain characteristics that distinguish it from other types of research. These characteristics include: a critique of gendered power relations; the study of everyday life/discourse; a representation of multiple voices; an understanding of historical context; and a practice called reflexivity.

Critique of gendered power relations. Gender is the construction and maintenance of certain beliefs about what is feminine and acceptable for women, versus what is masculine and acceptable for men, in work, in personal life, and in society. Ultimately, feminist research looks at how power is used or misused and the expected ways to believe and act as women and men. van Zoonen (1994) argued that "gender and power, although both very much in debate, form the constituents of feminist theory" (p. 4).

Study of everyday life. Lived experience is complex and messy, and it involves several layers of influences, from societies to individuals. Aschraft and Mumby (2004) suggested that a focus on the complex dynamics of everyday life draws attention to "irony, ambiguity and contradiction" in work and personal lives (p. 24). For public relations, this focus means that topics for study include everyday work practices, professional norms, and public and mediated discourses that enter and exit everyday life.

Multiple voices. Due to the complexities and messiness of lived experience and everyday discourse, feminist research looks at multiple perspectives, methods, and voices (Liao, 2006). As Wackwitz and Rakow (2004) argued, "lived experience is not always common experience" (p. 6). This means that multiple voices and texts are studied and understood, and that there can also be multiple feminist perspectives that can be debated. Mumby (1996) stated, "There are many modernist, postmodernist, and feminist positions, each of which interacts in a multiplicitous and dynamic fashion. Thus to talk about modernist versus postmodernist feminist perspectives does violence to the complex and nuanced debates that characterize feminist thought" (p. 262).

Historical context. Recently, feminists have begun to see the necessity of including historical contexts to their work (Ashcraft & Mumby, 2004). As Sjoberg (2006) indicated, "feminists see that history is the study of masculinity in global politics" (p. 892). Many feminists have argued that the typically ahistorical frame provided by U.S. and European feminists leave out the colonial oppression that many women have struggled under in various global communities (Aschraft & Mumby, 2004). Sjoberg (2006) asserted, "Gender analysis that does not take account of historical gender subordination suffers explanatory deficiency" (p. 890).

Reflexivity. One assumption of feminism is that all actions are politically driven and culturally situated. This means that every person brings to their work their own biases and understandings that will influence the outcomes of their work. Reflexivity is a way to expose and acknowledge personal biases that affect work outcomes. Feminists expect all researchers and communicators to be very aware of their own politics and culture, so that readers of communication materials and research studies are also made aware of the influences on the products.

Feminist Communication

Communication, argued Wackwitz and Rakow (2004), developed out of a "Western worldview" that universalizes white European male experience, and therefore, the field has failed to "recognize, support, and give voice to the great diversity of human experience" (p. 2). Furthermore, communication education rewards conformity and discourages difference of thought and experience. In communication and education, "gender tends to be reified, taken for granted, and controlled by the structures that benefit from it and prevent its examination" (Wackwitz & Rakow, 2004, p. 3). Feminist communication, then, attempts to uncover the controlling structures in media and in public relations used to discriminate according to gender. In other words, feminist communication wishes to show how media and public relations might be biased or discriminatory, and then help change the situation to a more equitable and empowering one.

Historically, any research in communication that looked at gender discrimination focused on simple sex differences in communication and its professions (Mumby, 1996; Stokoe & Smithson, 2001) and descriptions of media representations of women (Parameswaran, 2002, 2005). Aschraft and Mumby (2004) argued that little research has examined the ways in which organizations and communication are fundamentally gendered. In recent years, however, gender has been considered "a fundamental organizing principle" for communication practice and contexts (Ashcraft & Mumby, 2004, p. 19). Wackwitz and Rakow (2004) proposed that feminist communication "begins with an assumption that we are in need of deep structural change to produce new social relations and just societies" (p. 5).

Communication is not merely a channel that shows how women and men act, but rather it can actually create beliefs about gender norms and it can maintain these beliefs over time. We know that individuals and groups use media and public relations to articulate and interpret meanings (Aschraft & Mumby, 2004). This, in turn, helps them to construct their own identities, power relations, and organizational practices. Hence, if media and public relations are creating and maintaining stereotypical gendered norms, then students and professionals in public relations will relate to each other in stereotypically gendered ways and will produce public relations products in certain gendered ways. These dynamic enactments of gender and communication are focal points for feminist communication.

Feminist Public Relations

Feminist public relations has been less robust than that found in rhetorical studies, but it is growing ever more significantly in the field. "Feminization" of the field became a concern in the 1980s, when the number of women in the profession topped the number of men. The U.S. Department of Labor reported that in 1979 there were less than 44% women in public relations (U.S. Department of Labor Statistics, 1980, p. 174). In 2000, women comprised 70% of the public relations field (PRSA/IABC salary survey, 2000, p. 23).

Since then, there have been several studies that help explain gender problems in the field (for example, see Aldoory, 2003, 2005; Grunig, 2000, 2006; Vardeman & Aldoory, 2008). Some scholars have used differences between men and women in the field to promote the need for equity for women. This body of research has illustrated that while there are three times more women than men in the profession, men hold 80% of management and leadership positions (Grunig, Toth, & Hon, 2001; Toth, Serini, Wright, & Emig, 1998; Wright, Grunig, Springston, & Toth, 1991). Studies and professional audits continue to find a significant salary gap between women and men, where men make more average annual income. In 1999, Impulse Research for *PR Week* reported that in public relations, women earned 38% less than men. The average salary for men was $81,920, whereas the average salary for women was $59,026 (Leyland, 2000). Authors Seideman and Leyland (2000) asserted that there was a "distinct discrimination" (p. 29).

Some researchers have conducted content analysis to show that representations of women in public relations, in educational texts or in media and public relations campaigns, have not been accurate or equal (Brunner, 2006; Creedon, 1989). Brunner (2006), for example, analyzed introductory public relations textbooks and found that women are not represented proportionally to their numbers in the profession. Brunner concluded, "These results suggest that the contributions and importance of women to public relations may still be ignored despite the feminization of public relations" (p. 43).

A few feminist researchers in public relations have suggested more significant changes to be made to public relations education and practice (Aldoory, 2005; Grunig, Toth, & Hon, 2000; Hon, 1995; Toth, 2001). A basic premise is that equal numbers of women and men working in public relations will not eliminate gender discrimination. Ideological and organizational systems will continue to discriminate against women and put undue pressure on men at work (Choi & Hon, 2002; Creedon, 1991, 1993). Similar gendered systems are in practice in education, thus reinforcing in future practitioners stereotypical roles for women and for men in public relations. Transformation, therefore, of communication, organizational and education systems is required to improve public relations.

Feminist Criticism

Feminist criticism is a process of revealing underlying symbols and meanings in media, in public relations, and in public relations products such as campaigns. Dow (1996) adds to this definition the search for new and different meanings; she cites Modleski's (1991) definition of feminist criticism in this vein: "it has aimed, rather, at bringing into being *new* meanings and *new* subjectivities. . . . In this respect it may be said to . . . be *doing* something beyond restating already existent ideas and views, wherever these might happen to reside" (italics in original) (p. 49). There are two approaches to feminist criticism that are pertinent to public relations: (1) criticism of texts/discourse; and (2) criticism of organizational and professional practices and norms. Both of these are relevant in public relations, because on one hand, public relations products are gendered representations; and on the other hand, public relations professionals are gendered and work in gendered organizations.

Feminist criticism in public relations can potentially focus on the role of public relations and media in "mediating social change, in reproducing assumptions about women's appropriate roles, and in appealing to and constructing a subjectivity for women" (p. xix). According to Dow (1996), criticism of an organization or public relations practice can tell us something not just about that one situation, but also about the "kind of symbolic activity that [it] represents" (p. 5). Aschraft and Mumby (2004) constructed a "critical communicology of gendered organizing" that can be useful in public relations as well. It is the examination of "*how* work and gender become entwined, *how* this relationship is effectively sustained and altered over time and across arenas of human symbolic activity, and *how* communication functions as medium and outcome of institutionalized power" (emphasis in original) (p. 26). Barrett and Davidson (2006) described critical analyses that can point to the "emotional labour demands" of service sector work, and "the risks of renewed stereotyping and undervaluing of women at work through the focus on 'naturally female' skills" (p. 2).

Feminist criticism in public relations scholarship can incorporate both a textual approach to texts and an organizational approach. In fact, public relations as an applied body of knowledge creates the need for feminist criticism towards the profession as well as towards the professional, the organization, and the deliverable texts.

Related Studies

An extensive and broad search was conducted to find and offer here some examples of studies representing feminist criticism related to the field of public relations. The examples are categorized below into two areas of feminist criticism: (1) criticism of public relations materials and texts; and (2) criticism of public relations work and practice.

Feminist Criticism of Texts

Several studies were found that focused on U.S. campaigns, analyzing messages in order to uncover gendered and power dimensions (Abbott, 2007; Chowdhury, 2005; Kukla, 2006; Pace, 2005; Raheim, 1996). Kukla (2006) critically examined content and strategy of the breastfeeding advocacy campaign sponsored by the U.S. Department of Health and Human Services in 2004. She argued that the campaign's messages were insensitive to actual concerns that U.S. mothers have, and that the campaign was "well positioned to produce shame and compromise agency among the women it targets" (p. 157). Raheim (1996) analyzed the public service advertisements (PSAs) developed by the U.S. Centers for Disease Control and Prevention called "America Responds to AIDS." Raheim describes one group of the PSAs as appealing to women at different levels of comfort and experience in talking about AIDS. The messages address women's concerns about fear, embarrassment, sadness, and hardships related to AIDS. The ads also attempt to show that talking about AIDS is normal. Another group of PSAs challenge women to take assertive action and protect themselves against AIDS by terminating any risky relationships with male partners. Raheim (1996) argued, "For women who are neither economically, socially, nor emotionally prepared to separate from a partner whose behavior may be putting them at risk of HIV infection, this message is more likely to be disempowering than empowering" (p. 406).

Other studies attended to international campaigns and comparisons to U.S. norms for gender and power. Russo (2006), for example, analyzed the Feminist

Majority Foundation's Campaign to Stop Gender Apartheid in Afghanistan, which attempted to bring attention to the violence towards women in the Taliban-governed country post 9/11. Russo discovered what she called an "imperial feminist" framework used in the campaign that "ultimately serves to bolster U.S. world hegemony and empire" (p. 558). Chowdhury (2005) examined a campaign against acid violence in Bangladesh. The campaign began in the mid-1990s by local women activists of the organization Naripokkho, and over time, it was supported by international non-governmental organizations. Acid attacks are the splashing of car battery acid or sulfuric acid on the face or body of victims—at present, government reports claim that 300 incidents occur annually. In the 1990s, most of the victims were young women who had refused male proposals of sex or marriage. However, reasons for recent attacks predominantly involve land and family disputes. Chowdhury explored the "complicated transactions among victims, feminist organizers, the state, and international donor organizations," revealing the "multiple interests, agendas, and constraints governing the response to violence against women in the global South" (p. 165).

Some studies addressed individualized communication tactics (Barnett, 2005; French, Frasier, & Frasier, 1996; McKinley & Jensen, 2003). Barnett (2005) conducted an analysis of more than 100 news releases produced by the National Organization for Women (NOW). She found that NOW used certain frames about protection of women's rights in order to counteract the negative news frames that often ignored or disdained NOW's valuable work. In its news releases, NOW presented its opponents as "unpatriotic extremists and deviant from mainstream American society" (p. 41). French, Frasier, and Frasier (1996) examined print brochures and popular health guides to discern what these messages convey to women about alcohol consumption. The majority of their analyzed messages focused on pregnant women's sense of personal responsibility for fetal outcomes. The authors concluded that alcohol abuse messages overemphasized women's responsibility to their unborn fetus and underemphasized men's role in accountability, women's well-being, or long-term health issues. McKinley and Jensen (2003) examined the political and social implications of a feminist reproductive health radio program in Peru titled *Bienvenida Salud!* (Welcome to health!). The radio program was produced by the Amazonian Peoples' Resources Initiative, a reproductive rights organization in the U.S., in partnership with Minga Peru, a women's health and development organization in Peru. Authors found that "the emancipatory potential of consciousness-raising initiatives must be tempered by consideration of false consciousness and the inevitable will to power which surfaces among the more dominant members of supposedly similarly situated groups" (p. 197). However, they concluded that the program "fruitfully deployed personal experience as a basis for reflexivity, public debate, and social change" (p. 197).

A few studies focused on computer-mediated communication (Engstrom, 2008; Rodino-Colocino, 2006; van Doorn, van Zoonen, & Wyatt, 2007; Worthington, 2005). According to Worthington (2005), "the Internet has become increasingly popular among women seeking advice and information, especially among women whose financial situation affords easy access to computers and service providers" (p. 44). With websites a public relations tool often managed by public relations staff, analyses of websites have become more popular among feminist communication scholars. Engstrom (2008) engaged in a critical examination of the gendered messages constructed by The Knot, a website produced by a bridal media company of the same name. She argued that hegemony, which she defined as "common sense created by the media," was used towards an audience of unmarried women by The Knot to maintain status quo norms that reinforce requirements of femininity. These feminine requirements included use of cosmetics and consumerism. Rodino-Colocino (2006) analyzed news releases, ad campaigns, and websites for personal digital assistants marketed towards women. She argued that the computer industry reproduced and reinforced the gendered division of labor while simultaneously promoting products for women who work outside the home.

Feminist Criticism of Work

Instead of the tangible outputs produced by public relations, a few studies instead examined the process of working in public relations (Anderson, 2004; Dutta, 2006; Thomas & Zimmerman, 2007; Toll & Ling, 2005). For example, Anderson (2004) conducted a case study of the Women's Field Army, a branch of the American Cancer Society that comprised thousands of female volunteers during the years 1936 to 1945. These women used public relations to recruit volunteers, raise money, and promote the early detection of cancer. Anderson included both internal and external communication as data: internal documents, manuals, media pitch letters, public promotional materials, and national media. Anderson argued that the value of his study was that it "demonstrated the impact women had on the public relations efforts of one of the United States' largest non-profit organizations (American Cancer Society)" (p. 188). Toll and Ling (2005) studied tobacco industry documents describing how Philip Morris and its competitors developed promotional campaigns targeting women. Authors examined "previously secret" internal documents to provide a perspective on marketing decisions and strategies. The documents showed that Virginia Slims strategically borrowed women's liberation slogans to sell cigarettes to women.

Dutta (2006) interrogated the work of USAID, the federal agency responsible for development communication and planning in other countries. USAID often engages in what is called education-entertainment campaigns: campaigns that use television, radio, and other entertaining media for purposes of educating audiences about a health problem. Dutta looked at "the voices of marginalized people in the discursive space" (p. 222) to see how USAID communicated to its audiences. His goals were to challenge "elitist approaches" to constructing knowledge and to illuminate understandings "from below" (p. 222). Dutta concluded, "population control serves transnational hegemony by fostering conditions for sustainable development, which in turn, promotes economic growth and new opportunities for business" for the U.S. (p. 224). In other words, the campaigns developed by USAID not only serve the international audiences of women, but also serve U.S. interests in keeping population growth under control in certain countries.

Summary

The research in feminist criticism points to some overarching conditions that frame both the media and the work of public relations professionals. First, gendered oppression is perpetuated, globally and domestically, through governmental-sponsored media campaigns. Second, women's rights rhetoric is co-opted for purposes of financial gain. Third, feminism is used by organizations in order to continue to constrain both women and men in their work. Finally, racialized and marginalized groups of men and women continue to be invisible to campaign planners and researchers. These conditions mark the boundaries by which change needs to occur in public relations.

Lessons Learned

Culling together the findings from above and the philosophy and goals of feminist criticism, certain lessons can be learned that help inform and guide public relations professionals and future professionals. While readers may now understand that Steinem's comment about gender—as the most restrictive force in society—holds true for public relations, we might be able to address this force through research and practice.

Lesson 1. Feminist criticism can be applied to not only public relations materials, but also to public relations work itself and to the organizational structures that constrain men and women in the field. Feminist criticism is a watchful and active perspective used to evaluate whether all people are treated equitably. It is not limited as a way of doing research—it can be used by public relations students and professionals in their everyday interactions as they learn or work in public relations.

Lesson 2. Practitioners and students of public relations can begin to develop attuned, peripheral vision in order to see where they may be maintaining certain status quo norms themselves, in their studies and in the profession. As Russo (2006) reminded us, "Actions taken to challenge hegemony can in fact support and reify the hegemonic projects of the state" (p. 557). In other words, it may not be noticeable at first how we enact gendered expectations in ways that put pressure on colleagues. By thinking through ways women and men are expected to act versus ways they should be able to act might help reduce gendered norms prescribed by ourselves.

Lesson 3. When designing public relations campaigns, the real values and ideologies driving it are most evident in the objectives of the campaign (Dutta, 2006). While there are "overt" objectives that are often publicly shared and used to guide campaign development and implementation, there are also "implicit or covert" objectives, which "are almost always left out of the discursive space" and "refer to the broader objectives . . . that dictate the allocation of resources to the overt objectives" (Dutta, 2006, p. 223). When studying or when developing campaigns, these hidden agendas should be acknowledged.

Lesson 4. Public relations practitioners and students need to be aware of the unexamined nature of the whiteness in public relations. Whiteness is primarily an "unraced" social location (Rowe, 2000, p. 65) and hence, its culture and norms have become universally accepted. In her essay, Rowe (2000) equated silence with domination or privilege, in that the absence of white awareness illustrates its power position. Since feminist criticism aims to "unmask discourses of oppression," then we need to call attention to the "subtle ways in which whiteness functions" (Rowe, 2000, p. 65) in public relations.

Conclusion

The goals of feminism may seem unnecessary today, given the popular evidence of women's success in the U.S. The leadership roles and the economic power that many women have make gender oppression seem like a historical event rather than a current concern. Thus, for Gloria Steinem to suggest that today's society uses gender as a tool of oppression—more so than race, ethnicity, or class—seems radical. However, feminist criticism in public relations has indicated the following: (1) global gendered oppression through governmental-sponsored media campaigns; (2) co-optation of women's rights rhetoric for purposes of financial gain; (3) the appropriation of feminism by organizations in order to continue to constrain both women and men in their work; and (4) racialized and marginalized groups of men and women remaining invisible to campaign planners and researchers.

While it may at first be depressing to find support for Steinem's claim, the feminist researchers and their studies described in this chapter should also offer optimism—they model for readers the ways to expose discrimination and change current situations. For example, female public relations students are less likely to accept oppressing job contexts if they are aware of the symbolic and rhetorical expressions of gender discrimination. Male practitioners are less likely to feel pressured to put aside family responsibilities if they understand the organizational norms constraining them to do so. All practitioners are less likely to produce campaigns that are sexist when they acknowledge their own biases and stay aware of where gendered norms might come into play. Ultimately, these are lessons for public relations students and practitioners to engage in more liberating practices. Women and men in public relations are faced with both challenges and opportunities as they become aware of gendered norms that may constrain how they work. Knowledge and critique of ongoing problems will increase feelings of empowerment for public relations professionals, and thus help improve public relations texts and contexts.

References

Abbott, J. Y. (2007). The positive functions of "negative" rhetoric: Feminists' expository campaign against the Promise Keepers. *Women's Studies in Communication, 30,* 1–33.

Aldoory, L. (2003). The empowerment of feminist scholarship in public relations and the building of a feminist paradigm. *Communication Yearbook, 27,* 221–255.

Aldoory, L. (2005). A (re)conceived feminist paradigm for public relations: A case for substantial improvement. *Journal of Communication, 55,* 668–684.

Anderson, W. B. (2004). "We can do it": A study of the Women's Field Army public relations efforts. *Public Relations Review, 30,* 187–196.

Ashcraft, K. L., & Mumby, D. K. (2004). Organizing a critical communicology of gender and work. *International Journal of the Sociology of Language, 166,* 19–43.

Barnett, B. (2005). Feminists shaping news: A framing analysis of news releases from the National Organization for Women. *Journal of Public Relations Research, 17,* 341–362.

Barrett, M., & Davidson, M. J. (Eds.). (2006). *Gender and communication at work.* Hampshire, England: Ashgate.

Brunner, B. (2006). Where are the women? A content analysis of introductory public relations textbooks. *Public Relations Quarterly, 51*(3), 43–47.

Choi, Y., & Hon, L. C. (2002). The influence of gender composition in powerful positions on public relations practitioners' gender-related perceptions. *Journal of Public Relations Research, 14,* 229–263.

Chowdhury, E. H. (2005). Feminist negotiations: Contesting narratives of the campaign against acid violence in Bangladesh. *Meridians: Feminism, Race, Transnationalism, 6,* 163–192.

Creedon, P. J. (1989). Public relations history misses "her story." *Journalism Educator, 44,* 26–30.

Creedon, P. J. (1991). Public relations and "women's work": Toward a feminist analysis of public relations roles. *Public Relations Research Annual, 3,* 67–84.

Creedon, P. J. (1993). Acknowledging the infrasystem: A critical feminist analysis of systems theory. *Public Relations Review, 19,* 157–166.

Dow, B. (1996). *Prime-time feminism: Television, media culture, and the women's movement since 1970.* Philadelphia: University of Pennsylvania Press.

Dutta, M. J. (2006). Theoretical approaches to entertainment education campaigns: A subaltern critique. *Health Communication, 20,* 221–231.

Engstrom, E. (2008). Unraveling the knot: Political economy and cultural hegemony in wedding media. *Journal of Communication Inquiry, 32,* 60–82.

Few, A. L. (2007). Integrating black consciousness and critical race feminism into family studies research. *Journal of Family Issues, 28,* 452–473.

French, K. J., Frasier, T. D., & Frasier, C. J. (1996). Knowing when to say when and why. In R. L. Parrott & C. M. Condit (Eds.), *Evaluating women's health messages: A resource book* (pp. 190–199). Thousand Oaks, CA: Sage.

Grunig, L. A. (2000). A feminist phase analysis of research on women in postmodern public relations. In D. Moss, D. Vercic, & G. Warnaby (Eds.), *Perspectives on public relations research* (pp. 80–120). London: Routledge.

Grunig, L. A. (2006). Feminist phase analysis in public relations: Where have we been? Where do we need to be? *Journal of Public Relations Research, 18,* 115–140.

Grunig, L. A., Toth, E. L., & Hon, L. C. (2000). Feminist values in public relations. *Journal of Public Relations Research, 12,* 49–68.

Grunig, L. A., Toth, E. L., & Hon, L. C. (2001). *Women in public relations: How gender influences practice.* New York: Guilford Press.

Hon, L. C. (1995). Toward a feminist theory of public relations. *Journal of Public Relations Research, 7,* 27–88.

Kukla, R. (2006). Ethics and ideology in breastfeeding advocacy campaigns. *Hypatia, 21*(1), 157–180.

Leyland, A. (2000, March 27). Competition drives PR salaries up 8% in '99. *PR Week*, 1.

Liao, H. A. (2006). Toward an epistemology of participatory communication: A feminist perspective. *The Howard Journal of Communications, 17,* 101–118.

McKinley, M. A., & Jensen, L. O. (2003). In our own voices: Reproductive health radio programming in the Peruvian Amazon. *Critical Studies in Media Communication, 20,* 180–203.

Modleski, T. (1991). *Feminism without women: Culture and criticism in a "postfeminist" age.* New York: Routledge.

Mumby, D. K. (1996). Feminism, postmodernism, and organizational communication studies: A critical reading. *Management Communication Quarterly, 9,* 259–295.

Pace, L. (2005). Image events and PETA's anti-fur campaign. *Women & Language, 28,* 33–41.

Parameswaran, R. (2002). Local culture in global media: Excavating colonial and material discourses in National Geographic. *Communication Theory, 12,* 287–315.

Parameswaran, R. (2005). Journalism and feminist cultural studies: Retrieving the missing citizen lost in the female audience. *Popular Communication, 3*(3), 195–207.

PRSA/IABC salary survey 2000. (2000). Public Relations Society of America (http://www.prsa.org./salser/secure/tempfile/index.html).

Raheim, S. (1996). The reconstruction of AIDS as a women's health issue. In R. L. Parrott & C. M. Condit (Eds.), *Evaluating women's health messages: A resource book* (pp. 402–413). Thousand Oaks, CA: Sage.

Reinharz, S. (1992). *Feminist methods in social research.* New York: Oxford University Press.

Rodino-Colocino, M. (2006). Selling women on PDAs from "Simply Palm" to "Audrey": How Moore's Law met Parkinson's Law in the kitchen. *Critical Studies in Media Communication, 23,* 375–390.

Rowe, A. M. C. (2000). Locating feminism's subject: The paradox of white femininity and the struggle to forge feminist alliances. *Communication Theory, 10,* 64–80.

Rush, R. R., & Grubb-Swetnam, A. (1996). Feminist approaches. In M. B. Salwen & D. W. Stacks (Eds.), *An integrated approach to communication theory and research* (pp. 497–518). Mahwah, NJ: Lawrence Erlbaum.

Russo, A. (2006). The Feminist Majority Foundation's Campaign to Stop Gender Apartheid: The intersections of feminism and imperialism in the United States. *International Feminist Journal of Politics, 8,* 557–580.

Seideman, T., & Leyland, A. (2000, March 27). PR Week salary survey report 2000. *PR Week,* pp. 23–25, 27, 29, 31, 33, 35.

Sjoberg, L. (2006). Gendered realities of the immunity principle: Why gender analysis needs feminism. *International Studies Quarterly, 50,* 889–910.

Steinem, G. (2008, January 8). Women are never front-runners. *New York Times.* Retrieved January 9, 2008, from: http://www.nytimes.com/2008/01/08/opinion/08 steinem.html?scp=2&sq=gloria+steinem.

Stephen, T. (2000). Concept analysis of gender, feminist, and women's studies research in the communication literature. *Communication Monographs, 67,* 193–214.

Stokoe, E. H., & Smithson, J. (2001). Making gender relevant: Conversation analysis and gender categories in interaction. *Discourse and Society, 12,* 217–244.

Thomas, J. E., & Zimmerman, M. K. (2007). Feminism and profit in American hospitals: The corporate construction of women's health centers. *Gender & Society, 21,* 359–383.

Toll, B. A., & Ling, P. M. (2005). The Virginia Slims identity crisis: An inside look at tobacco industry marketing to women. *Tobacco Control, 14,* 172–180.

Toth, E. L. (2001). How feminist theory advanced the practice of public relations. In R. L. Heath & G. Vasquez (Eds.), *Handbook of public relations* (pp. 237–246). Newbury Park, CA: Sage.

Toth, E. L., Serini, S. A., Wright, D. K., & Emig, A. G. (1998). Trends in public relations roles: 1990–1995. *Public Relations Review, 24,* 145–163.

U.S. Department of Labor Statistics. (1980, January). *Employment and earnings.* Washington, DC: U.S. Government Printing Office.

van Doorn, N., van Zoonen, L., & Wyatt, S. (2007). Writing from experience: Presentations of gender identity on weblogs. *International Journal of Women's Studies, 14,* 143–159.

van Zoonen, L. (1994). *Feminist media studies.* Thousand Oaks, CA: Sage.

Vardeman, J. E., & Aldoory, L. (2008). A qualitative study of how women make meaning of contradictory media messages about the risks of eating fish. *Health Communication, 23*(3), 282–291.

Wackwitz, L. A., & Rakow, L. F. (2004). Feminist communication theory: An introduction. In L. F. Rakow & L. A. Wackwitz (Eds.), *Feminist communication theory: Selections in context* (pp. 1–10). Thousand Oaks, CA: Sage.

Worthington, N. (2005). Women's work on the World Wide Web: How a new medium represents an old problem. *Popular Communication, 3,* 43–60.

Wright, D. K., Grunig, L. A., Springston, J. K., & Toth, E. L. (1991). *Under the glass ceiling: An analysis of gender issues in American public relations.* New York: PRSA Foundation.

SECTION TWO

CREATING SHARED MEANING THROUGH ETHICAL PUBLIC RELATIONS PROMOTION AND PUBLICITY

Introduction: Rhetorical Rationale for Publicity and Promotion

Section Two undertakes the daunting challenge of offering thoughts that are useful to promotion and publicity. Five chapters offer insights, but don't offer formulae for how to be effective in these traditional public relations endeavors. In fact, the chapters tend to focus more on what failures plague successful efforts to achieve effective promotion and publicity.

Broadly defined, publicity and promotion are the timeless public relations functions that work to draw favorable attention to an organization, product, service, event, or other matter typically used to increase revenue. These strategic options are used to give voice to an organization, to make it public, to create interest in and understanding of its persona. Used well, the organization's character, what it does, the products it provides, and the services it can supply are brought into the community in constructive and reflective ways. To frame the topics discussed by the chapters let's recall the principles and theory previously explained.

Publicity and promotion are the timeless public relations strategies that work to bring attention to some matter and work to make that attention positive—and motivational. Having said that, we note first the need to beware of the paradox of the positive or paradox of the negative, and we realize that some publicity and promotion is devoted to overstate benefits or harms of some matter. These paradoxes occur when cases are so positive that they ignore negative aspects of some matter. Likewise, the paradox of the negative so focuses on negative aspects of some matter that it ignores what may reasonably be positive aspects. Is this, then, a call for balance? Is it a corrective against incentives practitioners have for clients to give a clouded lens as they build their cases on some matter?

Publicity requires efforts to create awareness, to shine a spotlight on some matter. Promotion is more likely to entail sustained publicity. Both have a narrative quality.

Publicity can capture the "once upon a time" theme, whereas promotion seeks to present a happily ever after story (see Heath & Coombs, 2006). Promotion plays out over time and features some positive outcome. These can include the use of a marathon to raise funds to fight a disease. The history of the marathon, its years, persons who participate, and those who benefit become the characters in the story. The goal is to create a happily ever after outcome.

Publicity and promotion work to create identification. For instance, describing the players, coaches, and other staff on a team helps fans to identify with the team—and motivating fans to attend games and root for the "home team." Such promotion should strive toward what Trujillo (1992) called *communitas* rather than *corporatas*. Corporatas is a perspective fostered for the narrow good of an organization, perhaps even to the actual detriment of fans. If the owner of a professional team features it as "my" team rather than a part of the community it is corporatas. The logic is that the community is more willing to support a team when it is their team. They identify with it (and buy souvenirs and attend games) because they identify with the team and other fans. The same is true of college and university teams. Is it any different for *our* symphony, *our* musical event, *our* parks, or whatever else might be the theme of the public relations campaign? Such logics also reinforce the theme that public relations must attend to the quality of community. Each organization should live the narrative of sharing social construction of meaning rather than manipulating people into believing the team is theirs only to move the team or change it in ways that benefit the owner rather than the community.

Products and services of all kinds are part of socially constructed and collectively enacted narratives. We identify with them. We identify with companies and other organizations. We identify with employers. They tell us stories, create narratives in cooperation, that people live as undirected plays. Such strategies require a solid commitment for products, services, and organizations to be what they claim to be, to walk the walk as they talk the talk. Such principles are as true for non-profits and governmental agencies as they are for businesses. People like events, such as the start and finish of some civic project. Should there be a ceremony to inaugurate the start of rebuilding the levees in New Orleans that failed during Katrina? When they are finished, should that fact be celebrated? Should key accomplishments be celebrated over time? During that time should their success be celebrated, especially during or after a major storm? In 2007, substantial media attention was devoted to the opening of the Skywalk over the Grand Canyon. Is it wise to do that if the intent is to create it as a tourist attraction to raise income for a very poor group of Native Americans? Can an overly positive presentation of the tourist attraction overwhelm the genuine concern by various members of the Native American community who view it as raping Mother Earth?

In all stories, we expect the details told to be true and coherent (Fisher, 1987). We expect organizations to stand and deliver, to be what they say they are, to do what they say they will. To the extent that they do not, their rhetoric and public relations fail because they were the telling of a false tale where reality was distant from and even contradictory to the story. For this reason, we are let down when we are encouraged to vote for a candidate who turns out to be a dud, buy a product that fails to produce as promised, or support a government project that is a waste of money. We expect businesses, non-profits, and government agencies to deliver, in fact to help us collectively manage risks. Those risks could be medicating a head-ache, curing a disease, or waging a just and effective war. We expect public rela-tions to solve rhetorical problems by bringing fact, value, and policy to prevail in a manner that is mutually beneficial. And, according to enactment theory, all of what the organization does has communicative impact. In that sense, the organization is and says what it does.

Given this foundation, what do the chapters that follow contribute to our dis-cussion? Chapter 7 reasons that publicity and promotion can only advance the image of organization if they are transparent, in ways that demonstrate consistency between statement and action, avoid hypocrisy, and reflect honest and responsible efforts to continually engage in constructive change that meets expectations of key publics.

Chapter 8 reasons that in sports and sports teams, brand equity depends upon achievement, often subject to empirical, statistical analysis. If such is the case, and it is, then what happens to the brand equity of a sport, team, or athlete if they achieve statistical distinction by "impure" means? That question presumes that purity of athleticism is the essence of achievement, not something else such as thrown games, corked bats, scuffed balls, or use of performance-enhancing substances, as in the case of baseball. It asks how a sport can responsibly balance its promotional messages with such tainted achievement.

Chapter 9 reasons that the Federal Drug Administration's approval is a vital regulatory hurdle to protect the public interest, and facts about products are the essence of the brand equity of the industry. Drugs—pharmaceuticals—are promoted and publicized to feature health benefits, conclusions that can be empirically assessed in probabilistic terms. What damage is done if the facts are manufactured, biased, and distorted to the benefit of a company, and poten-tial or actual harm of customers? Recall the continuing focus on the importance of responsibly demonstrating conclusions proposed through public relations. Product promotion and publicity call upon organizations to put facts before those who seek to make enlightened choices. What if those facts are crafted to the benefit of the sponsoring organization, and even against the health benefit outcomes of customers?

Chapter 10 features the theme that events such as the July 4th celebration can so positively assert some theme, such as freedom and liberty, that they ignore or marginalize instances where members of society do not actually enjoy those virtues of collective behavior. Such was the case of slavery (and, for instance, females' lack of franchise before an amendment to the Constitution granted them the right to vote). The great abolitionist and advocate of equality free from racism, Frederick Douglass, used the Fourth of July as a day to condemn the overly positive sense that liberty and freedom were universally enjoyed in America prior to the Civil War. His case demonstrates how activists use publicity and promotion to call attention to the case they are making, often by defining some problem, relating it to the ideals of a key public, and addressing how the problem needs to be solved despite hurdles to be overcome—classic rhetorical form and substance. Such advocacy can increase the thoughtful attention to the issue and motivate publics to learn more and take action. This chapter gives rationale for understanding and guarding against the paradox of the positive.

Chapter 11 addresses how the discourse of management can serve to create constructive or destructive relationships with employees. Climate and culture are vital to the full functioning of organizations. To that end, the quality of what is thought about work and workers, as well as the purpose of the work can define harmony or dysfunction within an organization.

As you read the chapters in this section, try to think of an organization with actions that match (or do not match) its rhetoric. Why do you think the organization has been successful in establishing its character well? When an organization faces an issue, such as the Native Americans who permitted the Skywalk to be built on sacred land, how do they reconcile their choice with public perceptions in what they do and why?

One last caveat, for those who assume that the voices of dominant organizations go unchecked, we offer these chapters to challenge students to consider the consequences suffered when organizations fail to engage in responsible and reflective promotion and publicity. And, we demonstrate (such as the case of Douglass) that activists can use the tools of publicity and promotion against some dominant voice in society in the pursuit of positive change.

References

Fisher, W. R. (1987). *Human communication as narration: Toward a philosophy of reason, value, and action.* Columbia: University of South Carolina Press.

Heath, R. L., & Coombs, W. T. (2006). *Today's public relations: An introduction.* Thousand Oaks, CA: Sage.

Trujillo, N. (1992). White knights, poker games, and the invasion of the carpetbaggers: Interpreting the sale of a professional sports franchise. In E. L. Toth & R. L. Heath (Eds.), *Rhetorical and critical approaches to public relations* (pp. 257–278). Hillsdale, NJ: Lawrence Erlbaum.

7

PUBLIC RELATIONS AND THE STRATEGIC USE OF TRANSPARENCY

Consistency, Hypocrisy, and Corporate Change

Lars Thøger Christensen
University of Southern Denmark

Roy Langer
University of Aarhus

In spite of considerable developments over the past century, the field of public relations continues to struggle with the issue of its proper position in the world. What is its role in the pursuit of a good or "full functioning" society? How can public relations add value to a global community? What are, in other words, its points of legitimacy in a world of growing complexity and interdependency (e.g., Heath, 2006)? These are complicated issues and public relations should not be blamed for failing to resolve them fully. The ongoing questioning, which has become part of the field's self-reflective institutionalization, holds some important merits in itself (cf. Holmström, 2005). While the discipline continues to have a widely acknowledged image problem (Callison, 2001; Edwards, 2006; Hutton, 1999; Newsom, Ramsey, & Carrell, 1993), the quest for an ethical public relations paradigm has been shaping the field for several decades (Grunig & Hunt, 1984; Grunig, 1993, 2000; see also Bowen, 2005; David, 2004; Edgett, 2002; Kent & Taylor, 2002; Woodward, 2000) to the effect that it is now considered central to the field's self-understanding (Seib & Fitzpatrick, 1995; Starck & Kruckeberg, 2003). Consequently, public relations has the potential to become a key driver towards a better society. The aim of this chapter is to add new dimensions to our understanding of that challenge and how it can be met in a society focused on increased information about organizations and their activities.

A recurrent theme in writings on public relations' contribution to a better society is the concept of "enlightened choice" (Heath, 2006, p. 108): the notion that public relations can and should participate in an ongoing provision of knowledge and insight and thus help citizens, consumers, and other stakeholders make decisions that are in the interest of the common good (e.g., Gallhofer, Haslam, & Roper, 2001; Heath, 2006; Motion & Weaver, 2005). Public relations, in these writings, is charged with the obligation of securing a steady flow of information about all matters of societal relevance concerning corporations and social institutions. In such perspectives, a crucial dimension of a good and just society is the availability of information, availability that limits opaqueness and complexity and thus helps reduce the potential for power abuse, fraud, corruption, and other types of corporate or institutional evil. Committing itself to support and facilitate the provision and circulation of information in order to build or rebuild trust and healthy stakeholder relationships, public relations places itself in the business of *transparency* (Jahansoozi, 2006). While transparency is a general managerial concern, holding promises of operational efficiency and control (e.g., Berggren & Bernshteyn, 2007), it has a special place in the context of contemporary public relations where transparency is often regarded as a precondition for trust, collaboration, dialogue, insight, accountability, rationality, and freedom (Kent & Taylor, 2002).

In the public relations literature, these issues have typically been phrased in terms of communication *symmetry*. With their model of excellent public relations, James Grunig and his colleagues have consistently argued that collaboration, trust, and accountability are based on genuine dialogue, negotiation and two-way relationships in which all parties are able to bring their interests and viewpoints to the table (e.g., Grunig, 1992; 2001). The model, thus, is essentially egalitarian, seeking to facilitate a balanced flow of communication and avoid the power relations that often shape debates and disputes between corporations and their stakeholders (see also, Toth, 2007). In spite of these qualities, the model has frequently been challenged from the epistemological, ontological, and geographical margins of the literature (e.g., Brown, 2006; Holtzhausen, 2000, 2002; Holtzhausen & Voto, 2002; Holtzhausen, Petersen, & Tindall, 2003; McKie & Munshi, 2005; Wehmeier, 2006). While some writers, for example, question the possibility for real power balance between two parties (e.g., Leitch & Neilson, 2001), others argue that the model promotes a "procedural correctness" that does not in itself guarantee that the decisions made in so-called two-way symmetrical forums are legitimate and socially or environmentally acceptable (Leeper, 2001; see also Cheney & Christensen, 2001b). Some critics even claim that the concept of symmetrical communication reflects a process of compromise designed to deflect criticism and uphold power relations rather than fostering open, collaborative negotiation (Roper, 2005a). These limitations and critiques notwithstanding, symmetry in communications continues to be a significant ideal in both theory and practice. Stacks and Watson (2007), for example, regard symmetry as a prerequisite for building relationships of mutuality and trust and ensuring a balanced flow of communication among all parties. While healthy symmetry may involve some asymmetric measures, symmetry, according to Stack and Watson, is essential in maintaining organizational credibility. In a similar manner, Heath (2007) refers to symmetry as a moving target, that is, a continuous management challenge of ensuring a healthy communication climate of arguments and counterarguments. Symmetry, thus, draws on the logics of systems (seeking balance), rhetoric (establishing balance in discourse), and social exchange theory (involving some evaluation of the quality of the exchange). These writings suggest that although full symmetry may be difficult to achieve and perhaps not even sufficient as a basis for a well-functioning dialogue, the quest for such a dialogue and a continuous exploration of its pitfalls and limitations is a worthy pursuit for public relations.

This chapter extends the interest in exploring the conditions for balanced communication between organizations and their stakeholders. To this end, we investigate the concept of *transparency*—a concept closely related to symmetry to which it adds meaning and content. Without some transparency, symmetry is pure form: balanced communication exchanges without insight or intelligibility. And without symmetry, transparency breeds power imbalances that potentially reduce collaboration and trust. First, we outline the role and institutionalization of organizational transparency. Drawing on Heald (2006a), we unfold the concept by discussing different types of transparency and their limitations in the context of corporate communications. In particular, we discuss transparency in the light of recent attempts to manage and control information and communication flows in response to increasing stakeholder pressure on organizations, as reflected in the concept of integrated communications. We argue that these developments result in a gap between the call for transparency on one hand, and the desire for consistency in corporate messages on the other. Extending these arguments, we explore and challenge the conventional assumption that differences between corporate words and corporate actions should at all times be avoided and eliminated. Such differences, we argue, are essential dimensions of social and organizational change. Thus, we advance Heath's (2001) "rhetorical enactment rationale for public relations" according to which symmetry is a dialogical and dynamic process where ideas, opinions, and truths are constantly negotiated and contested through an open and creative articulation of differences (see also, Heath, 2007). To stimulate such interaction, public relations needs a more subtle and nuanced understanding of transparency—and understanding that may imply more tolerance for inconsistencies and differences in corporate communications.

The Discourse and Institutionalization of Organizational Transparency

Transparency has become a prominent value and a powerful signifier in today's organizational world. While internal and external stakeholders expect to have unrestricted access to corporate information, legal restrictions force organizations to disclose information about their actions and plans, including the publication of annual reports (Riel, 2000). Business practices, for example, are inspected by media and business analysts (Deephouse, 2000) and organizations are increasingly held accountable for their strategic choices. In addition, investment policies of pension funds are regularly scrutinized by investors and other citizens. At the same time, organizations are expected to contribute to transparency themselves by sharing relevant information with their surroundings—a trend driven by the new communication technologies, especially the Internet. Given these trends, combined with a growing pressure from interest groups, media, legislators, business analysts, and other inquisitive stakeholders, it is not surprising to find that contemporary organizations feel more vulnerable and exposed than ever before (Backer, 2001).

Yet, this feeling does not necessarily imply that organizations are more transparent than they used to be.

Although organizational transparency has achieved renewed significance in today's world, neither the term nor the principles behind this movement are, as Hood (2006) pointed out, particularly new. In fact, Hood found important precursors to contemporary notions of transparency in legal doctrines of ancient China, in classical Greek ideas about stable laws, in the work of Adam Smith and his notion of non-discretionary rules of taxation, in the moral commentaries of Jean-Jacques Rousseau and his equation of opaqueness with evil, in the arguments of Immanuel Kant against secret treaties, in the candor and openness of reformed Christianity as opposed to the secrecy of Roman Catholic convention, in the town meeting of local governance, in statutory rights of access to government records, in the philosophy of surveillance by Jeremy Bentham and later Michel Foucault, and in feminist ethics of the 1960s and 1970s. Across these different ideas and practices, we find the conviction that openness and clarity—in the form of fixed, non-arbitrary, and predictable rules, candor and frankness in the organization of social affairs, and the application of rational and scientific principles in the investigation and analysis of the social world—is essential to secure an efficient, moral, and just society. To a large degree, this conviction still shapes the policies of contemporary, democratic societies.

During the past decade, the notion of organizational transparency has attracted increased managerial and public attention. While transparency is regarded as indispensable for accountability, it is gradually becoming a conscious strategy by corporations and institutions in their pursuit of respectability and social accreditation (e.g., Drucker & Gumpert, 2007). Thus we find that contemporary organizations not only describe their communication environment in terms of transparency but also *prescribe* transparency in communications as the proper managerial response. Transparency is not only a pervasive business jargon, it has also become a powerful dimension of business practice, institutionalized for example in anti-corruption organizations like Transparency International. Thus, we tend to concur with Hood (2006) who claimed that the notion of transparency has attained "quasi-religious significance" (p.3) in today's society where debates over corporate governance and organizational design are increasingly shaped by references to openness and transparency as the ultimate goal of modern management.

Still, as Hood pointed out, like other semi-religious terms, "transparency is more often preached than practiced, more often invoked than defined" (p. 3). To move beyond conventional perspectives, we take a closer look at transparency and its different meanings.

Unfolding the Notion of Transparency and its Developments

A commonsense understanding of transparency implies that everything is plainly revealed to us because we are able to see through the obstacles and clutter in our way. In a more concrete sense, something is transparent when it is capable of transmitting light so that objects, images, or behaviors can be seen as if there were no intervening material. Transparency, thus, invokes notions like clarity, lucidity, and translucency. A window, for example, is transparent, although it maintains an obvious distinction between inside and outside and thus some protection against exterior intrusion. With its big windows, the Dutch townhouse, for example, signals to passers-by that its dwellers have nothing to hide and live in accordance with social (Calvinist) norms and values. So, while transparency also implies some sort of openness, these terms are not completely synonymous. As we shall see in the following, transparency invokes a level of ethics beyond openness that takes the receiver end of the communication process into proper consideration.

In the context of modern organizations, transparency usually suggests openness and permeability—not only to light, but also to information, arguments, and ideas. Contemporary organizations, thus, are expected to be open in the sense of making available all sorts of information about their operations and decisions. Still, information availability and exchange may not constitute real transparency. While openness is a precondition for transparency, it is insufficient in itself to ensure the type of clarity and insight associated with the notion of transparency (Christensen, 2002). An organization may, for example, be very open about its decisions and documents without this openness transforming into intelligibility in the eyes of external audiences. As Heald (2006a) pointed out, openness only develops into transparency if relevant audiences are able to make sense out of the information thus made available: "transparency extends beyond openness to embrace simplicity and comprehensibility" (p. 26). Consequently, we cannot take for granted that sheer availability of information produces more sophisticated insight about an organization. While openness, as Heald emphasized, may be a feature of an organization, transparency entails a capability among receivers to actually process and handle the information available. And, as we know, this is often not the case. As Nobel Prize winner Herbert Simon and others have made clear, our ability to handle information is limited by our information processing capacity (Simon, 1997). Even if we imagine for a moment that the external audience had unlimited access to information about organizations, their images of the organizations in question would still be limited by their ability to *process* information—an ability shaped by their insight, time, and experience. Adding to this our propensity to reduce the complexity of new information to familiar schemes of interpretation (Manning, 1986), it would be a mistake to assume that information availability and corporate openness necessarily make organizations more transparent to their surroundings (see also Feldman & March, 1981).

Heald (2006a) contributed to a more sophisticated notion of transparency through an interesting discussion of its possible directions and varieties. His distinctions between transparency upwards, transparency downwards, transparency outwards, and transparency inwards allow us to discuss in more detail the different types of organizational processes that underlie the managerial ideal of "transparency." Transparency upwards means that a superior or principal can observe the behavior of his or her subordinates or agents. Conversely, transparency downwards implies that subordinates—or those being ruled—can observe the behavior of their rulers. The latter type of transparency is sometimes referred to as "accountability" although this term most often extends beyond organizational boundaries. In addition to these types of vertical transparency, Heald described two types of horizontal transparency: transparency outwards when organizational members

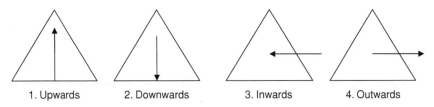

1. Upwards   2. Downwards   3. Inwards   4. Outwards

Figure 7.1 Organizational Transparency Directions

can observe events and developments outside the organization, and transparency inwards when people outside the organization can observe what is going on inside its formal boundaries. For logical consistency, we suggest a minor adjustment of Heald's two latter terms. While transparency outwards, in our discussion below, means that external audiences can observe what is going on inside the organization, transparency inwards refers to situations where organizational members can observe developments in the organization's environment. With this adjustment, the descriptors more accurately reflect the *direction* of information, as illustrated by the arrows in figure 7.1.

In contemporary discourse on organizational transparency, the term is typically used exclusively in its second and fourth senses—downwards and outwards—as referring to instances where management is open, visible to internal and external audiences. Interestingly, however, in their attempts to deal with these two types of transparency organizations tend to intensify the other two types—upwards and inwards. The organizational and social implications of this propensity will be addressed later.

In addition to transparency directions, Heald illustrated how the *focus* of transparency varies too. Transparency, for example, may pertain to discrete organizational *events* or results as opposed to organizational *processes*. Whereas the former are often measurable, the latter—which includes both procedural and operational components—may not be. In the ideal world, we might expect organizations to practice both types of transparency. Yet, event transparency and process transparency are not equally easy and cost-free to generate and maintain. As Heald pointed out, process transparency may in fact be damaging to efficiency and effectiveness. Another relevant distinction concerns the difference between transparency in *retrospect* and transparency in *real time*. Again, the organizational practices and resources involved differ considerably across these types. Whereas transparency in retrospect allows organizations to "oscillate" between periods of production and periods of reporting, transparency in real time involves continuous types of reporting or accountability that leaves out the possibility for the organization to focus exclusively on its productive activities. Finally, Heald emphasized the distinction between *nominal* and *effective* transparency. When transparency is merely a name or a label, we have a case of "transparency illusion" (see also Drucker & Gumpert, 2007). Effective transparency implies that receivers not only have formal access to information but also are able to process, digest, and use it. The notion of transparency, thus, is far more complex than conventional, commonsense understandings seem to indicate.

Limitations to Organizational Transparency

Some may justly claim that there are no valid arguments in a Western democracy for the opposite of transparency: secrecy and obfuscation (e.g., Welch & Rotberg, 2006). Yet, as we have already indicated, it may be rather difficult to achieve and sustain transparency in the context of an organization. For starters, organizations may not want transparency at all—even when they officially celebrate it. Branding, for example, can be thought of as an avoidance strategy designed to reduce effective transparency. Although contemporary organizations claim to embark on corporate branding programs in order to "sell" the organization *behind* the product, the general goal of branding is to add intangible dimensions to the product that obscure the process behind and the fact that products and processes are increasingly similar (Christensen, Morsing, & Cheney, 2008). Another type of avoidance strategy is undercover communication, which refers to covert campaigns by which organizations seek to influence (potential) consumers and other stakeholders. Although consumers are the primary target group of most covert campaigns—hence the more common term, undercover or stealth *marketing*—undercover communication involves as much public relations practices as advertising and marketing practices (Langer, 2003; Kaikati & Kaikati, 2004). Such campaigns have played a prominent role in the history of public relations: For instance, in 1929, Edward Bernays thrilled his tobacco client by staging a march of cigarette-puffing debutants at New York's annual Easter Parade. Of course, Bernays did not reveal his tobacco client, but launched the march as part of the womens' rights and liberation movement: women smoking cigarettes in public was thus framed and perceived as an expression of equality of males and females. Today, undercover communication has experienced a revival. The application of new media channels in commercial communication—among these interpersonal brand pushing channels—and the purposeful blurring of boundaries towards other social discourses and domains such as news, education and health information in order to promote product and corporate brands has led to a situation where many organizations seek to conceal their sender identity and/or the commercial interests. Prefabricated covert video news releases, for instance, seek to promote product and corporate brands by diffusing information into the media's news flow. Obviously, such attempts are criticized for their ethical stance (Langer, 2006). Still, undercover communication will probably continue as strategic attempts to avoid organizational transparency.

In addition to such avoidance strategies, the ideal of transparency is challenged by other social interests and concerns. Since information has a tendency to centralize power, limits on transparency may afford individuals some autonomy and protection against the intrusion of the political system or the media. Simultaneously, community and peaceful coexistence is often based on some level of ignorance. This is true not only for social systems founded on religious myths and principles, although such communities are especially vulnerable to increases in transparency. Ignorance may also be essential in a modern society where lack of transparency can help avoiding suspicion or jealousy (over, for example, unequal rewards) breaking into open conflict. Conflict resolution in times of war often involves sending differentiated messages to different parties—a strategy that can only work if transparency is limited (Heald, 2006b; cf. Cheney, 1991). Likewise, bargaining games often involve some level of dissimulation.

Tom McManus, by some described as a "guru" of transparency, has listed some of the difficulties associated with transparency (Lazarus & McManus, 2006, pp. 924–935):

- Openness and access to information is important, but so is privacy.
- The free flow of information is great, but security is a necessity.
- The right to own some information and restrict its distribution is a critical part of our system of commerce.
- The word "truth" is not part of the definition [of transparency, the authors] because truth implies objectivity but is so fundamentally subjective. Stakeholders are absolute experts on their perspective, but not on what is "true".
- Candor can be insulting and demeaning and may be beside the point in negotiation.

Hood (2006) referred to such difficulties as "rival doctrines," that is, competitive forces or concerns that challenge the ideal of organizational transparency. Freedom of information laws, thus, are often counteracted by privacy laws, bureaucracy, or doctrines of commercial confidentiality (see also, Heald, 2006b; Roberts, 2006). Outsourcing and privatization of functions previously carried out by public organizations, for example, potentially obscure the nature of these functions when transferred to the realm of a private enterprise. Similarly, the fight against terrorism has invoked notions of state security that increasingly oppose principles of transparency. And while technological advances have gradually limited the possibilities of managing different stakeholders through the use of multiple lines of communication, such differentiation in information flows may still be essential in order to uphold effectiveness and trust: too much transparency may encourage conformity to expectations or increase the propensity to deceive or "massage the truth" (O'Neill, cited in Heald, 2006b, p. 62). Given the need to retain some level of secrecy, upheld for example through gatekeeping and filtering, it is tempting to suggest, along with Drucker and Gumpert (2007), that full organizational transparency is an illusion:

> Transparency, the opposite of opacity, is a worthy, but unobtainable ideal in the social relationships of people, the workplace, and between governments and the governed. [...] The illusion of transparency is fostered by an ever-growing environment of informational access often bleeding into the realm of overload and message saturation. [...] The illusion of transparency is fostered by an ever-growing presence of press coverage of the governors, institutions and business coupled with more sophisticated use of media technologies to make these organizations appear more accessible and open.
>
> (Drucker & Gumpert, 2007, pp. 493ff.)

Even when some transparency is achieved, it is often one-sided or asymmetrical. Whereas Heald (2006a) mentioned examples of asymmetrical transparency between states and citizens (for example, in the former Deutsche Demokratische Republik), O'Neill (2006) discussed the tendency to impose transparency requirements on government or business organizations without enforcing similar requirements on the people and institutions that criticize them, e.g., journalists, media, or interest groups. Such asymmetry, according to O'Neill, produces suspicion and distrust: "This allows people who do not face the disciplines of transparency in their own working lives or institutions to criticize others for failing to meet standards which they need not and do not meet—sometimes, no doubt, with misplaced and unattractive self-righteousness" (pp. 80f.). O'Neill's objective is not to suggest that such asymmetries can be fully avoided, but to identify and discuss sources of distrust and suspicion in cases where rules for transparency are in fact implemented. Transparency requirements, according to O'Neill, are insufficient because they rarely take the needs and capabilities of their audiences into proper consideration. Consequently, transparency requirements tend to produce information without reception and openness without trust. In this situation, which corresponds to Heald's (2006a) notion of "nominal transparency" (see above), transparency is ritualized and decoupled from processes of communication and may, in contrast to professed intentions, produce confusion, prejudices and misleading beliefs.

Although it is generally considered a prerequisite for well-managed organizations to handle transparency strategically (e.g., Fombrun & Rindova, 2000; see also van Riel, 2000), it may well be argued that attempts to master transparency as a managerial competence is the major reason why organizational transparency has become decoupled from processes of real communication. Organizations carefully select, simplify, and summarize data. They selectively disclose or leak information, for example through "competitive signalling" (Heil & Robertsen, 1991, p. 403). And they shrewdly manage the timing of disclosure, often with the intention of deflecting critique or handling potential issues. Obviously, individual organizations do not control such processes fully themselves. Their attempts to manage levels and types of openness, however, imply that transparency is continuously staged, often through interorganizational enactments. While Rindova (2001) coined the notion of "polished transparency" to refer to forms of marketing aesthetics used to appeal to certain educated and inquisitive stakeholders, Baudrillard (1988, pp. 29ff) talked about "rituals of transparency" through which we simulate that our desire for information leads to more knowledge. This, he claimed, is hardly the case. When, for example, information about the side-effects of a particular drug is disclosed, the purpose of transparency is not to inform or assist the public but to protect the producers from blame and litigation. O'Neill (2006) talked about "defensive risk management" when transparency is reduced to strategic information disclosures designed to limit or transfer organizational liability and thus, in practice, avoid communication between organizations and their surroundings. Thus, from being an external condition to which organizations must adapt, transparency has gradually become an explicit strategy that *prescribes* transparency in all corporate communications. Such strategies may well be regarded as necessary in complex and critical environments. Yet, the process of taking charge of the information process allows organizations to establish a buffer between themselves and inquisitive stakeholders. Proactivity and (tacit) agreements between organizations as to what types of information to disclose help reinforce this buffer at the same time as transparency is promoted as an important managerial issue (Christensen, 2002).

The question of who benefits from organizational transparency, thus, is slightly more complex than we tend to assume. While foresighted and proactive organizations are able to turn external demands for information and transparency into strategic advantages, the type of information supplied and the form in which it is presented may only benefit insiders and experts who are familiar with the terminology used and, thus, able to unpack and digest it fully (O'Neill, 2006). Our ideals about organizational transparency therefore need to be qualified by the conditions under which transparency is evoked and enacted. At least we need to acknowledge, as Hood (2006) reminded us, that the town-meeting vision of transparency based on a direct and face-to-face type of interpersonal responsibility—a vision that underlies most celebrations of organizational transparency—is essentially in tension with the accounting vision of transparency that addresses primarily experts (regulators, auditors, financial markets, etc.) who are able to understand the often arcane bookkeeping rules and specialist terms associated with bureaucratic reporting practices.

To complicate matters, organizational transparency presumes a high degree of self-transparency (self-insight, self-knowledge) on the part of the organization. Without extensive insight into their own processes and practices, organizations cannot be expected to contribute much to transparency themselves beyond some minimal information disclosures required by agreements or law (Christensen, 2002). Although modernity has been shaped by the ideal of absolute self-transparency, self-transparency is—epistemologically and practically speaking—an unattainable goal (Vattimo, 1992). Societies and organizations are not transparent to themselves and even when leaders and managers claim to have the grand vision, such vision is only a partial—although often relatively powerful and privileged—account of reality (Andersen, 2003; Christensen et al., 2008). The limited and strategic versions of organizational transparency discussed above, thus, are not necessarily a product of conscious managerial attempts to withhold information and reduce transparency. Lack of transparency may occasionally be due to lack of organizational self-insight.

These limitations and paradoxes of transparency constitute a number of challenges for the self-understanding and practice of public relations: It is not just the concern of public relations to provide information about the organization to stakeholders, but also to protect organizational privacy and to ensure control about which information circulates about the organization. It is certainly the task of public relations to enhance trust in the organization by providing trustworthy information, but this does not mean that public relations presents the truth about an organization, as truth is always rhetorically negotiated (Heath, 2001). While public relations cannot provide full symmetrical transparency to all stakeholders, it has to take account of the situational interests, openness and reception of particular stakeholders, as well as their different and varying information needs. Moreover—and as transparency requires a high degree of self-insight—one of the major tasks of public relations is to contribute to increased organizational and societal self-knowledge. But even if and when public relations masters all these tasks, it is still challenged by the general quest for transparency. Its responses to this quest may lead to a reduction of transparency. In the next section, we elaborate on this point through a discussion of current trends in corporate communication.

Transparency and the Organization of Consistency

In spite of the practical and philosophical difficulties of producing and managing organizational transparency, contemporary organizations are deeply engaged in reorganizing themselves to adapt to the growing demand for information and stakeholder insight. In this process, discipline in the release of information plays a crucial role. And while there are several good reasons why organizations should avoid unauthorized disclosure of information (Heald, 2006b), discipline in its current form runs the risk of producing a new type of opacity.

Across sectors, a common reaction to transparency claims is a conspicuous professionalization of information and communication management (Kjær & Langer, 2005). Faced with pressures for more transparency, contemporary organizations intensify their endeavors to manage and control all information flows (Roberts, 2006). Managers of public and private sector organizations, thus, increasingly emphasize the need for messages to be mutually aligned and consistent. While transparency is seen as a general condition of contemporary markets, organizations regard consistency as a necessary organizational response: to adapt to increased transparency, organizations pursue consistency in everything they say and do (Christensen et al., 2008).

Although the ideal of consistency is shaping most managerial disciplines today, the field of integrated communications provides the most formalized vision of consistency in corporate messages. Christensen, Fırat, & Torp (2008) defined integrated communications as the notion and the practice of aligning symbols, messages, procedures, and behaviors in order for an organization to communicate with clarity, consistency, and continuity within and across formal organizational boundaries. The general rationale behind integrated communications is the conviction that increased complexity in today's market, due to message clutter, media fragmentation, globalization, and critical stakeholders, makes it indispensable for organizations to align and manage corporate messages consistently across different media and different audiences (e.g., Schultz, 1996; Schultz & Kitchen, 2000; see also, Aberg, 1990). While the philosophy behind integrated communications has an immediate commonsense appeal—what, after all, is the alternative?—it is often criticized for its prescriptive bias and its lack of practical implementation (e.g., Pettegrew, 2000–2001; Smith, 1996).

Still, it has achieved a tremendous impact on how organizations perceive, approach, and talk about their communications (Cornelissen, 2001). In fact, the vision of integrated communications has significant organizing properties (Cooren, 1999). With its persistent call for alignment and consistency—a call justified by ideals of clarity and transparency—the notion of integrated communications has produced a growing intolerance among managers towards differences and discrepancies in corporate communication. Differences, for example, between and among individual messages, between ideals and practices, between words and action, between the talk of managers and the talk of employees, etc. are increasingly regarded as unacceptable by organizations and their different audiences. This intolerance is exacerbated by inquisitive media, journalists, and interest groups on the search for inconsistencies in the messages and practices of, especially, large corporations and powerful politicians (Carroll & McCombs, 2003; DeLorme & Fedler, 2003; Kjær & Langer, 2005; Meijer & Kleinnijenhuis, 2006). And, since critical stakeholders often justify their existence trying to spot and publicize such inconsistencies, we are facing a communication environment in which managers and politicians feel a growing need to eliminate, reduce, or deny anything that can be regarded as departures from integrated and consistent behaviors. Given the power and impact of critical stakeholders, such efforts are understandable. Widely announced inconsistencies in corporate communications can be damaging to corporate reputations (Hutton et al., 2001).

Ironically, however, such professionalization of corporate communication may result in less transparency—or at least in a different type of transparency—than initially hoped for. This is true for a number of reasons. Externally, because most audiences lack the resources and expert knowledge needed to match corporate initiatives in the area of professional information management (Heald, 2006a). Internally, because organizations use transparency claims to discipline organizational voices. In their attempts to align all corporate messages, organizations have a tendency to regulate and control all communications, including both formal and informal dimensions of organizational life (Christensen, Torp, & Firat, 2005). Thus, contemporary organizations set out to discipline not only official messages like corporate design and promotions, but also the values, ideas, and aspirations of their members (Christensen et al., 2008; see also Kunda, 1992). In a practical manner of speaking, such regulation implies, as Heald (2006a) pointed out, a suppression of unofficial communication channels and attempts to prevent information "percolating the 'sides' of organizations" (p. 38). In many types of organizations, thus, we see an increase in workplace surveillance in the name of security and consistency. And often the surveillance is subtle and unobtrusive: "while the illusion of transparency is cultivated, the traces of surveillance and observation are obliterated" (Drucker & Gumpert, 2007, p. 496). Members of political parties, for example, are expected to articulate only the official voice of the party, and corporations often limit the voice to an official spokesperson, especially in times of crisis. The pursuit of consistency in corporate communications may, as a paradoxical consequence, prevent relevant information about corporate practices becoming accessible to the general public. In the name of openness, thus, organizations produce new types of closure. Simultaneously, the direction of transparency is altered dramatically. As a reaction to increased downwards and outwards transparency, that is instances where organizations are increasingly observable by internal and external audiences, management responds with strategies for more upwards and inwards transparency. One type of organizational transparency, in other words, is replaced by another. Figure 7.2 illustrates such transformations in organizational transparency caused by organizational attempts to manage and regulate all communication flows.

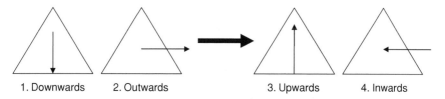

1. Downwards   2. Outwards   3. Upwards   4. Inwards

Figure 7.2 Transformations in Organizational Transparency

While upwards transparency is achieved through the application of rules and sur-veillance systems designed to make sure that all internal and external messages con-form to corporate standards, inwards transparency is manifested in the increased use of image analyses and institutionalized reputation programs that monitor and manage how the organization is perceived in its surroundings (Campbell, Herman, & Noble, 2006; Yang, 2007; Hatch & Schultz, 1997). Transparency, thus, can be considered a manifestation of what Foucault called a "disciplinary technology," a sophisticated version of earlier types of organizational surveillance (Heald, 2006a). In the name of legitimate external demands for more information and insight, contemporary organizations implement a host of disciplinary systems that formal-ize their accountability and simulate openness toward their surroundings. As it appears, accountability in this context refers less to the ability of organizations to answer questions and explain their decisions and behaviors to the general public than to their skillfulness at producing formalized and authorized accounts that succumb to official rules for openness and responsibility. Transparency, in other words, has become an *account* technology designed to discipline internal audiences and keep external audiences at bay (cf. Motion & Leitch, 2002).

In addition to its potential reduction of organizational flexibility, as discussed by Christensen et al. (2008), such disciplining of corporate communication practices produce a gap between the desire for consistency in corporate messages on the one hand and the call for transparency on the other. Although many organizations, including governments, are far more transparent than they used to be, this trend coexists, as Heald (2006a) pointed out, with an increased pressure on politicians, managers, and even lay organizational members to be disciplined or to speak with one voice. Effective transparency (in the sense discussed above), thus, is seriously challenged by the increased discipline of corporate communications. We cannot blame organizations for trying to professionalize their communication practices. However, when such professionalization implies tighter control of all communica-tion flows, presumably in the hope of avoiding inconsistencies and differences, we run the risk of reducing clarity and insight. We can only hope to approach some level of effective transparency if we acknowledge the significance and formative power of differences and discrepancies in organizational communication.

Differences, Hypocrisy, and the Potential for Corporate Change

Standard responses to transparency claims build on the assumption that differences and inconsistencies in corporate communications are problematic and should be avoided or eliminated. Differences and inconsistencies are disapproved because they are regarded as sources of hypocrisy. Yet, such differences and inconsistencies are inevitable in processes of human communication and organizing. First, differences are a fundamental dimension of language: The signifier *is* not the signified. Although some words bear a more "natural" or inevitable relation to the world than others (for example, onomatopoeia), language is mostly symbolic, that is, based on convention (Peirce, 1985; see also Campbell, Herman, & Noble, 2006). Just as the word "rose" in the English language refers to love only through conventional association, notions like "corporate social responsibility," "sustainability," or "credibility" have come to imply certain organizational activities (and exclude others) only through customary practices. And, as we know, such practices develop over time. Like other symbolic terms, they are essentially ambiguous and thus open for alternative interpretations (Morsing & Langer, 2006). Consequently, they are bound to be contested and renegotiated on a continual basis. And in such processes, differences between language, objects, and behaviors are both essential and inevitable.

Second, organizations produce differences and inconsistencies in their daily practices—even when they do not intend to do so. If all organizational stakeholders (including shareholders and customers) were articulating the same expectations, it would be relatively easy for organizations to reduce differences and come across as consistent (Brunsson, 2003). This, however, is rarely the case. In complex environments, organizations face many different stakeholders that express divergent and, often, conflicting goals and demands. While some stakeholders, for example, expect inexpensive automobiles, others call for solutions that reduce the emission of carbon dioxides. In the process of adapting to such differences in their environments, organizations unavoidably generate inconsistencies between their words and their actions, at least temporarily. Organizations, in other words, cannot avoid some level of hypocrisy. Without justifying deception and dishonesty, Brunsson (2003) argued that hypocrisy may be a transitory solution under conditions of complexity (see also, Brunsson, 1989; March, 1988). Trying to maneuver in a world of conflicting and incompatible demands and goals, organizations need to compensate action in one direction with talk and decisions in the opposite. While such practice of splitting words and action is usually regarded as insincere, cynical, and unethical, Brunsson's analysis of public sector organizations in Sweden illustrate that hypocrisy not only is inescapable to language, but integral to organizing.

In spite of these conditions, organizations and their managers are increasingly expected to "walk their talk"; that is, to practice what they preach. As a general rule, the "walk-the-talk" recipe provides, as Weick (1995) pointed out, a sensible buffer against the evils of hypocrisy. In this perspective, the philosophy behind integrated communications makes perfect sense: organizations need to integrate all communications in order to protect themselves against charges of hypocrisy. However, based on his notion that people and organizations act in order to think (see also Weick, 1979), Weick argued that the type of consistency prescribed by the walk-the-talk imperative seriously limits the possibility of discovering new solutions or ideas for which the previous words are inadequate. To fully benefit from the creative power of language use, organizations should not construe and implement the walk-the-talk imperative too tightly. Talk is action too and organizations learn from the ways they describe themselves and their surroundings—even when those descriptions are not fully accurate. If society only allows people and organizations to articulate and claim ideals, values, and intentions which they already practice, the creative and transformative power of language is left unused.

In line with this perspective, March (1988) recommended a relatively unrestricted articulation of corporate ideals. Like Brunsson, March does not condone hypocrisy as a strategy, but sees it as an inevitable byproduct of all organizing—not at least in situations where organizations try to improve their practices. A bad person with good intentions, March argued, *can* be a person who experiments with the possibilities of becoming a good person. Consequently, it would be more rational to make room for such experiments than to reject them. These observations speak in favor of more tolerance when observing and evaluating corporate communications. Such tolerance allows organizations to discover new solutions that benefit not only themselves but also their surroundings. Understandably, such tolerance is difficult to achieve today, in an era shaped by extreme cases of organizational fraud. In the aftermath of the "corporate meltdown" it is not surprising to find a widespread skepticism toward corporate messages and intensified calls for corporate transparency and consistency. In the context of financial deception, as we saw in the Enron scandal, the insistence on increased transparency and consistency makes perfect sense.

In the broader scheme of things, however, such calls ignore the fact that organizations change—and potentially improve—through communication. Scholars of communication have usually no trouble agreeing that communication is consequential, that it *does* things. And most would probably concur that this is true for *organizational* communication as well. Some will even argue that organizations *emerge* in communication; that communication, rather than being something superficial, distinct, and separate from organizational practice, is the "essential modality," as Taylor and van Every (2000) put it, of organizational life. Speech is action, just as our acts simultaneously speak. Accordingly, it is not possible to distinguish sharply between what an organization says and what it does. While this is certainly not to suggest a simple one-to-one correspondence between words and action, it is a reminder that communication has "organizing properties" (Cooren, 1999) that inevitably shape and generate organizational reality (see also Fairhurst & Putnam, 2004). Interestingly, however, when it comes to issues of, for example, corporate social responsibility, many of us tend to focus and insist on the *differences* between what organizations say and what they do. Some may even claim that the relationship between words and actions in this area is one of pretense or deceit (e.g., Peterson & Norton, 2007). And while it is not difficult to find examples of such behaviors, the potential for instigating organizational changes through new types of communication should not be underestimated.

An in-depth study of the Royal Dutch/Shell Group has led Livesey and Graham (2007) to argue that the talk of large corporations has the potential to transform the perceptions and the practices of social actors, including the organizations themselves. More specifically, their study illustrates how eco-talk emerged in the organization and how this talk gradually became a creative force in shaping the corporation's renewed identity. Instead of seeing eco-talk and corporate initiatives in the area of sustainable development as many critics would do, that is as autonomized communication or "cheap" public relations maneuvers, the study by Livesey and Graham focuses on the performative, pragmatic dimensions of language and communication: "Corporate eco-talk participates in (re)creating the firm and (re)constructing its relationship to nature, while opening up novel possibilities of understanding and action at the societal level" (Livesey & Graham, 2007, p. 336). Based on a thorough examination of select texts by Shell and its critics, Livesey and Graham illustrated the transformation of Shell's identity toward more sustainable practices. Simultaneously, they show how its new eco-talk at once reflected and shaped the understandings of environmental responsibility in society at large.

Other companies use the language of corporate social responsibility to spur corporate change and impel corporate action. For example, sportswear manufacturer Nike, once heavily criticized for using sweatshop child labor in Asia, now engages in the Nike Village Development Project. While its past makes it difficult for Nike to come across as sincere, the transformative potential of such initiatives should not be underestimated. That is, while companies like Nike do not become socially responsible simply by talking about it, their initiatives within that arena have reorganizing potential beyond the labels of "false advertising" (DeTienne & Lewis, 2005) or "greenwash" (Hamann & Kapelus, 2004). Although we should continue to be critical of what organizations say or do, we should simultaneously allow them to experiment with the ways they communicate. Such latitude not only allows them to find new solutions for themselves and their own organizational practices, but also—as Livesey and Graham suggest—helps society at large discover new ideals, goals, and productive discourses on responsibility and sustainability.

If the picture of how communication potentially shapes and transforms corporate behavior has any relevance beyond the case of Shell, the questions should be: How much latitude are we willing to grant organizations in experimenting with new ways of talking about their ideas, values, and plans? Can we allow them to articulate values they are not presently able to live up to? Or should we insist that their words always reflect their deeds? Rather than taking the conventional modernist approach where the task of the critic is to *unmask* and expose differences between what organizations say and do, we suggest taking a closer look at *the transformative potential of such differences.* Used with caution, differences can help stimulate and generate change in the interest of society. Such an approach is in line with the notion of auto-communication. Auto-communication takes place whenever people or organizations communicate with themselves through external media (Broms & Gahmberg, 1983; Christensen, 1994, 1997). By lending status and authority to self-messages, the external medium binds and commits the sender to do something about the proclaimed ideas, values, or plans. The external medium, in other words, is a "mirror" in which the sender sees and evaluates itself in the eyes of the generalized Other (Christensen et al., 2008). Self-evaluations are important sources of identity developments (Cooley, 1983; Mead, 1934). In such processes, accuracy and consistency are not the primary drivers. Just like the messages we deliberately convey about ourselves to significant others, corporate messages (advertising, corporate values, mission statements, etc.) are not perfect mirrors of reality. Rather, they are about the hopes, dreams, and visions of corporate actors. Interestingly, we tend to grant more leeway to some types of corporate communications than to others. Advertising, for example, has generally become accepted as a genre of communication with only marginal overlap with the reality it refers to. This attitude contrasts sharply to the expectations we have regarding statements about corporate social responsibility.

Having stressed the significance of differences and the limitations of conventional approaches to transparency, the central question, of course, is what big differences are we willing to accept in corporate communications and corporate behavior? How much inconsistency can we tolerate? What are the limits to hypocrisy? How can we rearticulate the standard of consistency in ways that do not preclude real transparency? And what is the role of public relations in this process?

Conclusion: Challenges to Public Relations

Believing that public relations' essential role is a provider of information about corporate matters, we have unpacked the notion of organizational transparency to explore its different meanings, directions, and implications for contemporary organizations and society. Although transparency is essential in generating trust, collaboration, dialogue, and accountability, its institutional forms tend to produce organizational closure rather than openness, control rather than insight, discipline rather than autonomy and freedom. With the current emphasis on consistency and alignment in all corporate communications—an emphasis often produced by a certain type of critique by journalists and media—such paradoxical and counterproductive consequences of transparency are bound to increase. Taking our point of departure in the organizing power of language, we call instead for more openness and curiosity toward, if not acceptance of, differences and discrepancies between corporate words and action. Our point is certainly not to justify corporate pretense and deceit, but to allow organizations to explore—through communication—their possibilities for change and improvements.

The role of public relations in this process is to throw light on differences and discrepancies rather than hiding them, denying them, or smoothing them out. Instead of contributing to illusions of full agreement, openness, and transparency between corporations and society, public relations can play an essential role in pointing out and clarifying important differences and inconsistencies in society. Although we frequently come across differences and inconsistencies in corporate messages and behaviors that we find troublesome, such differences and inconsistencies may appear more understandable if they are illuminated, explained, and contested rather than toned down. In line with Heath's (2007) ideal notion of advocacy, we argue that balanced communication is a work in progress that requires a willingness to highlight and explore differences between arguments and counterarguments. Attention to differences can be used as levers to mobilize internal and external audiences. Furthermore, it can be used to investigate limits and possibilities and to proactively creative better organizations. Therein lies a significant potential for change: in the open and creative articulation of differences. PR's role in facilitating such open and creative articulation is crucial. Rather than pressing organizations toward compromise and thus minimize, silence, or deny differences and inconsistencies, we suggest that organizations are urged and stimulated to use differences and inconsistencies proactively and creatively to highlight and debate their potentials for change and improvements (cf. Heath, 2001).

Such an approach implies a far more sophisticated approach to transparency. In contrast to the current business environment, where external transparency claims are transformed into disciplinary practices that potentially reduce transparency, we need to create conditions for another type of corporate transparency that allow organizations to share their limitations far more openly with their surroundings. Such transparency has both internal and external dimensions. Internally, it allows employees to openly address differences and inconsistencies instead of adapting their perceptions and utterances to the official corporate story (Christensen et al., 2008). This way, they can potentially contribute far more actively to organizational change. Externally, it allows and commits organizations to admit differences between stakeholders and their own perceptions.

Instead of insisting on agreement and consensus, as some renditions of the two-way symmetrical model tends to do (Grunig, 1993; Burkart, 2007), our notion of transparency implies that organizations make differences visible and clearly acknowledge their own stand on the issue. Interestingly, such an approach is far more ethically sound as it forces organizations to explain and justify their viewpoints and decisions more actively than when they aim for agreement and compromise. In fact, it is possible to argue that such an approach would have generated a better solution in the well-known Brent Spar case. By giving in to the pressure by Greenpeace and not dumping the former oil buoy Brent Spar in the North Sea, Royal Dutch Shell chose an approach of responsiveness rather than responsibility (Cheney & Christensen, 2001a). By contrast, an approach of responsibility would have implied a focus on facts and a persistent insistence on keeping the debate about the alternative—scrapping the buoy on land—alive. Such an approach, which acknowledges and accepts differences and disagreements, is not only more responsible, it also has the potential to generate more trust in the long run.

Such an approach implies a new professional role for the practitioner. Holtzhausen and Voto (2002) describe the public relations professional as an organizational activist, who is engaged in situational ethical decision making, has a desire for change, uses biopower to resist dominant power, and who is concerned with employee representation and the practice of disagreement and dissymmetry—thus confirming the emancipatory potential of public relations that challenges the managerial approach to the profession (see also Berger, 2005). In this vision, practitioners should not regard themselves as part of a dominant coalition, but as organizational activists, who represent and illuminate stakeholder interests vis-à-vis management. In addition to the activist role, the practioner could play the role of a "court jester" granted with the privilege of airing conflicting opinions and concerns without being punished. A jester's license would be of great advantage to the profession, as well as to organizations and society. It would enable public relations to facilitate and professionalize public debate and awareness in the sense of learning to listen to, understand, and incorporate multiple perspectives and nuances without downplaying or rejecting vital differences in perceptions. In this vision, it is not public relations' role to foster consensus and shared meaning but to illuminate fundamental differences in stakeholder perceptions and viewpoints. Such a role may well be regarded as a constructive step toward fostering community at a more sophisticated level; a community founded on a thorough understanding of the arguments that can be made against us (Heath, 2007). Finally, practitioners can be thought of as navigators that help organizations and society in gaining self-insight and knowledge. In all these roles, the mission of public relations is to educate both the corporation and society to deliver and expect more elaborate and complex accounts of issues and decisional situations.

To stay vibrant, public relations needs as a minimum to avoid becoming an account technology, that is, a technology that reduces transparency to formalized systems of accountability which big and powerful corporations can easily learn to master to their own advantage. Real and effective transparency involves keeping essential differences and discrepancies alive and visible for everybody to engage and judge. As Heath (2007, p. 62) puts it: "the competitive weight of views, ideas, or perspectives constitutes the true essence of symmetry." In this game, the focus on consistency is probably a bigger problem than hypocrisy. The insistence on consistency forces organizations to tighten their control measures, which potentially reduces real transparency. By allowing organizations to talk more freely about their ideals and good intentions without constantly reminding them that their behavior leaves much to be desired, we stand a better chance of discovering new modes of organizing that benefit society as a whole. Obviously, corporate ideals, initiatives, and claims need to be treated with caution. While a more sophisticated notion of transparency may teach us to tolerate some forms of emerging hypocrisy, we still need to condemn it when it is *deliberate*. If transparency is less one-sided (that is, more symmetric) there would probably be more tolerance for, or understanding of, inconsistency and differences in corporate communication—and thus greater potential for social learning. Practitioners in their roles as reflective organizational activists, court jesters, and navigators might well focus on developing such symmetric transparency as part of reflective communication management in future public relations (cf. van Ruler & Verčič, 2005).

References

Aberg, L. E. G. (1990). Theoretical model and praxis of total communications. *International Public Relations Review, 13*(2), 13–16.

Andersen, N. Å. (2003). The undecidability of decision. In T. Bakken & T. Hernes (Eds.), *Autopoietic organization theory, Abstakt, Liber* (pp. 235–258). Oslo: Copenhagen Business School Press.

Backer, L. (2001). The mediated transparent society. *Corporate Reputation Review, 4*(3), 235–251.

Baudrillard, J. (1988). Simulacra and simulations. In M. Poster (Ed.), *Jean Baudrillard: Selected writings* (pp. 166–184). Stanford, CA: Stanford University Press.

Berger, B. K. (2005). Power over, power with, and power to relations: Critical reflections on public relations, the dominant coalition, and activism. *Journal of Public Relations Research, 17*(1), 5–28.

Berggren, E., & Bernshteyn, R. (2007). Organizational transparency drives company performance. *Journal of Management Development, 26*(5), 411–417.

Bowen, S. A. (2005). A practical model for ethical decision making in issues management and public relations. *Journal of Public Relations Research, 17*(3), 191–216.

Broms, H., & Gahmberg, H. (1983). Communication to self in organizations and cultures. *Administrative Science Quarterly, 28*(3), 482–495.

Brown, R. E. (2006). Myth of symmetry: Public relations as cultural styles. *Public Relations Review, 32*(3), 206–212.

Brunsson, N. (1989). *The organization of hypocrisy. Talk, decisions and actions in organizations.* Chichester, Sussex, England: John Wiley.

Brunsson, N. (2003). Organized hypocrisy. In B. Czarniawska & G. Sevón (Eds.), *The northern lights—organization theory in Scandinavia* (pp. 201–222). Copenhagen: Copenhagen Business School Press.

Burkart, R. (2007). On Jürgen Habermas and public relations. *Public Relations Review, 33*(3), 249–254.

Callison, C. (2001). The good, the bad, and the ugly: Perceptions of public relations practitioners. *Journal of Public Relations Research, 16*(4), 371–389.

Campbell, F. E., Herman, R. A., & Noble, D. (2006). Contradictions in "reputation management." *Journal of Communication Management, 10*(2), 191–196.

Carroll, C. E., & McCombs, M. (2003). Agenda-setting effects of business news on the public's image and opinion about major corporations. *Corporate Reputation Review, 6*(1), 36–46.

Cheney, G. (1991). *Rhetoric in an organizational society. Managing multiple identities.* Columbia: University of South Carolina Press.

Cheney, G. (1992). The corporate person (re)presents itself. In E. L. Toth & R. L. Heath (Eds.), *Rhetorical and critical approaches to public relations* (pp.165–183). Hillsdale, NJ: Erlbaum.

Cheney, G., & Christensen, L. T. (2001a). Organizational identity. Linkages between "internal" and "external" organizational communication. In F. Jablin & L. L. Putnam (Eds.), *The new handbook of organizational communication* (pp. 231–269). Thousand Oaks, CA: Sage.

Cheney, G., & Christensen, L. T. (2001b). Public relations as contested terrain. A critical response. In R. L. Heath (Ed.), *Handbook of public relations* (pp. 167–182). Newbury Park, CA: Sage.

Christensen, L. T. (1994). Talking to ourselves: Management through auto-communication. *MTC Kontakten* (Marknadstekniskt Centrum, Stockholm), Jubilæumstidsskrift, 32–37.

Christensen, L. T. (1997). Marketing as auto-communication. *Consumption, Markets & Culture, 1,* 197–227.

Christensen, L. T. (2002). Corporate communication: The challenge of transparency. *Corporate Communications: An International Journal,* (3), 162–168.

Christensen, L. T., Fırat, A. F., & Torp, S. (2008). The organization of integrated communications: Toward flexible integration. *European Journal of Marketing, 42.*

Christensen, L. T., Morsing, M., & Cheney, G. (2008). *Corporate communications: Convention, complexity and critique.* London: Sage.

Christensen, L. T., Torp, S., & Fırat A. F. (2005). Integrated marketing communication and postmodernity: An odd couple? *Corporate Communication: An International Journal, 10*(2), 156–167.

Cooley, C. H. (1983). *Human nature and the social order.* New Brunswick, NJ: Transaction Books.

Cooren, F. (1999). *The organizing property of communication.* Amsterdam: John Benjamins.

Cornelissen, J. P. (2001). Integrated marketing communications and the language of marketing development. *International Journal of Advertising, 20*(4), 483–498.

David, P. (2004). Extending symmetry: Toward a convergence of professionalism, practice, and pragmatics in public relations. *Journal of Public Relations Research, 16*(2), 185–211.

Deephouse, D. L. (2000). Media reputation as a strategic resource: An integration of mass communication and resource-based theories. *Journal of Management, 26*(6), 1091–1112.

DeLorme, D. E., & Fedler, F. (2003). Journalists' hostility towards public relations: An historical analysis. *Public Relations Review, 29*(2), 99–124.

DeTienne, K. B., & Lewis, L. W. (2005). The pragmatic and ethical barriers to corporate social responsibility disclosure. *Journal of Business Ethics, 60*(4), 359–376.

Dozier, D. M., Grunig, J. E., & Grunig, L. A. (1995). *Managers' guide to excellence in public relations and communication management.* Mahwah, NJ: Lawrence Erlbaum.

Drucker, S. J., & Gumpert, G. (2007). Through the looking glass: Illusions of transparency and the cult of information. *Journal of Management Development, 26*(5), 493–498.

Edgett, R. (2002). Toward an ethical framework for advocacy in public relations. *Journal of Public Relations Research, 14*(1), 1–26.

Edwards, L. (2006). Rethinking power in public relations. *Public Relations Review, 32*, 229–231.

Fairhurst, G., & Putnam, L. (2004). Organizations as discursive constructions. *Communication Theory, 14*(1), 5–26.

Feldman, M. S., & March, J. G. (1981). Information in organizations as signal and symbol. *Administrative Science Quarterly, 26*(2), 171–186.

Fombrun, C. J., & Rindova, V. P. (2000). The road to transparency: Reputation management at Royal Dutch/Shell. In M. Schultz, M. J. Hatch & M. H. Larsen (Eds.), *The expressive organization* (pp. 77–96). Oxford: Oxford University Press.

Gallhofer, S., Haslam, J., & Roper, J. (2001). Problematising finance in practice: A case study of struggles over takeovers legislation in New Zealand. *Advances in Accountability: Regulation, Research, Gender and Justice, 8*, 121–155.

Grunig, J. E. (1992). *Excellence in public relations and communication management.* Hillsdale, NJ: Lawrence Erlbaum.

Grunig, J. E. (1993). Public relations and international affairs: Effects, ethics and responsibility. *Journal of International Affairs, 47*(1), 138–162.

Grunig, J. E. (2000). Collectivism, collaboration, and societal corporatism as core professional values in public relations. *Journal of Public Relations Research, 12*(1), 23–48.

Grunig, J. E. (2001): Two-way symmetrical public relations: past, present, and future. In R. L. Heath (Ed.), *Handbook of public relations* (pp. 11–30). Thousand Oaks, CA: Sage.

Grunig, J. E. (2006). Furnishing the edifice: Ongoing research on public relations as a strategic management function. *Journal of Public Relations Research, 18*(2), 151–176.

Grunig, J. E., & Hunt, T. (1984). *Managing public relations.* New York: Holt, Rhinehart & Winston.

Hamann, R., & Kapelus, P. (2004). Corporate social responsibility in mining in South Africa: Fair accountability or just greenwash? *Development, 47*(3), 85–92.

Hatch, M. J., & Schultz, M. (1997). Relations between organisational culture, identity and image. *European Journal of Marketing, 31*(5/6), 356–365.

Heald, D. (2006a). Varieties of transparency. In C. Hood & D. Heald (Eds.), *Transparency. The key to better governance* (pp. 25–43). Oxford: Oxford University Press.

Heald, D. (2006b). Transparency as an instrumental value. In C. Hood & D. Heald (Eds.), *Transparency. The key to better governance* (pp. 59–73). Oxford: Oxford University Press.

Heath, R. L. (2001). A rhetorical enactment rationale for public relations. The good organization communicating well. In R. L. Heath (Ed.), *Handbook of public relations* (pp. 31–50). Thousand Oaks, CA: Sage.

Heath, R. L. (2006). Onward into more fog: Thoughts on public relations' research directions? *Journal of Public Relations Research, 18*(2), 93–114.

Heath, R. L. (2007). Management through advocacy: Reflection rather than domination. In E. L. Toth (Ed.), *The future of excellence in public relations and communication management: Challenges for the next generation* (pp. 41–66). Mahwah, NJ: Lawrence Erlbaum.

Heil, O., & Robertson, T. S. (1991). Toward a theory of competitive marketing signaling: A research agenda, *Strategic Management Journal, 12*(6), 403–418.

Holmström, S. (2005). Reframing public relations: The evolution of a reflective paradigm for organizational legitimization. *Public Relations Review, 31*(4), 497–504.

Holtzhausen, D. R. (2000). Postmodern values in public relations. *Journal of Public Relations Research, 12*(1), 93–114.

Holtzhausen, D. R. (2002). Towards a postmodern agenda for public relations. *Public Relations Review, 28*(3), 251–264.

Holtzhausen, D. R., & Voto, R. (2002). Resistance from the margins: The postmodern public relations practitioner as organizational activist. *Journal of Public Relations Research, 14*(1), 57–84.

Holtzhausen, D. R., Petersen, B. K., & Tindall, N. T. J. (2003). Exploding the myth of the symmetrical/asymmetrical dichotomy: Public relations models in the new South Africa. *Journal of Public Relations Research, 5*(4), 305–341.

Hood, C. (2006). Transparency in historical perspective. In C. Hood & D. Heald (Eds.), *Transparency. The key to better governance* (pp. 3–23). Oxford: Oxford University Press.

Hutton, J. G. (1999). The definition, dimensions, and domains of public relations. *Public Relations Research, 25*(2), 199–214.

Hutton, J. G., Goodman, M. B., Alexander, J. B., & Genest, C. M. (2001). Reputation management: The new face of corporate public relations? *Public Relations Review, 27*(3), 247–261.

Jahansoozi, J. (2006). Organization-stakeholder relationships: Exploring trust and transparency. *Journal of Management Development, 25*(10), 942–955.

Kaikati A. M., & Kaikati J. G. (2004). Stealth marketing: How to reach consumers surreptitiously. *California Management Review 46*(4), 6–24.

Kent, M. L., & Taylor, M. (2002). Toward a dialogic theory of public relations. *Public Relations Review, 28*(1), 21–37.

Kjær, P., & Langer, R. (2005): Infused with news value: Management, managerial knowledge and the instutionalization of business news. *Scandinavian Journal of Management, 21*(2), 209–233.

Kunda, G. (1992). *Engineering culture*. Boston: Temple Press.

Langer, R. (2003). New subtle advertising formats: Characteristics, causes and consequences. In F. Hansen & L. Bech Christensen (Eds.), *Branding and advertising* (pp.
232–265). Copenhagen: Copenhagen Business School Press.

Langer, R. (2006). Stealth Marketing Communications—is it ethical? In M. Morsing &
S. C. Beckmann (Eds.), *Strategic CSR communication* (pp. 107–134). Copenhagen:
DJOEF Publishers.

Lazarus, H., & McManus, T. (2006). Transparency guru: An interview with Tom
McManus. *Journal of Management Development, 25*(10), 923–936.

Leeper, R. (2001). In search of a metatheory for public relations: An argument for
Communitarianism. In R. L. Heath (Ed.), *Handbook of public relations* (pp. 93–
104). Thousand Oaks, CA: Sage.

Leichty, G. (2003). The cultural tribes of public relations. *Journal of Public Relations
Research, 15*(4), 277–304.

Leitch, S., & Neilson, D. (2001). Bringing publics into public relations: New theoretical frameworks for practice. In R. L. Heath (Ed.), *Handbook of public relations* (pp.
127–138). Thousand Oaks, CA: Sage.

Livesey, S. M., & Graham, J. (2007). Greening of corporations? Eco-talk and the
emerging social imagery of sustainable development. In S. May, G. Cheney, & J.
Roper (Eds.), *The debate over corporate social responsibility* (pp. 336–350). Oxford:
Oxford University Press.

McKie, D., & Munshi, D. (2005). Tracking trends: Peripheral visions and public relations. *Public Relations Review, 31*(4), 453–457.

Manning, P. K. (1986). Signwork. *Human Relations, 39*(4), 283–308.

March, J. G. (1988). *Decisions and organizations.* Oxford: Basil Blackwell.

May, S., Cheney, G., & Roper, J. (Eds.) (2007). *The debate over corporate social responsibility.* Oxford: Oxford University Press.

Mead, G. H. (1934). *Mind, self and society.* Chicago, IL: University of Chicago Press.

Meijer, M. M., & Kleinnijenhuis, J. (2006). News and corporate reputation: Empirical
findings from the Netherlands. *Public Relations Review, 32*(4), 341–348.

Morsing, M., & Langer, R. (2006). CSR-communication in the business press:
Advantages of strategic ambiguity. In K. Podnar & Z. Jančič (Eds.), *Contemporary
issues in corporate and marketing communications: Towards a socially responsible
future* (pp. 26–34). Proceedings of the Eleventh International CMC-conference
on Corporate and Marketing Communications, Ljubljana, April 21–22. Ljubljana:
Fakulteta za družbene vede.

Motion, J., & Leitch, S. (2002). The technologies of corporate identity. *International
Studies of Management and Organisation, 32*(3), 45–64.

Motion, J., & Weaver, C. K. (2005). The discourse perspective for critical public
relations research: Life science networks and the battle for truth. *Journal of Public
Relations Research, 17*(1), 49–67.

Newsom, D. A., Ramsey, S. A., & Carrell, B. J. (1993). Cameleon changing II: A rep-
lication. *Public Relations Review, 19*(2), 33–47.

O'Neill, O. (2006). Transparency and the ethics of communication. In C. Hood &
D. Heald (Eds.), *Transparency. The key to better governance* (pp. 75–90). Oxford:
Oxford University Press.

Nichols, M. H. (1969). *Rhetoric and criticism.* Baton Rouge: Louisiana State University
Press.

Peirce, C. S. (1985). Logic as semiotic: The theory of signs. In R. E. Innis (Ed.),
Semiotics. An introductory anthology (pp. 4–23). Bloomington: Indiana University
Press.

Peterson, T. Rai, & Norton, T. (2007). Discourses of sustainability in today's public sphere. In S. May, G. Cheney, & J. Roper (Eds.), *The debate over corporate social responsibility* (pp. 351–364). Oxford: Oxford University Press.

Pettegrew, L. S. (2000–2001). If IMC is so good, why isn't it being implemented? Barriers to IMC adoption in corporate America. *Journal of Integrated Communication*, http://jimc.medill.northwestern.edu/JIMCWebsite/Archive2000/loyd.pdf

Plowman, K. D. (2006). Conflict, strategic management, and public relations. *Public Relations Review, 31*(1), 131–138.

Riel, C. B.M. van (2000). Corporate communication orchestrated by a sustainable corporate story. In M. Schultz, M. J. Hatch, & M. H. Larsen (Eds.), *The expressive organization* (pp. 157–181), Oxford: Oxford University Press.

Rindova, V. P. (2001). Panel on transparency: Condition or strategy in reputation building? Held at the Fifth International Conference on Corporate Reputation, Identity & Competitiveness, Paris, May 17–19.

Roberts, A. (2006). Dashed expectations: Governmental adaptation to transparency rules. In C. Hood & D. Heald (Eds.), *Transparency: The key to better governance* (pp. 107–125). Oxford: Oxford University Press.

Roper, J. (2005a). Symmetrical communication: Excellent public relations or a strategy for hegemony? *Journal of Public Relations Research, 17*(1), 69–86.

Roper, J. (2005b). Organisational identities, identification and positioning: Learning from political fields. *Public Relations Review, 31*(1), 139–148.

Ruler, B. van, & Verčič, D. (2005). Reflective communication management: Future ways for public relations research. In P. J. Kalbfleisch (Ed.), *Communication yearbook* (pp. 239–274). Mahwah, NJ: Erlbaum.

Schultz, D. E. (1996). The inevitability of integrated communications. *Journal of Business Research, 37*(3), 139–146.

Schultz, D. E., & Kitchen, P. J. (2000). *Communicating globally. An integrated marketing approach*. London: Macmillan Business.

Seib, P. & Fitzpatrick, K. (1995). *Public relations ethics*. Fort Worth, TX: Harcourt Brace.

Simon, H. A. (1997). *Administrative behavior, 50th anniversary edition*. New York: Free Press.

Smith, P. (1996). Benefits and barriers to integrated communications. *Admap*, February, 19–22.

Stacks, D. W. (2002). *Primer of public relations research*. New York: Guilford Press.

Stacks, D. W., & Watson, M. L. (2007). Two-way communication based on quantitative research and measurement. In E. L. Toth (Ed.), *The future of excellence in public relations and communication management: Challenges for the next generation* (pp. 67–84). Mahwah, NJ: Lawrence Erlbaum.

Starck, K., & Kruckeberg, D. (2003). Ethical obligations of public relations in an era of globalization. *Journal of Communication Management, 8*(1), 29–40.

Taylor, J. R., & Every, E. van (2000). *The emergent organization: Communication as its site and surface*. Mahwah, NJ: Lawrence Erlbaum.

Toth, E. L. (2002). Postmodernism for modernist public relations: The cash value and application of critical research in public relations. *Public Relations Review, 28*(3), 243–250.

Toth, E. L. (Ed.). (2007). *The future of excellence in public relations and communication management: Challenges for the next generation*. Mahwah, NJ: Lawrence Erlbaum.

Vattimo, G. (1992). *The transparent society*. Cambridge: Polity Press.

Wang, A. (2007). Priming, framing and position on corporate social responsibility. *Journal of Public Relations Research, 19*(2), 123–145.

Wehmeier, S. (2006). Dancers in the dark: The myth of rationality in public relations. *Public Relations Review, 32*(3), 213–220.

Weick, K. E. (1979). *The social psychology of organizing.* Reading, MA: Addison-Wesley.

Weick, K. E. (1995). *Sensemaking in organizations.* Thousand Oaks, CA: Sage.

Welch, T. C., & Rotberg, E. H. (2006). Transparency: Panacea or Pandora's box. *Journal of Management Development, 25*(10), 937–941.

Woodward, W. D. (2000). Transactional philosophy as a basis for dialogue in public relations. *Journal of Public Relations Research, 12*(3), 255–275.

Yang, S.-U. (2007). An integrated model for organization-public relational outcomes, organizational reputation, and their antecedents. *Journal of Public Relations Research, 19*(2), 91–121.

8

756*

The Legitimacy of a Baseball Number

Josh Boyd
Purdue University

Baseball is a game played "by the numbers." Managers make late-inning changes because they're "playing the percentages," and dedicated fans pore over statistics searching for explanations or hope. Certain milestones almost guarantee entrance into the Baseball Hall of Fame in Cooperstown, New York: 300 wins, 500 home runs, 3000 hits.

Baseball treasures its records as well. As the oldest continuous professional sport in America (the Cincinnati club began in 1869), baseball's oldest and loftiest records are revered and memorized: 56—number of games in the longest hitting streak, by Joe DiMaggio; 4256—career hit total of Pete Rose (who broke Ty Cobb's record of 4191). And until recent years, there were four numbers surrounding baseball's home run records: 714—Babe Ruth's career home run total, a record that stood until 1974; 755—Hank Aaron's total as the new home run king; 60—the number of home runs Babe Ruth hit in the single season of 1927; and the infamous 61*—the number of home runs Roger Maris hit in 1961, but with an asterisk because his total spanned a 162-game season while the Babe hit his in only 154 games (the schedule changed between 1927 and 1961).

In the past ten years, Ruth and Maris have been surpassed in single-season totals six times. Barry Bonds now holds that record, with 73 homers in 2001 (Baseball-Reference, 2007b).[1] On August 7, 2007, Bonds also captured the career record, hitting his 756th home run in front of the home fans in San Francisco. Despite the magnitude of this achievement, however, famed broadcaster Bob Costas had this to say: "I think ambivalence is the best possible way anyone outside San Francisco can feel about this" (Bell, 2007). "Ambivalence?" Why not "excitement," "awe," "joy?" Both Barry Bonds' records, including the career mark, are overshadowed by the cloud of suspicion that has surrounded him regarding steroid use in the latter half of his career (Fainaru-Wada & Williams, 2006). No one yet knows if these records will someday be subjected to the ignominious asterisk in the record books, but no waiting time is required to observe the way the legitimacy of these new records has been questioned. The Associated Press story announcing the historic home run even raised the issue—"Like him or not, legitimate or not, he is baseball's new home run king" (Associated Press, 2007b).

The concept of legitimacy, which is the consistency of organizational action with social norms (Epstein & Votaw, 1978), has been an important idea in public communication, from politics to management to public relations, for decades. And in public relations, legitimacy's two tenets of utility and responsibility (Boyd, 2000; Epstein, 1972) underpin almost all public relations efforts. Businesses with products no longer perceived as necessary go out of business, and organizations that fail to establish their responsibility (whether by polluting, engaging in discriminatory practices, or committing other ethical violations) find themselves dealing with complaints and negative regulatory or legal consequences.

Weber (1964) analyzed legitimacy as a characteristic of social order, attached to either persons or organizations, and Stillman (1974), Habermas (1979), and Francesconi (1982) pursued political applications. Epstein's (1972) focus on corporate legitimacy as a legal concept led to various management treatments of the concept in the 1970s (e.g., Dowling & Pfeffer, 1975; Epstein & Votaw, 1978; Pfeffer & Salancik, 1978; Sethi, 1977), and more recently, legitimacy has been identified as a concept central to the practice of public relations and crisis communication (e.g., Allen & Caillouet; Boyd, 2000; Bridges, 2004; Cheney & Christensen, 2001; Coombs, 1992; Hearit, 1995; Heath, 2006; Meisenbach & McMillan, 2006; Seeger, 1986). In these cases, however, the notion of "legitimacy" has been applied to organizations (e.g., NASA (Seeger, 1986), the Task Force on Food Assistance (Coombs, 1992)) or to organizational actions (Boyd, 2000). This chapter has a considerably narrower focus: the legitimacy of a number—756—as a new benchmark for baseball.

In order to explore the legitimacy of this number, the chapter will first provide background on Barry Bonds' career and alleged infractions, followed by a review of legitimacy literature. The analysis and conclusions that follow will then look at four key texts that illustrate the weak claims the number 756 has on legitimacy: the words and actions of the commissioner of baseball; the public comments of a noted broadcaster; and statements about Bonds from two other famous sluggers.

The Case of Barry Bonds

Barry Bonds grew up in baseball. Son of baseball star Bobby Bonds, godson of Giant great Willie Mays, and cousin of Yankee "Mr. October" Reggie Jackson (the latter two of whom are in the Hall of Fame), Bonds today owns an incredible career record in his own right, near the end of a career with the Pittsburgh Pirates and the San Francisco Giants. After St. Louis Cardinal slugger Mark McGwire broke the Roger Maris record that had stood for 37 years, the new home run record stood for only three years until Bonds shattered it with his 73.[2] But Bonds did not stop with a single-season record; he continued his assault on the hallowed career totals of Willie Mays (660), Babe Ruth (714), and eventually Hank Aaron (755). The single-season and career home run records go along with a series of other impressive records: most walks in a season, most career walks, and most times winning the Most Valuable Player award (7).[3]

One of the most amazing features of Bonds' career is that his best slugging statistics have come long after most ballplayers have passed their prime. Four of his top five home run seasons came after he turned 35, an age at which most professional baseball players' careers are in decline. His record-breaking season of 2001 came at what is, for baseball, the ancient age of 36. Such a counterintuitive surge in productivity is just one of the factors contributing to suspicions that Bonds, at some point later in his career, began using performance-enhancing substances including steroids.[4]

There is more direct evidence of drug abuse as well. During the 2006 season, Bonds tested positive for the use of amphetamines (Associated Press, 2007a), and he has also been connected to the Bay Area Laboratory Co-Operative (BALCO), apparently a clearinghouse for both legal nutritional supplements and illegal performance-enhancing drugs. In grand jury testimony regarding BALCO, Bonds insisted that he had never knowingly used steroids, but his own admissions and eyewitness testimony revealed that he had used the undetectable steroids known as "The Clear" and "The Cream" (Fainaru-Wada & Williams, 2006). Victor Conte and Greg Anderson, both eventually convicted of steroid-related felonies in the BALCO trial, provided statements and documents (including medication calendars) as evidence of Bonds' use of The Clear, The Cream, human growth hormone, and insulin (Fainaru-Wada & Williams, 2006). Fainaru-Wada and Williams also provide one other bit of circumstantial evidence for Bonds' use of performance-enhancing substances: the "Fat-Free Mass Index" (p. 274). According to this measure, the maximum naturally obtainable score is a 25. In 2002, based on Bonds' own reporting of his weight and body fat, his index was a 28, "well over the level of a 'presumptive diagnosis' of steroid use" (p. 275).

These pieces of circumstantial evidence all fit together to provide media publics, fan publics, and player publics with questions about the nature of Bonds' records in what sportscaster Bob Costas called bluntly "the steroid era . . . now an established notion" (Bell, 2007). Observations similar to the one that Gray Matthews (1995) made about Pete Rose have been made less eloquently about Barry Bonds: "there should be no doubts concerning [his] entitlement to membership in the baseball hall of fame, if such membership was determined by records only" (p. 279). But such membership is subjectively determined by sportswriter voters, influenced heavily by fan sentiment. And so the future question of Barry Bonds' Hall of Fame membership, as well as current questions about whether or not his record "counts," are all about legitimacy.

The Concept of Legitimacy

One complication of the question in this chapter is that the subject of legitimacy inquiry is not exactly an organization, though it is connected to Major League Baseball and the San Francisco Giants. The subject is not even an individual, though Barry Bonds is clearly central and responsible for the attributions of legitimacy or illegitimacy attached to his record. Instead, the subject is the record itself—a number. At each of these levels, the actor would be generally considered "private" as opposed to "public"—baseball is, after all, a business that operates independent of the government, though government intervention has been threatened to address steroid abuse, and though baseball has at times had brushes with federal regulation (Anderson, 2003, 2004). As Ulrich (1995) and Boyd (2001) have observed, however, even "private" organizations are "quasi-public institutions" (Ulrich,

1995, p. 2), and baseball, as the national pastime, is perhaps even more public in its perceived significance, an idea that baseball itself has promoted at various times in its history (Anderson, 2003, 2004).

Legitimacy is really the foundation of all effective communication with publics—without it, any organizational messages or actions will be looked upon with skepticism. Consequently, establishing and maintaining legitimacy is a necessary component of any kind of public relations. Meisenbach and McMillan (2006) identified legitimacy as one of four critical issues in the study of organizational rhetoric. Cheney and Christensen (2001) attach legitimacy more specifically to ethics; are organizational messages consistent and fair? And in a broader assessment of organizational discourse, do message sources possess integrity, and are the consequences of organizational messages positive? Do they represent "genuine public interests" (p. 260)? All of these questions, common to organizational rhetoric, focus on legitimacy as a central issue. In the case of Barry Bonds, the record itself is a message about which legitimacy and ethics have been called into question. For a series of messages to be legitimate, that series needs to be consistent, adaptive, and open "in response to challenges from outsiders" (Cheney & Christensen, 2001, p. 259). The need for legitimacy ideally acts as a constraint on organizational actions (Dowling & Pfeffer, 1975), motivating them to act in ways acceptable to their publics and to respond to challenges openly and honestly. Yet the lack of transparency from Bonds and baseball regarding the source of Bonds' late-career surge do not seem to meet fully legitimacy requirements.

Though legitimacy has several different facets, two seem to be central: in order for an organization to be seen as operating in a manner consistent with social norms, it must be perceived as useful (or competent) and responsible (Boyd, 2000; Epstein, 1972; Hearit, 1995). More broadly, legitimacy recognizes congruency between an organization, or its specific actions, with standards of socially acceptable behavior (Dowling & Pfeffer, 1975; Epstein & Votaw, 1978; Francesconi, 1982; Stillman, 1974). In the case of Barry Bonds' record, the organization is actually a single person (though Fainaru-Wada and Williams (2006) identify several members of Bonds' entourage that might qualify him as a quasi-organization); legitimacy attached to the record would find it both useful (that is, accurate and correct) and responsible (that is, obtained fairly). While many observers apparently have no "use" for this record, most discourse focuses on the "responsibility" aspect of legitimacy that this record struggles to fulfill.

As this instance illustrates, legitimacy can exist in varying degrees (Boyd, 2000; Brummer, 1991; Stillman, 1974). As Boyd (2000) observes, legitimacy does not demand unanimous agreement from all publics. At the same time, "although legitimation does exist in varying degrees, it is socially constructed and controlled by publics, and a significant portion of interested stakeholders must confer legitimacy for it to exist" (p. 346). Indeed, legitimacy is not controlled by organizations, but rather is conferred by publics (Pfeffer & Salancik, 1978). The method by which publics confer this quality upon an organization seems much less clear, but some scholars suggest criteria.

Brummer (1991) offers several criteria that must be met in order for a particular act to attain legitimacy. Two such criteria relevant to this case are that the action be performed appropriately, responsibly, and conscientiously, and that the act will engender the confidence of publics. Questions about organizational goals, organizational methods of operation, and organizational outputs can damage legitimacy (Dowling & Pfeffer, 1975). Legitimacy is particularly important to organizations (and, by extension in this case, persons and even records) heavily dependent on relationships with outsiders (Seeger, 1986); organizations depend on their environments for survival and success (Pfeffer & Salancik, 1978). A fan-driven sport such as baseball clearly needs favorable relationships with its supporters, but Bonds has not engaged in many of the tactics Heath (2006) suggests are effective at building legitimacy, particularly "being proactive and responsive to others' communication and opinion needs" (p. 100). Corporations seeking legitimacy usually bolster it by providing reasons why they are useful and responsible (Hearit, 1995). The difference between Bonds' non-committal grand jury testimony and his public denials is a particularly striking violation of these prescriptions for legitimacy building. As the texts in this study will show, these criteria have not been met adequately.

The Legitimacy of a Number

Baseball's checkered history certainly provides precedent for questioning the legitimacy of a particular result such as Barry Bonds' home run record. Bridges (2004), following Sethi (1977), explains the nature of legitimacy gaps. She argues that such gaps originate in one of two ways: either an organization changes the way it operates or has "an inappropriate behavior discovered," changing people's perceptions of its actions, or society changes its norms of evaluation and the organization, by not changing, violates changed social expectations (pp. 57–58).

In the first case, baseball's bad acts have been "discovered," most notably, in the cases of the 1919 so-called Black Sox gambling scandal (in which eight Chicago White Sox conspired with gamblers to throw the World Series to the Cincinnati Reds) and in the case of Pete Rose, who received a lifetime ban for allegedly betting on baseball games in which he was a participant (Anderson, 2003; Matthews, 1995). The second type of legitimacy gap has presented itself, for instance, when baseball's monopolistic practices (and anti-trust exemption) were investigated because of changing ideas about fair labor treatment (Anderson, 2004). The case of Barry Bonds' record is something of a hybrid; on one hand, allegations of performance-enhancing drug use fall into the first category, but the fact that baseball had no steroid policy until after the new millennium (long after, for instance, the Olympic movement had a strong anti-doping policy) indicates that part of the reason for this gap is that society changed its tolerance for such enhancements long before baseball did. In any event, baseball is no stranger to legitimacy-threatening controversies, even with stars as big as Barry Bonds.[5]

Four Legitimacy-Threatening Texts

To be sure, there have been legitimating actions: Major League Baseball hosts a special Barry Bonds page (www.barrybonds.com), Bonds himself speaks on his own behalf, and the Giants showed congratulatory video messages in the final days of the chase from other sports legends, including football's Joe Montana, basketball's

Michael Jordan, hockey's Wayne Gretzky, and boxing's Muhammad Ali (Kaplan, 2007). Rather than studying Bonds' or baseball's legitimating texts, however, this chapter will instead examine four texts that illustrate the legitimacy problems inherent in the number 756. There are certainly other such challenging texts (e.g., the journalistic exposé *Game of Shadows* (Fainaru-Wada & Williams, 2006) and public statements by other current and former players), but these four—only two of which are explicitly judgmental—nicely illustrate the legitimacy struggle that has been constructed around this record. The texts come from members of different but significant publics for baseball: (1) The televised statements of famed sportscaster Bob Costas; (2) The rhetorical actions of Commissioner of Baseball Bud Selig; (3) The well-publicized radio comments of retired Atlanta Braves slugger Dale Murphy; and (4) The congratulatory message released by former home run king Hank Aaron.

Bob Costas

Bob Costas is arguably the best sports broadcaster in the business today. He has won Sportscaster of the Year a record eight times, and he has earned 15 sports Emmy awards (HBO, 2007). He has been the primary network host for the Olympic Games seven times, and he has been involved in broadcasting all three major American sports. In short, he is a respected, recognized voice of American sports media. His public comments on the number 756 directly criticize both the manner in which the number was reached (responsibility) and how well the number represents a true baseball achievement (utility). In short, Costas has no "use" for the new record.

As Bonds approached the record total, Costas aired a program on his eponymous HBO show, *CostasNOW*, about Bonds' alleged drug use. In the program, Costas interviewed one of the drug makers who supposedly supplied Bonds. In response to this program, which clearly challenged the legitimacy of Bonds' achievements, Bonds replied, "Is that the story Bob Costas talked about? A little midget man, who doesn't know jack about baseball, who never played the game before?" Costas' response was clever: "As anyone can plainly see, I'm 5-foot-6½ and a strapping 150, and unlike some people, I came by all of it naturally" (Bloom, 2007a).

More significant than this exchange, largely online or to a specialized sports audience, is the interview between *Today Show* host Matt Lauer and Costas, which reached a much broader audience (Bell, 2007).[6] In this very public text, Costas called Bonds the very symbol of baseball's steroid era; he acknowledged Bonds as an excellent player pre-steroids, but added, "He then went into the stratosphere when he started juicing" (Bell, 2007). Lauer and Costas revisited Costas' earlier assessments of Bonds' record, and Costas did not back down, charging that Bonds would never have reached the record without chemical enhancement. At the same time he chastised Bonds, however, he was really addressing the record itself and the institutional structure that allowed it to come about: "There was an atmosphere in the game—the owners, the commissioner, the players' association, and the players themselves are all complicit in that" (Bell, 2007). So the legitimacy question is not so much about Barry Bonds specifically as it is about the record and how it does not fit with the baseball traditions it purports to surpass. Certainly the skepticism of the nation's top sportscaster casts a shadow of illegitimacy on Bonds' achievement. But Costas is not the only significant figure to weigh in.

Bud Selig

Bud Selig, former owner of baseball's Milwaukee Brewers, became the ninth commissioner of baseball in 1998. The first commissioner, Judge Kenesaw "Mountain" Landis, was appointed by the owners in 1921 to clean up baseball's image following the Black Sox scandal of 1919 (Anderson, 2003). Commissioners since then have included such colorful figures as A. B. "Happy" Chandler, former governor of Kentucky and commissioner when Jackie Robinson broke baseball's color barrier; Peter Ueberroth, who famously directed the 1984 Los Angeles Summer Olympic Games before becoming baseball's boss; and A. Bartlett Giamatti, former president of Yale University who banned Pete Rose from the game and then died suddenly a few days later. Though baseball's commissioners have had different degrees of power and fame, they all represent the "voice" of the game. Hired by team owners, they are the biggest baseball "officials" there are. In such a symbolically and practically significant role, Selig's response to Bonds' pursuit is noteworthy. Though Selig has little to say directly about the allegations of Bonds' drug use (responsibility), his omissions and ambiguities reveal definite reservations about the respect the new record deserves (utility).

Perhaps what is most noteworthy, as sports reporter Jayson Stark (2007) has observed, is what Selig has not said. In the days leading up to the big event, Selig was noncommittal about attendance, finally attending the game when Bonds tied the record, but not the game where Bonds broke the record. And when asked during this time whether Bonds' record would be "legitimate," Selig responded, "We're here to watch to see whether he does it. And whatever else happens, I'm not passing judgment—nor should I" (Stark, 2007). Though this falls short of condemnation, it falls squarely into "damning with faint praise." He could have endorsed the record wholeheartedly—"Of course it's legitimate; Barry Bonds is one of the greatest sluggers to play the game." He could have said, more neutrally, "It is certainly going to be an amazing achievement." But in refusing to pass judgment, his implication is that—at the very least—the question of legitimacy, and judgment about that legitimacy, is an open one. Selig did not even acknowledge the record at times when *not* acknowledging it seemed to send a clear message. When Bonds' Giants were playing in Selig's hometown of Milwaukee in late July, Selig went to a game because, in his words, it was "a beautiful night" and "a game that's important in the pennant race." In an eight-minute conversation with reporters, Selig never once mentioned the name "Barry Bonds" or the fact that he was within striking distance of Hank Aaron's record (Stark, 2007).

After the record-breaking home run, which Selig missed, ironically, because he was in New York to meet with the person heading up baseball's investigation of steroid use (ESPN, 2007), he released the following statement:

> I congratulate Barry Bonds for establishing a new, career home run record. Barry's achievement is noteworthy and remarkable. After Barry came out of the game, I congratulated him by telephone and had MLB executive

vice president Jimmie Lee Solomon and Hall of Famer Frank Robinson—both of whom were at the game and witnessed the record-breaking home run—meet with him on my behalf. While the issues which have swirled around this record will continue to work themselves toward resolution, today is a day for congratulations on a truly remarkable achievement.

(Bloom, 2007b)

In keeping with his reticence to talk about the achievement before it happened, this statement is again an endorsement so weak as to do almost nothing to build the record's legitimacy. Not only does the commissioner mention "the issues which have swirled around this record" in his congratulatory statement, but he also shows no optimism that Bonds or the record will be legitimated—rather than "innocence" or "justification," "resolution" is the best he can predict. Because the focus of this examination is on the legitimacy of a number, notice the descriptors Selig uses to characterize the record: "new," "noteworthy," and "remarkable" (twice). These carefully chosen adjectives in no way connote praise. That the record is "new" is uncontestable, and that it is "noteworthy" and "remarkable" are self-evident (the commissioner is "noting" and "remarking" on it). This statement, in fact, mirrors the careful statement Selig gave after he witnessed Bonds tie the record in San Diego. After offering congratulations, he immediately added, "No matter what anyone thinks of the controversy surrounding this event, Mr. Bonds' achievement is noteworthy and remarkable" (Doyel, 2007). In addition to again raising the specter of legitimacy in a congratulatory message, missing from both statements are any words that might add legitimacy to the record: "amazing," "impressive," "well-deserved," "earned," "wonderful." Selig's word choices could just as easily be applied to any interesting scandal. In Anderson's (2003) study of five key events affecting baseball's image, he concluded that Major League Baseball has actively employed public relations techniques in order to build legitimacy. With such an institutional history of legitimacy building, Selig's ambiguity about the nature of Bonds' achievement is even more striking.

In contrast to Commissioner Selig's tacit disapproval, former commissioner A. Bartlett Giamatti, who presided over the Pete Rose debacle, explicitly discussed his duty to protect baseball's integrity (Matthews, 1995). In meting out Rose's lifetime ban, Giamatti (1989) said, "I believe baseball is an important, enduring American institution. It must assert and aspire to the highest principles—of integrity, of professionalism, of performance, of fair play within its rules" (p. 10C). Such statements of baseball's values and the connection of those values to particular actions (in this case, the record of Barry Bonds) have been missing from the current commissioner. Rather than laying to rest whispers about legitimacy by making an official organizational pronouncement, Selig's seeming ambivalence has only allowed legitimacy questions to persist.

Dale Murphy

Dale Murphy is a retired baseball player. Though certainly not in the category of Barry Bonds, he played 18 seasons in the major leagues, winning two National

League MVP awards with the Atlanta Braves in 1982 and 1983. Murphy is famous enough in baseball that after he voiced his opinion about the record's legitimacy on Salt Lake City's 1280 AM radio station, it was national news. Murphy's comments addressed the question of what parents should tell their children about Bonds and the record. His answer? "You say, 'This is what happens when you take steroids. Your dad doesn't want to watch this, because it's drug abuse'" (Monson, 2007). Like Costas but with even more force, Murphy attacked both the manner in which the record was achieved (with an emphasis on the irresponsibility of drug use) and the value (utility) of the record itself.

Murphy disparaged the record's responsibility in comparison to another Atlanta Brave, Hank Aaron: "There is enough evidence to me to say without a doubt that [Bonds] used performance-enhancing drugs. He hit 73 home runs when he was 37. Hank would have hit 855 if he had the same advantage" (Monson, 2007). For support, he cited Bonds himself (alluding to Bonds' grand jury testimony in the BALCO case): "He hasn't denied it. He said he took it, but didn't know what it was. We found out later it was steroids. . . . I don't have a problem saying I know he [used performance-enhancing drugs]. It's obvious." As did Costas, Murphy acknowledged Bonds' natural skill, demonstrated before his alleged drug use began: "Barry's a great player, but he put an asterisk by his name on his own. He's deserved all the negative publicity that he's getting."

These comments again recognize the role that responsibility plays in the construction of legitimacy. The method of achieving the record is the primary source of illegitimacy—"he put an asterisk by his name on his own." The root of Murphy's complaint is the irresponsibility with which Bonds reached the mark. Interestingly, the lack of equal opportunity is another part of Murphy's assessment of illegitimacy. If all players used steroids, Murphy charged, then Hank Aaron's record would still be out of reach. He argued that the record is not legitimate because it is not a like comparison with home run records of old—drug-induced home run muscle can't be compared with non-drug-induced home run muscle.

Hank Aaron

The fourth key text, and the most neutral, comes from the man whose record Bonds broke: Hank Aaron. Aaron, in addition to holding the career home run mark for 33 years, still holds the career records for runs batted in, extra-base hits, and total bases. He is third on the all-time hits list, and he was inducted into the Hall of Fame in 1982. Currently an executive with the Atlanta Braves, Aaron was publicly silent through most of Bonds' pursuit of the record. On the record-breaking night, however, he broke that silence with a recorded message on the Giants' video screen. Aaron's diplomatic video message does not address the legitimacy question of responsibility, but a close reading reveals subtle jabs at the usefulness (value) of the record that undermine its overall legitimacy.

Though he did not attend the historic game in person, Aaron offered these words:

From the desk of Henry Aaron:

I would like to offer my congratulations to Barry Bonds on becoming baseball's career home run leader. It is a great accomplishment which required skill, longevity and determination. Throughout the past century, the home run has held a special place in baseball and I have been privileged to hold this record for 33 of those years. I move over now and offer my best wishes to Barry and his family on this historic achievement. My hope today, as it was on that April evening in 1974, is that the achievement of this record will inspire others to chase their own dreams.

(Associated Press, 2007c)[7]

This is much more complimentary than Selig's statement, but it also served a different purpose—Aaron was asked, and agreed, to offer a celebratory message as a fellow sports legend. Despite the grace with which he completed this task, however, close reading of the statement reveals some interesting ambiguity, ambiguity that does little to substantiate claims of legitimacy for the new record.

He begins with "I would like to offer my congratulations"—a common enough construction, to be sure, but indicating perhaps a bit of hesitation: "I would like to, but …." A stronger statement would have been simply, "I congratulate Barry Bonds." Aaron's adjectives are kinder—the achievement is "great," and "historic"; still not effusive, but better than Selig's. "Skill, longevity and determination" are positive attributes, to be sure; missing from the list is anything resembling "hard work" (presumably one of the things for which steroids lessen the need). Aaron's focus seems more on the record, however (and particularly the 33 years he held it) than on Bonds himself or on Bonds as a worthy holder of the record. Aaron does pass along "best wishes," but those are in part for Bonds' family. No praise of Bonds or any of his particular qualities is present—nothing like, "I am proud to hand the record off to such an outstanding ball player," or "Though it is on one hand sad to drop to number two, it is happy on the other hand that I can entrust the record to someone like Barry Bonds." The closing statement is interesting as well, in that it removes the focus from Bonds and his ownership of the record, reminding fans of Aaron's record-setting day and appealing to something larger than the game. The sentence has almost a surprise ending—Aaron hopes that the achievement of the record will . . . bring as much joy to Barry Bonds as it has to him? Stand for another 33 years? Be recognized for the outstanding accomplishment that it is? No—"inspire others to chase their own dreams." Aaron's statement meets the situational requirements, but does so in a very contained sort of way, acknowledging the record without lauding its new caretaker.

Conclusion

Legitimacy Lessons

Other events will affect the way baseball history judges this record. The federal perjury investigation, former Senator George Mitchell's investigation into steroid use, potential Congressional hearings, the final stages of Bonds' career—all of these things will affect the legacy of 756. But none of these things have to take place for the legitimacy of the record to remain an open and hotly debated issue. As the four statements examined in this chapter illustrate, legitimacy doubts have already dulled the luster of what should be one of the most treasured, exalted records in all of American sports.

One legitimacy application is that *responsible* action is always required for legitimacy. Whether an organization is looking to its overall persona (institutional legitimacy) or to a particular policy (actional legitimacy), it must attend to its publics' expectations for responsible execution. In the same way, a public figure (acting almost as an organization) should be concerned both about generally being accepted as acting in concert with social norms (institutional legitimacy) and with making individual choices that meet the same standards (actional legitimacy). As pop singing stars Michael Jackson and Britney Spears have demonstrated, the repeated failure to achieve actional legitimacy ultimately leads to questions of "institutional"/"individual" legitimacy. But in this chapter, a number itself is the subject of competing legitimacy claims. Barry Bonds, in baseball's "steroid era," seems to be only context for this number that is up for such a great legitimacy debate.

Like 756, other numbers and achievements, inside and outside of sports, require legitimation: record-shattering Olympic performances (such as Ben Johnson's later discredited 100-meter sprint at the 1988 Summer Olympic Games), surprising scientific claims (such as cold fusion), and performance-based milestones (such as incredibly productive political fundraisers) all lead to questions. In all of these cases, the number appears to speak for itself—the new record is up in lights, or on an official report. But questions about utility (should this achievement "count?" Do publics have any use for it?) persist. Closely connected to such misgivings is the question, "How was this spectacular result obtained?" In order to build legitimacy for the number/milestone/claim, the people who are the context for the number must provide evidence of responsibility that will bolster assessments of utility. What gave the athlete the ability to become higher, faster, or stronger? Can the scientific process be replicated? What is the secret to the fundraiser's success? Clear, thorough answers to these questions can establish the legitimacy of numbers and accomplishments that strain at credulity. When such legitimating actions are not taken, however, speculation and investigation often follow, leading to public, on-record statements such as the ones in this chapter, delegitimating the numbers because of a perceived irresponsible process in their achievement that makes them, though impressive, seem useless.

Commissioner Selig, whose statements have been shown to undermine the legitimacy of 756, is one of the few people in this case who had the power to end the legitimacy question by making a forceful decision one way or another. As Bridges (2004) argued, "legitimacy gap theory requires the organization to make certain its house is in order and that its behavior is perceived accurately by the many stakeholders in its environment" (p. 72). Selig's seeming ambivalence about the record neither enhances accurate stakeholder perception nor demonstrates to baseball fans that baseball's house is in order. In contrast to Selig's vague statements about the controversial record, Cutlip (1989) observed that the original baseball commissioner, Commissioner Landis, was hired to restore faith in the ideals of baseball. Matthews (1995) pointed out that in issuing a lifetime ban against Pete Rose for gambling, Commissioner Giamatti emphasized his duty to protect baseball's integrity. Again, Selig's lack of action, and persistent reminders of the controversy surrounding the record, fail to adequately address the record's legitimacy. In order to address the legitimacy of the record, Selig should have used available information to pursue one of two better options: either produce an adequate narrative to explain Bonds' late-career resurgence and strongly affirm the record's legitimacy, or acknowledge the mounds of circumstantial evidence pointing to the record's illegitimacy and prevent Bonds from ever reaching it. By failing to address the legitimacy of the record directly, the legitimacy of baseball more broadly may be threatened by questions about fair play. Mark Corallo, director of public affairs at the Justice Department when the BALCO investigation got underway, expressed the frustration felt by a lot of fans about Bonds' pursuit of the record and its ambiguous legitimacy. Exposing the truth about steroids, he said, "had to do with the guys who had been cheating Stan Musial and Mickey Mantle and Lou Gehrig and Hank Aaron and Willie Mays. . . . That's who they're cheating, they're cheating the baseball immortals and they're cheating the fans" (quote in Fainaru-Wada & Williams, 2006). Failure to address the legitimacy of a milestone may ultimately lead to an institutional legitimacy crisis. In this case, Selig had the power to affirm or reject legitimacy; he should have done one or the other.

Though the questions about 756* have not yet been officially resolved, one group of fans has made a permanent mark—of sorts—on the record. Marc Ecko, a designer who bought the record-breaking home run ball at auction, gave fans online options to determine what should happen to the ball. They could vote to shoot the ball into space, or they could send it to the Hall of Fame one of two ways: as is, or branded with an asterisk. Of 10 million online votes, 47% voted to brand the ball with an asterisk (compared to 34% who didn't want to change it and 19% who wanted to shoot it into space), and the Hall of Fame agreed to accept the ball in that condition (Curry, 2007). Part of the agreement to accept the ball is that the Hall will not hide the asterisk. So whether or not baseball's leaders ever make any kind of official move or pronouncement about the new record's legitimacy, there will be at least one sort of asterisk attached to it and on public display.

Extensions to Corporatas/Communitas Goals in Sport

Sport is a site of struggle between the values of "communitas" and "corporatas," where communitas values the teamwork and community building that ideally is found at the ballpark, and corporatas is its opposite, valuing structure, hierarchy, and individual achievement (Trujillo, 1992). Boyd and Stahley (2008) add that communitas ideals, such as enjoyment, experience, and means, contrast with more individualistic corporatas ideals of competition, profit, and ends.

Bonds, with all his individual achievements, records, and profits,[8] epitomizes the notion of the corporatas "star," not the communitas "hero" (Boyd & Stahley, in press). The allegations of Bonds' chemical pursuit of excellence reflect an emphasis on individual achievement and advancement, rather than the game of baseball, that demonstrates Heath's (2006) observation about the difference between corporatas and its opposite, communitas: "The concept of communitas features the symbolic and instrumental reality of community as transcending the structures and functions of individuals and organizations" (p. 106). Allegedly using steroids to break individual records (and become the highest-paid player in Major League Baseball) is bound very closely to individual, not community, structures and functions. As Trujillo (1992) observed, "corporatas is anti-communitas not because it seeks to destroy the community but rather because it reveals that community is ultimately powerless and clearly irrelevant" (p. 275).

And so the contrast between communitas and corporatas leads back to legitimacy. The baseball community, from sportscaster to players to executive authority, has shown itself powerless by not taking decisive action regarding the legitimacy of the number 756. As a result, the heritage and community of baseball, the oldest sport culture in America, is diminished. The results might not all be in, but the failure to affirm or deny the legitimacy of the home run record has resulted in reduced legitimacy for the record and, perhaps by extension, the sport. Legitimacy is not limited only to organizations and public figures—even numbers require legitimacy work from the entire community.

Notes

1 Unless otherwise noted, all baseball statistics (including salary data) are taken from www.baseball-reference.com.
2 Sammy Sosa, meanwhile, has the distinction of being the only player in baseball history to hit more than 60 home runs in a season three times, but he never won the home run title (he trailed Mark McGwire twice and Barry Bonds once).
3 Bonds won the award in 1990, 1992, 1993, 2001, 2002, 2003, and 2004 (Baseball-Reference, 2007a). No other player in professional baseball, basketball, or football has ever won as many as seven MVP awards.
4 The initial official ban was a 2002 policy that served as more of a fact-finding approach. After the first round of testing found 7% of major leaguers testing positive for only a limited group of banned substances, however (Bloom, 2003), the policy was strengthened, leading to automatic 10-game bans in 2005 for twelve players, most notable among them the Baltimore Orioles' slugger Rafael Palmeiro (Baseball-Almanac, 2007). In baseball's new collective bargaining agreement, the policy was made even tougher, with automatic 50-game suspensions for initial positive tests, 100-game suspensions for second positive tests, and lifetime bans for third positive tests (MLB, 2007). As part of this new policy, amphetamines were added to the banned list, but with milder repercussions.
5 Shoeless Joe Jackson, implicated in the 1919 Black Sox gambling scandal (Anderson, 2003), and Pete Rose, baseball's all-time hits leader under a lifetime ban since 1989 (Giamatti, 1989), in their eras certainly equaled Bonds in fame.
6 NBC's *Today Show* continues to be the dominant morning news program; for the week of July 30, the program drew 4.769 million viewers (mediabistro.com, 2007).
7 A reader comment posted after Aaron's statement creatively labels Bonds "Juicy McDruggerson."
8 Bonds has earned, by far, more money in his career than any player ever to play the game—more than $172 million.

References

Allen, M. W., & Caillouet, R. H. (1994). Legitimation endeavors: Impression management strategies used by an organization in crisis. *Communication Monographs, 61,* 44–62.

Anderson, W. B. (2003). Crafting the national pastime's image: The history of Major League Baseball public relations. *Journalism & Communication Monographs, 5*(1), 7–43.

Anderson, W. B. (2004). Major League Baseball under investigation: How the industry used public relations to promote its past to save its present. *Public Relations Review, 30,* 439–445.

Associated Press. (2007a, January 11). Report: Bonds failed amphetamine test. Retrieved September 11, 2007, from http://sports.espn.go.com/mlb/news/story?id=2727325

Associated Press. (2007b, August 8). Bonds moves into eternity, assumes MLB home run record. Retrieved September 5, 2007, from http://sports.espn.go.com/mlb/news/story?id=2965584

Associated Press. (2007c, August 8). Hank Aaron statement on Barry Bonds' achievement. *USAToday* online. Retrieved September 14, 2007, from http://www.usatoday.com/sports/baseball/2007-08-08-874656280_x.htm

Baseball-Almanac. (2007). Steroid suspensions. Retrieved September 11, 2007, from http://www.baseball-almanac.com/legendary/steroids_baseball.shtml

Baseball-Reference. (2007a). Barry Bonds. Retrieved Sept. 7, 2007, from http://www.baseball-reference.com/b/bondsba01.shtml

Baseball-Reference. (2007b). Single-season records & leaders for home runs. Retrieved Sept. 7, 2007, from http://www.baseball-reference.com/leaders/HR_season.shtml

Bell, J. (Executive Producer). (2007, July 30). Matt Lauer interview with Bob Costas. *The Today Show* [Television broadcast]. New York: National Broadcasting Company.

Bloom, B. M. (2003, November 13). Mandatory steroid testing to begin. MLB.com. Retrieved September 11, 2007, from http://anaheim.angels.mlb.com/news/article.jsp?ymd=20031113&content_id=603458&vkey=news_mlb&fext=.jsp&c_id=mlb

Bloom, B. M. (2007a, July 26). Bonds issues statement on Costas. MLB.com. Retrieved September 13, 2007, from http://mlb.mlb.com/news/article.jsp?ymd=20070726&content_id=2112020&vkey=news_mlb&fext=.jsp&c_id=mlb

Bloom, B. M. (2007b, August 8). BB king: Bonds hits home run no. 756. MLB.com. Retrieved September 14, 2007, from http://mlb.mlb.com/news/article.jsp?ymd=20070806&content_id=2133618&vkey=news_mlb&fext=.jsp&c_id=mlb

Boyd, J. (2000). Actional legitimation: No crisis necessary. *Journal of Public Relations Research, 12,* 341–353.

Boyd, J. (2001). Corporate rhetoric participates in public dialogue: A solution to the public/private conundrum. *Southern Communication Journal, 66,* 279–292.

Boyd, J., & Stahley, M. B. (2008). Communitas/corporatas tensions in organizational rhetoric: Finding a balance in sports public relations. *Journal of Public Relations Research, 20*(3), 251–270.

Bridges, J. A. (2004). Corporate issues campaigns: Six theoretical approaches. *Communication Theory, 14,* 51–77.

Brummer, J. J. (1991). *Corporate responsibility and legitimacy: An interdisciplinary analysis.* New York: Greenwood Press.

Cheney, G., & Christensen, L. T. (2001). Organizational identity: Linkages between internal and external communication. In F. M. Jablin & L. L. Putnam (Eds.), *The new handbook of organizational communication* (pp. 231–269). Thousand Oaks, CA: Sage.

Coombs, W. T. (1992). The failure of the Task Force on Food Assistance: A case study of the role of legitimacy in issue management. *Journal of Public Relations Research, 4,* 101–122.

Curry, J. (2007, September 27). Bonds baseball to be branded with asterisk. *New York Times* online. Retrieved September 28, 2007, from http://www.nytimes.com/2007/09/27/sports/baseball/27ball.html?em&ex=1191124800&en=aaa5 1188845a50c2&ei=5087%0A

Cutlip, S. M. (1989). A public relations footnote to the Pete Rose affair. *Public Relations Review, 15*(4), 46–48.

Dowling, J., & Pfeffer, J. (1975). Organizational legitimacy: Social values and organizational behavior. *Pacific Sociological Review, 18,* 122–136.

Doyel, G. (2007, August 5). The verdict is in: Selig thrives at showing incompetence. CBS Sportsline. Retrieved September 5, 2007, from http://www.sportsline.com/print/mlb/story/10281780

Epstein, E. M. (1972). The historical enigma of corporate legitimacy. *California Law Review, 60,* 1701–1717.

Epstein, E. M., & Votaw, D. (1978). Legitimacy. In E. M. Epstein & D. Votaw (Eds.), *Rationality, legitimacy, responsibility: Search for new directions in business and society* (pp. 69–82). Santa Monica, CA: Goodyear.

ESPN. (2007, August 8). Selig meets Mitchell, heads back to Milwaukee. Retrieved September 14, 2007, from http://sports.espn.go.com/mlb/news/story?id=2965348

Fainaru-Wada, M., & Williams, L. (2006). *Game of shadows: Barry Bonds, BALCO, and the steroids scandal that rocked professional sports.* New York: Gotham Books.

Francesconi, R. A. (1982). James Hunt, the Wilmington 10, and institutional legitimacy. *Quarterly Journal of Speech, 68,* 47–59.

Giamatti, A. B. (1989, August 24). Statement on Pete Rose. Reprinted August 25, 1989, in *USA Today,* 10C.

Habermas, J. (1979). *Communication and the evolution of society.* T. McCarthy, Trans. Boston: Beacon Press.

HBO. (2007). Bob Costas bio. CostasNOW. Retrieved September 13, 2007, from http://www.hbo.com/costasnow/bios/bob_costas.html

Hearit, K. M. (1995). "Mistakes were made": Organizations, apologia, and crises of social legitimacy. *Communication Studies, 46,* 1–17.

Heath, R. L. (2006). Onward into more fog: Thoughts on public relations' research directions. *Journal of Public Relations Research, 18,* 93–114.

Kaplan, D. A. (2007, August 9). The secret videotape: How the San Francisco Giants got Hank Aaron to record a video tribute to Barry Bonds. *Newsweek* online. Retrieved September 14, 2007, from http://www.msnbc.msn.com/id/20191137/site/newsweek/

Matthews, G. (1995). Epideictic rhetoric and baseball: Nurturing community through controversy. *Southern Communication Journal, 60,* 275–291.

Mediabistro.com. (2007). Morning show ratings: Week of July 30. Retrieved

September 13, 2007, from http://www.mediabistro.com/tvnewser/morning_show_ratings/default.asp

Meisenbach, R. J., & McMillan, J. J. (2006). Blurring the boundaries: Historical developments and future directions in organizational rhetoric. In C. S. Beck (Ed.), *Communication yearbook* (pp. 99–141). Mahwah, NJ: Lawrence Erlbaum.

MLB. (2007). MLB executives: Allan H. (Bud) Selig. The official site of Major League Baseball. Retrieved September 11, 2007, from http://mlb.mlb.com/mlb/official_info/about_mlb/executives.jsp?bio=selig_bud

Monson, G. (2007, August 8). MONSON: Murphy doesn't mince words about Bonds. *The Salt Lake Tribune* online. Retrieved August 29, 2007, from http://www.sltrib.com/sports/ci_6570668

Pfeffer, J., & Salancik, G. R. (1978). *The external control of organizations: A resource dependence perspective.* New York: Harper & Row.

Seeger, M. W. (1986). The Challenger tragedy and search for legitimacy. *Central States Speech Journal, 37,* 147–157.

Sethi, S. P. (1977). *Advocacy advertising and large corporations: Social conflict, big business image, the news media, and public policy.* Lexington, MA: Lexington Books.

Stark, J. (2007, July 20). Selig's non-statement about Bonds says plenty. ESPN.com. Retrieved September 5, 2007, from http://sports.espn.go.com/mlb/columns/story?columnist=stark_jayson&id=2944073

Stillman, P. G. (1974). The concept of legitimacy. *Polity, 7,* 32–56.

Trujillo, N. (1992). White knights, poker games, and the invasion of the carpetbaggers: Interpreting the sale of a professional sports franchise. In E. L. Toth & R. L. Heath (Eds.), *Rhetorical and critical approaches to public relations,* (pp. 257–277). Hillsdale, NJ: Lawrence Erlbaum.

Ulrich, P. (1995). Introduction. In P. Ulrich & C. Sarasin (Eds.), *Facing public interest: The ethical challenge to business policy and corporate communications* (pp. 1–10). Dordrecht, the Netherlands: Kluwer.

Weber, M. (1964). *The theory of social and economic organization.* A. M. Henderson & T. Parsons, Trans. New York: The Free Press.

9

THE DEVIL IN DISGUISE
Vioxx, Drug Safety, and the FDA

Jane Stuart Baker and Charles Conrad
Texas A&M University

Chris Cudahy
Atlantic Baptist University

Jennifer Willyard
The Justice Project, Austin, Texas

Contemporary research on organizational rhetoric (Cheney & Christensen, 2001; Cheney, Christensen, Conrad, & Lair, 2004; McKie, 2001) has done an excellent job of explaining how organizational rhetors draw upon cultural assumptions to develop positive images/reputations and manage crises. Our goal here is to extend that work by suggesting that organizations in regulated high-tech industries face a unique rhetorical situation, and have available a set of distinctive rhetorical strategies for managing the challenges they face.

Although Americans long have been deeply suspicious of government action in general and government regulation of private sector organizations in particular (Aune, 2001; Hirschman, 1991), the high "net catastrophic potential" (Perrow, 1984) of high-tech industries has generated more support for regulation than in less risky sectors of the economy. However, high-tech organizations also have a distinctive rhetorical advantage. Because they deal in "science," the key secular god term of the modern era (Burke, 1972; Lessl, 1989, 1999; Penrose, 2000; Weaver, 1953), industry rhetors have a powerful appeal available that other organizations do not. Science is central to modern life, and is necessary for continued social and economic progress: "The scientific culture embraces an ideology of progress that . . . reaffirm[s] an entirely familiar identification between science and the values that science's host culture attaches to modernity—progress, change, novelty and intellectual freedom" (Lessl, 1999, pp. 149, 151). We live, says Neil Postman, in a Technopoly that can be defined as "the submission of all forms of cultural life to the sovereignty of technique and technology. . . .Those who feel most comfortable in Technopoly are those who are convinced that technical progress is humanity's supreme achievement and the instrument by which our most profound dilemmas may be solved" (1992, pp. 52, 71).

As well as providing a technology-based "good life," science comforts us by seeming to provide a stable, unbiased, objective refuge in an uncertain and conflict-filled world. Since the Enlightenment, the certainty of science has supplemented, and for some people substituted for, the certainty of religious belief (Weaver, 2001, p. 1354). The scientist has replaced (or supplemented) the priest as the source of truth and/or the arbiter of competing value claims (Lessl, 1989, p. 183). Ironically, each of the key terms of scientific discourse— "science," "objectivity," and "unbiased"—are symbolic/rhetorical constructions (Kuhn, 1962; Feyerabend, 1978) and "miracles" are miraculous only if successfully defined as such. Debates about whether or not astrologists, psychoanalysts, economists, sociologists, environmentalists, and so on can legitimately claim the title of "scientist" are testimony to both the power of the term and to the contested nature of its definition; the popularity of books showing readers "how to lie with statistics" testify to the rhetorical nature of scientific methods.

A related issue involves ownership of the scientific enterprise. At its inception, people assumed that the promise of science would be best fulfilled if the scientific process was completely insulated from larger social concerns such as politics or profits (Gross, 1990). Because of the power that science holds to change societies, there was a consensus that it should not be used to fulfill narrow, special interests at the expense of the general public. However, by the middle of the nineteenth century, "scientific growth could no longer be sustained by the efforts of isolated amateurs, gentlemen scientists—and often clergy—who dabbled in experimentation . . . Science had outgrown this cradle. It needed the wealth and ideological support of institutions that were specifically tailored to meet the needs of organized laboratory research" (Lessl, 1999, p. 163). In order to obtain needed resources, scientists forged alliances with governments, politicizing the scientific process, and also with industry—conflating corporate profit with the ideals of discovery and public service.

The outcome was a very complicated rhetorical situation (Bitzer, 1970, 1980), both for spokespersons of high-tech organizations and for people whose trusted job it is to represent public interests. To the extent that organizations can persuade stakeholders that their actions are designed to create "miracles" for the common good, they will have high levels of legitimacy. But, to the extent that they are seen as seeking profit at the expense of society, they lose the support necessary to maintain their independence. Conversely, as long as critics are viewed as protecting the public, their efforts to "rein in" high-tech organizations are likely to be appealing; to the extent that they can be cast as unnecessary or unproductive interference in the production of scientific "miracles," they will be condemned. Using the U.S. pharmaceutical industry in general, and Merck's management of the recent Vioxx controversy in particular, we will examine this complex rhetorical situation.

Drugs, Rhetoric, and Crisis Management

In comparison to other industrialized countries, the U.S. relies heavily on regulation, and/or regulation plus government subsidies, to persuade organizations to act in ways that fulfill societal interests, instead of doing so through direct government ownership or control (Wilson, 1974). Political scientist James Wilson explains that this is because historically governments in the U.S. have not been politically strong enough to either control business or ignore popular pressure to do so (see also Perrow, 2002, on the relative power of state and federal government and its impact on the development of the "American system"). As a result, regulation is piecemeal, highly contested, often misunderstood, and constantly changing in focus and intensity as political pressures shift.

Although Americans generally believe that government regulations/regulatory agencies are created or strengthened in response to popular outcry, historically this has only rarely been the case (Llewellyn, 2007; Nadel, 1971; Wilson, 1974).[1] In those few cases when regulation has resulted from public pressure, the rhetorical strategies used to legitimize these government interventions in the free market are highly predictable: policy debates focus public attention on a moral "evil," personified in a corporation or industry, and illustrated by the evocation of "horror stories" that exaggerate the virtue of victims and the venality of perpetrators (Brown & Marmor, 1994; Conrad & Millay, 2000; Hackey, 1997; Stone, 1989). Proposed regulations are strong, stripped of substantive compromises in order to sustain public support long enough for the regulations to be enacted.

Of course the industries to be regulated have absolute economic incentives to fight measures that emerge in response to public outcry (Baumgartner & Leech, 1998; Cobb & Ross, 1997; Conrad 2004; Grossman & Helpman, 2001), but they often are unable to do so in public lest they further inflame popular indignation. Instead, they quietly negotiate procedural bargains with legislators that shift the political conflict from public debate over the regulations themselves to private deliberations about mechanisms of enforcement (Llewellyn, 2007; Wilson, 1974, pp. 145–146, 151). These bargains allow regulated organizations and industries to quietly lobby regulatory agencies in an effort to ultimately reduce the regulatory burden (Conrad & Abbott, 2007).[2] These arrangements may provide stability for a time, but when highly public "regulatory failures" occur, they can make it appear that the regulators have been "captured" by the industry they are supposed to regulate, engendering another round of popular outcry (Wilson, 1974).[3]

More often in U.S. history, regulation has emerged in response to pressure from industries themselves (Lipton & Harris, Sept. 16, 2007). Their goal usually is to obtain legal protections for themselves or to impose legal burdens on competitors, actions that typically are justified through a rhetoric of "reining in excessive" competition or rescuing the economy or an industry from "chaos."[4] Once the regulatory agency is created it will act to eliminate or reduce price competition in the industry and/or restrict the entry of new firms into the sector. The corporate beneficiaries will maintain strong influence over the agency, and the two will seek to maintain a low profile in order to escape the attention of the diffused-and-weakly-organized interests who pay the bills of regulation, primarily consumers and/or taxpayers (Stigler, 1971). Regulation that develops through these processes is likely to meet fierce resistance from advocates of "public responsibility" because the costs of regulation are largely borne by citizens while the benefits are accrued by few, concentrated, and politically well-organized corporate actors. In normal times, this opposition is unlikely to succeed, precisely because of differences in the capacity of the two sides to mobilize political pressure. However, in cases of apparent "regulatory failure," the relationship between regulators and the industries they regulate can "become controversial [and] will be defended by attempting to show that eliminating price competition is an appropriate means for ensuring safety, ending fraud, and promoting amenity (correcting evils allegedly caused by price cutters, who will be termed 'fly-by-night' operators") (Wilson, 1974, p. 142; see also Leiss, 2001; Perrow, 2002; and Powell & Leiss, 1997).[5]

Consequently, regardless of the origins of particular regulatory agencies, regulators and the organizations/industries they regulate face complex rhetorical problems. In order to legitimize themselves, regulators must appear to be sufficiently activist to forestall accusations that they have been "captured," but sufficiently responsive to industry needs to keep anti-regulation, free market advocates at bay.[6] Conversely, corporations in regulated industries must appear to be sufficiently "socially responsible" and "law-abiding" to undercut calls for increased regulation, but not so compliant that they excessively undermine growth, profitability, executive compensation, or share value. Fortunately, both parties have a number of rhetorical strategies available to help them deal with these dilemmas.

Some strategies are relatively simple—companies (or industries) can legitimize their actions by claiming to have followed all applicable laws, rules, and regulations (Elsbach, 1994; Watkins-Allen & Caillouet, 1994), while hoping that stakeholders forget or ignore the role that they played in crafting (and/or weakening) those regulations (Greider, 1993). Other strategies involve more complex, dramaturgical rituals. For example, regulators can impose or threaten to impose economically trivial demands on corporations while producing rhetoric that exaggerates the severity of the sanction(s). In turn, organizations/industries decry regulatory "activism," and exaggerate the economic impact of the regulatory agency's actions, while eventually acquiescing in order to demonstrate their cooperative attitudes and sense of social responsibility. Enlisting the media's help in exaggerating the severity of the conflict only strengthens the effect. Regulators then can congratulate the organization/industry for its flexibility, cooperativeness, and improved practices (Ritti & Silver, 1986). To make the dramaturgy credible, both sides must resist the temptation to use strategies that undermine the credibility of the other side.

The FDA and the Cox-2 Inhibitor (Celebrex/Vioxx/Bextra) Controversy

Pharmaceuticals is one of the most heavily regulated industries in the U.S. economy (Carpenter, 2004). Consequently, in the highly anti-regulatory political climate that has existed in the U.S. since the late 1970s (Kuttner, 1999), reputation management has been exceptionally important and exceptionally difficult for the industry's primary regulator, the U.S. Food and Drug Administration (FDA). Not only is a positive image necessary for the FDA to attract and retain qualified employees and adequate budgets, it also allows the agency to legitimize its actions in highly visible "life-and-death" decisions that carry significant political stakes (Carpenter, 2001; Hilts, 2004; Pew Research Center, 1998). The agency's rhetorical challenge is increased both by the presence of multiple stakeholder groups with very different values, interests, and expertise—the general public, politicians, pharmaceutical firms, and the scientific community—and by the nature of its key decisions. In the language of decision theory, the agency must avoid both "Type I" errors (approving a drug that subsequently is shown to be ineffective and/or have serious negative side effects) and "Type II" errors (rejecting a drug that should have been approved or delaying approval for too long a time).

Historically, avoiding Type I errors has been more important, because the public health effects and impact on the organization's reputation are both more significant and more permanent than avoiding Type II errors (Hilts, 2004). This changed with the AIDS epidemic of the 1980s and the impact of high-profile protests by patients who demanded "fast-tracking" drug approval. Under the Clinton administration, Congress passed two pieces of legislation to streamline the drug approval process. The Prescription Drug User Fee Act (PDUFA) allowed the FDA to charge drug companies application fees. By 2002 more than half of the FDA's approval budget was provided by drug company fees (Avorn, 2004; Moynihan & Cassels, 2005). The FDA Modernization Act of 1997 further accelerated the drug approval process. Between 1993 and 2003 the median time for drug approvals fell by 55% (Okie, 2005) and the number of drug recalls after approval rose from 1.6% between the years 1993 and 1996 to 5.4% from 1997 to 2001, in spite of the fact that during the same period a decreasing percentage of newly approved drugs actually had new active ingredients (Angell, 2005).[7] In spite of this more complicated rhetorical situation and increasing criticism of the agency (see, for example, Angell, 2005; Moynihan & Cassells, 2005; Willman, 2000), its credibility with the general populace remained exceptionally high, with poll data indicating 70% or more approval (Pew, 1998). However, the new century provided the agency with continued challenges. One of the most important involved pain medications called "Cox-2 inhibitors."

Act One: The Symbolic Creation of a "Miracle Drug"

Cox-2 inhibitors (Bextra, Celebrex, and Vioxx) fight pain by blocking an enzyme called cyclooxygenase, or "cox," which is known to cause inflammation. Although no more effective at reducing pain than older generation medications (the N-SAIDs Naproxen, Ibuprofen, and Diclofenac), Cox-2 drugs block cox selectively, leaving intact a form that helps protect the stomach lining (Cox-1). As a result, the drugs were believed to be less irritating to the stomach and therefore useful for people with peptic ulcer disease and other serious digestive tract problems (Duenwald, Oct. 5, 2004). Apparently the reduced gastrointestinal (GI) toxicity provided sufficient impetus for the FDA to approve Cox-2 drugs, even in the face of evidence indicating that the drugs increased cardiovascular clotting (Abramson, 2005).

Marketing Research

Immediately after receiving FDA approval, Celebrex' producers initiated an unprecedented marketing blitz for the drug, both direct ads with patients and indirect contacts with physicians. Within two years, sales of the drug topped $3.1 billion and accounted for one-third of all arthritis drug sales in the U.S. (Abramson, 2005).[8] However, a little less than a year later (September 13, 2000) *JAMA* published the results of a post-approval study of Celebrex that had been required by the FDA and conducted by its manufacturer (code-named CLASS).[9] The actual study ran for 12 months, but the *JAMA* article reported only the first six months of data, and the journal's accompanying very positive editorial was based on the 6-month data alone. However, during the *second* six months of the study, seven serious gastrointestinal complications occurred, six of which were in patients taking Celebrex.

In its report to the FDA, Celebrex' manufacturer claimed that the decision to not report the entire dataset was the result of differential subject dropout rates in the various study groups, an explanation that the FDA flatly rejected. The *JAMA* study also ignored complications other than upper-GI distress (for example, Coronary Heart Disease, or CHD). When all complications were included, Celebrex patients reported 11% more events than other patients, although the difference was not statistically significant. The *Washington Post* reported on the discrepancies between the complete study results and those included in *JAMA*, but overall they received scant media attention. The FDA did respond, however, with its third warning letter to the manufacturer, complaining of "unsubstantiated claims" in Celebrex ads, which also "minimize crucial risk information" and "promote Celebrex for unapproved uses" (cited in Abramson, 2005, p. 32).[10]

Soon after the *JAMA* article appeared, Merck's Cox-2 inhibitor, Vioxx, hit the market. As is typical of "me-too" drugs, marketing was even more intense, and more expensive. By the time it was withdrawn from the market, Merck was spending approximately $100 million per year in direct-to-consumer advertising, a tiny proportion of Vioxx' $2.5 billion per year sales (Meier, Oct. 1, 2004). Two months after the CLASS study was published in *JAMA*, the results of a post-approval study of Vioxx (VIGOR) compared to naproxen appeared in the *New England Journal of Medicine* (*NEJM*, November 23, 2000). The authors concluded that patients taking Vioxx had significantly fewer significant upper-GI events than those taking naproxen. However, a closer reading of the data indicated that the positive effects were limited to patients who also were taking steroids (for example, prednisone). Among patients not taking steroids, the observed differences were statistically nonsignificant (Abramson, 2005, p. 33), suggesting that for the vast majority of patients, Vioxx was no better at avoiding adverse GI events than much less expensive over-the-counter medications.

The original design of the VIGOR trial had a second component, one not reported in the *NEJM* article. A side effect of naproxen's effect of reducing Cox-1 levels is that, like aspirin, it makes blood platelets less "sticky," thus reducing the likelihood of cardiovascular "events." Since Vioxx does not have this effect, the study included a provision to have an independent committee examine the cardiovascular effects of the two drugs. The results revealed a significant increase in the number of myocardial events (n=27, as compared to 21 fewer upper GI events) in patients taking Vioxx. Abramson concludes (2005, p. 35): "Overall, the people in the VIGOR study who took Vioxx were 2.4 times more likely than those who took naproxen to experience a serious cardiovascular complication" (statistical significance of p=.0016). The FDA statistician who examined all cardiovascular events found that patients taking Vioxx were 1.9 times more likely to experience cardiovascular events than those taking naproxen (p=.041). However, neither the *NEJM* article, nor an accompanying highly favorable editorial (which also lauded Celebrex) examined these complications.[11] When pressured, Merck argued that these results stemmed from naproxen's favorable effects on coronary heart disease (CHD), not on any negative effects from taking Vioxx. One month later, the FDA sent Merck a warning letter about its "false, lacking in fair balance, or otherwise misleading" marketing of Vioxx, the second in a series of such letters, and implemented labeling changes for the drug, incorporating warnings relating to the results of the study ("Vioxx," p. 1287).

Subsequent research confirmed the adverse cardiovascular effects of Cox-2 inhibitors.[12] The largest relevant study (named TARGET, and involving 18,325 patients aged 50 or older with no history of CHD and who had been diagnosed with osteoarthritis) compared a second generation Cox-2 drug, lumiracoxib, to naproxen, and did so in a way that better controlled for alternate explanations of results (Schnitzer et al., 2004). However, *Lancet* concluded, "for patients taking low-dose aspirin, it is hard to justify the coxib: there is no benefit in ulcer complication reduction, but the risk of myocardial infarction and hepatotoxicity persist" (p. 640).

Six weeks after the publication of TARGET, Merck's final study of Vioxx side effects, code-named APPROVe, was halted prematurely after 18 months when regulators discovered that patients taking Vioxx were twice as likely to suffer myocardial infarction as those taking a placebo (Topol, 2004). Merck immediately pulled the drug from the market and notified the 2 million people taking it to consult their physicians.[13]

Analysis

In general, research on organizational crisis management suggests that organizational rhetors should move quickly to legitimize their actions in order to protect the organization's reputation. The optimal accommodation strategies seem to be ingratiation, acknowledgement, and, should those strategies fail or otherwise be unavailable, apologia. Watkins-Allen and Caillouet (1994) explain that

> ingratiation is designed to gain audience approval by conveying conformity to the normative institutional environment's rules. Speakers using ingratiation express beliefs, values and attitude similarity; attempt to persuade the target [audience] of the organization's positive qualities, traits, motives and/or intentions, and praise the target in order to gain approval. (Jones, 1964; Jones, Gergen & Jones, 1963, p. 48)

Acknowledgements admit that a negative event has taken place, but assert that "'it wasn't our fault,' or 'we had a good reason for our actions,' or 'the ultimate outcome was positive.'" Although they do not claim the same degree of innocence involved in ingratiation, they strive to "minimize the organization's responsibility for events or attenuate negative perceptions of events" (Elsbach, 1994, p. 65). The final acknowledgment strategy is an *apologia*, which attempts to distance institutional actors from their wrongdoing and reaffirm adherence to key social values (Benoit & Brinson, 1994; Coombs, 1995; Hearit, 1994) through dissociating the organization from the problem while claiming that corrective action has been or soon will be taken. Accommodation strategies are especially appropriate when a crisis portends to seriously damage an organization's reputation (Coombs & Holladay, 2002). The more severe the potential harm to organizational legitimacy, the more necessary it is to employ strategies that accommodate the victims in order to improve relations.

However, denial can be an effective strategy in cases of unambiguous corporate innocence (Benoit & Brinson, 1994; Coombs, 1995; Hearit, 1994, 1995) or when combined with an "institutional" defense—providing evidence that the organization has complied with all operant legal and regulatory requirements. For example, Elsbach found that the California cattle industry's claims that "all products are approved by the Food and Drug Administration on the basis of very stringent tests for safety" (p. 67) both deflected criticism and increased organizational legitimacy (see also Taylor & Bogdan, 1980).[14] Instead, Merck employed denial strategies when there was clear evidence that it had (at least) constructed misleading advertising, and without developing institutional legitimacy. Moreover, it failed to provide evidence refuting the conclusions of other studies. Questioning the methodology used in those studies became progressively less credible as study after study, using different research methods, drew similar conclusions, and as additional evidence that Merck had manipulated the results of its own studies was revealed.

Pharmaceutical organizations have two primary rhetorical advantages when their legitimacy is threatened: the modernist faith in the capacity of science, scientists, and high-tech organizations to produce modern miracles through objective, certain, trustworthy procedures, and their institutional ties to regulatory agencies. Merck had failed to exploit either advantage. Their creative approach to designing, conducting, and interpreting the results of research, combined with their strategic withholding of adverse data undercut their image as "scientists" and made it highly unlikely that any of their audiences would continue to see them as secular "guardians of truth."

In contrast, the FDA's multiple warning letters accusing the company of false advertising served to link the regulator to societal values and enhance its credibility as a guardian of public health. Critics continued to complain that the agency had been slow to act or had not acted forcefully enough, but it *had* acted, and in doing so it shifted the burden of legitimization to Merck while undermining its ability to employ institutional strategies.

Act Two: Merck Goes Public

On September 30, 2004, Merck ran an ad in many national newspapers which announced their withdrawal of Vioxx from the market. The advertisement consisted of a letter from Raymond B. Gilmartin, Chairman, President, and CEO of Merck, and included the company letter head, the CEO's signature, and Merck's company motto: "Where patients come first." The ad typically appeared in the business section of newspapers, but placing it in daily newspapers around the country suggests that it was meant to be viewed by the public at large. In a marked shift toward accommodative rhetoric, Gilmartin asserted that the decision to withdraw Vioxx demonstrated that Merck's "commitment to [its] patients is clear," and concluded that it was taking action "because we believe it best serves the interest of patients." Second, the ad claimed that the withdrawal was "voluntary," and repeated the claim four times in a one-page letter. Third, the company stated that it would "reimburse all patients for their unused VIOXX."

An exceptionally prominent ingratiation technique used by the company was that of social responsibility. Beginning with the title, "Merck Voluntarily Withdraws VIOXX," Merck frequently reminded its readers that the recall was voluntary. Voluntary action casts the organization as more in control of the situation than a recall forced upon them by the FDA, and it can begin the process of rebuilding trust with its stakeholder(s). It created the impression that Merck is a proactive company that takes necessary action by choice and is therefore socially responsible for the health of its patients. Merck also represented itself as socially responsible by proclaiming that sacrifices are being made for patients' welfare. First, the company urged patients to discontinue use of Vioxx and find alternative treatments for pain management. This statement contained two underlying assumptions that depicted Merck as socially responsible: by urging patients to stop use of the drug, Merck conceded future profits (from Vioxx) while simultaneously acknowledging the possibility that patients might find alternative medications with direct competitors. Merck made another monetary sacrifice by ensuring patients that they would receive reimbursement for any unused medication, causing a loss of *existing* profits. In each of these examples, the rhetorical stance implied that Merck is primarily committed to its customers and that profits are secondary.

The ad does acknowledge that *a* negative event had occurred (the CHD incidents in the APPROVe study), but claimed that the scientific import of these results was ambiguous and uncertain: "This decision is based on new data from a three-year clinical study. . . . The cause of the clinical study result is uncertain, but our commitment to our patients is clear." Like in Elsbach's cattle industry study, "spokespersons appeared to use acknowledgments to minimize their organization's responsibility for events or to attenuate negative perceptions of events" (p. 65; see also Dukerich & Carter, 2007; Dutton & Dukerich, 1991). Indeed, the ad continued, the APPROVe study was evidence of Merck's concern for its customers. Since it is standard industry practice to ignore FDA requirements to conduct post-approval trials, it was because of Merck's socially responsible values, Gilmartin could claim, that it (voluntarily) initiated the APPROVe study in order to "better understand the safety profile of VIOXX." Not only had the organization complied with all of the research requirements necessary to obtain FDA approval, they had initiated additional research *on their own volition*. In sum, with the withdrawal of Vioxx, Merck shifted from inappropriate denial strategies to potentially credible image-management strategies, and drew upon its relationship with the FDA to support its claims of social responsibility.

Act Three: The FDA Responds

The FDA's official response to Merck's withdrawal of Vioxx consisted of three press releases posted on the FDA webpage within a month of Gilmartin's letter. The first was an acknowledgment of Merck's actions and was issued on September 30, 2004. The second press release addressed the FDA's plans to "strengthen the safety program for marketed drugs" and was posted on the FDA's webpage on November 5, 2004. The third and final press release was posted on November 17, 2004, and addressed several topics.[15]

The September 30 press release is striking in two ways: its characterization of Merck's decision and the company's relationship with the FDA, and its description of the agency's actions. Like Gilmartin's ad, the FDA release focused on the voluntary nature of Merck's actions: the memo is entitled "FDA Issues Public Health Advisory on Vioxx as its Manufacturer Voluntarily Withdraws the Product"; its first sentence noted that "The Food and Drug Administration (FDA) today acknowledged the voluntary withdrawal from the market of Vioxx" and Acting FDA Commissioner Lester Crawford is quoted as saying, "Merck did the right thing by promptly reporting these findings to the FDA and voluntarily withdrawing the product from the market. . . . Although the risk that an individual patient would have a heart attack or stroke related to Vioxx is very small, the study that was halted suggests that, overall, patients taking the drug chronically face twice the risk of a heart attack compared to patients receiving a placebo" (para. 3). A follow-up paragraph notes that Merck initiated contact with the FDA regarding the APPROVe study on September 27, and on the following day "informed FDA of its decision to remove Vioxx from the market voluntarily." Through its use of ingratiation strategies, the agency invites the company to revive its previously strained relationship, and enhanced the credibility of Gilmartin's claims in the withdrawal memo/ad.

The remainder of the press release chronicles actions taken by the FDA regarding Vioxx. In June, 2000, Merck submitted the reports of the VIGOR study; the FDA consulted with its arthritis advisory committee in February 2001, and implemented labeling changes the following April. The FDA was in the process of "carefully reviewing" the results of additional studies to "determine whether further labeling changes were warranted" when Merck decided to withdraw Vioxx. Both the content and the tone of the release suggested that the Vioxx story was a routine case of a company and a regulatory agency working together to ensure the safety and efficacy of a product. There is no indication that the FDA was in the process of considering any sanctions other than label changes and no mention of the FDA's previous letters regarding false and misleading advertising.

A month later (November 5), the FDA released a second statement, notifying the public that it had acted "to strengthen the safety program for marketed drugs." The memo begins by clothing the FDA in the mantle of scientific miracles:

> Modern drugs provide unmistakable and significant health benefits, but experience has shown that the full magnitude of some potential risks have not always emerged during the mandatory clinical trials conducted before approval . . . This is what occurred recently with anti-depressants and Vioxx . . . FDA is determined to meet this challenge by employing

cutting-edge science, transparent policy, and sound decisions based on the advice of the best experts in and out of the agency.

The remainder of the memo announced that a number of changes would be made to the organization's operations and structure, and a set of risk-manage-ment guidelines that had been drafted the previous May would be finalized and published. These guidelines would "assist pharmaceutical firms in identifying and assessing potential safety risks before a drug reaches the market and also after a drug is already on the market using good pharmacovigilance practices and pharmacoepi-demiologial assessment." Acting Director Crawford concluded the memo:

> I am satisfied that these additional activities will strengthen the agency's program to greater ensure the safety of medical products that are mak-ing a major contribution to the health and quality of life of millions of Americans. Medicines that receive FDA approval are among the safest in the world; the measures we are taking are designed to strengthen this quality as well as our consumers' confidence that FDA's processes ensure the highest protection of the public health.

When read alone, the memo suggests that the Vioxx saga has ended, and the agency has turned a corner and is moving toward an even more positive future. However, four days before the FDA's second statement appeared, the *Wall Street Journal* (Matthew & Martinez, Nov. 1, 2004) reported that at the same time that Merck's management knew of possible CHD side effects, it was training its sales force in strategies of denying the link or avoiding comment on the issue. On the same day of the second FDA memo, an editorial was published by *Lancet* on its website which summarized the "Dodge Ball Vioxx" training memo, and concluded that "given this disturbing contradiction . . . it is hard to see how Merck's chief executive officer, Raymond Gilmartin, can retain the confidence of the public." *Lancet* also recalled that in 2001 the FDA had been "urged to mandate further clinical safety testing" of Vioxx, but refused to do so, an event that illustrated "the agency's built-in paralysis, a predicament that has to be addressed through funda-mental organisational reform" (p. 1995). Overall, *Lancet* concluded, "too often the FDA saw and continues to see the pharmaceutical industry as its customer—a vital source of funding for its activities—and not as a sector of society in need of strong regulation . . . For with Vioxx, Merck and the FDA acted out of ruthless, short-sighted, and irresponsible self-interest" (Dec. 4, 2004, pp. 1995, 1996).[16]

The *Lancet* editorial also took the FDA to task for its handling of a new meta-analysis of Vioxx, including a suggestion that an FDA scientist had been pressured to change his research conclusions in an internal FDA report, and subsequently pressured into withdrawing an essay containing his original, negative conclusions before it could be published in the journal. Further complicating the agency's efforts to put the Vioxx crisis behind it, on November 13, the *New York Times* reported that the FDA had withdrawn an invitation to Dr. Curt Furberg, Professor of Public Health at Wake Forest University, to serve on an advisory panel on Cox-2 inhibitors that was scheduled to meet during early 2005, because he had "publicly stated that he thought one of these drugs caused heart problems and that Pfizer, its maker, knew that and was covering [it] up" (Kolata, Nov. 13, 2004, p.1). FDA spokesperson Victoria Kao told the *Times* that the decision was routine: "They review [potential committee members] for each case to see whether they have a conflict of interest, financial or intellectual" (p. 1).

On November 17, Acting Commissioner Crawford responded to the new developments. He ignored *Lancet*'s assessment of the FDA's previous Vioxx efforts, and instead focused on the handling of the meta-analysis and Furberg issues. The FDA memo did not discuss the (negative) results of the study, but instead focused on the ways in which the scientist had failed to conform to established communication channels within the agency or follow long-institutionalized procedures for publishing research.[17] It used similar institutional strategies to respond to the Furberg controversy, arguing that no final decision had been made, but the makeup of the commission was being determined through standard bureaucratic procedures. Commissioner Crawford's subsequent testimony to Congress on November 17 used similar institutional appeals (Harris, Nov. 18, 2004; for a description of institutional appeals see Benoit & Brinson, 1994). Elsbach (1994), among others, has suggested that denials are generally less effective than acknowledgments, but the FDA in this case did not present a traditional denial. It stated that the "system is working," but it also tempered this conclusion by repeating a summary of the actions the agency was undertaking in order to remedy the problems that were causing the American public to lose confidence in the system.

In the process, the agency redefined the relationship between it and Merck. In contrast to the direct attacks involved in the agency's previous criticisms of Merck's Vioxx advertising, the post-withdrawal memos are cooperative in tone and conciliatory in content. The FDA made no demands of the company, and offered no apologies for its own performance or its relationship with Merck. Instead it focused on the steps that it was taking to improve an already-functioning regulatory process. It asserted that the agency's goal for the future is to strengthen its relationship with the industry, and to "assist manufacturers in the management and minimization of risks of pharmaceutical products throughout their life cycle" (FDA Acts, 2004, para. 11), and to "identify and assess potential risks before a drug reaches the market" (FDA Acts, 2004, para. 12). Statements such as these serve the purpose of demonstrating to the industry that the FDA's changes are not designed to incriminate drug companies but rather to help them produce medications that are both socially beneficial and highly profitable. Even after the Cox-2 withdrawals, public esteem for the agency stood at 50–75%, a decline from pre-Cox-2 levels, but still three to five times the 10–20% approval rate afforded the pharmaceutical industry or Congress (Lofstedt, 2007). The FDA's response also added credibility to Merck CEO Gilmartin's arguments, and it shifted the focus of attention from the company and the past to the agency and the future.

Post-mortem

Once Vioxx was removed from the market, the media became more interested in issues of drug safety. While some of this coverage, particularly in the business press (e.g., *Financial Times* or *Wall Street Journal*), was neutral, much of it was highly critical of the drug company(ies) for not being completely honest with regulators and with the public and of the FDA for its internal dissension and excessively cozy relationship with the industry. Even when press accounts were neutral, the bulk of the "high trust" experts quoted in stories took strongly critical positions. As the critics' credibility with the general public rose, industry (and Merck's) legitimacy plummeted (Lofstedt, 2007). Countries that ban direct-to-consumer drug advertising (e.g., Canada) celebrated the wisdom of their position; countries that had recently relaxed restrictions on DTCA (e.g., the U.K.) reconsidered their actions (Bowe, 2005; U.K. House of Commons Health Committee, 2005). As Watkins-Allen and Caillouet (1994) noted in their study of press coverage of environmental disputes, increased press coverage is self-reinforcing: investigative reporting on an issue leads to new negative revelations, which encourage more coverage, and so on.

Four months later, on January 31, 2005, Pfizer admitted that an unreleased 1990 internal study found that patients taking Celebrex suffered four times as many heart attacks as those taking a placebo and that the company had waited two months before releasing the study to the public (Berenson & Harris, Feb. 21, 2005; Harris, Feb. 17, 2005). Press coverage concluded, as did Psaty and Furberg in the *New England Journal of Medicine,* that "[f]ailure to publish the findings of these studies not only violates the trial participants' trust, but also misrepresents the evidence about risks and benefits for physicians" (2005). On February 5, 2005, the *New York Times* reported that in 2002 Merck had abruptly cancelled a major test of Vioxx's CHD risks (Meier); on June 23 the Canadian Press revealed that "Merck & Co. researchers privately sought to reformulate Vioxx in 2000 to reduce its cardiovascular side effects, even as the drug maker was publicly playing down a study [VIGOR] that highlighted the pain relief medication's potential heart attack risk"; on July 21 the *New York Times* reported that a training video based on the "Dodge Ball Vioxx" memo had been made for Merck sales representatives in 2000 showing them how to deny a link to myocardial infarctions (Berenson, July 11, 2005), and so on. The "drip, drip, drip" of negative publicity (Hawkes, 2005) had a devastating effect on Merck's public image: "It went from one of the most trusted companies in America (for a favorable portrait, see, for example, Vagelos & Galambos, 2004) to one that was accused of putting profits before public health" (Irving, 2005).

At the same time, Merck launched a counterattack designed to demonstrate its innocence. Two Merck scientists, Peter Kim and Alise Reicin, responded to the meta-analysis and hostile editorial published in the December 4 issues of *Lancet* by criticizing the methodology of the study, and by arguing that Merck had consistently forwarded its research results to the FDA, which subsequently made that information available on its website for any interested physician to read. The moment the company had unambiguous negative data available (the APPROVe study), it withdrew the drug from the market, an assertion that was shared by the Swedish drug regulatory agency (Jan. 1, 2005) and had been corroborated by the FDA's responses to the withdrawal announcement.[18] The positive claims made in Merck's letter to *Lancet* were echoed by additional letters from independent experts: Michel Lievre and Eric Abadie on behalf of the French Marketing Authorization Committee; Silvio Garanttini and Vittorio Bertele of Italy's Negri Institute for Pharmacological Research, and others (pp. 23–26). In short, the company claimed that it had cooperated with the FDA in precisely the way it should have, following all operant rules and regulations, and providing the oversight agency with all of the information it had at its disposal. Of course, Merck never mentioned the multiple FDA complaints about its false and misleading advertising, but neither did the FDA—in any of its post-recall rhetoric.[19]

Post-withdrawal pressure on the FDA also has been intense (see, for example, Harris, Sept. 28, 2007; *New York Times,* Feb. 17, 2005; Schultz, Dec. 12, 2004), but it has responded with a number of steps to solidify its image. It almost immediately forced Pfizer to withdraw Bextra, a rare case of the agency exceeding the recommendations of its advisory panel (Bowe, 2005), established the promised independent advisory board on drug safety (Berenson & Harris, Feb. 21, 2005), promised increased public input into its decision (Berenson & Harris, Feb. 21, 2005), and moved toward increased monitoring of approved drugs (*Houston Chronicle*, Jan. 31, 2007). The agency also successfully advocated for increased funding to support these steps in the 2007 renewal of PDUFA. However, charges of inadequate regulation persist, over the diabetes drug Avandia, cardiovascular stents, Cyberonics' pacemaker-like devise to treat depression, heartburn drugs Prilosec and Nexium, inadequate protection of human subjects during drug trials (Harris, Sept. 28, 2007), and others.

As a result, public opinion regarding the agency has become quite mixed. While 82% report that they trust the agency when it comes to overseeing prescription drugs, only 53% said that the FDA does an excellent or good job, with 47% rating its performance as fair or poor. The negative assessment is more pronounced among seniors. However, poll responses also reveal a widespread level of ignorance about the agency and its activities: only 54% knew that the FDA approves all new prescription drugs, and only 37% know that some of the agency's funds came from the industry (Reinberg, Sept. 20, 2007). When more specific questions are asked, and/or key information is provided, approval figures are much lower. A June 2006 poll by the *Wall Street Journal* and Harris polling found that 70% of respondents believed that the FDA had failed to protect the public from unsafe drugs and 82% believed that the agency placed politics above science in its decision making (Harrisinteractive, May 26, 2006). One year later, a *Consumer Reports* survey found that 60% believed the FDA had failed in its public protection duties and two-thirds were concerned that the agency received too much money from the industry (54% were very concerned). Ninety percent or more supported strengthening the agency's powers: mandating follow-up studies, requiring warning labels without having to negotiate with drug companies, and requiring companies to disclose all relevant research (June, 2007). The general public also widely approves of the agency shifting the balance toward increased regulatory "activism" and tighter regulation—in both 2006 and 2007 surveys more than 70% saying that drug safety was more important than getting new drugs to market quickly (Abraham & Smith, 2003; Kaufman, April 11, 2005 and April 25, 2006; Lofstedt, 2004; Pollack, Sept. 29, 2006). Somewhat ironically, while industry firms like Merck increasingly are drawing on their institutional ties to the FDA as a basis for their own legitimizing rhetoric, the agency's credibility now seems to depend on distancing itself from those organizations.

Implications

During the past twenty years, public relations scholars have called for the development of more complex theoretical frameworks which better reflect the power relationships (Leitch & Neilson, 2001) and political processes that characterize organizations' relationships among themselves and with multiple stakeholder groups (Grunig, 2001; Kersten, 1994; L'Etang, 1996; McKie, 2001; Seeger & Ulmer, 2002; Seeger, Sellnow, & Ulmer, 1998, 2001; Tyler, 2005). Drawing on contemporary perspectives on organizational rhetoric and political economy, we have argued that organizations in regulated, high-tech industries face a unique set of rhetorical challenges and possess a distinctive range of rhetorical strategies. The keys to managing those rhetorical situations are (1) recognizing and exploiting dominant cultural images of science as "objective" and "certain," and (2) maintaining a ritualized relationship with regulatory agencies that is mutually legitimizing. Similarly, regulatory agencies must enact rhetorical strategies that protect their credibility while managing the contradictory pressures they face from different stakeholders.

The Vioxx case study clearly indicates the complexity of these processes. The company's initial use of denial was strategically inappropriate and was undermined by what appeared to be a systematic process of withholding, distorting, and/or manipulating research on drug efficacy and side effects. Denial was especially unwise in this case because all of the evidence needed to undermine the company's claims was readily available on the FDA website to anyone willing to look hard enough for it (Abramson, 2005). Moreover, by offering no credible explanation or corrective action in response to the FDA's repeated criticisms of Merck's "false and misleading" advertising, and otherwise fostering an adversarial rhetorical relationship with the agency, the company severed its link to a relatively high-credibility avenue of legitimation. Even when the FDA went out of its way to rebuild Merck's credibility after Vioxx was withdrawn from the market, company rhetors ignored the agency's overtures. Consequently, the first "moral" of the Vioxx story is that organizational rhetors must be cognizant of both the relative effectiveness of different image-management strategies, and the advantages and constraints of their particular rhetorical situations.

The FDA more effectively managed the complex rhetorical situation it faced. By issuing warning letters, adding "black box" warnings, and requiring post-approval studies, it sustained an image of an activist, albeit imperfect, regulator while maintaining a cooperative relationship with the industry it oversees. Continued criticism suggests that these strategies have been less successful with stakeholders in Congress and the press than with the general public, and that the "drip, drip, drip" of adverse publicity about Vioxx eventually began to weaken the agency's overall credibility. However, the primary outcome of the continuing crisis has been the enactment of legislation that increases the agency's budget and provides it with enhanced legal power while not impinging on its freedom to act. Although it is too early to tell if the agency will be able to continue to legitimize itself with an increasingly suspicious public, it is clear that doing so will depend as much on the rhetoric of the pharmaceutical industry as on the agency's discourse.

The second implication of the Vioxx story involves the management of reputational crises over time. For decades politicians have recognized that they must think of political rhetoric as long-term campaigns within which every message is guided and constrained by previous appeals and sets the stage for subsequent rhetoric (Jamieson, 1975; Ulmer, 2001). This does not mean that rhetors cannot change strategies in the midst of a persuasive campaign. Organizational rhetors often do so, sometimes because of internal debates among the company's managers (Fombrun & Rindova, 2000) and sometimes because of changing external pressures. Sometimes the shift is to more appropriate and more persuasive strategies (Fombrun & Rindova, 2000); sometimes it makes the situation worse (Watkins-Allen & Caillouet, 1994). During the seven-plus years of the Vioxx crisis, Merck shifted from a rhetoric of denial to a rhetoric of accommodation after the results of the APPROVe study became available. While accommodation often is an optimal strategy, when it is "too little, too late" it cannot compensate for the loss of legitimacy created by previous inappropriate use of denial strategies.

At this point, public relations and organizational rhetoric scholars can confidently caution practitioners about the risks of strategy shifts. Unfortunately, we scholars have not yet conducted the kind of longitudinal research that would allow us to predict the effects of various combinations of strategies over time in different kinds of rhetorical situations. But, as public relations theory and research become more sophisticated, this kind of complex longitudinal research will emerge, eventually leading to reliable guidelines for strategic practice, even in situations like those faced by regulated high-tech industries.

Notes

1 The primary responsibilities of the contemporary FDA were developed and legitimized in precisely this way—the Pure Food and Drug Act and the Meat Inspection Act of 1906 (resulting in part from advocacy by Upton Sinclair), the Food, Drug, and Cosmetic Act of 1938, and the Kefauver drug probe of 1962. In these cases, public-interest regulation is designed to achieve what economic self-interest cannot, and regulation is enacted because "the imperfections of government action are [viewed as] preferable to the imperfections of the market" (Wilson, 1974, p. 137).

2 Sometimes these private negotiations break through into the public gaze, with almost comical results. For example, during the 2007 renewal of PDUFA, the Senate first added a provision allowing drug reimportation from Canada and other countries, and two days later made reimportation contingent on a certification of safety by the FDA, something that the Bush administration had made it abundantly clear would not happen until after they left office (Conrad & Jodlowski, 2008).

3 Political scientists argue persuasively that such cases rarely result from the actions of career regulators, although excessive caseloads in regulatory agencies make errors inevitable (see also Angell, 2005: 33; Posner, 1971; Venette, Sellnow, & Lang, 2003). Far more often, "regulatory failures" stem from actions by Congress

and/or the executive branch through the political appointees who are selected to head regulatory agencies. Evidently the term "regulatory capture" was coined by Bernstein (see Wilson, 1974). Critics argue that the potential for executive interference has been increased substantially by the Bush administration's recent directives to add a political appointee, in addition to those confirmed by Congress, to each regulatory agency in order to "make sure the agencies carry out the president's priorities" (Pear, Jan. 30, 2007, p. 1). At times presidential intervention also seems comical, as when Theodore Roosevelt, who had recently started using saccharin every day, retaliated against Bureau of Chemistry (the predecessor of the FDA) director Harvey Wiley's statement that the chemical might be harmful to health by creating a board to review and overturn many of the agency's decisions (Nadel, 1971, p. 24). Consider the two agencies examined in this chapter, the FDA and the NHTSA. *Congress* has required the FDA to rely almost completely on industry research regarding drug efficacy and side-effects; *Congress* has dictated that the FDA not conduct research on the relative cost-effectiveness of various drugs and/or treatment options or publicize existing research relative to cost-effectiveness; *Congress* passed the Hatch-Waxman Act, which extended patent protection for the pharmaceutical industry far beyond that afforded any other industry (Angell, 2005). Instead, *Congress* imposed the same provisions on our trading partners through NAFTA and other treaties (see Conrad & Jodlowski, 2008). *Congress* also passed the Bayh-Dole Act, which blurred the boundaries between academic and industry research; passed (and recertified and expanded) PDUFA, which at least creates the appearance that approval of new drugs is linked to industry funding; has repeatedly gutted efforts to bring nicotine under FDA control, and so on. In addition, because the FDA relies on other parts of the executive branch to enforce its decisions, industry lobbyists can avoid strict regulation by pushing for government inaction. For example, the Bayh-Dole Act allows the federal government to recapture government research grants that lead to highly profitable drugs, but no administration has ever enforced this provision of the act. The overall process does suggest that, like every other aspect of U.S. health care policymaking, regulation is a highly ideological process (Weissert & Weissert, 2003), one that requires all parties to continually legitimize their activities and the activities of other parties (Elder & Cobb, 1983; Stone & Marmor, 1990). Similarly, *Congress*, responding to the Reagan administration's anti-regulatory ideology, progressively reduced NHTSA's budget, so that in 2000 it was less than one-third as large as in 1980. NHTSA's efforts to upgrade tire standards were repeatedly blocked by a bipartisan coalition of Congresspersons from states with automobile and/or tire industries (led by John Dingell, D-MI; Michael Oxley, R-OH, and Billy Tauzin, D-LA) (Zagorin, Sept. 18, 2000); Congressional efforts to upgrade roof-crush (rollover) standards were stymied by pressure from the executive branch (Claybrook & Denard, 2002).

4 The "classic" case studies in this debate involve the creation of the Interstate Commerce Commission and the Federal Aviation Administration/Civil Aeronautics Board (Burkhardt, 1967; Cushman, 1941; Kolko, 1965; Kuttner, 1999). Recent revelations of safety problems with virtually everything imported from China by U.S. firms have even led industries to seek additional regulation, in order to protect themselves from themselves (Lipton & Harris, Sept. 16, 2007).

5 For a general analysis, see Baumgartner & Jones (1993); for extensions of "punctuated equilibrium" theories to health care, see Conrad & McIntush (2003) and Weissert & Weissert (2003). Wilson (1974) also argues that moribund regulatory agencies can suddenly be stimulated into expansion and increased activity by the appointment of leaders who are especially committed to social action and/or by the emergence of an especially zealous professional staff. This explanation often is used to explain the FDA's 1966 shift from having a "solicitous and benign attitude toward the pharmaceutical manufacturers" (Wilson, 1974,

p. 159) to a more activist position, and back again during the 1990s (Angell, 2005) and 2000s (Abraham & Smith, 2003; Moynihan & Cassells, 2005).

6 This challenge is especially difficult when a regulatory agency is charged with inconsistent goals. For example, the FDA must get needed drugs to market as quickly as possible *and* ensure the safety of the drugs it approves (Angell, 2005; Harris, June 11, 2007).

7 Similar systems are used in other countries, with Australia's 100% industry funding the highest percentage (Abraham & Smith, 2003). Industry and FDA rhetors have argued that the increase in recalls is inevitable and can be attributed to an increase in the number of new drug applications submitted to the FDA since PDUFA and FDAMA were enacted and to a reduction in approval time (Fontanarosa, Rennie, & DeAngelis, 2004; Friedman, Woodcock, Lumpkin, Shuren, Hass, & Thompson, 1999). Indeed, the ratio of withdrawals to approved formulas has not increased (Berndt, Gottschalk, Philipson, & Strobeck, 2005).

8 More than 70% of patients prescribed Cox-2 inhibitors during the first three years they were on the market were at low or very low risk of developing serious GI complications and should have been using low-cost alternatives instead (Kaufman, Jan. 25, 2005).

9 Because until recently the FDA had no enforcement powers short of withdrawing a drug that they had recently approved, drug companies have ignored requirements for post-approval testing about 70% of the time (Angell, 2005).

10 The FDA's previous warning letters were dated October 6, 1999 and April 6, 2000.

11 It was subsequently revealed that the authors of the *NEJM* editorial had financial ties to the industry that were sufficiently large to violate the journal's conflict-of-interest policies. After this information became public, *NEJM* loosened its policies.

12 For example, Wayne Ray, professor of preventive medicine at Vanderbilt University School of Medicine found that naproxen was not a superdrug for preventing heart attacks (Meier, 2004), and Cleveland Clinic's Eric Topol and his associates reported a 500% greater heart attack risk with Vioxx compared to naproxen in *JAMA* (Topol, 2004).

13 More than 200 million Americans took Vioxx while it was on the market (Berenson, July 11, 2005).

14 Similarly, Watkins-Allen and Caillouet (1994) found that denouncing one's critics also can increase legitimacy, especially with audiences who have a direct economic stake in the enterprise, but only if the targets lack political power or social legitimacy. However, it was difficult for Merck to attack the objectivity of "science" without undermining its own credibility. The solution was to critique the methodology of studies that revealed serious side-effects, while casting this kind of critique as an aspect of "good science."

15 These press releases were chosen because they referred directly to the Vioxx recall and were initial responses to the crisis facing Merck and the FDA. Subsequent FDA press releases addressed such topics as the Senate hearing on Vioxx, FDA and Pfizer actions regarding Celebrex, and implementation of the new policies addressed in the November 5 press release. These were not examined because they referred only indirectly to the Vioxx case or were reiterations of initial comments.

16 *Lancet* subsequently published its editorial as part of a regular issue. The page numbers we cite are from the "hard copy" (*Lancet*, Dec. 4, 2004). In a second editorial published in the December 4 issue, *Lancet's* editor excoriated the Bush administration for its widespread use of political pressure to alter scientific reports (p. 1994).

17 On January 4, 2005, the FDA reversed its decision and allowed the author, agency critic David Graham, to submit his research to *Lancet*. The study "shows that

88,000 to 139,000 people have had heart attacks that could be linked to Vioxx, with 30 per cent to 40 per cent of them fatal" (Canadian Press, Jan. 4, 2005).

18 Abramson's (2005, especially chapters 2 and 3) critical assessment of Vioxx and the FDA is based on this FDA data, although he also notes that it takes so much time and effort to gather and interpret it that it is unrealistic to expect practicing physicians to have been aware of the intricacies of the research.

19 When high-tech organizations select communication strategies, they have to be concerned both with maintaining a positive public image and with potential litigation. The latter considerations may lead its rhetors to use denial strategies when accommodation is the optimal means of repairing damaged public reputations (Arapan & Pompper, 2003; Arapan & Roskos-Ewoldsen, 2005; Marcus & Goodman, 1998). Merck has used the combination of denial and institutional appeals in Vioxx litigation, and has been much more successful in this different venue and rhetorical situation (LoPucki & Weyrauch, 2000; Wetlaufer, 1990) it has decided to fight each suit individually. Although Merck has benefited substantially from the effects of tort reform in key states (e.g., Texas) and by court decisions denying plaintiffs class-action status (Johnson, Sept. 7, 2007), Merck's claim that it "adequately warned patients and doctors of Vioxx's heart risks and that it never knowingly endangered patients" seems to have been judged credible by a number of juries (Berenson, August 21, 2007; for an analysis of the distinctive features of legal rhetoric, see Seeger & Hipfel, 2007). Jury awards have repeatedly been reduced by as much as 90% on appeal, the pace of lawsuits has slowed, and three years after the withdrawal the company had not paid a single dollar to claimants. As a result of these successes, Merck was able to settle 27,000 lawsuits for $4.85 billion, a fraction of the $10–15 billion costs initially estimated (Berenson, Nov. 9, 2007; Johnson, Nov. 7, 2007; *Lancet*, Dec. 4, 2004). Suits filed by states' Attorneys General on behalf of their citizens and Medicaid patients will be more difficult to manage by manipulating the structure of the legal system, but Merck seems to be committed to its institutional defense (Kershaw, 2007). Unfortunately, analyzing Merck's legal rhetoric is beyond the scope of this chapter.

References

Abraham, J., & Smith, H. L. (2003). *Regulation of the pharmaceutical industry.* Basingstoke, U.K.: Palgrave/Macmillan.

Abramson, J. (2005). *Overdo$ed America.* New York: Harper Perennial.

Angell, M. (2005). *The truth about the drug companies.* New York: Random House.

Arapan, L. M., & Pompper, D. (2003). Stormy weather. *Public Relations Review, 29,* 291–308.

Arapan, L. M., & Roskos-Ewoldsen, D. (2005). Stealing thunder. *Public Relations Review, 31,* 425–433.

Aune, J. A. (2001). *Selling the free market.* New York: Guilford Press.

Avorn, J. (2004). *Power medicines.* New York: Knopf.

Baumgartner, F., & Jones, B. (1993). *Agendas and instability in American politics.* Chicago: University of Chicago Press.

Baumgartner, F., & Leech, B. (1998). *Basic interests.* Princeton, NJ: Princeton University Press.

Benoit, W., & Brinson, S. L. (1994). AT&T: "Apologies are not enough." *Communication Quarterly, 42*(1), 75–88.

Berenson, A. (Aug. 21, 2007). Plaintiffs find payday elusive in Vioxx cases. Retrieved Aug. 21, 2007, from http://www.nytimes.com/2007/09/21/business/21merck.html

Berenson, A., & Harris, G. (Feb. 25, 2005). 10 voters on panel backing pain pills had industry ties. Retrieved Feb. 25, 2005, from http://www.nytimes.com/2005/02/25/politics/fda.html?pagewanted=print&position=

Berndt, E. R., Gottschalk, A., Philipson, T. J., & Strobeck, M. W. (2005). Industry funding of the FDA: Effects of PDUFA on approval times and withdrawal rates. *Nature Reviews Drug Discovery, 4,* 545–554.

Bitzer, L. (1970). The rhetorical situation. *Philosophy and Rhetoric, 1,* 1–14.

Bitzer, L. (1980). Functional communication. In E. White (Ed.), *Rhetoric in transition.* University Park, PA: Pennsylvania State University Press.

Bowe, C. (March 16, 2005). Doctors seek cure to rash of anti-drug advertising. *Financial Times,* 18.

Brown, L., & Marmor, T. (1994). The Clinton plan's administrative structure. *Journal of Health Politics, Policy and Law, 19,* 193–199.

Burke, K. (1972). *Dramatism and development.* Barre: Clark University Press.

Burkhardt, R. (1967). *The federal aviation administration.* New York: Praeger.

Canadian Press (Jan. 4, 2005). FDA gives whistle-blower scientist permission to publish Vioxx safety data. www.canada.com. Retrieved Jan. 4, 2005, from http://www.highbeam.com/doc/1P1-103935185.html

Carpenter, D. P. (2001). *The forging of bureaucratic autonomy, reputations, networks, and policy innovations in executive agencies, 1862–1928.* Princeton, NJ: Princeton University Press.

Carpenter. D. P. (2004). The political economy of FDA drug review: Processing, politics, and lessons for policy. *Health Affairs, 23,* 52–63.

Cheney, G., & Christensen, L. (2001). Organizational identity: Linkages between internal and external communication. In F. Jablin & L. Putnam (Eds.), *The new handbook of organizational communication* (pp. 231–269). Thousand Oaks, CA: Sage.

Cheney, G., Christensen, L., Conrad, C., & Lair, D. (2004). Organizational rhetoric as organizational discourse. In D. Grant, C. Hardy, C. Oswick, & L. Putnam (Eds.), *The handbook of organizational discourse* (pp. 79–104). Thousand Oaks, CA: Sage.

Claybrook, J., & Denard, R. (2002). Deadly Products. *Journal of Public Health Policy, 23,* 206–210.

Cobb, R., & Ross, M. (Eds.) (1997). *Cultural strategies of agenda denial.* Lawrence, KS: University of Kansas Press.

Conrad, C. (2004). The illusion of reform. *Rhetoric and Public Affairs, 7*(2004), 311–338.

Conrad, C., & Abbott, J. (2007). Corporate social responsibility from a public policymaking perspective. In May, S. K., Cheney, G., & Roper, J. (Eds.), *The debate over corporate social responsibility* (pp. 417–437). New York: Oxford University Press.

Conrad. C., & Jodlowski, D. (2008). Dealing drugs on the border. In H. H. Zoller & J. J. Dutta (Eds.), *Emerging perspectives in health communication.* Mahwah, NJ: Lawrence Erlbaum.

Conrad, C., & McIntush, H. (2003). Communication, structure and health care policymaking. In T. Thompson, A. Dorsey, K.I. Miller, & R. Parrott (Eds.), *Handbook of health communication* (pp. 403–422). Hillsdale, NJ: Lawrence Erlbaum.

Conrad, C., & Millay, B. (2000). Confronting free market romanticism: Health care reform in the least likely place. *Journal of Applied Communication Research, 29,* 153–170.

Consumer Reports (June 16, 2007). Consumer Reports survey finds strong backing for drug reforms. ConsumerReports.org. Retrieved Sept. 21, 2007, from http://www.

consumerreports.org/cro/health-fitness/news/2007/04/consumer-reports-survey-finds-strong-backing-for-drug-reforms-4-07/overview/consumer-reports-survey-finds-strong-backing-for-drug-reforms.htm.

Coombs, W. T. (1995). Choosing the right words: The development of guidelines for the selection of the "appropriate" crisis-response strategies. *Management Communication Quarterly, 8,* 447–476.

Coombs, W. R., & Holladay, S. J. (2002). Helping crisis managers protect reputational assets: Initial tests of the situational crisis communication theory. *Management Communication Quarterly, 16,* 165–186.

Cushman, R. (1941). *The independent regulatory commissions.* New York: Oxford University Press.

Duenwald, M. (Oct. 5, 2004). One lesson from Vioxx: Approach new drugs with caution. *New York Times,* late ed.: F5.

Dukerich, J., & Carter, S. (2007). Distorted images and reputation repair. In M. Schulz, M. J. Hatch, & M. H. Larsen (Eds.), *The expressive organization* (pp. 97–112). New York: Oxford University Press.

Dutton, J., & Dukerich, J. (1991). Keeping an eye on the mirror. *Academy of Management Journal, 34,* 517–554.

Elder, C., and Cobb, R. (1983). *The political uses of symbols.* New York: Longman.

Elsbach, K. (1994). Managing organizational legitimacy in the California cattle industry: The construction and effectiveness of organizational accounts. *Administrative Science Quarterly, 39,* 57–88.

Feyerabend, P. (1978). *Against method.* London: Verso.

Fombrun, C., & Rindova, V. (2000). The road to transparency: Reputation management at Royal Dutch Shell. In M. Schultz, M. Hatch, & M. Larsen (Eds.), *The expressive organization* (pp. 78–96). New York: Oxford.

Fontanarosa, P. B., Rennie, D., & DeAngelis, C. D. (2004). Postmarketing surveillance: Lack of vigilance, lack of trust. *Journal of the American Medical Association, 292,* 2647–2650.

Friedman, M. A., Woodcock, J., Lumpkin, M. M., Shuren, J. E., Hass, A. E., & Thompson, L. J. (1999). The safety of newly approved medicines: Do recent market removals mean there is a problem? *Journal of the American Medical Association, 281,* 1728–1734.

Jones, E. E., Gergen, K., & Jones, R. J. (1963). Tactics of ingratiation among leaders and subordinates in a status hierarchy. *Psychology Monographs, 77,* 566–588.

Greider, W. (1997). *Who will tell the people?* New York: Simon & Schuster.

Gross, A. (1990). *The rhetoric of science.* Cambridge: Harvard University Press.

Grossman, G., & Helpman, E. (2001). *Special interest politics.* Cambridge, MA: M.I.T. Press.

Grunig, J. (2001). Two-way symmetrical public relations: Past, present, and future. In R. Heath (Ed.), *Handbook of public relations* (pp. 11–30). Thousand Oaks: Sage.

Hackey, R. (1997). Symbolic politics and health care reform in the 1940s and 1990s. In R. Cobb & M. Ross (Eds.), *Cultural strategies of agenda denial* (pp. 141–157). Lawrence, KS: University of Kansas Press.

Harris, G. (Nov. 18, 2004). F.D.A. leader says study tied to Vioxx wasn't suppressed. Retrieved Sept. 12, 2007, from http://query.nytimes.com/gst/fullpage.html?res=9C01E0D7133FF93BA25752C1A9629C8B63&sec=health

Harris, G. (Dec. 6, 2004). At F.D.A., strong drug ties and less monitoring. Retrieved Dec. 6, 2004, from http://www.nytimes.com/2004/12/06/health/06fda.html

Harris, G. (Feb. 17, 2005). Medical panel poses pointed questions to drug makers over risks of painkillers. Retrieved Feb. 17, 2005, from http://query.nytimes.com/gst/fullpage.html?sec=health&res=9D0CE4D8133AF934A25751C0A9639C8B63

Harris, G. (Feb. 23, 2006). For generics, bumpy road to pharmacy. Retrieved Jan. 19, 2006 , from http://www.nytimes.com/2006/02/23/health/23drug.html

Harris, G. (June 11, 2007). Potentially incompatible goals at F.D.A. Retrieved June 10, 2007, from http://www.nytimes.com/2007/06/11/washington/11fda.html

Harris, G. (Sept. 28, 2007). Report assails F.D.A. oversight of clinical trials. Retrieved Sept. 28, 2007, from http://www.nytimes.com/2007/09/28/health/policy/28fda.html

Harrisinteractive (May 26, 2006). The FDA's reputation with the general public is under assault. www.harrisinteractive.com. Retrieved Sept. 21, 2007, from http://harrisinteractive.com/news/allnewsbydate.asp?NewsID=1060

Hawkes, N. (April 12, 2005). Warning as doctors turn back on arthritis drug. *Times*, 12.

Hearit, K. (1994). Apologies and public relations crises at Chrysler, Toshiba, and Volvo. *Public Relations Review, 20*, 113–125.

Hearit, K. (1995). "Mistakes were made": Organizations, apologia, and crises of social legitimacy. *Communication Studies, 46*, 1–16.

Hilts, P. (2004). *Protecting America's health.* Chapel Hill, NC: University of North Carolina Press.

Hirschman, A. O. (1991). *The rhetoric of reaction: Perversity, futility, jeopardy.* Cambridge, MA: Belknap Press.

Houston Chronicle (Jan. 31, 2007). FDA promises to step up oversight of approved drugs, A6.

Irving, R. (Jan. 15, 2005). Insurers cut cover to drug firms amid fear of lawsuits. *Times*, 52.

Jamieson, K. H. (1975). Antecedent genre as rhetorical constraint. *Quarterly Journal of Speech, 61*, 406–415.

Johnson, L. (Sept. 7, 2007). Merck wins major Vioxx ruling. *Houston Chronicle*, D3.

Jones, E. E. (1964). *Ingratiation.* New York: Appleton.

Kaufman, M. (April 11, 2005). Painkiller decision suggests shift in FDA's risk-benefit equation. *Washington Post*, A3, from http://www.washingtonpost.com/wp-dyn/articles/A42530-2005Apr10.html

Kaufman, M. (Jan. 25, 2005). New study criticizes painkiller marketing. Washingtonpost. com. Retrieved Jan. 25, 2005, from http://www.washingtonpost.com/wp-dyn/articles/A33786-2005Jan24.html

Kaufman, M. (April 25, 2006). Drug firms' deals allowing exclusivity. Washingtonpost. com. Retrieved Nov. 26, 2006, from http://www.washingtonpost.com/wp-dyn/content/article/2006/04/24/AR2006042401508.html

Kershaw, S. (Sept. 18, 2007). New York state and city sue Merck over Vioxx. Retrieved Sept. 18, 2007, from http://www.nytimes.com/2007/09/18/health/18vioxx.html?ref=health

Kersten, A. (1994). The ethics and ideology of public relations: A Critical examination of American theory and practice. In W. Armbrecht & U. Zabel (Eds.), *Normative aspekte der public relations* (pp. 109–130). Opladen, Germany: Westdeutscher Verlag.

Kolata, G. (Nov. 13, 2004). Scientist who cited drug's risks is barred from F.D.A. panel. Retrieved Sept. 12, 2007, from http://www.nytimes.com/2004/11/13/politics/13fda.html

Kolko, G. (1965). *Railroads and regulation, 1817–1916.* Princeton, NJ: Princeton University Press.

Kuhn, T. (1962). *The structure of scientific revolutions.* Chicago: The University of Chicago Press.

Kuttner, R. (1999). *Everything for sale.* Chicago: University of Chicago Press.

Lancet (August 21, 2004). A coxib a day won't keep the doctor away, *364,* 639–640.

Lancet (Dec. 4, 2004). Politics, spin, and science, *364,* 1994.

L'Etang, J. (1996). Public relations as diplomacy. In J. L'Etang & M. Pieczka (Eds.), *Critical perspectives in public relations* (pp. 35–53). London: International Thomson Business Press.

Leiss. W. (2001). *In the chamber of risks.* Montreal: McGill-Queen's University Press.

Leitch, S., & Nielson, D. (1997). Reframing public relations: New directions for theory and practice. *Australian Journal of Communication, 24,* 17–32.

Lessl, T. (1999). The Galileo legend as scientific folklore. *The Quarterly Journal of Speech, 85,* 146–168.

Lessl, T. (1989). The priestly voice. *The Quarterly Journal of Speech, 75,* 183–197.

Lipton, E., & Harris, G. (Sept. 16, 2007). In turnaround, industries seek U.S. regulation. Retrieved Sept. 16, 2007, from http://www.nytimes.com/2007/09/16/washington/16regulate.html

Llewellyn, J. (2007). Regulation: Government, business and the self in the United States. In May, S. K., Cheney, G., & Roper, J. (Eds.), *The debate over corporate social responsibility* (pp. 177–189). New York: Oxford University Press, 2007.

Lofstedt, R. (2004). Risk communication and management in the twenty-first century. *International Public Management Journal, 7,* 335–346.

Lofstedt, R. (2007). The impact of the Cox-2 inhibitor issue on perceptions of the pharmaceutical industry: Content analysis and communication implications. *Journal of Health Communication, 12,* 471–491.

LoPucki, L. M., & Weyrauch. W. O. (2000). A theory of legal strategy. *Duke Law Journal, 49,* 1405–1486.

Matthew, A., & Martinez, B. (Nov 1, 2004). E-mails suggest Merck knew Vioxx's dangers at early stage. *Wall Street Journal,* A1.

Marcus, A., & Goodman, R. (1998). Victims and shareholders. *Academy of Management Journal, 42,* 479–485.

McKie, D. (2001). Updating public relations: "New science," research paradigms, and uneven developments. In R.L. Heath (Ed.), *Handbook of public relations* (pp. 75–91). Thousand Oaks, CA: Sage.

Meier, B. (October 1, 2004). For Merck, defense of a drug crumbles at a difficult time. Retrieved August 10, 2007, from http://query/nytimes.com/gst/fullpage.html?res=9B03E3DE1338F932A35753C1A9629C8B63&sec=health

Moynihan, R., & Cassels, A. (2005). *Selling sickness.* New York: Nation Books.

Nadel, M. (1971). *The politics of consumer protection.* New York: Bobbs-Merrill.

New York Times (Editorial) (Dec. 8, 2004). Industry distortion of the F.D.A. Retrieved Dec. 8, 2004, from http://www.nytimes.com/2004/12/08/opinion/08wed1.html

New York Times (Editorial) (Feb. 17, 2005). Half a step on drug safety. Retrieved Feb. 17, 2005, from http://query.nytimes.com/gst/fullpage.html?res=9B04E2D7133AF934A25751C0A9639C8B63&sec=&spon=

Okie. S. (2005). What ails the FDA? *New England Journal of Medicine, 352*(11), 1063–1066.

Pear, R. (Jan. 30, 2007). Bush directive increases sway on regulation. Retrieved Jan. 30, 2007, from http://www.nytimes.com/2007/01/30/washington/30rules.html

Penrose, J. M. (2000). The role of perception in crisis planning. *Public Relations Review*, *26*, 155–171.

Perrow, C. (1984). *Normal accidents.* New York: Basic Books.

Perrow, C. (2002). *Organizing America.* Princeton, NJ: Princeton University Press.

Pew Research Center (1998). *Deconstructing distrust.* Washington, D.C.: Pew Research Center.

Pollack, A. (Sept. 29, 2006). New sense of caution at the F.D.A. *NY Times on the Web.* Retrieved Sept. 29, 2006.

Posner, R. (1971). Taxation by regulation. *Bell Journal of Economics and Management Science*, *2*, 22–50.

Postman, P. (1992). *Technopoly: The surrender of culture to technology.* New York: Vintage Books.

Powell, D., & Leiss, W. (1997). *Mad cows and mother's milk: The perils of poor risk communication.* Montreal: McGill-Queens University Press.

Pasty, B. M., & Furberg, C. D. (17 March, 2005). Cox-2 inhibitors—Lessons in drug safety. *New England Journal of Medicine*, *352*, 1133–1135.

Reinberg, S. (Sept. 20, 2007). Americans confused about FDA and drug safety. www.cbc.ca. Retrieved Sept. 21, 2007.

Ritti, R. R., & Silver, J. (1986). Early processes of institutionalization. *Administrative Science Quarterly*, *31*, 25–42.

Schnitzer, T., Burmester G., Mysler, E., Hochberg, M., Doherty, M., Ehrsam, E., Titton, X., Krammer, G., Mellein, G., Matchaba, P., Gimona, A., & Hawkey, C. (August 21, 2004). Comparison of lumiracoxib with naproxen and ibuprofen in the Therapeutic Arthritis Research and Gastrointestinal Event Trial (TARGET), reduction in ulcer complication: Randomised controlled trial. *Lancet*, *364*, 665–674.

Schultz, W. (Dec. 12, 2004). How to make the drugs we supply to the world safe again. *Houston Chronicle*, E6.

Seeger, M., & Hipfel, S. (2007). Legal versus ethical arguments: Contexts for corporate social responsibility. In S. May, G. Cheney, & J. Roper (Eds.), *The debate over corporate social responsibility* (pp. 155–166). New York: Oxford University Press.

Seeger, M., & Ulmer, R. (2002). A post-crisis discourse of renewal. *Journal of Applied Communication Research*, *30*, 126–142.

Seeger, M., Sellnow, T., & Ulmer, R. (1998). Communication, organization and crisis. In M.E. Roloff (Ed.), *Communication Yearbook 21* (pp. 231–275). Thousand Oaks, CA: Sage.

Seeger, M., Sellnow, T., & Ulmer, R. (2001). Public relations and crisis communication. In Robert Heath (Ed.), *Handbook of public relations* (pp. 155–166). Thousand Oaks, CA: Sage.

Stigler, G. (1971). The theory of economic regulation. *Bell Journal of Economics and Management Science*, *2*, 215–221.

Stone, D. (1989). *Policy paradox and political reason.* Boston: Little Brown.

Stone, D., & Marmor, T. (1990). Introduction. *Journal of Health Politics, Policy, and Law*, *15*, 253–257.

Taylor, S. J., & Bogdan, R. (1980). Defending illusions: The institution's struggle for survival. *Human Organization*, *39*, 209–218.

Topol, E. (Oct. 2, 2004). Good riddance to a bad drug. *New York Times*, late ed.: A15.

Tyler. L. (2005). Towards a postmodern understanding of crisis communication. *Public Relations Review*, *31*, 566–571.

Ulmer, R. (2001) Effective crisis management through established stakeholder relationships. *Management Communication Quarterly, 14,* 590–615

U.K. House of Commons Health Committee (2005). *The influence of the pharmaceutical industry.* London: The Stationary Office.

Vagelos, R., & Galambos. L. (2004). *Medicine, science and Merck.* New York: Cambridge University Press.

Venette, S., Sellnow, T., & Lang, P. (2003). Metanarration's role in the restructuring perceptions of crisis. *The Journal of Business Communication, 40,* 219–236.

Walker, J. (1991). *The mobilization of interest groups in America.* Ann Arbor, MI: University of Michigan Press.

Watkins-Allen, M., & Caillouet, R. (1994). Legitimation endeavors. *Communication Monographs, 61,* 44–62.

Weaver, R. (1953). *The ethics of rhetoric.* South Bend, IN: Henry Regency.

Weaver, R. (2001). Language is sermonic. In P. Bizzell & B. Herzberg (Eds.), *The rhetorical tradition: Readings from classical times to the present* (pp. 1351–360). New York: Bedford/St. Martin's.

Weissert, C., & Weissert, W. (2003). *Governing health* (3rd ed.) Baltimore, MD: Johns Hopkins University Press.

Wetlaufer, G. B. (1990). Rhetoric and its denial in legal discourse. *Virginia Law Review, 76,* 1545–1597.

Willman, D. (Dec. 20, 2000). How a new policy led to seven deadly drugs. *Los Angeles Times,* 1A.

Wilson, J. Q. (1974). The politics of regulation. In J. McKie (Eds.), *Social responsibility and the business predicament* (pp. 135–168). Washington, D.C.: Brookings Institution.

Zagorin, J. (Sept. 18, 2000). Blame Congress, not NHTSA. *Time.com.* Retrieved Oct. 1, 2000, from http://www.time.com/time/magazine/article/0,9171,997990,00.html

10

ACTIVIST PUBLIC RELATIONS AND THE PARADOX OF THE POSITIVE

A Case Study of Frederick Douglass' "Fourth of July Address"

Robert L. Heath
University of Houston

Damion Waymer
Virginia Tech

Public relations theory and best practices tend to focus primarily on companies, for-profit organizations, rather than on other types of organizations. This chapter examines activism, at least one case and one instance, to better understand some of the problems and the challenges for other organizations, often businesses or governments. If we think that public relations is limited to business promotion, we can ignore the promotional efforts by activists to call attention to, frame, and advocate one or many issue positions. In fact, we are likely to only obtain the democratic exchange long championed as the essence of public relations by seeing how and when activists engage in the dialogue that occurs on various issues. But, we would be remiss if we ignore the promotional aspects of activism by only addressing their issue engagement.

The nineteenth-century abolition movement gives us an opportunity to see organized activism engaging in what can be seen as constructive public relations. Abolitionist groups organized, sustained themselves, focused on key issues, and communicated their views on those issues in a variety of venues. They held local, regional, state, national, and international conferences to examine the issues related to slavery and in doing so even raised related issues such as those regarding the rights of women and universal suffrage. One of their promotional tactics included inviting noted guests to speak at their conferences. One such occasion motivated Frederick Douglass to deliver what has become known as his "Fourth of July Address."

This chapter gives brief discussion of non-profit activism as a genre and focuses on the comments of Douglass that are among the most famous of any speaker on abolition. This discussion helps understand the role of the activist organization in the issue dialogue that is a vital part of issues management. But, it also acknowledges the promotional aspects of activism. The chapter explains and applies the analytical concept of the paradox of the positive and incremental erosion. It features the premise that the statements of activism serve to frame issues in important ways forcing responses by other organizations. One of the most fundamental includes the attack on the paradox of the positive, the need to correct overly positive interpretations of various conditions that cause a strain between what is and what ought to be. The Fourth of July speech by Frederick Douglass demonstrates further evidence of the concept of the paradox of the positive, which in this case was attacked through what has been called incremental erosion (C. Condit & D. Condit, 1992). These issue debates can be a vital part of making society more fully functional.

Non-profit Public Relations

Non-profits organize to solve problems either not solved by other kinds of organizations, typically businesses or governmental agencies, or to raise money for some community benefit (Kelly, 1998, 2005). Friends of the Symphony would be the latter, as would the Red Cross. Other non-profits organize specifically to address public policy questions. This was the rationale for the many abolitionist groups that organized in the United States, Great Britain, and elsewhere. The Civil War ended chattel slavery and removed the need for champions of that cause in the United States. In all of these activities, public relations can be an asset, especially as a means for helping to manage image, build reputations, foster relationships, and generate revenue.

In 1992, L. Grunig argued a central theme in the excellence literature that activism can limit the effectiveness of organizations. This conclusion led to the advice that excellent public relations departments need to understand this limiting effect to respond properly. Such analysis is designed to direct and counsel businesses to better understand the dynamics of activism, listen to the complaints, and resolve conflict either by prevention or collaborative engagement. In a similar vein, Heath (1997) described non-profit activism as a crucial factor in the evolutionary history of issues management. He argued that activism creates or builds on the legitimacy gap between the activists and the target organization, whether business, government, or other non-profit. The activism may advance through five stages: strain, mobilization, confrontation, negotiation, and resolution. Likewise, Smith and Ferguson (2001) advanced the discussion of activism, largely for purposes of giving for-profits and governmental agencies a better understanding of the dynamics of their operating arena. Dozier and Lauzen (2000) called not only for a clearly articulated understanding of the role of activism in public relations theory but invited academics to join that activism to oppose a theoretical perspective grounded on a pro-business paradigm. That line of reasoning presumed that large organizations, through public relations, impose policies onto communities whose citizens would likely oppose those policies if not stymied by corporate public relations experts.

Given more attention in other bodies of literatures, NGOs (non-governmental organizations) have become a popular term, again to be discussed as a means for warning and preparing business public relations specialists to respond to activism proactively or reactively. This line of reasoning has recently extended to the discussion of terrorism, which is a specific kind of non-profit NGO.

Focusing less on the larger picture of activism and its social role, C. Condit and D. Condit (1992) addressed the strategy of incremental erosion, a generic activism tactic that was used by Coalition on Smoking OR Health against R. J. Reynolds Company. This activist group served as a case study to examine how activism positions itself to challenge the legitimacy of its target by chipping away at premises that are needed by the business to sustain its current means for generating revenue. In the history of the smoking controversy, many non-profits applied pressure on the industry and called for government regulation. Among these groups, the American Cancer Society and American Heart Association played primary and sustained roles in helping bring facts to the attention of key publics. In addition, various medical researchers engaged in the anti-smoking battle such as Alton Ochshner and Ernest Wynder. Each of these organizations and researchers in their own way chipped at the foundations of legitimacy that had sustained the industry's position on tobacco and health. In these ways, we have evidence of how such activists build platforms of fact and challenge premises that serve as the rationale for corporate policy.

Another substantial line of investigation has featured the manner in which activists position themselves to be credible (and attack their opponents' credibility) by seeking to take this high moral road in public policy battles. The discussion by Bostdorff (1992) is one of a few treatments of a non-profit (Planned Parenthood) engaged in public policy debate with other non-profits. Murphy and Dee (1996) observed how corporate and activist organizations may agree on key values, but differ on the policy means and organizational activities needed to achieve those values.

In this line of analysis, public relations is not only a key element in the effectiveness of activists, but it actually pressed academics to realize how long public relations (even if only by strategy or tactic if not by name) has been practiced. Textbook discussions have focused on the Catholic Church's use of communication to propagate the faith. The Church, as a non-profit, has been the target of attacks such as that by Martin Luther. In similar fashion, government has not only long used the strategies and tactics of public relations but has suffered the challenges of non-profit activism, such as that launched against King John by the barons; this forced conflict led to the Magna Carta. The spectacles of Roman emperors, the pageantry of fairs and knights, grandiose temples and burials of monarchs, the Great Wall of China: All of these fall into categories of functions, strategies, and tactics typical of public relations.

In the clash between activists and businesses and/or governmental agencies— and even other non-profits—the "other voice" featured in the rhetorical paradigm of public relations as statement and counterstatement is often that of one or more non-profit (Heath, 2001). As such, non-profit public relations features governmental relations, community relations, crisis communication, risk communication, and issues management. It entails the tactics of publicizing some matter of public interest, such as public health, to create strain. It calls for people to join together and fund the mobilization efforts that can force confrontation and may lead to negotiation and resolution. However, activists seek to raise standards of corporate performance and may refuse to negotiate because the resolution of conflict would establish a level of performance that might privilege the organization being attacked and weaken the power of the attacking organization.

With this history and analysis of non-profit strategic activity as a foundation, the next section focuses on the anti-slavery activity of the nineteenth century in the United States.

Anti-slavery Organizations and Activism

The civil rights movement is the longest sustained effort of its kind in the United States. Only a few years after the introduction of slavery, Quakers, motivated by their faith, petitioned slave owners to end this abomination. Activist groups dedicated to this cause came and went. The delegates who drafted the Declaration of Independence addressed slavery, a social institution that nearly doomed the eventual drafting of the United States Constitution. Slave owners populated every office in the federal government in the formative years of the United States. The institution of slavery was part of endless bargains and political horse wrangling including the definitions of territories and admissions of states as slave or non-slave.

What began as morally motivated petitioners grew into various anti-slavery organizations and civil rights groups, some of which continue into our day. However ineffective the anti-slavery groups had been prior to the nineteenth century, they gathered in full force and fury in the first six decades of the nineteenth century eventually leading to the Civil War. No telling of this story would be complete without recounting the publicity and terrorism efforts of John Brown. Abraham Lincoln and others credited the publicity efforts of Harriet Beacher Stowe and her *Uncle Tom's Cabin* with fomenting the eventual fury in the North that inspired secession. In the public relations tool pantheon, few individual communication tactics are more effective at demonstrating the power of publicity and promotion than Stowe's book. The book was intended to publicize the issue, but would not have been called a public relations tool since that specific term had not been coined. The book appeared in serial publication in 1852, the year of Douglass' July 4th indictment of America's hypocrisy on the matter of liberty.

Non-profit organizations devoted to anti-slavery agitation grew up across the U.S. and in Europe, especially Great Britain. Based on a shared sense of strain between the current policy on slavery and what its opponents preferred, many anti-slavery societies appeared in the United States and other countries, especially England. These societies understood, but also honed, the application of public relations tactics as they fought against the evil which they believed to blight the moral and legal underpinnings of the United States. As will be explained below, they were good at planning and executing events. During such an event, Frederick Douglass delivered his famous Fourth of July speech in Rochester, New York, at the invitation of the Rochester Ladies' Anti-Slavery Society. It was one of many such local groups affiliated in various ways with other state and national organizations as a network of such organizations.

William Lloyd Garrison's Massachusetts Anti-Slavery Society was one of the most effective. It publicized the strain of slavery and mobilized supporters not only to contribute financially, but also to participate at least by being audiences, readers, and protesters. He published the *Liberator*. Following Garrison's lead, Douglass joined the Massachusetts Anti-Slavery Society, spoke on its behalf as one of many operators in its speakers bureau, and eventually used that experience to launch his own anti-slavery publication, *North Star* (a metaphoric reference to the star slaves used to guide themselves into freedom), which grew into *Frederick Douglass' Paper*. Garrison's and Douglass' papers clearly were the equivalent of today's activist launch of a website or blog to blast their opposition and control the content of what is published and said. Activists learned long ago that they must play to the media coverage of standard news outlets, but they need their own voice to assure their messages are not distorted during news coverage. Print and public speaking were the communication tool staples of the era. Douglass wrote three versions of his autobiography, the sales of which helped sustain him and his cause. His paper attracted supporters and advanced his arguments against established thought, which he and others sought to chip away one premise at a time through incremental erosion (Condit & Condit, 1992).

In addition to serving the American Anti-Slavery Society, as well as associations in various states other than Massachusetts and towns other than Rochester, Douglass served as a featured speaker for the British Anti-Slavery Society and the international version of that organizational structure. Virtually every branch of the American Methodist Episcopal Church was a non-profit element of the anti-slavery movement. Other churches, even those with predominately white congregations, offered periodic sermons and allowed for the voices of the African American.

If speakers bureaus are a staple of the public relations practice, they were a necessity of the anti-slavery movement. Douglass and many other slaves/former slaves were cogs in the speakers bureaus supported by the many anti-slavery organizations and churches. Douglass, as were others, was featured as evidence of the cruel reality of slavery and the inherent humanity of members of his "race" (although he had a white father). Such speakers publicized their harrowing escapes, such as being smuggled to freedom in a box. Speakers or sometimes individuals who simply served as visual aids were valued to the extent they could demonstrate the cruelty of slavery. None of these confrontational publicity devices was more powerful than those who could bear backs scarred by the lash or necks marred from an iron collar. Men and women served in this capacity, opting to be photographed so their disfigured bodies could be displayed in print.

Speaking tours were arranged. They were publicized. They became well-staged events. The speakers as well as others in various anti-slavery societies became polished event planners and executers. As simple as that sounds, it was profoundly difficult because of the resistance against the anti-slavery movement. Speakers were harassed and discriminated against. In the winter, as well as during inclement weather in other seasons, they had to ride outside of carriages and coaches that carried white people. They were recognized and singled out for abuse. They were spat upon. Gangs would throw pepper into crowds gathered to hear them. They were threatened with violence. Police often assumed that the best way to maintain order was to prevent the speaker's performance. Lodging was hard to arrange during these tours. Inns and other establishments discriminated against these "featured speakers," thus giving them more ammunition when they spoke.

Societies of these sorts often were associated with those devoted to other causes, especially women's rights, primarily suffrage. These groups, individually and collectively, engaged in agitation to demonstrate the strain of their cause—to help others recognize the problems and see possible solutions. They lobbied; they created alliances to promote and oppose legislation, the most offensive of which was the Fugitive Slave Law. They raised money and mobilized forces; they created and sustained speakers bureaus and publications. In short, they strategically created conflict or the conditions for conflict. They defined and pressed issues, created platforms of fact, and advocated enlightened policy. They engaged in media relations and community relations, as well as offering testimonials and providing data for the (re)formation of public opinion.

One of the standard societal roles of non-profit activism has been to raise the value standards of society, to aspire, for instance, to higher environmental standards. This too was part of the anti-slavery effort, but it also worked to hold American public policy to the value standard espoused in two of the U.S.'s most hallowed documents: the Declaration of Independence and the Constitution. These documents and the celebration of the Fourth of July which honors them set the context for Douglass' Fourth of July speech which drew rhetorical force from the paradox of the positive.

Before applying this paradox to understand his speech as a vital strategy (in a standard public relations tool, the public address) in the public relations efforts of anti-slavery non-profits, the next section develops the logic of this rhetorical strategy and weakness in public opinion.

Theory of the Paradox of the Positive

By its nature and the consequent roles it plays in society—especially when practiced on behalf of businesses—public relations is a professional practice typically devoted to making positive claims. That tendency, unfortunately, leads to the aura of and rationale for claims that public relations relies heavily on "spin" and even is nothing but spin (Fall, 2005). By classical rhetorical standards, overly positive (or negative) claims stress or frame one perspective beyond the limits of being a fair and true representation of the relevant supporting material. These overly positive claims can focus so much on that perspective that they slight, at least, and even mask the negative side of the relevant case. Such bias results in the framing and supporting of issues in ways and to such a degree that those issues fail to meet the classical rhetorical standard that expects communicators to help audiences and publics make enlightened choices (Nichols, 1963).

During a marketing communication effort, the typical practitioner working for an organization, such as a business, is likely to feature positive interpretations of a product, service, or the organization. This framing may be designed to bolster the image or reputation of its products or services and even repair its image or reputation. But the claims made might be, by implication or actual statement, more positive than is supported by careful attention to the supporting data. As marketing concepts for instance, "new and improved" might stress positive improvement that masks flaws, failures, or inadequacies in the previous iteration of a product or service. This is a pervasive flaw in marketing lingo; however, only recently—and then only for pharmaceutical products, tobacco, and alcohol—the positive claims of what the product will do must be accompanied by acknowledged negative "side effects." In a crisis response, the positive elements of a lesson learned often overshadow or blur the negative impact of events and policies that led to the crisis. One clear case recently was the defense of Ken Lay, former CEO of Enron whose legal defense focused on the following proposition: If the business media, traders, and analysts had not made negative comments, the company would otherwise have survived and even thrived because it was founded on solid business principles.

Overly positive (or negative) statements violate central assumptions of responsible advocacy (Heath, 2007). The dialogue of society is best when it helps organizations to be reflective and work for legitimacy; it voices perspectives to help society be more fully functional (Heath, 2006). Distortions, intentional or merely a result of the nature of the language used, can result in perspectives that are deceiving rather than serving to facilitate the best understanding of some matter.

This challenge offers the exact point in a dialogue where activist non-profits are likely to engage those organizations being criticized. Activists tend to couch their arguments so they seek to correct the tendency of the positive to overcome the negative: the classic rhetorical model of problem solution. One of the inherent flaws of the efforts to make appropriate corrections is that the non-profit activist may be overly negative or overly positive in an attempt to balance the discussion of the issue. Thus, as we explore the public relations strategies for activism and social movement, the tensions between what is and what ought to be create the strain that motivates activists and leads them to stress what Sethi (1997) called the legitimacy gap. This gap occurs when what organizations do or believe differs in varying degrees or violates in myriad ways what their critics believe is a more legitimate perspective. Herein lies the rationale for issues management (Heath, 1997).

Whether people believe some organization is legitimate is likely to predict whether they identify with it or with those who criticize it. People tend to identify with perspectives they believe, or are convinced, to be the best available interpretation of some product, service, organization, or public policy issue. Thus, identification is a vital part of communication in general (Burke, 1969b) and public relations in specific.

Identification is an essential element of the positioning of activism that seeks to employ what Burke called the dialectic of division and merger. Cooperation and communion, sharing in common, is a theme central to Burke's approach to the most fundamental role public relations can play in society. Looking as he did so often and well for the chinks in the armor of communication, he warned: "If language is the fundamental instrument of human cooperation, and if there is an 'organic flaw' in the nature of language, we may well expect to find this organic flaw revealing itself through the texture of society" (Burke, 1934, p. 330).

This flaw was the centerpiece in the Fourth of July oration by Frederick Douglass. This theme, the central argument in this article, reasons that through highly positive statements—made publicly by the most prominent citizens of each community in adoration of the meaning of July 4th—persons of color residing in the United States in the early part of the nineteenth century were marginalized and alienated. The positive claims celebrating liberty, freedom, and equality were hollow to these people because they were excluded from the protection implied by those terms. Instead of providing protection of their interests, the terms were used to evaluate and protect the status of white male citizens whereas they were denied to slaves as well as freedmen (and even all women).

The quality of the themes and the approach to those themes is central to the nature of discourse which in turn helps us identify and consider the ethical and effective practice of public relations. By its nature and social role, public relations is a professional practice devoted to making positive claims. In recent years, scholars in that discipline have worked to develop a normative theory to critique and guide the practice. It centers on challenges to build community by fostering a fully functioning society (Heath, 2006). It entails efforts to achieve excellence through symmetry as opposed to asymmetry (J. Grunig, 1992). The analysis in this immediate article reasons that the paradox of the positive (or its negative counterpart) moves the continuum of the practice more toward asymmetry than toward symmetry. This view of public relations reasons that relationship building to enhance the quality of community requires that multiple interests be sought and worked into consensus through various approaches to conflict resolution. This process has as its centerpiece the daunting challenge of dealing responsibly with the problems of marginalization and alienation.

One source of marginalization and alienation is the definitional hegemony that occurs as positive claims are made, for instance, about the goals and processes of urban renewal which by implication point to the inner-city publics as being a contributing reason for urban blight (Waymer & Heath, 2007). Through ostensible improvement, rationale is given, through what are likely to be positive biases in analysis, whereby the privileged parts of society advance their claims for perfection—which is that most human motive as Burke (1968) reasoned in his "definition of man." The positive couched in perfection provides a mask for the negative aspects of some relevant issue. This imbalance in analysis features positive outcomes for one interest without effectively considering negative consequences for another interest.

Such symbolic tug of war, the wrangle of the marketplace, presupposes that all sides of some issue are given full and careful consideration. The quality of dialogue rests on the assumption that the full dialectic of perspectives receives consideration. Human experience witnesses a tug of war between various dominant dialectics. That logic supports Burke's (1973) claim that human existence is a dialectic of merger and division; in cooperation there is the essence of competition. In identification and association there is disassociation. Human struggle tends to pit "us" or "we" versus "them/they." Such dichotomy forces us to look for the origins of division and the potentiality of merger, the resolution of differences. As he explored the principles of economics and psychology, Burke (1973) found symbols of authority are fundamental to the rationale for acceptance and rejection. Taking an interpretive view that blended psychology and economics, Burke observed how those feeling alienation tend to reject the reigning symbols of authority. They do so because justification of authority often requires margin-alization of the victims of authority; they are marginalized by the terminology of authority. For instance, the creation and mobilization of an army results in and from the identification one group feels in opposition to some enemy. The ratio-nale for police is concern for criminals and murderers. Burke's thoughts on these matters reflected his concerns for social conditions in the United States during the 1930s:

> "Alienation" is thus also a concept clearly having both economic and psy-chological relevance. An increasing number of people become alienated by material dispossession. (p. 306)

Such alienation, the fodder of activist non-profit public relations, grows out of and can exploit the paradox of the positive. This claim is supported by the logics of linguistic relativism, that overarching theory of language that reasons meaning resides in words and paints reality, instead of merely naming reality as objective statements whereby the meaning of a term can be created by pointing to the thing to which it refers. This referential theory of language was posited by Ogden and Richards (1923), among others. (See Heath & Bryant, 2000, for a comparative dis-cussion of these two theories of language.) Referentialism rests on the fundamental proposition that the meaning of meaning occurs because of the mind's recall of an experience and the name associated with that experience. Words link things and the residue of the experience of those things. Ogden and Richards stated: "words are the meeting points at which regions of experience, which can never combine in sensation or intuition, come together" (pp. 130–131).

In his review of Ogden and Richards's theory of language, Burke argued that nothing could be further from reality than the words that are assumed to refer to it. This critique helped support and reflected Burke's views on linguistic relativ-ism which posits support for this revision, as Burke (1966) reasoned: "things are the signs of words" (p. 363). Instead of reflecting meaning, language defines and attitudinizes it. Such is the case, Burke argued, because "there will be as many dif-ferent worldviews in history as there are people" (p. 52). This is true because words as our instruments for knowing are nothing but structures of terms and therefore manifest the nature of the terminology, vocabulary (Burke, 1969a). The essence, as well as perceptual outcome, of this logic supports the fact that language, each idiom or vocabulary, is a reflection, selection, and deflection of how people see and act toward the world they name and experience.

Such is the case because words create terministic screens through which people perceive reality. Those perceptions distort, include, exclude, shade, enhance, dimin-ish, and such, depending on each word and the larger vocabulary and culture of the users of the word. Words constitute "a kind of photographic 'screen' which will 'let through' some perceptions and 'filter out' others" (p. 105). Thus, the logic of this widely acclaimed theory of language explained how people were subject to the whims and wiles of their culture, seeing nothing more or less than what it allowed. Perhaps no more brilliant statement exists on this theory than that articulated by the linguistic anthropologist, Sapir:

Human beings do not live in the objective world alone, nor alone in the world of social activity as ordinarily understood, but are very much at the mercy of the particular language which has become the medium of expression for their society. . . . We see and hear and otherwise experience very largely as we do because the language habits of our community pre-dispose certain choices of interpretation.

(Quoted by Whorf, 1956, p. 134)

This statement is the essence of the Whorf–Sapir principle of language and culture. Following this line of reasoning, Burke (1966) asserted that the verification of truth is problematic because the conclusions humans make imply "the particular terminology in terms of which the observations are made" (p. 46).

And, how do words relate meaning to the world of experience and thought, thus laying the rationale for understanding the flaws inherent in language, including the paradox of the positive? Burke (1973) reasoned that words are of three kinds: positive, dialectical, and ultimate. Positive terms, such as apple, need nothing to define them other than to know the category of thing to which they refer and the interpretations that arise from the culture or worldview of each observer. Thus, a positive word, cow, refers to a female bovine, and in American language suggests the eventuality of slaughter, a reality far from the Hindu meaning for the same physical reality. A second level of term is the dialectic, such as liberty or equality. Each dialectic term, such as liberty, has meaning only because of knowledge of its dialectical opposite, in this case slavery. Ultimate terms are those dialectical terms in whose names people act. On the field at Gettysburg during the American Civil War, soldiers for both sides appealed to the ultimate term, will of God for victory and freedom (whether for determination of states rights or for people caught in the linguistic vice of slavery). Perception is connected to language to such an extent that contact with reality "reveals only such reality as is capable of being revealed by this particular kind of terminology" (Burke, 1969a, p. 313).

Once such terms translate into action, they are likely to guide, motivate, and frame views and actions. As they tend to point to or away from attributes of perceived reality, words suffering the paradox of the positive may become more understandable but also more problematic. In marketing communication, purveyors of goods feature positive elements and dissociate from negative ones. This sort of verbal positioning establishes part of the rationale for crisis and risk management as well. When public relations practitioners battle over issues and even seek conflict resolution and foster collaborative decision making, they are prone to stress the positive side of their case and play down the negative aspects of the topic fundamental to the controversy.

The paradox of the positive is one of those flaws in language of which Burke warned us; it occurs, especially in the case study addressed in this chapter, when dialectic terms such as liberty, freedom, and equality were elevated to the ultimate stage through the Declaration of Independence and Constitution. Over many years and through myriad celebrations of July 4th, those terms had by 1850 become disconnected from their polar opposites in crucial ways. Such disconnection resulted in rhetorical problems facing anti-slavery activists. Activists, in turn, attempted to make incremental erosion (C. Condit & D. Condit, 1992) of the interpretations and applications of these terms in ways that caused rhetorical problems for those who supported slavery and racism or did not aggressively oppose them.

The rhetorical problem (Bitzer, 1968, 1987; Heath, 1992) facing Douglass on behalf of the anti-slavery societies was the singular application of the principles of the Declaration of Independence and Constitution to white males. Addressing this rhetorical problem, Douglass arose to address and expose this flaw as the condemnation of the terministic screen that supported slavery and disfranchisement (and other forms of discrimination). As long as it was in place, preventing people from seeing the irony and inconsistency of the celebration, it would be a wall to anti-slavery efforts. So, it had to be taken down, through incremental erosion (C. Condit & D. Condit, 1992), one unit of meaning or premise at a time.

Thus, linguistic relativity, which explains the paradox of the positive, established the theoretical foundation by which to analyze Frederick Douglass' Fourth of July oration which is a masterful instance of activist public relations. His simple theme, voiced eloquently, was that the positive celebration of the Declaration of Independence was hollow in the minds of those who realized that it excluded slaves and people of color who were free. It created the two-part mentality so central to diversity that marginalized people often feel the tugging of simultaneously being included, while being excluded.

As it promotes some preferred organizational perspective, public relations often features the positive, thereby suffering the paradox of that term. As non-profit activism, this aspect of the profession may feature the paradox as the basis for recognizing and diagnosing some issue-driven problem, the basis of a legitimacy gap, which consequently needs solution. Thus, we have the motive for activism and the grounds for strain, mobilization, confrontation, negotiation, and resolution—the key elements of activism.

Frederick Douglass and the Fourth of July Speech

The Declaration of Independence was a brilliant public relations document, an issues management, government relations masterpiece. It was designed and executed to accomplish vital issue communication, public opinion, and image management objectives. First, it explained in detail the reasons the King (not parliament) had violated principles of human rights and responsible sovereignty. Instead of making a purely enflamed case (or no case at all) against royal authority, it articulated the causes of grievance in a brief that would have pleased modern courts and lawyers in form and substance. It was dignified and high-minded, a clear statement of a higher sense of value that defined the legitimacy gap between colonists and the government, through the King; it indicted and tried the King. Second, it sought to galvanize colonists who opposed the King's tyranny so they could take up arms in "self-defense."

One of the three authors of the Declaration of Independence, John Adams (second president of the United States) believed it would be a vital part of the future of the new nation (assuming that it survived). Recall that the timing of the ratification of the Declaration might have made July 2 the national day of ceremony. That fact is important as we listen to the words of Adams, quoted by a biographer, foretelling the ceremony that would surround this ratification.

> The second day of July 1776 will be the most memorable epoch in the history of America. I am apt to believe that it will be celebrated by succeeding generations as the great anniversary festival. It ought to be commemorated as the Day of Deliverance by solemn acts of devotion to God Almighty. It ought to be solemnized with pomp and parade, with shows, games, sports, guns, bells, bonfires, and illuminations from one end of this continent to the other from this time forward forever more.
>
> (McCullough, 2001, p. 130)

Could any public relations professional operating in the twenty-first century describe more clearly the public relations event/publicity potential of this hallowed moment? Long before the celebration became a publicity or marketing communication spectacle, it was foretold as a public relations practitioner's dream. No professionals were ready to serve under that specific shingle for years to come; nevertheless, Adams grasped the public relations event possibilities of the document as it was being adopted and circulated.

As Adams predicted, the Fourth of July became much celebrated in many ways, including the most reverent and solemn. By the time Frederick Douglass was preparing to deliver his address, it was celebrated in cities, towns, and villages. One of the venues was the churches where day-long, quiet and thoughtful celebrations led to the praise of God for delivering the United States into freedom, liberty, and democracy (Colaiaco, 2006). In public relations, timing is important. For Douglass, not only the day but the occasion was essential to the depth of his argument and its effect on the audience. His central theme demonstrated the paradox of the positive. Colaiaco (2006) noted, "Douglass, the nation's leading gadfly, would hold a mirror up to his fellow Americans of the North, stirring them to examine their consciences and see their complicity in the sin of slavery" (p. 35).

As would be every subsequent and carefully positioned event, Douglass' speech was delivered in a time and place where it could achieve the greatest potential visibility. The speech was delivered before five to six hundred people in the Corinthian Hall in Rochester, New York. The date was July 5, 1852. The Fourth of July fell on a Sunday that year. The planners of this event wisely believed that the statement could be seen as offending the Sabbath despite the fact that slavery was rejected by many religions (but justified by some). The fifth was often chosen as the official day for protest speeches because that day was ideal for reflecting on the positive comments that typified the Fourth of July addresses that were made across the nation.

The event featuring Douglass was hosted by the Rochester Ladies' Anti-Slavery Society. It was advertised in papers and on placards to increase attendance and increase the likelihood that newspapers would carry it. Rochester was one of the major stations on the Underground Railroad. This was a public relations event, set carefully in the context of thousands of July 4th celebrations in this nation which was not yet 100 years old. The event was carefully staged. Douglass was carefully chosen for the task and given proper time to prepare. In his estimation of the impact of the presentation, Colaiaco (2006) probably over assumed the impact, but squarely nailed the approach to the rhetorical problem: "Frederick Douglass awakened the conscience of the nation, compelling Americans to confront the gravest moral dilemma in its history" (p. 6). Viewing the sense of July 4th at the time, Colaiaco called it America's "civil religion" (p. 7). The nineteenth-century abolitionist movement grew from a religious movement called the Second Great Awakening, but the defining "religious texts" for this civil religion were the Declaration of Independence and Constitution. Passages, short and long, were typically quoted from each or both by speakers and newspaper editorialists. July 4th was a day set aside to celebrate the ideals positively proclaimed in these texts. In such anthems, the United States was featured as the "city on the hill," the beacon of freedom for other peoples.

In a time long before 24-hour network news broadcasts and the Internet, such events could nevertheless generate substantial media coverage. Three leading papers gave Douglass' comments extensive front-page coverage: The *New York Tribune*, the *Chicago Tribune*, and the *New York Times*. It was also featured in abolitionist publications and mentioned in anti-slavery speeches that came in its wake.

The theme advanced by Douglass was not the unique gift of his critical intellect. Others had made statements of various kinds in which they had probed the inconsistency between the claims of the hallowed documents and the reality of slavery and rampant discrimination. But Douglass' unique gift, in the estimation of his peers, was the clarity and force of his presentation of this theme. It squarely focused on the narrowness of the definition of freedom, liberty, and democracy, a view clouded by the paradox of the positive. In that paradox, the dialectical opposites of these terms were obscured rather than illuminated to be prevalent throughout the nation. Some contemporaries of Douglass, such as Alexander Crummell, whose call for talented leaders to lift a people from slavery and despair preceded that theme made famous by W. E. B. DuBois.

On the dais with Douglass was the Reverend Robert R. Raymond of Syracuse. He delivered an opening prayer and read the entire Declaration of Independence replete with its lofty ideals of freedom and equality, the fundamentals of democracy.

> On the Fourth of July 1852, the abolition movement was in crisis. Using the power of his oratory, Frederick Douglass sought to energize the movement by calling upon the nation to resolve the American dilemma, the contradiction between the ideals of the Founders and the evil practice of slavery.
>
> (Colaiaco, 2006, p. 26)

A trademark of Douglass' activism was his rhetorical skill at addressing the positive respectfully, while giving the dialectic full opportunity to be revealed to his audience. He started by addressing "Mr. President (of the association), Friends, and Fellow Citizens" and set out three themes as part of his introduction. One was the deference he held for the concept of the Fourth of July as a matter of national spirit symbolic of "what the Passover was to the emancipated people of God" (Douglass, 1952, para. 4). A second was the maturing youthfulness of the nation which is needed in the darkening times:

> There is hope in the thought, and hope is much needed, under the dark clouds which lower above the horizon. The eye of the reformer is met with angry flashes, portending disastrous times; but his heart may well beat lighter at the thought that America is young, and that she is still in the pressible stage of her existence. (para. 4)

The third was his humble sense of himself as a critic, "the distance between this platform and the slave plantation, from which I escaped" (para. 3). These three themes frame the contrast between the positive ideals of independence and the dire conditions that constituted the strain pressed by the anti-slavery movement as the recognized problem that motivated collective action. The day to which his address referred marked that time when colonials sought to become a sovereign people. The founders have gone "so far in their excitement as to pronounce the measures of government unjust, unreasonable, and oppressive, and altogether such as ought not to be quietly submitted to" (para. 6). So too were the measures of government in regard to people of color, especially slaves, not to be "quietly submitted to" (para. 6). The precedent for Douglass was the actions of the founders whose risks were celebrated on July 4.

In detail he gave the audience reasons for feeling pride in what the founders had accomplished.

> Pride and patriotism, not less than gratitude, prompt you to celebrate and to hold it in perpetual remembrance. I have said that the Declaration of Independence is the ring-bolt to the chain of your nation's destiny: so, indeed, I regard it. The principles contained in that instrument are saving principles. Stand by those principles, be true to them on all occasions, in all places, against all foes, and at whatever cost. (para. 17)

One might assume that activism, often devoted to calling society to aspire to higher ideals, might have done so in this age. Douglass, however, realized that no higher ideals could be imagined. So, by reinforcing rather than critiquing the ideals, he set the foundation for pointing to the reality that in the positive attention to these ideals, the negative aspects of society—contrasted dialectically to those ideals—were rampant and painful, the more so because of the unfulfilled promise of the ideals.

After setting those opening themes, he offered more deferment: "I am not wanting in respect for the fathers of this republic" (para. 22). Set against the noble accomplishments of these founders, he asked: "What have I, or those I represent, to do with your national independence? Are the great principles of political freedom and of natural justice, embodied in that Declaration of Independence, extended to us?" (para. 35). Setting the contrast between the positive benefits of independence, and the condition of those not so benefited, Douglass stated bluntly: "I am not included with the pale of glorious anniversary! Your high independence only reveals the immeasurable distance between us." "The sunlight [of independence] that brought light and healing to you, has brought stripes [of the lash] and death to me. This Fourth of July is yours, not mine." Setting against the positive tone of July 4th, he forced the question: "Do you mean, citizens, to mock me, by asking me to speak today?" (para. 37).

Such challenges would not in that day force supporters of slavery to repent that sin. Nor would it cause civil or human rights to replace discrimination, but as C. Condit and D. Condit (1992) reasoned, each line focused on a premise that could be attacked to achieve incremental erosion. By taking stances comparing his (as an example) experience against the ideals of the Declaration of Independence, he augmented the strain necessary to motivate supporters of the abolition movement. Each argument, by contrast, set his and others' fate against that of those whose rights were protected by the Declaration of Independence.

Having used himself as a contrasting theme, the negative aspect of a society dedicated to liberty, he turned to details on slavery. He fleshed out the claim: "I hear the mournful wail of millions whose chains, heavy and grievous yesterday, are, to-day, rendered more intolerable by the jubilee shouts that reach them." He implored the audience to remember "those bleeding children of sorrow this day." "Standing there identified with the American bondman, making his wrongs mine, I do not hesitate to declare, with all my soul, that the character and conduct of this nation never looked blacker to me than on this 4th of July!" "Standing with God and the crushed and bleeding slave on this occasion, I will, in the name of humanity which is outraged, in the name of liberty which is fettered, in the name of the constitution and the Bible which are disregarded and trampled upon, dare to call in question and to denounce, with all the emphasis I can command, everything that serves to perpetuate slavery, the great sin and shame of America!" (para. 39). As Colaiaco (2006) observed, Douglass identified with those who sought to uphold the identity of the United States as stated explicitly and clearly in the foundational documents: "At issue for Douglass was the identity of America" (p. 36). Thus, for Douglass, "the abolitionist was the true descendent of the American Revolution and the slave . . . a glaring symbol of the nation's betrayal of its egalitarian promise" (p. 37).

The typical rhetorical stance of activism challenges the status quo by demonstrating through assertion and proof the weakness or hypocrisy of the ideals on which the status quo operates. For this reason, a case can be made that activists add value to the dialogue of society by seeking to raise standards, or values, on which public policy is founded. The first of the two options, to raise the standards of society, has been the hallmark of environmentalism, for instance. The second framing, stressing the failure to live up to hallowed values, is the essence of the rhetorical stance taken by Douglass. In terms of the discussion of civil rights, no documents more clearly define the character of U.S. citizens than do the Declaration of Independence or Constitution; they proclaim those values as the essence of the American spirit. Since, in their opinion, anti-slavery advocates believed that the values should be applied to all people embracing their human and civil rights, their activism pointed to the hypocrisy of the gap between the ideals of those documents and the reality of daily life for millions of people living in the U.S.

One could argue that the principles of liberty do not apply to non-humans. For that reason, other animals do not share the liberty appreciated by humans. Clearly no one would imagine that cows or horses should be allowed to exercise the vote because they do not have the capacity to cast a considered ballot. But if liberty is an inalienable right of humans, how can one in good conscience deny the principle to slaves? To exclude them from the blessing of liberty required a rationale. In this case, the argument for slavery stressed how they were not "as human" as others. To challenge that hypocrisy required an attack through incremental erosion. To that rhetorical end, Douglass asked,

> Must I undertake to prove that the slave is a man? That point is conceded already. Nobody doubts it. The slaveholders themselves acknowledge it in the enactment of laws for their government. (para. 40)

He offered proof from Southern statute books to demonstrate that those legal systems acknowledged "that the slave is a moral, intellectual, and responsible being" (para. 40). In their work, they are more like other humans than the brutes of the field. Can cattle raise a barn? Can sheep harvest and store hay? And thus, if they are humans and are to be treated as such by legal prescription, they have the right to liberty, to the service of their time and the ownership of themselves, to the stability of their families.

As these people serve in their labor, what do they believe their chance at liberty is? As Douglass asked, "What, to the American slave, is your 4th of July? I answer; a day that reveals to him, more than all other days in the year, the gross injustice and cruelty to which he is the constant victim" (para. 46). The dialectic between liberty and the tyranny of slavery, as well as the hypocrisy of the Declaration and Constitution as applied in a nation upholding slavery were the themes that forced the legitimacy gap, the strain between the ideal and the actual. Such challenges are vital to the strategic positioning and the corresponding messaging of the non-profit activism. Confrontation leading to conflict is a central purpose: Defining the issue so that it demands resolution. How was this strain articulated? Douglass set forth the theme:

> To him, your celebration is a sham; your boasted liberty, an unholy license; your national greatness, swelling vanity; your sounds of rejoicing are empty and heartless; your denunciation of tyrants, brass fronted impudence; your shouts of liberty and equality, hollow mockery; your prayers and hymns, your sermons and thanksgivings, with all your religious parade and solemnity, are, to Him, mere bombast, fraud, deception, impiety, and hypocrisy—a thin veil to cover up crimes which would disgrace a nation of savages. There is not a nation on earth guilty of practices more shocking and bloody than are the people of the United States, at this very hour. (para. 46)

Recall the quotation above in which John Adams extolled the virtue of the Fourth of July. Compare that to the way in which the hallowed event was damned as being

hollow by Douglass' analysis. Adams saw the day as the quintessential public relations event lauding the identity of America, the celebration of liberty, freedom, and
democracy. Through public display and religious ceremony, the hallowed day was
celebrated in ways designed to keep people focused on liberty, to refresh the meaning and salience of that value. That sort of publicity was made to sound hollow by
Douglass' counterstatements.

Douglass, premise after premise, eroded the foundations of liberty and justice for
all. He challenged and eroded each of the major arguments posed by those who were
against granting freedom and liberty to slaves and former slaves. Although there
are several established premises he sought to erode, two of the most prevalent are
highlighted in the following. He used the prevailing religious and Christian beliefs
that many Americans prescribed to as a means of highlighting the hypocrisy in the
positive term of liberty. Additionally, he also challenged those who argued that the
Constitution must be interpreted based on the intent of the framers; thus, slavery can
be justified. Each of Douglass' strategies is explained in greater detail.

Douglass, appealing to the strong Christian roots of Americans stated:

> The American church is guilty, when viewed in connection with what it is
> doing to uphold slavery; but it is superlatively guilty when viewed in con-
> nection with its ability to abolish slavery. The sin of which it is guilty is one
> of omission as well as of commission. (para. 63)

He further lamented the fact that most American churches did not challenge
the legitimacy of the Fugitive Slave Law. This fact implied that those churches
regarded "religion simply as a form of worship, an empty ceremony, and not a
vital principle requiring active benevolence, justice, love and good will towards
man" (para. 59). Douglass, appealing to the Christian desire to do good works as
illustrated in the story of the Good Samaritan, further argued that those churches
that endorse slavery esteem "sacrifice above mercy; psalm-singing above right
doing; solemn meetings above practical righteousness" (para. 59). Furthermore,
he argued that worship that can be performed by people "who refuse to give
shelter to the houseless, to give bread to the hungry, clothing to the naked, and
who enjoin obedience to a law forbidding these acts of mercy, is a curse, not a
blessing to mankind" (para. 59). Simply put, Douglass highlighted that the Holy
Bible refers to such people as "scribes, Pharisees, hypocrites, who pay tithe of mint,
anise, and cumin, and have omitted the weightier matters of the law, judgement,
mercy and faith" (para. 59). Thus Douglass, appealing to a higher moral ground
than the Constitution itself—Christian teachings—transcended issues of race and
incrementally eroded the positive associations of liberty based on a loftier, religious
ethic.

Additionally, Douglass addressed the argument raised by some that "the right
to hold and to hunt slaves is a part of that Constitution framed by the Illustrious
Fathers of this Republic" (para. 68). Douglass challenged his audience to interpret the Constitution as it ought to be interpreted: "as a GLORIOUS LIBERTY
DOCUMENT" (para. 71). Douglass stated: "Read its preamble, consider its purposes. Is slavery among them? . . . if the Constitution were intended to be, by its

framers and adopters, a slave-holding instrument, why neither slavery, slavehold-ing, nor slave can anywhere be found in it" (para. 71). Simply put, Douglass argued that if slavery and slaveholding were the intent of the framers of the Constitution, then he believed:

> your fathers stooped, basically stooped "To palter with us in a double sense: And keep the word of promise to the ear, But break it to the heart." And instead of being the honest men I have before declared them to be, they were the veriest imposters that ever practised on mankind. This is the inevitable conclusion, and from it there is no escape. (para. 69–70)

In such logic, Douglass cornered his critics and left them with only one rhetorical option. Critics must accept that blaming the "baseness [of slavery] on the fram-ers of the Constitution of the United States . . . is a slander upon their memory" (para. 70); thus, the Constitution must be viewed as a "GLORIOUS LIBERTY DOCUMENT" (para. 71).

In the rhetoric of public relations, each statement is likely to suffer the meaning expressed in one or more counterstatements. In this debate, clarity and meaning, proof and reasoning can be brought to the attention of publics. Such debate offers those publics the opportunity to make enlightened choice, the essence of rheto-ric (Nichols, 1963). Through messaging and positioning, Douglass and the New England Anti-Slavery Society sought to force attention to the shortcoming of a government that did not live up to its most hallowed ideals. By emphasizing the strain of this legitimacy gap, Douglass and his colleagues had the rationale needed to motivate people to mobilize in support of abolition, a means for confronting and forcing conflict that would demand resolution. To accomplish this end required careful analysis of the paradox of the positive, a vital strategic option available to leaders of social activism.

Conclusion

The purpose of this chapter is to build upon and advance the discussion of activist public relations. To that end, it examined the strategic positioning and messaging of one event during the nineteenth-century anti-slavery movement in the United States. The various elements of that movement challenged the status quo position on slavery and racial discrimination. To do so, it included events such as Frederick Douglass' Fourth of July oration. It was one of many instances that anti-slavery communicators worked to create strain by pointing to a legitimacy gap between hallowed values and the application of those values to the lives and conditions of people living and working in the United States. If sufficient, the strain between values and action could help anti-slavery organizers to achieve mobilization, confrontation, and perhaps engage in negotiation and resolution.

To do that, they engaged in many tactics. One of the most central includes the attack on the paradox of the positive, the need to correct overly positive inter-pretations of various conditions that cause a strain between what is and what ought to be. This strain is the motive that attracts followers and sustains activist non-profits in their efforts to correct what they target or frame as the evils of society. The Fourth of July oration delivered by Frederick Douglass in 1852 demonstrates further evidence for the concept of the paradox of the positive, which in this case was attacked through what has been called incremental erosion (C. Condit & D. Condit, 1992).

Careful analysis suggests the activist rhetoric of the anti-slavery movement supported the conclusion of Murphy and Dee (1996) who argued that corporations (or government agencies in this case) and activists may agree on one or more central values but differ substantially regarding how to achieve those values. Whereas Murphy and Dee used the case study of conflict between DuPont and Greenpeace, the examination above of Frederick Douglass' Fourth of July address demonstrates how key supporters of the Declaration of Independence and abolitionists agreed on the primacy of liberty as a defining value of civil society, but had substantially differing opinions as to whom, what categories of people, those values applied and in what manner. Slavery and liberty are dialectical terms. To focus on liberty and ignore or tolerate slavery was, Douglass argued, a crime against inalienable rights, a stance that demanded concerted efforts to correct this blight on the American ideals expressed in the Declaration. Such conclusions add depth to the theory of activist, non-profit public relations typical of social movement activism.

What is responsible advocacy? That question enlivens the discussion of the paradox of the positive and stresses the critical perspective that discourse of public relations is most ethical when it does not violate the paradox of the positive and helps people to make enlightened choices (Nichols, 1963). However much a person such as Douglass might want "public relations practitioners" who held key positions with the powerful forces of government and commerce of his time (Holtzhausen, 2007) to partner with his cause, one can only wonder whether that person could have so powerfully exposed the paradox of the positive by sharply contrasting the ideals of the Declaration of Independence to the reality of slavery and discrimination.

References

Bitzer, L. (1968). The rhetorical situation. *Philosophy and Rhetoric, 1,* 1–15.

Bitzer, L. (1987). Rhetorical public communication. *Critical Studies in Mass Communication, 4,* 425–428.

Bostdorff, D. M. (1992). "The Decision Is Yours" campaign: Planned Parenthood's characteristic argument of moral virtue. In E. L. Toth & R. L. Heath (Eds.), *Rhetorical and critical approaches to public relations* (pp. 301–314). Hillsdale, NJ: Lawrence Erlbaum.

Burke, K. (1934, May 2). The meaning of C. K. Ogden. *New Republic, 78,* 328–331.

Burke, K. (1964). On form. *Hudson Review, 17,* 103–109.

Burke, K. (1966). *Language as symbolic action.* Berkeley: University of California Press.

Burke, K. (1968). *Counter-statement,* Berkeley: University of California Press. (Originally published 1931.)

Burke, K. (1969a) *A grammar of motives.* Berkeley: University of California Press.

Burke, K. (1969b). *A rhetoric of motives.* Berkeley: University of California Press.

Burke, K. (1973). *The philosophy of literary form* (3rd ed.). Berkeley: University of California Press (originally published in 1941). The chapter entitled "Twelve Propositions" was reprinted from: K. Burke (1938). Twelve propositions by Kenneth Burke on the relation between economy and psychology. *Science & Society, 2* (Spring), 242–249.

Colaiaco, J. A. (2006). *Frederick Douglass and the Fourth of July Oration.* New York: Palgrave Macmillan.

Condit, C. M., & Condit, D. M. (1992), Smoking OR health: Incremental erosion as a public interest group strategy. In E. L. Toth & R. L. Heath (Eds.), *Rhetorical and critical approaches to public relations* (pp. 241–256). Hillsdale, NJ: Lawrence Erlbaum.

Douglass, F. (1852, July 5). What to the slave is the Fourth of July? Also, called "The meaning of July Fourth for the Negro." Retrieved, September 22, 2008 from http://web.archive.org/web/20060823232635/http://douglassarchives.org/doug_a10.htm

Dozier, D. M., & Lauzen, M. M. (2000). Liberating the intellectual domain from the practice: Public relations, activism, and the role of the scholar. *Journal of Public Relations Research, 12,* 3–22.

Fall, L. T. (2005). Spin. In R. L. Heath (Ed.), *Encyclopedia of public relations* (pp. 800–803). Thousand Oaks, CA: Sage.

Grunig, J. E. (1992). (Ed.). *Excellence in public relations and communication management.* Hillsdale, NJ: Lawrence Erlbaum.

Grunig, J. E. (2001). Two-way symmetrical public relations: Past, present, and future. In R. L. Heath (Ed.), *Handbook of public relations* (pp. 11-30), Thousand Oaks, CA: Sage.

Grunig, L. A. (1992). Activism: How it limits the effectiveness of organizations and how excellent public relations departments respond. In J. E. Grunig (Ed.), *Excellence in public relations and communication management* (pp. 503–530). Hillsdale, NJ: Lawrence Erlbaum.

Heath, R. L. (1992). The wrangle in the marketplace: A rhetorical perspective of public relations. In E. L. Toth & R. L. Heath (Eds.), *Rhetorical and critical approaches to public relations* (pp. 17–36). Hillsdale, NJ: Lawrence Erlbaum.

Heath, R. L. (1997). *Strategic issues management: Organizations and public policy challenges.* Thousand Oaks, CA: Sage.

Heath, R. L. (2001). A rhetorical enactment rationale for public relations: The good organization communicating well. In R. L. Heath (Ed.), *Handbook of public relations* (pp. 31–50), Thousand Oaks, CA: Sage.

Heath, R. L. (2006). Onward through the fog: Thoughts on public relations' research directions. *Journal of Public Relations Research, 18,* 93–114.

Heath, R. L. (2007). Management through advocacy: Reflection rather than domination. In E. L. Toth (Ed.), *The future of excellence in public relations and communication management* (pp. 41–66), Thousand Oaks, CA: Sage.

Heath, R. L., & Bryant, J. (2000). *Human communication theory and research: Concepts, contexts, and challenges* (2nd ed.). Mahwah, NJ: Lawrence Erlbaum.

Holtzhausen, D. R. (2007). Activism. In E. L. Toth (Ed.), *The future of excellence in public relations and communication management: Challenges for the next generation* (pp. 357–379), Mahwah, NJ: Lawrence Erlbaum.

Kelly, K. S. (1998). *Effective fundraising management.* Mahwah, NJ: Lawrence Erlbaum.

Kelly, K. S. (2005). Fundraising. In R. L. Heath (Ed.), *Encyclopedia of public relations* (pp. 353–357). Thousand Oaks, CA: Sage.

McCullough, D. M. (2001). *John Adams.* New York: Simon & Schuster.

Murphy, P., & Dee, J. (1996). Reconciling the preferences of environmental activists and corporate policymakers. *Journal of Public Relations Research, 8,* 1–33.

Nichols, M. H. (1963). *Rhetoric and criticism.* Baton Rouge, LA: LSU Press.

Ogden, C. K., & Richards, I. A. (1923). *The meaning of meaning.* New York: Harcourt, Brace, Jovanovich.

Sethi, S. P. (1997). *Advocacy advertising and large corporations: Social conflict, big business image, the news media, and public policy.* Lexington, MA: D. C. Heath.

Smith, M. F., & Ferguson, D. P. (2001). Activism. In R. L. Heath (Ed.), *Handbook of public relations* (pp. 291–300), Thousand Oaks, CA: Sage.

Waymer, D., & Heath, R. L. (2007, May). The paradox of the positive: A flaw in the practice of communication and public relations. Presented at the International Communication Conference, San Francisco.

Whorf, B. L. (1956). *Language, thought, and reality.* Cambridge, MA: MIT Press.

CONNECTING ORGANIZATIONS AND THEIR EMPLOYEE PUBLICS

The Rhetorical Analysis of Employee– Organization Relationships (EOR)

Damion Waymer
Virginia Tech

Lan Ni
University of Houston

Employee relations is an important area of public relations. Yet, it often goes understudied and undervalued because public relations does not have primary responsibility for internal communication. Moreover, public relations might not be expected to participate in the internal communication process at all. Employee relations is usually deemed as one of the primary responsibilities of human resources (HR); however, public relations professionals can and should play a role in helping HR to make the process more effective.

According to Heath (1997) a stake is "anything—tangible or intangible, material or immaterial—that one person or group has that is of value to another person or group" (p. 28). Stakes are valuable, and as such, organizations seek to establish relationships with the person, persons, or groups who possess valuable stakes. These stakeholders, in turn, are valuable to an organization as well.

Each scholar might define the concept of stakeholder a bit differently; however, each version of the definition generally stands for the same principle, namely that "corporations [and other organizations] should heed the needs, interests, and influence of those affected by their policies and operations" (Buchholz & Rosenthal, 2005, p. 137). Heath (1997), from an issues management perspective, defined stakeholders as "any persons or groups that hold something of value that can be used as rewards or constraints in exchange for goods, services, or organizational policies and operating standards" (p. 28). Typical stakeholders have been considered to include "consumers, suppliers, government, competitors, communities, employees, and of course, stockholders" (Buchholz & Rosenthal, 2005, p. 138). Thus, although employee relations has been deemed as the domain of HR, it is evident that from an issues management perspective public relations can and should play a role in this process.

Currently, in regard to dealing with employees and internal organizational members, public relations' role has been marginal at best. Public relations practitioners were often asked to provide help with the tools, such as the employee newsletter (now the intranet), of internal communication—not the training and development, change management, and the development of climate and culture. Though this internal tool is an important one, public relations scholars (Grunig, 1992; Grunig, Grunig, & Dozier, 2002) have argued extensively in the literature that public relations is more than the tools that it uses; it should be and is a strategic management function. As such, the authors argue that public relations should assist in the creation of productive work environments and happy employees; however, how exactly is this environment created? How can public relations, in concert with HR, work to create functional departments and employees who operate in a constructive culture and climate to make the organization successful and the employees empowered and fulfilled?

This chapter pursues these questions within the context of globalization. To adequately explore these questions, this chapter highlights and analyzes the told accounts of Chinese public relations managers and their employees who are employed by multinational corporations operating in their homeland. First, the authors establish how internal communication is rhetorical. Next, we discuss the concept of globalization, and how it impacts internal communication.

Internal Communication: A Symbolic, Rhetorical Construction

In an organizational context, communication has often been thought of as a tool or "conduit" used to convey thoughts and ideas between a sender and a receiver. People who view internal organizational communication in this vein are likely to see it as a tool used to transfer information from superiors to subordinates, and vice versa. However, this metaphorical viewing of communication is limited in scope and applicability. On the contrary, the authors argue that communication (both internal and external) constitutes and sustains organizations. Communicatively agreed upon and accepted practices and norms enable organizations to exist.

Organizations can be viewed as symbolic communicative constructions (see Morgan, 1997 for complete list of organizational metaphors), meaning that it is communication that creates and sustains organizations. Viewing an organization as symbolic means that the organization itself, its members, and all of its actions are semiotic creations. Organizations are often the sites where interactions among various stakeholders of organizations engage in activities to make meaning and to gain understanding. Simply put, there are no meanings in the words themselves, actions or activities, or any other "thing" that can take place in the organization; rather, meaning is attributed by individuals at the time in which they engage in activities or interact with one another or artifacts (such as a computer, a copying machine, or a door hanger).

To make this point more lucid, consider the following scenario. In accusations of sexual harassment in the workplace, a researcher viewing internal communication as symbolic may explore how men and women view sexual harassment differently.

Moreover, words and actions that may be viewed as harassment and offensive to some may not be viewed in the same way by others because the words and the actions themselves are symbols to be interpreted. In a similar vein organizational policies like paternity leave may be viewed as sound, fair practices, to some organizational members. What does it communicate to fellow employees and management if a male employee takes advantage of this policy? How will he be viewed? Do women feel marginalized by men who take advantage of these policies? More interestingly, although there is no formal statement or policy that says a male employee should not take leave, there might be an unstated culture in place that could prevent him from seizing this opportunity. There might be an unstated culture in place where any employee who wants to advance the career ladder must work at least 70 hours per week and limit his or her leave time. Employees who desire upward mobility might police themselves, and few employees—men or women—might decide to take advantage of these policies. This concept, in part, is known as unobtrusive control (Tompkins & Cheney, 1985).

This hypothetical example also illustrates the symbolic, rhetorical nature of organizations in general and internal communication specifically. Thus, by studying and understanding internal organizational communication, practitioners and scholars can better understand the ways in which people symbolically interact to provide meaning to their experiences as well as to understand the organizations that they are a part of. This increased understanding also enables individuals to recognize how these organizations impact their lives, and lived experiences. This chapter focuses specifically on the ways that globalization and multinational corporations impact internal communication between employees and public relations managers and how these challenges can be addressed communicatively.

Employee Relations in a Time of Globalization

Public relations scholars have accepted the challenge to develop normative theory to guide professional practice so multiple, legitimate interests and publics are simultaneously served rather than having only one interest advanced to the disadvantage of others (Heath, 2006). This view of public relations reasons that relationship building to enhance the quality of community requires that multiple interests be sought and worked to build consensus. No place is this more evident than in the analysis and criticism of large multinational companies that venture into foreign countries—shaping and influencing the indigenous culture in the name of globalization.

Globalization has been generating much controversy. Some maintain that it has broken down the barriers of national borders and facilitated exchange of products and knowledge, and these things should be taken into account in the current discussions about globalization (Feachem, 2001). According to the CATO Institute (2007)—which is the institute for trade policy studies—globalization can raise both the living standards and productivity of people in countries that "open" their borders up and embrace the global marketplace. Others argue that globalization has contributed to the further exploitation of markets and people and the widening of the gap between the rich and poor (Jenkins, 2003; Kentor, 2001).

In fact, firms make the choice of globalization based on the possession of excess and underutilized resources that can be used elsewhere in the world (e.g., Chatterjee & Wernerfelt, 1991). Many multinational companies entered foreign countries also because of resources in various forms, such as cheap labor and vast market opportunities, which are not always available in their home countries. When these multinational companies expand into foreign markets, they are applauded for creating more employment opportunities but at the same time criticized for taking advantage of people and resources in often less developed countries.

Faced with this, public relations scholars are questioning themselves about the "unspoken support for, and allegiance to corporate capitalist power" (Weaver, 2001) in the globalized economy. Weaver argued for bringing the "ethical obligations" to different cultures and social groups and for serving the interests of "those groups who perceive themselves as disempowered by globalization" (p. 280).

Employees at the overseas subsidiaries of multinational companies are an important group of such "disempowered" publics. They usually face a double power imbalance: one between employee and employer and the other between local branches usually in a developing country and powerful headquarters companies. Labor or human resources is one of the most essential resources for any organization and some multinational companies establish overseas subsidiaries for no other reason than to make use of the cheap labor in the overseas local market condition. Many times, conflicts between companies and employees arise because employees felt they were exploited.

In one report about the conflicts in multinational companies in China (Li, 2005), employees felt most strongly about three factors: unequal pay, lay-offs, and cultural differences. A typical example was with the famous accounting company, Pricewaterhouse Coopers, where the salary of non-local managers was more than 100 times higher than the local employees. The local Chinese accountants resorted to a strike to protest against such huge discrepancy in salary.

This Chinese accountant strike is not an aberration. Throughout history we have witnessed employees who mobilize (through professional organizations, trade associations, unions, or simply as a group of disgruntled workers) and challenge the organizations or industries that employ them. Due partially to its tendency of recurrence, scholars have studied this communicative tension. Exploring ways to grant voice to employees and theorizing about those efforts have been a focal point of organizational communication studies for more than a decade (see: Buzzanell, 1994; Mumby & Stohl, 1996). Moreover, theorizing in this vein has been sustained, in part, in more recent communication studies by scholars who have found that survey research can be a viable channel to voice employee attitudes and opinions (Edmondson, 2006), by scholars who study employee dissent strategies and tactics (Kassing, 2002; Kassing & Avtgis, 1999; Kassing & DiCioccio, 2004), by exploring emotional labor in the workplace (Miller, 2002; Tracy, 2005), as well as by exploring the role that identity plays in management/employee relations (Ashcraft, 2005; Jorgenson, 2002; Lucas & Buzzanell, 2004; Pepper & Larson, 2006).

Although internal communication, power, and control have traditionally been explored in the realm of organizational communication, this study contributes to the growing body of employee relations research that deals with boundary spanning and creating, maintaining, and fostering mutually beneficial relationships between organizations and their employee publics. For example, Holtzhausen and Voto (2002) asserted that public relations practitioners in some instances act as organizational activists, who desire change, resist dominant organizational power, and are concerned with matters of employee representation. This line of analysis is in alignment with Heath's (2006) notion that the role of public relations can and should be one of reflexivity—with its aim to make society more fully functioning. One way to achieve this aim is through the rhetorical empowerment of a major stakeholder group of any organization: its employees.

Employee relations is an important area of public relations, but at times this component of public relations has been limited to the top-down communication from management to employees. A lack of mutual understanding may bring about deteriorating relationships between organizations and their employee publics. Both parties in employee–organization relationships (EOR) should have a clear understanding of where the other party stands regarding essential issues in the relationships. Yet, is clear understanding possible? If it is not possible (and likely it is not) then what role can public relations—in concert with HR—play in this process?

Struggles over issues of power are at the heart of this globalization tension. Critical organizational rhetoric provides a lens through which to study organizational tensions, power struggles, and marginalization. At the core of organizational rhetoric is the all-important tenet that no matter which individuals speak on behalf of the organization, the organization is always speaking (Cheney, 1991; Cheney & McMillan, 1990; Crable, 1990; Meisenbach & McMillan, 2006).

Therefore, the purpose of this chapter is to explore, critically, how power differences influence the actual perceptions of different organizational members (employees) about employee relations under the globalization context. Then it makes some practical suggestions to empower the employees and improve employee–organization relationships (EOR).

Hegemony of Globalization

In any given society certain cultural beliefs, values, and practices prevail, while others are submerged or partially excluded. This, however, is the norm; Mumby (1989) asserted that by no means does culture function "in a smooth and cohesive fashion even a majority of the time . . . the construction of meaning . . . in a cultural system involves a struggle over the dominant interpretations of the myriad of discourses that make up a culture" (p. 293). The role of the critical scholar, however is to expose the ways that hegemony (Gramsci, 1971) or such prevailing cultural beliefs, values, and attitudes can control the ways that new ideas are accepted and rejected or become naturalized or even accepted on face value as common sense—even ideological (Cloud, 1996; Hall, 1985; Mumby, 1987, 1997).

In the context of globalization in public relations, the critical stance becomes paramount because powerful organizations and their spokespersons often speak out on dominant capitalistic issues. These issues include, but are not limited to, investment in developing and prospering foreign countries through globalization that often serve to privilege "the policies and operations of some organizations or industries and marginalizes others" (Heath, 1997, p. 196). In many cases, those who are marginalized are the native employees who are thought to be exploited by the incoming multinational corporation. According to Cheney and Dionisopoulos (1989):

> Such hegemony does not refer to simple or outright domination but rather to control over the premises that shape basic and applied policy decisions. In essence, corporate discourse seeks to establish public frames of reference for interpreting information concerning issues deemed important by Corporate America. (p. 144)

Thus, corporations through issues communication can shape and influence meaning (Heath, 1997) because meaning itself is "contingent not only on inter-subjective understanding within a community, but also on the process by which certain dominant groups are able to frame the interests of competing groups within their own particular world-view" (Mumby, 1989, p. 293).

A classic definition of power is provided by Robert Dahl: "A has power over B to the extent that he can get B to do something that B would not otherwise do" (1957, p. 203). Here A and B can refer to any individual, group, or organization. Power thus generally refers to the ability to influence and tends to be relational.

Mintzberg (1983) suggested five sources of power. Power can come from the control of (1) resource(s), (2) a technical skill, (3) a body of knowledge, (4) legal prerogatives or exclusive rights or privileges to impose choices, (5) access to those who can rely on the other four. The first three sources must also be essential to the function of organizations and are non-substitutable.

Reflected in the relationships employees have with their employers, power imbalance is inherent. Employees by nature are economically dependent upon the organizations. They have to obey certain rules and regulations, accept the hierarchical orders, and provide products or services the organizations need.

However, at the same time, organizations are also dependent upon employees, especially those employees whose work is essential to the organizations' operations and success. In Mintzberg's typology, they have more skills or a body of knowledge that constitute their bases of power. These employees do have bargaining power, even though perhaps not as much as the organizations.

This discussion of power differential is not new; however, this recognition of power differential between complex organizations and lay publics has led public relations scholars to date to focus on the ways that dialogue and two-way symmetrical communication between organizations and publics (Grunig, 1992, 2001) can offset the adverse implications associated with "big business" and lead to a more fully functioning society. To such an end, however, both dialogue and two-way symmetry between organizations and their publics may be limited because organizations and publics may be arguing from incompatible zones of meaning

(Heath, 1997). No matter how open the channels of communication may be, mutual understanding might never be reached. According to Heath (1997),

> Zones of meaning are the shared information and opinion that members of organizations and publics understand and hold dear. Zones are expressions of the meaning, the interpretation and judgment, groups and publics believe to be true representations of reality. Through their zones, groups and publics view reality. (p. 192)

Thus it is plausible that corporations that might very well have the best interest of society at heart can be deemed socially irresponsible and illegitimate because the zones from which they base their reality and articulate their positions might differ vastly from the zones of certain publics (note that different zones of meaning will likely exist, and there is no such thing as panacea in public relations that can solve every conflict or disagreement in the world; however, in many instances dialogue and two-way symmetry can and often should be used to find some common ground that the different parties might agree with. For example, see Murphy and Dee's 1996 study). This notion has been accepted by the scholarly community; the authors will further tease out this line of reasoning in the following example.

Major public universities around the United States have begun to launch major diversity initiatives. These programs are near and dear to many and have become quite the common practice in today's U.S. university system. These programs are designed to "broaden the pipeline" and extend educational opportunities to ethnic minorities, rural lower-class citizens, and other marginalized groups. One could argue that these universities' initiatives are expressions of their view of reality: (1) Students will benefit academically and socially from a diverse learning environment. (2) Many large universities are land-grant institutions—meaning that part of their responsibilities as an institution is to help the community which it inhabits; thus, giving marginalized groups access to the university is one way that they are adhering to the land-grant mission. (3) It is simply the right thing to do because they may feel that the only way to have a true democracy is by having an educated populace.

These appear to be noble causes; few would challenge the merit of these programs. However, there might be portions of the population who are operating from an incompatible zone of meaning. Consider those who might perceive that they have a great deal to lose if these programs are implemented. Consider those who might deem these programs unconstitutional and discriminatory on the bases of race. Consider those who might believe in the "American Dream"—those who believe in rugged individualism and that everyone should pull him- or herself up by the bootstraps. Finally, consider those who value the free market and little government interaction; they might deem these programs as a sort of governmental handout and might oppose them. (For a contemporary case, visit the transcripts of the Affirmative Action lawsuit filed against the University of Michigan.) How do these publics rhetorically combat the prevailing zone of diversity? How do they get their perspectives validated?

In a similar vein, employees may find themselves rhetorically battling against the dominant discourse of the organization that employs them. In the following section, the authors make this contestation more lucid.

EOR: The Rhetorical Wrangle in the Workplace

Organizations are choruses of diverse voices, and their members represent numerous voices and standpoints. Due to the increased complexity of organizations, their messages, and their diversity of members, multiple accounts of which organizational policies and procedures are acceptable, forwarded, and how these policies and procedures are viewed are of primary concern to the authors. Communication scholars, in their research, can and do address issues of power struggles within organizations and marginalization of members from the organization. In addition, scholars within the field often conduct research pertaining to the problematic of voice, which asserts that there are a variety of voices and standpoints present within organizations in general (Mumby & Stohl, 1996). They often expose issues of "hegemony, power, ideology, marginalization of voices, empowerment, legitimation and unobtrusive control" (Tompkins & Wanca-Thibault, 2001, p. xxvii). Moreover, according to Harding (1991)—a philosopher who has advanced standpoint theory among feminist researchers and scholars—"the perspective from the lives of the less powerful can provide a more objective view than the perspective from the lives of the more powerful" because marginalized persons have greater motivation to understand the perspective of the more powerful than vice versa, and marginalized publics have very little reason to preserve the existing structure that marginalizes them (pp. 269–270). To make this point more vivid, take for example the following.

Engineering students have very little reason to agree to tuition increases and the elimination of some of their available, affordable student parking. The students, however, understand that engineering programs are the staple at their university, and these programs give the school its reputation and prestige. Thus, they have a greater motivation to understand the perspective of university administrators—eliminating some parking for the construction of a state-of-the-art facility, as well as raising their tuition is necessary. However, how much "say" do the students really have in such matters? Conversely, the university administrators have less incentive to truly understand the perspective of the students on such matters. In short, although organizations are composed of a chorus of voices, some voices often wield more power than others.

In this chapter—in order to understand distinct voices and standpoints—the authors rhetorically analyze the discourse of Chinese employees who have been employed by multinational corporations that have come to their native land. More specifically, the authors critically analyzed the told accounts of employees and their public relations managers about their internal communication and work relationships. These texts are derived from a larger sample of interview data collected in China.

Interpretive Analysis of Employee Comments

The inherent power imbalance between upper-organizational management and lower-ranking employees is present in most if not all organizations; thus, it is not surprising that this power imbalance between the upper-organizational management and lower-ranking employees in a country that welcomed a foreign multinational company manifested itself. The employees seemed to talk almost exclusively in terms of contractual exchange, not in terms of viewing the organization as a warm, friendly, welcoming outlet from home. This distinction is important because although the Western notion of the family-friendly workplace has been deemed mythical, Western scholars studying family and work in the West have found that many employees deem work as a "social outlet" (Hochschild, 1997; Krouse & Afifi, 2007); in addition, the workplace can be a source of social support (Shin, Wong, Simko, & Ortiz-Torres, 1989), as well as play a "significant role in friendship development, coping processes, and organizational efficiency" (Krouse & Afifi, 2007, p. 109). Talk about these benefits of work was absent from the Chinese employees' work discourses.

Employees' Perspectives

Many employees, when first asked about the types of relationships they had with the companies, said "an employment relationship," or "a pure relationship of labor versus pay." One person called herself a "labor seller." A vivid description of this widespread mentality came from one employee of an insurance company, who used phrases such as "settling accounts" and said:

> You owe me nothing, I owe you nothing. I work here for one day, I get one day's pay. If you owe each other something, then you use the contract to formalize it. Otherwise, the account is not cleared. And [if you don't feel this way], any kind of job-hop doesn't make sense then. Because it will give you the feeling of betrayal by your lover or your family.

Related to contractual relationships where both parties agree on what each should do, many employees pointed out that most of the time, EOR boiled down to exchange. Other things, they argued, were just the means to achieve that exchange. Employees gave different accounts as to how they felt about such exchange.

From the employees' perspective, most things that companies did were for a purpose. For example, when talking about training or further education opportunities, many employees expressed the idea that they were happy about these opportunities, but at the same time they recognized clearly that the ultimate function of these opportunities was to enable companies to use employees' newly acquired skills for further service.

It was interesting to note that as long as employees felt that what they got and what they paid for were relatively equal, or the exchange was somewhat fair, they would still feel they have gained something. For example, one company made a relocation decision without notifying employees first. Almost all employees expressed disappointment and had the feeling of being "dumped." However, when they commented on this relationship, many of them still acknowledged that they had learned a lot. One employee described this purely exchange relationship:

> I think [company name] is a very practical company. . . . It's not like other companies which, after hiring some new employees, they will have a kind of learning process. Here, right after you come, you should be able to work.

However, given this almost naked exchange relationship, he still felt the relationship was valuable and might be a win-win because he received much career guidance and training. Through this relationship, he felt confident that he would be more competitive for any future jobs. This was echoed by almost all of his colleagues.

This finding led to more thinking about the nature of EOR. Many employees felt it natural to enter an exchange relationship with one particular organization, do what they can do to contribute to the organization, get what they expect to get, and then move on to another organization that might be a better fit for them. Employees had this kind of "stepping stone mentality" and regarded it as a win-win situation, even though it was exchange.

Worthy of note, even though these two types seemed to be most prominent, employees did mention other types of EORs. And these seemed to be similar to the management's perspective. Several employees commented that the perception of EOR might be different for themselves and for other employees. For example, one employee mentioned the feeling of growing together with the company and treating the organizational goal as her own mission and aspiration. This clearly indicated a covenantal relationship.

Another employee expressed a similar idea but then pointed out that although he himself felt good in this relationship, it might not be the same for others. Some employees also analyzed other factors that contributed to such difference in perceptions. Hence perceptions were based on relative standpoints within the organization. For example, one mentioned that more opportunities existed for those employees closer to the general manager than others. And different natures of departments might also play a role. For example, the employees in a quality control department in a company felt they were isolated and away from other parts of the company. Thus, they did not feel much connection to the company as a whole.

Commitment: Organization to Employees

Different positions generated differences in perspectives between managers and employees regarding the organizations' commitment to employees. Most managers believed that the companies did have commitment to the employees but not all employees felt the same.

Managers' perspectives. Almost all organizations studied had a strong commitment to their business in China. Participants suggested different indicators for such commitment, including the company moving essential functions such as R&D and production to China, having a long-term strategic plan for the subsidiary, or moving the focus of business from home country headquarters to China. That showed the companies wanted to maintain a long-term presence and growth in China. As a result, managers generally equated the company's commitment to the particular subsidiary in China with its commitment to the local employees. However, most employees made the distinction between the two, as discussed below.

Employees' perspectives. Sharing the managers' perspectives, some employees also considered that the commitment to business and that to employees were the same. For example, one employee looked at commitment in this way:

> If the company has long-term business here, and it does not close the office, then I feel it's a long-term commitment to us employees. . . . We are growing together with the company. I feel that as long as the company is growing in size and expanding the market here, it has commitment to the employees.

However, more employees showed different understandings about commitment. The organizations' strong commitment to their business in China did not necessarily translate into strong commitment to all local employees.

In particular, the distinction between core employees and non-core employees appeared to be a repeating theme. When asked about their organization's commitment to employees, more often than not, employees said things like "it depends on different types of employees." Many employees suggested that the organization's commitment to middle managers or core employees was totally different from that to non-core employees. More than one company studied employed temporary laborers or even "borrowed" laborers through the use of personnel agents or labor companies. Therefore, these people were not even their regular employees and the commitment to them was indeed limited.

However, for employees that were important to companies, these organizations did show strong commitment to retain them by using various methods. For example, one participant mentioned his company's plan for official reserve, meaning the organization had developed lists of outstanding employees and provided comprehensive training so that these people could later assume long-term and more important responsibilities.

Western managerial thought espouses the need to have connected, committed, and satisfied employees because it can be said that being or feeling connected to an organization could lead to satisfaction with that organization. This component—satisfaction—yielded the biggest discrepancy between management and employees in the organizations under study. While acknowledging that problems would always exist and that they still needed to work on improving the EOR, most employee relations managers felt the organization was more or less satisfied with the current EOR.

However, the responses from employees were different. They did not comment how they thought organizations were satisfied or dissatisfied. A common pattern appeared to be that companies did not really care about EOR because of power differences. Employees from different organizations expressed this similar idea when asked about how they felt the organization was satisfied with EOR. One response was representative of this idea:

> But in general, [company name] does not worry about not getting the people it wants, because of its fame. A lot of people are trying very hard

to get in, so it does not really care. . . . Every year, there are a lot of out-standing people who leave the company, but it seems we are still operating normally.

This opinion about an organization's attitude was echoed by many employees. In addition, a lot of employees also attributed this to the macro-environment and the change in time. One person, for example, said that the companies entering China were gradually assimilated. Many benefits or training opportunities that were available when the companies first arrived gradually disappeared. This was due to the external market condition of supply and demand. Employees, especially lower-level employees, said that the companies were not concerned about whether these employees were satisfied because these companies could easily get them replaced if they chose to leave. Hence although multinational companies are bringing employ-ment to nations like China, the relatively expendable nature of employees—at least the lower-level employees—manifested itself in the interviews.

Satisfaction

Findings suggested that managers and employees had similar ideas about employ-ees' satisfaction toward EOR. The managers were not too optimistic about employ-ees' satisfaction and the employees were also objective in their evaluations.

Managers also seemed to understand quite well what the employees were most and least satisfied with. For example, the manager in one company posited that employees might be satisfied with the company's future development, but not with their pay and benefits. Employees shared similar comments.

However, the two parties expressed differences in how they reached the conclu-sion and how they evaluated satisfaction. Managers usually used turnover rate to evaluate employees' satisfaction toward EOR. When asked about how they thought the employees were satisfied with the current EOR, managers used indicators such as "turnover not high," or "employee teams relatively stable" to support their evaluations.

On the other hand, employees had a clear idea of costs and benefits. Most people were most satisfied with the opportunities to learn skills and accumulate experi-ences useful in their career. Also they were able to analyze what they were paid and what they got, as well as their strengths and weaknesses. Many people would take into account their compensation and the stress at work or the amount of work load. If these two were somewhat balanced, they felt satisfied. One employee made this comment, demonstrating well what many had in mind:

> I feel it's o.k. based on the comparison with other companies. In addition, my own abilities, or the adjustment to the society. Like if I choose to leave, whether I can find a better job. I feel generally my value has been realized, as a whole, it's o.k.

Similarly, many employees talked about the case when even though they or their colleagues might not be totally satisfied with the relationship, they chose to stay because of the companies' brand names. Therefore, for them, whether to stay in a company or leave might not capture the satisfaction level as managers thought.

Conclusion

Although an inherent power differential exists between an organization's upper-ranking members and mid-range to lower-ranking employees, in countries where multinational companies have come to provide opportunities at lower operating costs, the power differential and its residual effects are more pronounced. From the texts, there is little reference to anything other than a contractual agreement between employee and employer; whereas, research about U.S. workplace environments show that ethnically diverse employees desire flexible policies and workplaces that cater to them and their cultural needs (Buzzanell, Waymer, Tagle, & Liu, 2007).

Multinational organizations bring with them the promise of bringing jobs and development to the countries in which they begin to operate. Additionally, in China multinationals must meet social responsibility requirements in order to operate in this expanding market (China View, 2005). This is very different from other practices in the developing world.

This chapter demonstrates that although power imbalance does exist between employees and organizations, conventional approaches to studying power may not be appropriate when studying this particular population. For example, employees may not be fully aware of the implications of this power differential because they can view themselves as willing, participating partners who have agreed to the terms of the work contract. As the employees' accounts indicate, employee satisfaction might ultimately be dependent upon whether the employees are getting what they expect or more from the contractual agreement (e.g., opportunities to learn new information, learn new skills, and the company keeping its reputable name).

This discussion highlights some of the consequences of the power difference in general and the different zones of meaning specifically. In the face of these differentials in power and meaning, employees have found a way to empower themselves. Many of these lower-level employees (usually young and with short tenure in companies) used the "stepping stone" or "settling accounts" mentality that emerged in this study to serve as a self-defense and self-empowering mechanism. By focusing more attention on what work experiences or skills they could gain rather than whether and how they could have much emotional attachment to their employing companies, these employees managed to achieve a mental balance and felt satisfied about better preparing themselves for their future career development. To some extent, this helped empower them professionally.

This form of empowerment, however, goes completely unnoticed and arguably unvalued by organizations that continually gauge employee satisfaction using a typically Western standard, such as turnover rates. As long as this approach to assessing satisfaction is taken, organizations can continually affirm that they are meeting the needs and wants of their employees simply if the turnover is low—when indeed this may not be the case. This mechanistic approach fails to address the humanistic aspects of work. Moreover, it provides organizations with a means and a rationale for continuing "business as usual" because "all is well" within the organization as it pertains to employees.

In a similar vein, the contractual nature of employment does not force organizations to be reflective in their management practices. If turnover is low, the organization has little to worry about because it evidently has met its contractual obligations. If turnover is high, employers are not necessarily to blame; employees might have voluntarily opted out of their contractual agreement. This too, is a mechanistic approach that does not give enough weight to the "relations" component of employee relations.

As many scholars in management have pointed out, power in organizations can be explained by the resource dependence theory; in short, the environment derives its power over the organization from the organization's dependence on certain resources. An organization is vulnerable because of its need for resources such as raw materials, labor, capital, knowledge, and outlets for its products and services. The employee publics obviously constitute a valuable resource in the internal environment for any organization. The more the organization needs the employees, the more power these employees have. However, this theory is limited in explaining the power that employees transfer to employers simply by viewing their employer/employee relationship as contractual and nothing more. As long as employees view their work relationships in this manner, their relationships with management will continue to be one where their needs and desires are categorized numerically in measures such as turnover. This contractual view of the employee/ employer relationship places the onus of employee satisfaction on the shoulders of the employees, and gives the organizations little reason or motivation to change the status quo.

This chapter has established the urgency for public relations and HR to form a meaningful partnership; there is no more time for battles over territory. Public relations scholars have worked toward the development of a normative theory that would urge scholars and practitioners to use public relations as a tool to create and to foster a more fully functioning society (Heath, 2006). Scholars have posited that encouraging two-way symmetrical communication between organizations and publics is one notable way to reach such ends (Grunig, 1992, 2001). Although competing zones of meaning may exist, "in a republic, can we be responsible if we conclude anything other than 'Let the dialogue continue?'" (Heath, 1997, p. 191). This chapter argues that although power imbalance does exist between employees and organizations, employee relations or internal communication practitioners—if properly motivated to do so—can serve as the bridge between the two to facilitate the development of mutually beneficial employee–organization relationships. With a better understanding of viewpoints from both parties, practitioners and HR professionals can work with employees to design strategies to empower the employees, as well as meet and address their work–life concerns. The practical suggestions raised below will help public relations practitioners serve as an "institutionalized mechanism" to truly consider employees' needs and empower them.

Employee relations practitioners need to identify the specific needs and wants of different employees and counsel the top management for corresponding compensations. For example, even though it is not possible to provide all employees equal level of involvement with the organizations' operations, organizations need to design strategies that will make employees at different levels feel they are somewhat connected to the organizations and that what they do will make a difference.

As mentioned earlier, empowerment can also come from the employees themselves. If management, public relations practitioners, and HR use internal communication as means to empower the organization and its members, then all involved parties will be able to look back at the organization and its actions with satisfaction at what the organization—defined by layers of engagement—has accomplished (Albrecht, 1988).

References

Albrecht, T. L. (1988). Communication and personal control in empowering organizations. In J. A. Anderson (Ed.), *Communication yearbook 11* (pp. 380–390). Newbury Park, CA: Sage.

Ashcraft, K. L. (2005). Resistance through consent? Occupational identity, organizational form, and the maintenance of masculinity among commercial airline pilots. *Management Communication Quarterly, 19,* 67–90.

Buchholz, R. A., & Rosenthal, S. B. (2005). Toward a contemporary conceptual framework of stakeholder theory. *Journal of Business Ethics, 58,* 137–148.

Buzzanell, P. M. (1994). Gaining a voice: Feminist organizational communication theorizing. *Management Communication Quarterly, 7,* 339–383.

Buzzanell, P. M., Waymer, D., Tagle, M. P., & Liu, M. (2007). Different transitions into working motherhood: Discourses of Asian, Hispanic, and African American women. *Journal of Family Communication, 7,* 195–220.

CATO (2007). Increasing public understanding of the benefits of free trade and the costs of protectionism. Retrieved August 24, 2007, from http://www.freetrade.org/issues/globalization.html

Chatterjee, S., & Wernerfelt, B. (1991). The link between resources and type of diversification: Theory and evidence. *Strategic Management Journal, 12,* 33–48.

Cheney, G. (1991). *Rhetoric in an organizational society: Managing multiple identities.* Columbia: University of South Carolina Press.

Cheney, G., & Dionisopoulos, G. N. (1989). Public relations? No, relations with publics: A rhetorical-organizational approach to contemporary corporate communications. In C. H. Botan & V. Hazleton, Jr. (Eds.), *Public relations theory* (pp. 135–157). Hillsdale, NJ: Lawrence Erlbaum.

Cheney, G., & McMillan, J. J. (1990). Organizational rhetoric and the practice of criticism. *Journal of Applied Communication Research, 18,* 93–114.

China View (2005, May 13). Corporate social responsibility in China. Retrieved July 25, 2007 from http://news.xinhuanet.com/english/2005-05/13/content_2952742.htm

Cloud, D. L. (1996). Hegemony or concordance? The rhetoric of tokenism in "Oprah" Winfrey's rags-to-riches biography. *Critical Studies in Mass Communication, 13,* 115–137.

Crable, R. E. (1990). "Organizational rhetoric" as the fourth great system: Theoretical, critical, and pragmatic implications. *Journal of Applied Communication Research, 18,* 115–128.

Dahl, R. A. (1957). The concept of power. *Behavioral Science, 2,* 201–215.

Edmondson, V. C. (2006). Organizational surveys: A system for employee voice. *Journal of Applied Communication Research, 34,* 307–310.

Feachem, R. G. A. (2001). Globalization: From rhetoric to evidence. *Bulletin of the World Health Organization, 79*(9), 804.

Gramsci, A. (1971). *Selection from the prison notebooks* (Q. Hoare & G. Nowell Smith, Trans.). New York: International.

Grunig, J. E. (1992). Communication, public relations, and effective organizations: An overview of the book. In J. Grunig (Ed.), *Excellence in public relations and communication management* (pp. 1–28). Hillsdale, NJ: Lawrence Erlbaum.

Grunig, J. E. (2001). Two-way symmetrical public relations: Past, present, and future. In R. L. Heath (Ed.), *Handbook of public relations* (pp. 11–30), Thousand Oaks, CA: Sage.

Grunig, L. A., Grunig, J. E., & Dozier, D. M. (2002). *Excellent public relations and effective organizations: A study of communication management in three countries.* Mahwah, NJ: Lawrence Erlbaum.

Hall, S. (1985). Signification, representation, ideology: Althusser and the poststructuralist debates. *Critical Studies in Mass Communication, 2,* 91–114.

Harding, S. (1991). *Whose science? Whose knowledge? Thinking from women's lives.* Ithaca, NY: Cornell University Press.

Heath, R. L. (1997). *Strategic issues management: Organizations and public policy challenges.* Thousand Oaks, CA: Sage.

Heath, R. L. (2006). Onward through the fog: Thoughts on public relations' research directions. *Journal of Public Relations Research, 18,* 93–114.

Hochschild, A. R. (1997). *The time bind.* New York: Henry Holt.

Holtzhausen, D. R., & Voto, R. (2002). Resistance from the margins: The postmodern public relations practitioner as organizational activist. *Journal of Public Relations Research, 14,* 57–84.

Jenkins, R. (2003). Globalization, production, employment and poverty: Debates and evidence. *Journal of International Development, 16,* 1–12.

Jorgenson, J. (2002). Engineering selves: Negotiating gender and identity in technical work. *Management Communication Quarterly, 15,* 350–380.

Kassing, J. W. (2002). Speaking up: Identifying employees' upward dissent strategies. *Management Communication Quarterly, 16,* 187–209.

Kassing, J. W., & Avtgis, T. A. (1999). Examining the relationship between organizational dissent and aggressive communication. *Management Communication Quarterly, 13,* 100–115.

Kassing, J. W., & DiCioccio, R. L. (2004). Testing a workplace experience explanation of displaced dissent. *Communication Reports, 17,* 113–120.

Kentor, J. (2001). The long term effects of globalization on income inequality, population growth, and economic development. *Social Problems, 48,* 435–455.

Krouse, S. S., & Afifi, T. D. (2007). Family-to-work spillover stress: Coping communicatively in the workplace. *Journal of Family Communication, 7,* 85–122.

Li, Q. (2005). Same work, different pay: Frequent conflicts facing multinational companies. Retrieved on May, 19, 2006, from http://finance.news.tom.com/1535/1644/2005131-157036.html

Lucas, K., & Buzzanell, P. M. (2004). Blue-collar work, career, and success: Occupational narratives of sisu. *Journal of Applied Communication Research, 32,* 273–292.

Meisenbach, R. J., & McMillan, J. J. (2006). Blurring the boundaries: Historical developments and future directions in organizational rhetoric. In C. Beck (Ed.), *Communication yearbook, 30* (pp. 99–104). Mahwah, NJ: Lawrence Erlbaum.

Miller, K. (2002). The experience of emotion in the workplace: Professing in the midst of tragedy. *Management Communication Quarterly, 15,* 571–600.

Mintzberg, H. (1983). *Power in and around organizations.* Englewood Cliffs, NJ: Prentice Hall.

Morgan, G. (1997). *Images of organization.* Thousand Oaks, CA: Sage.

Mumby, D. K. (1987). The political function of narrative in organizations. *Communication Monographs, 54,* 113–127.

Mumby, D. K. (1989). Ideology and the social construction of meaning: A communication perspective. *Communication Quarterly, 37,* 291–304.

Mumby, D. K. (1997). The problem of hegemony: Rereading Gramsci for organizational communication studies. *Western Journal of Communication, 61,* 343–375.

Mumby, D. K., & Stohl, C. (1996). Disciplining organizational communication studies. *Management Communication Quarterly, 10,* 50–72.

Murphy, P., & Dee, J. (1996). Reconciling the preferences of environmental activist and corporate policymakers. *Journal of Public Relations Research, 8,* 1–33.

Pepper, G. L., & Larson, G. S. (2006). Cultural identity tensions in a post-acquisition organization. *Journal of Applied Communication Research, 34,* 49–71.

Shinn, M., Wong, N. W., Simko, P. A., & Ortiz-Torres, B. (1989). Promoting the well-being of working parents: Coping, social support, and flexible job schedules. *American Journal of Community Psychology, 17,* 31–55.

Tompkins, P. K., & Cheney, G. (1985). Communication and unobtrusive control in contemporary organizations. In R. D. McPhee & P. K. Tompkins (Eds.), *Organizational communication: Traditional themes and new directions* (pp. 179–210). Beverly Hills, CA: Sage.

Tompkins, P. K., & Wanca-Thibault, M. (2001). Organizational communication: Prelude and prospects. In F. M. Jablin & L. L. Putnam (Eds.), *The new handbook of organizational communication: Advances in theory, research, and methods* (pp. xvii–xxxi). Thousand Oaks, CA: Sage.

Tracy, S. J. (2005). Locking up emotion: Moving beyond dissonance for understanding emotion labor discomfort. *Communication Monographs, 72,* 261–283.

Weaver, C. K. (2001). Dressing for battle in the new global economy: Putting power, identity, and discourse into public relations theory. *Management Communication Quarterly, 15,* 279–288.

SECTION THREE

ACTIVISM, ISSUES, CRISIS, AND RISK
Rhetorical Heavy Lifting

Rhetorical Rationale for Issues, Crisis Response, and Risk Management

However timeless public relations is, and some of us think it reaches back far beyond nineteenth-century mass media, it has been engaged in the discussion of public policy issues for centuries. It has also played a vital role in crisis response and risk management. These topics have taken on new life over the past three decades. Issues began to become a renewed theme during the turbulent 1960s, leading to the coining of the term issues management in the 1970s. At about the same time crisis emerged with enthusiasm as a featured part of the discipline, made very popular by the Johnson & Johnson response during the Tylenol crisis. Another crisis, the release of deadly methyl isocyanate from a Union Carbide plant in Bhopal, India, gave more support for the crisis trend, and helped make risk an important topic. That topic, by that name, had become popular, and was given currency by the nuclear energy crisis at Three Mile Island generating facility in Pennsylvania. These trends demonstrated how public relations is part of the rhetorical and critical heavy lifting. In fact, it is easy to justify the role of public relations in such matters if we conclude that the rationale for society is the collective management of risk.

First, let's agree that an issue is a contestable matter of fact, value, or policy. A crisis is a risk manifested. A risk is an event the likelihood of which (probability) can be estimated, the magnitude of the impact can be calculated, and the reasonableness of which can be debated.

Having made those broad points in opening, we can connect the discussion in Section Two with themes in this section. If a product turns out to harm people (or their pets, for instance), the company encounters a crisis. Such an event can lead people to doubt that the company is willing and able to exercise proper control over product quality to serve its customers, to help them manage some risk that made the product attractive. (Recall how this theme was discussed in chapter 9.) Crisis is a predictable event that tests the ability of the organization (and thus its reputation) to be as effective as it claims and is expected to be.

The rhetorical problems associated with crisis focus on the cause of the crisis, the responsibility for it, the ability to learn from it, and the skills and commitment of the organization to implement the lessons learned. We make attributions about crisis, such as a company was not vigilant and effective in protecting employees when an explosion occurred because of faulty maintenance that killed or injured several employees or other individuals in and around operations. A business might have a security policy that anyone wearing apparel that is currently sold there must have on them a sales receipt or they will be arrested for shoplifting. If a young man is arrested for wearing apparel currently sold, says he bought the apparel, and even says he can call his parents to bring a sales receipt, should the company demand that the receipt be produced? Should they take his word? Will the credence of his story depend on the color of his skin?

We assume that crisis can lead to issues. We know that issues can create a crisis. The issue related to the health hazard of tobacco or alcohol use creates crisis for industries that produce and advertise/promote those products. If the way the issue developed affects the organization's ability to generate profit, it encounters a crisis. Likewise, a crisis, such as a mining disaster that kills several workers will necessarily generate an issue where debate is likely to focus on ways to increase mine safety. Thus, we expect companies and other organizations to help manage risks.

The logic of risk as a scientific matter is captured in the statement: How safe is safe enough? That scientific question, subject to principles of sound science, is challenged by a cultural interpretation framed in the question, how fair is safe enough (Tansey & Rayner, 2009)? The logic of that question contrasts the scientists' ability to calculate risk with the opinions of those who may bear the risk or mitigate its impact on risk bearers. The logics of sound science can be challenged by those who may, have, or will suffer the risk; they may ask who or what privileges these scientists to draw the conclusions they do.

These brief glimpses into issues, crisis, and risk management are only a tantalizing aspect of this section. It suggests how discourse serves various ends and should do so in ways that lead to mutually beneficial outcomes, but necessarily requires input from many voices including academic (and managerial) voices. In that way, the organization is good and communicates well and engages responsibly in public dialogue on these very serious matters. This standard also becomes the essence of the critical judgment of public relations as a rhetorical process. As you read the chapters in this section, recall an organization in your experience that engaged successfully in public dialogue about a crisis or a high-risk situation. You are also encouraged to think of an organization that "pretended" or postured to engage in cooperative dialogue but so skewed the case that only its interest truly emerged to the more introspective critic.

Chapter 12 features a discussion of the rhetorical implications and challenges for crisis communication to serve the interests of various publics and address the reputation of the offending, or ostensibly offending, organization. This chapter builds on well-established social scientific foundations to advance the understanding of how meaning, as well as process, is a vital part of a successful or failed crisis response. The attributions that various publics, including the media, make are about how responsible and responsive an organization was to a crisis and how the response to it can affect reputation and lead to various issues that linger during the post-crisis phase. Rhetorical options can offer insights into ways that the dialogue can be most constructive to outcomes relevant to crisis.

Chapter 13 focuses on the quality of dialogue and the discourse ethics of the Disney Company. To a large extent, this discussion focuses on internal public relations although the debate was very public as major management level players in the history and future of the Disney Empire debated its future through careful analysis of its mission, vision, and management philosophy. It's interesting to note how public relations can play out not only between an organization and an external activist critic, but also within the management (shareholder and management team) ranks. Similar challenges occurred, for instance, during 2008 when members of the Rockefeller company (John D. Rockefeller created the companies that have shaped ExxonMobil today) fought publicly with ExxonMobil management over the mission and vision of that vast company.

Chapter 14 addresses the role and responsibility of trade associations. Some have, at least in specific instances, called trade associations fronts. So, one key question is when is an organization a front versus a worthy trade association? Or, can trade associations be worthy voices in society, or are they always fronts? Powerful and huge industries have for over a century created trade associations. Does the presence of such associations distort messages, dialogue, and bring even deeper pockets into the public policy issues debates, or can these organizations actually enhance the quality of discourse? What is the rhetorical challenge and the ethical responsibility of such powerful associations in a society dedicated to the free and open exchange of issue positions?

Chapter 15 takes a sharp look at the impact that multiple voices have on an organization's ability to engage in constructive and proactive crisis and issues response. In keeping with its mission to advance the interests of those of its faith, has the Catholic Church—at least in various venues—failed to meet this challenge as it has or has not responsibly and responsively engaged in issue debate and crisis response following allegations of Roman Catholic clergy sexual abuse of those most vulnerable, the children of the faith? Does the presence of multiple victim voices change the rhetorical challenge of its crisis response?

Chapters in this section are not the only ones that address crisis, issues, and risks. Those themes are embedded in discussions throughout this book as they are in so much of what practitioners do and organizations must prepare for and respond ethically in the event of their occurrence. For instance, one is able to suggest that Frederick Douglass added to the emerging national crisis as he discussed the issue of slavery in a society dedicated to the principles championed in the most glorious of national events, the celebration of the Fourth of July (see chapter 10). Baker and her colleagues in chapter 9 clearly address crisis and reputational damage as they examine the struggles surrounding approval and promotion of regulated drugs. This codicil is designed to suggest that however we have separated chapters into sections for purposes of focused discussion, the many aspects of organizational functioning expose themselves to multiple and complex public relations challenges.

Reference

Tansey, J., & Rayner, S. (2009). Cultural theory and risk. In R. L. Heath, & H. D. O'Hair (Eds.), *Handbook of crisis and risk communication* (pp. 53-80). New York: Routledge.

12

CRISIS, CRISIS COMMUNICATION, REPUTATION, AND RHETORIC

W. Timothy Coombs
Eastern Illinois University

> People think I'm crazy, 'cause I worry all the time
> If you paid attention, you'd be worried too
> You better pay attention
> Or this world we love so much might just kill you
> I could be wrong now, but I don't think so
> It's a jungle out there.
> From Randy Newman's (n.d.) "It's a Jungle out There"

People who watch the television show *Monk* will be familiar with this song. I feel the song is the perfect way to introduce crisis management. Crisis managers could be seen as the people in organizations that sing this song. Any management team that feels its organization is impervious to a crisis risks a serious and painful realization some day. Crises can happen to any organization.

Crises are a rhetorical challenge for organizations. The crisis itself generates uncertainty and the need for information. Management must provide messages related to public safety, the status of production, and effects of the event on the environment to name but a few. Managers say and do things after a crisis designed to reduce the negative effects of the crisis. It is only natural that rhetoricians would be attracted to what can be called "crisis rhetoric." Rhetoricians have a long tradition of studying the effects of words and deeds on publics. The communicative responses generated by a crisis fits well with their research eye. This chapter explores the contributions of the rhetorical approach to crisis communication and views it as a function of public relations. The chapter begins by defining key concepts, moves to an analysis of crisis communication as rhetoric, examines the strategic uses of crisis responses and post-crisis communication, and concludes with a review of the contributions and shortcomings of a rhetorical approach to crisis communication.

Defining the Key Concepts

It is important to define and explicate the three central concepts in this chapter: crisis, crisis communication, and reputation. How all these elements intersect is the basis for examining the rhetorical contributions to crisis communication.

Defining Key Terms

A crisis is an event that threatens important stakeholder expectations about an organization and can significantly affect an organization's performance. Stakeholders are people who are affected by and who can affect an organization (Bryson, 2004). Their perceptions are important in a crisis because stakeholder perceptions help to define a crisis event. A crisis exists if enough stakeholders believe a crisis exists. Crisis managers must view events from the perspective of stakeholders if they are to effectively manage a crisis (Coombs, 2007a). The crisis is a threat to disrupt operations and generate negative outcomes including injuries, property damage, and financial loss. In addition, all crises inflict some damage on the organization's reputation (Barton, 2001; Dilenschneider, 2000).

Crises can pose rhetorical problems for managers. A rhetorical problem is a perceived or actual gap between what stakeholders believe or how they behave and what stakeholders should believe or how they should behave. A "rhetorical problem is a gap in agreement, alignment of interests, cocreated meaning, shared understanding, shared facts and their interpretation, motivation, interests, evaluations, behavior, or conclusions" (Heath & Coombs, 2006, p. 118). Crises generate uncertainty, hence, the initial rhetorical problem in a crisis is the lack of understanding by stakeholders. Stakeholders need to know what has happened and how it might affect them. In turn, other rhetorical problems can be spawned including gaps in reputations or purchase intentions. Crisis communication is used to redress these rhetorical problems.

Crisis communication is actually a very broad concept encompassing any step in the crisis management process. The basic process of crisis management involves the pre-crisis stage concerned with preparation and prevention, the crisis phase where the immediate needs generated by the crisis must be addressed, and the post-crisis phase where lingering crisis concerns are redressed and attempts are made to learn from the event (Coombs, 2007a). There is an internal focus to the pre-crisis phase on promoting the need for preparation and growing interest in the application of risk communication. The pre-crisis phase has drawn virtually no attention from rhetorically based researchers. Therefore, this chapter concentrates on the rhetorical contributions for the crisis and post-crisis phases of crisis management.

Rhetorical contributions have focused on the crisis response (crisis phase) and post-crisis communication (post-crisis phase). Crisis response and post-crisis communication include what management says and does after a crisis occurs. The crisis response consists of the initial messages used to manage the immediate crisis. In the crisis stage, the crisis management team actively addresses the crisis which itself is the focal point of organizational activity. The crisis response uses communication to help those affected by the crisis and the organization in crisis itself, thereby making it a reactive form of communication (Hearit, 2006).

In crisis phase, the rhetorical problems center on the health and well-being of the stakeholders. Crisis managers must protect them from harm, help them cope psychologically with traumatic events, and try to remove the uncertainty created by the crisis. Crisis managers try to protect stakeholders from physical harm and financial harm. This includes attempts to prevent structural and environmental damage. Consumers must not use dangerous products. Employees need proper evacuation and care. Customers and suppliers need to know how the crisis will impact the supply chain and their operations. Investors must know the effect on their finances. Community members must be kept safe, their property secure, and their environment healthy. The media need information for stories about what just happened. The crisis response is used to address some very significant rhetorical problems.

The crisis response can be subdivided into instructing information, adjusting information, and reputation management (Sturges, 1994). Instructing information warns stakeholders by telling them what they should do to protect themselves physically from the effects of a crisis. A siren warning people to shelter-in-place or a news story telling people which peanut butter or dog food is contaminated are examples of instructing information. Adjusting information helps stakeholders to cope psychologically with the crisis. Expressions of concern and corrective actions (steps taken to prevent a repeat of the crisis) are examples of adjusting information. Adjusting information tries to convince stakeholders that they will be okay. Crisis managers should provide instructing and adjusting information before addressing reputational concerns.

The instructing and adjusting information will have some effect on an organization's reputation, although the primary focus of instructing and adjusting information is helping stakeholders and any benefits to the organization's reputation are a welcome side benefit. In fact, many crises may need no additional attention to reputation management beyond instructing and adjusting information. Reputation repair may start with the crisis response but is more likely to be used in post-crisis communication.

In the post-crisis phase, the rhetorical problems center on promises for closure of the crisis. Communication promises are made during the crisis phase. Stakeholders are promised information when it is known and updates on recovery efforts, corrective action, and investigations of the crisis. There will be some communication promises in every crisis, thus, a post-crisis phase exists for each crisis. It is relatively easy to fulfill communication promises by delivering the promised information when management receives it. The fulfillment of communication promises is complicated when the information is negative and can hurt the organization in some way. Then management is much less inclined to deliver the information. However, all communication promises should be fulfilled or the organization will suffer additional reputational damage from the crisis.

An organization receives closure when the operations have returned to near normal. Post-crisis communication is used as the crisis moves from being a focal point to just another concern in the organization. The organization is returning to business "near normal," the crisis team stands down, and the remaining crisis management needs are handled by managers in relevant areas of the organization.

Stakeholders, however, may not feel the same closure. Instead, there are lingering rhetorical problems in the form of reputation damage, litigation, and legislation. A lingering reputational threat occurs when the media and/or other stakeholders through online communication may keep discussing the negatives from the crisis. When the reputation remains a lingering rhetorical problem, reputation management becomes an important part of crisis response and/or post-crisis communication. Post-crisis communication typically includes updates on repairs and investigations or information promised during a crisis. But reputation management can be a part of post-crisis communication when reputational concerns haunt an organization's post-crisis phase. For instance, Cadbury had to manage its reputation well after recalling its salmonella-infected chocolate in June 2006.

Reputation management includes crisis managers' efforts to repair/restore the reputational damage from a crisis (Hearit, 2006; Sturges, 1994). Stakeholders holding a less favorable reputation of an organization following a crisis can be a rhetorical problem. While all crises inflict some reputational damage, not all crisis managers try to repair this damage. A reputation is an aggregate evaluation stakeholders make about how well an organization is meeting stakeholder expectations based on its past behaviors (Rindova & Frombrun, 1999; Wartick, 1992). Because they involve evaluations, reputations vary from favorable to unfavorable. Reputations are widely recognized as a valuable, intangible asset (Carmeli & Tishler, 2005; Davies, Chun, da Silva & Roper, 2003). A wide array of stakeholders are adversely affected by a crisis including community members, employees, customers, suppliers, and stockholders. Crises threaten to damage reputations because a crisis gives people reasons to think badly of the organization and violates stakeholder expectations about how an organization should act (Coombs, 2007a; Hearit, 1994). Reputation management efforts are designed to protect this valued, intangible asset and represent the bulk of the rhetorical post-crisis communication research.

Litigation and legislation are additional rhetorical problems related to lingering reputational concerns but worthy of individual discussion. In the U.S., crises are likely to breed lawsuits. Victims want compensation and lawyers see an opportunity to make money. However, beyond the financial concern is a punitive motivation. Awards in such cases are called punitive because they are meant to punish the offender. Victims may not feel closure until the organization is punished in some way and held accountable. Litigation is one way to punish an organization. Legislation is another form of punishment. Organizations are forced to change and must bear the cost of those changes. But legislation is more than punishment, it is a form of corrective action. If the organization will not take the proper steps to prevent a repeat of the crisis, the government can force them to take the necessary corrective measures. Both litigation and legislation help to promote closure for a crisis.

A final element of closure is the continued treatment of the psychological trauma from a crisis event. The efforts to help stakeholders cope psychologically continues from the crisis to the post-crisis phase. Stakeholders may not realize there is a problem until well after the crisis: delayed stress syndrome. Providing counseling and in some instances a symbolic healing gesture may be required in the post-crisis phase. Consider how West Pharmaceuticals created a memorial for the employees · killed at its Kinston, N.C., facility in 2003. Most organizations will have fairly simple post-crisis phases that only require delivering on informational promises rather than coping with lingering reputational problems, litigation, legislation, and psychological trauma.

Crisis Communication as Rhetoric

So, does a rhetorical perspective provide a useful vantage point for understanding crisis response and post-crisis communication? The short answer is yes and the balance of this chapter will support this conclusion. The crisis response and post-crisis communication research raises a series of critical questions: "What makes an effective crisis response or post-crisis communication?" and "Why should those responses be effective?" It is my contention that rhetoric has been instrumental in answering both questions.

The crisis response and post-crisis communication seeks to inform stakeholders (instructing information) and to persuade stakeholders (adjusting information and reputation management). Hence, post-crisis communication is consistent with Bryant's definition of rhetoric as the "rationale of informative and suasory discourse"(Bryant, 1953, p. 408). Crisis communication is a form of rhetoric because it involves both information and persuasion. Stakeholders need to be informed about what happened in a crisis and actions they need to take to protect themselves from the crisis (Sturges, 1994). Crisis managers also seek to persuade stakeholders to see the crisis and/or the organization in crisis from a certain perspective. Put another way, crisis communication uses persuasion to protect organizational assets. Moreover, the crisis response and post-crisis communication is a form of public discourse designed to redress rhetorical problems.

A quick review of the development of crisis response and post-crisis communication provides an excellent foundation for understanding rhetorical contributions to crisis communication. The crisis response literature began as simple lists of what to do or not to do after a crisis hit. These lists were based on the experiences of practitioners. In other writings I have referred to this as the *form approach* that explains how an organization should respond (Coombs, 1999, 2007a). Practitioners agreed that form recommendations should include: be quick, be consistent, and be open. Being quick means a crisis response should be fast, ideally within the first hour of a crisis. Being consistent means to speak with one voice about the crisis to avoid conflicting statements. Being open means organizational members are available to the news media, are willing to disclose information, and are honest in their responses (Coombs, 1999). These three elements of form help an organization to present its side of the story in the crisis.

The form recommendations can be called accepted wisdom. Although the three actions are effective, no one really knew why. Researchers attempted to explain why these actions should be beneficial in crisis management. Rhetorical theory was used to address the question of why these crisis responses were effective. A crisis demands information be supplied to fill the vacuum a crisis creates. Crises create vacuums by raising questions about what happened and why—a rhetorical problem arises. An organization uses the three form recommendations to fill the information vacuum with its side of the story. Silence is a passive response because it allows others to take control of the situation (Brummett, 1980). A quick response is aggressive and demonstrates that the organization has some control over the situation (Hearit, 1994). Later studies used experimental methods to prove the value of an organization quickly presenting information about the crisis, what was termed "stealing thunder" (Arpan & Pompper, 2003; Arpan & Roskos-Ewoldsen, 2005).

Rhetoricians know it takes more than a message to create an effective response. The credibility of the source plays an important role as well. Consistency and openness help to establish the credibility of the organization. Inconsistent messages will quickly erode credibility (Clampitt, 1991) while honesty is a key component in credibility (McCroskey, 1997). Openness can build pre-crisis credibility by establishing a history of being open and honest with the news media.

The early applications of rhetoric did not specifically seek to explain why the form recommendations worked but provided explanations nonetheless. In other words, the rhetorical approach to crisis communication explained why managers should use the form recommendations. The focus of the rhetorical approaches to crisis communication was on the strategic use of the crisis response and post-crisis communication, the next topic in this chapter.

Strategic Use of Crisis Response and Post-crisis Communication

The form recommendations were fairly simplistic, seeking to describe how to communicate after a crisis. The more complex question involves message content: what crisis managers need to say and do to address the rhetorical problems generated by a crisis. Again, the rhetorical approach was addressing the question of why. Why should certain crisis response strategies be used in particular crisis situations? The rhetorical approach was very strategic by concentrating on the use of communication to achieve the crisis response objectives of helping victims cope physically (instructing information) and psychologically (adjusting information) as well as some movement toward reputation repair. But instructing and adjusting information have received little attention with the focus being on reputation repair. This focus reflects an emphasis on the strategic value of crisis management to an organization. To support this contention the key rhetorical works in post-crisis communication are reviewed.

Two Seminal Works of 1988

The year 1988 is an important one for rhetorical approaches in crisis communication. Two works set the tenor for this field. One is Dionisopolous and Vibbert's (1988) book chapter in *Oratorical Encounters: Selected Studies and Sources of 20th Century Political Accusation and Apologies* which justified the application of apologia (the genre of self-defense) to corporate rhetoric. The central argument was that organizations, like people, have a public persona (reputation) that is subject to attack and requires defense. Organizations can experience and respond to character attacks. Hence, it is logical that organizations can engage in self-defense rhetoric. While the book chapter detailed the parameters of corporate apologia, it did not apply them directly to crisis communication (Dionisopolous & Vibbert, 1988).

However, a number of other researchers took up the mantel of corporate apologia and applied it to crisis communication, a point that will be detailed shortly.

Also published in 1988 is Benson's article about crisis communication involving Johnson & Johnson's response to the second Tylenol product tampering. Benson's work helped to explain the value of a quick response. He noted a quick response was somewhat proactive by helping crisis managers take control of and present their side of the story. More importantly, Benson (1988) called for future research in the area of crisis communication that examined crisis response strategies available to crisis managers and to understand when each of these crisis response strategies would be the most effective. This article established a foundation for using the situation to guide the crisis communication.

Corporate Apologia as Crisis Communication

A crisis can be viewed as a challenge to an organization's character—it is a threat to its reputation (Dilenschneider, 2000). It was natural for researchers to follow Dionisopolous and Vibbert (1988) and apply apologia to crisis communication. Ice (1991) was among the first to publish an article that applied apologia to crisis communication. His research centered on four strategies from apologia: denial, claim there is no crisis; bolstering, connect the audience to something the publics view favorably; differentiation, move the crisis out of its current, negative context; and transcendence, place the crisis in a broader context to make it appear less negative. The work by Ice (1991) and Hobbs (1995) represent more of a generic, rhetorical analysis than an examination of crisis communication. However, apologia was being adapted to explain crisis communication.

It is in the work of Hearit (1994, 1995a, 1995b, 2001, 2006) that corporate apologia becomes transformed into a distinct line of crisis communication research rather than an additional application of apologia. Hearit focuses on the crisis and response to the crisis and adapts apologia to this specific field of study. Hearit views corporate apologia (self-defense) as a subset of crisis communication. Hearit has developed a unique perspective for integrating corporate apologia into crisis communication. Hearit built his crisis communication work around social legitimacy, the consistency between organizational values and stakeholder values. Social legitimacy can be threatened by a crisis because a crisis can make an organization appear incompetent and/or in violation of stakeholder expectations. Hearit (1994, 1995a) uses the violation of social legitimacy (the rhetorical problem) as the character attack that warrants the application of apologia.

Hearit (1996, 2001) infuses dissociation into corporate apologia as part of his shift from generic criticism to crisis communication. Hearit breaks the bonds of genre with dissociation. A communicator uses dissociation to split a single idea into two parts. Crisis managers employ dissociation in an effort to reduce the reputation risk posed by a crisis. Hearit (1995b, 2006) discusses three dissociation tactics relevant to post-crisis communication: (1) opinion/knowledge, (2) individual/group, and (3) act/essence. Opinion/knowledge seeks to deny a crisis exists. The crisis manager states that the reports of a crisis or the organization's connection to the crisis are just opinion and do not match the facts of the situation. When stakeholders look at the facts, they will see there is no crisis or no connection to the organization. If the organization is not involved in a crisis, there can be no damage from the crisis. The individual/group dissociation seeks to deflect some responsibility from the organization. A specific part of the organization is blamed for the crisis. Typically some person or group is said to be responsible for the crisis, not the entire organization, and the organization will then punish them. The argument is that the organization has acted responsibly and should not be punished by stakeholders. Finally, the act/essence dissociation accepts responsibility for the crisis but argues the crisis does not represent the "real" organization. The crisis was an anomaly, not a true reflection of the organization's character. Stakeholders should forgive the organization the lapse if stakeholders believe the claim that the organization generally is "good" (Hearit, 1996; Ihlen, 2002).

Hearit's (2006) later work draws the connection between corporate apologia and the need to address guilt, responsibility for a crisis, and liability. Five prototypical stances of apologia are identified: denial, counterattack, differentiation, apology, and legal. Table 12.1 provides definitions for these strategies. Ultimately,

Table 12.1 Post-crisis Response Strategies

Hearit

Denial: the organization denies any wrongdoing.

Counterattack: the organization denies wrongdoing and claims the accuser is the one at fault.

Differentiation: the organization attempts to distance itself from guilt for the crisis. There is an admission of responsibility but factors are identified that limit the organization's responsibility.

Apology: the organization accepts responsibility and promises not to do it again. This is a form of dissociation.

Legal: the organization allows the legal team to handle the crisis and avoids public statements.

Benoit

Denial
    Simple denial: did not do it.
    Shift the blame: blame someone or thing other than the organization.

Evading Responsibility
    Provocation: response to someone else's actions.
    Defeasibility: lack of information about or control over the situation.
    Accidental: did not mean for it to happen.
    Good intentions: actor meant well.

Reducing Offensiveness
    Bolstering: remind of the actor's positive qualities.
    Minimize offensiveness of the act: claim little damage from the crisis.
    Differentiation: compare act to similar ones.
    Transcendence: place act in a different context.
    Attack accuser: challenge those who say there is a crisis.
    Compensation: offer money or goods.

Corrective Action: restore situation to pre-act status and/or promise change and prevent a repeat of the act.

Mortification: ask for forgiveness; admit guilt and express regret.

Hearit (2006) concludes that corporate apologia is a type of ritual. Its utility lies not in addressing guilt and forgiveness but in meeting audience expectations for properly enacting the ritual. A successful apologia meets the requisite criteria for an apologia—the expectations for a post-crisis response (Hearit, 2006).

It should be noted that others have applied the rhetorical concept of genre to crisis communication and have moved beyond apologia. This research reflects a "hunt" to find new genres in post-crisis communication. However, there are serious flaws to these genre hunts. The generic perspective "looks at naturally occurring instances of persuasive discourse with a view toward formulating rules of discourse of that type" (Simons, 1986, p. 36). In other words, researchers look for patterns in how people communicate in specific types of situations. To develop a genre, a large number of very similar cases need to be examined for patterns. The genre hunts in post-crisis communication use one or two cases to make claims of a genre. That violates the core premises of the generic perspective and calls the "findings" of these studies into question. Therefore I have not included a detailed discussion of these genre hunts in this chapter.

Image Restoration Theory

Benoit's (1995) Image Restoration Theory (IRT) is built on two assumptions: (1) communication is a goal-directed activity and (2) maintaining a positive reputation (Benoit uses the term image) is one of the central goals in communication. IRT examines how communication is used to maintain a positive reputation. IRT begins when an unfavorable act that will threaten reputation (image) is committed. If an actor is believed to be responsible for that act, there is a need for image restoration. An actor then uses one or a combination of five image restoration strategies: denial, evading responsibility, reducing offensiveness, corrective action, and mortification. Table 12.1 provides definitions of the strategies and the sub-strategies. The development of these strategies reflects the rhetorical roots of IRT. Benoit's list of image restoration strategies was informed by apologia, Burke's idea of guilt and purification, and the accounts research (what is said after an event) from interpersonal communication and psychology (Benoit, 1995).

IRT is a general framework for addressing reputation (image) threats across a variety of situations. IRT has been applied post hoc to political, entertainment, and corporate crises. The political applications include President Clinton (Benoit, 1999) and Kenneth Starr (Benoit & McHale, 1999). The entertainment applications include Hugh Grant (Benoit, 1997) and Queen Elizabeth (Benoit & Brinson, 1999). The corporate crisis applications include AT&T (Benoit & Brinson, 1994), Sears (Benoit, 1995), and USAir (Benoit & Czerwinski, 1997). While amenable to post-crisis communication, IRT was not developed specifically for applications to either crises or to corporate actions. However, the nature of the threat crises pose to reputations makes IRT a logical adaptation for crisis communication, especially post-crisis communication. IRT has generated a large number of case studies dominated by post-crisis communication from corporations. IRT's thoroughly developed list of potential crisis response strategies is an important contribution to post-crisis communication. These post hoc case studies help to illuminate the rhetorical actions taken by crisis managers and attempt to draw implications about the effects of the crisis responses on the organization's reputation.

Rhetoric of Renewal

It has been argued that crisis communication, especially post-crisis communication, is too focused on defensive communication and issues of blame and legal liability. This should not be taken as a criticism but an observation. There are many different crises and a wide variety of crisis response strategies are necessary. Rightly some of those strategies will be defensive (designed to focus on and protect the organization) (Coombs, 2006). The rhetoric of renewal chooses to focus on the more positive and accommodative (victim-centered) actions of post-crisis communication. Renewal provides a new direction and purpose to an organization that is discovered after the crisis occurs (Ulmer, Sellnow, & Seeger, 2006).

The rhetoric of renewal is evolutionary rather than revolutionary. It is rooted in previous crisis communication research that recognizes the use of accommodative strategies to help victims including the utilization of adjusting information and the compensation strategy. Renewal extends the notion of accommodation by making a positive view of the future as the centerpiece of the crisis communication, typically post-crisis communication. As such, renewal represents a subset of the larger array of crisis communication and is not appropriate for all crises. As Ulmer et al. (2006) observe the opportunity for renewal depends on what the organization has done prior to the crisis.

Ulmer (2001) began the exploration of renewal with his insightful case study of the Malden Mills fire. Not all organizations can use renewal and renewal would not be appropriate for all crisis situations. But, there are times when the optimistic discourse of renewal makes for an effective crisis response. Through a number of case studies, four criteria have emerged for the use of renewal: (1) a strong ethical standard for the organization pre-crisis; (2) strong stakeholder relationships for an organization pre-crisis; (3) a focus on life beyond the crisis rather than seeking to escape blame; and (4) engaging in effective crisis communication (Ulmer et al., 2006).

As a newer approach, the rhetoric of renewal provides two important contributions to post-crisis communication. First, it highlights the value and nature of a positive crisis communication. Second, it reinforces the value of the situation for the crisis response and post-crisis communication. The nature of the crisis event and organization in crisis (the crisis situation) determine whether or not a rhetoric of renewal can be used effectively. However, the rhetoric of renewal is a more restricted approach because it seems to only be applicable in certain situations.

Situational Crisis Communication Theory

Situational Crisis Communication Theory (SCCT) fuses concepts from rhetoric and Attribution Theory to develop a systematic method for evaluating the reputational threat of a crisis and selecting crisis response and post-crisis response strategies designed to maximize the reputational protection of the response. SCCT incorporates social science methods and extends beyond the roots of rhetoric. Threat refers to the amount of damage a crisis could inflict on the organization's reputation if no action is taken. SCCT holds crisis communication should begin with instructing and adjusting information as a baseline. The threat will determine if post-crisis responses are needed to address lingering rhetorical problems for the reputation. From rhetoric, SCCT derives the crisis response strategies and a focus on the situation determining the most effective response (Coombs, 1995, 2007b). From Attribution Theory, SCCT derives people's need to assign responsibility for a crisis and the three factors used to asses the reputational threat of a crisis situation: (1) initial crisis responsibility, (2) crisis history, and (3) prior relational reputation. It also borrows instrumentation and assessment methods from social scientific Attribution Theory. This allows for a more systematic test of crisis messages.

Initial crisis responsibility is based on stakeholder attributions of personal control for the crisis by the organization, what SCCT terms crisis responsibility. Crisis responsibility reflects how much stakeholders believe organizational actions caused the crisis (Coombs, 1995). Research demonstrates that increased attributions of crisis responsibility by stakeholders produce lower reputational scores among those same stakeholders. The reputational threat to an organization increases as stakeholders' attributions of crisis responsibility to the organization intensifies (Coombs, 1998; Coombs & Holladay, 1996, 2002, 2004). The initial crisis assessment is based upon the crisis type. The crisis type is how the crisis is being framed. Table 12.2 defines and categorizes the crisis types in SCCT.

Table 12.2 Crisis Types by Attribution of Crisis Responsibility

---

Victim Crises: Minimal Crisis Responsibility

    Natural disasters: acts of nature such as tornadoes or earthquakes.

    Rumors: false and damaging information being circulated about your organization.

    Workplace violence: attack by former or current employee on current employees on-site.

    Product tampering/malevolence: external agent causes damage to the organization.

Accident Crises: Low Crisis Responsibility

    Challenges: stakeholder claim that the organization is operating in an inappropriate manner.

    Technical-error accidents: equipment or technology failure that causes an industrial accident.

    Technical-error product harm: equipment or technology failure that causes a product to be defective or potentially harmful.

Preventable Crises: Strong Crisis Responsibility

    Human-error accidents: industrial accident caused by human error.

    Human-error product harm: product is defective or potentially harmful because of human error.

    Organizational misdeed: management actions that put stakeholders at risk and/or violate the law.

Crisis history is whether or not an organization has had a similar crisis in the past. Prior relational reputation is how well or poorly an organization has or is perceived to have treated stakeholders in other contexts. Prior relational reputation is unfavorable if the organization has a history of treating stakeholders badly. An unfavorable prior relational reputation suggests an organization shows little consideration for stakeholders across a number of domains, not just in this crisis. Both factors demonstrate a direct and indirect effect on the reputational threat posed by the crisis. Either a history of crises or an unfavorable prior relational reputation intensifies attributions of crisis responsibility thereby indirectly affecting the reputational threat. Moreover, the two factors have a direct effect on the reputational threat that is separate from crisis responsibility (Coombs, 2004a, 2004b).

A two-step process is used to assess the reputational threat. The first step requires an assessment of the initial crisis responsibility attached to a crisis by determining the crisis type being encountered. By identifying the crisis type, the crisis manager can anticipate how much crisis responsibility stakeholders will attribute to the organization at the onset of the crisis thereby establishing the initial crisis responsibility level. The second step involves evaluating the crisis history and prior relationship reputation, the two intensifying factors. Crisis history and an unfavorable prior relationship reputation increase the initial assessment of the reputational threat (Coombs & Holladay, 2001, 2004). The crisis manager then determines if a post-crisis response is needed and, if so, which post-crisis response strategy(ies) will fit the reputational threat of the crisis. A reputational threat is likely to linger when the crisis poses a strong reputational threat. Table 12.3 presents an overview of the main recommendations from SCCT.

Table 12.3 Attribution Theory-based Crisis Communication Best Practices

---

1. All victims or potential victims should receive instructing information, including recall information. This is one-half of the base response to a crisis.
2. All victims should be provided an expression of sympathy, any information about corrective actions, and trauma counseling when needed. This can be called the "care response." This is the second-half of the base response to a crisis.
3. For crises with minimal attributions of crisis responsibility and no intensifying factors, instructing information and care response is sufficient.
4. For crises with minimal attributions of crisis responsibility and an intensifying factor, add excuse and/or justification strategies to the instructing information and care response.
5. For crises with low attributions of crisis responsibility, and no intensifying factors, add excuse and/or justification strategies to the instructing information and care response.
6. For crises with low attributions of crisis responsibility and an intensifying factor, add compensation and/or apology strategies to the instructing information and care response.
7. For crises with strong attributions of crisis responsibility, add compensation and/or apology strategies to the instructing information and care response.
8. The compensation strategy is used any time victims suffer serious harm.
9. The reminder and ingratiation strategies can be used to supplement any response.
10. Denial and attack the accuser strategies are best used only for rumor and challenge crises.

Summary of Rhetorical Approaches to Crisis Communication

Logically, researchers have drawn upon rhetoric to examine the crisis response and post-crisis communication as both are rhetorical problems. The various rhetorical approaches share two characteristics. First, each research line identifies crisis response strategies that could be used by crisis managers and offers some advice on their use. The prescriptive nature of the advice ranges from suggestions to guidelines. The post-mortem case studies are more suggestive while SCCT favors prescriptive guidelines. Second, each research line has a strong focus on the crisis situation. The crisis situation is viewed as a driver of post-crisis communication. It is by understanding the situation and the post-crisis response strategies that crisis managers make proper decisions about post-crisis communication.

Conclusion: Contributions and Shortcomings

We now return to the question, "Has rhetoric been a useful perspective for crisis communication?" Useful is taken to mean that crisis managers can learn from the research and can craft more effective responses to a crisis as a result of the rhetorically based research. The rhetorical approach provides guidance on the range of crisis response and post-crisis communication strategies and the exigencies that affect their strategy choices.

Returning to the questions asked earlier in the chapter, the rhetorical approach has helped crisis managers understand what makes for effective crisis responses and post-crisis responses and why those responses are effective. Ideas from rhetoric have explained why the early form recommendations are effective. The rhetorical perspective aided the strategic aspect of crisis responses by helping to identify the content (instructing and adjusting information) necessary for an effective crisis response. But content can be more than instructing and adjusting information.

The greatest strength of the rhetorical approach to crisis communication lies in the application of reputation repair as part of the crisis response and post-crisis communication. Researchers drew upon rhetoric to create a list of options for reputation repair. The list is an important resource for crisis managers. Some researchers have gone further and made suggestions for when each crisis response strategy might be the most effective in redressing the rhetorical problem. Such advice helps crisis managers develop their post-crisis communication strategies.

The greatest strength of the rhetorical approach to crisis communication is also a shortcoming. With the focus on reputation (perceptions of the organization), we know precious little about how crisis responses and post-crisis communication affect subsequent behaviors such as purchase intention or negative word-of-mouth stimulated by a crisis. These are important concerns because they indicate how stakeholders may alter their interactions with an organization thereby impacting the organization in meaningful ways. Some researchers in marketing and public relations have begun to examine these concerns and that is a useful direction for future research. It may be time to combine the rhetorical approach with social scientific approaches, as in SCCT, to broaden our field of view and to systematically test our recommendations for crisis response and post-crisis communication

(Coombs, 2007a). However, we should not forget that the rhetorical approach has been one of the keys to unlocking crisis communication. Wherever the field may evolve from here, the rhetorical approach has created a solid foundation for the understanding of crisis communication.

References

Arpan, L. M., & Pompper, D. (2003). Stormy weather: Testing "stealing thunder" as a crisis communication strategy to improve communication flow between organizations and journalists. *Public Relations Review, 29*(3), 291–308.

Arpan, L. M., & Roskos-Ewoldsen, D. R. (2005). Stealing thunder: An analysis of the effects of proactive disclosure of crisis information. *Public Relations Review, 31*(3), 425–433.

Barton, L. (2001). *Crisis in organizations II* (2nd ed.). Cincinnati, OH: College Divisions South-Western.

Benoit, W. L. (1995). *Accounts, excuses, and apologies: A theory of image restoration*. Albany: State University of New York Press.

Benoit, W. L. (1997). Hugh Grant's image restoration discourse: An actor apologizes. *Communication Quarterly, 45*, 251–267.

Benoit, W. L. (1999). Clinton in the Starr chamber. *American Communication Journal*. Retrieved August 15, 2007 from http://www.acjournal.org/holdings/vol2/Iss2/editorials/benoit/index.html

Benoit, W. L., & Brinson, S. (1994). AT&T: Apologies are not enough. *Communication Quarterly, 42*, 75–88.

Benoit, W. L., & Brinson, S. L. (1999). Queen Elizabeth's image repair discourse: Insensitive royal or compassionate Queen? *Public Relations Review, 25*, 145–156.

Benoit, W. L., & Czerwinski, A. (1997). A critical analysis of USAir's image repair discourse. *Business Communication Quarterly, 60*, 38–57.

Benoit, W. L., & McHale, J. (1999). "Just the facts, ma'am": Starr's image repair discourse viewed in 20/20. *Communication Quarterly, 47*, 265–280.

Benson, J. A. (1988). Crisis revisited: An analysis of strategies used by Tylenol in the second tampering episode. *Central States Speech Journal, 39*, 49–66.

Brummett, B. (1980). Towards a theory of silence as a political strategy. *Quarterly Journal of Speech, 66*, 289–303.

Bryant, D. (1953). Rhetoric: Its functions and its scope. In D. Ehninger (Ed.), *Contemporary rhetoric: A coursebook* (pp. 15–38). Glenview, IL: Scott, Foresman.

Bryson, J. M. (2004). What to do when stakeholders matter: Stakeholder identification analysis techniques. *Public Management Review, 6*, 21–53.

Carmeli, A., & Tishler, A. (2005) Perceived organizational reputation and organizational performance: An empirical investigation of industrial enterprises. *Corporate Reputation Review, 8*(1), 13–30.

Clampitt, P. G. (1991*). Communicating for managerial effectiveness*. Newbury Park, CA: Sage.

Coombs, W. T. (1995). Choosing the right words: The development of guidelines for the selection of the "appropriate" crisis response strategies. *Management Communication Quarterly, 8*, 447–476.

Coombs, W. T. (1998). An analytic framework for crisis situations: Better responses from a better understanding of the situation. *Journal of Public Relations Research, 10*, 177–191.

Coombs, W. T. (1999). Information and compassion in crisis responses: A test of their effects. *Journal of Public Relations Research, 11,* 125–142.

Coombs, W. T. (2004a). A theoretical frame for post-crisis communication: Situational crisis communication theory. In M. J. Martinko (Ed.), *Attribution theory in the organizational sciences: Theoretical and empirical contributions* (pp. 275–296). Greenwich, CT: Information Age Publishing.

Coombs, W. T. (2004b). Impact of past crises on current crisis communications: Insights from situational crisis communication theory. *Journal of Business Communication, 41,* 265–289.

Coombs, W. T. (2006). The protective powers of crisis response strategies: Managing reputational assets during a crisis. *Journal of Promotion Management, 12,* 241–259.

Coombs, W. T. (2007a). *Ongoing crisis communication: Planning, managing, and responding* (2nd ed.). Los Angeles: Sage.

Coombs, W. T. (2007b). Protecting organization reputations during a crisis: The development and application of situational crisis communication theory. *Corporate Reputation Review, 10,* 163–176.

Coombs, W. T., & Holladay, S. J. (1996). Communication and attributions in a crisis: An experimental study of crisis communication. *Journal of Public Relations Research, 8*(4), 279–295.

Coombs, W. T., & Holladay, S. J. (2001). An extended examination of the crisis situation: A fusion of the relational management and symbolic approaches. *Journal of Public Relations Research, 13,* 321–340.

Coombs, W. T., & Holladay, S. J. (2002). Helping crisis managers protect reputational assets: Initial tests of the situational crisis communication theory. *Management Communication Quarterly, 16,* 165–186.

Coombs, W. T., & Holladay, S. J. (2004). Reasoned action in crisis communication: An Attribution Theory-based approach to crisis management. In D. P. Millar & R. L. Heath (Eds.), *Responding to crisis: A rhetorical approach to crisis communication* (pp. 95–115). Mahwah, NJ: Lawrence Erlbaum.

Davies, G., Chun, R., da Silva, R. V., & Roper, S. (2003). *Corporate reputation and competitiveness.* New York: Routledge.

Dilenschneider, R. L. (2000). *The corporate communications bible: Everything you need to know to become a public relations expert.* Beverly Hills, CA: New Millennium.

Dionisopolous, G. N., & Vibbert, S. L. (1988). CBS vs Mobil Oil: Charges of creative bookkeeping. In H. R. Ryan (Ed.), *Oratorical encounters: Selected studies and sources of 20th century political accusation and apologies* (pp. 214–252). Westport, CT: Greenwood.

Hearit, K. M. (1994). Apologies and public relations crises at Chrysler, Toshiba, and Volvo. *Public Relations Review, 20,* 113–125.

Hearit, K. M. (1995a). "Mistakes were made": Organizations, apologia, and crises of social legitimacy. *Communication Studies, 46,* 1–17.

Hearit, K. M. (1995b). From "we didn't do it" to "it's not our fault": The use of apologia in public relations crises. In W. N. Elwood (Ed.), *Public relations inquiry as rhetorical criticism: Case studies of corporate discourse and social influence.* Westport, CT: Praeger.

Hearit, K. M. (1996, Fall). The use of counter-attack in apologetic public relations crises: The case of General Motors vs. Dateline NBC. *Public Relations Review, 22*(3), 233–248.

Hearit, K. M. (2001). Corporate apologia: When an organization speaks in defense of itself. In R. L. Heath (Ed.), *Handbook of public relations* (pp. 501–511). Thousand Oaks, CA: Sage.

Hearit, K. M. (2006). *Crisis management by apology: Corporate response to allegations of wrongdoing.* Mahwah, NJ: Lawrence Erlbaum.

Heath, R. L., & Coombs, W. T. (2006). *Today's public relations: An introduction.* Thousand Oaks, CA: Sage.

Hobbs, J. D. (1995). Treachery by any other name: A case study of the Toshiba public relations crisis. *Management Communication Quarterly, 8,* 323–346.

Ice, R. (1991). Corporate publics and rhetorical strategies: The case of Union Carbide's Bhopal crisis. *Management Communication Quarterly, 4,* 341–362.

Ihlen, O. (2002). Defending the Mercedes A-class: Combining and changing crisis response strategies. *Journal of Public Relations Research, 14,* 185–206.

McCroskey, J. C. (1997). *An introduction to rhetorical communication* (7th ed.). Boston: Allyn & Bacon.

Newman, R. (n.d.). It's a jungle out there. Retrieved July 31, 2007 from: http://www.usanetwork.com/series/monk/theshow/music/music.html

Rindova, V., & Fombrun, C. (1999). Constructing competitive advantage: The role of firm-constituent interactions. *Strategic Management Journal, 20,* 691–710.

Simons, H. (1986). *Persuasion: Understanding, practice, and analysis* (2nd ed.). New York: Random House.

Sturges, D. L. (1994). Communicating through crisis: A strategy for organizational survival. *Management Communication Quarterly, 7*(3), 297–316.

Ulmer, R. R. (2001). Effective crisis management through established stakeholder relationships. *Management Communication Quarterly, 14,* 590–615.

Ulmer, R. R., Sellnow, T. L., & Seeger, M. W. (2006). *Effective crisis communication: Moving from crisis to opportunity.* Thousand Oaks, CA: Sage.

Wartick, S. (1992) The relationship between intense media exposure and change in corporate reputation. *Business & Society, 31,* 33–49.

13

DIALOGUE, DISCOURSE
ETHICS, AND DISNEY

Rebecca J. Meisenbach
University of Missouri-Columbia

Sarah Bonewits Feldner
Marquette University

Scholars suggest that public relations research is moving away from or beyond J. Grunig and L. Grunig's (e.g., 1992) well-known and much-discussed symmetrical model of public relations and toward cocreational models (Botan & Taylor, 2004). In particular, they suggest that dialogic theories, processes, and procedures best define the study and practice of public relations. One of the first to discuss dialogue, Pearson (1989b), argued that "the goal of public relations is to manage these communication systems such that they come as close as possible to the standards deduced from the idea of dialogue" (p. 128).

His untimely death kept him from further pursuing his standards of dialogue, but his writings make the worth of the pursuit clear:

> The important question becomes, not what action or policy is more right than another (a question that is usually posed as a monologue), but what kind of communication system maximizes the chances competing interests can discover some shared ground and be transformed or transcended.
> (Pearson, 1989a, p. 206)

The idea of maximizing participation of all competing voices runs parallel to Jurgen Habermas's theory of communicative action and the resulting discourse ethics as has been mentioned by communication scholars, including Pearson (1989b) (see also, Kent & Taylor, 1998; Leeper, 1996; Meisenbach, 2006). Continuing interest in Habermas's theories can assist scholars in the pursuit of dialogic standards. In that tradition, we seek to develop Habermas's (1990, 1993) concept and procedure of discourse ethics as one such standard for dialogic public relations.

Leeper (1996) and Meisenbach (2006) offered entry points into the dialogic potential of public relations by employing Habermas's discourse ethics. Despite these and other theoretical discussions (e.g., Kent & Taylor, 2002), actual examples of dialogic public relations are very difficult to find. The question remains then, what obstacles prevent organizations from enacting a truly dialogic model of public relations and further what might that model look like?

We begin by discussing recent public relations research on the developing dialogic roles of publics and review relevant concepts of Habermas's communicative action and discourse ethics. We then consider these issues and methods in relation to a recent corporate controversy between the Walt Disney Company and the shareholder-focused revolt known as the Save Disney campaign. We apply Habermas's (1990, 1993, see also Leeper, 1996; Meisenbach, 2006) concept and procedure of discourse ethics as a standard for dialogic public relations, using it to analyze the successes and failures of the rhetorical moves made by both the Walt Disney Company and Save Disney campaign from 2002 to 2005. This case provides an opportunity to identify obstacles, opportunities, and strategies for enacting discourse ethics within dialogic public relations practice.

Publics and Dialogue

Public relations scholars are reconceptualizing publics with increasing frequency. First, there are the progressively more blurred lines between individual and organizational rhetors (Cheney & McMillan, 1990; Crable, 1990). In addition, Botan and Taylor (2004) pointed out that early public relations scholarship took a functional approach to publics, viewing them as a means for achieving an organization's goals. However, they noted a turn in the research toward a cocreational perspective of organization–public relations (e. g., Leitch & Neilson, 2001). Publics in this sense are not passive recipients of public relations strategies, but are active and engaged "as producers and reproducers of the community of discourse" (Chay-Nemeth, 2001, p. 2).

Vasquez and Taylor (2001) provided additional direction for how scholars might begin to advance the ways in which publics are addressed. Publics should be framed as rhetorical communities. This perspective brings a communicative framework to the forefront, viewing "a public as a rhetorical community that emerges over time through communication interactions such that a group consciousness is developed around an issue or a concern" (Vasquez & Taylor, 2001, p. 147; see also Springston & Keyton, 2001). The public envisioned here also parallels what Botan and Taylor (2004) referred to as a cocreational public that is actively involved in a meaning-making process. It suggests a form of public relations that embraces the presence of rhetoric in organization–public relations (R. L. Heath, 2001).

The challenge is to view publics and organizations in a dialogic perspective both theoretically and practically (Botan, 1997; R. L. Heath, 2001). Because of the difficulty of operationalizing dialogue, most research fails to incorporate a strong sense of the back and forth between organizations and publics. Many public relations studies focus on how the organization defends itself against challenges with very little consideration of the rhetorical positions of publics, except as obstacles that must be overcome (e.g., L. Grunig, 1992). On the other side is activist research, which has focused primarily on the rhetoric of the non-organizational challengers (e.g., Reber & Berger, 2005). Scholars are still looking for integrated considerations of the rhetoric of both sides, and how that can or fails to engage in dialogic consideration of the contested issues (Edwards, 2006). Perhaps, the best example of this kind of work is found in Brimeyer, Eaker, and Clair's (2004) study of the agitation and control typologies present in a labor union and employing company's rhetoric during a crisis. However, they focused on classifying the strategies of each party rather than on defining the connections between them or the procedure through which they sought to persuade each other. So while public relations scholars recognize the need for a dialogic perspective (R. L. Heath, 2001; Pearson, 1989a, 1989b), most research in the area has failed to examine what this dialogue might look like in practice. We turn to discourse ethics as a way of seeing and understanding public relations dialogue in action.

Communicative Action and Dialogue

Habermas's promotion of communicative action as a process in which all stakeholders have access to public deliberation resonates with calls for dialogic public communication. Because of the complexity and value of Habermas's work for pursuing and understanding dialogue in public relations, we first provide an introduction to his communicative action and then explore how communicative action provides for his theory of discourse ethics.

Habermas's (1984, 1987) theory of communicative action focuses on how people act within the lifeworld, which is the context and background of meaning that humans inherit through culture and which defines how they see the world. The lifeworld comprises three rationalization structures: personality, culture, and society. Each rationality represents a divergent way of seeing and making sense of the lifeworld, and Habermas argued that all three structures of rationality should be maintained and balanced in modern society. Personal rationality addresses internal concerns, how we talk to ourselves. Cultural rationality focuses on social concerns that are publicly considered, while societal rationality circumvents discussion and is driven by forces of power and profit.

Habermas's discussion of societal and cultural rationalities leads to his discourse ethics. Stemming from modern society's increasing bureaucratization, societal rationality's forces of power and profit problematically dominate or colonize the lifeworld. Whereas cultural rationality entails open discussion and debate about claims, societal or system rationality does not involve this type of discussion; it sidesteps discussion. Often today's corporations employ a form of societal rationality and bypass public deliberation of issues and decisions that publics believe they should be involved in discussing. That is, publics often call for the type of debate entailed in communicative action while corporations ignore this call (see Deetz, 1992).

In contrast to the corporate tendency toward societal rationality, Habermas focused on and promoted cultural rationality developed through communicative action. Habermas (1984) defined communicative action as "the type of interaction in which *all* participants harmonize their individual plans of action with one another and thus pursue their illocutionary aims *without reservation*" (p. 294). Furthermore, communicative action is based on the debate of criticizable validity claims.

The bases of validity claims include: the truth, normative rightness, and sincerity of the claim being made (Habermas, 1984). In communicative action the publics must be able to take a stance of yes or no in relation to these claims and judge to what extent they see the speaker's statement as true, right, and sincere. First, claims are judged by whether they are true or untrue, that is, a speaker asserts and a listener may challenge whether a statement is true. In addition to the truth or falsity of statements, validity of claims is also judged by rightness. In other words, by saying some statement p, the speaker asserts that "It is right that p" (1987). Finally, the validity of claims is judged by the standard of sincerity. These claims to sincerity address "the truthfulness that the speaker claims for expression of a subjective experience to which he has privileged access" (1984, p. 309). Judging this claim requires knowledge of the speaker's intention (J. Heath, 2001), which participants judge by available contextual information.

Habermas (1990) argued that all three validity claims are present in every utterance. Every time a speaker makes an utterance within the framework of cultural rationality, she wants the audience to accept the truth, rightness, and sincerity of her statement. As Meisenbach (2006) noted:

> The appealing suggestion of the copresence of the validity claims is that the truth or falsity of a statement does not stand separate from its right-ness and sincerity. If I say, "I give money to the United Way," I am argu-ing (cognitively) that it is true that I donate money to the United Way. On a moral level, I am also claiming that donating to the United Way is right or just in this situation and that it is ethical for me to present such an argument. Finally, I am claiming on the aesthetic level to be truthful or sincere (rather than sarcastic or contradictory to my other statements and actions) in my utterance. All three claims are present in my utterance, ready to be defended. (p. 42)

Thus, truth, rightness, and sincerity of utterances remain necessarily connected and ideally are considered together. When placed in the context of public relations, if they discuss their claims at all, corporations often limit themselves to focusing on the truth or falsity of their claims, while overlooking discussion of whether the utterance promotes something good or is sincerely offered. It is worthy of mention that consideration of the truth and rightness validity claims is very similar to how the issues management literature (e.g., R. L. Heath, 1997) considers gaps in organization–public perceptions of questions of fact and value relating to issues. In addition, the third validity claim, sincerity, can be linked to discussions of the management of credibility or ethos. Habermas argues that these three points of contest are simultaneously part of decisions about whether to accept the policy suggested by an utterance.

While believing that this debate of validity claims occurs via communicative action, Habermas argued that one of the primary reasons that communicative action is disrupted is the colonization of the lifeworld. This colonization occurs when the non-discursive steering mechanisms of profit and power infiltrate the cultural rationality value spheres, corrupting and halting the process of communicative action. This stance is distinct from R. L. Heath's (2001) suggestion that a process of statement and counterstatement will continue after the introduction of a profit motive. Habermas suggests that the introduction of a societal rationality statement into public discourse is colonizing because it short-circuits the debate of validity claims, leading to automatic support for whatever action enhances efficiency and profit. Societal rationality stops the conversation. For example, in the colonized lifeworld, if someone offers free computers for every student at a university, the university would automatically accept the gift because doing so fits the profit steering mechanism. The lack of discussion means that questions about whether students need the same computers, what impact the computers will have on education, or how the university might become obligated to the donor will not be considered; communicative action is bypassed.

For Habermas, the goal is not to eliminate societal rationality. Rather, a balance between cultural and societal rationality is needed. Within today's modern corporations, tendencies toward societal rationality are strong. In particular, public relations practice, which seems geared toward the promotion of cultural rationality, mutual understanding, and agreement, is often stymied by the profit and power motives of today's corporate culture.[1] However, in an age of increasingly stronger calls for corporate social responsibility, organizations should attend to their roles as a part of both the societal (i.e., profit making centers) and the cultural (i.e., socially responsible entities) spheres.

Habermas's discourse ethics can be seen as an attempt to keep societal rationality and its nondiscursive steering mechanisms of power and money in check. This perspective can guide organizations toward dialogic public relations and help scholars and practitioners understand how publics react to the actions and statements of organizations.

Discourse Ethics

Habermas's (1990, 1993, 1996) discourse ethics outlines a procedure for moral deliberation based on his Principle of Universalization (Principle U), which states that all affected by an utterance can accept those consequences. Leeper (1996) pursued discourse ethics as an alternative to the relativism of the situational perspective in public relations. He discussed how Habermas's conceptualization of the ideal speech situation and validity claims could be used to generate codes of ethics for public relations practitioners. He concluded that Habermas's work could be used to both evaluate and guide public relations practices. However, while providing an excellent background on the antecedents to discourse ethics, Leeper's work did not fully address the procedural implications of Habermas's development of Principle U.

Meisenbach (2006) explicated the implications of discourse ethics for scholars by breaking down Principle U into five practical steps:

1. identify an utterance for deliberation,
2. identify all stakeholders who would be affected by the implementation of this utterance,

3. articulate the utterance to all identified as affected,
4. discursively debate among affected parties the consequences and value of the utterance, and
5. form judgment of the validity and acceptability of the proposed utterance.

These steps are presented as the procedure for enacting Habermas's discourse ethics and thus as a framework for assessing the rhetorical moves of organizations and publics.

Through this discourse ethics procedure, various norms and individual ethical standards are established, challenged, and altered. The universal aspect of Principle U in fact suggests that this procedure occurs universally and naturally, regardless of culture or willingness of individual participants. As such it means that even when a particular organization resists the procedure or skips steps in it, that as long as societal rationality has not completely eliminated cultural rationality then Principle U is salient. If concerns of corporate responsibility and accountability to shareholders belong to the realm of cultural rationality, this means that even when organizations choose to ignore these steps they remain relevant terms of debate.

Meisenbach (2006) used this procedure as an analytical framework for understanding and assessing public resistance to the American Red Cross's (ARC) establishment and use of the Liberty Fund after the terrorist attacks in 2001. She found that while the ARC had violated (skipped some of) the steps inherent in Principle U, publics still followed the procedure and criticized the ARC's private decision about handling the funds. This example focused on the relevance of the principle to the rhetoric of a non-profit organization. Because of its universality, discourse ethics has much explanatory and analytical potential for those interested in understanding and assessing relations among publics and all kinds of organizations. To demonstrate and expand this potential, we examine how the policies and practices of the Walt Disney Company (WDC) were challenged first by internal board members and then by an ad hoc activist organization known as Save Disney. Specifically, we analyze the relevant and accessible rhetoric from these parties from 2002 to 2005 seeking their enactment and/or denial of a discourse ethics procedure.

The Bid to Save Disney: The Case of the Save Disney Campaign

Many people have long been fascinated by the operations and seeming magic that is the Walt Disney Company (WDC) empire. The company and its trademark characters are known worldwide. WDC is the second largest media and entertainment company in the world. Its enterprises include its theme parks, movie and television studios, and consumer products (Hoover's, 2007). In 2006, the company had over 130,000 employees, nearly one million shareholders, and revenues in excess of $34 billion (Hoover's, 2007; Walt Disney Company, 2006a, 2006b). The "magic" that surrounds the company's history and current operations explains why this organization garners worldwide interest.

Many have tried to capture the lore of Disney through narratives of the company's history and biographies about its leaders. Beyond telling the story of Disney, business, sociology, media, and organizational communication scholars have long been interested in Walt Disney (the founder) and the WDC. Much of the scholarly work analyzes the content of the movies and characters produced by the company (e.g. Hoerrner, 1996; Lacroix, 2004). Other work addresses the mythology of the company and juxtaposes the constructed story of Walt Disney and the magical company that he created with the "reality" of the man and the company's existence (Boje, 1995; Wasko, 2001). These investigations address what Disney means in society.

Disney's magical culture is a large part of the success of the larger organization. However, efforts to create and preserve magic are juxtaposed with the practices needed to maintain profitability. Smith and Eisenberg (1987) analyzed the specific communicative practices and metaphors tied to the company's culture as they addressed how WDC management and employees created and negotiated a conflict during the 1980s at the southern California theme park, Disneyland. The authors highlighted the degree to which management's focus on the need to cut corners conflicted with employee desires to retain the family focus of the company. Specifically the connotations of the family metaphor in the WDC culture (primarily articulated by employees) conflicted with the profit and efficiency focused needs associated with the drama metaphor (primarily used by management). The authors did not focus on the ways in which this conflict exemplifies the tension that Habermas highlighted between the system and the other spheres of the lifeworld. However, such a parallel exists and could be explored further.

Disney's challenge of maintaining a balance between societal and cultural rationality is highlighted in the shareholder-driven revolt known as the Save Disney campaign. While this particular campaign and the events surrounding it brought these issues to light, the culture of the WDC had already created the conditions for these problems. In what follows, we outline the communicative stance adopted by the company leading up to the campaign and analyze the particular rhetorical strategies employed by the WDC and the managers of the Save Disney campaign. In so doing, we seek to identify both moments in which the principle of discourse ethics was employed and those in which opportunities for engaging in dialogue were missed.

Analyzing the WDC/Save Disney Dialogue

In this analysis we focus on how the rhetoric of the WDC and Save Disney campaign seeks, denies, and contributes to dialogue, specifically comparing it to a discourse ethics procedure. We begin with the WDC culture and rhetoric just prior to the formation of the Save Disney campaign, focusing on how it relates to dialogue and discourse ethics.

Disney's Corporate Culture of (Non) Dialogue

To understand the goals and strategies of the Save Disney campaign, it is helpful to first understand the communicative culture at the WDC. The board of directors at the WDC had a history of limiting open discussion of company practices long before Save Disney began (see Smith & Eisenberg, 1987). The analysis that follows suggests that similar issues affected the board of directors of the WDC in the 1990s and beyond.

In the 1990s, two WDC board members, Roy Disney, Walt Disney's nephew, and Stanley Gold, Roy's lawyer and friend, began to challenge the decision-making processes of the board and particularly the leadership of Michael Eisner, WDC CEO and chair of the board. According to Stewart (2005), for several years Roy and Gold felt that their verbally expressed concerns had been ignored. Both men had spoken directly to Eisner about their concerns and tried unsuccessfully to remind him of a promise he had allegedly made in the 1980s that he would step down if the two men ever questioned that he was still right for the job. In 2002, Gold began sending letters to the board members expressing the same concerns.

In August 2002, Gold wrote a letter to fellow board member Ray Watson who had been quoted in a news article suggesting that the whole board supported Eisner. Gold, who recently had been harshly reprimanded by Eisner for allegedly talking to the media himself (an accusation Gold vehemently denied), wrote:

> We, the Directors, are guilty of not discussing the real issues affecting the company. We have not fully and critically addressed the failed plans of our executives or the broken promises that management has made to the Board and the shareholders. . . . We are too polite, too concerned with hurting each other's feelings, when our real job is (a) to protect the shareholders and (b) to coalesce around a management team and a plan that we believe will get us out of our current malaise.
>
> (quoted in Stewart, 2005, p. 404)

Gold was arguing that the board was guilty of squashing dissent and ignoring problems.

Board members and investors began challenging Gold over allegations that he had been taking his grievances to the press, that is, to those outside of the WDC board of directors. The day after Gold spoke with a *New York Times* reporter (after gaining Eisner's permission to do so) influential investor Sid Bass wrote a letter to Gold and copied it to all of the board members:

> every board member has a fiduciary duty not to make statements to investors, investment bankers, and the press which will damage the company. . . . I am not addressing the merits of either side of a debate, but how a debate is properly waged . . . you must play by the rules or step down.
>
> (as cited in Stewart, 2005, pp. 406–407)

Bass's words make clear that the norms inside WDC promoted a very narrow definition of acceptable debate, much less dialogue. The assumption was that the only appropriate place for debating the management of the Company was the boardroom. Bass's letter also suggested that board members are not supposed to share any negative information, even with the shareholders. In a response to Bass, Gold argued: "The problem at the Walt Disney Company is not Stanley Gold, it is not leaks (real or imagined) or unprofessional conduct, but instead it is poor performance, lack of credibility and accountability and poor capital allocation" (p. 408). This statement sums up the arguments and utterances that Gold and Roy had been trying to present to the board and became the cornerstone of the Save Disney campaign that was to come.

Amidst this contentious communicative environment, a September 2002 board meeting loomed. Gold continued to try to generate support for his stance. Gold's arguments centered on his contention that the CEO was not providing even the board with all of the financial information it needed to make responsible decisions in the interest of shareholders. So at the September board meeting, Gold formally presented his case. However, there was no discussion afterward, and his subsequent request to call for a vote on whether to hire outside consultants to better assess the situation was resisted and tabled. At the same meeting, Eisner presented his own action plan and urged a unanimous vote of support for the plan to show board unity to the outside world. Roy refused and that vote was also tabled to avoid formalizing the board's split to outsiders. The "decisions" to avoid making decisions appeared to be a norm and established a culture that clearly violated the discourse ethics procedure. In a letter of April 3, 2003 to director George Mitchell (copied to all directors) Gold challenged this procedural issue, saying: "I fear that our inability to discuss difficult problems and make hard decisions is an abdication of our fiduciary duty" (as cited in Stewart, 2005, p. 431). But such statements made little difference.

The issue came to a head in November 2003, when a board member met with Roy to tell him that the board members had decided that he would not be renominated to the board. In response, Roy resigned from the board and his position in animation. Gold resigned soon afterward and his resignation letter, posted on the original December 2003 Save Disney website, noted that the decision to remove Roy from the board was "yet another attempt by this board to squelch dissent by hiding behind the veil of 'good governance.' What a curious result." He also questioned the recent WDC policy "barring board members from communicating with shareholders and the media" and suggested that by acting "independently" perhaps "I can have greater success in shaping the policies, practices and operations of [WDC] than I had as a member of the board." Eisner reportedly did not consider Roy and Gold to be a great threat; however, history proved him wrong because these events led to Roy and Gold launching the ad hoc organization and Internet-based activist campaign known as Save Disney.

The Save Disney campaign is interesting not only for its magnitude and unique approach, but in this context it marks a turning point in how WDC issues are discussed. Of interest here is a turn from practices that clearly violated discourse ethics procedures by preventing open debate to interaction that allowed space for the rhetorical arguments of multiple stakeholders. It is this turn that is the focus of the rest of this analysis.

Save Disney's Contribution to Dialogue

While the Save Disney campaign used multiple tools, including an email list-serv and in-person visits to proxy services, the focal point of the campaign was a website launched in December 2003. The original website was very simple, with a one-paragraph introduction and links to Roy's and Gold's resignation letters along with a thank you message/explanation from Roy to all Disney cast members.[2] A disclaimer at the bottom of the page noted: "This website has been established to provide a forum for discussing, analyzing and critiquing the performance, direction, and management of The Walt Disney Company." In contrast to the culture of the board, which served to stifle discussion and debate, Roy and Gold were creating a forum through which they could share and debate existing WDC communication as well as their own communication that had been silenced by the Disney board. Thus, Roy and Gold reasserted the need for the WDC to engage in dialogue.

In early January 2004, Roy and Gold introduced a more sophisticated website. There, they laid out the primary goal of the campaign. This stated goal represents the central utterance and first step in the discourse ethics procedure that we focus on for the remainder of this analysis (see Table 13.1). In a letter on January 27, 2004, they urged shareholders to vote "NO on the reelection of Michael Eisner, George Mitchell, Judith Estrin, and John Bryson as directors," because "they symbolize, respectively, the poor management, poor governance, poor compensation practices, and lack of board independence that are impeding the development of long-term shareholder value at The Walt Disney Company." This was the same goal Roy and Gold worked to achieve from within the board.

Table 13.1 Steps of Discourse Ethics for the Save Disney Campaign

Steps	Description	Save Disney Case
Step 1	Generate an utterance	"Vote No" on election of Eisner and other board members
Step 2	Identify those potentially affected by the enactment of the utterance	Employees, board members, shareholders, consumers
Step 3	Articulate the utterance to all affected by the utterance	Message communicated via Save Disney website, emails, presentations, and rally
Step 4	All parties discursively debate the consequences and their acceptability	Occurred through website postings, emails, and press releases
Step 5	Judge the validity and acceptability of the proposed utterance	Shareholder vote held at the WDC annual meeting

The launch of the Save Disney campaign represented a new opportunity to move through a discourse ethics procedure. Beginning with the selection of the utterance, instead of suggesting an external review of the board's processes, the Save Disney campaign argued for the removal of the individuals who seemed most closely linked to the lack of debate occurring on the board, that is, to the shutting down of a discourse ethics procedure. They then considered all who were being and would be affected by the implementation of this utterance and came up with a broad set of stakeholders. In stark contrast to the narrowly defined appropriate public as determined by the WDC board, on December 10, 2003, a posting on the site explained that the SaveDisney.com website was "devoted to those concerned about the welfare of The Walt Disney Company and its future direction." Next we turn to how the primary claim was publicly debated.

The Save Disney website actively invited public discussion and participation. It provided colorful graphics, streaming audio and video, extensive links to stories on the company, interactive poll questions, an invitation for any site visitor to join the SaveDisney.com mailing list, personal and frequently updated statements from Roy, and postings of news and commentaries relating to the company from around the world. There were also distinct sections for different categories of stakeholders including: families, consumers, and employees. As such, the website invited participation by company shareholders, but also a wide range of external stakeholder groups. Comments and stories from visitors to the site frequently became highlighted contributions to the website and campaign.

While a wide variety of Disney stakeholders were publicly participating in discussions about the contested practices of the WCD and its leadership via the SaveDisney.com website and its list-serv, finding relevant public discussion and responses from the WDC board and/or Eisner is more challenging. In December 2003, a brief WDC press release announcing new board members was the only official statement that even implied Roy's and Gold's departures. Much more visible were Roy's and Gold's in-person and video-conference presentations of their positions and reasoning to proxy advisory services in early 2004. On February 2nd, they made a particularly important presentation to Institutional Shareholder Services (ISS). Shortly after the presentation, ISS issued a public report questioning WDC's strength and the blending of management and board positions. ISS recommended that shareholders vote "withhold" on Eisner, and that they should wait and see what changes that vote generated in the company before voting no on other board members (Stewart, 2005).

Such moves may have finally prodded the WDC board into entering public discussion of the contested issues. On February 6, 2004, the board of directors issued a statement to shareholders acknowledging and refuting the challenges being generated through the Save Disney campaign. In addition to highlighting current Disney successes, several lines were devoted to rebutting Save Disney arguments about the poor governance and lack of board independence. However, the overall message of the statement was that Roy and Gold were wrong to be challenging the company: "You may have heard recently about the attack being waged by two former directors against the chief executive officer and certain members of the Board of Directors of your company. You should be disturbed by this attack" (Walt Disney Company, February 6, 2004). The letter went on to characterize Roy's and Gold's actions as "trying to distract the Board and management." These statements from the WDC board highlight the degree to which the board was still operating under the assumptions that dissent was unhelpful and that non-board members had no business trying to engage in debate about company policies. Also, while a response to the Save Disney campaign, these comments do not directly respond to the content of Roy's and Gold's claims. Rather, in their statement, board members were challenging Roy's and Gold's right to make such claims. Couched in the scheme of communicative action, the board was challenging the rightness and sincerity of the Save Disney claims, while leaving alone the issue of the truth of the campaign's statements.

In an open letter to shareholders posted on the SaveDisney.com website on February 12, 2004, Roy and Gold responded to the accusations of being an inappropriate distraction:

> We disagree with the Board's attitude that this is not the time for dissent. In our view, open discussion is essential to good corporate governance and the creation of shareholder value, regardless of whether the stock price is up or down. We made every effort as Board members to engage the Board in a constructive dialogue regarding the crucial issues facing Disney in the past few years, when Disney's stock price traded in the teens. Our efforts were deprecated and rebuffed. If it was not the time to challenge management then, and it is not the time to challenge management now, when is the time?

They then restated their position on the WDC: "We believe Disney needs a Board and senior management who will approach difficult issues head-on, after giving careful consideration to disparate points of view." In contrast with the statements offered by the WDC board, these comments speak directly to the truth, rightness, and sincerity of the board's claim. Roy and Gold addressed the argument that they are not sincere or the appropriate people to address these issues. In part they respond by making an implicit call for a discourse ethics procedure, approaching issues, hearing various stakeholders, and facing them head on. They concluded by saying: "We believe that Disney's current senior management seeks to avoid this type of dialogue and our Board experience has confirmed that the Board is unwilling to pursue this type of exchange." The focus of the Save Disney campaign was the failure of the current leadership; however, in advancing this argument, the campaign managers also asserted the need for dialogue.

The WDC board responded to the Save Disney campaign's efforts with its own letter, on February 17th. The directors argued that the company was on strong financial ground, but did not address any of the challenges about a lack of dialogue on the board. Instead, most of the letter again tried to undermine the credibility of Gold and Roy: "In the face of this significant recovery, it is unfortunate that Stanley Gold and his client Roy Disney persist in waging their distractive propaganda campaign against The Walt Disney Company and its Board of Directors." Under a subheading of "The bottomline for Disney shareholders" the directors declared, "You have every right to be concerned that [Roy and Gold] are putting their own interests ahead of yours." However, nowhere did the board state what Roy's and Gold's interests were or how they might differ from the reader's own interests.

The day before the shareholder meeting on March 2nd, board member Mitchell argued in the *Wall Street Journal* that "The changes we have made have resulted from our listening. We listened to the concerns that have been expressed about the company and about all of corporate America" (Mitchell, 2004). However, the concerns the board "heard" were about boards that are too large, and lacking in independence, diversity, and expertise, and not about the actual leadership of the company. By this time, the Save Disney list serv had approximately 35,000 registered members who received regular email updates from Roy and the campaign (Magill, 2004), but Mitchell did not directly address the campaign and its claims about WDC leadership.

At the official shareholder meeting, Gold and Roy spoke to 3000 shareholders (Orwall, Steinberg, & Lublin, 2004). Roy reasoned: "We need to install a new management team, one that understands and believes in the enormously valuable legacy that's been entrusted to us." As usual, Gold's rhetoric was harsher: "Let me be clear. No half measures, no excuses, no amount of spinning will be tolerated. Michael Eisner must leave now" (as cited in Stewart, 2005, p. 509).

At the end of the meeting, the initial voting tallies were announced. Whether accidental or not, Stewart (2005) reported that Eisner attempted to adjourn the meeting without announcing any voting results. When attendees chanted "vote, vote," Eisner said, "I almost got away with that, didn't I?" (Ahrens, 2004). While only the initial raw numbers were read at the meeting, according to final official numbers released in April 2004, Michael Eisner had received a no confidence vote from 45.37% of shareholders, and board member George Mitchell received a 25.69% no confidence vote ("Walt Disney Co.," 2004). On the surface, the vote demonstrated a near split. But in the context of the typical full support recorded in shareholder board elections, and the realization that the 45% withhold vote represented the largest withhold vote ever received by a CEO, the will of the oppositional voice was clear.

Later that evening, the WDC issued a press release announcing the decision to separate the positions of CEO and chairman of the company, creating a new position of Chairman of the Board, to which George Mitchell was appointed (Walt Disney Company, March 3, 2004). This move did not end the disagreements among the company stakeholders, but it was a catalyst for significant changes in WDC governance over the ensuing five years. Six months later, Eisner announced he would resign as CEO of the WDC effective September 2006. The Save Disney campaign praised the decision, but argued that the change was not occurring soon enough, and continued to call for Eisner's immediate resignation. At this point, yet another utterance went through the discourse ethics procedure.

Eventually, Eisner agreed to step down in September 2005, and to not seek reelection for his board position in 2006 (Marr, Mangalindan, & Lublin, 2005). Eisner's own choice for his successor, Bob Iger, was appointed as CEO of WDC. After several meetings with Iger in July 2005, the WDC, Roy, and Gold issued a joint statement that they had come to a resolution and the Save Disney campaign would come to an end (Orwall, 2005). Time will tell how much this incident will influence public relations practice at the WDC.

Discourse Ethics Procedure and the Save Disney Campaign

The events and discourse surrounding the Save Disney campaign are intriguing in their own right as a historic and successful challenge to corporate management practice. Beyond this, these events provide a compelling example for considering opportunities and challenges for dialogue between corporations and their stakeholders. This outcome warrants our offering of several generalizations that help define dialogic public relations.

In considering the "Vote No" utterance in the context of the second step (identifying who would be affected by the implementation of this utterance), we have established how the WDC board generated a very narrow assessment of the relevant stakeholders (the board members) and allowed Roy's and Gold's arguments to be shared only with this select group. The board then refused to engage in discussion and debate about the consequences of the utterance even among its members and avoided making a judgment about the utterance, thus straying from the discourse ethics procedure.

The launch of the Save Disney campaign represented an attempt to expand the debate to a wider audience of stakeholders, and consequently, restart the discourse ethics procedure. In stark contrast to the narrowly defined appropriate publics as determined by the WDC board, the Save Disney website was "devoted to those concerned about the welfare of The Walt Disney Company and its future direction" (December 10, 2003 website). The website included comments directed at WDC board members, employees, shareholders, and consumers. The creation of the Save Disney campaign and website allowed Roy and Gold to enact step three (articulating the utterance to everyone they had identified as potentially affected by it). While the prevailing communication culture of the board was one that stifled debate, the tactics of the Save Disney campaign forced the WDC board members to participate in step three (albeit in limited terms).

The fourth step of the discourse ethics procedure entails debate among the parties about the consequences and value of the utterance. Shareholder concerns were articulated and discussion was allowed. During this fourth step of debate, the conditions of communicative action become most relevant. Communicative action prescribes specific criteria for debate among stakeholders. The statements offered by the campaign and the resulting responses from the WDC represent the bulk of the discussion and debate in this campaign. A focus on the various bases of validity that communicative action entails helps to explain in part the way in which this debate played out. Rather than addressing the truth (factual validity) of the Save Disney claims, the WDC board members focused on the rightness and sincerity of these claims. In contrast, the Save Disney campaign focused on the factual truth of the WDC statements and emphasized the degree to which the board was not being sincere in its communication. The end result is that the two parties were not engaged in productive debate or dialogue.

While the focus here has been on the debate between the Save Disney campaign managers and the WDC board, other stakeholders did participate in this debate. The investor proxy services participated through public statements supporting the Save Disney campaign's advocacy for withholding support for Eisner. Employees, shareholders, and consumers voiced their support for the arguments made by Roy and Gold. However, only direct WDC shareholders could participate in the formal vote about the utterance under consideration.

Finally, the fifth step, forming judgment on the validity and acceptability of the norm, was enacted through the vote at the annual shareholder meeting. The results sent a clear message that many stakeholders believed that Eisner and his fellow board members should be removed, thus supporting the initial claims made by Roy and Gold.

In the end, the arguments of the Save Disney campaign prevailed, but not without a long and difficult fight. The success of the Save Disney campaign can be attributed in part to the degree to which its actions embraced the discourse ethics procedure. While its participation in discussions with the WDC did not always directly address the claims made by the company, it did remain true to the ideal of involving a broad range of stakeholders and allowing for open exchange. This is perhaps the greatest failure and missed opportunity of the WDC. Eisner and the board clearly overlooked the potential impact of such a public dialogue, and as such, participated in the dialogue in a limited sense. It is unclear if outcomes would have been different had the WDC fully participated in the discussion. However, this stands as a missed opportunity for the company. What remains to be seen is if the corporate governance at WDC will now follow a deliberation procedure with its publics that is more in line with discourse ethics.

Discussion

Corporations today are more likely to acknowledge their accountability to their shareholders and the board members who represent them, particularly given the recent corporate scandals. However, the case covered here occurred after the Enron, WorldCom, and Tyco scandals and yet the WDC's CEO, Eisner, appeared to forget that he needed to engage in dialogue even with the company's board members. The blurred lines between internal and external publics also became clear in this case as rhetorical discussions that were originally limited to a very internal locus, eventually became front page news across the country, playing out for both internal and external publics.

What is also significant to note about the events leading up to the campaign is the degree to which the board action parallels Habermas's description of the colonization of the lifeworld and failure to create conditions of communicative action. Board members such as Roy and Gold found that even in their privileged internal company position, when they had an utterance to share, they did not get to decide who the stakeholders in that utterance were (step two), had to seek Eisner's permission before they could share the utterance with most stakeholders (step three), debate of the utterance was often squelched (step four), and judgments of many utterances were not allowed (step five). According to such accounts, Eisner and the board had created a communicative culture that cut off dialogue. In contrast, Pearson (1989b) argued that "dialogue is a precondition for any legitimate corporate conduct that affects a public of that organization" (p. 128).

This case serves as a cautionary tale to managements that might still be inclined not to pursue or even to stop dialogic relations with their publics. Habermas's discourse ethics suggests that even when someone or something attempts to circumvent the procedure, the principle of universalization is just that, universal. The principle and its procedure will be pursued by interlocutors. Just as board members, victims' families, donors, and elected officials found a path to enact a discourse ethics procedure in the Liberty Fund case, so did stakeholders of the Disney company. Once it became clear that presentations of positions and arguments that ran counter to Eisner's would not be entertained or heard, that is, that a process even remotely resembling a procedure of discourse ethics was not in place on the board, Roy and Gold left the boardroom and found an alternative path for enacting a discourse ethics procedure. Thus, the current chapter demonstrates how Principle U plays out in public relations. These days, corporations are increasingly aware of their accountability to a wide range of publics, and further research can explore how a discourse ethics procedure plays out among a wider range of organizational stakeholders. This procedure offers a useful plan for organization–public communication as well as a scholarly tool for assessing such relationships.

It should also be noted that the recent development and impact of the Internet played a significant role in facilitating the discourse ethics procedure in this case, but had both strengths and weaknesses. On the positive side, it clearly allowed Roy and Gold to interact with a wide range of stakeholders. Anyone who could access the Internet and felt a linkage to the WDC, could become a member of the campaign and participate in discussions through the site. However, the Save Disney web team carefully controlled the website and our analysis of the extensive website found only one letter posted from an employee that was mildly critical of the Save Disney stance. It is unclear if voices of opposition to the campaign were censored from or simply were not submitted to the website.

This uncertainty reminds us that while the Save Disney campaign might have been clamoring for more dialogic public relations between the WDC and its publics, the campaign website itself was not a fully dialogic site. It offered a voice for a stance that was not being allowed within the WDC, but didn't provide much divergence on its own pages. While the campaign encouraged debate, only one choice was advocated on the website. Thus, it took the input from the WDC, the Save Disney campaign, other websites, the formal press, and untold others to generate a truly dialogic space.

This finding points to a final contribution of this case study, which is to highlight the degree to which dialogue exists in a much broader space than previously imagined. Dialogue does not simply entail exchanges between two parties in a single interaction. Rather, it seems in today's ever-changing communication climate that dialogue entails participation from multiple parties, in a variety of forums. Further rhetorically based research could focus on websites that claim to be (and may be) a forum for all sides of an issue. Studies and examples like these can further enhance our understanding, pursuit, and analysis of dialogic public relations.

Notes

1 While some scholars suggest that agreement is the ideal goal of public relations, we suggest that even when agreement is not possible, understanding of divergent positions can still be beneficial for organization–public relations.
2 All Disney employees are known as cast members.

References

Ahrens, F. (2004, March 4). Eisner loses one title in Disney shake-up. *Washington Post*, A01.

Boje, D. M. (1995). Stories of the storytelling organization: A postmodern analysis of Disney as "Tamaraland." *Academy of Management Journal, 38*, 997–1035.

Botan, C. H. (1997). Ethics in strategic communication campaigns. *Journal of Business Communication, 34*, 188–202.

Botan, C. H., & Taylor, M. (2004). Public relations: The state of the field. *Journal of Communication, 54*, 645–661.

Brimeyer, T. M., Eaker, A. V., & Clair, R. P. (2004). Rhetorical strategies in union organizing: A case of labor versus management. *Management Communication Quarterly, 18*, 45–75.

Chay-Nemeth, C. (2001). Revising public: A critical archaeology of publics in the Thai HIV/AIDS Issue. *Journal of Public Relations Research, 13*, 127–161.

Cheney, G., & McMillan, J. J. (1990). Organizational rhetoric and the practice of criticism. *Journal of Applied Communication Research, 18*, 93–114.

Crable, R. E. (1990). "Organizational rhetoric" as the fourth great system: Theoretical, critical, and pragmatic implications. *Journal of Applied Communication Research, 18*, 115–128.

Deetz, S. (1992). *Democracy in an age of corporate colonization: Developments in communication.* Albany: State University of New York Press.

Edwards, H. H. (2006). A rhetorical typology for studying the audience role in public relations communication: The Avon 3-Day disruption as exemplar. *Journal of Communication, 56*, 836–860.

Grunig, J. E., & Grunig, L. (1992). Models of public relations and communication. In J. Grunig (Ed.), *Excellence in public relations and communication management* (pp. 285–326). Hillsdale, NJ: Lawrence Erlbaum.

Grunig, L. (1992). Activism: How it limits the effectiveness of organizations and how excellent public relations departments respond. In J. E. Grunig (Ed.), *Excellence in public relations and communication management* (pp. 503–530). Hillsdale, NJ: Lawrence Erlbaum.

Habermas, J. (1984). *Theory of communicative action: Volume 1: Reason and the rationalization of society* (T. McCarthy, Trans.). Boston: Beacon Press.

Habermas, J. (1987). *The theory of communicative action: Volume II: Lifeworld and system: A critique of functionalist reason* (T. McCarthy, Trans.). Boston: Beacon Press.

Habermas, J. (1990). *Moral consciousness and communicative action* (C. Lenhardt & S. Weber Nicholson, Trans.). Cambridge, MA: MIT Press.

Habermas, J. (1993). *Justification and application: Remarks on discourse ethics* (C. P. Cronin, Trans.). Cambridge, MA: MIT Press.

Habermas, J. (1996). *Between facts and norms* (W. Rehg, Trans.). Cambridge, MA: MIT Press.

Heath, J. (2001). *Communicative action and rational choice.* Cambridge, MA: MIT Press.

Heath, R. L. (1997). *Strategic issues management: Organizations and public policy changes.* Thousand Oaks, CA: Sage.

Heath R. L. (2001). A rhetorical enactment rationale for public relations: The good organization communicating well. In R.L. Heath (Ed.), *Handbook of public relations* (pp. 31–50). Thousand Oaks, CA: Sage.

Hoerrner, K. L. (1996). Gender roles in Disney films: Analyzing behaviors from Snow White to Simba. *Women's Studies in Communication, 19*, 213–228.

Hoover's. (2007, July 24). *The Walt Disney Company.* Hoover's Company Records— In-Depth Records. Retrieved July 27, 2007, from LexisNexis Academic database.

Kent, M. L., & Taylor, M. (1998). Building dialogic relationships through the World Wide Web. *Public Relations Review, 24*(3), 321–334.

Kent, M. L., & Taylor, M. (2002). Toward a dialogic theory of public relations. *Public Relations Review, 28*(1), 21–37.

Lacroix, C. (2004). Images of animated others: The Orientalization of Disney's cartoon heroines from the Little Mermaid to The Hunchback of Notre Dame. *Popular Communication, 2*(4), 213.

Leeper, R. V. (1996). Moral objectivity, Jurgen Habermas's discourse ethics, and public relations. *Public Relations Review, 22*, 133–150.

Leitch, S., & Neilson, D. (2001). Bringing publics into public relations: New theoretical frameworks for practice. In R. L. Heath (Ed.), *Handbook of public relations* (pp. 127–138). Thousand Oaks, CA: Sage.

Magill, K. (2004, March 5). Power of Disney's deaniacs grows. *New York Sun*, 11.

Marr, M., Mangalindan, M., & Lublin, J. S. (2005, March 14). Cast change: Disney turns to insider Iger to take CEO reins from Eisner; longtime chief to leave early and give up board seat; critics call search "sham"; Meg Whitman withdraws. *Wall Street Journal* (Eastern Edition), A.1. doi: 807186411.

Meisenbach, R. J. (2006). Habermas's discourse ethics and principle of universalization as a moral framework for organizational communication. *Management Communication Quarterly, 20*, 39–62.

Mitchell, G. J. (2004, March 2). Disney character. *Wall Street Journal* (Eastern Edition), A18.

Orwall, B. (2005, July 11). Disney, dissidents reach accord. *Wall Street Journal* (Eastern edition), B2.

Orwall, B., Steinberg, B., & Lublin, J. S. (2004, March 4). Disney's Eisner steps down from chairman post after protest garners 43% of voted shares. *Wall Street Journal*, A1.

Pearson, R. (1989a). A theory of public relations ethics. Unpublished doctoral dissertation, Ohio University.

Pearson, R. (1989b). Business ethics as communication ethics: Public relations practice and the idea of dialogue. In C. H. Botan & V. Hazleton, Jr. (Eds.), *Public relations theory* (pp. 111–131). Hillsdale, NJ: Lawrence Erlbaum.

Reber, B. H., & Berger, B. K. (2005). Framing analysis of activist rhetoric: How the Sierra Club succeeds or fails at creating salient messages. *Public Relations Review, 31*, 185–195.

Smith, R. C., & Eisenberg, E. M. (1987). Conflict at Disneyland: A root-metaphor analysis. *Communication Monographs, 54*, 367–380.

Springston, J. K., & Keyton, J. (2001). Public relations field dynamics. In R.L. Heath (Ed.), *Handbook of public relations* (pp. 115–126). Thousand Oaks, CA: Sage.

Stewart, J. B. (2005). *Disney war.* New York: Simon & Schuster.

Vasquez, G. M., & Taylor, M. (2001). Research perspectives on "the Public." In R.L. Heath (Ed.), *Handbook of public relations* (pp. 139–154). Thousand Oaks, CA: Sage.

Walt Disney Company. (2004, February 6). Letter to Disney shareholders from the board of directors, The Walt Disney Company [press release]. Retrieved from http://corporate.disney.go.com/files/2004_0206_shareholder1.pdf

Walt Disney Company. (2004, February 17). Letter to shareholders from the board of directors, the Walt Disney Company [press release]. Retrieved from http://corporate.disney.go.com/news/corporate/2004/2004_0217_shareholderletter2.html

Walt Disney Company. (2004, March 3). Statement from the board of directors of the Walt Disney Company [press release]. Retrieved from http://corporate.disney.go.com/news/corporate/2004/2004_0303_board.html

Walt Disney Company. (2006a). *2006 Annual Report*. Retrieved from http://corporate.disney.go.com/investors/annual_reports/2006/index.html

Walt Disney Company. (2006b). *Form 10–K September 30, 2006*. Retrieved from Thomson ONE Banker database.

Wasko, J. (2001). Challenging Disney myths. *Journal of Communication Inquiry, 25*, 237–257.

14

SECRET PERSUADERS

Ethical and Rhetorical Perspectives on the Use of Public Relations Front Groups

Michael J. Palenchar
University of Tennessee

Kathy R. Fitzpatrick
Quinnipiac University

Imagine you are a public relations practitioner intensely working to represent your client—a manufacturing company, a non-profit organization, your local school district, or the county hospital. How challenging would it be to be part of a conversation, such as advocating your organization's interests as part of the solution to a problem your town faces, when you don't know who you are speaking with? How much does it matter who says what? Who is being paid what to speak on its behalf? And if they mention an organization that takes a position on some matter, will you really know the character of the organization? What is their interest in the matter, and what does their interest and the values they associate with it do to strengthen or weaken their "voice" and to help solve the problem?

According to Aristotle (Apostle, 1984), the full realization of our rational powers is not something we can individually achieve or maintain. Humans need to engage in discourse that challenges us to think more and to achieve greater understanding. Rational activity performed in political community (*polis*) includes transparency of source and character of source, to make the best life and society. The goal of community deliberation is to determine and promote the conditions under which citizens can be fully active and are fully aware of how those decisions are made. Institutions should be set up so as to promote the development of citizens' powers to think and to know (Apostle), including openness in the deliberation process.

The rhetorical and critical tradition's contribution to academic research in and the practice of public relations has been addressed throughout this volume. One new facet in this discussion is the utilization and function of front groups in the sphere of public discourse and in particular public relations. Public relations front groups involve third-party organizations that are typically fashioned by public relations agencies on the behalf of undisclosed organizations that are strategically created to be something they appear not to be. These groups involve deliberate financial, source, membership, and informational misrepresentations designed to persuade in a purportedly open communication context where interests are at stake for the advantage of the undisclosed special interest or commercial purpose. Open dialogue and advocacy on behalf of client or organization interests to make society more fully functioning is the hallmark of ethical public relations practice, not to function fully as a result of being shadowy and engaged in advancing hidden agendas.

At the core of any discussion about front groups within public relations is the role of public relations practitioners in creating shared meaning in support of public affairs and public policy efforts and the sales of products and services for organizations and clients, and the role of ethics and responsible advocacy within these efforts. The purpose of this chapter is to review what constitutes a front group and provide a brief review of the evolution and contemporary practices of front groups in public relations, to review applicable public relations associations' ethical guidelines, and ultimately to provide a rhetorical argument for the discontinued use of front groups as a public relations strategy and tactic. The authors make the case that front groups as a public relations strategy and tactic contradict both contemporary standards of ethical public relations practice and the rhetorical tradition of advocacy and, therefore, should be abolished.

This research area is significant because it addresses a very public and controversial technique for public communication, a subject that has received sparse attention in the public relations literature with only three articles in the *Journal of Public Relations Research* and one article in *Public Relations Review* that even mentioned the words *front groups*. The *Encyclopedia of Public Relations* (edited by Heath, 2005) doesn't even have an entry for this contentious and often-used technique. This discussion also is enhanced by consideration of how research in and the professional practice of public relations can add value to the organizations who hire public relations services and to society as a whole. As Heath (2006) stated, "we need a paradigm of public relations that features it as being capable of adding value to the full functioning society, one that relishes research and reflective soul searching to define the ethical status of what public relations practice does but does not destroy its soul" (p. 95).

Evolving Front Group Practices

Third-party groups, coalitions, special interests groups, and trade associations formed and structured to advocate an explicit policy interest have always been part of the U.S. political and economic landscape. Such groups range from union and non-union workers' rights, religious ideology, veteran affairs, manufacturing associations, students' rights, and environmental conservancy, to the for-profit promotion of products and services.

One effective communication and management strategy frequently used by organizations that operate in the public policy arena is a coalition. According to Tucker and McNerney (1992), coalitions are temporary constructs of individuals, groups, and organizations that band together and advocate for an intended purpose. Coalitions derive their power from their size (individuals and/or groups represented) and the credibility attached to those numbers and the standing of those who comprise the coalition (1992). Their power is indicated by their ability to pressure policy makers and affect discourse and behavioral outcomes related to issues and policy decisions. For example, trade associations can be legitimate coalitions that have banded around a product, service, or typically an industry to openly advocate and promote the interests of the association's organizational membership. Legitimate trade associations' membership lists are public, funding mechanisms transparent, and mission and vision statements openly operationalized. While particular actions of certain trade associations are questionable or outright deceptive, the fundamental nature of trade associations, like other legitimate third-party groups and special interests groups, is not deceptive.

A twentieth-century outgrowth of coalitions is the controversial technique called front groups. There are numerous challenges to defining a front group. What differentiates legitimate third-party techniques or coalitions from a front group? Are single-issue advocacy groups under the banner of front groups? According to SourceWatch, a project of the Center for Media & Democracy (2007), "a front group is an organization that purports to represent one agenda while in reality it serves some other party or interest whose sponsorship is hidden or rarely mentioned" (p. 1). Although these groups appear to represent citizen involvement in public policy debates, they are actually created and funded by outside organizations to advocate for issues or causes that benefit the silent partner. According to Beder (1998), the creation and use of front groups is permitting a process whereby organizations are able to take part in public discourse and government hearings "behind a cover of community concern" (p. 20).

A stronger definition of front groups and more appropriate for this chapter is one advocated by Fitzpatrick and Palenchar (2006): "Controversial public relations techniques used by organizations to influence public opinion and public policy on behalf of undisclosed special interests. The groups are created to pursue public policy objectives for organizations that disguise their connection (e.g., financial support) with the effort while attempting to appear independent. The typical objective of front groups is to convince public policy makers that citizen support skews in a particular direction or to influence outcomes in local, state and national elections" (p. 203).

Not all organizations involved in propaganda, manipulative control of public policy issues, or efforts to conceal true intentions can be categorized as front groups. There are varying degrees of financial disclosure, misrepresentation, and manipulation. A front group's funding, control, and membership are managed by the special interests of the secret sponsor. Front groups are typically transient by nature, reflecting their often single-issue focus. In addition, according to Megalli and Friedman (1992) and Beder (1998), many front groups operate out of public relations agencies with employees of the firms acting as directors and managers as well as the membership of the group.

A typical objective of front groups is to convince public policy makers that citizen support for a particular action or policy leans toward a particular direction. Toward that end, front groups usually are given high values-laden, noble-sounding names, such as "Citizens for [Something Good]." There is a rhetorical cleverness to creating and naming front groups. Industry and other front groups are often named to appear like non-profits in attempt to create an appealing front while hiding their true character, which is the opposite of asserting their character and virtue. There is nothing wrong with using a name that asserts your character as long as the words match the mission and vision of the organization.

The average person reading a report from "Citizens for [Something Good]" often takes the name at face value and assumes that this is a grassroots organization of citizens from their local, regional, state, or national community. Other tactics of front groups, according to Megalli and Friedman (1992) and Fullwood (1996), are the use of scientific sounding names, such as the Council for Agricultural Science and Technology, or names that suggest a concern for the public interest, such as the National Wetlands Coalition. Many front groups have innocuous sounding names that give no indication of their relationship to any issue, product, service, or organization.

Consumer Reports (1994) labeled front groups as "public-interest pretenders [that] work in so many ways—through advertisements, press releases, public testimony, bogus surveys, questionable public-opinion polls, and general disinformation—that it's hard to figure out who's who or what the group's real agenda might be" (p. 316). Former U.S. Treasury Secretary Lloyd Bentsen coined the term "Astroturf" in 1994, distinguishing manufactured front groups that impersonate lobbying coalitions from genuine grassroots lobbying efforts involving legitimate coalitions representing individuals and organizations they openly represent (Pires, 1994). Beder (1998) described Astroturf grassroots coalitions as the instant manufacturing of public support.

Third-party groups, coalitions, special interests groups, trade associations, and single-issue advocacy groups also are distinguished from front groups by the deceptive nature of the source of the front group effort. All these approaches are used by profit and non-profit organizations and involve the utilization of financial resources, the mobilization of human resources and rely on the development of public and behind-the-scenes political resources. Legitimate advocacy groups transparently do so exposing financial backers, intended purposes, and memberships. Front groups, on the other hand, are instruments designed to intentionally mislead the public and policy makers on policy matters (Bodensteiner, 1997).

Pfau, Haigh, Sims, and Wigley (2007) used the term *front-group stealth campaigns* to describe this public relations endeavor. "Front-group stealth campaigns involve sponsors, sometimes individually, but much more often collectively through interest groups, seeking to influence public opinion using deceptive names" (p. 74). Their experimental research demonstrated that front groups may be effective in the short term, eroding publics' attitudes toward the issue under debate while increasing positive perceptions of the front group, though not its non-disclosed sponsor. More importantly, however, when front groups were exposed, the positive effects originally identified in the experiment went away and negative perceptions increased toward the previously concealed sponsoring organizations. The research also suggested that the use of front groups in support of commercial activities is a more serious concern than its use in public policy because the names of front groups in commercial affairs are more likely meant to deceive as opposed to hiding true intentions, and that commercial front groups are less regularly questioned than political front groups by the very nature of their role in public discourse.

Others have noted through case studies and other methodologies that front groups damage the credibility of organizations that create false fronts in cases in which the hidden special interests are exposed by media, competition, non-governmental organizations, or government representatives. For example, in one of the few published studies concerning front groups, Bodensteiner (1997) found that Citizens for Riverboat Gambling, a front group created by a public relations firm to gain approval for riverboat gambling in Iowa, was unable to accomplish its guarded objective when it was disclosed that the group, funded primarily by a gaming company, was made up primarily of members of the public relations firm.

The use of deceptive public relations practices—particularly those perceived to interfere with the efficient functioning of government—also invites greater scrutiny of public relations conduct by legislators and the courts. As Fitzpatrick and Palenchar (2006) concluded in their review of U.S. Supreme Court decisions involving third-party practices, if front group practices continue unabated, it might be only a matter of time until the Court expands its view of constitutionally permissible *legal* restrictions on public relations communication. If that happens, the field of public relations will have only itself to blame.

A comprehensive list of front groups or even an exhaustive typology is beyond the scope of this chapter, but for example, nine front groups or Astroturf organizations were recently outed by Common Cause (2006), a non-profit civic watchdog association in their report *Wolves in Sheep's Clothing: Telecom Industry Front Groups and Astroturf.* These included Consumers for Cable Choice, FreedomWorks, Keep it Local NJ, Progress and Freedom Foundation, American Legislative Exchange Council, New Millennium Research Council, Frontiers of Freedom, Internet Innovation Alliance, and MyWireless.org. Former Common Cause President Chellie Pingree and Jeff Chester, founder and executive director for the Center for Digital Democracy, argued for full disclosure from these and other front and Astroturf groups within the telecommunications industry, suggesting they are a danger for democracy by deliberately misleading citizens and lawmakers (Moss, 2006).

Research on the modern history of front groups suggests that the use of deceptive third-party techniques that eventually translated into front groups was initiated with public relations pioneer Edward Bernays (Cutlip, 1994). Bernays provided public relations and talent agent services for an actor client who was unable to secure funding for a play called *Damaged Goods.* The play, described by Bernays as a "propaganda play that fought for sex education," was unable to attract funding "because of its strong content for the period" (p. 162). Bernays described his created false front organization as a "prestigious sponsoring committee" to legitimize the play through the issue of sex education, and ultimately was able to acquire funding through this representation.

Bernays arguably might have been the first public relations practitioner to use the front group or third-party technique (Cutlip, 1994). Bernays, in a 1959 interview, said "We used it (the idea of a prestigious sponsoring committee) many times since then because I think it is still the most useful method in a multiple society like ours to indicate the support of an idea of the many varied elements that make up our society. . . . I might add, however, that when this was done, we did it in an open or overt way" (p. 163). While the level of transparency is open to debate, according to Cutlip, Bernays probably stressed the overt character of the technique because by 1959 the use of third-party practices "had come under heavy fire from the critics of public relations" (p. 163).

Another famous creation of front groups in the 1920s and 1930s by Bernays, along with the Onondaga Silk Company and the America Tobacco Company, was the Color Fashion Bureau to promote the purchase of Lucky Strike cigarettes (see Coombs, 2005). The flagship brand of American Tobacco was Lucky Strike, but one problem was the product's green packaging—survey research determined that women did not buy the product because the green packaging clashed with their clothes. This front group was created to bring the color of green to consumers' homes so their green clothing (the purchase of green clothing was promoted by another American Tobacco Company campaign developed by Bernays) and most importantly the green-colored packaging of Lucky Strike cigarettes didn't clash. According to Coombs (2005), the Color Fashion Bureau conducted a media relations campaign that presented the coming green trend in home furnishings and overall home decor. In a period of a few months, the bureau received requests for information from 77 newspapers, 95 magazines, 83 furniture and home decoration manufacturers, 301 department stores, 175 radio stations, and 64 interior designers. While the front group within an overall public relations campaign addressed the primary reason as to why women were not purchasing Lucky Strikes, according to Coombs there is no evidence that the promotion of green actually led to women buying more Lucky Strikes, though the popularity of the brand skyrocketed.

Public opinion, communication, and persuasion research during World War I and II helped to advance public relations practices, as well as many other communication practices. For example, the success of the Creel Committee on Public Information, which successfully helped to mobilize U.S. public support for World War I and to promote the United States' interests in Europe, led numerous public relations practitioners to add the third-party technique to their public relations portfolio of services. Carl Byoir, one of those practitioners, played an important role in the work of the Creel Committee, and it is Byoir who is often credited with the development of the actual front group technique.

The Carl Byoir & Associates' firm created a front group called the Pennsylvania State Association of Township Supervisors that helped lead to the veto of some trucking legislation, resulting in lawsuits based primarily on the railroads' use of front groups (Cutlip, 1994). In this landmark case, known as the "Noerr Decision" (Eastern Railroad Presidents Conference et al. v. Noerr Motor Freight, Inc. et al., 1961), the courts for the first time addressed the use of public relations techniques directly, considering whether the railroads' use of the third-party technique in a publicity campaign to oppose legislation constituted a violation of the Sherman Anti-Trust Act, which prohibits trade restraints and monopolizations (Fitzpatrick & Palenchar, 2006).

The trial and appellate courts ruled for the plaintiffs, finding that the industry's campaign was "malicious in that its only purpose was to destroy the truckers as competitors, and fraudulent in that it was predicated upon the deceiving of those authorities through the use of the third-party technique" (Eastern Railroad Presidents Conference v. Noerr Motor Freight, 1961, p. 133). But, in reversing the decision, the U.S. Supreme Court found that the right of the people to petition the government does not depend on their intent in doing so. With regard to the use of front groups, the Court wrote:

> [T]he third-party technique, which was aptly characterized by the District Court as involving "deception of the public, manufacture of bogus sources of reference, [and] distortion of public sources of information," depends upon giving propaganda actually circulated by a party in interest the appearance of being spontaneous declarations of independent groups. We can certainly agree with the courts below that this technique, though in widespread use among practitioners of the art of public relations, is one which falls short of the ethical standards generally approved in this country.
>
> (p. 141; see Fitzpatrick & Palenchar, 2006)

The practice was not only criticized as unethical by the U.S. Supreme Court but became the focus of a number of lawsuits. Byoir was fined $5000 in a different court for his use of false fronts with a different client (Olasky, 1987). Ultimately however, according to Cutlip (1994), Byoir learned that the deceptive tactic that had worked so well in time of war was less acceptable on the domestic political front. Gower and Lamme (2003), in their insightful review of Noerr, argued that the public relations industry, and related industry trade publications, unfortunately did not confront the issue of front groups and its ramifications to the field at this ideal time nor debate the merits of the controversial practice in its early stage. "Although the lawsuit can be considered a clever public relations strategy in its own right, it essentially put public relations tactics on trial. Unfortunately, the trial shone a light on the seedier side of public relations" (p. 18).

Front groups continued as a public relations practice following Noerr though it was not widely reported until the 1990s when it made a comeback (Pires, 1994). In a 1992 speech to the Public Relations Society of America's (PRSA) Chicago chapter, industry leader Daniel Edelman (1992) observed that the practice of front groups that was routine in the public relations field in the 1950s and 1960s had become discredited for a while. "Unfortunately," he said, "it has come back with a vengeance" (p. 32).

As an example, in the 1990s, international public relations firm Hill & Knowlton created a prominent and highly controversial front group called Citizens for a Free Kuwait. The group was not funded by concerned citizens as the name implied, but by the exiled Kuwait monarchy to secure American support during the first Gulf War. The effort was widely viewed as a corruption of the public information system and remains one of the most widely cited examples of front groups used by public relations practitioners (e.g., Cutlip, 1991; Fitzpatrick & Palenchar, 2006).

Other contemporary uses of front groups represent a variety of industries ranging from petrochemical to tobacco to real estate to pharmaceuticals. For example, Mintz (2000) reported that some of the nation's largest utility companies "secretly funneled millions of dollars" (p. A10) through two front groups called Citizens for State Power and Electric Utility Shareholders Alliance, specifically formed to stop Congress from deregulating their industry. According to their own internal documents, the efforts of the groups were described as "discreet, guarded and highly confidential" (p. A10).

Another issue that is inundated with front groups is tobacco regulations. According to Americans for Nonsmokers' Rights (n.d.), "it has been a common practice of Big Tobacco to use third parties or to create front groups 'to be out in front fighting' smokefree policies, while the industry remains behind the scenes, protecting its public image" (p. 1) because the industry has no credibility with the public. Castleman (1996) conducted an investigation of the role and strategies of American tobacco companies in the public policy debates regarding tobacco regulation. Among other strategies uncovered through industry documents is the creation and funding of phony grassroots campaigns. "Since there are no natural grassroots movements to protect tobacco profits, the companies have to invent them" (p. 34). According to Castleman, these included the creation of front groups to make pro-tobacco legislation handed down by state and national politicians appear to be the public's will. "The irony is that while the tobacco industry spouts 'local control' rhetoric, it is cynically using front groups and statewide pre-emption laws to snuff out genuine grassroots initiatives to control smoking" (p. 55). Cutlip (1994) identified as a front group the Tobacco Industry Research Committee (TIRC), which was organized by the tobacco industry in 1954 and later renamed in 1964 as the Council for Tobacco Research—United States. However, with the inclusion of the term "tobacco industry" in the organization's title, by the standards of Fitzpatrick and Palenchar's (2006) definition earlier cited, among others, it fails to meet the negative standards of a front group. While the TIRC's motives, strategies, and tactics can be questioned, the name demonstrates a clear link to the tobacco industry.

Although corporations are the most frequent targets of criticism, religious and other non-profit organizations also use front groups. According to Young (1993), for example, the Church of Scientology International has created multiple front groups for a variety of purposes, such as creating health and education organizations whose undisclosed objective is to educate people about scientology as well as deceptive third-party techniques to influence public policy. Another example is Planned Parenthood, which was identified by the *New York Times* as engaging in Astroturf practices by disseminating form letters to editors at publications throughout the country "that look like authentic grassroots responses from readers but are not" (Lee, 2003, p. C10).

The exponential rise of issue or product front groups in the United States is a relatively recent occurrence in the past few decades that is a direct result of the rising importance of the consumer, citizen, and environmental movement. With the increase in public interest groups and their increasing power, according to Megalli and Friedman (1992), new mechanisms were needed to deliver the corporate message. "Every day, groups with deceptive names, groups that represent major U.S. corporate powers, seek to dupe journalists and citizens into believing that the reports they produce and the positions they advocate are something other than the usual corporate propaganda" (p. 21). The presence of front groups is ubiquitous.

Public Relations Industry Ethical Guidelines

In the absence of source disclosure laws requiring special interests to reveal their participation in public policy efforts at the time of communication (see Fitzpatrick & Palenchar, 2006), the policing of front groups falls to the public relations industry and its practitioners. Public Relations Society of America (PRSA), the field's leading U.S. professional association, requires its approximately 28,000 members to conform to a code of ethics based on open and honest communication that promotes the "free flow of information" (2000). As early as 1959, the PRSA Code of Ethics included a section devoted to third-party techniques, and though the earlier codes didn't use the term "front groups," the standards urged members not to create false fronts via third-party techniques.

The current PRSA code directly addresses the use of front groups under a provision that outlines what members shall do: "reveal the sponsors for causes and interests represented" and "avoid deceptive practices" (2000). Examples in the PRSA code of *improper* conduct also address the use of front groups and grassroots lobbying practices: "Front groups: A member implements 'grass roots' campaigns or letter-writing campaigns to legislators on behalf of undisclosed interest groups," and "A member deceives the public by employing people to pose as volunteers to speak at public hearings and participate in 'grass roots' campaigns." According to the code, such behavior does not contribute to open communication that "fosters informed decision making in a democratic society" (2000).

In August 2004, in preparation for national elections in the United States, PRSA issued Professional Standards Advisory PS-3 entitled *Front Groups*. In the advisory, PRSA acknowledged that as the political process intensifies a variety of front group organizations will surface on behalf of issues and candidates blindly sponsored by industries, organizations, and individuals. PRSA's recommended practice is that "members should recognize that assisting front groups that represent undisclosed sponsorships and/or deceptive or misleading descriptions of goals, causes, tactics, sponsors or participants constitutes improper conduct under the PRSA Member Code of Ethics and should be avoided" (p. 2).

In April 2007, a set of common principles for a code of conduct for European public relations practitioners was developed by the European Public Affairs Consultancies' Association (EPACA), International Public Relations Association (IPRA), and the Society of European Affairs Professionals (SEAP). The code's ten core principles addressed related issues such as being transparent about interests represented, being truthful, and ultimately the fundamental concept of true dialogue is the acknowledgment of the rights of all parties involved to state their case and express their views (IPRA, 2007). SEAP's (n.d.) own code of conduct, under Article 2—Transparency and Openness, advocates that when "making representations to the EU institutions they shall be open and transparent in declaring their name, organization or company, and the interest they represent," that they will "neither intentionally misrepresent their status nor the nature of their inquiries to the EU institutions nor create any false impression in relation thereto," and that they will "take all reasonable steps to ensure the truth and accuracy of all statements made or information provided by them to the EU institutions" (p. 1). Similarly, the Global Alliance of Public Relations and Communications Management Association's (2002) review of national codes of ethics for public relations associations around the world demonstrated a consistent acknowledgment to the fundamental ethical requirement of transparent communication, including by those whom public relations practitioners represent.

Concerns about front groups also are addressed by other national and international associations. Developed in 1961, the International Public Relations Association's code of ethics talks of such deceptive practices: "A member shall at all times seek to give a faithful representation of the organization which he/she serves. A member shall not create any organization to serve some announced cause but actually to serve an undisclosed special or private interest of a member or his/her client or employer, nor shall he/she make use of it or any such existing organization" (p. 1).

The Arthur W. Page Society (n.d.), a professional association for senior public relations and corporate communications executives who seek to enrich and strengthen the profession, advocates the Page Principles, seven guiding principles to guide public relations practitioners' actions and behaviors. While all are worthy topics of discussion, three principles stand out directly in relation to front groups: (1) *Tell the truth*—ensure that the public know what is happening and provide an accurate picture of among other things the company's practices; (2) *Manage for tomorrow*—anticipate public reaction and eliminate practices that create difficulties; and (3) *Realize a company's true character is expressed by its people*—responsibility of corporate communications to support each employee's capability and desire to be honest, knowledgeable ambassadors to customers, friends, shareowners, and public officials. All three principles suggest actions and behaviors that contradict the use of front groups in public relations.

The Public Relations Coalition (2003), a partnership of 19 major U.S.-based organizations representing corporate public relations, investor relations, public affairs, and related communications disciplines, challenged corporate America to do three things: adopt ethical principles, pursue transparency and disclosure in everything that they do, and make trust a fundamental precept of corporate governance. Within its report *Restoring Trust in Business: Models for Action*, the Coalition argues for creating an open company based on numerous steps including, "Be willing to disclose all of your business, social and political activities, as long as doing so does not raise legal issue or jeopardize your competitive position in the marketplace" (p. 8).

Although these codes clearly prohibit front group practices, adherence to the codes is strictly voluntary. Public relations professional associations, which operate within a self-regulated industry, have no real authority to compel the ethical behavior of their practitioners. Additionally, the PRSA code has been broadly interpreted by some to mean that practitioners must reveal the identity of organizations served only if asked (Fitzpatrick & Palenchar, 2006).

Overall, neither code of ethics, industry standards and guidelines, nor the risks of being revealed as a front group sponsor seems to have had any significant effect on the continuing use of such practices. One reason may be that the results of the detailed investigative reporting sometimes required to link political messages to their financial sponsors may be reported too late to allow citizens and/or lawmakers to consider the source before taking action (Goldberg & Kozlowski, 2002). Another may be that front group backers perceive the rewards of winning as outweighing any potential risks.

Rhetorical Perspective on Front Group Practices

Public relations is a way for people and organizations to be involved in the marketplace of ideas, the free exchange of ideas. Part of the free exchange of ideas includes knowledge of source, funding, and intent of discourse within the marketplace of ideas. A foundational component for this discourse through advocacy is Burke's (1969a) iconic wrangle in the marketplace or the human barnyard. For rhetoric, advocacy is a fundamental concept within humanity, and that wrangle is the point, the counterpoint of advocacy, negotiation, discourse, conversation, or more broadly communication.

Advocacy from this perspective is an ethical, strategic management and communication approach to addressing public relations problems. According to Heath (2007), advocacy is based on engaged dialogue where participants discover and learn the merits of others' positions, and how the interplay and refinement of these ideas transpire in public communication. "This paradigm assumes that ideas grow in quality through dialogue as a win-win outcome" (p. 43). According to Heath (2007) and Fitzpatrick (2006), the challenge for public relations practitioners is the utilization of advocacy and related skills so that it serves society as opposed to only narrow interests who look to position their perspective central and superior to others for their own advantage.

Within this call is the larger purpose of rhetoric, as opposed to distortion or win at any cost, and at the core of any discussion of rhetoric within public relations lies the fundamental call by Quintilian (1951) to be a good person who can therefore speak well. According to Heath (2006), organizations have at times replaced individuals as key figures in society and the public relations field must address what it means to be a good organization communicating well.

Rhetoric is a process for the free exchange of ideas and one of the fundamental communication theoretical orientations that guides public relations research and practice. Rhetoric is fundamentally about persuasive speech, a product of intensive systematic reflection (study of what works and why) for identifying best arguments for (and against) one's position. According to Burke (1966), rhetoric is the use of language as a symbolic means of creating cooperation in beings that by nature respond to symbols. When we seek agreement there is a bilateral emphasis on open communication. There are a great many rhetorical situations in which communicators are likely to conceal some aspects of their views while emphasizing others (advocacy). Cultural norms regulate what are permissible omissions. But fundamental to advocacy is that we do not expect them (in this instance the sponsoring organization of a front group) to deliberately misrepresent the fact that they are partisan advocates. The speaker (sponsor of the front group) within discourse and drama should be known to the audience.

Rhetoric is instrumental in that one person engages another in an exchange of symbols to accomplish some goal. It is an attempt to coordinate social action, but not manipulate social action (Hauser, 1986). Aristotle (1932) defined rhetoric as the art of discovering the available means of persuasion in any given circumstance—in general a method to think about communication.

Ethics plays a fundamental component within rhetoric, though not as an attached element or theory but as an inseparable, intertwined construction. Philosophers and scholars have defined ethics as the study of what is right or wrong, fair or unfair, just or unjust. Others have argued that ethics is in essence morality. While a thorough review of ethical orientations is not the scope of this chapter, such models are based on historical philosophical perspectives such as Aristotle's golden mean.

Aristotle's golden mean advocates that a person of moral maturity would naturally seek the action that would further moral character. Moral maturity is defined as one who is of good character, which comes about by developing the habits of good character, thus gaining sound moral reasoning. This moral mean lies somewhere between excess and deficiency, though does not advocate starting with extremes and identifying the mean—this would lead to mediocrity rather than excellence. The moral mean is different for each person, and is acquired through good character, moral maturity, and the ability to perceive a situation accurately as it pertains to the individual (Apostle, 1984). Within public relations, this approach can be taken to form the basis of a good organization communicating well based on developing the habits of good character and behavior (Palenchar & Heath, 2006). This rhetorical heritage of Western civilization offers rationale for the ethical practice of public relations (Heath, 2000, p. 69):

> It explains how public relations participates in the creation and implementation of value perspectives that shape society. It supports the practice of public relations in the marketplace and public policy arena, where values are brought to bear on economic and sociopolitical matters. The rhetorical heritage of public relations features the role of public discourse through which ideas are contested, issues are examined, and decisions are made collaboratively. In this way, concurrence is achieved to guide personal and societal decisions.

Within the field of public relations, scholars and practitioners advocate various perspectives on incorporating ethics into the study, pedagogy, and practice of public relations. For example, Fitzpatrick and Gauthier (2001) modeled their own professional responsibility theory of public relations ethics that is based on practitioners' dual obligations to serve client organizations and the public interest. Bivins (1980) and Pearson (1989) advocated for an ethical paradigm for public relations based on moral philosophy.

Palenchar and Heath (2006) suggested that at the core of public relations, rhetoric, and ethics is the individual and community right to know, to involve stakeholders in risk assessment and decision-making processing. They identified public partnership, shared control, uncertainty environment, community decision making, trust and collaboration, individual values, community relativism, and community narratives as at the heart of ethical and responsible public relations. Responsible advocacy occurs when public relations practitioners make a case that reflects the arguments and claims of concerned citizens and employees. This is an internal voice for external interests. This management positioning of public relations does not demand that it is contentious toward management preferences but gives fair and honest vetting to concerns voiced by employees, customers, and neighbors.

Organizational standards should be based on genuine attitudes and actions of the organization, and resulting behaviors that are perceived and recognized by stakeholders and the market as credible, ethical, and beneficial, rather than an image that is inconsistent with organizational operations (Palenchar & Heath, 2006). "The character of this market recognition is therefore largely one of social agreement, i.e., one constructed by shared communication." (Spickett-Jones, Kitchen, & Reast, 2003, p. 69). This perspective is consistent with Pearson's (1989) contribution to public relations ethics that maintaining a communication relationship with the public is essential and that the quality of those relationships is improved through dialogue.

Front groups fail the tests of rhetorical tradition and the ethical organization communicating well on several levels. First, public relations practitioners are in a unique position within the organizations they represent, and part of their function is to appreciate which behaviors, issues, and policies are supported by their stakeholders and other members of the public and which are not, and maybe more importantly the reasons why. What organizational behaviors elicit community support, donations, repeat customers, voters, and content employees should be continually researched, and once these standards are observed, strategic efforts to reach them are a requirement of the good organization communicating and behaving well. As Bowen and Heath (2005) discussed, the goal is to help make the organization deserving of stakeholders' support by thinking and adjusting behaviors from the inside out and from the outside in to know and aspire to standards of moral rectitude.

A second ethical and rhetorical tradition is the concept of listening, which is a fundamental function of public relations: to listen to what other members of society have to say and what they are engaging and expending their social, economic, political, and cultural capital upon. Listening requires responsibility and responsiveness, as well as the transparent dialogue of sharing and advocating an organizational perspective that may be similar or different from multiple stakeholders' perspectives. According to Heath and Coombs (2006), "an understanding of rhetoric helps practitioners recognize and analyze the strategic communication choices they have in light of the messages set forth by the organization's critics" (p. 21).

A third area of failure for front groups in the rhetorical tradition is the role of two-way communications, and one public relations model that receives considerable attention is the two-way symmetrical model, identified as one of the four models of public relations practice by J. Grunig (1984) and J. Grunig and Hunt (1984), which more recently has been described since 1992 (J. Grunig & L. Grunig) as the excellence model for public relations practice. Even though the two-way symmetrical model has undergone various alterations since its debut as a noted historical development in the field of public relations, what has held true is what J. Grunig and White (1992) noted, that "public relations should be based on a worldview that incorporates ethics into the process of public relations," (p. 57) and what J. Grunig and Hunt (1984) summarized—that public relations and social responsibility are interconnected. "Public relations managers should be 'inside the door' of management in all kinds of organizations where they can provide internal social reports on the organization's public performance" (p. 59).

Fourth, and maybe most important in terms of this chapter, is the idea of building community through shared meaning. Rhetoric is fundamentally the act of shared, cocreated meaning, constructed through two-way communication in an effort to engage public discourse, create understanding, refine positions, and alter opinions through point and counterpoint discourse, advocacy, and persuasion. Bryant's (1953) definition of rhetoric as "the function of adjusting ideas to people and people to ideas" (p. 413) is fundamental to the role that public relations practitioners perform for the organizations they represent as part of a larger society.

Fifth is the concept of shared similarities called identification, a key element of Burke's (1969b) theory of rhetoric. People typically want to identify with others individually or in groups, to feel a part of something beyond themselves yet part of themselves. As a powerful motivator of change, public relations practitioners are called upon to consider identification in their research about and practice with stakeholders. Quesinberry's (2005) work focused on identification as a continuing challenge for public relations practitioners, suggesting that companies that fail to maintain identification with audiences are in danger of failing.

Leichty (2003) applied a cultural theory of rhetoric to discourse about public relations and within his discussion of public relations' egalitarian critics is noted a particular criticism for front groups and Astroturf social movements that "deprive social movements of their natural advantage in public debates: public skepticism about the intentions of corporate interests" (p. 287). Callison (2004), in his work on perceptions of public relations practitioners, noted that if sources, including public relations practitioners, are viewed as lacking credibility, then common sense suggests public relations practitioners filter organizational information through a source not directly attached to the organization. He goes on to suggest that unaffiliated sources will not take up arms for an organization of which they have no connection, and thus wonders "should an organization make efforts to communicate through perceived outside sources, and more importantly, is it ethical to do so" (p. 387). Callison suggested that "[T]he fact that collections of people assembled by organizations to represent them have become so pervasive signals now it would seem the public relations industry answers these questions" (p. 387). Callison hit on an important point that organizations may fare best by enlisting outside experts who support their issue or cause or product or service simply because the organization is in the right.

The Arthur W. Page Society's 2007 report entitled *The Authentic Enterprise,* based on a survey of chief executive officers, examined the rapidly changing context for global businesses and society. The CEOs surveyed for this report "underscored these converging forces—technology, global integration, multiplying stakeholders and the resulting need for transparency—as the most important communications challenges facing their companies" (p. 14). The report's acknowledgement for *authentic* business practices underscores a fundamental element of rhetoric.

Rhetoric helps to foster truth and solve problems within the limitations of human discourse and cocreated meaning. The role of front groups only further exemplifies the limitations of organizations to manage communication effectively within the constructs of good organizations communicating well in the rhetorical tradition. What is the balance between the public's right to know and the prevailing interests of the corporation? How does one assess the ethical dimensions of front groups? Many of the Greek philosophers, especially Plato and Aristotle, chose not to ask what is the right thing to do. Instead, they focused on what traits of character makes one a good person (Apostle, 1984). For the purpose of this chapter, a better question may be what traits of character make an organization a good member of the community, and what traits of strategic public relations make one a good organization communicating well.

Meeting the Challenge

Let's return to the opening paragraph of this chapter where you were asked to imagine yourself as a public relations practitioner and asked the importance of knowing who is speaking. How much does it matter who says what? Who is being paid what to speak on its behalf? And if they mention an organization that takes a position on some matter, will you really know the character of the organization? At the core of these questions and the discussion within this chapter is transparency of source and source funding (and membership within grassroots advocacy campaigns). Do you think that hiding the source of information is the best way to arrive at solutions for both your client and society? These types of questions are fundamental to the free exchange of ideas, the marketplace of ideas, and to the ethical practice of public relations.

Front groups as a public relations strategy and tactic contradict both contemporary standards of ethical public relations practice and the rhetorical tradition of advocacy. Such practices, which also fail to meet the expectations of a good organization communicating well, should be eliminated as an ethically acceptable option within third-party and coalition-based strategies. Front groups also fail to achieve dialogue from a rhetorical perspective because it fails in the achievement of common meaning. Common meaning is not possible without knowing who you are speaking with, who or what are they advocating for and to what purpose, and the financial support of such efforts.

As Heath (2007) noted, public relations practitioners are inherently public communicators, different yet no different than Aristotle or Isocrates from ancient Greece and Rome. Public communicators' dialectic, as part of the rhetorical heritage, challenges communicators to inspect the norm and not grant it as an assumption. Like Plato attacking the poets for teaching the Greek youths in ways that did not encourage critical examination of premises, researchers and practitioners in the field of public relations who fail to question the use of deceptive tactics such as front groups should be similarly challenged. Front groups should not be allowed unless those who create such organizations are able to withstand critical examination of their use.

The implications of engaging in unethical front group practices are significant. As Bodensteiner (1997) observed, "Since it is the reputation of the public relations person/firm which is damaged if a coalition goes astray, then the public relations practitioner must stand firm as the ethical guard on coalition conduct" (p. 43). Clearly, it is in the interest of the public relations profession to safeguard the credibility of its practices and to preserve the trust of its publics.

References

Americans for Nonsmokers' Rights (n.d.). Front groups & allies. Retrieved July 24, 2007, from http://www.no-smoke.org/getthefacts.php?dp=d21|d23

Apostle, H. G. (1984). *Aristotle's Nichomachean ethics.* Grinnell, IA: Peripatetic Press.

Aristotle. (1932). *Rhetoric.* (L. Cooper, Trans.). Englewood Cliffs, NJ: Prentice-Hall.

Arthur W. Page Society. (2007). *The authentic enterprise.* New York: Author.

Arthur W. Page Society. (n.d.). Page principles. Retrieved August 21, 2007, from http://www.awpagesociety.com/site/about/page_principles

Beder, S. (1998). Public relations' role in manufacturing artificial grass roots coalitions. *Public Relations Quarterly, 43*(2), 20–23.

Bivins, T. H. (1980). Ethical implications of the relationship of purpose to role and function in public relations. *Journal of Business Ethics, 8,* 65–73.

Bodensteiner, C. A. (1997). Special interest group coalitions: Ethical standards for broad-based support efforts. *Public Relations Review, 23,* 31–47.

Bowen, S. A., & Heath, R. L. (2005). Issue management, systems, and rhetoric. Exploring the distinction between ethical and legal guidelines at Enron. *Journal of Public Affairs, 5,* 1–15.

Bryant, D. C. (1953). Rhetoric: Its function and its scope. *Quarterly Journals of Speech, 39,* 401–424.

Burke, K. (1966). *Language as symbolic action.* Berkeley: University of California Press.

Burke, K. (1969a). *A grammar of motives.* Berkeley: University of California Press.

Burke, K. (1969b). *A rhetoric of motives.* Berkeley: University of California Press.

Callison, C. (2004). The good, the bad, and the ugly: Perceptions of public relations practitioners. *Journal of Public Relations Research, 16*(4), 371–389.

Castleman, M. (1996, May/June). Tobacco strikes back. *Mother Jones,* pp. 32–69.

Center for Media and Democracy. (2007). Front groups: From Source Watch. Retrieved January 26, 2008, from http://www.sourcewatch.org/index.php?title=Front_groups

Common Cause. (2006, March). *Wolves in sheep's clothing: Telecom industry front group and Astroturf.* Washington, DC: Author.

Consumer Reports. (1994, May). *Public-interest pretenders,* pp. 316–317.

Coombs, W. T. (2005). Lucky Strike Green Campaign. In R. L. Heath (Ed.), *Encyclopedia of public relations* (pp. 495–498). Thousand Oaks, CA: Sage.

Cutlip, S. M. (1991, April 10). *The historic legacy of public relations*. 5th Annual Harold Burson Distinguished Lecture, Raymond Simon Institute for Public Relations, Utica College of Syracuse University.

Cutlip, S. M. (1994). *The unseen power: Public relations: A history*. Hillsdale, NJ: Erlbaum.

Eastern Railroad Presidents Conference et al. v. Noerr Motor Freight, Inc. et al., 365 U.S. 127 (1961).

Edelman, D. J. (1992). Ethical behavior is key to field's future. *Public Relations Journal, 48*(11), 32.

Fitzpatrick, K. (2006). Baselines for ethical advocacy in the "marketplace of ideas." In K. Fitzpatrick & C. Bronstein (Eds.), *Ethics in public relations: Responsible advocacy* (pp. 1–17). Thousand Oaks, CA: Sage.

Fitzpatrick, K., & Gauthier, C. (2001). Toward a professional responsibility theory of public relations ethics. *Journal of Mass Media Ethics, 16*(2/3), 193–212.

Fitzpatrick, K. R., & Palenchar, M. J. (2006). Disclosing special interests: Constitutional restrictions on front groups. *Journal of Public Relations Research, 18*(3), 203–224.

Fullwood, C. (1996). Alar report right from the start, but you'd never know it. *Public Relations Quarterly, 41*(2), 9–12.

Global Alliance of Public Relations and Communications Management Associations. (2002, February). Benchmarking of codes of ethics in public relations—Phase 2. Retrieved September 13, 2007, from http://www.globalpr.org/knowledge/ethics/ethics-Benchmarking.pdf

Goldberg, D, & Kozlowski, M. (2002). Constitutional issues in disclosure of interest group activities. *Indiana Law Review, 35*, 755–766.

Gower, K. K., & Lamme, M. O. (2003). Public relations on trial: "The railroad truckers brawl." *Journalism History, 29*(1), 12–20.

Grunig, J. E. (1984). Organizations, environments, and models of public relations. *Public Relations Research & Education, 1*, 6–29.

Grunig, J. E., & Grunig, L. A. (1992). Models of public relations and communication. In J. E. Grunig (Ed.), *Excellence in public relations and communication management* (pp. 285–326). Hillsdale, NJ: Erlbaum.

Grunig, J. E., & Hunt, T. (1984). *Managing public relations*. Fort Worth, TX: Holt, Rinehart and Winston.

Grunig, J. E., & White, J. (1992). The effect of worldviews on public relations theory and practice. In J. Grunig (Ed.), *Excellence in public relations and communications management* (pp. 31–64). Hillsdale, NJ: Erlbaum

Hauser, G. A. (1986). *Introduction to rhetorical theory*. Prospect Heights, IL: Waveland Press.

Heath, R. L. (2000). A rhetorical perspective on the values of public relations research: Crossroads and pathways toward concurrence. *Journal of Public Relations Research, 12*(1), 69–91.

Heath, R. L. (Ed.). (2005). *Encyclopedia of public relations*. Thousand Oaks, CA: Sage.

Heath, R. L. (2006). Onward into more fog: Thoughts on public relations' research directions. *Journal of Public Relations Research, 18*(2), 93–114.

Heath, R. L. (2007). Management through advocacy: Reflection rather than domination. In E. L. Toth (Ed.), *The future of excellence in public relations and communication management: Challenges for the next generation* (pp. 41–65). Mahwah, NJ: Erlbaum.

Heath, R. L., & Coombs, W. T. (2006). *Today's public relations: An introduction.* Thousand Oaks, CA: Sage.

International Public Relations Association. (1961, May). Code of conduct. Retrieved January 19, 2007, from http://www.ipra.org/detail.asp?articleid=210

International Public Relations Association. (2007, April 27). EU lobbyists agree joint principles for codes of ethical conduct. Retrieved November 2, 2007, from http://www.ipra.org/detail.asp?articleid=143

Lee, J. (2003, January 27). Editors and lobbyists wage high-tech war over letters. *New York Times,* C10.

Leichty, G. (2003). The cultural tribes of public relations. *Journal of Public Relations Research, 15*(4), 277–304.

Megalli, M., & Friedman, A. (1992, March). Fronting for business [Electronic Version]. *Multinational Monitor,* 21–27.

Mintz, J. (2000, May 11). Utilities secretly lobbied Congress: Electric firm gave millions to left and right to halt deregulation. *Washington Post,* A10.

Moss, L. (2006, April 3). Civic gadfly steps on "Astroturf" groups. *Multinational News,* 30.

Olasky, M. (1987). *Corporate public relations: A new historical perspective.* Hillsdale, NJ: Erlbaum.

Palenchar, M. J., & Heath, R. L. (2006). Responsible advocacy through strategic risk communication. In K. Fitzpatrick & C. Bronstein (Eds.), *Ethics in public relations: Responsible advocacy* (pp. 131–153). Thousand Oaks, CA: Sage.

Pearson, R. (1989). Beyond ethical relativism in public relations: Co-orientation, rules, and the idea of communication symmetry. In J. E. Grunig & L. A. Grunig (Eds.), *Public relations research annual* (Vol. 1, pp. 67–86). Hillsdale, NJ: Erlbaum.

Pfau, M., Haigh, M. M., Sims, J., & Wigley, S. (2007). The influence of corporate front-group stealth campaigns. *Communication Research, 34*(1), 73–99.

Pires, M. A. (1994, June). Lobbying: The ethical challenge. *Impact,* 1–3.

Public Relations Coalition. (2003, Sept. 17). *Restoring trust in business: Models for action.* New York: Arthur W. Page Society.

Public Relations Society of America. (2000). *PRSA 2000 member code of ethics.* New York: Author.

Public Relations Society of America. (2004, August). Professional standards advisory PS-3. Retrieved September 28, 2007, from http://www.prsa.org/aboutUs/ethics/psaPS3.html

Quesinberry, A. A. (2005). Identification. In R. L. Heath (Ed.), *Encyclopedia of public relations* (pp. 403–405). Thousand Oaks, CA: Sage.

Quintilian, M. F. (1951). *The institution oratio of Marcus Fabius Quintilianus* (C. E. Little, Trans.). Nashville, TN: George Peabody College for Teachers.

Society of European Affairs Professionals. (n.d.). Code of conduct. Retrieved January 26, 2008, from http://www.seap.eu.org/linkdocs/code_conduct.pdf

Spickett-Jones, J. G., Kitchen, P. J., & Reast, J. D. (2003). Social facts and ethical hardware: Ethics in the value proposition. *Journal of Communication Management, 8*(1), 68–82.

Tucker, K., & McNerney, S. L. (1992). Building coalitions to initiate change. *Public Relations Journal, 48*(1), 28–30.

West, H. R. (2004). *An introduction to Mill's utilitarian ethics.* Cambridge: Cambridge University Press.

Young, R. V. (1993, November/December). Scientology from the inside out. *Quill,* pp. 38–41.

15

INTER-ORGANIZATIONAL CRISIS COMMUNICATION

Exploring Source and Stakeholder Communication in the Roman Catholic Clergy Sex Abuse Case

Suzanne Boys
University of Cincinnati

The Case

In the winter of 2002, the *Boston Globe* published an unprecedented exposé on clergy sexual abuse in the Roman Catholic Church. Although this was not the first time U.S. Catholic priests were accused of sexual exploitation, this was the first time that substantive allegations of systemic complicity were levied publicly against the Roman Catholic hierarchy in the United States. During the weeks and months following the initial exposé, there was a swell of media attention, a growing public outcry, increasing litigation over alleged abuse and cover-ups, and the emergence of issue-driven grassroots organizations. Escalating public involvement with the issue of clergy sexual abuse challenged the U.S. Catholic bishops' attempts to internalize and thus retain exclusive control of the situation.

As the U.S. Roman Catholic hierarchy lost exclusive jurisdiction over the situation, it became clear that sexual exploitation by priests could no longer be delimited as a few isolated incidents in the Boston Archdiocese. By the end of 2002, approximately 500 individuals had come forward alleging abuse and approximately 1200 priests had been accused; further, at least six U.S. prelates had resigned due to abuse-related issues by 2003 (*Boston Globe*, n.d., "Scandal and Coverup"). By November 2004, the Archdioceses of Portland, Tucson, and Spokane had filed for bankruptcy in response to multimillion dollar claims levied against each of them. By June 2005, the Boston Archdiocese had paid $150.8 million to settle sex abuse claims (Simpson, 2006). Rather than receding in response to the hierarchy's management, the situation had escalated into a large-scale organizational crisis.

Not only was the hierarchy repeatedly confronted with allegations of systemic complicity with abuse, but its attempts to manage the crisis were contested vigorously by a variety of stakeholders. The early *Globe* articles paved the way for an increasingly audible public discourse on the phenomena of clergy sexual abuse. Key stakeholders weighing in on the issue include grassroots groups focused on supporting those victimized by clergy (advocacy groups) and on changing the Church (dissent groups), individuals alleging sexual exploitation (victims/survivors) and their families, civil and criminal courts, members of the Roman Catholic hierarchy and the laity, and a wide variety of media. While some stakeholders were either internal or external to the Church, others had a complex alignment with the Church (e.g., secular groups composed of (ex)Catholics or groups of Catholics disowned by the Church). This cohort of stakeholders has found expression in many venues including but not limited to depositions, press releases, promotional materials, newsletters, books, conferences, media releases, personal letters, court briefs, news reports, protests, petitions, as well as movies and interviews.

Despite the vocal involvement of numerous stakeholders in the crisis, the hierarchy's communicative response to the situation has followed relatively traditional crisis management strategies (i.e., apologia [Hearit, 1994 & 1996] and image restoration discourse [Benoit, 1997]) with the goal of single-handedly "resolving" the crisis. This communication (in the form of policies, homilies, surveys, press releases, self-audits, meetings, apologies, etc.) has sought to deny, minimize, remediate, and control the crisis, all under the exclusive auspices of the Roman Catholic hierarchy. This discursive position stands in contrast to other stakeholders' attempts to defer closure, draw out underlying issues, amplify non-dominant voices, contest dominant interpretations, and collaborate on possible solutions. What has emerged, then, since the winter of 2002 is an ongoing situation in which an organization's attempts at strategic communicative crisis management are being contested publicly by a variety of stakeholders.

This situation provides an excellent opportunity for expanding current understandings of how source and stakeholder organizations rhetorically co-construct a crisis. As will be shown in the next section, early research explores how source organizations use crisis communication (e.g., Hearit, 1994, 1996; Benoit, 1997). More recent research investigates how emergent voices (e.g., stakeholders/stakeseekers) respond to a source organization's crisis communication (i.e., Waymer & Heath, 2007). However, it remains to draw the two into a single frame, rigorously engaging the contested nature of crisis communication. This chapter responds by drawing into a single frame the crisis-specific press releases/statements of three key organizations in the U.S. Roman Catholic clergy sex abuse crisis (a "source" organization and two stakeholder organizations). This approach yields insights into two key questions regarding the rhetorical construction of crises. First, (how) do stakeholder organizations engage a source organization's crisis communication? Second, (how) do stakeholder organizations engage one another through crisis communication? Before engaging these questions, a closer look at extant rhetorical approaches to understanding crisis communication contextualizes the study.

Rhetorical Analyses of Crisis Communication

According to early research, crises are marked by public scrutiny, high intensity, image-threats, and financial threats (Fink, 1986). More particularly, a crisis is "a specific, unexpected and non-routine organizationally based event or series of events which creates high levels of uncertainty and threat or perceived threat to an organization's high priority goals" (Seeger, Sellnow, & Ulmer, 1998, p. 233). Reflecting across the growing body of crisis research, Heath and Millar (2004) noted that a crisis is typically conceptualized as "an untimely but predictable event that has actual or potential consequences" for both a source organization and its stakeholders (p. 2). They went on to note that standard definitions often focus on crisis damage, consequences, and response options.

Important depth is added to these standard understandings through rhetorical conceptualizations of crises (Heath & Millar, 2004). Rhetoric, which addresses "the ways in which discourse functions in various social contexts" has been applied to the field of public relations since the early 1980s (Cheney & Christensen, 2001). From this perspective, a crisis gives rise to a rhetorical problem (Heath, 2004; Heath & Millar, 2004), or a situation which mandates a response (Bitzer, 1968). According to Heath (2004), a crisis breaches an organization's narrative of control and continuity, thus requiring the organization to reassert order through "a series of statements that is expected to present a factually accurate, coherent, and probable account for the event and its proper resolution" (p. 168). However, this is complicated by the ambiguous meanings and outcomes of a crisis (Penrose, 2000, p. 157; Sellnow & Seeger, 2001; Ulmer & Sellnow, 1997), which make discursive framing and interpretation central to crisis management (Heath & Millar, 2004). Rhetorical approaches engage the communicative complexity of crises. From this perspective, organizational crises may be defined as unexpected, destabilizing situations marked by ambiguity and threat which emerge and are contested communicatively.

The tradition of organizational rhetoric has been brought to bear on crisis communication in several ways, including apologia theory (Hearit, 1994), kategoria-based apologia (Hearit, 1996), and image restoration theory (Benoit, 1997). Each of these schools of thought builds on the others. The most developed and closest to the roots of classical rhetoric is that of apologia. Hearit (1994) described apologia as a "discourse of defense" which reframes organizational actions in a more compelling light (pp. 114–115). He saw apologia as serving three goals for a source organization. First, *persuasive accounts* "reassert terminological control over the interpretation of the act with a counter-interpretation of events" (p. 115). Second, *statements of regret* allow an organization to express sorrow while downplaying responsibility. Third, *dissociation* allows the organization to distance itself from the situation, thus appearing in a more favorable light (p. 121). Although the defensive nature of apologia indicates some degree of communicative interactivity among stakeholder organizations (i.e., attack and defense), apologia theory is largely used as an analytical lens for understanding a source organization's response to a threat.

On the heels of his (1994) terminological approach to apologia, Hearit (1996) proposed the notion of kategoria-based apologia. Since apologia is inherently defensive, Hearit noted that organizations may respond to an attack with a counterattack. This essentially shifts an accused organization from the defensive (the situation of traditional apologia) to the offensive. There are three forms of kategoria: levying new charges, challenging the validity of charges by reframing them, or challenging the ethics of the accuser (pp. 235–236). Given the inherent power differentials among stakeholders in an organizational crisis, an organization can only use kategoria on an opponent of equal or larger power without appearing to bully its accuser (p. 244) or distract stakeholders from key issue(s) (pp. 244–245). Although kategoria apologia derives from the communicative interplay among stakeholder organizations, it presumes a combative orientation, thus obscuring the possibility of collaborative strategies.

Benoit's typology of image restoration strategies might be considered the next development in crisis rhetoric. According to Benoit (1997), his focus on message options builds on, and is more exhaustive than, apologia theory. Essentially, he offered a typology of strategies organizations may use to restore their image. Organizations may deny the act with a simple denial or a shifting of blame. They may evade responsibility by claiming that they were provoked, alternative actions were not feasible, the situation was an accident, or they acted out of good intentions. Organizations in crisis may also work to reduce the offensiveness of the act by bolstering their image, minimizing the act, differentiating the act from more negative acts, pointing to some transcendent aspect of the context or outcome, attacking the accuser, or offering compensation to victims. Finally, they may take corrective action or offer an apology. Although insightful, this approach is clearly biased toward the source organization, framing the concerns of stakeholders as "obstacles or costs to be quickly resolved, minimized and overcome" (Seeger & Ulmer, 2002, p. 129).

While augmenting basic assessments of crisis communication strategies with a focus on sense-making and enactment, standard rhetorical perspectives on crisis communication remain constrained by the riding managerial bias in the literature (Waymer & Heath, 2007). This bias emerges perhaps most tellingly where scholars fail to challenge the source organization as the primary focus or agent of public relations. When publics are considered, they are generally considered in relation to, and from the perspective of, the source organization (Botan, 1997; Botan & Taylor, 2004; Leichty & Warner, 2001; Leitch & Neilson, 2001). They are, in essence, made Other, and viewed from the standpoint of the source organization. The assumption that public relations discourse flows from an organization to "its" publics obscures the contested nature of many PR situations. The result is that "public relations theory has been unable to come to terms with the power relationships between discourse participants or with ethical issues relating to power differentials" (Leitch & Neilson, 2001, p. 127). This managerial bias undoubtedly constrains research on crisis communication. According to Waymer and Heath (2007), "the crisis communication literature is largely void of the other voices and views present in particular situations and the possible ways that these voices can influence public discourse and opinion" (p. 95).

Clearly it is time to challenge the source organization as the primary rhetor in an organizational crisis. Although there has been some treatment of PR from critical perspectives (as this volume and its predecessor shows), further explorations of PR as a contested practice are necessary. One way to engage this bias is by exploring how alternative voices (e.g., stakeholders and the media) challenge a source organization's narrative of control during a crisis (Waymer & Heath, 2007). According to this line of thought, organizations are essentially narrative (Heath, 1997), and their primary narratives are narratives of control (c.f., Conrad, 1992). In these narratives, organizations "work hard to enact the persona that they are in charge of their destinies and aware of the interests and concerns of the other characters . . . in the narrative" (Heath, 1997, p. 317). A crisis, however, serves to breach this narrative of control. As such, it creates a rhetorical exigency for multiple entities. On one hand, it necessitates the generation of a crisis narrative by the source organization (Heath, 1997). On the other hand, it creates a platform for alternative voices (e.g., stakeholders, various publics, the media) to exert influence on the source organization and the crisis (Waymer & Heath, 2007).

As may be expected given the managerial bias of the discipline, early research into organizational crisis narratives focused primarily on management goals in the source organization. For example, Heath (1997) uncritically presumed that organizational "control is a dominant cultural archetype" which serves and is desired by both organizations and stakeholders (p. 319). Heath (2004) went so far as to describe a crisis as a loss of organizational control, and positioned his work as an effort to help organizations "struggle to regain control over their operations and practices" (p. 170). He conceptualized crisis communication as a narrative designed to persuade key publics that the source organization "is willing and able to shoulder responsibility for its activities and their consequences as well as maintain or regain control over its operations" (pp. 169–170). From this perspective, crisis narratives are subnarratives used to reestablish the larger narrative of organizational control. Although restoring the narrative of control may guide a source organization's crisis response, this goal is not necessarily shared by salient publics.

Despite its focus on organizational/managerial ends, Heath's (2004) work opened the door for tracing the contested nature of narratives of control. At the most basic level, by noting the potential for conflict between an organization and its stakeholders over the very existence and nature of a crisis, he highlighted key areas in which a crisis is contested. In noting that the source organization's narrative emerges in concert with other narratives (e.g., those generated by media, stakeholders, government entities, or other publics), he opened the door for an exploration of the polyvocal narrativization of crises. In his assertion that every narrative emerges from a set of preferences and moves toward a desired ending, one might infer a multiplicity of desired outcomes for a given crisis. Even more to the point, he described the convergence and divergence possible among competing crisis narratives, arguing that "the narrative of one group can be a counterstatement and perhaps a corrective to the narrative of another group" (p. 173).

The door opened by Heath was walked through by Waymer and Heath (2007), who listened to the crisis communication generated by emergent voices. By focusing on peripheral responses to Hurricane Katrina, the authors challenged the riding managerial bias in crisis research. Key here is their assertion that a crisis creates a portal for non-dominant voices to "challenge the frame that the organization is . . . in control" (p. 95). By conceptualizing a crisis as a means to enter the larger "crisis dialogue" or to influence the communicative construction of the crisis, Waymer and Heath inverted the traditional notion of crisis communication. That is, rather than exploring the managerial efficacy of crisis communication, they explored a rhetorical tool (i.e., transcendence) stakeholders use to "challenge the narrative of control, gain exposure for their positions, influence public opinion, and shape responses to a crisis" (p. 105). This response-based analysis offers an essential rebalancing of managerial understandings of crisis communication. It also points to two additional questions. First, what rhetorical tactics (beyond transcendence) do stakeholders use to engage a source organization? Second, what rhetorical tactics do stakeholders use to engage one another?

In light of these questions and Heath's (2004) recommendation to compare crisis communication generated by several organizations across a single crisis, this chapter explores the PR generated by three key organizations in the U.S. Roman Catholic clergy sex abuse crisis. Specifically, it analyzes the crisis-relevant press releases/statements posted on each organization's website from January 2002 (when the case broke to the public through the *Boston Globe*'s exposé) through June 2005 (when data collection occurred, and at which time each organization was poised to discuss the crisis at its own national conference). Both stakeholder organizations emerged in direct response to clergy sex abuse and focus on some aspect of the crisis, so all of their press releases were crisis-specific. However, the source organization has a history that precedes and a purpose that supersedes clergy abuse, so only a percentage of its press releases directly focused on the crisis. (Approximately 10% of the 886 press releases posted on the source organization's website during the specified time frame were case-specific.) When compiled, relevant press releases from the source organization comprised a 140-page document; relevant press releases/statements from the two stakeholder organizations comprised a 635-page document. An introduction to the three organizations and their crisis goals follows.

Three Organizations, Three Crisis Goals

When tracking the recent clergy sex abuse crisis in the United States, three organizations emerge as central: the United States Council of Catholic Bishops (USCCB), Voice of the Faithful (VOTF), and the Survivors Network of those Abused by Priests (SNAP). As the primary governing body of the U.S. Roman Catholic Church, the USCCB may be seen as the Church's organizational representative in this crisis. Its goals include engaging and coordinating Catholic activities in the U.S. (USCCB, n.d.). Its decision-making power is evident throughout the crisis, namely in the creation of the Charter for the Protection of Children and Young People and the establishment of the National Review Board. The USCCB has clearly served as the voice of the American arm of the institutional Catholic Church, and has had high visibility in managing the crisis. It has power to represent and manage the global Catholic Church in the United States.

Both VOTF and SNAP were formed by (ex)Catholics in direct response to the phenomena of clergy abuse. VOTF's mission is to provide a voice through which the laity can share in Church governance. The organization's goals include supporting victims, survivors, and priests of integrity and shaping structural change within the Church (VOTF, n.d., b.). Although it situates itself as a mechanism for bridging the laity and the hierarchy, Church officials contest VOTF's position as a Catholic organization. SNAP is a "volunteer self-help organization of survivors of clergy sexual abuse and their supporters" which works to educate its members and their communities in order to prevent clergy abuse (SNAP, n.d.). Their goals are healing and justice (SNAP, n.d.). Although members of SNAP may be (or have been) Catholic, the organization does not identify itself as Catholic.

A survey of each organization's crisis-specific press releases/statements shows that each organization has a distinct goal for the crisis. The USCCB's prime objective seems to be gaining control of the crisis and moving past it. VOTF's purpose is to gain enough organizational legitimacy to become influential in the Church. SNAP's chief intent is putting an end to systemic clergy sexual abuse. While a traditional rhetorical analysis would measure how (un)effective the USCCB was in reestablishing its narrative of control, and an assessment of emergent agents would trace non-dominant responses to the source organization's narrative, the following analysis traces how source and stakeholder organizations' differing approaches to crisis communication work together to affect the emerging crisis.

Drawing the press releases/statements of the three organizations into a single frame shows a general disconnection between the source and each stakeholder organization. Early in the crisis, the hierarchy involves SNAP symbolically (inviting members to address the bishops at the 2002 General Assembly in Dallas) and VOTF conflictually (banning them from meeting on Church premises). These overtures quickly fade from the hierarchy's PR and are replaced with attempts to preclude source–stakeholder interaction. This shift, however, does not stymie stakeholder attempts to affect the crisis and engage the source organization. The following sections explore the rhetorical tactics used by the USCCB to reestablish its narrative of control and by two stakeholder organizations to engage that narrative.

Source–Stakeholder Tactics

Defensive Initiatives

Despite its defensive position in the crisis, the USCCB's PR is predominantly proactive. This is the case as it announces meetings, rolls out new policies, marks organizational changes, and narrates its managerial strategies. Its PR is comprised of what might be called *defensive initiatives*, a preemptive defense which might be compared to "stealing thunder" (Arpan & Roskos-Ewoldsen, 2005). This tactic is marked by such words as *announced, resolved, named,* and *appointed.* Although these strategic actions are taken in response to the larger crisis situation, they are communicated in a proactive, declarative way. For example, early in the crisis, the USCCB announces "that the convened membership of the conference . . . approved a new Charter for the Protection of Children and Young People" (USCCB, 2002, June 15). Later it notes that "Two hundred ten priest canon lawyers received training in the canonical procedures for implementing the Essential Norms for Diocesan/Eparchial Policies Dealing with Allegations of Sexual Abuse of Minors by Priests or Deacons" (USCCB, 2003, February 27).

Note the declarative tone in these quotes. It is as if the USCCB is rolling out a new policy and training its priest canon lawyers of its own accord. The larger context of crisis slips away in such language, the proactive tone almost outweighing the defensive stance of the organization. Similar language permeates the USCCB's press releases. The predominance of such language clearly serves the goal of reestablishing the USCCB's narrative of control. This tone is set from the earliest days of the crisis, as the hierarchy effectively launched its crisis campaign by highlighting "two decades of efforts by the nation's Catholic bishops to address the problem of sex abuse in the Church and to assist those who have been affected by it" (USCCB, 2002, February 15).

According to feedback embedded in stakeholder PR, another prominent tactic used by the hierarchy is *silence* or *non-responsiveness*. An example of how stakeholder organizations call attention to this tactic follows.

> [Cardinal] Mahony did not respond to SNAP's letter. . . . SNAP is troubled by Mahony's silence and non-responsiveness to their request. . . . "Surely, the Cardinal can do SOMETHING. . . . We are convinced that he can find a way to help these men and other victims", says Manny Vega, SNAP Leader.
>
> (SNAP, 2004, December 22)

The bishops' reliance on the tactic of non-responsiveness is further indicated by stakeholders' criticisms that the bishops hampered internal audits, refused to open documents or publish the names of the accused, and operate within a "culture of secrecy." (Note: Although beyond the scope of this analysis, additional context would be added by an exploration of how Roman Catholic culture(s) have affected the crisis.)

By consistently applying defensive-initiative language and largely avoiding responsive language, the USCCB strategically downplays the crisis situation and frames its actions as positive and proactive. The USCCB's attempts to reassert unilateral control, however, are shadowed by consistent challenges by the stakeholder organizations. In particular, VOTF's press releases are marked by attempts to engage the hierarchy.

Defensive and Offensive Responses

VOTF's attempts to engage the hierarchy are fueled by an assumption that the crisis will be resolved through dialogue. According to VOTF:

> Solutions must involve collaboration among the laity, priests, religious, and hierarchy. . . . Healing requires listening to one another, to survivors and their families, to priests, religious, and to the laity—women and men of good will who share a responsibility for the well-being of the Church. We must listen to one another; we must have real and honest dialogue; we must cooperate in shaping solutions.
>
> (VOTF, 2002, December 13)

This quest, however, is met by an overt rejection of VOTF by the hierarchy. As VOTF is banned from meeting on Church property in many dioceses and excluded from discussions and decision making, it faces a prioritization between its paradoxical goals of changing and affirming the Church. A closer look at VOTF's PR reveals how this tension plays out.

Although VOTF claims an offensive position for itself in the crisis (i.e., working to change the Church), it is forced into a defensive position by its inability to legitimate itself as part of the Church. This defensive orientation is clear in the following quote.

> Voice of the Faithful is profoundly concerned by the recent bannings from church property . . . the very parishioners who have been erroneously labeled as "anti-Church and ultimately, anti-Catholic" are the same mainstream Catholics welcomed to Sunday morning Mass and encouraged to financially support the very properties from which they have been banned. . . . We must also remind our bishops that as an association of Catholic laity, Voice of the Faithful has formed properly under the meaning of Canon 215. . . . In addition, the teachings of Vatican II clearly articulate the right—and even the obligation—of laypersons to form associations and make their voices heard on matters concerning the good of the Church.
>
> (VOTF, 2002, October 11)

Clearly, VOTF is on the defensive here, using *defensive-responsive* language to establish itself as a legitimate Catholic organization. This tactic is a mechanism for responding defensively to the hierarchy's attack, and may be compared to Hearit's (1994) apologia.

Despite being on the defensive about its identity as a legitimate Catholic organization, VOTF attempts to be an offensive force on other issues in the crisis (e.g., naming systemic complicity with abuse, addressing financial mismanagement). Even its offensive maneuvers, however, are couched as a response to the hierarchy. The tactic of *offensive response* (i.e., responding to another's discourse with an attack) may be compared to Hearit's (1996) kategoria apologia. By situating itself as responsive to the hierarchy, though, VOTF undermines the power of its offensive tactics. Its PR is marked by passive, low power words like *call on, has learned,* and *seeks.* Its identity as "an organization . . . formed in response to the sexual abuse crisis in the Catholic Church" is underscored by its consistent use of responsive tactics. For example:

> [VOTF] announced today that the Archdiocese of Boston Policies and Procedures for the Protection of Children are welcome, if overdue. The long delay in issuing these policies is regrettable, but these provisions can move the Archdiocese of Boston in the right direction if they are implemented aggressively.
>
> (VOTF, 2003, May 30)

This is typical of VOTF's blow-by-blow responses to the USCCB's actions. Such deferential critique accords with VOTF's position as an internal dissent organization.

Throughout the crisis, then, VOTF uses responsive language both to defend its identity and to critique the hierarchy. Its use of responsive language for both offense and defense marks VOTF's submission to the hierarchy. The apparent effect of this approach is that, in order to be acknowledged by the hierarchy, VOTF submits its goal of democratizing the Church to the hierarchy's goal of reasserting control over the Church.

Offensive Responses and Offensive Initiatives

Although SNAP shares VOTF's quest to engage the hierarchy, its motivation is different. For SNAP, the pursuit is fueled by an awareness that the hierarchy has access to unidentified abuse victims among the laity, one of SNAP's primary publics. Although this leads SNAP to retain a relatively respectful posture toward the USCCB, its pursuit to engage the hierarchy is more tempered and strategic than VOTF's. In fact, SNAP's attempts to elicit a response from the hierarchy rival the USCCB's rhetorical power at times by echoing the hierarchy's powerful, declarative language.

SNAP uses more initiatives in its PR than VOTF does, and largely relies on an offensive orientation in its communication. Interestingly, where SNAP does respond, it often responds to incriminating behaviors of the hierarchy rather than to the claims of the hierarchy. The following is an example of SNAP's *offensive response* to behaviors of the hierarchy.

> The problems in Springfield reflect decades of mismanagement, cover up, protection of perpetrator priests and their criminal behavior, and possible destruction of diocesan documents. Let us not be naive in assuming that this could be rectified quickly by the right bishop. The problems in the diocese reflect the actions of its former leader, Bishop Thomas Dupre, but also his inner circle. The diocese was not the domain of one corrupt man, and cannot be "cleaned up quickly" by one honest man.
>
> (SNAP, 2004, March 9)

In this quote, SNAP leverages its response to a bishop's resignation as an opportunity to point out the corruption permeating a particular diocese. This is clearly an *offensive response*. At another point, SNAP turns its response to a cardinal's use of the statute of limitations into an attack on the hierarchy's legal tactics, arguing that Church officials are fighting on "technicalities and loopholes" (SNAP, 2005, January 5). So, where VOTF uses responses to defend itself against the hierarchy, SNAP uses responses to attack the hierarchy, pointing out discrepancies between the Church's rhetoric and its actions.

Across time, SNAP levies an increasingly forceful stream of *offensive initiatives* (i.e., being the first to levy an attack) on a multitude of issues. This approach accords with SNAP's identity as an activist organization, and exemplifies what one might think of as a typically offensive orientation to crisis communication. Initiating attacks against the source organization is a key function in any crisis. By naming a variety of potential issues, SNAP attempts to broaden the scope of the crisis. However, the introduction of new topics into the larger crisis discourse is dependent on some response or engagement by other participants. In this case, many of the themes SNAP introduces are not picked up (at least in this PR venue) by the other organizations, decreasing the likelihood that they gain traction as key issues. (More will be said about the effect of non-collaboration on the creation of issues in the next section.)

In summary, each organization seems to take a different approach to crisis communication. The USCCB favors defensive initiatives, VOTF uses defensive responses on identity and offensive responses on crisis issues, and SNAP alternates between offensive initiatives and offensive responses. These rhetorical approaches have interesting implications for each organization's individual crisis goals. In order to reassert control of the situation, the USCCB offsets the vulnerability of its defensive position with a masterful, proactive language. Less strategically, VOTF undermines its attempt to change the Church by positioning itself as fundamentally responsive to the hierarchy. SNAP seeks to put an end to clergy sexual abuse by leveraging specific criticisms against the hierarchy. Although the hierarchy's monological crisis rhetoric effectively roadblocks stakeholder–source communication, it does not stop stakeholder-to-stakeholder communication. The next section takes a closer look at some tactics that VOTF and SNAP use (with varying success) to influence the rhetorical framing of the crisis.

Stakeholder-to-Stakeholder Tactics

Collaboration

Despite the hierarchy's attempts to control the crisis and silence stakeholders, crisis-specific stakeholder communication crescendos across the time studied. In fact, within a year of the crisis breaking into public consciousness, VOTF and SNAP are each producing more crisis-specific press releases/statements than is the USCCB. A survey of this stakeholder PR shows the two stakeholder organizations using a series of collaborative communication tactics throughout the crisis, which may be grouped into three main categories, as follows.

First, *they speak and act together*. They attend the same meetings, use quotes from one another as sound bites, speak at one another's events, and disseminate nearly identical statements. For example, early in the crisis, VOTF notes that it joined SNAP in a meeting with Governor Keating, the chair of the National Review Board (i.e., an internal audit panel). In describing that meeting, VOTF quotes a SNAP representative as saying that, "The governor heard and seemed to agree that victims need to be listened to by the bishops, in the same way we have been listened to by Voice of the Faithful" (VOTF, 2002, October 4). Not only are the organizations at the same meeting, but SNAP serves as a sound bite for VOTF. In this instance (one among many examples), VOTF and SNAP underscore one another's voices.

A similar effect occurs when representatives from one organization speak at an event sponsored by the other organization. This happens regularly, and is marked in each organization's PR. In these instances, the organizations showcase one another's voices and messages. They also emphasize the overlap between the organizations, essentially narrating their interdependence. Note the following excerpt of a speech given by then-president of VOTF, James Post, at a SNAP conference:

> I wanted to be here with you in Chicago this weekend for two reasons. First, I want to say to each of you . . . that we stand together in the fight for social justice for survivors of clergy sexual abuse. Voice of the Faithful and SNAP continue to cooperate in a fight to rid the Catholic Church of one of the great evils of our lifetime—clergy sexual abuse.
> (VOTF, 2005, June 11)

Here, the organizations are shining the spotlight on one another in order to highlight their collaboration and unity.

At other times, VOTF and SNAP essentially echo one another's voices. On more than one occasion, the organizations post nearly identical paragraphs in their press releases/statements (e.g., as the organizations attempt to influence the USCCB's 2004 national meeting and as the groups call for independent audits of the hierarchy). Clearly, posting the same content on the same day indicates that the two organizations are working in concert. Similar collaboration happens when they co-sign a letter to Bishop Skylstad about the crisis management strategy of bankruptcy (SNAP, 2004, December 1).

Second, *they mark one another's actions and advance one another's goals.* Although the latter is not the most common use of coordinated speaking and acting between VOTF and SNAP, several excellent examples emerge in their press releases/statements. In one, VOTF encourages its members to participate (as activists) in a 2003 Lenten prayer service in Boston. One of the things they ask members to do is to prepare a donation for SNAP or another survivor support group (VOTF, n.d., a). By asking VOTF members to bring a check made out to a survivor support group, VOTF is simultaneously rerouting money away from the archdiocese and supporting the work of SNAP (and other survivor support organizations). In another example, SNAP restates, affirms, and extends a local VOTF chapter's agenda regarding an abusive situation. Similarly, immediately after SNAP successfully stops a Ford truck ad that played on the issue of sexually abusive clergy, VOTF affirms SNAP's action and extends it, "calling on" Ford officials to meet with clergy sex abuse survivors (2005, February 3). By affirming and/or extending one another's organizational goals, both VOTF and SNAP show a responsive awareness of one another.

They also use their press releases/statements to draw attention to one another's actions. For example, SNAP describes the increasing engagement of the laity by saying: "We are also hopeful because regular Catholics are doing more. . . .through organizations like Voice of the Faithful, they're supporting survivors in more ways than we ever dared hope five or ten years ago" (SNAP, 2003, June 18). In this statement, SNAP traces VOTF's actions and their effects. Similarly, VOTF notes when members of SNAP meet with the National Review Board and the lack of closure that meeting engenders (VOTF, 2004, December 13). Selectively marking one another's actions is an indirect way to publicize, affirm, and advance one another's goals.

Third, *they defend and honor one another*. Here, the organizations exemplify an empathetic awareness of one another that is marked actively and symbolically. For example, when VOTF found out that the Diocese of Worcester had subpoenaed SNAP's records of all those alleging abuse in the diocese, it expressed "deep disappointment" and decried the subpoena as a disturbing tactic that would "only serve to inflict more pain on the survivors of sexual abuse" (VOTF, 2002, September 23). By publicizing the action of the diocese, VOTF makes a passive defense of SNAP. Similarly, SNAP offers a defense of VOTF in light of the bannings. In July 2003, the organization calls on the new archbishop of Boston (Sean O'Malley) to "immediately lift the ban on Voice of the Faithful. Doing this will show that he understands the value of genuine, independent lay voices in healing this fractured, dispirited church" (SNAP, 2003, July 1). Each organization shows an awareness of and willingness to publicly defend the other's vulnerabilities.

They are also willing to publicly celebrate one another. For example, VOTF introduces two key SNAP leaders as "honored guests" at a press briefing before the June 2003 USCCB general assembly (VOTF, 2003, June 19). Then, in September 2004, SNAP gives its "Survivors Lifeline Award" to Jim Alvord, Regional Director of VOTF in the Bridgeport Diocese. They applaud him "for his work on behalf of survivors" and describe him as "a strong and vigilant voice in support of survivors" (SNAP, 2004, September 21). Perhaps the best example of VOTF honoring SNAP comes from a speech given by James Post at SNAP's June 2005 conference. There, Post, then president of VOTF, is quoted as saying:

> My second reason for being here today is to publicly thank SNAP. . . . Your participation in the work of VOTF has made a great difference to us. You have told the story of your experience. . . . Thank you. . . . You have also helped us mobilize and motivate thousands of people. . . . You have stirred the conscience of Catholics across this nation, and set in motion processes of change that will help us one day achieve justice for survivors and safety for all children and adults in our Church.
>
> (VOTF, 2005, June 11)

Not only does this illustrate how the organizations speak and act together (as noted in the previous paragraphs), but it also illustrates how they honor one another. By expressing gratitude for SNAP, Post clearly honors the organization's role in the crisis.

While this is not an exhaustive review of the stakeholder organizations' collaborative tactics, it hints at the potential for a typology of tactics by which stakeholder organizations function in concert. Through the use of such co-oriented tactics, stakeholder organizations may seek to influence the rhetorical construction of a crisis. At the same time, given stakeholder organizations' separate identities and distinct crisis goals, the use of collaborative tactics seems likely to be bounded.

Non-collaboration

An examination of VOTF's and SNAP's press releases/statements does, in fact, indicate this to be the case. One of the noteworthy missed opportunities for collaboration is in influencing what issues emerge as widely salient to the crisis (as alluded to in the previous section). In the clergy sex abuse crisis, numerous issues introduced by either VOTF or SNAP are not picked up by the other stakeholder organization. This lack of collaboration raises questions about how stakeholder organizations may (inadvertently) affect emergent conceptualizations of a crisis.

In the current case, each stakeholder organization introduces potential issues that are ignored by the others. One such area is the storyline of each organization's growth. These stories, found in each organization's PR, serve to narrate key events, milestones, and struggles in each organization's life cycle. For the most part, however, they are not engaged by the other key stakeholder. Although this oversight may seem inconsequential, it is not. In order to affect the crisis, each organization must establish itself as a legitimate voice in the larger crisis discourse. When the crisis burst into public consciousness in 2002, however, VOTF did not exist and SNAP was largely unknown to the general public. By publicly affirming one another (not an unlikely occurrence, given the similarity of their goals and their generally collaborative orientation), the organizations could have lent credence to one another's position in the crisis. This opportunity to legitimate one another's organizational existence, however, largely slips by in the current case.

Another area which is not consistently collaborative is a running commentary (either criticisms or commendations) on the hierarchy's actions. Each stakeholder organization makes a selective notation of those actions of the hierarchy that are particularly salient to that organization, and many of these comments stand as one-time statements. The effect, when taken together, is a laundry list of disparate notations about the hierarchy which are named by one organization, but ignored by the other. This becomes important in light of the collaborative nature of issue construction. That is, for a potential issue to take root, it must be addressed by multiple voices across time. At stake here is how non-dominant voices can move beyond buckshot crisis commentary to strategic issue management. It appears stakeholders must balance between introducing their own concerns into the general crisis discourse (and hoping another voice will engage those concerns) and using their PR to affirm and extend another stakeholder's concerns. (Selective) mutual attention to one another's issue pitches may be a powerful mechanism for challenging dominant conceptualizations of a crisis.

Perhaps more important than stakeholder organizational narratives and commentary on the source organization is SNAP's attempt to reframe the crisis. In its press releases/statements, SNAP gives a running commentary on legal aspects of the case, almost like a sports announcer giving a play-by-play. (See Table 15.1 for a list of items introduced by SNAP in 2004 alone.)

Table 15.1 Items Introduced by SNAP in 2004

- A relevant report by the Maine Attorney General
- Allegations against and criminal investigation of a Massachusetts bishop
- Legal restrictions in Wisconsin against prosecuting Church leaders
- What victims/survivors want out of a mediation process in Milwaukee
- The freeing of convicted sex offender in St. Louis
- Bishop Gregory's use of "hardball legal tactics" against victims/survivors
- Bishops being found in contempt of court for refusing to turn over documents
- A former Brooklyn priest given a life sentence
- Sentencing/plea agreement of a Cincinnati priest
- The release of documents in a Massachusetts case
- A Missouri ruling opening the door for delayed prosecution of child molesters
- Two former seminarians settling a civil suit against their abuser (Missouri)
- A Stigmatine priest's guilty plea
- The lifting of a Nevada priest's probation
- The dismissal of a suit against the Rochester, NY diocese
- The arrest of a Wisconsin abuser
- A priest who loses his slander suit against his accuser (Tulsa)
- 14 victims/survivors who settle Chicago lawsuits
- Two civil suits settled against the St. Louis Archdiocese and one of its priests
- The Missouri Supreme Court decision not to hear an appeal by alleged abuser
- Wisconsin Supreme Court precedent treating clergy abuse differently from other types of molestation
- A Michigan court ruling in favor of statute of limitations
- The bankruptcy of the Diocese of Spokane.

One could look at each of these topics individually, noting that none of them is addressed in USCCB or VOTF press releases. One could also look at them as a comprehensive attempt to reframe the crisis within the juridical arena. (Note that SNAP generally positions the crisis within the legal arena rather than in the Church.) Either way, SNAP is caught in a double bind as it attempts to expand the crisis in ways that neither the source organization nor the other key stakeholder organization engages fully. Obviously, the lack of response from the hierarchy is strategic, since dropping this frame may decrease the attention and thus credibility the legal jurisdiction gains in the larger discourse. Non-responsiveness from VOTF seems less strategic, since it downplays one of the most significant arenas for contest in the crisis. (Reframing the crisis in the judicial arena would legitimize the claims each organization makes about the systemic nature of clergy abuse. It would also underscore their shared challenge to the Church's exclusive authority in the crisis.) This adds an additional layer to Waymer and Heath's (2007) argument for the existence of competing frames for a crisis.

Items in each of the three areas described above (stakeholder organizational narratives, commentary on the source organization, and attempts to reframe the crisis) are mentioned in a single press release/statement, ignored by the other stakeholder organization, and dropped from the larger crisis discourse. This indicates that crisis issues may require a joint construction, leaving a single organization recourse only to naming a possible issue. Without engagement from another voice, a named issue is likely to drop. It also shows that an organization can influence the construction of a crisis by either dropping or by taking up an issue named by another organization. That is, by failing to acknowledge or respond to a potential issue, an organization reduces the chance that issue has of becoming a full-fledged issue. Conversely, taking up an issue named by another organization gives momentum to the agenda of the naming organization. The clergy sex abuse crisis shows how organizations can miss opportunities for strategic issue management. In this case, stakeholders drop opportunities to legitimate one another, to sustain one another's topics, and to collaboratively reframe the crisis.

This exploration of proposed (but dropped) issues is essential to understanding how organizations co-construct a crisis. Although not taken up by other parties, these pitches may reveal key or strategic issues for an organization. If a given issue or theme is repeatedly introduced by an organization and ignored by others across the crisis, this may indicate a point of resistance, frustration, or intractability. In such a case, the initiating organization may be attempting to persuade the other organizations to engage an issue it finds particularly salient. This may also indicate the flow of power in a crisis, if one addresses whose issue pitches are picked up and whose dropped.

In this case, most potential topics are introduced by the USCCB and SNAP. In time, however, those that gain the attention of more than one stakeholder organization (at least across the organizations' press releases/statements) are generally those presented by the USCCB. Despite its capacity for collaborative PR, VOTF seems more likely to take up the USCCB's threads than SNAP's, which might indicate the alignment of power in the crisis. Further, it is not surprising that VOTF and SNAP have more dropped pitches than does the USCCB. Given the USCCB's non-responsiveness, the only way VOTF and SNAP can engage the USCCB (which each hopes to do) is to respond to issues it introduces. This constrains VOTF's and SNAP's ability to reframe the crisis, since their primary access to communication with the hierarchy requires them to engage its agenda.

Although there is more work to do in exploring stakeholder crisis communication, this extends current understandings of how emergent voices individually or collaboratively challenge a source organization's narrative of control. It also highlights ways in which stakeholder organizations miss opportunities for strategic collaboration. The next section highlights areas for future research emerging from this approach.

Conclusion

The focus of this chapter has been on the polyvocal nature of crisis communication. By approaching crisis communication as an inter-organizational phenomenon, this chapter indicates how differing approaches to crisis rhetoric interact and affect the co-creation of a crisis. In the Roman Catholic clergy sex abuse case, it is clear that key organizations employ different types of crisis communication in hopes of meeting different crisis outcomes. The hierarchy uses a monological orientation to seek a quick return to organizational control; VOTF uses a responsive orientation to seek legitimacy and influence in the Church; and SNAP uses a critical orientation to end systemic clergy sexual abuse. Interestingly, at this writing (October 2007), the hierarchy still has not regained full control of the crisis, VOTF remains a marginalized entity in the Church, and SNAP continues to unearth abuses in the Church. As the crisis continues, it is clear that none of the organizations has fully met its goal. This may be due, in part, to the way in which each organization's rhetoric affects that of the others.

In this case, there is a conflict between the source organization's traditional rhetorical approach (i.e., apologia and image restoration attempts) and the stakeholder organization's attempts at invitational or critical engagement. This effectively derails communicative interaction between the source organization and stakeholder organizations. Further, by refusing to engage any alternative framing of the crisis, the source organization implicitly bounds the impact stakeholder organizations can have on the crisis. By refusing to countenance any crisis framework but its own, the source organization leaves stakeholder organizations only two courses of action: they can engage the source organization's rhetorical treatment of the crisis (which VOTF does), or they can cultivate alternative understandings of the crisis in alternative arenas (which SNAP does).

On the level of stakeholders, there is a bounded amount of collaborative crisis communication. In their PR, the stakeholder organizations studied here speak and act together; mark one another's actions and advance one another's goals; and defend and honor one another. The use of these tactics shows a dialogical orientation to crisis rhetoric, and allows the organizations to cooperate in crafting an alternative understanding of the crisis. However, a survey of their press releases/statements reveals that (at least in this medium) the organizations fail to leverage this collaborative potential to its full extent. Not only do they independently narrate their organizational histories and offer individual commentaries on the source organization's crisis management, but they fail to collaborate on a strategic and substantive reframing of the crisis in the legal arena.

This study has three main implications for researchers and practitioners. First, by augmenting current understandings of rhetorical strategies with a focus on initiatives and responses, this study offers a mechanism for tracing the flow of attack, apologia, kategoria apologia, and stealing thunder across a crisis. Second, the preliminary typology of stakeholder tactics indicates a need for continuing assessment of tactics and their strategic value. Third, this study indicates the effect of non-collaboration on a crisis outcome. Although further study is necessary in each of these areas, they open the door to greater reflection on recommended best practices for emergent voices in crisis situations.

This study's most important contribution may be turning the power of a rhetorical lens onto the communicative practices of emergent voices in a crisis. The resulting insights are key for non-dominant voices that want to affect an unfolding crisis; they are also important for source organizations that either value inclusive crisis communication or fear potential damage from ignoring emergent voices. As Waymer and Heath (2007) noted, appreciating the potential power of emergent voices "can inform and enhance crisis communication research and best practices" and enhance the quality of crisis planning (p. 96). This benefit must certainly be offered to marginalized voices as well as managerial voices.

Despite the limitations of exploring crisis communication through the press releases/statements generated by select organizations in a single case, this analysis indicates the importance of critiquing crisis communication as a contested form of organizational communication. Inasmuch as crisis communication is a tool used by organizational rhetors to gain desired ends, it is a rhetorical practice. To understand this practice, it is essential to sift competing voices against one another, exploring how their communicative tactics affect the emerging crisis. Only in this way will scholars begin to understand the recursive effect organizational rhetors have on one another in the construction of a crisis.

References

Arpan, L., & Roskos-Ewoldsen, D. (2005). Stealing thunder: Analysis of the effects of proactive disclosure of crisis information. *Public Relations Review, 31*, 425–433.

Benoit, W. (1997). Image repair discourse and crisis communication. *Public Relations Review, 23*, 177–186.

Bitzer, L. (1968). The rhetorical situation. *Philosophy and Rhetoric, 1*, 1–15.

Boston Globe. (n.d.). Scandal and coverup. Retrieved July 1, 2005, from: http://www.boston.com/globe/spotlight/abuse/scandal/

Botan, C. (1997). Ethics in strategic communication campaigns: The case for a new approach to public relations. *Journal of Business Communication, 34*(2), 188–202.

Botan, C., & Taylor, M. (2004). Public relations: State of the field. *Journal of Communication, 54*, 645–661.

Cheney, G., & Christensen, L. (2001). Public relations as contested terrain: A critical response. In R. Heath (Ed.), *Handbook of public relations* (pp. 167–182). Thousand Oaks, CA: Sage.

Conrad, C. (1992). Corporate communication and control. In E. Toth & R. Heath (Eds.), *Rhetorical and critical approaches to public relations* (pp. 187–204). Hillsdale, NJ: Lawrence Erlbaum.

Fink, S. (1986). *Crisis management: Planning for the inevitable.* New York: American Management Association.

Heath, R. (1997). *Strategic issues management.* Thousand Oaks, CA: Sage.

Heath, R. (2004). Telling a story: A narrative approach to communication during crisis. In D. Millar & R. Heath (Eds.), *Responding to crisis* (pp. 167–187). Mahwah, NJ: Lawrence Erlbaum.

Heath, R. & Millar, D. (2004). A rhetorical approach to crisis communication: Management, communication processes, and strategic responses. In D. Millar & R. Heath (Eds.), *Responding to crisis* (pp. 1–17). Mahwah, NJ: Lawrence Erlbaum.

Hearit, K. (1994). Apologies and public relations crises at Chrysler, Toshiba, and Volvo. *Public Relations Review, 20*(2): 113–125.

Hearit, K. (1996). The use of counter-attack in apologetic public relations crises: The case of General Motors vs. Dateline NBC. *Public Relations Review, 22*, 233–248.

Leichty, G., & Warner, E. (2001). Cultural topoi: Implications for public relations. In R. Heath (Ed.), *Handbook of public relations* (pp. 61–74). Thousand Oaks, CA: Sage.

Leitch, S., & Neilson, D. (2001). Bringing publics into public relations. In R. Heath (Ed.), *Handbook of public relations* (pp. 127–138). Thousand Oaks, CA: Sage.

Penrose, J. (2000). The role of perception in crisis planning. *Public Relations Review, 26*(2), 155–171.

Seeger, M., Sellnow, T., & Ulmer, R. (1998). Communication, organization, and crisis. In M. Roloff (Ed.), *Communication yearbook 21* (pp. 230–275). Thousand Oaks, CA: Sage.

Seeger, M., & Ulmer, R. (2002). A post-crisis discourse of renewal: The cases of Malden Mills and Cole Hardwoods. *Journal of Applied Communication Research, 30*(2), 126–142.

Sellnow, T., & Seeger, M. (2001). Exploring the boundaries of crisis communication: The case of the 1997 Red River Valley flood. *Communication Studies, 52*(2), 153–168.

Simpson, A., Jr. (2006, April 20). Insurers paid $43 million of $150 million Boston clergy abuse settlements. *Insurance Journal.* Retrieved January 1, 2006, from www.insurancejournal.com/news/east/2006/04/20

Survivors Network of those Abused by Priests. (n.d.). SNAP mission statement. Retrieved December 1, 2006, from: http://www.snapnetwork.org/links_homepage/mission_statement.htm

Survivors Network of those Abused by Priests. (2003, June 18). One year later. Retrieved July 1, 2005, from: http://www.snapnetwork.org/snap_statements/2003_statements/061803_one_year_later.htm

Survivors Network of those Abused by Priests. (2003, July 1). 3 steps new Boston archbishop should take on day 1, according to SNAP. Retrieved July 1, 2005, from: http://www.snapnetwork.org/snap_statements/2003_statements/070103_steps_for_omalley.htm

Survivors Network of those Abused by Priests. (2004, March 9). Statement regarding appointment of new bishop to Springfield, MA diocese. Retrieved July 1, 2005, from: http://www.snapnetwork.org/snap_statements/2004_statements/030904_new_bishop_springfield.htm

Survivors Network of those Abused by Priests. (2004, September 21). Clergy abuse survivors host CT conference. Retrieved July 1, 2005, from: http://www.snapnetwork.org/snap_press_releases/2004_press_releases/092104_snap_ct_conference.htm

Survivors Network of those Abused by Priests. (2004, December 1). Sex abuse victims and lay Catholics urge bishop to meet. Retrieved July 1, 2005, from: http://www.snapnetwork.org/snap_press_releases/2004_press_releases/120104_skylstad_urged_tomeet.htm

Survivors Network of those Abused by Priests. (2004, December 22). Sex abuse victims urge cardinal to "rein in" parishioners. Retrieved July 1, 2005, from: http://www.snapnetwork.org/snap_press_releases/2004_press_releases/122204_mahony_reign_in_parishioners.htm

Survivors Network of those Abused by Priests. (2005, January 5). Sex abuse victims want Detroit church official deposed. Retrieved July 1, 2005, from: http://www.snapnetwork.org/snap_press_releases/2005_press_releases/010505_want_detroit_official_deposed.htm

Ulmer, R., & Sellnow, T. (1997). Strategic ambiguity and the ethic of significant choice in the tobacco industry's crisis communication. *Communication Studies, 48*, 215–233.

United States Council of Catholic Bishops. (n.d.). About us. Retrieved December 1, 2006, from: http://www.usccb.org/whoweare.shtml

United States Council of Catholic Bishops. (2002, February 15). USCCB web site details bishops' efforts to address sex abuse. Retrieved July 1, 2005, from: http://www.usccb.org/comm/archives/2002/02-026.shtml

United States Council of Catholic Bishops. (2002, June 15). U.S. Bishops approve Charter to Protect Children and Young People. Retrieved July 1, 2005, from: http://www.usccb.org/comm/archives/2002/02-111.shtml

United States Council of Catholic Bishops. (2003, February 27). Training held on "Essential Norms"; Vatican official took part. Retrieved July 1, 2005, from: http://www.usccb.org/comm/archives/2003/03-035.shtml

Voice of the Faithful. (n.d., a). Massachusetts VOTF members encouraged to attend Bishop Lennon's lenten prayer service. Retrieved July 1, 2005, from: http://www.votf.org/Press/pressrelease/stjames.html

Voice of the Faithful. (n.d., b). Who we are: Mission, goals, and identity statement. Retrieved December 1, 2006, from: http://www.voiceofthefaithful.org/Who_We_Are/mission.html

Voice of the Faithful. (2002, September 23). Voice of the Faithful deeply disappointed at Worcester diocese's subpoena decision. Retrieved July 1, 2005, from: http://www.votf.org/Press/worcester.html

Voice of the Faithful. (2002, October 4). Voice of the Faithful joins survivors in meeting with Gov. Keating on clergy sexual abuse crisis. Retrieved July 1, 2005, from: http://www.votf.org/Press/pressrelease/keating.html

Voice of the Faithful. (2002, October 11). VOTF statement regarding bannings in Newark and Camden, NJ. Retrieved July 1, 2005, from: http://www.votf.org/Press/pressrelease/njbanning.html

Voice of the Faithful. (2002, December 13). Statement from Jim Post on the resignation of Cardinal Law as archbishop of Boston and the appointment of Bishop Lennon as apostolic administrator. Retrieved July 1, 2005, from: http://www.votf.org/Press/pressrelease/1213.html

Voice of the Faithful. (2003, May 30). Voice of the Faithful responds to Boston Archdiocese's child protection policies & procedures announcement. Retrieved July 1, 2005, from: http://www.votf.org/Press/pressrelease/0530.html

Voice of the Faithful. (2003, June 19). Voice of the Faithful calls for disclosure, accountability at bishops' conference. Retrieved July 1, 2005, from: http://www.voiceofthefaithful.org/bishopsconference/0619pr.html

Voice of the Faithful. (2004, December 13). Voice of the Faithful and Survivors Network of those Abused by Priests ask for credible church audits. Retrieved July 1, 2005, from: http://www.votf.org/Press/pressrelease/121304.html

Voice of the Faithful. (2005, February 3). Voice of the Faithful offers to facilitate meeting with Ford Motor Company, survivors over controversial ad. Retrieved July 1, 2005, from: http://www.votf.org/Press/pressrelease/030305.html

Voice of the Faithful. (2005, June 11). Remarks by James E. Post, Voice of the Faithful President. Retrieved July 1, 2005, from: http://www.votf.org/Press/pressrelease/061305.html

Waymer, D., & Heath, R. (2007). Emergent agents: The forgotten publics in crisis communication and issues management research. *Journal of Applied Communication Research, 35*(1), 88–108.

SECTION FOUR

CHARACTER, ETHICS, AND LEGITIMACY IN THE PRACTICE OF PUBLIC RELATIONS

The Good Organization Communicating Well

Carroll (1991) suggested that organizations must meet their responsibilities at all levels. This includes generating profits for investors and abiding by both economic and legislative laws. Moreover, organizations must in one way or another "meet the expectations of consumers, employees, and the community while promoting welfare and goodwill at the ethical and philanthropic levels" (Albinger & Freeman, 2000, p. 243). Thus, in order for corporations to retain their privileges of operation they need to respond to the social pressures applied from multiple stakeholders: discerning customers, discerning job seekers, discerning investors, and discerning employees.

Corporate audiences and publics routinely rely on the information provided by organizations, information provided through the media, and the reputations of said organizations when making investment decisions, career decisions, and product choices. Moreover, "reputations signal publics about how a firm's products, jobs, strategies, and prospects compared to those of competing firms. Favorable reputations can therefore generate excess returns for firms by inhibiting the mobility of rivals in an industry" (Fombrun & Shanley, 1990, p. 233). Reputations, however, may provide other potentially favorable outcomes such as allowing firms to charge premium prices, attract better applicants, retain employees, enhance their access to capital markets, and attract investors (Fombrun & Shanley, 1990). These outcomes are clear benefits of an established, favorable reputation. Yet, establishing a favorable reputation—being deemed a legitimate, ethical organization of sound character, is in many ways a rhetorical effort.

As discussed in chapter 1, Aristotle believed that the character or what he considered "ethos" of public speakers was essential to their success or failure as a speaker. In a similar vein, organizations of high character, in part, enjoy the benefit of being deemed legitimate organizations. For example, Ben & Jerry's ice cream enjoyed success in part due to its commitment to being philanthropic and community-oriented.

Chapter 16 gets at the heart of public relations and character from a historical perspective. This chapter looks at the works and the legacy of two iconic public relations figures, John W. Hill and Arthur Page, as a means of extending our discussion of what it means to be ethical, of good character, and deemed legitimate in the practice of public relations. Both believed that public relations could not—and should not—defend organizations that were not of good character. One could argue that their case was based on what might be called public relations ethics, but for them the larger ethic was the responsibility of organizations to society from which they obtained their franchise to operate.

Chapter 17 helps to explain public relations activities that violate conventional rules of public discourse, as well as why and how organizations employ such actions that may seem counterproductive, clumsy, or even offensive. Many might consider such public relations efforts unethical, of little character, and "ends justify the means" oriented; however, this chapter—through a postmodern lens—sets the stage for legitimizing such "extreme" activists' public relations efforts and tactics. As students and practitioners of public relations consider the following:

- What codes—legal and/or moralistic—guide your interpretation of corporate messages and corporate social responsibility efforts?
- In a global marketplace which you inhabit, are codes of ethics still to be considered situational? Are there universal codes of ethics?

For these questions, take for example a recent Absolut Vodka advertisement that was withdrawn. The intended audience was Absolut Vodka consumers in Mexico. This advertisement, entitled "In an Absolut World" idealized an early nineteenth-century map that showed California, Arizona, and other U.S. states as Mexican territory. Many U.S. citizens were angered by this advertisement.

Finally, consider this question:

- Assuming Absolut Vodka was an organization of weak character, how would its character impede its ability and rhetorical options to deal with the backlash to this advertisement?

Organizations of questionable character face constant challenges and threats to their legitimacy. For example, as discussed in chapter 18, organizations such as Wal-Mart (criticized for its questionable organizational practices) encountered activist pressures because organizational operations were questionable and at times deemed unethical. This chapter used digital cinema as a means to constitute an activist public in opposition to an issue or organization. Additionally, this chapter analyzes the ways that activists employed a documentary to constitute an anti-Wal-Mart identity, as well as highlighted the ways that new media such as digital cinema and the Web give activists more methods to challenge and confront organizations that they deem are engaged in questionable practices.

Most, if not all, organizations that have been subject to activists' pressures, have had their legitimacy questioned, or are trying to avoid such threats, recognizing the benefits of being deemed socially responsible—that is in essence being an organization of good character. Chapter 19 highlights the ways that organizations, through rhetoric, attempt to be considered environmentally responsible citizens, and it analyzes the environmental social responsibility, consciousness, and the "Green Rhetoric" of three of the most successful corporations to date: General Electric, Starbucks, and Toyota. Clearly, these organizations believe that "going green" is good for their images; it helps to paint them as considerate, legitimate, caring, and responsible citizens. The chapter, however, poses the following question: Why should we believe these companies and their environmental claims—especially if such attempts at "character-building" (i.e. Wal-Mart's recent commitment to being environmentally friendly) are considered shams, phony, and non-genuine because the organization's character has been in question for such a long period of time or if its corrective efforts are narrowly self-serving disguised as altruism?

Both character and legitimacy have narrative qualities. Organizations earn a favorable reputation and are considered legitimate by being ethical and by meeting their social responsibilities for extended lengths of time. Some might argue that character, ethics, and legitimacy compose the cornerstone of public relations. Without them, it is difficult to conceive of brand loyalty and organizational trust. Stated another way, who wants to be in public relations(hips)—unless coerced or manipulated—with partners who are untrustworthy, of weak character, and completely self-serving? The following chapters extend this logic and further establish the import of character, ethics, and legitimacy to the study and practice of public relations.

References

Albinger, H. S., & Freeman, S. J. (2000). Corporate social performance and attractiveness as an employer to different job seeking populations. *Journal of Business Ethics, 28*, 243–253.

Carroll, A. B. (1991). The pyramid of corporate social responsibility: Toward the moral management of organizational stakeholders. *Business Horizons, 34*(4), 39–48.

Fombrun, C., & Shanley, M. (1990). What's in a name? Reputation building and corporate strategy. *Academy of Management Journal, 33*, 23–258.

16

CHARACTER AND THE PRACTICE OF PUBLIC RELATIONS

Arthur W. Page and John W. Hill

Karen Miller Russell
University of Georgia

The importance of Arthur W. Page and John W. Hill in U.S. public relations history cannot be exaggerated. Page, the first American public relations practitioner to serve as vice president and director of a major corporation—AT&T—was ranked the third most important practitioner of the twentieth century by *PRWeek* in 1999, behind only Ivy Lee and Edward Bernays, and a society for senior counselors is named for him (Page Society, 2007). Hill, the head of the world's largest and most influential agency of his time—Hill and Knowlton, H&K—has been called the best-regarded person in the field during his time, known for having "just a very plain, decent honesty about him" (Burger, 1993), and in surveys of PR practitioners and journalists alike, Hill and Knowlton ranked first and best ("Public Relations," 1960).

A strong emphasis on "character" defined the public relations philosophy of both Page and Hill. Both men had high standards for the practice of public relations. Both were recognized by their contemporaries as ethical in their practice and in the leadership they provided to the growing field. Both emphasized the need for integrity and the importance of sound public relations in a democratic society, which both connected to counseling on policy: it was important to both that public relations should have a seat at the management table.

However, the way these shared beliefs played out in practice was not the same. Page saw the public relations department as the conscience of the corporation. "This particular department of ours," he told AT&T's Publicity Conference in 1927, "is not pressed with the commercial end of this business; it is not engaged in the immediate money making, the physical preparation of plant, and it is freer, if it has the brains and perspective and intention, to be the custodian of the ideals of the company" (Page, 1927). This role contributed to the development of a spirit of service that permeated the company. Hill, on the other hand, believed that the most important ethical decision was made the moment an agency accepted a client: if the client was ethically acceptable, it was the agency's job to advocate its interests in any ethically appropriate manner. "I have seen John Hill decline an exceedingly lucrative new account because the would-be client impressed him as wanting to shade the truth in dealing with the public," wrote Edward Barrett, a former H&K executive who was the dean of the graduate school of journalism at Columbia University (Hill, 1963, p. vi). Hill also thought it important to influence client policy, but as an independent counselor, client selection came first.

This historical study will compare and contrast what Page and Hill wrote and said about character and will illustrate how their ethical standards played out in important episodes in the practice of public relations. In so doing, this chapter will show that Page and Hill illustrate two competing models of public relations ethics, but that they were united in their emphasis on character as the key to ethical PR. Finally, it evaluates the role of character, demonstrating that while character is necessary, it cannot guarantee the practice of public relations in the public interest.

The Question of Character

"Character" is important in public relations because it influences an individual's ability to persuade. As Heath (2000) states, "To be good precedes being an effective communicator" (p. 80). Noting that such classical rhetoricians as Quintilian, Aristotle, Cicero, and Plato all accepted the notion that "goodness" or "virtue" underlies oratory, Brandenburg (1948, p. 23) explains, "Most people agree that a speaker's success in a given situation depends significantly upon the opinion of his character which the audience has or acquires."

Moreover, Aristotle's emphasis on *ethos*, "the character of the individual speaker," (Rahoi, 1994, p. 93) has become an important concept in the literature on public relations ethics. Bostdorff (1992) points out that character and morals are etymologically related, derived from the same Greek word, and that the concepts of moral virtue and character are intertwined. Many public relations scholars have therefore incorporated *ethos* in discussions of PR ethics. For example, Martinson (2000) asks, "What would Aristotle say?" about ethical decision making in public relations. He argues that "Aristotle would counsel the public relations practitioner that he or she will respond ethically when faced with the 'big ethical crunch' only if the practitioner has trained the will to habitually respond ethically to the everyday choices the practitioner is called to make" (p. 19). Martinson concludes that practitioners must not choose between serving the client or employer and serving the public interest; they must do both. Page and Hill would have agreed.

Page's Conception of Character

When Arthur W. Page became vice president and head of the Information Department at AT&T in 1927, his prior experience had given him many opportunities to think about the role of publicity and propaganda in influencing public opinion (Russell, 2005a). He had served for a number of years as editor of *World's Work* magazine, which published several editorials relating to the public relations of big business—some of which he probably wrote (Page, 1959). For example, one editorial suggested that the best publicity men were former reporters and editors, "because a man who has not had experience in 'handling news' generally makes a mess of it when he has information to impart to the press" ("The 'publicity men,'" 1906). Another editorial declared in 1908 that "public opinion rules us at last," so the only wise policy was one of frankness ("The passing," 1908). In addition, during the last months of World War I, Page served as a propagandist for the Allied Expeditionary Force's Psychological Subsection in France. He helped to prepare leaflets which the Army dropped by the millions from airplanes during the last two or three months of the war in hopes of convincing German soldiers to surrender (Griese, 2001). Thus, although he had no experience in corporate publicity, when he arrived at AT&T in 1927, he had already put some thought into how it should be conducted.

Character was important to Page because of the Information Department's role in the corporation. He positioned character in reference to professionalism and public service, describing it as "running a business so that the more the employees know about it the better they feel about it, and running it with people who know what they are doing, have a pride in their profession and want that profession held in high esteem by other people because it deserves to be" (Page, 1938). In Page's view, good character led to a spirit of service that defined a new professionalism among business executives. In a 1928 draft for a graduation speech, Page predicted an increased sense of professionalism in American business, a movement away from a pure profit motive and toward providing a service to the public and taking money only to assure continued service to the public. He wrote that "big business can afford the research and study to do right and in the long run it cannot afford to neglect the professional spirit," which included relegating "the money motive to its proper place" (Page, 1928). Good character was also necessary to the successful practice of public relations: "To build an organization that has neither the confidence of those who make it up nor the character in its dealings with the public, is so much harder than doing it honestly that very few people succeed in it for any length of time" (Page, 1943). Page worked to create an Information Department that upheld his standards for character and effectiveness.

Hill's Conception of Character

Like Page, John W. Hill's career began in journalism, and like Page he moved to public relations in 1927 (Russell, 2005b). Hill worked for several newspapers and even tried to start up one of his own before both developing a newsletter for Cleveland, Ohio, business executives and becoming financial editor of the *Daily Metal Trade* in 1920. He observed corporations relaying financial news with "incredible ineptitude" (Hill, 1963, p. 17), which motivated him to open a corporate publicity office in Cleveland in April 1927. His first clients included Union Trust, Otis Steel, United Alloy Steel, Standard Oil of Ohio, and Republic Steel. In March 1933 Hill took a partner, Don Knowlton, director of advertising and publicity at Union Trust, when it, like so many other banks, failed during the Depression (Miller, 1999). Little is known about Hill's early work until the agency opened its New York branch in 1933, but Hill stated that he was inspired by reading a collection of speeches by Ivy Lee, like Hill a news reporter who had "come to look with exasperation on corporate executives who ignored or spurned the press." Lee's approach — "not just talk, but action"—"kindled in me a determination to go into his kind of endeavor," Hill wrote (1963, p. 16).

When speaking of character, Hill typically referred to integrity and made comparisons with the law. In providing counsel, he noted, "lawyers can cite statutes, judicial precedents, and established legal procedures." But "public relations people in the main must rest their counsel on experience plus opinions and judgment that are binding on no one" (Hill, 1963, p. 134). Therefore, he asserted, "the most important single element" in providing counsel "is integrity, which is a matter of character" (Hill, 1963, p. 135). Because he saw ethics as a personal matter, Hill did not see a counseling code of ethics as a workable, enforceable solution to ethical problems. "Unlike law or medicine, public relations cannot be defined in precise terms," he wrote (1963, p. 139). Instead, he said, "the greatest hope for the future lies in the fact that the number of strong responsible firms is increasing year by year."

To Hill, choosing an ethical client and contributing to that client's policy were paramount in ethical public relations practice. Newsom (1992) explains that there are two schools of thought on public relations client representation: "One says you shouldn't work for someone you don't believe in. The other says that clients deserve representation in the court of public opinion" (p. 4). Hill landed firmly in the first school. "There can be no substitute for honest dealing with the people by any enterprise which wants to keep the respect of the public," he wrote. A company's "image" began with its attitudes toward its publics, which were made manifest in policies and intrinsic values. "The rightful purpose of public relations is to confirm, strengthen, and defend those values," Hill explained. "Without integrity this cannot be accomplished." An effective public relations program was based not on "insidious and mysterious powers," but on policy decisions made "in the light of what is genuinely believed to be in the public interest" (pp. 161–162). Hill saw no point in working for a client who would not operate in this manner.

Character and Ethics in Public Relations Practice

Page and Hill thus embody two of the models identified by Fitzpatrick and Gauthier (2001) in their analysis of theoretical bases for public relations ethics. Hill's approach was the Attorney Adversary model, which sees public relations as performing "the socially necessary role of professional advocacy within the adversary process essential to free enterprise and competition" (Fitzpatrick & Gauthier, 2001, p. 196). The authors describe this model as inadequate because the court of public opinion fails to offer participants protections in the manner of the judicial system. Yet John Hill's frequent references to attorneys, precedents, and the law certainly indicate that he believed in a parallel.

Page's approach was most closely associated with what Fitzpatrick and Gauthier (2001) call the model of Partisan Values Versus Mutual Values. Based on Sullivan (1965), this model suggests that practitioners must balance mutual values, which take into account the interests and rights of others (the public interest), with partisan values (those of the client or employer). "Balancing the special interests of the institutions represented with those affected by those institutions is the issue that seems to defy resolution," Fitzpatrick and Gauthier (2001, p. 200) assert. Yet Page honestly believed that AT&T could benefit both consumers and shareholders. He wrote, "We believe that, in removing the limitations of time and space from the words of man, we are giving him the ability to make a more effective civilization. And particularly we believe that it is important to increase the influence of his brain by facilitating human intercourse, for it is by the origination and spread of ideas that progress is made" (Page, 1932b, pp. 23–24). Such benefits far outweighed the cost of a telephone call.

Although their approaches reflect different models of public relations ethics, the primary difference may be contextual. Hill, who ran an agency that depended on clients, simply had a different perspective from Page, who worked for a single employer for 20 years. Each man recognized deficiencies in his model of public relations ethics, and both sought to overcome those deficiencies with the concept of character. For John Hill, the counselor's character and integrity provided the protections that the bar of public opinion might fail to offer. For Arthur Page, character engendered a professional spirit of service that put the profit motive in its proper place. In fact, there are more similarities than differences in their think-ing—and in their reputations, for both were known as highly ethical in their prac-tice of PR (Cutlip, 1994; Golden, 1968).

Public Relations and the Public Interest

Page and Hill each recognized public opinion as the final arbiter in a democracy. "All business in a democratic country begins with public permission and exists by public approval," Page (1941, p. 154) wrote. Hill likewise said that "public opin-ion has been recognized as the ultimate human force throughout history" (Hill, 1963, p. 156). And both recognized that corporations had to pass what Page called "the political test." The test, Page (1932a) explained, "is whether or not we have attained a position in which a man would lose votes and a newspaper would lose circulation by attacking the New York Telephone Company or the Bell System in any part." The only reason for politicians, editors, or others to criticize Bell was that "they believe when they criticize large corporations they are voicing a general public opinion" (Page, 1932a). Thirty years later, Hill (1963) echoed this idea: "Sound policy, then, must pass the public-approval test, along with the profit-pro-ducing test, if a corporation is to feel itself secure on every front" (p. 166).

It was this connection between public relations and public interest that led both Page and Hill to believe that public relations must be a management function. Page later said that he would not have gone to work for AT&T unless he was convinced that the company's president, Walter Gifford, meant for him "to sincerely study the public's needs and serve them" (quoted in Griese, 2001, p. 93). Hill likewise demanded and got a seat at his clients' tables: he attended virtually every meeting of the directors of the American Iron and Steel Institute and Avco Manufacturing for decades, and his top executives had the same close relationships with other H&K clients (Miller, 1999). As Hill pointed out, public relations must have something to offer. "The extent to which public relations counsel influences policy depends on whether he can demonstrate capacity for giving sound, practical and objective advice on policy matters. If he can do so, there will be little question about his role in policy decisions" (Hill, 1963, p. 141).

Page and Hill each saw a relationship between sound public relations (character) and public interest (the democratic functioning of society). Therefore, this section will describe an important incident from each man's career that reveals how his ideas functioned in practice: AT&T's response to the Depression in the 1930s, and Hill and Knowlton's representation of the tobacco industry during the decade and a half following the health scare in 1954. In both instances, the public relations function's contributions to policy were vital, and corporate values and ethics were called into question. What part did character play?

AT&T and the Great Depression

AT&T's public relations policies under Page were driven by a commitment to the company's Financial Policy, a speech written by Page and delivered before the National Association of Railroad and Utilities Commissioners by AT&T president Walter S. Gifford in 1927, just a few months after Page joined the company. In the speech, Gifford (quoted in Page, 1941, pp. 11–13) pointed out that AT&T's stock ownership was "widespread and diffused," and conceded that AT&T was a monopoly. The company's many far-flung stockholders and consumers depended on Bell, giving the System serious obligations. "Obviously, the only sound policy that will meet these obligations is to continue to furnish the best possible telephone service at the lowest cost consistent with financial safety." He spoke also of the "spirit of service" that marked Bell's history, a tradition that continued with "several thousand people whose sole job it is to work for improvement," "scientists and experts devoted exclusively to seeking ways and means of making the service better and cheaper." Then, quoting statistics on the growth and improvement of the System in the 20 years since states had generally begun regulating the telephone, Gifford noted that "practically any one anywhere can talk by telephone with any one else, anywhere else in the country." "With your sympathetic understanding we shall continue to go forward," Gifford told his company's regulators, "providing a telephone service for the nation more and more free from imperfections, errors or delays, and always at a cost as low as is consistent with financial safety."

The stock market crash in October 1929 and the subsequent Depression provided the first major challenge to the Financial Policy. AT&T's stock, which sold for more than $300 before September 1929, hit bottom in 1932, at a low of just under $70, and telephone business declined steadily from 1931 to 1935 (Griese, 2001). AT&T made a series of decisions in response. Executives chose to maintain rates for customers, wages for employees, and the traditional $9 dividend for shareholders. However, someone had to pay the price. At the bottom of the economic trough, more than 2.5 million customers had stopped service, the labor force had been slashed by as much as one-third, and as many as half of the employees who remained were working only part-time (Griese, 2001; Long, 1937; Gifford, 1930). In addition, the company's retained surplus fell from $234 million to $93 million, a drop of more than 60% (Baida, 1985).

AT&T also maintained its commitment to service, which Page had connected so closely with character. Throughout the Depression officials repeatedly emphasized the importance of research and development to reduce the cost of service. "Stated briefly, our job is to furnish tens of millions of people with the best possible telephone service at all times," Gifford (1937) said at AT&T's annual meeting. "The continued success of the Bell System will continue to depend on how we do that job. Telephone service was never better than it is today and we expect not only to maintain its present high level but to make it still better." AT&T improved service in a number of ways during the Depression. In 1931 the company introduced the TWX, teletypewriter exchange service, which "consists of the establishment and operation of central switching exchanges for teletypewriters. Any subscriber to this service can obtain immediate a two-way written communication with any other subscriber to the service within the same city or in a distant city." The Associated Companies also continued conversion from manual operation to the dial telephone (begun in the 1920s), another way that technology could help save money (AT&T, 1931).

AT&T figures showed that service gradually improved in almost every imaginable way before and during the Depression. In 1924, it took an average of 7.9 minutes to establish a long distance toll board connection; in 1933 it took just 1.5 minutes. The percentage of both local and long distance calls completed on the first attempt rose slowly but steadily. The number of days required to establish new service dropped. In 1933 almost 94% of "troubles" were cleared on the same day they were reported. Installation, repairs, speed of service—all improved. The following year the company was able to report that "Criticisms per 1,000 telephones were the lowest on record. More than nine out of every ten long distance calls were completed while the customer remained at his telephone" (Andrew, 1934).

The 1935 annual report offered reasons that service would continue to get better—the continuing growth of the American population, the waning of the Depression, and a trend toward higher living standards, but most of all, systematic research "to assure that service is continuously adapted to the developing needs of the public" (AT&T, 1935). In 1931 the company had stated that "there has been no substantial reduction in development and research activity other than that occasioned by the closing of Bell Telephone Laboratories on Saturday mornings beginning in August" (AT&T, 1931). Eventually even Bell Labs employees faced layoffs, but AT&T managers protected the company's research arm as best they could. Page would recall the commitment to research as one of the outstanding accomplishments of the Gifford era: when asked to enumerate the most important decisions made during the years that Gifford ran AT&T, Page included "The decision not to weaken the future by losing our nerve and damaging research by excessive cuts during the depression" (Page, 1948).

Public reaction to AT&T's decisions was decidedly muted. Although there were some rates protests, none were particularly earnest. An AT&T (1932) report concluded, "Considering the natural reaction of human nature towards paying full price for anything in a time of depression, unemployment, falling incomes and rising taxes the public's attitude towards the Bell System is extraordinarily friendly." This does not mean people were happy about rates. But the company found that consumers were most likely to agitate for lower rates only when one or all of the other utilities—gas, electric, water—had reduced rates in the area. Most people seemed to view the telephone differently from other utilities: "people can get on without a telephone," the report noted, which constituted a "considerable safeguard to our rates" (AT&T, 1932). Rather than protesting, people simply cancelled their telephone service—2.5 million of them by 1937 (Gifford, 1937).

Hill and Knowlton and the Tobacco Industry

Hill and Knowlton faced not national economic disaster but industry-wide calamity. During the early 1950s, scientific evidence increasingly linked cigarette smoking with lung cancer, heart disease, and other health problems. Doctors and scientific researchers rang warning bells, consumption began to decline, stock prices fluctuated as the news media reported bad news about smoking, and the tobacco companies took notice (Miller, 1999). In December 1953, tobacco manufacturers met with top executives from Hill and Knowlton to discuss a public relations response. During this meeting, John Hill and Bert Goss, an H&K vice president and Hill's right-hand man, asked a series of key questions that indicate how important the client selection process was to the agency.

According to H&K records (H&K, 1953), Hill and Goss asked tobacco company representatives if they would openly sponsor their public relations activities; if they accepted "the principle that public health is paramount to all else"; if they considered their own advertising and competitive practices part of the problem; if they would agree to sponsor new research on the problem; if they saw the problem as "extremely serious and worthy of drastic action"; and if they were primarily concerned with cigarettes as opposed to other forms of tobacco. These questions were carefully calculated to help Hill and Goss determine not only tobacco company ethics but also their executives' willingness to accept counsel and to change policies and practices based on H&K's advice and recommendations. Only after these questions had been satisfactorily answered, and after they met with tobacco company research directors, did Hill and Knowlton agree to work with the tobacco industry.

Hill and Knowlton's first public statement on behalf of the tobacco manufacturers was an institutional advertisement that ran in almost 450 newspapers in more than 250 cities across the United States on January 4, 1954. Titled "A Frank Statement to Cigarette Smokers," the ad was signed by the members of the Tobacco Industry Research Committee (TIRC), a group that included a number of manufacturers' and growers' organizations. The ad included three strong statements that formed the basis for H&K's defense of the industry: "We accept an interest in people's health as a basic responsibility, paramount to every other consideration in our business. We believe the products we make are not injurious to health. We always have and always will cooperate closely with those whose task it is to safeguard the public health" (reproduced in Glantz et al., 1996, p. 34).

In its public relations campaign, as Miller (1999) has shown, Hill and Knowlton argued that the case against tobacco had not been proven, and that by sponsoring research on tobacco, pollution, cancer, heart disease, and other related topics, the cigarette manufacturers were upholding their promise to the public. By insisting that a medical controversy existed, H&K guaranteed that a journalist seeking objectivity and balance would always quote a TIRC representative in news reports that were negative toward tobacco, further perpetuating the idea that there was a medical controversy. Additionally, the manufacturers remained in the news with stories about the amount of money they provided for cancer research, and TIRC officials worked to shed doubt on research negative toward the industry (Courtwright, 2005). The TIRC campaign, combined with the introduction of filtered cigarettes, advertising, and other measures, resulted in an abatement of the tobacco controversy, at least until the U.S. Surgeon General's report in 1964 implicated smoking without question or exception (Miller, 1999).

Five years after the release of the Surgeon General's report, Hill and Knowlton resigned the tobacco account. However, it did not do so because of the availability of more or better medical evidence against smoking. By the 1960s, companies like Brown and Williamson, Liggett and Myers, and Philip Morris knew from their own research that nicotine is addictive and that cigarette tars are carcinogenic (Glantz et al., 1996). In fact, there is evidence to suggest that H&K urged the industry to stick with its contention that a medical controversy existed even as it was becoming more and more clear that one did not exist (American Tobacco, n.d.).

Rather, as described by Miller (1999), the agency resigned because it had lost the ability to contribute meaningfully to policy making. In 1966, the tobacco companies began to fund "special projects" that were awarded by lawyers rather than through peer review and that were focused on producing results for legal defense rather than scientific inquiry. The companies ignored H&K's advice on public statements, an advertising code, and cigarette warning labels. At least as late as 1966, John Hill, by then retired and himself a smoker, continued to defend the tobacco industry by citing the millions of dollars it had devoted to research since the 1950s. But eventually, the client's lack of cooperation made it impossible for H&K to continue advocating for tobacco, so the agency resigned in 1969. Recently, the agency revealed that it has a policy not to serve tobacco-related clients anywhere in the world (Garcia, 2007).

Comparison

In both of these situations, detractors have criticized corporate decision making. AT&T should have paid its employees more, or reduced rates, or cut the dividend during the Depression. H&K should have refused to represent the tobacco industry, or used different strategies and tactics, or resigned sooner. But in each case, the counselor's actions are wholly consistent with his character and model of public relations ethics.

In balancing Partisan Values Versus Mutual Values, AT&T's actions during the Depression reveal a sincere commitment to the Financial Policy, which Page had not only publicized but had helped to craft. Employees complained about AT&T management's decisions, arguing that no more job cuts should occur until the dividend was decreased and executive salaries reduced (AT&T, 1933a, 1933b). As historical observers, we might disagree with the policy, or believe that its effects were at times detrimental to employees and consumers, or even dispute how much profit constitutes "financial safety." But no one can deny that AT&T officials, including Page, did what they said they would do: improve service, reduce costs, and put aside money during good times to be used in bad economic times. Bell executives were not heartless in their decisions to maintain wages, rates, and the dividend at the expense of many employees and consumers; they were simply trying to fight their way through an economic calamity that no one really understood. Following the dictates of the Financial Policy was not only a logical response but gave truth to Page's reflection that "The statements of policy made publicly and reiterated are hostages for performance" (Page, 1941, p. 163).

Similarly, Hill and Knowlton has been roundly criticized for its participation in the tobacco industry's response to the health scare (Pollay, 1990). Courtwright (2005, p. 423), for example, called the TIRC a "smoothly running disinformation machine." H&K, applying Hill's Attorney Adversary model of public relations ethics, saw tobacco as a legal product and promoted it as best it could. If we accept that H&K executives at least at the outset truly believed what the manufacturers told them in the initial client meeting, the agency's response was ingenious—it worked for many years and has since been duplicated in other situations like global warming (see, for example, Vergano, 2005). Nonetheless, when the client companies stopped accepting counsel on policy, H&K could no longer advocate for them and therefore resigned.

Conclusion

Did Page and Hill act ethically, placing public interest before client/employer interest when faced with these dramatic challenges? To answer that, we must first determine what the public interest is. Heath (2000) points out that "What constitutes the good is a question that is contested rhetorically" (p. 77). In essence, he argues that no one can determine the public interest but the public:

> Public relations adds value to the extent that it accommodates to and shapes the values that foster and sustain marketplaces. It acknowledges that customers and benefactors are the ultimate critics of statements that are used to convince them that a product or charity, for instance, will satisfy their needs, wants, and interests. Other voices make conflicting and competing appeals. The target of such efforts makes the ultimate choice—rejection or concurrence. (p. 87)

However, knowing this does little to help the individual practitioner determine what the public interest might be. Lippmann (1955, p. 42) argued that the public interest is what people "would choose if they saw clearly, thought rationally, acted disinterestedly and benevolently." How is a practitioner to predetermine what the public would choose if it could? Page and Hill thought the answer was character.

Did character help Page balance Partisan Values Versus Mutual Values? The question is too simple. In truth, Page and AT&T encountered not one public interest but multiple interests, with different publics being harmed or benefited by various policy decisions. Page and other AT&T executives tried to balance many competing values, and the Information Department never lied or covered up the facts about AT&T's policies and decisions. However, consumers and employees who disagreed with AT&T's decisions had little recourse except to cancel their telephone service or quit their jobs.

Did character overcome for Hill and Knowlton the limits of the Attorney Adversary model? Whether or not Hill and his executives intended it, their campaign did harm people who continued to smoke during the 1950s and especially the 1960s because of the information they received suggesting that the case against smoking had not been proven. Hill and Knowlton's representation of the tobacco industry had muddied public discussion about an important issue, saving the client by confusing the jury. The Attorney Adversary model can provide justification for H&K's actions, though, in that tobacco was, and remains, a legal product which the companies had a legal right to sell—and promote.

The analysis of Page's and Hill's work supports Fitzpatrick and Gauthier's (2001) contention that both the Partisan Values Versus Mutual Values and the Attorney Advocacy models are flawed. Character is an important basis for ethical public relations practice. But even people of good character can be faced with ethical dilemmas (being forced to choose to serve one public at the expense of others) caused by being responsible to competing interests. Page and Hill both recognized the supremacy of public opinion, played important roles in the policy-making process, and believed that character was the basis for not only ethical but effective public relations. In spite of that, both AT&T and the tobacco companies caused suffering by their actions. Good character alone does not guarantee that the interests of all publics will be, or can be, served.

Fitzpatrick and Gauthier (2001) conclude that public relations people owe their primary loyalty to their client or employer, but that professional responsibility "requires public relations professionals to consider the interests of all affected parties and make a concerted effort to balance them to the extent possible while avoiding or minimizing harm and respecting all of the persons involved" (p. 205). In other words, public relations professionals must serve as advocates, but as responsible advocates. Fitzpatrick and Bronstein (2006) argue that the dimensions of responsible advocacy include individual accountability, informed decision making, multicultural understanding, relationship building, open communication, dialogue, truth and transparency, and integrity. Good character, then, provides an important foundation for ethical and effective public relations practice, but the public relations person must make a steadfast effort to consider, and balance, the good of the clients and the publics they serve to avoid or minimize causing them harm.

References

American Tobacco. (n.d.). Meeting at TIRC offices. Downloaded August 29, 2007, from: http://ltdlimages.library.ucsf.edu/imagesw/w/a/m/wam06a00/Swam06a00.pdf

Andrew, S. L. (1934, September). "Illustrative Material," General Publicity Conference notes. Box 1310; AT&T Corporate Archives, Warren, NJ.

AT&T. (1931). Annual Report.

AT&T. (1932). Bell System Public Relations as indicated by conferences of March, 1932. Box 1310; AT&T Corporate Archives, Warren, NJ.

AT&T. (1933a). Some Employee Attitudes and Reactions Indicated in Joint Discussions Under Employee Representation Plans, January 1933. Box 58, Unemployment Problems, 1931–1934; AT&T Corporate Archives, Warren, NJ.

AT&T. (1933b). Some Employee Attitudes and Reactions Indicated in Joint Discussions Under Employee Representation Plans, July 1933. Box 58, Unemployment Problems, 1931–1934; AT&T Corporate Archives, Warren, NJ.

AT&T. (1935). Annual Report.

Baida, P. (1985, June/July). Breaking the Connection. *American Heritage, 36*(4), 65–80.

Bostdorff, D. M. (1992). "The decision is yours" campaign: Planned Parenthood's characteristic argument of moral virtue. In E. L. Toth & R. L. Heath (Eds.), *Rhetorical and critical approaches to public relations* (pp. 301–313). Hillsdale, NJ: Lawrence Erlbaum.

Brandenburg, E. (1948). Quintilian and the good orator. *Quarterly Journal of Speech, 34*(1), 23–29.

Burger, C. (1993, 1 March). Personal interview. New York City.

Courtwright, D. (2005). "Carry on smoking": Public relations and advertising strategies of American and British tobacco companies since 1950. *Business History, 47*(3), 421–432.

Cutlip, S. M. (1994). *The unseen power: Public relations, a history.* Mahwah, NJ: Lawrence Erlbaum.

Fitzpatrick, K., & Bronstein, C. (2006). *Ethics in public relations: Responsible advocacy.* Thousand Oaks, CA: Sage.

Fitzpatrick, K., & Gauthier, C. (2001). Toward a professional responsibility theory of public relations ethics. *Journal of Mass Media Ethics, 16*(2&3), 193–212.

Garcia, T. (2007, 7 August). Union calls on UC to cut ties to H&K. *PRWeek.* Retrieved August 31, 2007, from: http://www.prweek.com/us/news/article/730078/AFSCME-urges-University-CA-cut-ties-Hill---Knowlton/

Gifford, W. S. (1930). Statement at the Annual Meeting. AT&T Corporate Archives, Warren, NJ.

Gifford, W. S. (1937). Statement at the Annual Meeting. AT&T Corporate Archives, Warren, NJ.

Glantz, S. A., Slade, J., Bero, L. A., Hanauer, P., and Barnes, D. E. (1996). *The cigarette papers.* Berkeley: University of California Press.

Golden, L. L. L. (1968). *Only by public consent: American corporations search for favorable opinion.* New York: Hawthorn Books.

Griese, N. L. (2001). *Arthur W. Page: Publisher, public relations pioneer, patriot.* Atlanta: Anvil.

Heath, R. L. (2000). A rhetorical perspective on the values of public relations: Crossroads and pathways toward concurrence. *Journal of Public Relations Research, 12*(1), 69–91.

H&K. (1953, 15 December). Background on the Cigarette Industry Client, Box 24, TIRC-Program 1954; Papers of John W. Hill, State Historical Society of Wisconsin, Madison, WI.

Hill, J. W. (1963). *The making of a public relations man.* New York: David McKay.

Lippmann, W. (1955). *Essays in the public philosophy.* Boston: Little, Brown.

Long, N. E. (1937). The public relations policies of the Bell System: A case study in the politics of modern industry. Ph.D. diss., Harvard University.

Martinson, D. L. (2000, Fall). Ethical decision making in public relations: What would Aristotle say? *Public Relations Quarterly,* 18–21.

Miller, K. S. (1999). *The voice of business: Hill and Knowlton and postwar public relations.* Chapel Hill: University of North Carolina Press.

Newsom, D. (1992). PR practitioners question client choice and representation. *PR Update.* March, 4.

Page, A. W. (1927, April). Publicity conference. Record Group 2, Series 2, Box 1, Folder 7; Page Society Archives, New York.

Page, A. W. (1928, 12 June). Proposed speech for commencement at Randolph-Macon College, Box 62; Papers of Arthur W. Page, State Historical Society of Wisconsin, Madison, WI.

Page, A. W. (1932a, 28 March). "Talk on public relations," Public relations course. Record Group 2, Series 2, Box 1, Folder 7; Page Society Archives, New York.

Page, A. W. (1932b). Social aspects of communication development. In Page et al., *Modern communication.* Boston: Houghton Mifflin.

Page, A. W. (1938, 20 September). "Fundamentals of a public relations program for business," speech before the Seventh International Management Congress, Box 62; Papers of Arthur W. Page, State Historical Society of Wisconsin, Madison, WI.

Page, A. W. (1941). *The Bell Telephone System.* New York: Harper and Brothers.

Page, A. W. (1943, 24 February). Letter to Julian Street, Box 9; Papers of Arthur W. Page, State Historical Society of Wisconsin, Madison, WI.

Page, A. W. (1948, 24 August). Letter to Walter Gifford, Box 18; Papers of Arthur W. Page, State Historical Society of Wisconsin, Madison, WI.

Page, A. W. (1959). The reminiscences of Arthur W. Page. Oral History Collection, Columbia University, 1959, New York.

Page Society (2007). Background and history. Downloaded August 20, 2007, from: http://www.awpagesociety.com/site/about/background

The passing of corporate secrecy. (1908, February). *World's Work,* 9837–9838.

Pollay, R. W. (1990). Propaganda, puffing, and the public interest. *Public Relations Review,* 16(3), 39–55.

Public relations: A communication system ripens. (1960, 25 November). *Printer's Ink,* 273, 66–68.

The "publicity men" of corporations. (1906, July). *World's Work,* 7703.

Rahoi, R. L. (1994, Spring). Connecting with the truth: The rhetorical responsibility for ethical concerns—an historical review. *Journal of the Northwest Communication Association,* 22, 91–103.

Russell, K. M. (2005a). Arthur W. Page. In *Encyclopedia of Public Relations* (Vol. 2, pp. 599–603). Thousand Oaks, CA: Sage.

Russell, K. M. (2005b). John W. Hill. In *Encyclopedia of Public Relations* (Vol. 1, pp. 387–391). Thousand Oaks, CA: Sage.

Sullivan, A. J. (1965). Values in public relations. In O. Lerbinger and A. Sullivan (Eds.), *Information, influence, and communication: A reader in public relations* (pp. 412–439). New York: Basic Books.

Vergano, D. (2005, 12 June). The debate's over: Globe is warming. *USA Today.* Downloaded August 28, 2007, from: http://www.usatoday.com/news/world/2005-06-12-global-warming-cover_x.htm

17

OUTLAW DISCOURSE AS POSTMODERN PUBLIC RELATIONS

Josh Boyd
Purdue University

Sarah Hagedorn VanSlette
John Carroll University

The concept of "outlaw" is both old and new—from Wild West desperados to satirists to terrorists, there have always been pockets of resistance to convention that go beyond simple activism in unusual and seemingly irrational ways. Conventional activists are still alive and well, of course: people still write letters to editors. Protesters still picket and carry huge signs with slogans and demands. Public meetings attract people to support and oppose controversial proposals. Interest groups still publish position papers, perhaps expanding their reach by publishing those papers on the Internet (Coombs, 1998).

Coombs (1998) describes conventional activism to manage issues as "frequently a mix of lobbying to change public policy and agitating management to alter organizational policies" (p. 290). This direct, action–reaction kind of activism, even if it makes use of new technologies (as do his examples of the Flaming Fords website and the Free Burma Coalition website), relies on standard argument–response methods. In contrast, some activists eschew such conventional, recognizable methods on the Internet and beyond. Some, for instance, have made satirical videos available on the Web critiquing entrenched corporate targets (e.g., Spiridellis [2005] critiques so-called "big box" retailers such as Wal-Mart). Others have created websites such as www.dowethics.com that look genuine but actually mock corporate practices with a tone of ironic realism. The dowethics website, in fact, looks so authentic that BBC World TV once went through the site to try to recruit an actual Dow Chemical spokesperson to participate in a BBC story (Ossinger, 2006). While these techniques, though unusual, may seem innocuous, terrorism is a much more consequential manifestation of the same unconventional approach to activism.

From funny to deadly, what is the thread connecting these disparate approaches to activism? Some of these approaches, while opposing powerful organizations or ideas, do not lay out anything recognizable as "counterarguments" at all; even though in some ways twenty-first-century activists employ Weiss's (1993) "intrusive scenarios," they do not always hold to his requirements of "detailed, cognitively satisfying causal stories" with "vivid evidence that supports the stories" (p. 225). Coombs (1998) argues that activists need to possess urgency, issue legitimacy, and power before they can really exert influence on the management of issues, but some activists choose to proceed without the issue legitimacy (and often power) perceived to be required. Instead, these new activists often emphasize not arguments countering the established order, but attention-getting appeals, whether humorous or terrifying, lacking the details or substance of conventional counter-argument and protest. What do these developments mean, and how do they fit in with traditional ways of doing public relations? This chapter argues that these kinds of approaches to public relations activism illustrate how outlaw discourse (Sloop & Ono, 1997)[1] is best explained through a postmodern lens. Going a step beyond Brown's (2006) postmodern-influenced description of public relations as cultural styles, we discuss situated public relations practices that reflect a postmodern perspective. And answering the call for communication and public relations theorists to examine the practical impacts of postmodernism (e.g., Gower, 2006; Holtzhausen, 2000; Holtzhausen & Voto, 2002; Mumby, 1997; Toth, 2002), this chapter examines how the concept of "outlaw discourse" (often enacting Brown's [2006] "performance" and "activist" public relations styles) might represent a type of postmodern public relations argument.

First, a caveat: a purely postmodern approach to almost anything is inconceivable. The need for closure, certainty, and control (Stewart, 1991) is a modernist imperative that allows daily life to continue. Without modernist assessments, accountability, and answers, it is hard to imagine what the world might look like. As a perspective, however, postmodernism can provide a helpful lens through which to understand rhetorical action that does not seem to make sense from a purely modernist perspective—the "outlaw discourse" that doesn't answer or question its opposition, but approaches it from an altogether different angle. In the postmodern interest of disclosure, we locate ourselves at the "critical modernist" point on Mumby's (1997) continuum from modernism to postmodernism: interested in issues of power and resistance and suspicious of surface meanings (in a postmodern sort of way), but still desiring closure, willing to make judgments, and preferring right over wrong.

The purpose of this examination, then, is not to promote outlaw discourse as a solution to the blend of modernism and postmodernism present in contemporary culture (Taylor, 2005). The purpose instead is to help explain public relations activities that break the rules, seem counterproductive, and in many cases call attention to themselves for their clumsiness or offensiveness. Why and how do organizations employ such actions? In what context can such public relations efforts be understood? And what situations might prompt people to employ public relations that is "outlaw?" This chapter aims to explain a postmodern approach to public relations in order to sharpen critical thinking about unconventional—and often offensive—public relations campaigns.

First, the chapter will explore the very possibility of postmodern public relations, acknowledging the inherent paradoxes in such an enterprise, and will then touch on the need for understanding more postmodern approaches to public relations. The chapter then offers an overview of outlaw discourse, with an emphasis on how it seems to present a postmodern alternative to conventional activism and argument and why some activists employ it. After offering two brief applications, the chapter concludes with implications of outlaw discourse for public relations theory and practice.

Postmodern Public Relations

Postmodernism

Postmodernism, like public relations, is a term that many people feel strongly about but have difficulty defining consistently. Any attempt to define the postmodern is inherently paradoxical, because "any such effort is a (modernist) attempt to impose order" (Mumby, 1997, p. 2). Because it is against the nature of postmodernism to pin a static definition on it, we present here some themes that are important to the intersection of postmodernism and communication.

People who study postmodernism are usually interested in "the complex relationships of power, knowledge, and discourse created in the struggle between social groups" (Taylor, 2005, p. 113). A postmodern perspective rejects consensus as a value or worthy goal; it sees all knowledge as political and all audiences as localized in time and space (Lyotard, 1979/1984). It is superficial and disconnected from history (Jameson, 1991). Mumby (1997) calls postmodernism "a discourse of vulnerability" (p. 14) in that the scholar must recognize how little he or she really knows or, perhaps, can know. The separation of signifier and signified is virtually eliminated, creating further vulnerability by allowing for the possibility that signs—words, symbols, images, campaigns—don't necessarily possess an agreed-upon meaning. As Taylor (2005) sums up postmodernism's outcomes, postmodernism is "maddeningly both urgent and playful. It uses the strategies of blankness, irony, and reflexivity to heighten our awareness of paradox, ambiguity, uncertainty, emergence, and difference" (p. 118). In other words, postmodernism creates a situation in which the more we know, the more we understand we don't/can't know.

This bleak perspective on postmodernism is tempered by the fact that the world has not yet been conquered by the postmodern condition. Both Mumby (1997) and Taylor (2005) agree that modernism and postmodernism are not a dichotomy, but rather extremes existing at opposite ends of a continuum. Practice exists somewhere in the middle. No matter how much the dominance of the sign/image demonstrates the influence of postmodernism, there are still certainties that govern many aspects of daily life—bills to be paid, decisions to be made, values to be upheld as true and right. Inside or outside of public relations, most people still seem to care about the modernist value of fairness and the modernist orientation toward measurable results. But certainly the encroachment of postmodernism into territory long dominated by modernism does create a degree of uncertainty and even vulnerability, to use Mumby's term, about communication.

Possible?

Trying to point out the practical value of a postmodern approach is also an inherently modernist (and therefore paradoxical) pursuit (Toth, 2002). And writing about it seems counter to postmodern commitments when the audience is a hierarchically organized academic field, the essay itself uses a highly structured documentation system, and the whole process acknowledges a metanarrative in which the production and dissemination of ideas is valued. Yet at the same time, Mumby (1997) argues that "far from marginalizing communication as a human activity, postmodernism contributes to a more insightful understanding of the processes through which communication, identity, and power intersect" (p. 23). Perhaps there is hope for this endeavor. But because postmodernism coexists with many commitments of modernism, this chapter will proceed to (modernistically) explore the nature of postmodernism and two applications of it in public relations. It is also in this spirit that this chapter will help readers make sense of public relations practices that seem nonrational and perhaps even counterproductive. While it is possible that some readers might someday employ outlaw strategies of public relations, it is even more likely that readers might someday be on the observing or receiving end of outlaw discourse and have to understand and respond to it.

An additional problem for seeing public relations through a postmodern lens is that traditional public relations takes a very modernist approach (Gower, 2006; Holtzhausen, 2000; Holtzhausen & Voto, 2002), illustrated plainly in the models and theories that lead the practice of public relations toward the ideals of measurable objectives, two-way communication, and clear ethical judgments. If postmodernism rejects consensus as a worthy goal (Lyotard, 1979/1984), then building mutually beneficial relationships with publics seems anachronistic. So why take on the project of trying to understand public relations from a postmodern perspective (or vice versa)?

One recent work frames the practice of public relations in terms more consistent with the commitments of postmodernity. Brown (2006) proposes a non-hierarchical and sometimes overlapping approach to public relations as cultural styles, reflecting a postmodern frame that allows for "both/and" classifications of public relations. Instead of assessing the quality of the different frames, he simply presents them as different alternatives to the practice of public relations, similar to postmodernism's embrace of different and sometimes conflicting worldviews. His activist public relations, oratorical public relations, narrative public relations, and performance public relations models each connect classical antecedents to contemporary enactments, providing a view of public relations that allows for some of the uncertainty and paradox accompanying postmodernism.

Necessary?

Toth (2002), admitting the paradoxical nature of her request, nevertheless calls for postmodern approaches to public relations that have practical significance. Holtzhausen (2000) and Gower (2006) join in the call for an examination of how postmodern theories can help scholars and practitioners. Holtzhausen sees the need for postmodern approaches as particularly pressing because of public relations' traditional role in "the maintenance of metanarratives and domination in society" (p. 100), priorities which fly in the face of the postmodern condition that is, at least to some extent, now a part of everyday communication. She suggests public relations in which practitioners recognize the politics inherent in their public relations and are direct about their (lack of) objectivity. Scholars can join practitioners in adapting to postmodernism by "being critical and by exposing the irony and contradictions of public relations practice" (p. 111). One way that irony and contradictions can be exposed is through identifying them, and another is actually violating the norms that they highlight—one of the common tactics employed in outlaw discourse.

Outlaw Discourse as Postmodern Public Relations

"Outlaw discourse" is not the only label applied to unconventional or unacceptable forms of public relations. Berger and Reber (2006) write about "unsanctioned influence tactics" they call "Omega approaches" to public relations (p. 152). Unlike the generally external focus of outlaw actors, however, Berger and Reber's quasi-outlaws are public relations professionals working to exercise influence within their own organizations. In this situation, "leaking information is the most controversial and complex unsanctioned influence tactic in the public relations field" (p. 167). As the examples and brief cases to follow will illustrate, outlaw discourse takes "unsanctioned" public relations tactics much further.

Let us be clear that "outlaw discourse" and "activist discourse" (in the conventional sense or in Brown's [2006] sense) are not synonymous. As the following section will explain, outlaw discourse is not composed simply of counterarguments or oppositions, but of tactics that reflect different ways of thinking; they espouse what might be seen as a "third option" in a controversy—not a compromise, but an alternative logic or way of approaching the problem that might seem simply disruptive or rude, lacking the clear kind of clash upon which traditional argument depends. When Coombs (1998) describes the activities of Greenpeace, for instance, he is clearly describing activist public relations: "For instance, Greenpeace might push for new regulation on chemical discharges into the air while simultaneously asking companies to voluntarily implement lower discharge levels" (p. 290). This kind of direct clash ("Reduce your air pollution; change your organizational policy") is not indicative of outlaw discourse, which might instead create a funny YouTube video of the company choking on its own fumes, sabotage company operations in some way, or (seemingly tangentially) accost company executives about personal problems. And so Greenpeace, as Coombs describes a typical action, is definitely activist, but not outlaw.

Outlaw groups come in all shapes and sizes. Some may be laudably democratic and some manipulative and undemocratic, but both engage in public relations that requires attention (Gower, 2006) and critical thought. As Brown (2006) observed, "it is no longer useful to insist that everything we disapprove must be excluded from our conception of public relations" (p. 211). Countering the modernist emphasis on progress, a student of postmodern public relations must embrace the "both/

and" possibilities of public relations battles, even those involving actors that might be described as unsavory. Outlaw discourse is a concept that illuminates these complex relationships, particularly as they apply to activist public relations.

So why do organizations turn to outlaw approaches to activism that reflect postmodern values and priorities (such as they are)? The concept of outlaw discourse draws from Goodnight's (1982) description of discourse that "overturns" societal norms and assumptions. Ono and Sloop (2002) classify and analyze discourse on a normative continuum, ranging from dominant discourse (which fosters political, cultural, and social norms, and maintains the most commonly accepted norms and behaviors, typical of many public relations efforts) to outlaw discourse (which challenges the political, cultural, and social norms of a system). The term "outlaw" has been used in the literature to describe either a group or an individual that breaks the rules of the dominant system and refuses to act in accordance with the normative assumptions of his or her system (e.g., Boyd, 2002; Doxtader, 2000; Ono & Sloop, 2002; Sloop & Ono, 1997). Outlaw discourse employs a logic that, when translated into the dominant system, is deemed illogical, immoral, or illegal. The groups and individuals who enact outlaw discourse have either been positioned or have positioned themselves outside of what is viewed as normal or rational. Sloop and Ono (1997) point out that no one is always entirely in or out of the law, because actors constantly work together to construct social discourse and, at the same time, be defined by that discourse.

For Sloop and Ono (1997), outlaw discourse is a set of loosely shared logics of justice, ideas of right and wrong that are different from a culture's dominant logics of judgment. Boyd (2002) adds that outlaw discourse intentionally flaunts conventional standards. It is important to point out, though, that "outlaw discourses are not simple inversions of dominant discourses; they do not refute or counter dominant positions; rather, they are discourses outside the logics of dominant ones" (Ono & Sloop, 2002, p. 15). Since they are not simple inversions of dominant discourse, "there can be, and indeed are, multiple outlaw discourses" (p. 142).

Outlaw discourse provides an opportunity for public relations scholars to explore the ways in which changing societal norms and assumptions shape public discourse as some ideas are accepted and others are marginalized, particularly in the context of activist efforts to challenge dominant organizations. Outlaw discourse provides an explanation for those activist voices that are subaltern, or outside what is typically normal and acceptable for public dialogue. For practitioners, outlaw discourse presents a challenge to understand these voices; outlaw discourse reflects some sort of disenfranchisement. As such, it should alert practitioners to work harder to gain understanding of these publics and their rationales for their seemingly irrational logics.

By studying outlaw discourse, public relations critics expose and call attention to voices that fall outside of society's norms and assumptions about what is good, fair, and sometimes even lawful. Goodnight (1982) said that studying the practices of personal, public, and technical spheres of argument is one useful way of identifying society's assumptions and beliefs related to argumentation and discourse. As Boyd (2002) found in a study of an activist group's opposition to Procter & Gamble's fat substitute olestra, outlaw discourse in regulatory controversy intentionally disregards the personal/public/technical standards of argument in order to disrupt the modernist march of progress.

Though Goodnight (1982) certainly advocates adherence to the different knowledge standards of the different spheres, he also acknowledges the possibility of strategically violating the dictates of the spheres. He writes that

> an arguer can accept the sanctioned, widely used bundle of rules, claims, procedures and evidence to wage a dispute. Or, the arguer can inveigh against any or all of these "customs" in order to bring forth a new variety of understanding. (p. 217)

The idea that a public relations campaign could strategically ignore publics' norms and expectations clearly flies in the face of the modernist "universal audience" advocated by Perelman and Olbrechts-Tyteca (1958/1969). Again, this shift is consistent with postmodern thinking as illustrated by Lyotard's (1979/1984) localized audience. Adhering to the self-consciously marginalized character of the "outlaw," Holtzhausen and Voto (2002) affirm that postmodern PR involves ethics that emphasize "the situational and local nature of ethical decision making" (p. 77), the kind of localized ethics that can lead to outlaw logics perceived as immoral and unethical by those outside that decision-making process (i.e., outsiders viewing the results of the activism).

There is no limit to the disruptive, transgressive forms outlaw discourse can assume. Part of its postmodern character means that its components cannot be comprehensively included or excluded—situational requirements will affect the kind of "outlaw" an organizational actor might choose to be. Boyd (2002) suggests at least two specific incarnations of outlaw discourse, however: objection and counteranalysis. Outlaw objection strategies are used to question the methods and assumptions of the dominant system, but not their conclusions directly. Counteranalysis, on the other hand, happens when one side in a debate cannot meet the standards of argumentation within that sphere, so that party presents an alternative to the accepted logics and conclusions of their opponent. The two parties within this argument are in starkly different power positions, with the less powerful party acting according to logics that are considered irrational or abnormal by the more powerful party. Boyd says that outlaw discourse is necessary and even invited in some cases when the standards for argument are not flexible enough to accommodate dissent and may leave no other place for dissent other than outside the previously established norms and logics of argumentation—this provides another glimpse of the motivation and explanation of outlaw discourses.

An activist group's outlaw discourse can be enacted in several different ways. It might mean that the group chooses not to participate in "official" forums for expressing dissent. It might also mean that the group participates in these forums, but not in conventionally acceptable ways (e.g., making superficial claims or attacks without evidence; using inappropriate language or wearing inappropriate clothes). It might even mean choosing new media not controlled by dominant organizations or ideologies in order to spread a message of counteranalysis or objection without being subject to the control of organizations and systems being protested (e.g., outside the control of Bagdikian's (2004) "media monopoly" corporations).

Ono and Sloop (2002) argue that once outlaw discourse does enter the public sphere (such as it is), it faces three possible fates: First, it can become popularized and lead to social change. Second, if the argument of the outlaw discourse is fairly conventional or something that poses little threat to social norms, it might simply become part of the dominant discourse and lose what little is resistant and challenging about it. Finally, it might remain an outlaw discourse, unacceptable and unaccepted, but that means that it "never becomes part of the larger civic discourse and is, in a sense, remarginalized" (p. 18). Ono and Sloop (2002) believe that only the first outcome is worthwhile: "a successful outlaw logic must change the way normative judgments are made" (p. 143). While an interest in "outcomes" may seem counterintuitive, remember that outlaw discourse is not devoid of goals or logics; rather, its goals and logics emanate from a localized community of like-minded thinkers whose perspective may be drastically different from the perspective of larger and more powerful publics and organizations.

Outlaw discourse has taken many forms for both individuals and groups (Sloop & Ono, 1997). In one study, outlaw activists emerged in media coverage of the immigration issue of California's Proposition 187, which proposed preventing undocumented immigrants from receiving medical care and education in the United States (Ono & Sloop, 2002). The outlaw voices, present in both traditional and new media, "problematize[d] fixed binaries between citizen/immigrant and between legal/illegal immigrant" (p. 159), and brought about "noncompliance resolutions of K-12 school boards as well as University of California campuses and faculty [who refused] to accept legitimacy of the government to enact or rule on Proposition 187" (p. 159). Ono and Sloop conclude that the various strategies by which outlaw discourse reconfigures immigration do indeed present productive counter-logics to the binary character of the dominant immigration discourse. Their conclusion, then, is that not only is this outlaw discourse different, but (assessed modernistically) even a useful contribution to public discussions.

Further extending the reach of outlaw discourse, Boyd (2002) uses Sloop and Ono's conceptualization of outlaw discourse to analyze the controversy surrounding the FDA's approval hearings for the P&G fat substitute olestra (brand name Olean). The outlaw in this case is a more established activist group, the Center for Science in the Public Interest (CSPI). It enacted outlaw discourse by refusing to follow the highly structured rules of the technical sphere and challenging the assumptions of the dominant regulatory system. When P&G brought olestra before the FDA's Food Advisory Committee, CSPI was there to object. Granted a six-month extension to find scientific evidence of olestra's potential harm, CSPI returned six months later with . . . nothing. CSPI not only violated, but intentionally ignored the carefully defined (modernist) standards of the FDA's technical sphere. Though unsuccessful in causing the FDA to deny the petition, CSPI did alienate FDA officials (by traditional standards an undesirable result); the organization received a special unflattering mention in the FDA's final rule. But despite losing this battle, CSPI's outlaw discourse could be argued to have won the war. Olestra won regulatory approval in the technical sphere, but meanwhile CSPI had been making the same allegations of olestra's danger in the public sphere—a sphere with lower standards of evidence and plenty of reporters hungry for stories.

Perhaps not coincidentally, olestra limped through regulatory approval and to market, but never became the juggernaut product for which Procter & Gamble had hoped, forever linked (due to CSPI's outlaw rule-breaking) to terms like "anal leakage" and "fecal urgency" (Boyd, 2002). The public relations consequences of CSPI's outlaw tactics can actually be found in a public relations journal article. Two years after FDA approval, Worley (2000) asked rhetorically, "Was the publicity surrounding the WOW! potato-chips (which introduced us to Olean) an example of 'good' public relations because it spurred tremendous sales in the product despite the fact that it made many people sick?" (p. 376) Worley clearly accepted CSPI's outlaw message, both parts of which are false—olestra generated only small sales, and CSPI never provided evidence more recent than the mid-1970s to show any ill effects of the additive. In fact, a modernist judgment of the different logics involved in this debate would point out that a double-blind study with over 1000 subjects actually found that people reported more negative digestive side effects after eating full-fat potato chips than they did after eating chips made with olestra (Cheskin, Miday, Zorich, & Filloon, 1998).

In examining the case as an illustration of an organization pushed to outlaw discourse, Boyd (2002) argued that because the FDA operates in such a tightly bounded technical sphere, any group lacking the resources to make offers of proof that meet the requirements of that sphere must rely upon outlaw discourse even to interrupt the FDA approval process. As in Ono and Sloop's (2002) example, this outlaw discourse created a consequential "other" logic; in this case, an outlaw rhetor broke with the dominant norms of the appropriate sphere and called attention to the narrow standards of argumentation that were accepted in that system. And so olestra provides another explanation for why outlaw discourse exists.

The objection strategy of interruption employed by CSPI is only one implement in the outlaw toolkit. Another way outlaws might resist dominant organizations is by prioritizing dissymmetry and dissensus (Holtzhausen, 2000), operations in stark contrast to public relations' traditional emphasis on cooperation and consensus as telos. In terms of power relations, outlaw discourse depends on exactly this kind of dissent and dissymmetry—what Mumby (1997) calls "transgressive style" (p. 19). In a scholarly context that illustrates the potential for activism even within organizations (as Holtzhausen and Voto [2002] advocate), he offers the controversial article by Blair, Brown, and Baxter (1994) published in *Quarterly Journal of Speech*. In it, the authors make public anonymous reviews they received on a journal submission, reviews that they argued revealed a masculinist bias in the scholarly review process. Turning the tables and putting the reviewers' words under public scrutiny definitely violated expectations and interfered with expectations regarding who could influence whom. Mumby's explanation of the postmodern character of the article seems to correspond directly to the character of outlaw discourse: "Not only does the article violate normal conventions of academic writing through its self-reflexive structure, but it also invokes a stark reversal of the normalized power relations characteristic of academia" (Mumby, 1997, p. 19). By laying bare the review process in scholarly journals, this article achieves what outlaw discourse often achieves in the hands of activists: a pulling back of the curtain to reveal domination that was concealed or unknown to relevant publics.

The Ultimate Outlaw Discourse: Terrorism

Brown (2006) observes that "in the war for public opinion, some of our era's theatricality has crossed the boundary from special effects to horrific ones" (p. 211). Nowhere is this horrible extreme of outlaw discourse more evident than in the case of terrorism. Acts of terror attack publics' consciousness by favoring "awe over evidence" (Brown, 2006, p. 211), relying on what Picard (1989) described as the "propaganda of the deed"—"the violent terrorist act itself conveys messages that the terrorists are effective, that they must be feared, and that they must be taken seriously" (p. 12). Anyone who has passed through airport security or attempted to engage in any number of everyday activities now closely scrutinized since 9/11 recognizes that terrorists are being taken seriously as a consequence of their outlaw discourse. Richards (2004) echoes this perspective on the terrorist act as public relations in claiming that "the purpose of the theatrical element of terror is to have impact, to shape the political climate" (p. 171). Perhaps in the case of the Unabomber and his distinctive mode of attire, some of the lasting impact is incidental; in cases such as 9/11, however, terrorism "seeks spectacular impact; it constructs an audience that is awestruck, whether in fear or admiration" (p. 175). Rada (1985), though claiming a distinction between public relations and terrorism because of differing attitudes about social responsibility, acknowledges the shared goals of public relations and terrorism: "commanding attention, delivering a message, and influencing opinion" (p. 26).

Though terrorism has employed what today might be called "outlaw" tactics since long before the existence of the term "postmodernism" (e.g., the Boston Tea Party or John Brown's raids), the logics behind such acts seem to have drifted even farther from simple modernist explanations (e.g., "Reduce taxes in the colonies" or "Abolish slavery"). Even as recently as the 1970s, a time to which Picard (1989) and Rada (1985) responded, the performance public relations of terrorist "outlaws," though offensive and illegal to most publics, still had relatively linear aims. Hijackers threatened to blow up airliners unless they were taken to Cuba or destinations in the Middle East. Hostages were offered their freedom in exchange for the freedom of political prisoners. In contrast, what would be a modernist explanation for the 9/11 attacks? Or ongoing suicide bombings in Iraq? Though outlaws may well have existed at some level for centuries, a postmodern perspective is an increasingly useful tool for making sense of outlaw discourses' subaltern publics and their logics. And terrorists, whatever the localized logics for their acts, reflect the outlaw attitude that no legitimate, powerful rhetorical action is available to them in traditional types of argument.

The deadly results of terrorism make it no less important to study as an outlaw discourse that is a postmodern application of public relations. If anything, the consequences of terrorism make understanding it and how it operates as public relations of paramount importance. Picard (1989) observes that larger, more established groups with terrorist affiliations use more traditional public relations tactics, such as press conferences, press releases, and interviews, in addition to their outlaw acts. Small groups even farther outside the mainstream, however, are more likely to depend only on tactics such as the "propaganda of the deed" and the forced publication of manifestos. Whether traditional or not, however, the message of terror is outside the realm of what is traditionally acceptable for persuasion. Coercion by force or threat of force is clearly an application of outlaw discourse, and just as clearly has a public relations impact, as Richards (2004) notes, by combining crime, politics, and theatre.

A Lighter Case Study: *The Wittenburg Door*[2]

Not all outlaw discourse is a life-and-death matter. One lighter instance of outlaw discourse can be found in *The Wittenburg Door*, the self-proclaimed "world's pretty much only religious satire magazine." Alluding to Martin Luther's 95 theses nailed to the door of the Wittenberg church, the magazine's motto is "still nailing it to the church." Published by Christians, the magazine nevertheless eschews traditional arguments about various elements of Christian practice in favor of a boundary-crossing, taboo-breaking outlaw discourse that aims to enlighten as it offends. It has designated Buffy the Vampire Slayer as "Theologian of the Year," and designated such notables as televangelist Pat Robertson, Santa Claus, and even Mother Teresa "Losers." It blasted a book titled *Killed Cartoons: Casualties from the War on Free Expression* for ironically refusing to publish a cartoon, and went ahead and published it in *The Wittenburg Door*.[3] In one recent issue, the magazine published a fake interview with Christian family authority James Dobson—and it does not make Dobson look good (Briggs, 2007).

The goals of *The Door*, due to the splintered nature of Christian faith traditions, are daunting: to bring about "course corrections" and to point out hypocrisy in "ANY religious persuasion" ("About," 2007). If the magazine addressed these goals conventionally, they would have to gain influence in unnumbered religious institutions. They would then have to press their positions through various different ecclesiastical structures and traditions. Without such power, and with a humorous tone that might well be deemed sacrilegious, *The Door*'s conventional public relations options are limited. It could certainly issue press releases and create a non-profit foundation (likely with limited attention or influence), but instead, it has taken on the mantle of outlaw, taking private and internal religious matters public with satire that takes on a whole herd of sacred cows and needs not stay within the constraints of any particular convention or logic.

The magazine is very self-reflexive about its mission and its status as outsider: "You've heard us say it before: Satire is lining up 100 sacred cows and shooting them all with a machine gun. Whichever one yelps the loudest, you shoot 10 more times" (Darden, 2005). This statement was followed by a summary of recent complaint letters which would naturally lead to more satire directed at the same targets. But Darden acknowledges that shooting sacred cows has had only limited effectiveness:

> We've failed in virtually everything we've attempted over the past 200 issues.
> We've failed in virtually every cause we've championed.
> We've failed in our numerous attempts at relevancy.

We've failed in our numerous attempts at solvency.

We've failed because some of the articles we've published were published for the wrong reasons.

We've failed because we rejected some of the articles we should have published.

. . . No joke. What's better now than it was when *The Wittenburg Door* started 200 issues ago? We haven't changed a thing. At least America was in the midst of the so-called "Jesus Movement" back then. Today it is in the death throes of the Evangelical Church. The sacred has been replaced by a powerful heresy that equates political power with righteousness; simple, easy answers now substitute for hard-won truth; idol worship now masquerades as true devotion.

Despite these "failures," however, *The Wittenburg Door* continues to shoot sacred cows and generate numerous subscriber cancellations each month, all part of an outlaw plan to tear down idols taking the place of true faith. As Darden adds, "when it comes to making a change in the Status Quo, about all that's left to us *is* satire and humor. It's a cheap—but dangerous—weapon" (italics in original). Irony. Violating norms. Shooting sacred cows. Operating from the margins. Being a little bit dangerous. *The Wittenburg Door* exemplifies a postmodern approach to problematizing church traditions, and it does so with the tool of outlaw discourse.

Implications for Public Relations Theory and Practice

Outlaw discourse opens a window on public relations that shows how activists operating at the margins of acceptable public dialogue have adapted to and adopted communication styles in ways that defy convention but can be understood through a postmodern lens. For scholars and mainstream practitioners, the notion of "outlaw discourse" provides an explanation for activism that doesn't seem to fit traditional conceptualizations of public relations and what it means to manage relationships with publics. For activists lacking power and legitimacy, outlaw discourse provides, if not a quick fix, at least a high-risk, potentially high-reward opportunity to take advantage of changes in the practice of communication in the twenty-first century.

Mumby (1997) admits uneasiness about the occasional excesses of postmodernism, with its extremes of relativism and self-indulgence, and we share these concerns. And indeed, both activists and scholars can fall prey to these excesses. A number of years ago, one of us witnessed a professorial candidate talk about how destruction of property might be an acceptable way to gain attention for a cause. This approach certainly fits the general parameters of outlaw discourse, but we believe many public relations scholars would be uncomfortable teaching it as an appropriate tactic (the candidate was not hired). Even farther out on the margins of activism (if we use a modernist visual-spatial sort of modeling), racist speech and action or terrorism, as described above, certainly qualify as "outlaw discourse" but bring with them consequences deemed unacceptable by most publics. So "outlaw discourse" needs to be seen as a postmodern turn in public relations activism, with the caveat that, like the rest of postmodernism, it can (even as it purposefully transgresses norms and rules) be taken to extremes about which public relations scholars and practitioners may be justifiably uneasy. Rather than breaking through the strictures of convention in order to open up conversation among publics (its utopian conceptualization), it can create harm. From that harm, however, students of public relations with a more modernist orientation can still find productive applications by examining that outlaw discourse to understand marginalized publics and their perceived helplessness.

In addition to recognizing the blurred line between constructiveness and destructiveness that outlaw discourse straddles, public relations scholars also need to expound upon what kinds of organizations and people can employ outlaw public relations. The examples mentioned in this chapter all come from non-corporate organizations with varying degrees of structure. What other outlaws might play a role in contemporary public relations? Can corporations be outlaws (Hagedorn, 2006)? Can minority party or third-party politicians who actually get elected? Or does positioning within a hierarchy automatically exclude a public relations actor from the possibility of acting as (or being recognized as) an outlaw? Because corporations are generally within dominant hierarchies and power structures, however, the question of whether it is even possible for a corporation to be an "outlaw" is an open one. Perhaps future work on postmodern public relations will take up the question of exactly who can enact true outlaw speech.

It seems that activist public relations will continue to confound conventional expectations for public relations. So various online and offline media will continue to provide attention to anti-corporate Internet-circulated video (video is, after all, postmodernism's most distinctive new medium [Jameson, 1991]). Lonely satirists will continue executing sacred cows. Osama bin Laden may continue to air his grainy desert home videos. Sweatshop protestors will employ unconventional, irrational, seemingly counterproductive acts. But as these unconventional, seemingly disconnected examples of activism will persist, they will challenge and violate norms of public relations practice, demonstrating the need for public relations observers and practitioners to borrow a postmodern lens to make sense of it all. The concept of outlaw discourse provides one promising point of entry for a discussion of the implications of the postmodern condition on the study and practice of public relations.

Notes

1 Sloop and Ono (1997) originally spelled the word "outlaw" with a hyphen, but in their more recent work on the subject (Ono & Sloop, 2002) they removed the hyphen. Consequently, except in the reference list (where references will use their exact original forms), "outlaw" will be unhyphenated in this piece.

2 Yes, "Wittenburg" is misspelled in the title. In the magazine's typical irreverent style, it has carried forward a misspelling from the publication's early days as a self-referential type of self-deprecation.

3 The cartoon mixes WWJD (What would Jesus do?) with WMDs (Weapons of Mass Destruction) to come up with What Would Mohammed Drive? (WWMD),

featuring an Islamist driving a Ryder truck carrying a nuclear weapon. The cartoon is available at http://www.wittenburgdoor.com/archives/loser212.html

References

About the Wittenburg Door. (1997). *The Wittenburg Door* online. Retrieved September 25, 2007, from: http://www.wittenburgdoor.com/about_the_door.html

Bagdikian, B. H. (2004). *The new media monopoly.* Boston: Beacon Press.

Berger, B. K., & Reber, B. H. (2006). *Gaining influence in public relations: The role of resistance in practice.* Mahwah, NJ: Lawrence Erlbaum.

Blair, C., Brown, J. R., & Baxter, L. A. (1994). Disciplining the feminine. *Quarterly Journal of Speech, 80,* 383–409.

Boyd, J. (2002). Public and technical interdependence: Regulatory controversy, out-law discourse, and the messy case of olestra. *Argumentation and Advocacy, 39,* 91–109.

Briggs, J. B. (2007, July/August). James Dobson teaches Luke 14:26. *The Wittenburg Door,* no. 212, pp. 10–11.

Brown, R. E. (2006). Myth of symmetry: Public relations as cultural styles. *Public Relations Review, 32*(3), 206–212.

Cheskin, L. J., Miday, R., Zorich, N., & Filloon, T. (1998, January 14). Gastrointestinal symptoms following consumption of olestra or regular triglyceride potato chips. *Journal of the American Medical Association, 279*(2): 150–152.

Coombs, W. T. (1998). The Internet as potential equalizer: New leverage for confronting social irresponsibility. *Public Relations Review, 24,* 289–303.

Darden, R. (2005, July/August). Special 200th anniversary loser: Us! *The Wittenburg Door,* no. 200. Retrieved Aug. 30, 2007, from: http://www.wittenburgdoor.com/archives/loser212.html

Doxtader, E. W. (2000). Characters in the middle of public life: Consensus, dissent, and ethos. *Philosophy and Rhetoric, 33*(4), 336–369.

Goodnight, G. T. (1982). The personal, technical, and public spheres of argument: A speculative inquiry into the art of public deliberation. *Journal of the American Forensic Association, 18,* 214–227.

Gower, K. K. (2006). Public relations research at the crossroads. *Journal of Public Relations Research, 18,* 177–190.

Hagedorn, S. C. (2006). Linking dissent, incivility, the trickster myth, and outlaw discourse: Exploring and expanding outlaw discourse. Unpublished doctoral dissertation, Purdue University, West Lafayette, IN.

Holtzhausen, D. R. (2000). Postmodern values in public relations. *Journal of Public Relations Research, 12,* 93–114.

Holtzhausen, D. R., & Voto, R. (2002). Resistance from the margins: The postmodern public relations practitioner as organizational activist. *Journal of Public Relations Research, 14,* 57–84.

Jameson, F. (1991). *Postmodernism, or, the cultural logic of late capitalism.* Durham, NC: Duke University Press.

Lyotard, J. (1984). *The postmodern condition: A report on knowledge* (G. Bennington & G. Massumi, Trans.). Minneapolis: University of Minnesota Press (original work published 1979).

Mumby, D. K. (1997). Modernism, postmodernism, and communication studies: A rereading of an ongoing debate. *Communication Theory, 7,* 1–28.

Ono, K. A., & Sloop, J. M. (2002). *Shifting borders.* Philadelphia: Temple University Press.

Ossinger, J. L. (2006, Feb. 13). The problem with parody. *Wall Street Journal,* R7.

Perelman, C., & Olbrechts-Tyteca, L. (1969). *The new rhetoric: A treatise on argumentation* (J. Wilkinson & P. Weaver, Trans.). Notre Dame, IN: University of Notre Dame Press (original work published 1958).

Picard, R. G. (1989). Press relations of terrorist organizations. *Public Relations Review, 15*(4), 12–23.

Prassel, F. R. (1993). *The great American outlaw.* Norman: University of Oklahoma Press.

Rada, S. E. (1985). Trans-national terrorism as public relations? *Public Relations Review, 11*(3), 26–33.

Richards, B. (2004). Terrorism and public relations. *Public Relations Review, 30,* 169–176.

Sloop, J. M., & Ono, K. A. (1997). Out-law discourse: The critical politics of material judgment. *Philosophy and Rhetoric, 30,* 50–69.

Spiridellis, G. (Director). (2005). Big box mart (video). Retrieved Aug. 7, 2007, from: http://www.jibjab.com

Stewart, J. (1991). A postmodern look at traditional communication postulates. *Western Journal of Speech Communication, 55,* 354–379.

Taylor, B. C. (2005). Postmodern theory. In S. May & D. K. Mumby (Eds.), *Engaging organizational communication theory and research: Multiple perspectives* (pp. 113–140). Thousand Oaks, CA: Sage.

Toth, E. L. (2002). Postmodernism for modernist public relations: The cash value and application of critical research in public relations. *Public Relations Review, 28,* 243–250.

Weiss, A. (1993). Causal stories, scientific information, and the ozone depletion controversy: Intrusive scenarios in the policy process. In T. Brante, S. Fuller, & W. Lynch (Eds.), *Controversial science: From content to contention* (pp. 225–240). Albany, NY: SUNY Press.

Worley, D. A. (2000). Public relations as postmodern: Reply to Margaret E. Duffy. *Critical Studies in Media Communication, 17,* 374–377.

18

DOCUMENTARY AS AN ACTIVIST MEDIUM
The Wal-Mart Movie

Ashli Quesinberry Stokes
University of North Carolina, Charlotte

Rachel L. Holloway
Virginia Tech

In his work, *Death of a Thousand Cuts*, Jarol B. Mannheim (2001) identified the "corporate campaign" as an increasing phenomenon in American business. Using the strategies and tactics developed in political campaigns, corporate campaigns are designed to undercut the relationship between a corporation and its key stakeholders—investors, customers, community leaders, and employees—in an effort to influence corporate practice. Corporate campaigns often attack the "very corporateness" of their targets (Mannheim, 2001). Fueled by the decline of organized labor in the late twentieth century and the rise of anti-corporate political and ideological sentiments, corporate campaigns (perhaps more appropriately called "anti-corporate campaigns") now draw on the knowledge and expertise of campaign professionals schooled in methods of research, financial analysis, media strategy, and grassroots activation. Public relations strategies once considered within the primary purview of corporations are now used by opponents to undercut a corporation's reputation and thereby move corporations toward change.

Few organizations in the United States represent "corporateness" more than the Wal-Mart Corporation. It employs 1.3 million people or roughly 1% of the American workforce and its sales are equal to 2.5% of the U.S. gross domestic product ("Hot Topic," 2005). Its Superstores dot the American landscape. Once primarily centered in the rural south of the United States, Wal-Mart expanded into urban centers in the north and west and into small towns across the Midwest. Given its sheer size and economic impact, it's not surprising that Wal-Mart is the target of organized attacks on multiple fronts, including labor and employment practices, economic impacts on small town America, and environmental consequences of its big box stores. Wake Up Wal-Mart, an advocacy group funded by the United Food and Commercial Workers, and Wal-Mart Watch, a group affiliated with the Service Employees International Union, organize activists to attack Wal-Mart's reputation. Experienced political campaign operatives from the presidential campaigns of John Kerry and Howard Dean lead the Washington, D.C.-based anti-Wal-Mart groups, applying everything learned about the Internet and grassroots organizing in presidential campaigns to an ongoing effort to change Wal-Mart.

In 2005, anti-Wal-Mart activists received a boost from a different kind of advocacy professional—documentary filmmaker Robert Greenwald. Known for his previous efforts attacking Fox News and the Bush Administration's justification for the war in Iraq, Greenwald's production company, Brave New Films, released the documentary, *Wal-Mart: The High Cost of Low Price* in November 2005. Greenwald partnered with more than 150 churches, issue organizations, unions, and progressive political organizations, including Moveon.org, to organize film screenings in more than 7000 locations across the country (Smith, 2005). The film also received extensive national and international media coverage upon its release. Integrating best practices of movie publicity with grassroots organization and the power of narrative persuasion, the film exemplifies a new tactic available to organizations with a primary purpose of challenging institutionalized power.

The symbolic struggle to define Wal-Mart in its political, social, and economic context exemplifies the contemporary "wrangle of the marketplace"(see chapter 2). Increasingly, the exchange of ideas, opinions, and values is an organizational dialogue (Crable, 1990). Issue advocacy organizations and activists engage the institutionalized voices of corporations and government in competition for supporters. The organizations not only propose an interpretation of reality, but also work to build constituencies through creation of positive shared identifications. Wal-Mart needs satisfied customers, productive and loyal Wal-Mart associates, and supportive local government officials, among others. Anti-Wal-Mart organizers seek the opposite. They want individuals to identify *as* "anti-Wal-Mart" and then to act on the basis of that shared identity.

The purpose of this chapter is to explore digital cinema as a means to constitute an activist public in opposition to an issue or organization. The power of video to create shared identity is not new to corporate public relations. Videos and television advertising are standard approaches for building organizational identification with employees, investors, and consumers. Activists traditionally have struggled to gain access and influence equal to their corporate opponents, due to their marginalized status and limited financial and human resources. Relatively inexpensive new communication technologies, however, create new opportunities for both organization and influence (Coombs, 1998; Heath, 1998; Taylor, Kent, & White, 2001). Digital cameras, relatively inexpensive editing software available for home computers, and cheap DVDs combined with the power of the Internet open the realm of digital cinema to activist organizations.

Using *Wal-Mart: The High Cost of Low Price* as the exemplar, we employ Whiteman's (2004) coalitional model of documentary film to demonstrate how both the documentary form and its content invite participation in the anti-Wal-Mart movement. We draw also on a constitutive theoretical framework that conceptualizes how audiences may come to view themselves as possessing the identity of an anti-Wal-Mart activist as a result of participating in and with the documentary. Using the rhetorical strategies of *cohortatio*, which amplifies viewer indignation, identification, which creates common ground among viewers, and enactment, which helps viewers take action, we analyze how activists employed the film to constitute an anti-Wal-Mart identity. That is, they helped frame, form, and determine the variety of ways viewers could collectively express and unite over their disapproval of the Wal-Mart corporation. On a tactical level, new media such as digital cinema and the Web give activists more methods to constitute anti-corporate identities outside traditional media channels. This constitutive approach to understanding how public relations publics are created also goes beyond a tactical purpose. We note also how constitutive theoretical frameworks have implications in determining and establishing standards of public relations practice. In terms of broader public relations practice, the types of constitutive challenges seen in the Wal-Mart movie prompt similar responses from those who they attack, both in message and media. After analysis of the medium and its message, we discuss the implications for documentary in modern public relations.

Independent Documentary Film, Coalition Building, and Constituting Activist Identity

Studies exploring the potential for film, video, or television to influence political attitudes and beliefs are central to the study of media effects. While research on political campaign advertising, candidate political videos, issue advertising, and other video forms is extensive, few studies have focused on the impact of video outside election campaigns, or more specifically the influence of documentaries on public opinion. Whiteman (2004) noted that studies that report positive effects investigated a broader sense of impact. In his analysis of Feldman and Sigleman's (1985) study of the made-for-television film *The Day After* and Lenart and McGraw's (1989) study of the impact of the television broadcast, *Amerika*, Whiteman (2004) noted that both studies highlight the context of the viewing, the influence of interpersonal discussion surrounding the viewing, and media coverage of the films.

On this basis, Whiteman (2004) proposed a coalition model of political impact for documentary film and video. His coalitional model includes three contextual factors. First, he considered the entire filmmaking process, including production and distribution, as an element of the film's potential impact. He also extended the model to include the larger political context, including the activists and elites associated with issues raised in the film. He also called for "a more extensive range of effects," including "community activists using screenings as a tool to produce changes in local communities or elites taking action on an issue raised by a film" (Whiteman, 2004, p. 54). Finally, he considered the film's discourse as "discourse outside the mainstream," an alternative sphere of discourse through which activists might be educated and mobilized outside of typical communication channels.

Whiteman's model of documentary as a form of political activism is enhanced by viewing the film's various forms of influence through a constitutive theoretical lens. The Wal-Mart movie goes beyond creating traditional constituencies of activist publics to create a multivocal discursive space. Although it does not really offer any "new" critiques about Wal-Mart and its practices, the movie and its supporting website create a "place" where all types of people can express their grievances and encourage a dialogue about Wal-Mart. As a result, the Wal-Mart movie can be seen as both reaffirming and creating new types of activist identity as well as reconstituting new types of activist public relations practice.

To illustrate how the movie's content, production, and distribution builds an anti-Wal-Mart identity that cuts across various social and class lines, we draw on Charland's (1987) constitutive rhetorical theory that argues that a person's identity is shaped through persuasion. Rhetoric calls subjects into being by reframing their worlds and providing them with a new collective understanding of themselves and their identities. Constitutive rhetoric facilitates the development of a more activist identity because it does more than address people; it attempts to remake them by replacing one reality with another. By telling a story that is generalizable to a broad group of people, viewers can become identified with a larger activist community. For Charland (1987), constitutive rhetorical narratives create three ideological effects that hasten the development of activist community. Activist stories create a collective subject, position it toward taking action because people believe in the transhistorical nature of their identities, and resolve contradictions arising from different subject positions. That is, by participating in a collective identity, the tensions and differences between activists can become masked (Charland, 1987). Although subjects face challenges from other subject positions vying for their acceptance, constituted subjects have a history, motives, and a telos, or end (Charland, 1987). As a result, the movie enacts a collective subject position that deflects other appeals for viewer attention and efforts and unifies their disparate histories, motives, and desire for solutions into a more unified front.

In terms of broader constitutive implications, documentary has an important generative function. Activists can use a documentary to "create a public space within which citizens and decision makers can encounter, discuss, and decide to act on the issues raised" (Whiteman, 2004, p. 66). The impact of the documentary depends on the number of groups involved, their resources, and the creativity and aggressiveness groups use in reaching audiences (Whiteman, 2004, p. 66). Even with these constraints, documentary helps create a public space for the discussion of issues, stimulating social change (Whiteman, 2004). It also helps activist groups "develop and sustain an alternative public discourse that will both mobilize their supporters and challenge the dominant discourse" (Whiteman, 2004, p. 55). A documentary's constitutive potential expands exponentially when combined with discursive spaces on the Internet. A constitutive perspective also highlights the notion that types of communicative activities can influence others to adopt the same practices. Even as we communicate to win resources, our rhetorical choices collectively establish norms that govern communicative practice (Burke, 1950; Charland, 1987; Giddens, 1984; Stein, 2002). That is, we may achieve our communicative goals, but in the process, these goals are often unintentionally surpassed and influence future discourse. Jasinski (1998), for example, argued that communication achieves instrumental goals but also shapes "a culture's experience of time and space, the norms of political culture and the experience of communal existence (including collective identity), and the linguistic resources of the culture" (p. 75). Communicators shape culture through the success or, occasionally, failure of their efforts. In other words, what counts as good communication is often developed through what is accepted as good communication. For example, because Metabolife, a diet drug manufacturer, employed a preemptive communication strategy to deflect newsmagazine criticism, future targets of newsmagazine exposés may use a similar strategy in an attempt to avoid critique (Stokes, 2005). Likewise, Howard Dean's unprecedented success with online political organizing in his presidential bid in 2004 established new standards for political campaign communication on the Internet.

The Wal-Mart movie and ones like it can also direct audience thinking about organizations. A constitutive approach looks at how the movie shapes general activist discursive activity by framing our perceptions of, as well as our discussions and expectations about, activism. Such films help populate our culture with messages that encourage certain meanings over others. Repeated use of a particular idiom allows people to conceive of events in a particular way (Jasinski, 1997, 1998). For example, if public relations experts influence the media to discuss "corporate downsizing," rather than "firing," then the media text encourages audiences to conceive of corporate policies in this way (Stokes, 2005). We illustrate how the Wal-Mart movie helps to influence these activist communication patterns and strategies. Whether intentionally or not, the movie's rhetorical choices shape expectations for audience members confronted with the opportunity to organize against Wal-Mart and for those activists facing similar challenges. We first discuss broadly how the film can serve a generative function in activist public relations activity. We then detail how the movie cultivates an activist identity through the use of the rhetorical strategies of *cohortatio*, identification, and enactment. Finally, we note the larger implications of digital technology in producing new opportunities and challenges in public relations practice.

Constituting an Activist Public through Collaborative Production

The unique production and distribution model of *Wal-Mart: The High Cost of Low Price* demonstrates the impact of cinema beyond individual effects on individual viewers. Unlike other recent documentaries like *Supersize Me* and *An Inconvenient Truth*, for example, Greenwald and Brave New Films engaged existing networks of activists and expanded the networks through strategies that tapped into the alternative sphere of discourse made possible through digital technology. In fact, Greenwald opened up the process of filmmaking to build the anti-Wal-Mart coalition from the earliest stages of the film's production. Although these other documentary films certainly share an activist viewpoint, Greenwald's film is unique in terms of collaborating with activists in order to create the film itself.

A visit to the website devoted to *Wal-Mart: The High Cost of Low Price* (Wal-Martmovie.com) reveals the constitutive production strategy used to create the Wal-Mart movie. Under "Meet the Wal-Mart Movie Team," the website lists producers, co-producers, editors, and the other standard roles expected in the credits of any film. What is unusual is the team of 850 volunteer field producers who assisted in the movie's creation. Field producers for Brave New Films are activist-producers. They conduct research, shoot video, raise awareness, and assist with distribution (Brown, 2006). Greenwald credits one "Super Field Producer" with driving 40 miles to get a shot of a Wal-Mart at night in the rain (Brown, 2006). Greenwald also allowed field producers to remix the movie after release, incorporating their own footage back into the film, creating an even stronger sense of involvement and creating a local angle for screenings sponsored by field producers ("Filmmaker Lures Shoppers," 2005). Activists named the film through online voting at the movie website. Greenwald explained his approach: "the way I look at it is, it's a conversation. It's interactive, so it's not preaching and it's not a speech" (Brown, 2006, p. 37). Recall that in constitutive terms, activists develop a history, common motives, and a telos, or end they seek. The film's production process facilitates the constitutive process. Activists are part of the movie's history; they have their own personal story to tell. They work together with the film's creator to create a compelling attack on the corporation. They become more committed to the cause by viewing various aspects of the movie, and having input into the "solution" proposed in the film. It literally is, in part, "their" film.

The film's promotion strategy produced similar opportunities to create anti-Wal-Mart identities among activists. Brave New Films used some traditional public relations techniques, including a press release announcing the upcoming release; an announcement of the limited theatrical release; a release announcing Greenwald's offer to screen the film at Wal-Mart headquarters in Arkansas; and an announcement of the sales figures for the DVD.

However, less traditional strategies drew greater interest and fueled mainstream media coverage. Greenwald and friends produced a series of "parody ads" along with the trailer and posted them on the movie's website, the website iFilms, and on YouTube.com. The spots were downloaded 100,000 times ("When Viral Marketing Attacks," 2005). Organizations supporting the film provided links from their websites. Bloggers wrote about the movie, for example, Killer Movies, Old Hippie's Groovy Blog, At last..., Pulpmovies Trailer Park, Higher Pie, Z3bl0g, Evolve Happy, ladyoceanstar, My own Backyard, Blog for Democracy, Burp, and Cinema Confidential (links can be accessed at http://www.Wal-Martmovie.com). Greenwald wrote his own blog about the movie with an available RSS feed. Moveon.org promoted the film through its website and listserv. Brave New Films launched a MySpace group for "Evil Smiley." These multiple alternative spaces connected anti-Wal-Mart activists before the film's very limited theatrical release.

Initially the film was scheduled for theatrical release only in New York and Los Angeles. However, the "buzz" created about the film expanded theatrical release to San Francisco and Boston. Clinton McClung, Program Director of the Coolidge Corner Theater in Boston said,

> "Wal-Mart: The High Cost of Low Price" initially flew under our radar, at least in terms of a theatrical release. That is until the calls and email started from patrons who had heard about the film and couldn't wait to see it, not just in their homes but in the theatre. The appeal of this film for theatrical showings is not just seeing it on the big screen, but the sense of community and empowerment that comes from watching the film in a group. It not only sparks discussion, but forges connections between

like-minded individuals and—we hope—helps spread the message of the
film to a larger audience.

(Brave New Films, 2005)

The sense of connection created through watching a film is essential to the constitution of a shared anti-Wal-Mart identity. Brave New Films consciously created
opportunities for face-to-face interactions among activists through its grassroots
distribution strategy.

Greenwald began his distribution efforts by contacting individuals who had pur-
chased his previous documentaries. Then "outreach producers" created a network
of associated organizations to plan 7000 screenings in private homes, schools,
family businesses, community centers, and churches. The movie website reports
the producers' explicit intent. Under a link called "organizing with film," Lisa
Smithline, the film's outreach producer, wrote: "Film holds a unique and special
place in American culture, and as such, provides the perfect tool to organizations
looking to build popular support for social change" (http://www.Wal-Martmovie.
com). The conscious decision to use film to create an alternative discourse outside
the mainstream is reflected in the opening paragraph of the outreach webpage: "In
a media age dominated by celebrity trials and missing children, it is a constant battle
to break through the noise. Brave New Films targets under-reported issues that
are ripe for a larger audience" (http://www.Wal-Martmovie.com). The website
provided promotional support for local screenings, including print and radio ads,
a press release template, website graphics, t-shirts, a discussion guide and action
items to guide interaction after the film screening, and much more.

The combination of participative production, cyber/viral promotion, and grassroots distribution constituted a broad-based activist network. People of similar
interests and concerns were brought together within their local communities to
share a media experience. Equally important, of course, was the film itself and its
invitation to form an anti-Wal-Mart public.

Rhetorically Constituting an Anti-Wal-Mart Identity

An analysis of the constitutive power of advertising discourses demonstrates most
clearly how the content of the Wal-Mart movie can strengthen activist identity
and help form an anti-Wal-Mart public. Stein (2002) built on Charland (1987) to
argue that audiences are constructed by advertising texts because these and other
discourses present a "second persona," or an idea of the audience, which may be
appealing (Black, 1970). As Black (1970) explained about the nature of this "second persona" implied by texts, "rhetorical discourses, either singly or cumulatively
in a persuasive moment, will imply an auditor" (p. 109). In other words, the Wal-
Mart movie and other texts invite the audience "to be" someone or something.
These texts address or "hail" an audience to further a particular persuasive goal.
In this way, a constitutive framework suggests that "the critic can see in the auditor implied by a discourse a model of what the rhetor would have his real auditor
become" (Black, 1970, p. 113). Critiques of Nike's advertising could examine how
the company's ads invite young women athletes to tell their observers to "Judge

me as an Athlete" and how stressing "Female Athlete=Athlete. Period." encourages them to envision themselves as fit, confident, empowered supporters of the brand. Similarly, in her examination of Macintosh's "1984" ad, for example, Stein explained how the ad helped change how consumers thought about such emerging technologies and transformed them into personal computer users. Before the ads, these roles had been viewed with skepticism and anxiety (Stein, 2002, p. 175). Fortified by the ad, consumers utilized the tropes of freedom and revolution in their discourse about the personal computer; subsequently, a market was created that continues to have influence in our lives today. Advertising and public relations discourses thus "establish frames of reference and mark the boundaries of public discussion as an integrative common language" (Stein, 2002, p. 175).

In constitutive terms then, the producers of the Wal-Mart movie invite viewers to organize to collectively pressure the corporation to change its policies. The movie invites viewers to boycott, disparage, and otherwise push Wal-Mart to listen to activist criticism and change accordingly. To create this more united activist identity, the movie engages in rhetorical strategies that connect viewers' experiences with Wal-Mart and encourage discussion and action. The Wal-Mart movie cuts across activist identity lines, bringing people as varied as pastors to suburban mothers together in the expression of dislike for the corporation. In essence, the movie stakes out three themes which particularly condemn the company and cultivate a pan-anti-Wal-Mart activist identity, including: (1) the company's treatment of its employees, (2) Wal-Mart's destroying of American business and way of life, and (3) activist efforts in resisting Wal-Mart's entry into their communities. Each theme weaves together many different strands of research and reporting, personal stories and testimony from a variety of people, and a particular rhetorical strategy. This technique of "connecting the dots" among, across, and between various community experiences with Wal-Mart cultivates a more unified activist identity and may help build this identity among uncommitted viewers.

A large portion of the movie contrasts Wal-Mart's claims that it treats employees well with stories and research that argue that the company flagrantly mistreats its workers. From issues ranging from its wages, its healthcare and insurance policies, and its discriminatory behavior toward illegal immigrants and minorities, ex-Wal-Mart employees paint a damning portrait of the company. A rhetorical strategy evident in the employee rights and treatment portion of the film is *cohortatio*, or amplification that moves the hearer's indignation. In classical rhetorical terms, *cohortatio* is a type of intensification that can fuel outrage. Fueling this sense of anger is important in constituting a broader anti-Wal-Mart identity. As Black (1970) explained, "Actual auditors look to the discourse they are attending for cues that tell them how to view the world" (p. 192). Here, audiences watching the film are guided into viewing Wal-Mart's corporate policies and behavior with indignation rather than with indifference or complacency. If the film helps audiences begin to see Wal-Mart's policies as unacceptable, they may then be motivated to tell others and take action, strengthening the collective activist response to the Wal-Mart Corporation.

This strategy is seen, for example, when ex-workers discuss their struggles to pay their bills and feed their families on Wal-Mart's wages. As two women sit in a kitchen discussing their experiences with the company, they argue that their wages could not cover their families' basic needs such as food and medical care. They also express frustration that much of their check goes straight back into the company's coffers[1]: "It was just impossible for me to pay my bill and pay for day care and work . . . the money that I did get went right back into Wal-Mart." Because the movie juxtaposes these ex-employee comments with images of them working hard and struggling to get by, the comments can build anger without alienating the viewers. Workers become indignant that Wal-Mart's efforts to keeps its costs down leaves them without enough working hours to cover their expenses. "I was just getting about 19 hours a week and there's just no way you can pay bills with that. It's just not right at all," one woman, silhouetted in darkness, laments. Another adds, "Your dignity is not there, your pride is not there and you go to work knowing that you're not making enough to make ends meet . . . but yet you gotta go with a smile on your face and fake it. Yeah, that's pretty bad." Between the number of people complaining and the building anger in their comments, *cohortatio* can cultivate indignation among viewers. In fact, especially in light of the documentary's style of combining various scenes or clips of different people in different scenarios throughout the movie in this way, the volume of complaints about the company helps to constitute what it means to be "anti-Wal-Mart" in orientation.

Of particular concern in provoking viewers' anger against the company is the cost of Wal-Mart's medical insurance program. The movie amplifies Wal-Mart's culpability through a number of ex-employee comments. Ex-employees are frustrated with their inability to stay in Wal-Mart's medical program rather than relying on state programs. One points out, for example, "there's no way I can afford to have $75 taken out of each check for medical." Many ex-employees express a type of confusion as to why the healthcare program costs so much, but others directly accuse the company of being too focused on profit: "But they're a billion dollar company so I don't see why they can't offer a better medical package for their associates so that we can afford to get our families on insurance." One woman accuses the company outright of manipulating its employees:

> You talk about using the system, look at the way Wal-Mart is using the system—they're promoting people to go to healthy kids and to get food stamps and section 8 housing. *They're* the ones that are using the system.

Further, as a company facing the largest gender discrimination suit in history, several women also angrily share their negative experiences with Wal-Mart's discriminatory practices. One stops working in her yard to tell the camera, for example, "Bottom line, if you were a female, you just weren't worth the time, you weren't worth the money, you weren't worth the effort, nothing." Another woman recounts her experience with a male manager about her efforts to join the management program: "There's no place for people like you in management," he said. And I said, "Well, what do you mean people like me—is it that I am woman or that I'm Black?" And he said, "Well, two out of two ain't bad."

As the movie presents claim after employee claim through *cohortatio,* the volume of outrage expressed works to create the impression that ex-employees have witnessed similar circumstances. As a result, the leap from being just angry at a personal experience with Wal-Mart can coalesce into something much broader because ex-employees hear how others have suffered the same indignities. As one ex-manager complained, "And the worst part about this is that no one will ever know how big this is . . . what happens to people . . . there's gotta be more people like me out there but they are too afraid to say anything." As the documentary medium poignantly reveals, there are other people out there with these similar experiences who have also been brave enough to conquer their fear and talk. The documentary's ability to provide this forum thus works in a cultivating, unifying, constitutive fashion. Through this strategy, isolated personal stories can coalesce into people working together.

Another rhetorical strategy clearly at work in the film is that of identification, or the process of persuading movie audiences that they share values and norms with the people featured. This strategic process of communicating common ground is crucial to the constitutive process, because for the film to be successful in creating a collective anti-Wal-Mart identity, audiences must recognize themselves in the movie's stories (Charland, 1987). Identification is a rhetorical strategy that can happen, as Burke explained, "spontaneously, intuitively, or even unconsciously," but it is important because audiences must participate and relate to a story or person in order to be persuaded by it (Burke, 1966, p. 301; Charland, 1987). First articulated by scholar Kenneth Burke, identification is a rhetorical concept focused on audience recognition of shared characteristics or interests. As Burke (1969) described it, "A is not identical with his colleague, B. But insofar as their interests are joined, A is identified with B" (p. 20). Less overt than some persuasive strategies, without the ability to convince audiences of shared interests, the movie's anti-Wal-Mart message is likely to fail. On the other hand, if people believe their views and beliefs overlap with the movie's, it becomes much easier to successfully persuade them to take action against the corporation, as approving of the film's message is akin to approving of themselves. Further, as Burke (1969) saw identification as "compensatory to division," creating rapport between the movie and its viewers necessarily involves showing viewers how *they* are alike but different from Wal-Mart (p. 22). The movie's messages work to include audience members as part of a certain group, while at the same time excluding those who support Wal-Mart from this community.

Prominent in the film is the theme that being anti-Wal-Mart does not mean being anti-American. Identification through antithesis, which works by demonstrating and uniting against a common enemy, creates this theme. This strategy functions by cultivating an "us versus them" mentality. In the movie, the strategy works with a twist, however, because Wal-Mart, once seen as part of the American ethos, becomes the enemy. The movie contrasts "Americans" with "Wal-Mart." In the process it revises the perception of who typically works for "activist" causes. Folksy, traditional American imagery, values, and stories abound in several chapters of the film. By letting average, "red blooded" Americans critique Wal-Mart, the film makes a more persuasive case against the company. Common stereotypes might predict that people from small town, red-state America might be in favor of Wal-Mart's approach to free enterprise and its American business success story, but the people on camera tell a different tale. In a variety of scenes, several small business people and small town employees make a number of statements that stress how Wal-Mart is un-American in its approach to business. One says, for example, "I'm all for free enterprise but when you look at the company, it has the richest people in the world so in reality, I think they could spread that out." Another adds, "To even use America and Wal-Mart in the same sentence is just—I don't agree with it at all." Another differentiates his belief in the American system from Wal-Mart's abuse of it:

> I'm not at all in favor of any kind of communism and socialism. I believe that America should always and forever remain free—however, I think there should be regulations established wherein . . . you know, they busted up Standard Oil and Ma Bell but Wal-Mart seems to be going on a rampage through the American economy and nobody's even paying attention.

All of these statements unite similar people against the Wal-Mart enemy. In essence, these statements strengthen the movie's credibility because they feature people who viewers might assume to be in support of the company and its values clearly articulating why the company does not represent their values.

Closely related to the efforts of establishing Wal-Mart as un-American in its business practices are poignant stories and images of how Wal-Mart is ruining the distinctive rural American way of life. In doing so, the film employs the assumed or transcendent "we," an implicit identification strategy, which uses this pronoun and its derivatives to call audiences to see themselves as part of the anti-Wal-Mart community (Cheney, 1983). When "we" are called to act against the company, for example, "we" unite on the basis of this particular strategy's evocation of our anti-Wal-Mart identity. As the speakers express their frustration at the closing and shuttered streets of their hometowns due to Wal-Mart's entry into the community, viewers see images of American flags waving, kids playing in fountains, and majestic homes standing proudly; these images are contrasted with overgrown lots, littered Main streets, and deserted town squares. Bruce Springsteen's haunting version of "This Land is My Land" plays in the background. In one scene, an interviewee remarks about the devastated communities upon the arrival of Wal-Mart, "It's like a neutron bomb hit it." Several participants lament the loss of their way of life. One angrily warns, "When we start talking about quality of life they (Wal-Mart) start talking about cheap underwear. You can't buy small town quality of life at Wal-Mart, they don't sell it. But once they steal it from you, you can't get it back at any price."

Similarly, Red Esry, a former soldier, former independent grocer, and grand-father denounces Wal-Mart's devastating effect on rural business: "it's not the competition we're up against . . . it's the competition being helped from one level to the other . . . Wal-Mart is getting all the breaks." While being interviewed, he never ceases working in his former store while telling the story of how he lost his business. He argues his loss is due in part to the subsidies given to Wal-Mart, but not to independent businesses like his. Esry wonders, "if Wal-Mart gains ground and has a monopoly where will our families and children be? What will they have to do to work and be competitive?" His comments are juxtaposed with images of his teary wife, granddaughter, and son lamenting the loss of their store, which they call a "family member." Taken together, these statements are easy for viewers to relate to because they may be representative of many viewers' experiences. It may be easy for viewers to appreciate Wal-Mart's low prices but these stories may cause them to question what may happen to their communities in the process.

As people can identify, or relate, to messages when they see that they are alike in some fashion, it follows that these various identifications also work to provide portions of a person's identity. In this sense, identification can function beyond just persuading a person of a message; rather, areas of initial overlap can filter out and constitute portions of how a person views him or herself. Indeed, as Cheney (1983) noted, "our corporate (or organizational or institutional) identities are vital because they grant us personal meaning" (p. 145). When a person feels she belongs to a certain group, or accepts a particular name or label for herself, parts of her identity become constituted. In other words, it is possible to become consubstantial with the movie's messages, meaning that people in the movie and its audience can act together since they share common motives. As Heath (2001a) explained, "Through identification, people develop various collective identities with which they govern themselves and form human relations" (p. 376).

It is in this way that individual identities can broaden collectively and strengthen activism against Wal-Mart. The last section of the film deals specifically with illustrating how activists have been successful in keeping Wal-Mart out of their communities and how and why viewers should similarly organize. Along with showing how people share dislike for the company, the movie relies on a type of rhetorical enactment to urge viewers to take action against the company. Rhetorical enactment acknowledges that what Wal-Mart says and does becomes meaningful only because of the interpretations—meaning—that people place on the company's actions and statements (Heath, 2001b). That is, by showing a variety of different interpretations of why Wal-Mart does not belong in a given community, the movie can build on identification to call for viewers to enact their beliefs and fight against the company. Whereas the *cohortatio* strategy fueled anger against the company and identification strategies helped viewers from various walks of life to see themselves in the film's story, the enactment strategy puts the last piece in the constitutive puzzle in place. As discussed, with constitutive rhetoric, "to be constituted as a subject in a narrative is to be constituted with a history, motives, and a *telos*" (Charland, 1987, p. 140). The first two strategies helped cultivate a common history for activist claims and offered motives to encourage their common distaste for the company. The last strategy helps urge them toward a telos, or end, once they are thus constituted. After all, the movie seeks to do more than show viewers that people like them do not like Wal-Mart; rather, it urges them to do something about their dislike and take action.

To do so, the movie shows that people from all walks of life find reason to organize against the company. This last segment juxtaposes affluent gated communities with impoverished communities coming together in their opposition. The music becomes uplifting. We see Chandler, Arizona, with its stately homes, lakes, and golf courses contrasted with urban, reviving communities in central Los Angeles. These people are invited to interpret their reasons for opposing Wal-Mart through a variety of prisms. For example, one provides a political interpretation as she looks up at the American flag hanging above her doorstep, "that flag represents our right to fight for our freedoms and our freedoms include the freedom to fight against Wal-Mart." This woman relied on her neighbors to write letters, to move from 1500 to 4000 petition signatures, and to paint signs and hold rallies to keep Wal-Mart out of her community. Another woman provides a religious interpretation of why Wal-Mart does not belong in her community of Inglewood, California. Inside a much more modest home, she argues "I'm sure there are a lot of companies who think they are good Christian companies, but not if they are going to make money on the back of the workers. As Christians, we're not about capital, we're about people." Another argues against Wal-Mart's entry into Inglewood by differentiating it from other more traditional Wal-Mart markets: "It is not like they came into the small towns in the South and towns that have no business and they brought in business. No, no, no, this is something completely different—they represent plantation capitalism." This woman, then, takes a different position and objects to Wal-Mart from the perspective of racial justice.

When viewers can see that a number of different meanings are used to justify keeping Wal-Mart out of a given area, they learn that they can all become united, no matter their own particular issue with the company. In light of many images of grassroots activism with people making handmade signs, protesting on the sides of roads, holding press conferences, and mailing letters, resisting Wal-Mart also becomes attainable and realistic. Several participants expressed surprise about the willingness of people to organize against Wal-Mart: "We were absolutely amazed and all of them wanted to do something." About the Inglewood success story, a lawyer offers:

> The lesson learned in Inglewood is that we have the ability, through our democracy, to take power and take control and actually hold the company accountable. It's a hard process and there are a lot of things that have to be put in place, but when you put those things in place you can win. It includes the ability to organize regular people, small business owners, workers.

These comments illustrate that it is possible for David to beat Goliath, as several participants note. By sharing the different interpretations of why they believe it is important to fight against Wal-Mart and then showing that the process can be successful, grassroots community activism is enacted on the screen and can motivate and inspire those watching the movie. The film's content is reinforced through its viewing context. Screenings organized by church leaders for church members, by community volunteer groups for active citizens, and by the local environmentalist organization for like-minded individuals provide social support for identity and action the film invites.

Implications and Conclusions

The Wal-Mart movie demonstrates the potential for the documentary to open up new ways of organizing, participating, and identifying to create broad constituencies in opposition to corporate (and other) power. The combination of the rhetorical range available in a documentary with grassroots production and distribution taps into a new alternative realm of political discourse—the community and social network constituted in the blogosphere, MySpace, and YouTube—while simultaneously creating a discursive space in local communities.

In constitutive terms, documentary and/or digital cinema may possess more power in cultivating an anti-Wal-Mart identity than more traditional public relations attacks against the company. The movie's combination of remarks from people of various walks of life, its visual imagery, and its carefully selected music may provide more ways for audiences to share in the perspective offered by the film. Clearly, many public relations tactics have moved beyond the standard news release and entered the digital age, but the Wal-Mart movie addresses stakeholders in a unique manner, providing them with a variety of almost tangible, living, breathing expressions of dislike against the corporation. In fact, since the release of the movie, other corporations have adopted this tactic when communicating with various stakeholders. Fireman's Fund Insurance, for example, created a DVD called "Into the Fire," to raise consciousness about the many challenges firefighters face. Proceeds from the sale of the DVD will be used to help purchase needed equipment for fire departments across the nation. This savvy technique may also help engender positive feelings toward Fireman's Fund. Similarly, Centocor, a biomedicine company, created a documentary called "Innerstate" to raise chronic disease awareness and inspire patients to take action about their conditions. Most tellingly, Wal-Mart itself released a movie "Why Wal-Mart Works and Why that Drives Some People C-R-A-Z-Y," to respond to its critics using documentary film. What this trend may suggest, then, is the ability of film to speak to various audiences in a more constitutive fashion, helping them to band together and identify in response to a variety of corporate initiatives.

In addition to its constitutive ramifications, the movie's impact demonstrates what *Time* magazine calls an intersection of three cultural revolutions with significant implications for public relations practice (Grossman, 2006). The first is in digital video production. Without cheap digital video recorders and simple editing software, Greenwald could not activate 850 field producers or make a 90-minute documentary for a fraction of what it would have cost just 10 years ago. The second revolution is Web 2.0, the explosion of websites such as MySpace, Flickr and YouTube where people around the world share information in multiple forms in a "self-stoking mass collaboration" (Grossman, 2006, p. 65). The parody ads distributed without a single media purchase, the Evil Smiley group, the website linkages essential to the film's success are all part of Web 2.0. This kind of activity is indicative of the micropolitics of the postmodern era. Holtzhausen (2000) noted that publics will "be in a continuous state of flux as people form and disband activist groups that serve their needs in the short term" (p. 102) and they are doing so on Web 2.0.

The third revolution, perhaps the most important for public relations, is an increasing rejection of mainstream media: "the idea of a top-down culture, in which talking heads spoonfeed passive spectators ideas about what's happening in the world, is over. People want unfiltered video from Iraq, Lebanon, and

Darfur—not from journalists who visit there but from soldiers who fight there and people who live and die there" (Grossman, 2006, p. 65). The authenticity of the voices in the documentary and its integration of personal identification with broader issues meet the expectations of potential activists. Indeed, James McEnteer (2006) attributed the rise of political documentary since 2000, in part, to the "corporatization and trivialization of the news" (p. xii). Greenwald created a hybrid form combining the expertise of professional filmmakers with the unfiltered, participative collaborative community of Web 2.0 and local activists, totally bypassing media organizations.

As such, the Wal-Mart movie's "anti-corporateness" extends to the media industries, especially the film industry known for stifling independent voices and tightly controlling film distribution. Greenwald demonstrated that a film could reach a large audience without Hollywood backing. The movie's website reported 100,000 DVD sales in the first month after release and a Nielsen Videoscan rating of no. 5 on the documentary video charts in its first weeks of release, without the assistance of the largest retailer for DVDs, Wal-Mart. The grassroots screenings equaled or surpassed many blockbuster releases. In its first week, the Wal-Mart movie was scheduled for 7000 screens. *Shrek 2*, the biggest opening release ever in the U.S., was released on 4163 screens (Brown, 2006). Greenwald's ability to effectively bypass "big media" is significant and indicative of the shifting power differentials in the contemporary issue environment.

While innovative activists quickly embrace the technological and media revolution to build audiences and activists, corporate public relations is struggling to catch up with its savvy political counterparts and opponents. Wal-Mart hired public relations and marketing firms to respond to the movie, but must find a way to enter the dialogue created in local communities and on the Internet and Web 2.0. This case demonstrates the need for public relations practice to continually reconceptualize publics, to recognize the local as global, and to reconsider the power of interpersonal influence in a multi-mediated, postmodern world. At the very least, it demonstrates the power of activists to reshape the realm of political influence in a postmodern rhetorical age.

Note

1 All text samples are taken directly from the Wal-Mart movie (*Wal-Mart: The High Cost of Low Price,* 2005, Brave New Films).

References

Black, E. (1970). The second persona. *Quarterly Journal of Speech, 56,* 109–119.

Brave New Films. (2005). Independent documentary takes on Hollywood. Retrieved November 1, 2006, at: http://www.walmartmovie.com/wm_sales.php

Brown, K. (2006, January 1). Greenwald's grassroots gospel. *Realscreen, 37.* Retrieved November 1, 2006, from: http://web.lexis-nexis.com

Burke, K. (1950). *A rhetoric of motives.* Berkeley: University of California Press.

Burke, K. (1969). *A rhetoric of motives.* Berkeley and Los Angeles: University of California Press.

Charland, M. (1987). Constitutive rhetoric: The case of the People Quebecois. *Quarterly Journal of Speech, 73,* 133–150.

Cheney, G. (1983). The rhetoric of identification and the study of organizational communication. *Quarterly Journal of Speech, 69,* 143–158.

Coombs, W. T. (1998). The internet as potential equalizer: New leverage for confronting social irresponsibility. *Public Relations Review, 24,* 289–303.

Crable, R. E. (1990). "Organizational rhetoric" as the fourth great system: Theoretical, critical and pragmatic implications. *Journal of Applied Communication Research, 18,* 115–128.

Feldman, S., & Sigelman, L. (1985). The political impact of prime-time television: "The Day After." *Journal of Politics, 47,* 557–578.

Filmmaker lures shoppers for Wal-Mart doc. (2005, October 28). *Daily Variety, 289*(20), 2. Retrieved November 3, 2006, from: Lexis Nexis Academic (0011-5509).

Giddens, A. (1984). *The constitution of society: Outline of the theory of structuration.* Berkeley: University of California Press.

Grossman, L. (2006, November 13). Invention of the year. *Time, 168*(20), 64–65.

Heath, R. L. (1998). New communication technologies: An issues management point of view. *Public Relations Review, 24,* 273–288.

Heath, R. L. (2001a). Identification. *Encyclopedia of rhetoric.* New York: Oxford University Press.

Heath, R. L. (2001b). A rhetorical enactment rationale for public relations: The good organization communicating well. In R. L Heath (Ed.), *Handbook of public relations* (pp. 31–50). Thousand Oaks, CA: Sage.

Holtzhausen, D. R. (2000). Postmodern values in public relations. *Journal of Public Relations Research, 12,* 93–114.

Hot topic: Is Wal-Mart good for America? (2005, December 3). *Wall Street Journal,* A10. Retrieved September 25, 2008 from: http://web.factiva.com

Jasinski, J. (1997). Instrumentalism, contextualism, and interpretation in rhetorical criticism. In W. Keith and A. Gross (Eds.), *Rhetorical hermeneutics* (pp. 195–224). Albany: SUNY Press.

Jasinski, J. (1998). A constitutive framework for rhetorical historiography: Toward an understanding of the discursive (re)constitution of "Constitution" in *The Federalist Papers.* In K. J. Turner (Ed.), *Doing rhetorical history: Concepts and cases* (pp. 72–92). Tuscaloosa: University of Alabama Press.

Lenart, S., & McGraw, K. (1989). America watches "Amerika": Television docudrama and political attitudes. *Journal of Politics, 51,* 697–712.

McEnteer, J. (2006). *Shooting the truth: The rise of American political documentaries.* Westport, CT: Praeger.

Mannheim, J. B. (2001). *The death of a thousand cuts: Corporate campaigns and the attack on the corporation.* Mahwah, NJ: Lawrence Erlbaum.

Smith, D. (2005, November 20). Filmmaker fires a shot at a corporate giant; Greenwald turns his activist eye on Wal-Mart. *Boston Globe,* N14. Retrieved on November 3, 2006, from: http://web.lexis-nexis.com

Stein, S. (2002). The "1984" Macintosh ad: Cinematic icons and constitutive rhetoric in the launch of a new machine. *Quarterly Journal of Speech, 88,* 169–192.

Stokes, A. Q. (2005). Metabolife's meaning: A call for the constitutive study of public relations. *Public Relations Review, 31,* 556–565.

Taylor, M., Kent, M. L., & White, W. J. (2001). How activist organizations are using the Internet to build relationships. *Public Relations Review, 27,* 263–284.

When viral marketing attacks: Taking a whack at Wal-Mart. (2005, October 24). *Brandweek*, n.p. Retrieved November 3, 2006, from: http://web.lexis-nexis.com

Whiteman, D. (2004). Out of the theaters and into the streets: A coalitional model of the political impact of documentary film and video. *Political Communication, 21,* 51–69.

19

GOOD ENVIRONMENTAL CITIZENS?

The Green Rhetoric of Corporate Social Responsibility

Øyvind Ihlen
University of Oslo

In March 2007, *Fortune* magazine summed up the distinguishing features of the three most admired companies in the U.S. that year. The verdict was clear: "Green" had come to mean something more than money. The magazine concluded that the list toppers General Electric, Starbucks, and Toyota had at least partly built their success on environmental strategies (Fisher, 2007). The integrated company General Electric touted its so-called "ecomagination" campaign; the coffee company Starbucks argued that it has taken an environmental leadership role; and Toyota's hybrid engine models made inroads in the automobile market. The green theme has been echoed elsewhere too, as larger companies have paid increased attention to the environmental aspect of corporate social responsibility (CSR) (Bullis & Ie, 2007). The world's largest company, Wal-Mart, has also joined in (Wal-Mart, 2006). Still, only a few rhetorical studies of CSR have been conducted (i.e., Llewellyn, 1990; McMillian, 2007; Saiia & Cyphert, 2003). Furthermore, to this author's knowledge, no one has published rhetorical studies of how corporations try to come across as "good environmental citizens."

This chapter pursues the latter question in light of theories regarding ethos. The rhetoric of General Electric, Starbucks, and Toyota is examined by looking at three publications that are available on their respective websites: *Delivering on Ecomagination: GE 2006 Ecomagination Report* (General Electric, 2007), *My Starbucks: Corporate Social Responsibility/Fiscal 2006 Annual Report* (Starbucks, 2007), and *Embracing the Environment: The Toyota Way 2006* (Toyota, 2007). First, however, the concept of CSR is discussed briefly along with its link to public relations. Then an overview is provided of the treatment the ancient and modern literature gives to ethos and credibility.

The Good and Believable Corporate Citizen

Corporate Social Responsibility and Public Relations

Most definitions of CSR revolve around the idea that CSR is about minimizing the negative and maximizing the positive effects of organizational activity in relation to people, society, and the environment. The literature on CSR is also vast and growing fast (e.g., Habisch, Jonker, Wegner, & Schmidpeter, 2005; May, Cheney, & Roper, 2007). In public relations, it has been posited that public relations practitioners should adhere to a professional set of ethics that is designed to maximize what is considered as the public good. CSR might be the way in which this ideal is realized (L'Etang, 1994). Some public relations scholars actually conflate CSR with public relations, or argue that CSR should be at the heart of what public relations is all about, namely balancing of the interests of organizations and their stakeholders (Boynton, 2002).

Still, some see CSR as thinly disguised "business as usual" practice, and there is widespread skepticism towards CSR messages (i.e., Christian Aid, 2004; Cloud, 2007). The fact that attempts to strengthen legitimation can backfire has been dubbed "the self promoter's paradox": "The more problematic the legitimacy of a company is, the more skeptical are constituents of legitimation attempts" (Ashforth & Gibbs, 1990, p. 191). The purpose behind CSR acts as reputation-building efforts might become too apparent and the company thus enters a vicious circle. Consequently, some urge companies to choose a minimalist approach to communicating about CSR (Morsing & Schultz, 2006).

Although CSR is by far the most common phrase used in practice and academia, it might be questioned whether the word "social" should be dropped and the phrase shortened to CR. Some argue in favor of the latter stating that environmental issues, business ethics, and socio-economic issues are just as important as social issues (Ruud, Jelstad, Ehrenclou, & Vormedal, 2005). Others question whether there is a difference between doing the socially responsible act or the responsible act (Robert L. Heath, personal communication, August 30, 2007).

Many advocates of CSR see it as a form of "enlightened self-interest" that secures long-term profit by building reputation, forestalling regulation, securing a more stable societal context for business, and reducing operating costs by avoiding conflict (Carroll, 1999; Davis, 1973). Research indicates that although companies might pay lip service to their duties toward society, the main goal for CSR activities is to improve reputation (Gjølberg & Ruud, 2005; Pollach, 2003). If this is the general case, then companies should not be surprised if public sentiment towards CSR is lukewarm or negative. Self-interest feeds skepticism and cynicism. This means that a company's success in relation to CSR will rest on its "ability to meet the rhetorical demands of civil discourse" and that others are convinced of the company's sincerity (Saiia & Cyphert, 2003, p. 48).

Llewellyn (1990) argued that CSR rhetoric often is theological at root and separated in sect and church discourse. In the former, fundamentalist form, companies are "true believers" and issues are considered in black and white terms. The church-like discourse, however, is more nuanced. Here companies express the faith that CSR will pay in the long run.

Other authors have also directed attention to the importance of a morality discourse to demonstrate legitimacy: Bostdorff (1992) has posited that an organization needs to demonstrate the positive values of its act, the purity of its purpose, and how it has embraced a highly valued social role. McMillian (2007), however, questions whether companies currently are up to this task. In her view, the rationality of companies is too narrow and their CSR rhetoric is characterized by traits such as "instrumentality, exclusivity, attribution, monologue and narcissism" (p. 22). For the rhetoric to be aligned with the basic idea of CSR, there needs to be emphasis on connection, reciprocity, and trust. Other scholars have emphasized the need to create involvement, rather than to rely on self-absorbed, one-way communication strategies (Morsing & Schultz, 2006). Corporations should aim for the creation of "mutual dwelling place[s]" (McMillian, 2007, p. 25). This is also another way to understand the concept of ethos.

Ethos: The Controlling Factor in Persuasion

Rhetoric is often defined as "an ability, in each case, to see the available means of persuasion" (Aristotle, trans. 1991, 1.2.1). Aristotle argued that the rhetor has three types of appeal or proofs at his or her disposal: logical arguments, appeals to emotions, and ethos—ethical appeals to portray the rhetor as trustworthy.

Although he only devoted one chapter to ethos in his book *On Rhetoric,* Aristotle held that ethos was the first and "controlling factor in persuasion" (Aristotle, trans. 1991, 1.2.4). The importance of ethos becomes clear when rhetoric is thought of as the province of areas where no exact knowledge exists. In such cases we are left to trust or not trust those that speak. Ethos can thus be shown to trump logos, as we do not automatically adhere to valid logical arguments (Jasinski, 2001).

Ethos in general manifests itself to the audience whether the rhetor likes it or not, and is concerned with the character of the rhetor. Briefly defined it is "character as it emerges in language" (Baumlin, 2001, p. 263). In other words, it is considered as the elements of a speech or a text that presents the rhetor as trustworthy. This is called direct or invented ethos.

In addition to direct ethos, there is also an indirect route through other aspects of discourse (Kinneavy & Warshauer, 1994). That is, emotional appeal might strengthen ethos: "the hearer suffers along with the pathetic speaker, even if what he says amounts to nothing" (Aristotle, trans. 1991, 3.7.5). Similarly, using the logos appeal of enthymemes and maxims works well since audiences "are pleased if someone in a general observation hits upon opinions that they themselves have about a particular instance" (Aristotle, trans. 1991, 2.21.15).

A recurring theme in *On Rhetoric* is the need to take into account the specific audience's predispositions. It was important, Aristotle maintained, that the rhetor must exhibit qualities that the community, and not the individual, defines as virtue. Some thus argue that the rhetor is triggering the "audience's projection of authority and trustworthiness onto the speaker" (Baumlin & Baumlin, 1994, p. 99). In line with this, Craig R. Smith (2004) argues that ethos "dwells in the character of the audience; and . . . in the speaker's style" (p. 3). Smith thus urges us to see ethos, not as only tied to the rhetor, but also to the text and to the audience; in short, the rhetorical situation has to be accounted for.

Aristotle argued that it was sufficient if the audience *believed* the rhetor possessed certain qualities like loyalty or honesty. In this sense, *On Rhetoric* has been seen as an unsentimental and amoral manual on public discourse that details what works and what doesn't. This viewpoint can be contrasted to that of Plato, who thought that ethos "defines the space where language and truth meet and are made incarnate within the individual" (Baumlin, 2001, p. 264). From an analytical viewpoint, the Aristotelian perspective is interesting enough, although critics are of course also interested in the question of sincerity in communication. Here, however, it seems that the most viable option for the critic is to compare what is said, with what is done. This falls beyond the focus of this chapter.

Some liken ethos to *character* (Bostdorff, 1992). Character is discussed in relation to another point as well: Aristotle argued primarily that ethos concerned what was said in the speech itself (invented ethos), not the rhetor's status or reputation in the community (Aristotle, trans. 1991). A highly influential rhetorician like Cicero, however, held that a rhetor's history might color the impression that the audience receives: "The character, the customs, the deeds, and the life, both of those who do the pleading and of those on whose behalf they plead, make a very important contribution to winning the case" (Cicero, trans. 2001, 2.182). Cicero thus saw ethos and pathos as intertwined (Baumlin, 2001). In fact he did not write about ethos per se, but about a rhetor's *persona*.

Some writers have tried to differentiate persona and ethos by defining the former as the audience's perception of a source of communication. Ethos, by contrast, is "the sum of particular intellectual and moral qualities that an audience recognizes in the rhetor's message, for instance, the determination that a speaker is acting as a competent and responsible scientist" (Ulman, 1996, p. 50). Hence persona can be understood as the wider category of the two, while ethos pertains to actual texts and inventional strategies.

How to Strengthen Ethos

Aristotle suggested a threefold approach to strengthen direct and invented ethos: the rhetor should demonstrate practical wisdom, virtue, and goodwill towards the audience (Aristotle, trans. 1991). These aspects have a complex interrelation and correspond to the theme, the speaker, and the audience respectively (Kinneavy & Warshauer, 1994):

Practical wisdom (phronesis): This has been taken to mean that the rhetor should inhabit good sense, sagacity, expertise, and come across as intelligent and knowledgeable. An obvious strategy is to prepare well and gain knowledge about the subject and the audience. That the wisdom should be practical implies that it is knowledge of *the right action*, something "that is distinct from technical knowledge and that cannot be learned in the same way as technical knowledge" (Kinneavy & Warshauer, 1994, p. 179).

The rhetor might also try to use specialized language or add details to a balanced and well thought-out text. A rhetor could, for instance, attempt to describe an environmental problem by using scientific expressions. *Phronesis* is also bolstered by the use of logos and stylistic appeals. The latter entails, for instance, choice of grammatical person, verb tense, and voice. The rhetor could strive for an intimate distance to create identification with the audience or, conversely, use a formalistic distance in order to give an impression of seriousness and objectivity—of following what is considered as appropriate style for the occasion. Word length and qualifiers are also features that can give the impression of a high level of accuracy and that the rhetor is knowledgeable (Crowley & Hawhee, 1999).

Virtue (arête): The rhetor should show virtue, that is, be of good moral character. For Aristotle the virtues included "justice, courage, self-control, liberality, magnanimity, magnificence, prudence, wisdom, and gentleness" (Smith, 2004, p. 9). Cicero argued that if the rhetor had experienced difficulties, these should be elaborated upon to strengthen the audience's estimate of his or her ability to bear suffering (Cicero, trans. 2001).

The virtues were seen as "moving targets established by the audience" (Smith, 2004, p. 7). This again points to how the rhetor has to adapt to the audience; virtues valued by one audience might be despised by another. Still, in general, the virtues most appreciated by the audience are often those that are most useful to society (Kinneavy & Warshauer, 1994).

Cicero pointed out that citing approval from respected authorities would be very valuable (Cicero, trans. 2001). This "third party technique" was also extolled by Aristotle: "Since there are sometimes things to be said about oneself that are invidious or prolix or contradictory . . . it is best to attribute them to another person" (Aristotle, trans. 1991, 3.17.16). Today, industry and businesses will typically cite "partnerships" with environmental organizations to strengthen their environmental ethos.

Goodwill (eunoia): The rhetor should also show goodwill towards the audience. This should not be understood as *befriending* the audience, since friendship requires reciprocation. If the audience detects the latter, the credibility of the rhetor is not enhanced (Smith, 2004). Rather, goodwill is wishing good for others for their sake. Like Aristotle writes in *The Nicomachean Ethics*: "Goodwill is inoperative friendship, which when it continues and reaches the point of intimacy may become friendship proper—not the sort of friendship whose motives is utility or pleasure, for these do not arouse goodwill" (Aristotle, trans. 1996, 9.5.3).

To demonstrate goodwill, the rhetor should "somehow identify with the audience, by for instance holding some of their basic aspirations, speaking their language, and if necessary sharing and affirming their prejudices" (Kinneavy & Warshauer, 1994, p. 177). Goodwill might thus be indirectly supported by pathos.

Another technique suggested is to show how the needs of the audience have been taken into consideration. The rhetor can try to give adequate explanations so that no member of the audience is alienated for lack of background information or insight. A rhetor could for instance take care to explain scientific expressions regarding environmental problems in colloquial terms.

As pointed out, several of the techniques mentioned above are useful for corporate rhetors. Still, some challenges arise from the shift from individual rhetors to collectives as rhetors; from ancient time to present day.

Modern Conceptions of Ethos and Credibility

The present-day rhetorical situations are necessarily different from the ones in ancient Greece or Rome. The modern audience appreciates other virtues than the ancient audience; among these is probably the need for authenticity. The rhetor has to be perceived as being him- or herself since our culture ties value to what is authentic, real, and genuine (i.e., Johansen, 2002).

It has also been argued that the list of credibility factors should be expanded to include power (that the audience perceives that the rhetor might reward or punish them), idealism (the audience members see qualities in the rhetor to which they aspire), and similarity (the audience sees the rhetor resemble themselves) (Hart & Daughton, 2005).

The latter factor, "similarity to the audience," also invites use of the term identification like Burke (1950/1969) postulated it, and the way it was later adapted to organizational discourse by Cheney (1983). Techniques pointed out are demonstrating common ground between the rhetor and the audience, use of an antithesis, and, finally, the use of the personal pronoun "we" to create identification. Examples of these techniques include how an environmental organization underscores how people share one Earth, and thus must care for it in the best possible way. The same environmental organization might also paint a picture of greedy companies that do not care about the environment, but just clamor for profits. The audience is thus invited to identify with the environmentalists that fight such companies. And finally, the environmental organization might emphasize how *we* share one Earth, how *we* need to fight greedy polluting companies, and so forth.

The latter study is an example of how rhetorical theory might be fruitfully extended and used on organizational discourse. Still, the direct transfer of ancient rhetorical theory to the study of such texts might be awkward, particularly in light of how an organization is a collectivity with many selves and many realities (Cheney, 1992; McMillian, 2007). This gives all the more reason for theory development drawing on modern writings on, for instance, reputation.

The literature on reputation management argue that organizations wishing to build a good reputation should be authentic, distinctive, transparent, visible, consistent, and responsive (van Riel & Fombrun, 2007). Factors such as these and the concern for reputation have obvious links to being perceived as a trustworthy organizational rhetor. Discrepancies between what is said and done are typically highlighted and criticized in the media. It is expected that companies *walk the talk*. If not, the reputation suffers.

In a reputation textbook by Doorley and Garcia (2007), companies are urged to implement three principles in their CSR communication: (1) accuracy: they need to know what is happening in the field; (2) transparency: the stakeholders should be given sufficient, relevant, comparable, intelligible information to be able to judge the company's performance; and (3) credibility: companies should bring in independent, credible third parties to verify or give testimonials, adopt recognized standards for conduct (human rights, worker's rights, etc.), admit problems, and engage with stakeholders informally and formally, for instance through partnerships. In other words, this operationalizes some of the advice from ancient rhetoric and adapts it to the modern organization.

In an empirical study of how companies present corporate ethics on their websites, the author found that companies relied on several of the techniques mentioned above, including third-party endorsement and mentioning links to NGOs. In addition, concrete examples of fulfilling CSR commitment were often highlighted, and the company's history and "heritage" of integrity used as ethos proofs (Pollach, 2003).

An ethical use of these strategies could involve "the construction of a speaker's ethos as well as construction of a 'dwelling place' (ethos) for collaborative and moral deliberation" (Hyde, 2004, p. xviii). This, as argued by McMillian (2007), could help address the fundamental problems of current CSR discourse and corporate practice. McMillian sees the creation of mutual dwelling places as replacing corporate monologue with dialogue; including *all* stakeholders, not only a few privileged ones; adding new measures of success, like human and social capital; "replacing external attribution with corporate accountability and disclosure"; and fundamentally altering and de-centering the corporations' "self-adoring gaze" (p. 25). This might also help organizations to reach the ideal of being the "good organization communicating well" (Heath, 2001, p. 31).

In the following, the ancient and modern writing on credibility will be applied to CSR texts that attempt to build an environmental ethos for the corporate rhetor.

Environmental Ethos in Play

"Talking green, acting dirty," read a headline in the *New York Times* when General Electric rolled out its "ecomagination" campaign in 2005 (Sullivan & Schiafo, 2005, p. 23). The newspaper argued that General Electric has a history of actively opposing environmental regulation and claimed that the company has dragged its feet cleaning up its toxic legacy. Starbucks, for its part, has been accused of greenwashing since the company is only selling a token amount of certified organic coffee beans. The company has also had its share of trouble in relation to fair trade and labor disputes (e.g., Kamenetz, 2005, http://www.starbucksunion.org). As for Toyota, the *New York Times* used the headline "The Hybrid Emperor's New Clothes" in 2005, and claimed that the tested hybrid model did not provide any tangible economy benefits (Sabatini, 2005). A division of Friends of the Earth took out ads asking: "Is Toyota a wolf in sheep's clothing?" The company was also taken to task for lobbying against stricter environmental regulations (http://www.bluewaternetwork.org/telltoyota/).

In other words, the environmental ethos of General Electric, Starbucks, and Toyota is contested. The question the public might ask is: Why should we believe these companies and their environmental claims? The following analysis points to four broad strategies used by these corporate rhetors to come across as good environmental citizens: The companies claim they improve the world, they state that they clean up their own act, they point to acclaim from others, and they try to pose as friendly and caring.

Claim 1: "We Improve the World"

The theological tone of CSR rhetoric (Llewellyn, 1990) is rather evident in the way that all three companies directly or indirectly claim that they improve the world. General Electric points to its "commitment to invest in a future that creates innovative solutions to environmental challenges and delivers valuable products and services to customers while generating profitable growth for the Company [*sic*]" (p. 1). The company has identified and set out to exploit a market for technology that can be promoted as environmentally friendly. A range of products are developed under the moniker "ecomagination," a term provided the company by the public relations firm Edelman (http://www.edelman.com/about_us/awards/, retrieved July 10, 2007). The company thus seems to be on the verge of having its own environmental CSR denomination so to speak. The brochure *Delivering on Ecomagination* is filled with examples bearing witness and ranging from carbon capture to water use and purification initiatives. It is also pointed out how the company works together with "world-recognized" research centers around the globe (p. 11). The word "research" in fact figures 48 times in the 38-page brochure. Combined with phrases like "double our investment in R&D" (p. 6), these are good indicators of how the company attempts to demonstrate its knowledge or *phronesis* (Aristotle, trans. 1991).

Toyota is about technology and believing too. The carmaker claims that its hybrid models "represent a revolution in the history of the automobile and in the development of automobile environmental technology" (p. 1). Throughout the 16-page brochure, the company points to how it cares for the environment and how this commitment "does not end until the vehicles have been retired from use in an eco-friendly manner" (p. 1). The religious tone of CSR rhetoric (Llewellyn, 1990) is mirrored in the title of Toyota's brochure—*Embracing the Environment*.

General Electric and Toyota both use the topic of comparison and figures to emphasize the environmental value of their products. For instance: A new locomotive engine from General Electric uses "less fuel and [generates] up to 40% less nitrogen oxide and particulate matter emission" (p. 16). Choosing a hybrid like Prius from Toyota "saves up to 352 gallons/year (1,332 L/yr) versus the average midsize car" (p. 14). This logos argumentation serves to bolster the ethos claim of improving the world. Again, it is the technique of *phronesis* that is employed (Aristotle, trans. 1991).

Starbucks obviously has to choose another strategy since its products are not about technology. Starbucks won't improve the world with the help of its products, but rather by the way it conducts its business and the way it takes on a *leadership role*. It is explicitly argued that the way to strengthen the relationship with stakeholders is by focusing the communication on "Starbucks commitment and passion to improve the world and the ways in which we are demonstrating this" (p. 1). Examples are provided showcasing "improvement" and that the company helps "create a more sustainable approach to high-quality coffee production" and "contribute positively to local communities" (p. 1). The former is done through, for instance, paying "premium prices for premium quality coffee" (p. 8). The company claims a leadership position "in both our industry and within our global society through our participation in organizations such as the United Nations Global Compact" (p. 1). Starbucks promotes collaborative action on climate change and explicitly agrees "with the consensus of the scientific community that climate change could pose an enormous threat to the future of the planet" (p. 16). The report also states that the company has taken out six full-page ads in the *New York Times* arguing for collective action. Here, it might be said that Starbucks tries to demonstrate *arête* or virtue (Aristotle, trans. 1991) or the type of idealism (Hart & Daughton, 2005) that an environmentally friendly audience might appreciate.

In other words, the environmental ethos of the three companies is indirectly strengthened through logos arguments relying on examples and comparisons, highlighting qualities of its *products* and its *leadership role* respectively. Taken together, the companies thus claim legitimacy by taking on the highly valued social role of improving the world (Bostdorff, 1992).

Claim 2: "We Clean Up Our Own Act"

Companies' CSR rhetoric is typically filled with examples of how they fulfill their CSR commitments (Pollach, 2003). In the same way, the three companies in this study point out how they make efforts to minimize their environmental footprint. Starbucks, for its part, purchases renewable energy, cuts energy consumption, and promotes use of "post-consumer recycled fiber" in its cups; in the U.S. and Canada 20% of the energy use of its stores comes from wind energy (p. 17). General Electric, on the other hand, highlights energy efficiency in its own plants: "To make ecomagination truly 'sustainable' from a business perspective, GE set very real, aggressive targets, one of which is to improve the energy efficiency of Company [*sic*] operations and reduce the Company's [*sic*] greenhouse gas (GHG) emission" (p. 28).

In the brochure from Toyota, the company argues that its environmental efforts extend to the whole life cycle of the vehicles, from design, to manufacturing and distribution. The carmaker says it "achieved zero landfill at our manufacturing facilities in North America as a whole, defined as a 95% or greater reduction in landfill waste from 1999 levels" (p. 7). Toyota also reports that it achieved its stated goal of "reducing energy consumption 15% two years ahead of schedule" (p. 8). The carmaker furthermore points to reduction of waste, as well as recycling, as evidence of internal environmentally friendly practices.

All three companies thus strengthen their environmental ethos indirectly by logos arguments that build on examples, facts, and figures. They are not only improving the world through their products and leadership roles, but also by getting their own house in order. In this way, it might be said that the companies also are demonstrating practical wisdom or *phronesis* (Aristotle, trans. 1991), and thus strengthen their environmental ethos directly as well. The companies attempt to walk the talk, like the reputation literature urges (Doorley & Garcia, 2007; van Riel & Fombrun, 2007).

Cleaning up its own act, might also be called a type of virtue, or *arête* (Aristotle, trans. 1991), that the audience might appreciate. Still, given the skepticism of CSR messages (i.e., Christian Aid, 2004; Cloud, 2007), the demonstration of such virtue has to rely on approval of others to avoid the "self-promoter's paradox" (Ashforth & Gibbs, 1990, p. 191).

Claim 3: "Others Approve of Us"

All three companies use the third-party strategy to strengthen their ethos, as advocated by the ancient rhetoricians (Aristotle, trans. 1991; Cicero, trans. 2001), as well as reputation scholars (Doorley & Garcia, 2007; van Riel & Fombrun, 2007). There is no need to rely solely on the companies' own claims. General Electric invites its audience to read what the Indian Minister for Science and Technology and the Chinese Vice Premier have to say in this regard. The company has also drafted a larger statement from the President of the Pew Center on Global Climate Change (p. 36), and the company has set up an advisory council comprised of so-called "industry thought leaders with expertise in energy and the environ-ment" (p. 34). A knockout quote from the Acting Assistant Administrator for the U.S. Environmental Protection Agency's (EPA) Office of Air and Radiation reads: "Partners like GE are outstanding leaders in protecting our environment through energy efficiency. . . . As one of the 2007 ENERGY STAR Sustained Excellence winners, GE has taken energy efficiency to new heights year after year and we all benefit" (p. 35).

In 2006, Toyota took home the first prize in the latter competition. The car-maker also highlights its ranking by the American Council for an Energy-Efficient Economy (ACEEE) "Greener choices of 2006" list (p. 6). Starbucks, too, can boast about awards and its link to the EPA. The coffee company mentions that it is a member of the EPA's so-called Green Power Partnership, and that it has been "recognized by the EPA with a 2005 Green Power Leadership Award" (p. 17).

General Electric also tries to further its credibility by getting a formal verification from the sustainability and marketing firm GreenOrder, and by citing its member-ship on indexes like the Dow Jones Sustainability Index, KLD Global Climate 100 Index, and Innovest Global 100 "Most Sustainable Corporations in the World" index (p. 33). A Toyota dealership in Texas has also been "the first auto dealership in the nation to apply for LEED certification (the U.S. Green Building Council Leadership in Energy and Environmental Design [LEED] Green Building Rating System)" (p. 9).

Furthermore, General Electric and Starbucks state that they have adopted industry standards such as the World Resources Institute (WRI)/World Business Council for Sustainable Development (WBCSD) GHG Protocol, and the Global Reporting Initiative (GRI). This follows one of the credibility points given in the literature on reputation management (Doorley & Garcia, 2007).

In summing up, like other empirical studies have shown (Pollach, 2003), a common ethos strategy is to employ third parties to testify to the virtue of the company. This might also be the most important *direct* ethos strategy of corporations.

Claim 4: "We Care About You"

Aristotle (trans. 1991) pointed to how a rhetor could strengthen ethos by showing goodwill towards the audience. General Electric, Starbucks, and Toyota, all employ different versions of this strategy. The latter does it by providing "tips on how you can play your part to reduce the environmental impact of your vehicle, and save money at the same time" (p. 2). Here it is detailed how drivers can "achieve additional savings and reduce [their] vehicle's impact on the environment" by, for instance, accelerating smoothly (p. 14). The appeal to the wallet is of course interesting here. This is obviously a need of the audience. In this particular text, however, the company does not heed the advice from the literature on the importance of creating a dialogue and involving the audience (Morsing & Schultz, 2006). In this respect, the other two companies come closer by issuing direct invitations to comment and dialogue. Both companies direct stakeholders to their websites, and Starbucks points to an online survey for feedback.

General Electric also seeks to create identification by using lines such as "When we engage diverse stakeholders we're better able to understand *our* mutual challenges and identify opportunities for improvement" (emphasis added) (p. 32). Starbucks, on the other hand, repeatedly declares that it wants to be "*your* Starbucks" (original emphasis) (p. II). The coffee company literally works to create mutual dwelling places. Metaphorically too, the company goes some way to do that. By printing pseudo-handwritten notes from, for instance, "a coffee supplier to Starbucks" (p. 8), the president of the National Trust for Historic Preservation (p. 14), and a principal of "a law firm specializing in community-based renewable energy projects" (p. 17), the company gives room to outside voices. These voices do, however, only function to adorn Starbucks with accolades. This seems a far cry from the advice given in the literature that dissenting voices should be heard as well and that shortcomings should be professed (Morsing & Schultz, 2006).

As for the General Electric text, the president of the Pew Center on Global Climate Change is pictured alongside the printed letter where she pays tribute to the company. The only other people to figure prominently are the president and CEO, and the vice president for the "ecomagination" program. The rest of the people pictured remain nameless, just like they do in the brochure of Toyota. In fact, the latter text does not identify any management figures either.

Taken together: Although the companies attempt different techniques to create goodwill (*eunoia*) and thus strengthen ethos (Aristotle, trans. 1991), it might be asked how well positioned these rhetors are if a goal is to create identification (Cheney, 1983) or metaphorically "mutual dwelling place[s]," (McMillian, 2007, p. 25). No dissenting voices are allowed to disrupt the pastoral environmental image these corporations attempt to paint of themselves.

Conclusion

In the late 2000s, the concept of CSR is everywhere and it is indeed a management fashion (Zorn & Collins, 2007). Still, research on CSR communication is in its infancy. Often publications point out that corporations need to conduct two-way communication and take into account all stakeholders. In this chapter, I have attempted to move beyond this advice to discuss the ethos strategies of companies that want to come across as good environmental citizens. A suggestion from this chapter is that companies will typically rely on four strategies, and that they can be assessed accordingly on the claims they put forward: (1) Do they really improve the world? As is to be expected, the companies seldom address the fundamental issues underlying the environmental problem. (2) Do they really clean up their own environmental act? It is noteworthy that the companies attempt to cash in on their win–win strategies on energy conservation. It certainly makes good business sense to save money, and it is without a doubt a good thing for the environment too. The question remains, however, if companies should be able to pat themselves on the back because of this. (3) Who certifies the environmental efforts of the companies? Are they really approved by credible third parties? Are the codes and standards of conduct the companies prescribe to really followed? (4) Do the companies care? Do they invite dissenting voices and create a common dwelling place? Or is the CSR rhetoric one-way, self-absorbed, and celebratory (McMillian, 2007; Morsing & Schultz, 2006)? The companies researched for this chapter seemed to fail in the latter respect. The fact that they *did* top the *Fortune* ranking, as mentioned at the beginning of this chapter, might be a consequence of how they have attempted to integrate CSR in their core activity and to make it a strategic advantage (Porter & Kramer, 2006). The business-minded constituents polled by *Fortune* might appreciate these attempts.

Some scholars appear to argue that companies should be given more slack, and that the insistence on how they should walk the talk and always behave consistently is misplaced. The value of strategic ambiguity is highlighted (Eisenberg, 2007). Managers should *talk the walk*: Corporations should be allowed to "talk about their ideals and good intentions without constantly" being reminded "that their behavior leaves much to be desired" (Christensen, 2007, p. 454). Still, it might be hypothesized that extolling the virtues of ambiguity and the power of language to transform corporate action do not cancel out the call for consistency that prevails. Hence corporations stand to hurt their reputation if they fall back on glaring strategic ambiguities. More importantly from a public viewpoint: It is probably the old mixture of "stick and carrot strategies" that can keep "the externalizing machine" (Bakan, 2004) that is the modern corporation in check. Civil society will have to follow corporate activities closely, laud those that take positive steps, but also speak out against manipulation and other ethical violations. In this respect, it is important to recognize the narrow and instrumental rationality that necessarily characterizes companies and the economic system they operate within.

Further research needs to be conducted to assess whether the findings above hold for the rest of the text corpus of the researched companies. Furthermore, the three texts that have been analyzed in this chapter are primarily written with a North American audience in mind. However, many scholars have pointed to the importance of cultural differences (Beckmann, Morsing, & Reisch, 2006). More research needs to be conducted along such lines, in order to get a better grasp of the green rhetoric of CSR.

References

Aristotle. (trans. 1991). *On rhetoric: A theory of civic discourse* (G. A. Kennedy, Trans.). New York: Oxford University Press.

Aristotle. (trans. 1996). *The Nicomachean ethics* (H. Rackham, Trans.). London: Wordsworth.

Ashforth, B. E., & Gibbs, B. W. (1990). The double-edge of organizational legitimation. *Organization Studies, 1*(2), 177–194.

Bakan, J. (2004). *The corporation: The pathological pursuit of profit and power.* London: Constable.

Baumlin, J. S. (2001). Ethos. In T. O. Sloane (Ed.), *Encylopedia of rhetoric* (pp. 263–277). New York: Oxford University Press.

Baumlin, J. S., & Baumlin, T. F. (1994). On the psychology of the *pisteis*: Mapping the terrains of mind and rhetoric. In J. S. Baumlin & T. F. Baumlin (Eds.), *Ethos: New essays in rhetorical and critical theory* (pp. 91–112). Dallas, TX: Southern Methodist University Press.

Beckmann, S. C., Morsing, M., & Reisch, L. A. (2006). Strategic CSR communication: An emerging field. In M. Morsing & S. C. Beckmann (Eds.), *Strategic CSR communication* (pp. 11–36). Copenhagen: Jurist- og Økonomforbundets Forlag.

Bostdorff, D. M. (1992). "The decision is yours" campaign: Planned Parenthood's characteristic argument of moral virtue. In E. L. Toth & R. L. Heath (Eds.), *Rhetorical and critical approaches to public relations* (pp. 301–314). Hillsdale, NJ: Lawrence Erlbaum.

Boynton, L. A. (2002). Professionalism and social responsibility: Foundations of public relations ethics. *Communication Yearbook, 26,* 230–265.

Bullis, C., & Ie, F. (2007). Corporate environmentalism. In S. K. May, G. Cheney, & J. Roper (Eds.), *The debate over corporate social responsibility* (pp. 321–335). New York: Oxford University Press.

Burke, K. (1950/1969). *A rhetoric of motives.* Berkeley: University of California Press.

Carroll, A. B. (1999). Corporate social responsibility: Evolution of a definitional construct. *Business & Society, 38*(3), 268–295.

Cheney, G. (1983). The rhetoric of identification and the study of organizational communication. *Quarterly Journal of Speech, 69,* 143–158.

Cheney, G. (1992). The corporate person (re)presents itself. In E. L. Toth & R. L. Heath (Eds.), *Rhetorical and critical approaches to public relations* (pp. 165–183). Hillsdale, NJ: Lawrence Erlbaum.

Christensen, L. T. (2007). The discourse of corporate social responsibility: Postmodern remarks. In S. K. May, G. Cheney, & J. Roper (Eds.), *The debate over corporate social responsibility* (pp. 448–458). New York: Oxford University Press.

Christian Aid. (2004). *Behind the mask: The real face of corporate social responsibility* (Report). London: Christian Aid.

Cicero. (trans. 2001). *On the ideal orator* (J. M. May & J. Wisse, Trans.). New York: Oxford University Press.

Cloud, D. L. (2007). Corporate social responsibility as oxymoron: Universalization and exploitation at Boeing. In S. K. May, G. Cheney, & J. Roper (Eds.), *The debate over corporate social responsibility* (pp. 219–231). New York: Oxford University Press.

Crowley, S., & Hawhee, D. (1999). *Ancient rhetorics for contemporary students* (2nd ed.). Needham Heights, MA: Allyn and Bacon.

Davis, K. (1973). The case for and against business assumption of social responsibilities. *Academy of Management Journal, 16*(2), 312–322.

Doorley, J., & Garcia, H. F. (2007). *Reputation management: The key to successful public relations and corporate communication.* New York: Routledge.

Eisenberg, E. M. (2007). *Strategic ambiguities: Essays on communication, organization, and identity.* Thousand Oaks, CA: Sage.

Fisher, A. (2007, March 5). How to get a great reputation. *Fortune.*

General Electric. (2007). Delivering on ecomagination: GE 2006 ecomagination report. Retrieved June 4, 2007, from: http://ge.ecomagination.com/

Gjølberg, M., & Ruud, A. (2005). *The UN Global Compact: A contribution to sustainable development?* (Working paper 1/2005). Oslo, Norway: ProSus.

Habisch, A., Jonker, J., Wegner, M., & Schmidpeter, R. (Eds.). (2005). *Corporate social responsibility across Europe.* Berlin: Springer.

Hart, R. P., & Daughton, S. (2005). *Modern rhetorical criticism* (3rd ed.). Boston: Allyn & Bacon.

Heath, R. L. (2001). A rhetorical enactment rationale for public relations: The good organization communicating well. In R. L. Heath (Ed.), *Handbook of public relations* (pp. 31–50). Thousand Oaks, CA: Sage.

Hyde, M. J. (2004). Introduction: Rhetorically, we dwell. In M. J. Hyde (Ed.), *The ethos of rhetoric* (pp. xiii–xxviii). Columbia: University of South Carolina.

Jasinski, J. (2001). *Sourcebook on rhetoric: Key concepts in contemporary rhetorical studies.* Thousand Oaks, CA: Sage.

Johansen, A. (2002). *Talerens troverdighet: Tekniske og kulturelle betingelser for politisk retorikk [The credibility of the speaker: Technical and cultural conditions for political rhetoric].* Oslo, Norway: Universitetsforlaget.

Kamenetz, A. (2005, May 30). Baristas of the world, unite! *New York,* from: http://www.nymag.com/nymetro/news/features/12060

Kinneavy, J. L., & Warshauer, S. C. (1994). From Aristotle to Madison Avenue: Ethos and the ethics of argument. In J. S. Baumlin & T. F. Baumlin (Eds.), *Ethos: New essays in rhetorical and critical theory* (pp. 171–190). Dallas, TX: Southern Methodist University Press.

L'Etang, J. (1994). Public relations and corporate social responsibility: Some issues arising. *Journal of Business Ethics, 13,* 111–123.

Llewellyn, J. T. (1990). The rhetoric of corporate citizenship. Unpublished Ph.D. dissertation, University of Texas at Austin.

McMillian, J. J. (2007). Why corporate social responsibility: Why now? How? In S. K. May, G. Cheney, & J. Roper (Eds.), *The debate over corporate social responsibility* (pp. 15–29). New York: Oxford University Press.

May, S. K., Cheney, G., & Roper, J. (Eds.). (2007). *The debate over corporate social responsibility.* New York: Oxford University Press.

Morsing, M., & Schultz, M. (2006). Corporate social responsibility communication: Stakeholder information, response and involvement strategies. *Business Ethics: A European Review, 15*(4), 323–338.

Pollach, I. (2003). Communicating corporate ethics on the World Wide Web. *Business & Society, 42*(2), 277–287.

Porter, M. E., & Kramer, M. R. (2006). Strategy & society: The link between competitive advantage and corporate social responsibility. *Harvard Business Review,* (December), 78–92.

Ruud, A., Jelstad, J., Ehrenclou, K., & Vormedal, I. (2005). *Corporate responsibility reporting in Norway: An assessment of the 100 largest firms* (No. 9/05). Oslo, Norway: Program for Research and Documentation for a Sustainable Society (ProSus).

Sabatini, J. (2005, July 31). The hybrid emperor's new clothes. *New York Times,* 1.

Saiia, D. H., & Cyphert, D. (2003). The public discourse of the corporate citizen. *Corporate Reputation Review, 6*(1), 47–57.

Smith, C. R. (2004). *Ethos* dwells pervasively: A hermeneutic reading of Aristotle on credibility. In M. J. Hyde (Ed.), *The ethos of rhetoric* (pp. 1–19). Columbia: University of South Carolina.

Starbucks. (2007). My Starbucks: Corporate social responsibility/Fiscal 2006 annual report. Retrieved June 4, 2007, from: http://www.starbucks.com/aboutus/

Sullivan, N., & Schiafo, R. (2005, June 12). Talking green, acting dirty. *New York Times,* 23.

Toyota. (2007). Embracing the environment: The Toyota way [brochure]. Retrieved June 4, 2007, from: www.toyota.com/environment

Ulman, H. L. (1996). "Thinking like a mountain": Persona, ethos, and judgment in American nature writing. In C. G. Herndl & S. C. Brown (Eds.), *Green culture: Environmental rhetoric in contemporary America* (pp. 46–81). Madison: University of Wisconsin Press.

van Riel, C. B. M., & Fombrun, C. J. (2007). *Essentials of corporate communication.* London: Routledge.

Wal-Mart. (2006). Wal-Mart 'greening' could have huge impact. Retrieved January 15, 2008, from: http://www.walmartfacts.com/articles/1618.aspx

Zorn, T. E., & Collins, E. (2007). Is sustainability sustainable? Corporate social responsibility, sustainable business and management fashion. In S. K. May, G. Cheney, & J. Roper (Eds.), *The debate over corporate social responsibility* (pp. 405-416). New York: Oxford University Press.

INDEX